The
Alexander Pope
Encyclopedia

The
Alexander Pope
Encyclopedia

❧ ☙

Pat Rogers

GREENWOOD PRESS
Westport, Connecticut • London

Library of Congress Cataloging-in-Publication Data

Rogers, Pat, 1938–
    The Alexander Pope encyclopedia / Pat Rogers.
      p.   cm.
    Includes bibliographical references (p.   ) and index.
    ISBN 0–313–32426–3 (alk. paper)
    1. Pope, Alexander, 1688–1744—Encyclopedias.   2. Poets, English—18th century—Biography—
Encyclopedias.   3. Great Britain—Intellectual life—18th century—Encyclopedias.   I. Title.
PR3632.R64   2004
821'.5—dc22   2003061266

British Library Cataloguing in Publication Data is available.

Library of Congress Catalog Card Number: 2003061266
ISBN: 0–313–32426–3

First published in 2004

Greenwood Press, 88 Post Road West, Westport, CT 06881
An imprint of Greenwood Publishing Group, Inc.
www.greenwood.com

Printed in the United States of America

∞

The paper used in this book complies with the
Permanent Paper Standard issued by the National
Information Standards Organization (Z39.48–1984).

10 9 8 7 6 5 4 3 2 1

Copyright Acknowledgments

The author and publisher gratefully acknowledge permission to use excerpts from the following material:

The Correspondence of Alexander Pope, edited by George Sherburn, 5 vols. (Oxford: Clarendon, 1956).
Reprinted by permission of Oxford University Press.

Joseph Spence, *Anecdotes, Observations, and Characters of Books and Men*, edited by J.M. Osborn, 2 vols.
(Oxford: Clarendon, 1966). Reprinted by permission of Oxford University Press.

The Twickenham Edition of the Works of Alexander Pope, edited by J. Butt et al., 11 vols. (London:
Methuen, 1938–1968). Reprinted by permission of Taylor & Francis.

for Adrienne

❧ Contents ❧

⇥ List of Entries ⇤

List of Entries

List of Entries

List of Entries

✵ Acknowledgments ✵

The author's warmest thanks are due to the following.

Dr. George Butler, of Greenwood Press, for commissioning the volume and for his support during its writing.

Michelle Lattanzio, for invaluable help in processing the disks on which the text was written and in printing them out, as well as for many other services willingly performed.

Dr. Paul Baines, who gave the benefit of his deep knowledge of Pope and his massive understanding of the early eighteenth century. He selflessly undertook the grueling task of reading through the entire set of entries and saved me from innumerable mistakes and oversights.

Nathan Hein, for drawing the maps.

Others who kindly checked individual entries to ensure that gross errors of omission or commission were weeded out: Julius Bryant, Anna Eavis, Michael McGarvie, Jim McLaverty, and Anthony Beckles Willson.

Dr. Adrienne Condon, who has contributed most of all, with her intellectual guidance and with her moral support and self-abnegating promotion of the work.

✺ Introduction ✺

The aim of this book is to bring together in a single volume all the most material facts about Alexander Pope. It covers his life, his writings in prose and verse, his correspondence, his friends and enemies, his main themes and concerns, and his literary techniques.

The primary business of an encyclopedia lies in the area of facts rather than speculative notions. This work seeks simply to provide the reader with a reliable and up-to-date compendium of the essential data. It does not attempt to supply long, discursive treatment of general issues such as Pope's place in the landscape gardening movement or his attitude toward women. There is an abundance of worthwhile commentary on such matters already, and the encyclopedist's role in this volume is best confined to summarizing major trends and citing appropriate references. Those who desire an extensive survey of modern secondary literature on such broad topics should consult *A Complete Critical Guide to Alexander Pope* (2000) by Paul Baines. The *Encyclopedia* concentrates, rather, on setting out the facts so far as they can be ascertained at present. It devotes a high proportion of the entries to what is called in the German language *Realien*, that is, persons, places, dates, events, and entities such as groups and institutions. In the Bibliography at the end will be found a wide selection of the major editions and the most important writings on every aspect of Pope and his work. While the scope of the *Encyclopedia* does not extend to every aspect of the early Hanoverian age, a large number of entries contain material on the events of the time and the running ideological concerns of the period (see, for instance, **Treaty of Utrecht** or **Ancients and Moderns**),

where these impacted Pope in some significant way.

Encyclopedias necessarily feed off other works of reference. However, it is possible to aim at extending the reach of existing knowledge in limited ways. In this work some of Pope's connections with the Catholic gentry are set out more fully than before, and a small number of individuals who have not been properly identified before are given a more secure role in Pope's life or works. New information is supplied in a number of entries.

In some ways Pope has been lucky. He never lost all his readers, even when he became unpopular with critics in the nineteenth century. Tag lines and hackneyed quotes from his poetry have always made up a hefty section in dictionaries of familiar sayings (see **stock quotations**). They have been used to point numerous morals and adorn endless tales and turn up in formal and informal contexts, sometimes as titles of books, movies, and popular songs ("A little learning," "To err is human," "Fools rush in," "Where angels fear to tread," "Who breaks a butterfly upon a wheel," "Damn with faint praise," "Consult the genius of the place in all," "Nature and nature's laws," "Nature to advantage dressed," "Whatever is, is right," "Hope springs eternal," "The proper study of mankind," and countless others). In the last century he has bowed before successive waves of new critical ideology but has never broken. Today he remains a controversial and contentious figure—not admired by all but central to any serious account of the development of poetry in English.

Pope figures in almost all undergraduate literature programs and is ubiquitous in graduate courses on the eighteenth century. He remains the subject of extensive research and scholarship, with books on him, as well as numerous articles, appearing every year. Recent criticism has fired new debates in the 1990s and 2000s. However, so far there has never been a comprehensive reference work on Pope. No single work approaches this function, so that students and readers have to access numerous sources to locate information and commentary. There is an urgent need for a volume that will fill this gap, comprehensively but concisely.

CATEGORIES OF ENTRY

The scope of entries may be summarized as follows:

1. *Pope's works*. Entries are supplied for all major works in prose and verse and for the great majority of Pope's shorter poems. Books that he edited or to which he made a perceptible contribution are included, as are all collaborative items. There are some general headings by genre providing cross-references, for example, **ballads** and **epistles**. Entries provide the following information, where it can be ascertained: details of the earliest publication, listing date, format, pagination, price, and the standard bibliographical references (see "Griffith" and "Foxon" in the Abbreviations); and a brief history of later editions. Then come payments to Pope; date and process of composition and revision; and a short summary of contents and aims, with a note on reception history. Fuller entries are provided for Pope's most famous and most discussed works, *The Rape of the Lock* and *The Dunciad*, broken down under various headings such as "Literary Sources and Models" and "Analysis of the Narrative." These items are so complex, both in their internal organization and under their bibliographical aspects, that it has seemed necessary to make an exception here.

2. *Personal entries*. The subjects here include biographic materials, as well as entries on subjects in which Pope took a particular interest or explored in his work. Examples chosen at random are **ancestry**, **birth**, **education**, **gardening**, **library**, **ombre**, **religion**, and **will**.

3. *Topical entries*. A large and diverse group. Included are historical events such as the **South Sea Bubble**; groups and movements, such as **nonjurors**; cultural terms and categories, such as **opera** and **publishers**; and key literary terms with a relevance to Pope's work, for instance, **georgic** and **mock-heroic**.

4. *Biographical entries*. These cover over 300 individuals whom Pope knew or wrote about. All those with whom he had any sort of significant contact are included, among them everyone with whom he exchanged letters (other than cases of just one or two isolated business communications). Longer entries are provided for Pope's closest friends, such as members of the **Scriblerus Club**. Elsewhere treatment is graduated according to the length and depth of Pope's relations with the figure in question. The form of entries varies slightly but normally starts with basic biographic facts (except in the case of individuals so well known that this would be redundant, as with **Sir Isaac Newton** or **Voltaire**). These are followed by matters such as the date of first contact with Pope, where known, and an indication of views expressed by the subject about Pope, and vice versa.

In addition, there are more than sixty entries for critics and scholars who have made an important contribution to the study and understanding of Pope. Living individuals are not given an entry, but the contributions of many in this category will be found in **reputation**.

5. *Places*. All locations with which Pope is identified in some respect. These include his places of residence; birth and burial place; his haunts in London and elsewhere; country houses where he called on his **rambles**, or where he gave advice on landscape planning; towns and districts he visited; and places with a significant presence in his work, for example, **Hampton Court**.

READING LIST

Each substantial entry is followed by a short reading list. This is confined to major treatments of the topic in question and generally includes only books. Where specialist findings have been absorbed into standard authorities, for example, the **Twickenham edition**, the earlier source is not normally listed. Books on a general topic or biographies of a given figure are excluded unless they throw light on Pope personally. Thus, the reader will find under **Voltaire** only material explicitly related to this writer's attitude toward Pope. Short entries carry a reading list only where at least one important work has been devoted to the subject. In the case of persons, items such as biographies or critical monographs are omitted if they are out of date or otherwise irrelevant to contemporary study of Pope. The aim is to give a list of selected reading that adds to the understanding of Pope and is not accessible in other ways.

FORMS OF REFERENCE

A consistent form of reference has been adopted within the entries. Cue-titles have been allocated to the main sources (see Abbreviations). Quotations from the poems are taken from the standard *Twickenham Edition*, in the form *TE* 2: 345. Other cue-titles refer to the *Prose Works*, cited in the form *Prose* 1: 222; to the collected *Correspondence*, cited as *Corr* 4: 333; and to the older **Elwin and Courthope edition**, found in the form *EC* 6: 111. References to the main biographic sources are to the collection of personal memorabilia assembled by **Joseph Spence**, as *Anecdotes* 2: 333; to the work by George Sherburn, as *Early Career* 210; and to the standard biography by **Maynard Mack**, as *Life* 456. Other short forms used for the most frequently cited sources will be found in Abbreviations.

Other information has been drawn from hundreds of disparate sources, including contemporary books and pamphlets, later studies, and modern scholarly texts. These are named only where a direct quotation is made. Routinely no reference is supplied (again where there is no quotation) from standard works of reference, that is, the *Complete Peerage; Dictionary of National Biography*; the *History of Parliament*; the *Oxford English Dictionary*; and the *Victoria County History*. It scarcely needs to be said that

these works have provided the basis for countless statements throughout the text, though they have been checked where appropriate.

Quotations are normally given verbatim, except that errors have been corrected and punctuation occasionally normalized where the original pointing might be misleading. Proper names, for persons or places, are normally given outside quotations in their accepted modern form. However, where the title of an individual used a spelling no longer in use for the place in question, the form employed in Pope's day is retained: thus, **Countess of Winchilsea**, not "Winchelsea." Entries for peers are made in their most familiar form through Pope's lifetime: thus, **Viscount Bolingbroke**, and not Henry St. John, and **Robert Walpole**, not the Earl of Orford. In borderline cases an arbitrary decision has been made: thus, the **first Earl of Oxford**, not Robert Harley, and **George Granville**, not Baron Lansdowne. Those ennobled after Pope's death, such as **George Lyttelton**, are entered under their earlier name. Cross-references have been given under the alternative name in these latter instances. Throughout the text, outside quotations, "AP" is used for Alexander Pope.

Cross-references are given to other entries in a systematic way. Any major reference to a topic covered elsewhere in the *Encyclopedia* is shown by a citation of the entry in bold type, for example: see **Jacobites**. Such a bolding occurs only in the first reference within a given entry. Other cross-references may be found at the conclusion of an entry. Readers should look for the significant word in the title of an entry. Thus, a statement "see **Judith Cowper**" prompts a search under the letter C, while "see the **Duchess of Buckinghamshire**" should be followed up under B. Where the context means that ambiguity is impossible, some familiar surnames are used without a given name (as **Swift** or **Addison**).

CHRONOLOGY

This lists the main events of Pope's life, together with his major publications and the most significant incidents bearing on his career (e.g., publications of his close friends, such as *Gulliver's Travels;* national events with a personal relevance, such as the **South Sea Bubble**). The chronology does not seek to cover the entire public history of the time.

BIBLIOGRAPHY

The full Bibliography appears at the conclusion of the text. It is divided into sections covering reference works (including bibliographies and catalogs); editions (collected, selected, individual works, manuscripts, letters); biographies; critical studies (including anthologies of published criticism, collections of essays, monographs, specialized studies, and work on individual poems); local studies; and background materials. The last section is confined to books that contain explicit commentary on Pope. There is no attempt to provide a full reading list for every aspect of Pope's age. Secondary work on aspects of the period is cited where appropriate under individual topics within the main entries. Within each section or subsection of the Bibliography, items are listed alphabetically under the name of the author or the work.

With one exception, the Bibliography is limited to full-length books. A vast array of articles and Web sites now exists, and it would require a volume of double this length to list them all. It can be said, nevertheless, that all the most influential writing on Pope appears in one or other of the items in the Bibliography.

INDEX

This is intended as an integral part of the *Encyclopedia*. It has been designed to operate in conjunction with the system of cross-referencing described above. Entries are provided for all topics, works, persons, and places in the main text. Within the entry for Pope, there is a detailed breakdown of subjects.

It has been an immense pleasure to compile this *Encyclopedia*, and I hope it will give both profit and pleasure to readers. Inevitably, there will be errors and culpable omissions, despite all the efforts made to eliminate them. This is a pioneering attempt, with no earlier example to serve as a guide. Any indications from readers of such blunders on my part will be gratefully received, and the database from which the text has been put together will be corrected.

✲ *Abbreviations* ✲

Anecdotes	J. Spence, *Anecdotes, Observations, and Characters of Books and Men*, ed. J.M. Osborn, 2 vols. (Oxford: Clarendon, 1966)
AP	Alexander Pope
Ault	N. Ault, *New Light on Pope* (London: Methuen, 1949)
Book Trade	D. Foxon, *Pope and the Early Eighteenth-Century Book Trade*, ed. J. McLaverty (Oxford: Clarendon, 1991)
CIH	M. Mack, *Collected in Himself: Essays Critical, Biographical, and Bibliographical on Pope and Some of His Contemporaries* (Newark: University of Delaware Press, 1982)
Corr	*The Correspondence of Alexander Pope*, ed. G. Sherburn, 5 vols. (Oxford: Clarendon, 1956)
EA	*Essential Articles for the Study of Alexander Pope*, ed. M. Mack, rev. ed. (Hamden, CT: Archon, 1968)
Earls of Creation	J. Lees-Milne, *Earls of Creation: Five Great Patrons of Eighteenth-Century Art* (London: Hamish Hamilton, 1962)
Early Career	G. Sherburn, *The Early Career of Alexander Pope* (Oxford: Clarendon, 1934)
EC	*The Works of Alexander Pope*, ed. W. Elwin and W.J. Courthope, 10 vols. (London: John Murray, 1871–89)
Foxon	D.F. Foxon, *English Verse, 1701–1750: A Catalogue of Separately Printed Poems with Notes on Contemporary Collected Editions*, 2 vols. (Cambridge: Cambridge University Press, 1975)
FRS	Fellow of the Royal Society
Garden and City	M. Mack, *The Garden and the City: Retirement and Politics in the Later Poetry of Pope 1731–1743* (Toronto: University of Toronto Press, 1969)
Gardening World	P. Martin, *Pursuing Innocent Pleasures: The Gardening World of Alexander Pope* (Hamden, CT: Archon, 1984)
Griffith	R.H. Griffith, *Alexander Pope: A Bibliography*, 2 vols. (Austin: University of Texas Press, 1922–27)
Guerinot	J.V. Guerinot, *Pamphlet Attacks on Alexander Pope 1711–1744: A Descriptive Bibliography* (London: Methuen, 1969)
JTS	J. Swift, *Journal to Stella*, ed. H. Williams, 2 vols. (Oxford: Clarendon, 1948)
L&GA	*The Last and Greatest Art: Some Unpublished Poetical Manuscripts of Alexander Pope*, ed. M. Mack (Newark: University of Delaware Press, 1984)

Abbreviations

Life	M. Mack, *Alexander Pope: A Life* (New Haven, CT: Yale University Press, 1985)
MP	Member of Parliament
"New Anecdotes"	G. Sherburn, "New Anecdotes of Alexander Pope," *Note & Queries*, 5 (1958), 343–49
P&AGE	M.R. Brownell, *Alexander Pope and the Arts of Georgian England* (Oxford: Clarendon, 1978)
Portraits	W.K. Wimsatt, *The Portraits of Alexander Pope* (New Haven, CT: Yale University Press, 1965)
Prose	*The Prose Works of Alexander Pope*, vol. 1, *The Earlier Works 1711–1720*, ed. N. Ault (Oxford: Blackwell, 1936); vol. 2, *The Major Works 1725–1744*, ed. R. Cowler (Hamden, CT: Archon, 1986)
PRE	*Pope: Recent Essays by Several Hands*, ed. M. Mack and J.A. Winn (Hamden, CT: Archon, 1980)
Social Milieu	H. Erskine-Hill, *The Social Milieu of Alexander Pope: Lives, Example and the Poetic Response* (New Haven, CT: Yale University Press, 1975)
Swift *Corr*	*The Correspondence of Jonathan Swift*, ed. H. Williams, 5 vols. (Oxford: Clarendon, 1963–65)
TE	*The Twickenham Edition of the Works of Alexander Pope*, ed. J. Butt et al., 11 vols. (London: Methuen, 1938–68)
This Long Disease	M.H. Nicolson and G.S. Rousseau, *"This Long Disease, My Life": Alexander Pope and the Sciences* (Princeton, NJ: Princeton University Press, 1968)
Women's Place	V. Rumbold, *Women's Place in Pope's World* (Cambridge: Cambridge University Press, 1989)

➤ Chronology ≪

Year	Age	Events in AP's Life
1688	Birth	AP born in London (21 May). James II flees to France, prior to accession of William III and Mary.
1692	4	AP's family moves to Hammersmith, outside London.
1698	10	AP's father acquires house at Binfield, in Windsor Forest: the family in residence there by 1700.
1702	14	Accession of Queen Anne.
1704	16	Swift, *A Tale of a Tub* and *The Battle of the Books*.
1705	17	AP's first surviving letters; now acquainted with Sir William Trumbull.
1707	19	AP met Martha and Teresa Blount about this time.
1709	21	*Pastorals* and other early work published.
1711	23	*Essay on Criticism. The Spectator* begins (AP occasional contributor).
1712	24	First version of *The Rape of the Lock* in two cantos.
1713	25	*Windsor-Forest*, celebrating end of the War of the Spanish Succession. Addison's *Cato*. AP now familiar with the Scriblerus group, including Swift, Arbuthnot, Parnell, and Gay.
1714	26	*The Rape of the Lock* in five cantos. Death of Queen Anne; succession of George I.
1715	27	*The Temple of Fame*. First installment of the *Iliad*. Jacobite rising. Bolingbroke flees to France.
1716	28	Pope family leaves Binfield and moves to Chiswick, outside London.
1717	29	Death of AP's father. *Collected Works* published.
1718	30	AP leases house at Twickenham, his home for the rest of his life. Death of Parnell.
1719	31	Defoe, *Robinson Crusoe*.
1720	32	Last installment of the *Iliad*. South Sea Bubble.
1721	33	Edition of Parnell.
1723	35	Edition of Buckinghamshire's works. Atterbury plot; the bishop exiled to France. AP's in-laws implicated in Waltham Blacks affair.
1725	37	First installment of the *Odyssey*. Edition of Shakespeare.
1726	38	*Odyssey* completed. Swift visits England; *Gulliver's Travels* published.

1727	39	First two volumes of *Miscellanies* published. Death of George I; succession of George II.
1728	40	*The Art of Sinking* published in third volume of *Miscellanies*. Gay, *Beggar's Opera*. First version of *The Dunciad*.
1729	41	*The Dunciad Variorum* published.
1730	42	Cibber becomes Poet Laureate.
1731	43	*Epistle to Burlington*.
1732	44	*Miscellanies*, fourth volume. Death of John Gay. Death of Atterbury. Hogarth, *The Harlot's Progress*.
1733	45	First of the *Imitations of Horace* published (to 1738). *Epistle to Bathurst*. *Essay on Man* I–III published. Death of AP's mother.
1734	46	*Essay on Man* IV published. *Epistle to Cobham*.
1735	47	*Epistle to Arbuthnot*, followed by death of Arbuthnot. *Epistle to a Lady*. Second volume of AP's *Works*. Curll's edition of the *Letters*.
1737	49	*Epistle to Augustus* published. Authorized edition of *Letters*. Death of Queen Caroline.
1738	50	*Epilogue to the Satires*. Samuel Johnson, *London*.
1740	52	AP's health worsens.
1741	53	*Memoirs of Scriblerus* published.
1742	54	Fourth book of *The Dunciad* published separately. Fielding, *Joseph Andrews*.
1743	55	*The Dunciad* in four books.
1744	56	AP working on deathbed edition. Dies (30 May). Johnson, *Life of Savage*.
1745		Death of Swift. Death of Robert Walpole. Jacobite rising.

The
Alexander Pope
Encyclopedia

A

Abberley. Estate northwest of Worcester, owned by the Walsh family from the time of Henry VIII. The brick core of the old house lies beneath the present Victorian structure. AP visited his friend **William Walsh** there in August and September 1707 and consulted him on an early version of the *Essay on Criticism*. Another friend, **Edward Blount**, who was a second cousin of Walsh, visited Abberley in 1719 and wrote to AP from there, informing him that Walsh's sisters recalled the poet and his complimentary line on their brother (*Corr* 2: 10–11). The house passed to William's sister Anne, who married Francis Bromley, and remained in the Bromley family for some generations.

Abbott, Edwin (1808–82). Teacher and writer on education. Compiled *A Concordance to the Works of Alexander Pope* (1875). Although it omits the translations, this was a serviceable reference tool for a century. See **concordances**.

Abscourt or App's Court. A large estate near Walton in Surrey. It is mentioned in AP's Horatian poem *The Second Epistle of the Second Book*, l. 232. Its occupant was then apparently Col. Anthony Browne, who leased the property with Jeremiah Browne from the Earl of Halifax. In 1742 the gardening writer Stephen Switzer noted that the *ferme ornée* was now enjoying great popularity, as evidenced by the creation of such parks at Apps Court, **Riskins**, and **Dawley**. Around April 1743 AP paid a visit to the house, which was a large Jacobean mansion. The estate was acquired about 1900 by a water company, who created two reservoirs on the site.

accidents. According to **Joseph Spence**, "Mr. Pope's life, was in danger several times, and the first so early as when he was a child in coats." While he was playing with a toy cart, at the age of about three, a wild cow struck him with her horns, wounded him in the throat, and trampled over him. The informant is **Magdalen Rackett**, the poet's half sister, who witnessed the incident (*Anecdotes* 1: 3–4). When he was about twenty-two, the driver of a coach in which he was riding attempted to ford the Thames at night. After entering the water, the horses stopped and refused to go further. It turned out that the river was not passable at this point, and if the coach had continued, it would have been swallowed up. The best-known incident occurred in September 1726, when AP was returning from a visit to **Viscount Bolingbroke**'s home at **Dawley**. The coach was descending a steep bank beside the Crane river, near **Whitton**, when it overturned. AP was trapped in the partially submerged coach, until rescued by one of Bolingbroke's footmen, who broke the window and pulled him out. He was taken to the nearby home of the lawyer **Nathaniel Pigott**. In the process AP received a bad cut to his right hand, which could have resulted in the loss of two fingers. Fortunately he escaped without permanent damage, although he was forced to use **John Gay** as an amanuensis for a time. The event became well known, and even **Voltaire** heard about it and wrote to commiserate. In 1740 AP wrote to ask a place for the footman who had saved his life: his name was Philippe Hanaus, of Brussels. See G. Sherburn, "An Accident in 1726," *Harvard Library Bulletin*, 2 (1949), 121–23, as well as *Corr* 2: 399–408; 4: 289.

In August 1736 there was a final accident.

AP was leading a young lady, Miss Talbot, down the stairs (landing stage) near his house at **Twickenham**, when she slipped and fell into the river. The poet was dragged into the Thames along with her. They floundered in the water for some time before they could be rescued (see *Corr* 4: 28).

Acis and Galatea. Musical drama in one act composed by **George Frideric Handel**, variously described as a masque, a serenata, and a pastoral entertainment. It was probably first performed in the summer of 1718 at **Cannons**, where Handel was director of music for the **Duke of Chandos**. A revised version in three acts was performed at the **Haymarket Theatre** in 1732.

The libretto is based on a story told in the *Idylls* of **Theocritus** and the *Metamorphoses* of **Ovid**, Book 13. Its authorship has not been certainly established, but contemporary sources name AP and **Gay** as responsible; we know that their friend **John Arbuthnot** was in very close touch with Handel and with Chandos at this juncture. Some material was added by **John Hughes**. Two items have commonly been associated with AP: the words for a trio, "The flocks shall leave the mountain," derive in part from "Autumn" in AP's *Pastorals*; while a chorus "Wretched lovers" (opening Act 2 in the revised version) echoes verses in Book 13 of AP's *Iliad* translation. For the text of these lines, see *TE* 6: 215–17. For general background on the work, see W. Dean, *Handel's Dramatic Oratorios and Masques* (Oxford: Clarendon, 1990), 153–90; and D. Burrows, *Handel* (New York: Schirmer, 1994), 80–82, 96–97.

Adderbury. House near Banbury in Oxfordshire. It had formerly belonged to the poet Rochester (see *On Lying in the Earl of Rochester's Bed at Atterbury*). In 1717 it was leased by the **Duke of Argyll**, who planned alterations to the irregular Jacobean mansion. The remodeling was carried out by Roger Morris in the 1730s. Most of the house was demolished in 1808. AP visited the seat in 1739, as revealed in a letter to the Duke dated 11 July (*Corr* 4: 189).

Addison, Joseph (1672–1719). Author and politician. Educated at Charterhouse school and Oxford, as was his friend and colleague **Richard Steele**. Fellow of Magdaken College, Oxford, 1698–1711. Gained notice of **John Dryden** as a result of his Latin poems. Traveled in Europe, 1699–1703, with a view to preparing himself for government service. Patronized by leading Whigs including **John, Baron Somers** and **Charles Montagu, first Earl of Halifax**. Member of the **Kit-Cat Club**. Celebrated the battle of Blenheim, and particularly the **Duke of Marlborough**, in his most popular poem *The Campaign* (1704). Another well-known work in verse was *A Letter from Italy* (1704). Under-Secretary of State, 1706; secretary to Lord Wharton, the Lord-Lieutenant of Ireland, 1709, where he had contacts with **Jonathan Swift**. Elected MP from 1708. His *Whig Examiner* papers in 1710 set out the contrary position to Swift's *Examiner*.

With the fall of the Whigs in 1710, Addison lost official favor. He had already contributed to Steele's **Tatler** and now joined with his friend in setting up the hugely influential *Spectator*. In 1713 his tragedy *Cato* enjoyed a tremendous success. After the arrival of **George I** in 1714, he returned to a place in the sun. In 1715–16, at the time of the **Jacobite rising**, he produced a pro-Hanoverian paper called *The Freeholder*. In 1716 he married the Countess of Warwick, whose son the **seventh Earl of Warwick** was a companion in pleasure of AP. As Secretary of State, 1717–18, he was regarded as going outside his area of natural competence, and steadily declining health made his resignation personally as well as politically necessary. His works were posthumously published by his protégé **Thomas Tickell** in 1721.

AP was probably introduced to Addison by Richard Steele in 1712, although several of the early mentors who surrounded AP were in fact well known to the other man. AP contributed to *The Spectator*, where Addison praised *An Essay on Criticism*. It was Addison who first encouraged AP to undertake his translation of the *Iliad* (*Prose* 1: 256). However, by the time the work started to appear, Addison had shifted his loyalties and supported the rival version of his friend Tickell. He seems also to have encouraged some of the pamphleteers in their assaults on AP. Although relations remained outwardly cordial, a deep split (based partly on political differences) had opened up. An attempt to mend fences came too late, in the shape of the verses *To Mr. Addison*, written perhaps in 1715 but not published until after the addressee's death. AP had already started to draft the damaging portrait of his onetime friend as **Atticus** and may have given Addison a sight of this passage in order to deter him from further acts of hostility. The lines were first published in 1722 and were reprinted by **Edmund Curll** in the following year. Later AP expanded the passage and included it in the *Miscellanies* in 1728. They then formed the basis of the character sketch of Atticus in the *Epistle to Arbuthnot*, ll. 193–214.

As this history suggests, the relations of Addison and AP were tangled. According to AP, "He was very kind to me at first but my bitter enemy afterwards." Some of the factors that played into this situation can be studied in comments made by AP to **Joseph Spence** (*Anecdotes* 1: 60–82). They include AP's slightly reserved encouragement of *Cato*; Addison's links with the circle at **Button's** coffeehouse, who wrote against AP; and his support of Tickell's projected translation (which AP suspected was actually carried out by Addison). There was also a "clerical" streak in Addison, which led **Jacob Tonson senior** to suggest that he would some day be made a bishop, and possibly a belief on AP's part that Addison and Steele were homosexual (see under **Steele**). In AP's estimation, Addison prided himself unduly on *Cato* and *The Campaign*, whereas in reality his forte lay in his prose, which he wrote with "so great ease, fluency and happiness." This last is a judgment with which most modern readers would concur. There were of course faults on both sides and a measure of jealousy and suspicion in both men. Despite all his reservations, AP recognized that Addison was a talented and important writer. The *Epistle to Augustus* describes the good influence he had exerted on English letters:

> And in our own (excuse some Courtly stains)
> No whiter page than Addison remains.
> He, from the taste obscene reclaims our Youth,
> And sets the Passions on the side of Truth;
> Forms the soft bosom with gentlest art,
> And pours each human Virtue in the heart. (*TE* 4: 213)

The fullest biography is P. Smithers, *The Life of Joseph Addison*, 2nd ed. (Oxford: Clarendon, 1968). On relations with AP, see Ault 101–27; and *Early Career* 114–48. For background on the break between the two men, see B.A. Goldgar, *The Curse of Party: Swift's Relations with Addison and Steele* (Lincoln: University of Nebraska Press, 1961). A useful bibliographical source is C.A. Knight, *Joseph Addison and Richard Steele: A Reference Guide 1730–1991* (New York: G.K. Hall, 1994).

Aden, John Michael (1918–93). Scholar at Vanderbilt University who worked principally on **Augustan satire**, including **Dryden**. His publications on AP include a number of articles, as well as two books: *Something Like Horace: Studies in the Art and Allusions of Pope's Horatian Satires* (1969) and *Pope's Once and Future Kings: Satire and Politics in the Early Career* (1978).

Aitken, George Atherton (1860–1917). Critic and biographer. He wrote a life of **Richard Steele**, 2 vols. (1889), and produced a pioneering study of the *Life and Works* of **John Arbuthnot** (1892). Among the many works he edited were the poems of **Thomas Parnell** (1894); novels of **Daniel Defoe**; *The Spectator*; and the *Journal to Stella* (1901). He also contributed many lives of figures in the world of AP to the *Dictionary of National Biography* and wrote sections on **Swift** and Arbuthnot for the *Cambridge History of English Literature*. Probably the best informed of the commentators on this period who were active at the turn of the nineteenth century.

Allen, Ralph (1693–1764). Businessman and philanthropist. He entered the postal service as a young man and came to **Bath** by 1710. In 1712, at the age of seventeen, he assumed responsibility for the cross-post system and in the years to come obtained a grant to control the mail in western England. Around 1730 he became an important supplier of stone to the building industry from his quarries on the edge of Bath. His stone was used in major London construction projects as well as in the growing city of Bath. Allen was active in a number of local enterprises and in charitable foundations such as Bath General Hospital.

It is not certain when Allen first met AP, although it was certainly no later than 1734. In 1736 he provided the money to issue the "authentic" edition of AP's letters. By this time he had embarked on his elegant new mansion, **Prior Park**, and AP was enlisted to advise on the creation of the gardens. In return Allen gave materials from his stone quarries to be used in AP's **grotto**. He also visited the poet at **Twickenham**. After Allen took up residence at Prior Park, AP became a frequent visitor, although a quarrel in 1743 involving **Martha Blount** led to a temporary estrangement. In AP's **will** he left his books to be shared between Allen and **William Warburton**. He also ordered a debt of £150 to be discharged, which Allen justifiably considered a serious underestimation of the financial help he had given the poet. Warburton was another regular visitor to Prior Park, and after AP's death he married Gertrude Tucker, Allen's niece and heiress. However, the most important literary figure in Allen's later life was **Henry Fielding**, who complimented his patron discreetly in *Joseph Andrews* (1742) and then made Allen the principal model for Squire Allworthy in *Tom Jones* (1749). Later Fielding dedicated *Amelia* (1751) to his patron. There were also many contacts between Allen and Henry's sister, the novelist Sarah Fielding (1710–68).

AP was cautious in bestowing public praise on Allen, who felt some awkwardness in the area of literary patronage. The poet's most open tribute occurs in the *Epilogue to the Satires*, where his friend is celebrated as "low-born," later amended to "humble," Allen, doing good "by stealth" (*TE* 4: 308). Over eighty letters from AP to Allen, written between 1736 and 1744, are known to survive.

See B. Boyce, *The Benevolent Man: A Life of Ralph Allen of Bath* (Cambridge, MA: Harvard University Press, 1967); and *Social Milieu* 204–40.

Amesbury. The seat of the **Duke** and **Duchess of Queensberry**, eight miles north of Salisbury in Wiltshire, where **John Gay** lived for long periods prior to his death in 1732. The house was designed by John Webb in the middle of the seventeenth century; it had three storeys with seven bays in addition to wings. AP visited the Duke and Duchess there in 1734 and 1743.

"Amica." Pseudonym of an unknown lady who preserved her letters and poems directed to AP, written c. 1737–44. This curious fanmail is preserved in private hands. It was first made public by **Maynard Mack** in *Life* 796–801.

ancestry. AP's ancestry has been traced back for several generations on both sides. On the maternal side, his **Turner** ancestors have been located as far as the fifteenth century. The family was settled around York until shortly before the poet's day. Some of the siblings of AP's mother, **Edith Pope**, clung to the Roman Catholic faith; others were Protestants. For a detailed account, see Rumbold (as below). On the paternal side, the Popes derived from Hampshire. AP's great-grandfather was an innkeeper at Andover, in the north of the county, and this man's son, an Anglican parson, held a living in the same district. The clergyman's son was AP's father, **Alexander Pope senior**, who was a Catholic convert. Edith was his second wife.

The most famous individual in the family tree was the painter **Samuel Cooper**, who married AP's maternal aunt. AP did not know any of his uncles, but Christiana Cooper, his godmother, survived until he was almost five and bequeathed him her books, pictures, and medals (subject to a life interest on the part of her sister Elizabeth). In turn, Elizabeth Turner lived until

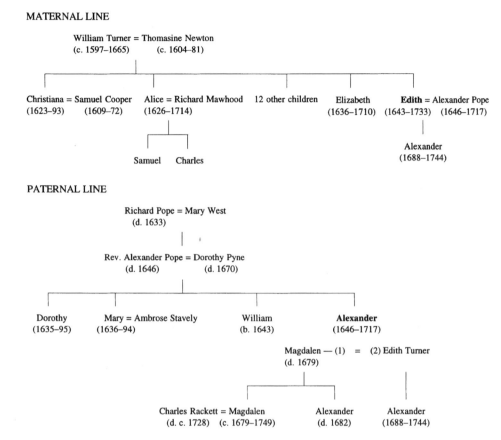

MATERNAL LINE

William Turner = Thomasine Newton
(c. 1597–1665) (c. 1604–81)

Christiana = Samuel Cooper   Alice = Richard Mawhood   12 other children   Elizabeth   **Edith** = Alexander Pope
(1623–93)   (1609–72)   (1626–1714)   (1636–1710) (1643–1733) (1646–1717)

Samuel   Charles

Alexander
(1688–1744)

PATERNAL LINE

Richard Pope = Mary West
(d. 1633)

Rev. Alexander Pope = Dorothy Pyne
(d. 1646)   (d. 1670)

Dorothy   Mary = Ambrose Stavely   William   **Alexander**
(1635–95)   (1636–94)   (b. 1643)   (1646–1717)

Magdalen — (1)   =   (2) Edith Turner
(d. 1679)

Charles Rackett = Magdalen   Alexander   Alexander
(d. c. 1728)   (c. 1679–1749)   (d. 1682)   (1688–1744)

Alexander reached manhood, and she was probably the "old aunt" who taught AP to read (*Anecdotes* 1: 8–9). Another sister, Jane, seems to have survived until after Christiana's death in 1693. From AP's aunt Alice descended a prominent Catholic family, the Mawhoods. In the poet's own lifetime, his most significant contacts were with the family of his half sister **Magdalen Rackett**.

In the table above, only the most directly relevant figures are included. For a more complete genealogical table, see *Life* 22–23; Rumbold 18.

See *Life* 3–27; and V. Rumbold, "Alexander Pope and the Religious Tradition of the Turners," *Recusant History*, 17 (1984), 17–37. A pioneering study by J. Hunter, *Pope: His Descent and Family Connections* (1859), London: privately printed, provides some of the basis for these sources.

Ancients and Moderns. A highly charged "quarrel" at the end of the seventeenth century

and the beginning of the eighteenth. It concerned the nature of intellectual achievement, as this was identified either with the triumphs of the classical world (passed on by the Renaissance) or with the discoveries of the modern world (drawing on the empiricist tradition established by Francis Bacon). The areas of learning covered ranged from science to philosophy and religion. Debate at first raged most fiercely in the French Academy, with **Nicolas Boileau** at the head of the "Ancients" ranged against Charles Perrault, now best known for his fairy tales. In England, partisans of the Ancients included Sir William Temple, patron of **Jonathan Swift**, as well as the "Christ Church wits" led by **Francis Atterbury** and William King. Devotees of the modern were Bernard de Fontenelle and Charles Perrault in France, while their number in England included **Richard Bentley** and William Wotton.

Swift's *The Battle of the Books* (1704) replays the quarrel in allegorical form, taking the side of Temple and his allies against Bentley. At the same time, Swift published *A Tale of a Tub*, another work over which the shadow of the battle lies heavily. AP deals with the issues frontally in *An Essay on Criticism* and mockingly in *The Dunciad*: in some regards, his translations of **Homer** also serve as a commentary on the issues.

See R.F. Jones, *Ancients and Moderns* (1936; rev. ed., St. Louis: Washington University Press, 1961); and J.M. Levine, *The Battle of the Books: History and Literature in the Augustan Age* (Ithaca: Cornell University Press, 1991), esp. chapters 6 and 7 on AP.

Anecdotes. A collection of reported conversations assembled by **Joseph Spence**. He gave the collection various names as time went by, including "Miscellaneous Thoughts, Anecdotes, and Characters of Books & Men," "Conversazione," and so on. The largest single group comprises material concerning AP, who was a close friend of Spence during the poet's later years. AP knew of Spence by 1726, and soon afterward the younger man started to record interviews with AP. Spence spent a number of years on the Continent, but when in England he continued to transcribe sessions with AP right up to the end of the poet's life. Spence provides a detailed description of his last days.

The manuscripts were made available at different times to **William Warburton**; **Owen Ruffhead**; **Joseph Warton**; **Samuel Johnson**; Hester Lynch Thrale; and the Duchess of Portland (daughter of AP's friend, the **second Earl of Oxford**). Among those Spence had consulted for information were **Anne Arbuthnot**, daughter of AP's friend; **Martha Blount**; **Lord Bolingbroke**; **William Cheselden**; **Lady Mary Wortley Montagu**; **Colley Cibber**; **Nathaniel Hooke**; and **Edward Young**.

Extensive manuscripts reporting these conversations survive. The most important materials came down in the care of Bishop Robert Lowth and passed to Samuel Weller Singer (1783–1858), who published a selection in 1820 as *Anecdotes, Observations, and Characters of Books and Men*. They were later acquired by the Duke of Newcastle. A transcript of one manuscript had been made for an earlier member of the Duke's family: portions of this were copied out in 1794 by the great Shakespearean scholar Edmond Malone (1741–1812), and after his death they formed the basis for another selection, also published in 1820.

The Newcastle manuscripts were sold in 1938 to the scholar **James M. Osborn**. He devoted much of the next thirty years to preparing an authoritative edition, published in 1966. This supplants all previous versions. The edition also uses manuscripts preserved at the Huntington Library, the British Museum, and elsewhere.

Along with AP's own correspondence, the *Anecdotes* represent the fullest source of biographic knowledge on the poet. They exhibit his views, often candid and indiscreet, on a wide range of literary and personal matters. Osborn's edition is organized topically and enables readers to see how the poet's opinions sometimes developed over time. No other major figure in English literature before the time of Boswell left so many intimate traces of his or her being—not even diarists such as Samuel Pepys and John Evelyn, who seldom analyze their artistic and intellectual preferences in detail, however closely they narrate events.

Spence did not confine himself to AP. His anecdotes cover many other individuals, notably **Dryden, Addison**, Cibber, and Young. There are important entries on **gardening** and on figures whom Spence met during his foreign travels.

See J. Spence, *Observations, Anecdotes, and Characters of Books and Men*, ed. J.M. Osborn, 2 vols. (Oxford: Clarendon, 1966).

Anne, Queen (1665–1714). The last Stuart monarch, daughter of **James II** and Anne Hyde and half sister of the **Pretender**. She was firmly Protestant in her sympathies, and her rooted affection for the Church of England led her naturally to support moderate Tory measures and to eschew the cause of **Jacobites**. However, her reign was dogged by serious divisions over the succession from the time she came to the throne in 1702. The loss of all her twelve live-born children meant that a foreign princess, the Electress of Hanover, stood in line to succeed. Deep political and social conflicts were mirrored in the party battles of this period. The long-running **War of the Spanish Succession** invaded many areas of domestic politics, and the Union with Scotland in 1707 provoked further dissension. Anne tried to keep a steady course through her ministers, including the Whiggishly inclined Lord Godolphin and the **Duke of Marlborough**, as well as Robert Harley (later the **first Earl of Oxford**), but the climate remained unstable until her death. In 1682 she had married Prince George of Denmark (1653–1708), a well-intentioned but ineffectual figure.

There is no evidence that AP knew the Queen personally. However, he moved on close terms with the leading members of the **Harley administration** and, but for his Catholic faith, would have been acceptable at court. His poem *Windsor-Forest* offers a review of major aspects of the Queen's reign, celebrating her success (as the Tories viewed it) in achieving the **Treaty of Utrecht**. This is the only time AP composed an unreserved panegyric to any monarch. She appears as the Stuart monarch reigning over a land of peace and plenty; as the Diana-like guardian of the forest and the seas; as the sovereign who favors men of virtue; and above all as "great Anna," who decrees that peace shall supplant war and banishes discord. She is, too, the "*British* QUEEN" who will revive the glories of the Elizabethan age and preside over a beneficent world order based on trade. Sadly, all AP's hopeful prophecies came to nothing. Little more than a year after *Windsor-Forest* appeared, the Queen died on 1 August 1714, worn out by persistent ill health and the cares of her troubled reign.

See D. Green, *Queen Anne* (London: Collins, 1970); E. Gregg, *Queen Anne* (London: Routledge, 1980). Episodes of direct relevance to AP are described in J. Sutherland, *Background for Queen Anne* (London: Methuen, 1939). Day-to-day life and politics are illustrated from contemporary newspapers in W.B. Ewald, Jr., *The Newsmen of Queen Anne* (Oxford: Blackwell, 1956).

Annus Mirabilis. Subtitled *Or, The Wonderful Effects of the Approaching Conjunction of the Planets Jupiter, Mars, and Saturn.* An eight-page pamphlet, attributed to "Abraham Gunter Philo., a Well-wisher to the Mathematicks," bearing the imprint of **James Roberts**, and published in December 1722, with a Dublin reprint following. Sometimes assigned to **John Arbuthnot**, perhaps on the grounds indicated by **George Sherburn**: "Its medical details suggest, but do not establish, collaboration with Arbuthnot" (*Early Career* 272). There is nothing in the text beyond the reach of AP's medical knowledge, and the vein of humor is distinctly his own. Arbuthnot may have been a collaborator.

The work is a parody of astrological predictions along the lines of **John Partridge** and draws on a particular strand of providential prophecy going back to **Dryden**'s poem on the year 1666, also called *Annus Mirabilis*. In this case the prodigious happenings relate to a sudden universal sex change, causing embarrassments to members of each gender. There are abundant opportunities for sexual innuendo and obscene double entendre, all duly taken. The use of "Abraham Gunter Philo[math]" as putative author recalls the use by the Scriblerians elsewhere of **Esdras Barnivelt** and **E. Parker**. According to a notice at the end of the *Memoirs of Martin Scriblerus*, it was Martin himself who was responsible for *Annus Mirabilis*.

Anstis, John (1669–1744). The leading heraldic figure of his day, who became Garter King of Arms in 1718 after a long battle with **Sir John Vanbrugh**, a less qualified herald supported by the Whig establishment. Anstis was a Tory MP for Cornish boroughs controlled by **George Granville**. In September 1715 he was arrested for suspected involvement in the Jacobite plans for a rising in the West Country, led by Lansdowne and **Sir William Wyndham**. He was released soon afterward, having allegedly destroyed incriminating evidence.

Anstis was a notable antiquarian scholar who helped **Humfrey Wanley** in assembling for AP's friend the **second Earl of Oxford** the splendid **Harleian library**, to which he gave a large collection of deeds in 1716. He subscribed to over thirty books by his fellow Jacobite **Tho-**

mas **Hearne**. It was he who provided a copy of the grant of arms to John Shakespeare (father of the dramatist), when AP was at work on his **Shakespeare edition**. AP refers to him twice in the *Imitations of Horace* in a neutral manner, and it is likely the relations of the two men were distant if friendly.

See A. Wagner and A.L. Rowse, *John Anstis: Garter King of Arms* (London: HMSO, 1992).

antiquarians. Like his friends in the **Scriblerus Club**, AP enjoyed mocking the pretensions of foolish dabblers in subjects such as antiquarianism, archeology, collecting, and the pursuit of virtù, that is, the cult of fine objects of art. His regular targets included men like the doctor and geologist **John Woodward** and the collector of artistic trophies, the **ninth Earl of Pembroke**. A broad sweep of such individuals, ranging from virtuosi to numismatists and butterfly collectors, can be found in Book 4 of *The Dunciad*. A similar vein of satire is found in some of the collaborative works, notably the *Memoirs of Martinus Scriblerus*, where the hero is a pretender to learning in medicine, science and antiquities.

All this is true, yet AP himself had some of the instincts and interests of these men. His own **grotto** resembled in some ways the cabinets of curiosities that were created by men like Woodward. Moreover, he was on good terms with collectors such as **Dr. Richard Mead** and **Sir Hans Sloane**, while the coin expert Sir Andrew Fountaine (possibly the model for "Annius" in *The Dunciad*) was a longtime friend of **Swift**. AP's own interest in coins went back many years: see also *To Mr. Addison*. The explanation seems to be that he was working out a somewhat conflicted attitude and in some manner contrived a strategy to allow himself to pursue his own tastes without embarrassment. By exposing the absurdities of the collectors in *The Dunciad*, AP was able to cleanse his own doings at **Twickenham** of any imputation of antiquarian folly.

For background, see G. Parry, *The Trophies of Time: English Antiquarians of the Seventeenth Century* (Oxford: Oxford University Press, 1995); and B.M. Benedict, *Curiosity: A Cultural History of Early Modern Inquiry* (Chicago: University of Chicago Press, 2001).

Arbuthnot, Anne (d. 1751). Daughter of **Dr. John Arbuthnot** and a close friend of AP in later years. She visited the poet shortly before his death. AP used a legacy of £100 that he received in the will of Alderman **John Barber** in 1741 to send her to **Bath** for the sake of health. He left £200 to Anne in his own **will**, to be paid after the death of **Martha Blount**, who in the event outlived her. She gave **Joseph Spence** a number of anecdotes for his collection.

Arbuthnot, George (1703–79). Son of **Dr. John Arbuthnot** who after the death of his father became one of AP's closest friends. He assisted the poet in a number of business affairs, especially in contacts with members of the book trade. A lawyer, he had an office in Castle Yard, Holborn, adjoining the main legal quarters of London. He was clerk to the King's Remembrancer in the Exchequer, dealing with the recovery of debts due to the Crown. He was unmarried. George resisted the publication of spurious works later issued as written by his father. At least twice he accompanied AP on visits to **Bath**. He acted as one of the executors for AP's **will** and drew up in July 1745 a list of the securities AP owned at his death. The list is preserved at **Mapledurham** (see *Corr* 4: 340). AP left George £200 after the decease of **Martha Blount**. Fourteen letters that AP wrote to him survive.

Arbuthnot, Dr. John (1667–1735). Scottish physician and writer. Studied at **Oxford** before graduating M.D. at St. Andrews University in 1696. Taught mathematics in London. FRS, 1704. Attended on Prince George of Denmark and gained the favor of his wife, **Queen Anne**. Physician to the Queen, 1709, with lodgings in St James's Palace, and attended her in her last illness, 1714. Lost favor under the new regime. Lived subsequently on Dover Street and Cork Street off Piccadilly. Reappointed physician to

Queen Caroline in 1730. His patients included **William Congreve**.

Arbuthnot was a man of broad cultivation who wrote on many subjects. He published works on probability, ancient units of measure, mathematics, diet, geology, and other topics. He was well versed in music and served as one of the directors of the Royal Academy of Music: Here he came into close contact with **Handel** and the **Duke of Chandos** at **Cannons** and **Burlington House**. His main literary forte lay in satire and witty polemics, which brought him into a collision with figures such as the physician **John Woodward**. In 1712 he produced his best-known work, *The History of John Bull*, as well as a shorter piece, *The Art of Political Lying*, both of which were much admired by his friend **Jonathan Swift**, whom he met about 1711.

In politics Arbuthnot seems always to have been a Tory. His father, a minister in Kincardineshire, was ejected for resistance to the Presbyterian orthodoxy that came in after the arrival of **William III**. His brother **Robert Arbuthnot** was an important figure in the financial affairs of the **Pretender**, acting as banker for the Stuart supporters; while another brother, George, took part in the **Jacobite rising**. However, the doctor remained aloof from the movement, and his precise sympathies are hard to gauge.

In all probability, AP was introduced to Arbuthnot by Swift in 1713. They were soon good friends and linked before long in a common purpose with the establishment of the **Scriblerus Club**. At the outset Arbuthnot seems to have been the most active member of the group in prosecuting their main enterprise, the composition of what became *The Memoirs of Martin Scriblerus*: indeed, his colleagues sometimes addressed the doctor under the name of Scriblerus. He was almost certainly responsible for much of the medical and scientific satire in this work, although finally it was left to AP to put the material into shape and publish it. In addition, Arbuthnot wrote some shorter Scriblerian items, some printed in the *Miscellanies* several years later. He had a hand in the collectively written farce *Three Hours after Marriage*, in which AP and **John Gay** also took some part.

Humorous, humane, and articulate, Arbuthnot was one of AP's most respected friends, as well as a trusted medical adviser. Only about twenty letters that passed between them are known to survive, fewer than in the case of Swift (who was, of course, settled at a much greater distance from London). The doctor's skills in diplomacy sometimes came in useful when AP was embroiled in a dispute. He was a subscriber to the *Iliad* and the *Odyssey*. In *A Farewell to London* (1715) the poet makes his adieu to "Arbuthnot's raillery / On every learned Sot" (*TE* 6: 129). The epitaph to Colonel **Francis Charteris** that is cited in a note to the *Epistle to Bathurst* was by Arbuthnot (*TE* 3.ii: 85–86). He may also have written *Virgilius Restauratus*, which was attached as an appendix to *The Dunciad*. He, **Thomas Parnell**, and AP seem to have collaborated on the *Origine of Sciences*.

It cannot be doubted that AP's friendship with Arbuthnot extended his social contacts. The doctor had known individuals such as **George Clarke**, the **Earl of Peterborough**, and **Sir Hans Sloane** before they had come into the poet's orbit. As his final illness took hold, Arbuthnot wrote a letter on 17 July 1734, offering a "Last Request" that AP would continue to write satire but would "study more to reform than chastise" (*Corr* 3: 417). It is not surprising that AP addressed one of his most personal and heartfelt poems to his longtime friend. The *Epistle to Arbuthnot* chiefly celebrates the physician, whose "Art and Care" had prolonged the poet's life, but at the end the verse movingly evokes the frail human being, whose last days will (AP hopes) be "social, chearful, and serene" (*TE* 4: 127). This phrase precisely captures some of Arbuthnot's most noteworthy qualities. He survived publication of the *Epistle* by no more than eight weeks. He died on 27 February 1735: AP and the **Earl of Chesterfield** had visited him on the previous evening. AP was grief stricken, but it is typical that he managed to write a letter of sympathy to the doctor's son, **George Arbuthnot**, that focuses not on his own distress but on the needs of the dead man's children (*Corr* 3: 452). Others such as Swift expressed their sorrow at the news (*Corr* 3: 456). AP's poem provides a worthy monument to a long and intimate alliance, as it meditates on family and friendship. In his obituary list AP describes him as "a very learned man, remarkable for his honesty and piety" (*EC* 1: x). Arbuthnot's was among a group of small portraits framed together at **Twickenham** (*Garden and City* 248).

Serious work on Arbuthnot must still begin with two older works: G.A. Aitken, *The Life and Works of John Arbuthnot* (Oxford: Clarendon, 1892; reprint, New York: Russell & Russell, 1968); and L.M. Beattie, *John Arbuthnot: Mathematician and Satirist* (Cambridge, MA: Harvard University Press, 1935; reprint, New York; Russell & Russell, 1967). A more recent introduction is R.C. Steensma, *Dr. John Arbuthnot* (Boston: Gale, 1979).

Arbuthnot, Robert (1669–1741). Brother of **Dr. John Arbuthnot**. A prosperous banker in Rouen and Paris who was on friendly terms with AP and **Jonathan Swift**. AP was impressed by his mercurial nature (*Corr* 3: 253). Robert was an undisguised Jacobite, who helped in fund-raising campaigns for the **Pretender**. He subscribed to the *Odyssey* and to the poems of **John Gay**. Another brother, George Arbuthnot (1688–1733), was an army officer who seems to have taken part in the **Jacobite rising** in 1715. He later married Peggy, sister of the singer **Anastasia Robinson**. Subsequently George worked as supercargo in an East India Company vessel and died in China.

Argyll, John Campbell, second Duke of (1680–1743). Often spelled "Argyle." Soldier and politician. As Lord High Commissioner of the Scottish Parliament, he played an important role in furthering the Union of the two Parliaments in 1707. He served under the **Duke of Marlborough** at Ramillies and Malplaquet but later broke with the Duke. He gained further advancement under the **Harley administration**. In another timely move at the death of **Queen Anne**, he proposed the appointment of the **Duke of Shrewsbury** as Lord Treasurer,

helping to ensure a smooth transition to the new Hanoverian dynasty. As commander in chief of the forces in Scotland, he was charged with crushing the **Jacobite rising** of 1715–16; his success in holding at bay the larger Jacobite army at Sheriffmuir helped to destroy Stuart hopes. During the reign of **George I** he went in and out of favor, mainly because of his attachment to the cause of the Prince of Wales (later **George II**) against his father, the King. He eventually in 1736 achieved the rank of field marshal. In later years, he became an ally of the **opposition to Walpole**.

AP had numerous and complicated relations with Argyll. On the whole these are not reflected very clearly in his major poetry, except for a stirring couplet on "ARGYLE, the State's whole Thunder born to wield, / And shake alike the Senate and the Field" in the *Epilogue to the Satires* (*TE* 4: 318). He figures directly or indirectly in many of the shorter poems, as, for example, *The Court Ballad*. The two men were certainly on good terms around 1717, when AP stayed with Argyll. A supposed hostile reference in *The Sixth Epistle of the First Book of Horace Imitated* (*TE* 4: 243) is not very likely to be to the Duke. In later years the pair were in correspondence: AP visited **Adderbury**, the Duke's seat, in 1739 and may have written a poem there (see *On Lying in the Earl of Rochester's Bed at Atterbury*). Earlier, in 1726–28, **James Gibbs** had designed for Argyll a large house at Sudbrook, across the Thames from **Twickenham**. Moreover, the Duke's brother and successor, the **Earl of Islay**, was another peer close to AP, as well as a neighbor of the poet at **Whitton**. It was Argyll who most quickly perceived on the first night of *The Beggar's Opera* that the play would have a resounding success: a tribute, as AP remarked, to his acute sense of the public taste (see *Anecdotes* 1: 107–8).

There is as yet no adequate study of AP's dealings with the Duke: See the essay "Pope and Argyle" in Ault 172–85 for some details. In the same way, an up-to-date and scholarly biography is needed. Meanwhile, see P. Dickson, *Red John of the Battles: John, 2nd Duke of Argyll and lst Duke of Greenwich 1680–1743* (London: Sidgwick and Jackson, 1973).

Aristarchus. The character of a pedantic verbal critic in *The Dunciad* (4: 198–274) in a passage satirizing undue emphasis in study of the classics on the literal and the trivial, rather than broad humane issues. The name is taken from a Greek scholar who was head of the Alexandrian Library in the middle of the second century B.C. He is regarded as one of the founders of textual scholarship, especially in his work on **Homer**. AP's characterization is based chiefly on the redoubtable figure of **Richard Bentley**.

Arnold, Matthew (1822–88). Poet and critic. One of the most influential Victorian commentators on AP. He discussed the Homeric translations in his book *On Translating Homer* (1861), faulting AP because "he does not render [Homer's] plainness of style and diction" and because he unduly ornaments the descriptive passages in the original. A more general assessment appears in his essay "The Study of Poetry," the introduction to *The English Poets*, ed. T.H. Ward (1880), reprinted in *Essays in Criticism: Second Series* (1889). Arnold describes **Dryden** as "the puissant and glorious founder" and "Pope as the splendid high priest" of what he terms "our age of prose and reason, of our excellent and indispensable eighteenth century." Their verse fails the test of ultimate value, which calls for a "criticism of life," deriving from a "high seriousness" on the part of the writer. Effective within their own limits, Dryden and AP are excluded from the truly great. "Though they may in a certain sense be masters of the art of versification, Dryden and Pope are not classics of our poetry, they are classics of our prose."

Art of Sinking, The. More formally, Περὶ βάθους: *or, Martinus Scriblerus His Treatise of the Art in Sinking in Poetry*. It first appeared in the so-called "last" volume (actually the third of four) of the Pope–Swift **Miscellanies**, published on 8 March 1728 (dated 1727). The work occupies the opening pages of this volume: It replaced *The Dunciad*, which was originally

planned to appear in this book for the first time. It was reprinted a number of times and eventually found its way into AP's *Works* in 1741. At this date the words "Written in the Year 1727" were added to the title.

It is likely that the treatise has its origins in the early schemes of the **Scriblerus Club** around 1713–14, when the members projected "an account of the works of the unlearned." It is possible that each of the group contributed something to the works in its infancy. However, nothing emerged for the next fifteen years; and it is certain that AP was the main author of *The Art of Sinking* in its published form. The reasons are: (1) AP oversaw publication of the *Miscellanies* and had sole control of what went into these volumes; (2) the work shows a consistent overlap with the themes and ideas of *The Dunciad*; and (3) the individual targets are essentially those that AP, rather than his colleagues, had come to fix on as his own. In particular, it was AP who had devoted years of his life to translating **Homer** and who had made a special study of the theory of the epic. There is some sketchy evidence, produced by AP's opponents, suggesting that **Swift** never saw the item before publication and that **Arbuthnot** wished to reduce the amount of personal satire in it (see *TE* 5: xvi).

The Art of Sinking is a cod version of a familiar Augustan genre, the "art" or guide to a given subject. Specifically, it parodies the influential Greek treatise, *Of the Sublime*, attributed to an unidentified author of the first century A.D. known as Longinus. Since a translation into French by **Boileau** in 1674, this had become a classic work of criticism and provided a touchstone for impassioned or emotional writing of all kinds. AP does not follow very closely the organization of the Greek work, but he systematically undercuts its definition of the "profound" (= deep, i.e., lofty) by describing the way to achieve "profound" effects in literature (= abysmal, obscure, unfathomable).

The work consists of sixteen chapters. Of these the first twelve constitute the direct parody of a rhetorical treatise along the lines of Longinus. The remaining four were described as an "Appendix" in the first edition, and they represent more general advice on how to produce bad literature. Chapter 13 embodies "A Project for the Advancement of the Bathos," suggesting some institutional ways of promoting bathos in the nation. Chapter 15, "A Receipt to Make an Epic Poem," is taken almost whole from an early essay by AP in *The Guardian* (1713). The last chapter contains "A Project for the Advancement of the Stage," in which AP airs some of his prejudices on theatrical matters.

The earlier chapters provide amusing illustrations of bad writing, produced by pretension, ignorance, bad taste, and general ineptitude. AP divides the "profound" authors into various classes, distinguished by their characteristic failings—example, parrots (plagiarists) and porpoises (clumsy authors addicted to big words). Abundant quotation is provided to illustrate the ways in which poets can fall into "bathos" (in the modern sense), and the use of initials purposely fails to disguise the identity of some of AP's favorite butts, such as **Sir Richard Blackmore**, **Ambrose Philips**, **John Dennis**, **Laurence Eusden**, and **Leonard Welsted**.

See the edition by E.L. Steeves (New York: King's Crown Press, 1952; reprint, New York: Russell & Russell, 1968); as well as *Prose* 2: 171–276.

Ashe, Sir James (1683–1733). A baronet, son of a prominent Royalist, who lived on one of the largest estates in **Twickenham**, later known as Cambridge House. The mansion originally dated from c. 1610–20; it was demolished in the 1930s, but most of the land had already gone to construct the development known as Cambridge Park. It stood not far from the Middlesex bank of the Thames, just above **Richmond**. Only one letter survives from Ashe to AP, dating perhaps from 1725, at the time of the poet's involvement with the proposed monument to **Sir Godfrey Kneller**. Ashe was a churchwarden of **Twickenham parish church** and one of the trustees for its rebuilding when the chancel collapsed in 1713.

Atossa. Character sketch of a capricious, emotionally violent, and quarrelsome woman in AP's *Epistle to a Lady*, which has caused controversy of various kinds ever since it was written. In the form now known, it first appeared in a suppressed version of the poem prepared in 1744 (see **deathbed edition**). However, the passage is also found, with a slightly different text, in a single surviving copy of the *Works*, vol. 2 (1735), which was privately presented by AP to **Frederick, Prince of Wales** in 1738. This volume contained over eighty lines of daring satire on contemporary women (some relating to **Queen Caroline**) that had been omitted from early printings of the poem and cancel leaves substituted. It is not certain what stage of composition is represented by the additional lines, but they may come from an early draft. After the suppression of the 1744 edition, the lines on Atossa appeared in a pamphlet published two years later by **Lord Bolingbroke**, who claimed that they referred to Sarah Churchill, **Duchess of Marlborough**. He also accused AP of accepting £1,000 from the Duchess to keep the verses out of the public eye, yet allowing them to creep into the world. This raises many problems. There is no evidence that such a bribe was offered or taken. Moreover, AP himself did not actually publish the deathbed edition, merely distributing a very few copies to friends (none survive). Finally, it is by no means certain that the lines ever related to Sarah. From 1751 the passage was restored in editions of AP's *Works*.

The identity of "Atossa," if indeed she has a single model, remains open to conjecture. It is clear that some contemporaries besides Bolingbroke thought they were aimed at the Duchess of Marlborough, even though she had established good relations with AP by the end of his life. The other candidate is Katharine Sheffield, **Duchess of Buckinghamshire**, who has been generally supported in more recent years. One reason for this is the choice of name: Atossa was a Persian princess, daughter of Cyrus the Great and sister of Cambyses. This appears to glance at Katharine Sheffield, who was the illegitimate daughter of **James II** and a half sister of the **Pretender**. She is also a more plausible candidate in that (contrary to the case with Sarah) her relations with AP had declined markedly in the 1730s. Moreover, she had died in 1743, mentally unstable. It would make much more sense for AP to set about releasing the lines after her death, no matter at what date they were composed: again, this consideration does not apply in the case of the Duchess of Marlborough, who outlived AP by four months. There are signs that AP may have composed a satire on Sarah, as he did on her late husband, perhaps in the guise of "Orsini"; and it is possible that Bolingbroke had seen such an item in AP's papers. However, as the character sketch stands, it appears to relate much more closely to the Duchess of Buckinghamshire. A story related by **William Warburton**, which cannot be corroborated, has it that the poet read the character of Atossa to the Duchess of Marlborough "as that of the Duchess of Buckingham." However, Sarah said "she knew very well whom he meant" (*Anecdotes* 1: 166).

The complicated issues involved are explored in *TE* 3.ii: 159–70. See also V.A. Dearing, "The Prince of Wales's Set of Pope's Works," *Harvard Library Bulletin*, 4 (1950), 320–38, partially reprinted in *EA* 368–81; and *Life* 746–50.

Atterbury, Francis (1662–1732). Churchman. Educated at Westminster school and Christ Church, **Oxford**, where he became a tutor. Took orders, 1687. Engaged in the controversy over the letters of Phalaris, which sparked the contest of the **Ancients and Moderns** in England. He rose to prominence as a preacher and as a leading figure in Convocation, the Parliament of the Church of England. Doctor of Divinity, 1701. Dean of Carlisle, 1704, and of Christ Church, 1712. Despite some reservations on the part of **Queen Anne**, he was promoted in 1713 to the important posts of Bishop of Rochester and Dean of Westminster, which gave him jurisdiction over the Abbey. At the time of the **Hanoverian accession**, he flirted with the possibility of leading a Jacobite coup but acquiesced in the new regime. However, he continued to hold communications with the Stuart court, as at the time of a planned invasion in 1717. Five years later, shortly after Atterbury had conducted the funeral service for the **Duke of Marlborough**, he was arrested for his share in a new attempt to restore the **Pretender** to the throne (see **Atterbury plot**). He was imprisoned in the Tower of London, where AP visited him. The House of Lords mounted a show trial against him in May 1723. Despite some dubious forms of evidence, the prosecutors had little difficulty in establishing Atterbury's guilt, and a verdict was given against the bishop. He was deprived of all his offices and banished from the country. In June he left for the Continent, and he spent most of his remaining years in France, initially in the service of the Stuart court.

AP may have met Atterbury through a friend such as **Swift**, who had been a neighbor at Chelsea in 1711. The prelate's uncompromising High Church politics made him a controversial figure even in Tory circles, but AP treated him with something approaching reverence. The first surviving item in their correspondence is a letter from Atterbury dated 8 November 1717, in which he urges AP to convert to the Anglican faith. AP wrote a respectful but firm letter declining to take this step (*Corr* 1: 451–54). After this the two men kept in regular touch, even when the bishop went into exile—though this was technically a felony. AP sent him many poems in manuscript and wrote some touching letters of sympathy. When Atterbury came in front of the Lords, AP was called to give evidence, which he did in the face of extreme nervousness. After the bishop's death, AP wrote an epitaph jointly on Atterbury and his beloved daughter, Mary Morice (see **William Morice**), which was first printed in 1735 but then canceled in the press: it first appeared in 1751. In his register of departed friends, AP noted "a man renowned in all branches of knowledge, of great courage, who was banished from England in the year 1723." About forty letters survive between the two men.

See G.V. Bennett, *The Tory Crisis in Church and State, 1688–1730: The Career of Francis*

Atterbury, Bishop of Rochester (Oxford: Clarendon, 1975), which is in effect a biography of the public man.

Atterbury plot. The name given to a scheme to invade Britain and install the **Pretender** on the throne. A leading role in England was taken by AP's close friend **Francis Atterbury**, the Bishop of Rochester. Also involved were a number of Tory peers such as Lord North and Gray, **Lord Orrery**, and the **Earl of Strafford**; on the French side, **George Granville**, Lord Lansdowne, occupied an important role along with the **Duke of Ormonde**. The plot was discovered and suspects watched by government agents directed by **Robert Walpole**. On 24 August 1722 Atterbury was arrested and sent to the Tower of London, where he was visited by AP. His trial before the House of Lords took place on 6–11 May 1723. AP was called to give evidence, and despite considerable nervousness, he managed to speak to the Lords on 8 May on behalf of the bishop. However, the House convicted Atterbury on 16 May, sending him into exile. AP had a final meeting with his friend on 17 June, prior to the bishop's journey to France. In the years to come, AP kept up a correspondence with Atterbury and often celebrated his friend in verse.

The episode brought out conflicting feelings in the nation. Loyal Hanoverians congratulated Walpole on his efficiency in rooting out what was undoubtedly a serious attempt to overturn the regime. Those identified with Tory or Stuart sympathies deplored the use of informers to obtain convictions against some of the minor figures, including the lawyer Christopher Layer, who was executed. The affair cast its shadow on *Gulliver's Travels* three years later.

See G.V. Bennett, *The Tory Crisis in Church and State, 1688–1730: The Career of Francis Atterbury, Bishop of Rochester* (Oxford: Clarendon, 1975).

Atticus. The name given to **Joseph Addison** in AP's ruthless portrait of his former friend and colleague. The earliest version of the lines, written around 1716, does not use the oblique form of naming and refers to "A—n." This version, which survives in a manuscript text, was first published in a newspaper on 15 November 1722, three years after Addison's death. It was reprinted in the following year by **Edmund Curll**. Later the poet regretted that it had been leaked to the world (*Anecdotes* 1: 73). AP kept on tinkering with the lines and published a longer version in the *Miscellanies* (1728). With minor alterations this appeared in its most familiar form as part of the *Epistle to Arbuthnot* in 1735.

AP borrows the name from Titus Pomponius Atticus (110–32 B.C.), the friend and correspondent of Cicero. Atticus was a neutral in politics who managed to stay on good terms with both Antony and Emperor Augustus. He was himself a writer, although his works are lost. Most relevantly, he kept a staff of slaves whom he employed to prepare manuscripts that he then circulated. But it is obvious that the sound and shape of the name suited AP's immediate poetic needs.

Auden, Wystan Hugh (1907–73). Poet and critic. Although Auden wrote only one sustained essay on AP, there are many references both in his verse and in his prose. In his *Letter to Lord Byron* (1937), Auden gives a brief and polemical account of the history of English poetry. AP and the dissenting hymn writer Isaac Watts (1674–1748) are seen as representative of their age, in their close relation to their readers: "Each poet knew for whom he had to write." (Wittily, Auden mentions "Two arts as different as Jews and Turks," recalling AP's favorite coupling of these words.)

Auden's essay on AP originally appeared in *From Anne to Victoria*, ed. B. Dobrée (London: Cassell, 1937), 89–107. It was reprinted in *Essays in Criticism*, 1 (1951), 208–24; and in *EA* 22–37. The discussion ranges across AP's personality, the age in which he lived, the philosophical and theological assumptions of the age (here the argument overlaps with that of the *Letter to Lord Byron*), the status of authors, the **heroic couplet**, and other stylistic features of AP's verse.

Augustanism. A contended term, especially in recent times. From the era of **Dryden**, comparisons with the age of the Emperor Augustus in Rome (27 B.C.–A.D. 14) had generally carried positive overtones, evoking comparisons with the achievement of **Virgil**, **Ovid**, and **Horace**. A more skeptical attitude developed after the **Hanoverian accession**, and Tories in particular seized on the fact that the full name of **George II** was Georg August, or "George Augustus." It was AP more than anyone else who helped to undermine the "Augustan" pretensions of his kingship, with his ironic encomium of George in his *Epistle to Augustus*. Many of AP's other works are relevant to the issue: see in particular the *Epistle to Burlington*. Others continued to see the reign of Augustus in a favorable light, and as late as 1759 Oliver Goldsmith could still happily apply the expression "The Augustan Age in England" to the reign of **Queen Anne**. In casual usage the concept is applied to the period between Dryden and **Johnson** and connotes a variety of literary qualities—regularity, balance, allusive classicism, and humane learning, for example. Its opposite typically lies in the Romantic or Gothic and sometimes in the plebeian. The term is more seldom applied to **Defoe** than to **Swift**, and to Samuel Richardson than to **Fielding**.

For differing views of the historical bearings of the term, see H. Weinbrot, *Augustus Caesar in "Augustan" England: The Decline of a Classical Norm* (Princeton, NJ: Princeton University Press, 1978); and H. Erskine-Hill, *The Augustan Idea in English Literature* (London: Arnold, 1983).

Augustan satire. A useful if imprecise term, employed to cover a variety of work in prose and verse, written from approximately 1660 to 1760. It can most easily be defined by specifying the authors most commonly covered under this rubric. The first great master was **John Dryden**, and other Restoration writers such as Samuel Butler, the Earl of Rochester, and John Oldham are often included. A second phase begins with **Jonathan Swift** and embraces AP along with other members of the **Scriblerus Club**, that is, **Arbuthnot**, **Gay**, and **Parnell**. In the last phase the mode extends to satiric novels

and may be seen in the works of **Fielding** and (at the end of the period) Laurence Sterne. Parallels can be detected with the graphic satire of **William Hogarth**.

The term has obviously been affected by the usage **Augustanism** and tends to be applied to polished literature with high formal values. It indicates a fondness for parody, **imitation** of classical models, and play with generic conventions, as exemplified by **mock-heroic**. Less frequently, the concept is extended to cover rougher and more extemporaneous writing, as exemplified by some of the satires of Andrew Marvell, the poems of **Defoe**, and the fiction of Tobias Smollett. So far the expression has not generally been applied to women writers such as Jane Collier, although **Lady Mary Wortley Montagu** may be included on the basis of her methods and generic choices (see *Court Eclogues*). AP's achievement is central to the course of Augustan satire, most obviously in *The Rape of the Lock*, *The Dunciad*, the *Moral Essays*, and the *Imitations of Horace*.

An excellent introduction is I. Jack, *Augustan Satire: Intention and Idiom in English Poetry, 1660–1750* (Oxford: Clarendon, 1952).

Ault, Norman (1880–1950). Mainly known as an anthologist who also worked as artist, he became one of the leading Popian scholars of his time. His contributions include an edition of AP's *Prose Works*, vol. 1 (1936), and of a collection AP issued in 1717 as *Pope's Own Miscellany* (1935). He coedited with **John Butt** the *Minor Works* for the **Twickenham edition**, vol. 6 (1954). Studies by Ault that still retain a good deal of interest were assembled as *New Light on Pope* (1949).

Author to be Lett, An. A pamphlet of twelve pages written by **Richard Savage**, published in 1729. The subtitle runs: "Being a Proposal Humbly Address'd to the Consideration of the Knights, Esquires, Gentlemen, and other . . . Members of the . . . Society of the Bathos. By . . . Iscariot Hackney." The supposed writer's name suggests the treacherous dealings of unscrupulous "authors for hire." An amusing satire on **Grub Street**, the pamphlet anatomizes the methods of the notorious publisher **Curll**, who employs "Hackney" to do his dirty work: "It was in his service that I wrote Obscenity and Profaneness, under the Names of Pope and Swift. Sometimes I was Mr. Joseph Gay. . . . I abridg'd Histories and Travels, translated from the French, what they never wrote, and was expert at finding out new Titles for old Books." In the pages of this work, as **Samuel Johnson** noted, "are related many secret histories of the petty writers of that time, but sometimes mixed with ungenerous reflections on their birth, their circumstances, or those of their relations; nor can it be denied that some passages are such as Iscariot Hackney might himself have produced." AP may well have supplied material to Savage. The notes to *The Dunciad Variorum*, published in the same year, make use of a similar array of facts.

The pamphlet has been reprinted with an introduction by J. Sutherland (Los Angeles: Augustan Reprint Society, 1960).

Ayre, William. Putative author of some posthumous memoirs of AP, published in two volumes on 8 January 1745. The full title is *Memoirs of the Life and Writings of Alexander Pope, Esq; Faithfully Collected from Authentic Authors, Original Manuscripts, and the Testimonies of Many Persons of Credit and Honour: Adorned with the Heads of Divers Illustrious Persons*. The work provoked a riposte titled *Remarks on Squire Ayre's Memoirs* (1744), with sketchy memoirs of **Edmund Curll**. The biography is a typical Curll performance: garrulous, digressive but never uninteresting. No new material of substance is provided. "Ayre" may be a pseudonym for Curll himself: nothing is known of an individual with that name, though books around this period are attributed to him. See also **biographies of Pope**.

B

Balaam, Sir. A brief exemplum at the end of AP's *Epistle to Bathurst*, ll. 349–402. The story tells of the rise and fall of a businessman in the City of London. He starts off as a sober merchant, makes money, and is knighted. Next Balaam gains power as a corrupt company director, achieves social standing, and enters Parliament. A bribe from France leads to his disgrace and downfall, with his property forfeited to the Crown and his life curtailed by a sentence of death.

The character is remotely based on the Old Testament prophet Balaam, in Numbers 22–24. However, AP may have an individual in mind in composing what is for the most part a generalized parable of money and society. The leading candidate is Thomas Pitt (1653–1726), grandfather of the "great Commoner" William Pitt. He served in the East India Company and was Governor of Fort St. George (Madras) from 1697 and 1709. He made a huge fortune by selling the famous 144-carat "Pitt diamond" to the Regent of France in 1717 for £100,000 (at least). He acquired an estate in Cornwall and became MP for the tiny rotten borough of Old Sarum. Many of these details fit the story of Sir Balaam in the poem, although other references seem to point to other contemporaries. Pitt lived at Swallowfield in **Berkshire**, eight miles from **Binfield**, and close enough to the poet's home territory to be a familiar topic of conversation. AP's main object was to satirize the links between commerce and high politics in the world of **Robert Walpole** and especially the rise of unscrupulous men in the wake of the **South Sea Bubble**. He narrates the life history with speed, rich allusiveness, and sometimes raw colloquial language.

ballads. A main vehicle of political and social satire in early modern history was the broadside ballad. The name refers to the habitual mode of publication, which was a single sheet, most often printed on one side only. It might carry crude wood-cut illustrations. Until the end of the seventeenth century such ballads were generally printed in black letter, that is, Gothic, type. From around 1700 this practice was discontinued. In most cases, the sheet did not carry any music: instead, the work was said to be set "to the tune of - - - - -," giving the title of a well-known song. The ballads are therefore restricted to a familiar set of metrical and stanza forms. The most common is the so-called ballad stanza, which consists of quatrains rhyming ABAB, with the A lines consisting of iambic octosyllabics (^-^-^-^-) and the B lines in iambic trimeter (^-^-^-).

In the seventeenth century, accomplished literary writers such as Marvell, Rochester, and **Dryden** learned to turn this form to more sophisticated ends. They retained the formal properties of the ballad, along with its fondness for folk wisdom in the guise of proverbs and mottos. Frequently such poems contained ribald comments on the great, though the identity of the victim in these onslaughts was regularly disguised by the use of initial letters only, as in "the D—— of M——." The best-known series of *Poems on Affairs of State* appeared from 1697: AP owned and annotated a volume published in 1705 (see *CIH* 136–37). The influence of this genre on his mature style remains to be fully explored, since it extends well beyond the "ballads," in the narrow sense, which he composed. His ballads are in the traditional vein, but their wit, ingenious obscenity, deft wordplay, and subtle rhythmic effects are all far beyond the attainment of most writers in the form. Unsurprisingly, these items appeared anonymously. For examples, see *The Court Ballad*, *The Discovery*, *Duke upon Duke*, *Moore's Worms*, and *Sandys's Ghost*.

Banister, John. See **Edward Taverner**.

Barber, John (1675–1741). Printer. An important friend of both AP and **Swift**, Barber provided a link with the city of London and with active Jacobite circles.

Born in London, he was a godson of the writer **Elkanah Settle**. Apprenticed to a printer in 1689, with his premium of £20 paid by Settle; freed in 1696. Began to run his own business, c.1700; one of his first successes came with a poem by **Daniel Defoe** in 1705. City Printer, 1709. Became intimate with Henry St. John, later **Viscount Bolingbroke**, and through him gained the acquaintance of leading Tories, including the **first Earl of Oxford**, **Francis Atterbury**, and Swift. When the Tory government came to power in 1710, Barber became the official printer of the *London Gazette* and the votes of the House of Commons, as well as serving the South Sea Company from its inception. Together with Benjamin Tooke, he gained the reversion of the post of King's Printer. He also printed the journal the *Examiner*, written by Swift and then by Delarivier[e] Manley (1663–1724). Eventually Manley went to live with Barber and stayed with him until her death. There are frequent references in the *Journal to Stella* to Barber, who printed some of the Dean's best-known pamphlets and saw him at one time almost on a daily basis. "There is an intimacy between us," Swift reported (*JTS* 1: 140). When *The Public Spirit of the Whigs* (1713) incurred the suspicions of the House of Lords, it was Barber who managed to shield Swift from punishment. In the years following, Barber was responsible for some major books, including the poems of **Matthew Prior** in 1718.

He was one of the few to do well out of the **South Sea Bubble**, emerging with a sizable fortune of at least £20,000, together with a town house in Bloomsbury and a country home at East Sheen, near **Richmond**. He had joined the Common Council of the city of London in 1711 and became an Alderman in 1722. For the next two decades, Barber played a major role in city government, as one of the leading Tories in a fiercely contentious municipal body. He had jousts with other members of the book trade, including **Edmund Curll** and Nathaniel Mist.

At the time of the **Atterbury plot**, Barber went on a visit to Naples and Rome. It is generally believed that the aim of this trip was not to recoup his health, as was claimed, but to carry to the **Pretender** a sum of about £50,000 that English Jacobites had raised to support the cause. He may have been sent on this mission by the **Duchess of Buckinghamshire**. On his return he agreed to give up his printing business, perhaps in order to escape punishment for his activities on behalf of the Stuarts. In 1725 he became Sheriff of London, and one of his tasks was to supervise the management of the corrupt Newgate prison. Some of the things he learned in this capacity may have been passed on to **John Gay** for use in *The Beggar's Opera*. Gay was invited to city feasts with the Alderman, who subscribed to Gay's poems in 1720 (as he did to the *Odyssey*). In 1729 Barber himself is thought to have packed the jury in a trial of the printer of *The Craftsman* and ensured that the accused was acquitted. He also received some of the forfeited assets of the rapist **Francis Charteris**. Through his influence **Charles Jervas** was commissioned to paint **George I** for the Guildhall in London. Later he presented a portrait of Swift by Jervas to Oxford University. Barber was in close touch with the Dean and took charge of both of his Irish protégées, **Mary Barber** (no relation) and **Laetitia Pilkington**, when they came to England. In 1732–33 Barber served as Lord Mayor of London. Here he played a prominent role in the defeat of the Excise scheme promoted by **Sir Robert Walpole**. In 1734 he unsuccessfully stood as a parliamentary candidate for the city of London. In his will he left £300 to Bolingbroke, £200 to Swift, and £100 to AP, a fair reflection of the poet's less intimate friendship with the printer.

In fact, AP was directly involved in literary business with Barber only once. This came as a result of *The Works of Buckingham* in 1723, where Barber owned the rights, although the publisher (unmentioned on the title page) was **Jacob Tonson junior**. It was Barber's former journeyman, **John Wright**, who took over as AP's main printer. Only one short letter survives from Barber to AP. However, there is no doubt that Barber was an exceedingly useful man for the poet to know, and their hidden connections remain to be unraveled. AP uses Barber's name for comic purposes in the apparatus of *The Dunciad*.

The most important source is C.A. Rivington, *"Tyrant": The Story of John Barber 1675 to 1741, Jacobite Lord Mayor of London and Printer and Friend to Dr. Swift* (York: William Sessions, 1989). This title accurately indicates a long-winded, digressive, and excessively detailed quality in the work, but it is a mine of useful information.

Barber, Mary (c. 1690–1757). Poet. She was probably born in England but married a Dublin draper named Jonathan Barber. She had four children. One of her sons became a prominent surgeon in Dublin. She herself was treated by **Dr. Richard Mead** for what was then called "gout." From 1728 Rev. Patrick Delany brought her into the circle of **Jonathan Swift**, who described her as "a virtuous, modest gentlewoman, with a great deal of sense." One of her works was "A True Tale" in tribute to the *Fables* of **John Gay**. She was also a friend of the writers Constantia Grierson and **Laetitia Pilkington**. Among her patrons were **Lord Carteret** and the **Earl of Orrery**.

She acted as an intermediary between Swift and his English contacts and was briefly arrested in January 1734 for carrying with her into England some of his poems that the authorities regarded as seditious. Swift was one of those who encouraged her to bring out her *Poems on Several Occasions* (1734). There was a prefatory letter from Swift to Orrery, followed by a dedication by Mrs. Barber to the Earl. The volume contains several neat and witty poems in various forms. Barber prints poems addressed to Swift, Orrery, **John Barber** (probably no relation), **Mary Caesar**, and others. Along with passing references to AP, there are lines "To Alexander Pope, Esq; Intreating him to write Verses to the Memory of Thomas, late Earl of Thanet." Despite this flattering invitation, AP does not appear to have complied. The impressive subscription list of more than 800 names includes the Archbishop of Dublin (John Hoadly); Alderman John Barber; **Lord Bathurst** and members of his family; the Bishop of Cloyne (**George Berkeley**), along with six other bishops; Mary Caesar and her husband Charles; **William Cleland**; no less than twenty-nine countesses; **George Bubb Dodington**; Anne Donellan, the friend of **Handel**; General **James Dormer**; Sarah, **Duchess of Marlborough**; the **Duchess of Buckinghamshire**; the **Duchess of Queensberry**, fifteen other duchesses, and thirteen dukes, several well known personally to AP; the second **Earl of Oxford**, together with his wife, and twenty-three more earls; **Nathaniel Hooke**; **Erasmus Lewis**; Dr. Mead; **Robert Nugent**; **William Pulteney**; Samuel Richardson; Elizabeth Rowe; **Rev. James Stopford**; **Thomas Tickell**; William Trumbull, son of AP's patron; **Sir Robert Walpole** (five copies); **Sir William Wyndham**; and **Edward Young**. This array of Anglo-Irish worthies could not have been assembled without energetic lobbying among the well-connected in both countries. The list naturally includes, besides Swift, "James Arbuthnott, M.D." (actually **Dr. John Arbuthnot**); John Gay; and AP and his mother.

In 1737 Barber was given the manuscript of Swift's *Polite Conversation* to publish for her own benefit, something that helped to alleviate her circumstances, now that she was apparently widowed. While in England in 1731 she had attempted to get AP to revise her poems, but he was reluctant to do this. See *The Poetry of Mary Barber*, ed. B. Tucker (Lampeter: Mellen, 1993), which reproduces the contents of the 1734 volume. See also A. Carpenter, " 'Our Chief Poetess': Mary Barber and Swift's Circle," *Canadian Journal of Irish Studies*, 19 (1993), 31–44.

Barnivelt, Esdras, Apoth. The putative author of *A Key to the Lock* (1715), a Scriblerian pamphlet offering to explicate AP's recent success, *The Rape of the Lock*. It was written by AP himself.

Baron, The. Character in *The Rape of the Lock*, based on the real-life Catholic nobleman **Robert, seventh Baron Petre.**

Bateson, Frederick Wilse (1901–78). Fellow of Corpus Christi College, Oxford. A trenchant critic who wrote widely on English poetry and edited the *Cambridge Bibliography of English Literature*, 5 vols. (1940). Founding editor of the journal *Essays in Criticism* from 1951. Together with N.A. Joukovsky, he edited the Penguin Critical Anthology on AP (1971). His main contribution to the study of AP came with an innovative treatment of the *Moral Essays* in a volume of the **Twickenham edition** in 1951.

Bath. City in the west of England that achieved its greatest celebrity as a spa from the time of **Queen Anne** and became a crucible for architectural and social innovation during AP's lifetime. He visited Bath in the autumn of 1714; in 1715; in 1716, with the **Earl of Burlington**; in 1728 (an extended stay for health reasons); and in 1734. There were probably other trips, and the city was also a favorite destination of friends such as **Gay, Arbuthnot, Parnell, Congreve, Chesterfield, Bolingbroke**, and others. From the mid-1730s AP became friendly with **Ralph Allen**, one of the most important figures in Bath, and he made visits almost every year, often in the course of one of his **rambles** through the West. From 1741 he was able to stay with Allen at the fine new mansion **Prior Park**. The last such visit took place in 1743. Among other residents of the city known to AP were the medical men **George Cheyne, William Oliver**, and Jeremiah Pierce, as well as the famous Master of Ceremonies, Richard "Beau" Nash (1674–1761). There is no extensive tribute to Bath in AP's poetry; his fullest description of life there occurs in a letter to **Martha Blount** on 6 October 1714 (*Corr* 1: 259–61).

Bathurst, Allen, Lord (1684–1775). One of AP's most important friends among the aristocracy and one of the executors named in the poet's **will**. The son of a courtier under **Queen Anne**, he served as MP for **Cirencester**. He was then created a Baron at the end of 1711, in a move by the government of the first **Earl of Oxford** to ensure passage in the House of Lords of the peace terms. A great survivor, he was made an Earl in 1772: his son Henry had just become Lord Chancellor. His sympathies were always strongly Tory and in earlier years unquestionably Jacobite: he supported the 1715 rising and later gave £1,000 to a campaign to support another invasion by the **Pretender**. From 1711 he was a member of the **Brothers Club** along with many of AP's closest friends and associates, including **Swift** and **Arbuthnot**. His good relations with **Lady Mary Wortley Montagu** continued even after she quarreled violently with AP. Lady Mary's witty *Epistle* to Bathurst (c. 1725) portrays her friend as irresolutely shifting from architectural schemes and landscaping projects to womanizing and dreams of favor at court.

It is not certain when he and AP first met; they were good friends by 1718, when AP made his first visit to Bathurst's seat at Cirencester and began his involvement in the design of the park there. In addition, Bathurst had inherited a house at **Riskins**, near Iver in Buckinghamshire, which AP often visited and where he worked on his translation of **Homer** and probably gave advice on improving the garden. Some joking "Lines to Lord Bathurst" appear in a letter of 1718 (*Corr* 1: 477). In all, some thirty letters between the two men are known to survive. Late in AP's life Bathurst helped him to revise *The Idea of a Patriot King*, the work of another noble friend, **Lord Bolingbroke**. He subscribed to the *Iliad*, the *Odyssey* (ten copies), and the **Shakespeare edition**.

AP liked Bathurst for his geniality, his spontaneity, and his worldly sophistication. The two men also shared a delight in landscape **gardening**. When AP came to address the peer in his *Moral Essays*, the **epistle** is couched in an idiom of racy vigor, quite unlike the accents of formal distance that he adopted in his *Epistle* *to Burlington*. The texture of the writing expresses AP's easy and confident relations with Bathurst. Again, in *The Second Epistle of the Second Book*, AP issues a blunt caution to Bathurst on overweening attempts to defeat the power of nature in his schemes at Cirencester. In many ways Bathurst comes across as an attractive man, despite loose sexual morals and a sometimes casual attitude toward social responsibilities. He lived long enough to meet in his eighties another hedonist, the novelist Laurence Sterne, who found in him "a disposition to be pleased, and a power to please others beyond whatever I knew." Portraits by **Kneller** and **Dahl**: it was probably a copy of the former that hung at the poet's house (*Garden and City* 249). He was an executor of the **will** of AP, who left him three statues.

See *Earls of Creation* 21–56.

Bathurst, Charles (1709–86). Bookseller. He was apprenticed to **Benjamin Motte** in 1727 and after being freed went into partnership with his master, c. 1735. When Motte died in 1738, he took over the business. In 1739 he married Motte's sister-in-law Mary Brian. He became a successful publisher, with a 5 percent share in the valuable rights to **Warburton**'s edition of AP from 1751. Late in life AP began to deal with Bathurst on a regular basis: in fact, he "seems to have had a much more satisfactory relationship with Bathurst than he did with Motte" (David Foxon). On occasions the bookseller visited AP at **Twickenham**. Their contacts had chiefly to do with the *Miscellanies*, where Bathurst had inherited rights held by Motte. He also aided AP with materials for the **grotto** (*Corr* 3: 349). Ten letters from AP to Bathurst survive.

Battersea. AP's friend **Viscount Bolingbroke** inherited Battersea manor house on the death of his father in 1742: the St. John family held the lordship of the manor from 1627 to 1763. The house was situated across the Thames from Chelsea and adjoining the parish church of St. Mary's. Most of it was demolished in 1778 and the remainder in the early twentieth century. Bolingbroke did not immediately take posses-

sion and is said to have lent the property to the **Earl of Marchmont**. However, the property lent may have been the new Dower House, built nearby in 1698 and still surviving. By late 1743 Bolingbroke was installed at the Manor House. AP visited Bolingbroke and Marchmont there in November 1743 and February 1744, during the final months of his life. Later the house boasted what was known as "Pope's room."

Battle of the Books, The. Prose satire by **Jonathan Swift**, written in the late 1690s and published anonymously in 1704 along with *A Tale of a Tub*. The full title reads: *A Full and True Account of the Battel Fought last Friday, between the Ancient and the Modern Books in St. James's Library*. This formula parodies the standard title page of a pamphlet on contemporary events such as a military campaign. It is a pungent contribution to the quarrel of the **Ancients and Moderns**, mounted on behalf of the Oxford wits who had supported the cause of the Ancients in the wake of Swift's mentor Sir William Temple. At the heart of the satire as champion of the Moderns is the scholar **Richard Bentley**, whom AP would later enshrine as the fatuous "explicator" of the text of *The Dunciad*. Improbably cast as the hero of the Ancients is the Hon. Charles Boyle, father of AP's friend the **fifth Earl of Orrery**. The *Battle* is a textbook example of **mock-heroic**, although it draws also on allegory and exemplum.

See *A Tale of a Tub, to which is added The Battle of the Books, and The Mechanical Operation of the Spirit*, ed. A.C. Guthkelch and D.N. Smith, 2nd ed. (Oxford: Clarendon, 1958).

Battle of the Frogs and Mice. The short mock-epic in ancient Greek, titled Βατραχομυομαχια. It probably dates from the fifth century B.C. and is based on one of Aesop's fables. In early times this parody of epic was often attributed to **Homer** himself, and it was still included in editions of the poet in AP's day. It consists of three comically brief books. For the genre, see **mock-heroic**.

A translation of the work was published by **Thomas Parnell** in 1717, together with a life of Zoilus, the carping critic of antiquity. It has always been recognized that Parnell undertook the task as a pendant to AP's translation of the *Iliad*, then under way, and that the material on Zoilus was inspired by hostile comments on AP's version. Indeed Zoilus is probably meant as an antetype of AP's modern scourge **John Dennis**. The origins of the work go back to the summer of 1714, when AP and Parnell were working together at **Binfield**. On 13 September AP wrote to his friend, "I have receivd your Batrachomuomachia" (*Corr* 1: 253). However, in March 1715 he was again asking for the translation and the life of Zoilus; Parnell told him the life was completed in June of that year, but in February 1716 AP still apparently did not have a copy either of his or of the poem. It was not until the early part of 1717 that AP could inform Parnell that he had put the book "into the press" (*Corr* 1: 395). Finally the long-expected work came out on 16 May 1717, as *Homer's Battle of the Frogs and Mice. With the Remarks of Zoilus. To which is Prefix'd, The Life of the said Zoilus*. There were two issues (Griffith 74–74a; Foxon P73–74). The publisher was **Bernard Lintot**, who paid the copy money of £16.2s. 6d. (£16.125) to **John Gay** at the request of Parnell. In later years the poem "corrected by Mr. Pope" was added at the end of some editions of AP's translation of the *Odyssey*. It is uncertain how much of the 1717 version owed to AP. When AP published the poems of Parnell in 1722, he included the verse portion only. The translation of the poem is written in heroic couplets, running to 490 lines in all.

For the text of the entire work (preface, life, poem, and remarks), see *Collected Poems of Thomas Parnell*, ed. C. Rawson and F.P. Lock (Newark: University of Delaware Press, 1989), 64–108; commentary appears on 442–79.

Beach, Mary (c. 1648–1725). AP's nurse. Sometimes spelled "Beech" and sometimes named as "Mercy." She joined the household of AP's father at an unknown date, perhaps in the 1670s. She looked after the poet from the time of his birth, originally as a wet nurse, and remained with the family until her death. It is possible, though not certain, that AP contracted **Pott's disease** from her during infancy. AP recorded the passing of "his most faithful nurse" on 5 November 1725 (*EC* 1: ix). In a letter to the **second Earl of Oxford** shortly afterward, he wrote that "she having been tryd, & found, kind & officious so long, thro so many accidents and needs of life, is surely Equal to a meer Natural Tye" (*Corr* 2: 337). He thought so well of Mary that he set up a memorial to her on the outside of the northeast wall of **Twickenham parish church**, with an inscription in English paying tribute to her constant service for "thirty-eight" (actually thirty-seven) years. Her burial took place at the church on 7 November 1725.

Beattie, Lester Middleswarth (d. 1969). Scholar who taught at Carnegie-Mellon University. He is chiefly known for his useful study *John Arbuthnot: Mathematician and Satirist* (1935; reprint, New York: Russell & Russell, 1967).

Bedingfield, Sir Henry (d. 1760). Member of an ancient family in Norfolk, well known to AP through many connections with other Catholic gentry. He married Lady Elizabeth Boyle (d. 1751), sister of the **Earl of Burlington**. In the previous generation his father, Sir Henry, the second baronet, had died in 1704, while his aunt Johanna married Richard Caryll and was the mother of AP's close friend **John Caryll senior**. His uncle Edward was in contact with AP and helped to distribute *The Rape of the Lock* to the real-life originals of Belinda and the Baron (*Corr* 1: 141–42). Both Sir Henry and his uncle subscribed to the *Iliad*. Edward's daughter Mary (d. 1761) married Sir John Swinburne (1698–1745), whose own mother **Mary, Lady Swinburne** was the daughter of Anthony Englefield and herself a correspondent of the poet. Sir John was thus a first cousin of **Teresa** and **Martha Blount**. With so many familial links, it is not surprising that the Bedingfields and their kin were often involved in AP's life.

Bedlam. More formally, Royal Bethlehem or Bethlem Hospital. Founded in 1247 as the Priory of St. Mary Bethlehem, it had begun to treat insane patients by the early fifteenth century. Originally located in Bishopsgate, it moved a short distance to London Wall, on the south edge of Moorfields, in 1675. The hospital was removed again in 1815, to what is now the site of the Imperial War Museum in Kennington, and then in 1936 it took up its present home in Beckenham, Kent. It is now part of the Maudsley Hospital.

Eighteenth-century Bedlam is most familiar through its depiction by **William Hogarth**, especially in the last scene of *The Rake's Progress* (1735). AP locates the secret cell of the dunces close to Bedlam in the second version of *The Dunciad*. He refers to the two figures of "Raving Madness" and "Melancholy Madness," corresponding broadly to mania and depression, which were placed over the gates of the hospital. They were carved by Caius Gabriel Cibber, father of the leading dunce **Colley Cibber**, around 1680. He also mentions Dr. James Monro (1680–1752), physician to the hospital 1728–52, one of a line of distinguished practitioners in the family. In the *Epistle to Arbuthnot*, AP identifies the urge to write with madness in the couplet "The Dog-star rages! nay 'tis past a doubt, / All *Bedlam*, or *Parnassus*, is let out" (*TE* 4: 96). In his correspondence he sometimes uses the term "Bedlam" or "Moorfields" for a similar purpose.

Beggar's Opera, The. Play by **John Gay**, the most lastingly popular dramatic work to emerge from AP's circle. Initially rejected by the managers at **Drury Lane Theatre**, headed by **Colley Cibber**, it was later accepted by **John Rich** and first performed at **Lincoln's Inn Fields Theatre** on 29 January 1728. A fashionable audience, including AP and his friends, was in attendance. At first it seemed uncertain whether the piece would succeed, but gradually the house warmed and the final curtain brought a clamor of applause, as AP noted (*Anecdotes* 1: 107–8). The play had a phenomenal run, with royal command performances and bringing Gay at least £700 in the first few weeks. In the end he probably made something like £2,000 all told. The *Opera* was about the most popular

play on the English stage in the eighteenth century and is regularly revived in the theater up to the present day, quite apart from performances on film and television.

The play has its roots in Scriblerian ideas of generic transformation. **Swift** wrote to AP in 1716, suggesting a "Newgate pastoral" as a possible subject for Gay's dramatic talents (*Corr* 1: 360). That Gay was the sole author of the play was stressed by AP, though he admitted that appearances were against this, "for 'twas writ in the same house with me and Dr. Swift [in 1726]. He used to communicate the parts of it, as he write them, to us, but neither of us did more than alter an expression here and there" (*Anecdotes* 1: 57). As the play headed toward its premiere, AP and Gay kept Swift apprised of its progress.

Gay's great coup was to find suitable words to match both the story line and the music of some familiar music, principally **ballads**, which were set by Johann Christoph Pepusch (1667–1752). The play initiated a taste for ballad opera, which lasted for many years. Subsequent arrangements have been made by Benjamin Britten and others, while Kurt Weill supplied original music for Bertolt Brecht's topical adaptation *Die Dreigroschenoper*, or *Threepenny Opera* (1928). In the course of the play, the author has fun with many contemporary topics, including the rage for **opera** and the cult of superstar performers. It is generally agreed that the key figure in the action, the thief-taker Peachum, stands for both the gang boss **Jonathan Wild** and the prime minister **Sir Robert Walpole**.

Useful background is provided in *Contexts 1: The Beggar's Opera*, ed. J.V. Guerinot and R.D. Jilg (Hamden, CT: Archon, 1976). See also C. Winton, *John Gay and the London Theatre* (Lexington: University Press of Kentucky, 1993). W.E. Schultz, *Gay's Beggar's Opera: Its Content, History and Influence* (New Haven, CT: Yale University Press, 1923; reprint, New York: Russell & Russell, 1967), retains considerable interest.

Belinda. The heroine of *The Rape of the Lock* whose real-life model was **Arabella Fermor**.

AP also wrote a set of verses "To Belinda on the Rape of the Lock," consisting of thirty lines in heroic couplets. It was first published anonymously in the collection **Poems on Several Occasions** (1717) and given in a slightly different form in the biography by **Owen Ruffhead** (1769). In the poem AP contrives neatly to do some salvage work on Arabella's reputation, yet risking compounding the scandal by jokingly comparing her to Lucretia. At the end AP repeats the claim expressed at the end of the *Rape*, to the effect that Arabella will be immortalized by his verse: "Who censure most, more precious hairs would lose, / To have the *Rape* recorded by his Muse." For the text and commentary, see *TE* 6: 107–10.

For AP's choice of name, see the comments of **Geoffrey Tillotson**: "The short form of Arabella is 'Belle,' which smoothly links with fashionable 'Belinda' and allows the pun on the newly imported Gallicism, 'belle' (= pretty young lady). . . . (Pope does not use this word elsewhere in his poems)" (*TE* 2: 143). The word also makes a kind of Franco-Spanish union, *belle* + *linda* ("pretty" in Spanish), which hints at affectation. It might be added that the name "Belinda" was fashionable chiefly because of its use in the literature of highfalutin' romance, a genre in which the heroine might be expected to be well read. Her name thus links her with Florio, Damon, and the other smart socialites of the poem. Finally, Belinda was a vulnerable young woman seduced by the hero Dorimant in George Etherege's comedy *The Man of Mode* (1676)—a classic of the Restoration stage that would have been familiar to AP and his readers.

Beljame, Alexandre (c. 1843–1906). Pioneering French student of AP. He was the first Professor of English language and literature at the Sorbonne in Paris (1881). He edited *Robinson Crusoe* (1883) and together with Émile Legouis an anthology of English writing (1905). His major contribution to the field was *Le public et les hommes de lettres en Angleterre au dix-huitième siècle 1660–1744 (Dryden, Addison, Pope)* (1881; rev. ed., 1897). This was already a little out of date when translated by Edith O.

Lorimer as *Men of Letters and the English Public in the Eighteenth Century* (1948), with an introduction by **Bonamy Dobrée**. However, it remains an original attempt at cultural criticism and the sociology of the book, which contains some materials that are still valuable.

Bellenden, Mary, later Campbell (1685–1736). One of the **maids of honor** well known to AP, at the court of the Prince and Princess of Wales. She served the Princess (later **Queen Caroline**) from 1715 to 1720. She figures in several of AP's shorter poems around 1716 and occurs in his correspondence. Noted alike for beauty and wit, Mary is described in *Mr. Pope's Welcome from Greece* as "soft and fair as down," while her sister Margaret (b. 1684) is "the tallest of the land." They were the daughters of a Scottish peer, the second Baron Bellenden (d. 1707). Mary subscribed in 1718 to the poems of **Matthew Prior**. In 1720 she married Colonel John Campbell (1693–1770), also a friend of AP and **John Gay**: he was a groom of the bedchamber to the Prince (later **George II**) from 1714, and after her death, in 1761, he became fourth Duke of Argyll. Caroline, daughter of Mary and John Campbell, married **Baron Bruce** in 1739 as his third wife.

Benson, William (1682–1754). Politician, writer, and architect. A Whig MP from 1715, he managed to get himself appointed Surveyor-General in 1718, as successor to **Sir Christopher Wren**, to the amazement of almost everyone. His slender claim rested on the possible design in 1710 of a villa, Wilbury in Wiltshire, which anticipated the fashion for **Palladianism**. He had also carried out improvements at nearby **Amesbury**, which he leased in 1708, and curried favor with the Hanoverian regime by providing ornamental waterworks for their palace at Herrenhausen (claiming falsely that he had originated the design). Soon after taking over the Board of Works, he lost whatever credibility he might have had by alleging that the House of Lords was in imminent danger of falling down, with the result that the peers were told to find another chamber for their own safety. Competent architects soon found that the props Benson had erected as a protective measure were more dangerous than any decay of the structure. Benson was dismissed, but he had acquired a reversion to the post of Auditor of the Imprest and eventually succeeded to this lucrative job in 1735. He erected a monument to **John Milton** in Westminster Abbey in 1737, with a bust by **Michael Rysbrack** and an inscription describing his own achievements at greater length than those of the poet. In his last years he became seriously deranged. Despite some ability, as well as knowledge of botany and classical literature that came in useful for his *Letters concerning Poetical Translations and Virgil's and Milton's Arts of Verse* (1739), he had always been eccentric and self-seeking at best.

AP refers in *The Dunciad* to the two most famous occasions on which Benson committed a faux pas. The first occurs in Book 3, where a vision of the world ushered in by the new "Augustus" (here **George I**) foresees that Benson will sit as "sole Judge of Architecture." A detailed note spells out the blunder that the Surveyor-General had made over the House of Lords (*TE* 5: 188). In Book 4, "bold Benson" emerges to thrust aside competitors for political favor. The note refers to Benson's efforts to boost his own standing as a patron, notably with regard to the Milton monument (*TE* 5: 352).

See A. Eavis, "The Avarice and Ambition of William Benson," *The Georgian Group Journal*, 12 (2002), 8–37.

Bentley, Richard (1662–1742). Scholar and clergyman. The greatest classical scholar of his day and a despotic master of Trinity College, Cambridge, from 1700. He had been Keeper of the Royal Libraries, 1694, and intervened decisively in the quarrel over the **Ancients and Moderns** in opposition to the Oxford wits who were friends of **Jonathan Swift**. This earned him a derisory role in *The Battle of the Books* (1704) as a champion of the defeated Moderns. His later works included an innovative edition of **Horace** (1711) and an ill-fated attempt to apply the principles of classical editing to the text of *Paradise Lost* (1732).

It is possible that AP had private reasons for attacking Bentley, although it is not certain they had more than the slightest personal contact, if that. A well-known story has it that Bentley gave a magisterial rebuff to the poet, after the publication of his translation, with the words, "A pretty poem, Mr Pope, but you must not call it Homer." The anecdote is doubly suspect, because in its most familiar form it refers to a subscription by Bentley: in fact, he did not subscribe to either of AP's Homeric versions. In any case, AP had probably taken against Bentley long before this, on account of his role in the affair of Ancients and Moderns. Still, Bentley had no real place in the earliest version of *The Dunciad*. It was only after the scholar turned his attention to **Milton** that he came right into the sights of AP's satiric artillery. The *Imitations of Horace* contain a number of jokes at the expense of "slashing *Bentley*" (*Epistle to Arbuthnot* l. 164), and *Sober Advice from Horace* claims to offer a reconstruction by Bentley of the Latin text. This satiric technique was developed in the later versions of *The Dunciad*. The poem in four books (1743) has extended the attack on pedantic scholarship, and "Richard Aristarchus" has become one of the architects of its preposterous apparatus. Many notes are signed "BENTL.," who represents an absurd hypertrophy of verbal criticism. Within the poem itself Bentley enters as a character in Book 4, with some damaging recollections of the troubled history of Trinity College under his watch. He advances the cause of Queen Dulness in the role of **Aristarchus**: "Thy mighty Scholiast, whose unweary'd pains / Made Horace dull, and humbled Milton's strains" (*TE* 5: 363).

Without doubt, AP was unfair to Bentley, whose learning, precision, and energy did much to convert textual editing into a rigorous modern discipline. But Bentley was also a combative and bumptious man, whose judgment lapsed when he strayed into areas outside his technical mastery. The lines "Where Bentley late tempestuous wont to sport / In troubled waters, but now sleeps in Port" (4: 201–2) brilliantly evoke a combination of ideas. There is the calm River Cam, ruffled by the academic infights promoted by Bentley, as well as an episode mentioned in AP's note, when the visiting scholar **Scipione Maffei** was offered a superfluity of drink. "He told us," Maffei's companion reported, "that he no longer engaged in study, and that having had his fill of work and glory, he was now taking his ease. He then had *punch* brought in (a strong liquor of which the English are very fond), and begged the company to partake of it, after drinking it very freely himself, not from a glass, but from a pitcher which contained more than seven or eight mugs of this liquor." Besides, Bentley was known to have a great liking for port wine.

The standard account is J.H. Monk, *The Life of Richard Bentley D.D.*, 2 vols. (London: Rivington, 1833), which is authoritative but infuriatingly vague on dates. R.J. White, *Dr. Bentley: A Study in Academic Scarlet* (London: Eyre & Spottiswoode, 1965), is a brisk treatment.

Berkeley, Hon. George (1692–1746). Not to be confused with the philosopher. A minor politician who came into AP's orbit mainly as a result of his marriage to **Henrietta Howard** in 1735. He was a brother of the third Earl of Berekeley and of Lady Elizabeth Germain, a friend of **Swift**. AP seems to have maintained good relations with Berkeley, who was a pallbearer at **John Gay**'s funeral and who subscribed to the *Odyssey*.

Berkeley, Rev. George (1685–1753). Irish churchman and philosopher, friend of AP and **Swift**. He is best known today for his philosophical works, including the *Treatise Concerning Human Knowledge* (1710), and for his stay in Rhode Island, while he attempted to set up a college in Bermuda (1728–32). To contemporaries he would have been just as recognizable as Dean of Derry (from 1724) and Bishop of Cloyne (from 1734). Author of *An Essay towards Preventing the Ruin of Great Britain* (1721), deploring the lassitude and depression of the country in the wake of the **South Sea Bubble**.

Like Swift, Berkeley was educated at Kilkenny school and Trinity College, Dublin, where he later was a Fellow. Ordained, 1709; Doctor of Divinity, 1721. He came to know the group of wits in London in 1713, including **Addison** and **Steele**, and he attended the first night of *Cato*, sending a well-known description of the event to his friend John Perceval, later **Earl of Egmont**. Berkeley then went to Italy as chaplain to the **Earl of Peterborough**. From Leghorn he wrote AP an amusing letter on 1 May 1714 (*Corr* 1: 221–22), one of four items of surviving correspondence between the two men. Another, in 1717, gives a vivid description of the island of Ischia. In fact, the two men had extensive contacts, and AP once invited Berkeley to stay a week at **Twickenham**. Berkeley is said to have persuaded AP to translate an episode of **Horace**, which could be applied to the Bermudan project, but if it was carried out, the poem is lost (*Anecdotes* 1: 153). The poet survived long enough to read Berkeley's *Siris, a Chain of Philosophical Reflections and Enquiries concerning the Virtues of Tarwater* (1744), although this was too late for the regimen to effect a miraculous improvement in AP's health. Berkeley subscribed to both the *Iliad* and the *Odyssey*.

The standard biography is A.A. Luce, *The Life of George Berkeley* (London: Nelson, 1949; reprint, New York: Greenwood, 1968).

Berkeley Street. Around August 1743 AP began to negotiate for the lease of a house in the West End of London for twenty-six years, through the agency of **George Arbuthnot** (as a Catholic, AP was strictly unable to act). It stood at the northern end of Berkeley Street, near Berkeley Square, in a fashionable area that had been developed at the end of the seventeenth century and augmented by the building of Berkeley Square from 1739. Only a stone's throw away was Bolton Street, where **Martha Blount** had been living with her sister. AP spent £90 on repairs but was unable to complete the transaction before his death in the following year. It is clear that the house was always intended for Martha's occupancy, and she completed the purchase for £315 (plus interest) in 1746. She lived there for the rest of her life. **Magdalen Rackett**, AP's half sister, resented the care her brother had taken for Martha's future and refused to allow the lease to be paid for out of his estate. See *Women's Place* 287–90.

Berkshire. In effect, AP's home county, since he lived through most of his childhood and youth at **Binfield** and had numerous contacts with residents of this shire for the rest of his life. Known as the "royal county" on account of the presence of Windsor, near its eastern edge, and **Windsor Forest**, occupying much of its eastern portion. The Thames formed the northern border for much of its course across the county. The major town was Reading, with a population of 6,000 to 7,000, although it shared the role of administrative center with Abingdon: assizes alternated between these towns and Newbury. Similarly the county members of Parliament were nominated at Reading and elected at Abingdon. Berkshire contained two other boroughs of Wallingford and Windsor; the incorporated market towns of Maidenhead, Newbury, and **Wokingham**; and the market towns of Faringdon, Hungerford, East Ilsley, Lambourn, and Wantage. As well as the knights of the shire, there were MPs for each of the boroughs.

AP had relatives in this district, that is, his half sister **Magdalen Rackett** and her family; neighbors such as **John Dancastle**; old friends of his parents such as the **Englefield family**; patrons such as **Sir William Trumbull** and **Lord Bolingbroke**; and a variety of contacts with Berkshire folk—thus, Richard Pottenger (1690–1739), a judge, justice of the peace for Berkshire, and MP, was a relation on his father's side. **Arabella Fermor** lived after her marriage at Ufton Court. Late in life AP became friendly with the **Duchess of Marlborough**, then often resident at Windsor Lodge.

See also **Easthampstead**; **Letcombe Bassett**; **Waltham Blacks**; and **Whiteknights**.

Bethel, Hugh (1689–1748). One of AP's closest friends. A Whig country gentleman, who lived at Beswick near Beverley in Yorkshire, although he also had a house in London. From 1715 to 1722 he served in Parliament. Shortly

before AP died, he and Bethel agreed to exchange portraits, but only the picture of Bethel was executed: it hung at AP's house. For some reason **William Kent**'s portrait of AP fell through. Bethel's portrait, hung in a gold frame, was the only one in AP's bedroom at the time of his death (*Garden and City* 255). AP presented to Bethel a copy of his *Poems* (1717) with a Latin inscription.

It is not certain when the two men met: AP's first extant letter dates from 1723. AP also knew Hugh's brother **Slingsby Bethel**, a merchant in Tower Hill, London, and his four sisters (see **Lady Codrington**). Hugh suffered from asthma, and his visit to Italy in 1741–43 seems to have been made on grounds of health. He lent AP money, lent practical assistance to **Martha Blount**, aided the poet's sister **Magdalen Rackett**, and gave him financial advice. An early **will** actually listed Bethel as an executor. Over forty letters survive to Bethel from AP, who regarded him as "the soul of friendship" and as a "male bawd" who brought people together. Among his own friends was **William Cleland**. He also took a keen interest in the visual arts and stood at the center of a group of Yorkshire connoisseurs linked to the local magnate, the **Earl of Burlington**. On his death in February 1748, his estate of £2,000 per annum passed to his brother Slingsby.

AP celebrates Bethel as an open, upright, and unpretentious figure. In the *Essay on Man* he appears as "blameless Bethel" (*TE* 3.i: 140). Later AP cast him in the role of Ofellus, in his imitation of *The Second Satire of the Second Book of Horace* (1734): The character represents a blunt and observant commentator, drawn to the simple life, who deals in down-to-earth language and colloquial idioms. The vocabulary is concrete and even gross, particularly in respect of food and digestion. See *TE* 4: 51–69.

Bethel, Slingsby (1695–1758). An African merchant in London who was an Alderman, Sheriff, and finally Lord Mayor in 1755–56. MP for the city of London, 1747–58. He was the brother of AP's close friend **Hugh Bethel** and acted as intermediary for the poet when

Hugh was abroad. In addition, he helped to handle AP's investments and bought wine for him. Sixteen letters from AP to Slingsby survive, all dating from 1736 onward.

Bettenham, James. Printer. A former apprentice and son-in-law of **William Bowyer senior**. His political sympathies seem to have lain with the High Church. Starting out c.1718 as a publisher of mainly Tory tracts, he became known as a printer from c. 1720, specializing in producing Greek and Latin texts, as well as theological works and the highly successful almanacs known as *Vox stellarum*, attributed to Francis Moore. He was used as the printer of the first version of *The Dunciad* in 1728, and although he did not hold the rights, he entered the book into the register of the Stationers' Company on 30 May 1728.

Betterton, Thomas (1635–1710). Actor and dramatist. The last of the major figures of the Restoration theater, he had known **John Dryden** well, in addition to **Shakespeare**'s supposed godson, Sir William Davenant. Generally regarded as the greatest actor of his day, and termed by AP "the best actor I ever saw" (*Anecdotes* 1:23). He is said to have had a farm near Reading in his later days, and a reference by AP in a letter to Anthony **Englefield** in 1707 suggests that he was familiar with the gentry of **Berkshire** among whom the poet grew up. AP claimed to have been acquainted with Betterton from boyhood, and the experienced man of the theater was probably one of the many father figures on whom the young poet modeled himself. He may have encouraged AP to consider writing for the stage.

When Betterton died in April 1710, AP proposed a possible inscription for his **epitaph**. Other friends of the actor were **William Wycherley** and **John Caryll senior**, who was glad to find that the widow had entrusted Betterton's literary remains to AP (*Corr* 1: 142). As it turned out, AP inserted two translations of **Chaucer** in a miscellany published by **Bernard Lintot** in 1712—the volume that saw the first appearance of *The Rape of the Locke*—and assigned them to Betterton. For these the actor's

widow was paid just over five guineas by Lintot. There is reason to believe, however, that they had been composed by AP himself. The only surviving oil painting that can be attributed with certainty to the hand of AP is a portrait of Betterton, copied from **Kneller**: for a reproduction, see *Life* 91. A portrait of the actor was kept at AP's house. AP mentions Betterton's "grave Action" on the stage in the *Epistle to Augustus*, l. 122. In his private obituary list, AP marked the actor's death with the entry, "The Roscius of his age, made his exit to the applause of all good men" (*EC* 1: ix).

There is no comprehensive study of Betterton. R.W. Lowe, *Thomas Betterton* (London: Longman, 1891; reprint, New York: Blom, 1991), focuses on the actor, while J. Milhous, *Thomas Betterton and the Management of Lincoln's Inn Fields, 1695–1708* (Carbondale: Southern Illinois University Press, 1979), concentrates on an aspect of his career as a manager.

Bevis Mount. Home of the **Earl of Peterborough** and one of the most important places of retirement for AP to gain health and refreshment. It was situated in the Portswood area of Southampton, northeast of the city center. The Earl first acquired property there in 1730, on land that had belonged to the medieval priory of St. Denys. He extended his holdings, and by the time of his death in 1735 he had purchased about seventy acres of land. The house was a modest two-story building with a portico, about the size of AP's own **villa**. The garden occupied less than ten acres between the house and the River Itchen. The main feature of the property was the hill after which it was named (deriving from the legendary local hero "Sir Bevis [Bevois] of Hampton"). A tomb fancifully described as that of Sir Bevis was located near the Earl's "wilderness." Peterborough created a terrace with a picturesque view over the valley below and placed a variety of garden furniture, including statues, grottos, and alcoves around the site. Winding paths led to a prospect of the river, while a vineyard and a bowling green diversified the landscape. A near neighbor was Peterborough's physician **Nathanael St. An-**

dré. Peterborough's widow, **Anastasia Robinson**, remained at Bevis Mount until she died in 1755; it was then occupied by the Earl's nephew, Sir John Mordaunt. The site was turned over to residential development in the middle of the nineteenth century, and the house itself was demolished early in the twentieth century. Today the extent of the former grounds is marked by the Avenue to the west, Avenue Road to the north, Bevois Valley Road to the east, and Rockstone Lane to the south.

AP's first visit may have occurred in 1731. For the remainder of the Earl's life, Bevis Mount served as a favorite spot for AP to recoup his energies and to work on his poetry. Here he put together the *Epistle to Arbuthnot* and composed *Sober Advice from Horace*. As he told Arbuthnot in August 1734, "I write this from the most beautiful Top of a Hill I ever saw, a little house that overlooks the Sea, Southampton, & the Isle of Wight; where I study, write, & have what Leisure I please" (*Corr* 3: 424). Other visits took place in 1733 and 1735. AP had been involved in Peterborough's **gardening** plans from the start (see also **Parson's Green**). After the Earl died, he made further visits to supervise work on the landscape, the last probably in August 1737. The Countess was a devout Catholic, and her home became known as "the nursery for Southampton's Catholicism" (*CIH* 489). This combined with the monastic origins of the property to invest Bevis Mount with a unique aura of reverence for the poet. In addition, he was able to make some of his most adventurous "**rambles**" while based here. In particular, his trip to the ruins of the nearby Cistercian monastery of Netley Abbey in August 1734 inspired one of the finest of all his letters, addressed to **Martha Blount**. See G.S. Rousseau, "A New Pope Letter," *Philological Quarterly*, 45 (1966), 409–18.

See *Gardening World* 180–205 for the most detailed and perceptive review of this subject.

bibliography. Serious work on the bibliography of AP can scarcely be said to have begun prior to the twentieth century, although previous editors had made a start in defining the canon and in teasing out the publishing history. Early work includes an article by **George Atherton Aitken** in the *Transactions of the Bibliographical Society*, 12 (1911–13), 113–43.

Everything that had gone before was supplanted by the work of **Reginald Harvey Griffith**, published as *Alexander Pope: A Bibliography*, 2 vols. (1922–27). The first volume covers AP's works up to 1734, and the second volume those published from 1735 to 1751. A projected continuation, on books about AP, never appeared. Griffith also supplied the entry for AP in *The Cambridge Bibliography of English Literature* (1940), 2: 294–304. Contributions by **Arthur Ellicott Case** and **George Sherburn**, among others, clarified the position further. However, readers should beware of the unreliable compilation by **Thomas James Wise**, *A Pope Library: A Catalogue of Plays, Poems, and Prose Writings by Alexander Pope* (1931; reprint, 1973). In more recent years, **Maynard Mack** has done most to bring order to the subject, while significant contributions have been made by Vinton A. Dearing, among others. **David Foxon** supplies some new details in his catalog *English Verse, 1701–1750*, 2 vols. (1975). AP's own works can be found in the *English Short Title Catalogue (1473–1800)*. A preliminary listing of his works, compiled as part of this project, will be found in R.C. Alston and M.J. Jannetta, *Bibliography Machine Readable Cataloguing and the ESTC* (1978).

Secondary work on AP can be traced in J.E. Tobin, *Alexander Pope: A List of Critical Studies Published from 1895 to 1944* (1945); and C.L. Lopez, *Alexander Pope: An Annotated Bibliography, 1945–1967* (1970). Recent additions are reported each year in *The Scriblerian*.

Bickford, Edmund (1685–1732). Lawyer at the Inner Temple. A Devon friend of **John Gay** and **William Fortescue** whose estate at Buckland Filleigh bordered on his family home. He became a Commissioner for Bankruptcy. Subscribed to the *Iliad* and to Gay's *Poems*. One of those to greet AP in the poem *Mr. Pope's Welcome from Greece*. He witnessed the agreement for AP's translation of the *Odyssey*.

Bicknell, Margaret (c. 1690–1723). Actress and dancer. Together with her sister Elizabeth Younger (c. 1699–1762), also an actress, singer, and dancer, she became friendly with AP, **John Gay**, and their circle.

Binfield. Village in **Berkshire**, which was AP's home from about 1700 to 1716, when his family moved to **Chiswick**. It lies in the hundred of Cookham, northwest of the town of Bracknell, which was itself a small settlement with a single street in AP's day, and about three miles from **Wokingham**. The parish occupied 3,500 acres, situated in the heart of **Windsor Forest**, with a mixture of woodland and arable land. Some common land survived, later to be enclosed. The village lies on a ridge with an elevation mostly between 200 and 300 feet above sea level. At the beginning of the eighteenth century the population stood at around 500 to 600 people.

The Popes had their home at **Whitehill House**, on the southern edge of the parish. It stood near the southern end of what is now Murrell Hill Lane, north of the road from Wokingham to Bracknell (which ran approximately on the line of the present-day B3408 route). This road carried on to Staines and London, and it would have been well known to AP. Nearby, to the northeast, was a small grove of beech trees to which the young AP liked to retreat. A site of natural protection named Pope's Meadow has been maintained by Bracknell Forest Council in this area since 1984. Today the community of Popeswood nearby is in effect a suburb of Bracknell, which bills itself as "the borough of innovation in the high-tech heart of Britain." On the other side of AP's home the parish was crossed by the Forest Road, leading from Reading to Windsor. Since 1597 the lords of the manor had been members of the Dancastle family, represented in the poet's time by **John Dancastle**: their home lay on the eastern side of the village. (The present house on the site dates from around 1754, when William Pitt, later Earl of Chatham, bought it.) The most notable topographic feature is perhaps a stream or "cut" that runs from south to north through the parish.

The parish church of All Saints is situated at the other end of the village from the Popes' residence. It was built of local stone from c. 1350, with considerable renovation during the nineteenth century. Among the monuments in the church was that of Judith, Countess of Salisbury, mother-in-law of **Sir William Trumbull**, AP's principal mentor during his early years at Binfield.

biographies of Pope. In his lifetime AP was the subject of numerous brief notices in newspapers and pamphlets, but only one attempt at biography as such seems to have been undertaken. This was the entry in *The Poetical Register*, published by **Edmund Curll** in two volumes (1718–20) and written by **Giles Jacob**. AP apparently corrected the proofs for this entry, but there is no evidence to support the claim of **John Dennis** that he had written the laudatory article himself.

Two short biographies appeared straight after the death of AP. Both were titled *The Life of Alexander Pope, Esq.*, and each furnished a copy of his **will**. One was published by Charles Corbett; the other, issued by Weaver Bickerton, is a little longer, less facetious, and more informative. Neither work adds much to what could have been gleaned from previous sources, such as Curll's annotations to Pope's letters. The dauntless publisher was soon entering the field himself, with a two-volume compilation titled *Memoirs of the Life and Writings of Mr. Pope*, which came out in January 1745. It is attributed to "**William Ayre**," generally thought to conceal, most imperfectly, the authorship of Curll himself. The last of such early efforts comes in the collective biography *Lives of the Poets of Great Britain and Ireland, to the Time of Dean Swift*, 5 vols. (1753). This was nominally the work of Theophilus Cibber, but it was mainly compiled by Robert Shiels. The author of the entry on AP had the advantage of consulting the edition of 1751 by **William Warburton**, and all in all, it is the most competent work to date.

In 1756 appeared the first volume of the *Essay on the Genius and Writings of Pope* by **Joseph Warton**. This made use of the unpublished notes of Warton's friend **Joseph Spence**, later to form the basis of the celebrated *Anecdotes*. By now, more was beginning to emerge about AP's previously obscure early years. The next attempt came in 1759, with a perfunctory life by W.H. Dilworth, who was also responsible for a biography of **Swift** in the previous year. Despite the promise of "many curious anecdotes of his noble patrons," not much new about AP emerges. More substantial was *The Life of Alexander Pope, with a Critical Essay on his Writings and Genius* (1769). This was the work of the political writer **Owen Ruffhead**, but it owes its being to Warburton, who had long been assembling materials and was displeased by the first volume of Warton's *Essay*. Ruffhead's book was reprinted in London and Dublin, included in an edition of the *Works* of AP, and later translated into French. While the work serves a polemical end, to reinstate Warburton's views as the authoritative line on the poet, it does contain a considerable amount of interesting matter.

A further decade passed before the appearance of the famous study of AP by **Samuel Johnson**, which came out in the *Lives of the Poets* in 1781. It was the longest item in the series and was thought by Sir Joshua Reynolds to be the finest of them all. What may not be apparent today is that Johnson was in some measure responding to the earlier biographers, especially Warton and Ruffhead. Johnson had the advantage of knowing some of AP's friends, including **Richard Savage**. Moreover, he was able to consult other survivors from AP's day, including the **third Earl of Marchmont**, one of the executors AP had appointed in his will. He makes sustained use of Spence's *Anecdotes*; and he enjoyed the benefit of aid from John Nichols (1745–1826), a printer, historian, and editor with a deep knowledge of the literary byways of the eighteenth century. In combination with Johnson's superior power of analysis and his skill as a writer, these factors help to explain the fact that his life is regarded as the best that had yet appeared. In the opinion of the great Popian scholar **George Sherburn** it was still in 1934 "easily the most satisfactory life of the poet yet written" (*Early Career* 13).

Judged purely on grounds of biographic coverage, as distinct from critical insight, it would scarcely be possible to maintain this view today. But Johnson's treatment remains an epoch in the understanding of AP as man and writer.

There was no significant independent biography for several generations. Johnson's life was commonly appended to editions of AP's works, while editors such as **William Lisle Bowles** (1806) and **William Roscoe** (1824) added new letters and unoriginal memoirs. Warton completed his *Essay* with a second volume, published in 1782, and edited the *Works* in 1797. Scholars such as Nichols unearthed new materials. However, the most important development came with the publication of Spence's *Anecdotes* by Samuel Weller Singer in 1820. (An edition by Edmond Malone appeared in the same year.)

The most thorough life for many years was produced by **Robert Carruthers** (1853), but this was partially overtaken soon afterward by the researches of **Charles Wentworth Dilke**, incorporated mainly in notes and scholia dispersed about the academic press. Dilke's revelations concerning the publication of AP's letters caused massive rethinking of the entire literary career and led to many hostile comments on AP's moral standing. One of the most extreme reactions to the new information came in the famous **Elwin and Courthope edition** (1871–89). Elwin was unable to conceal his growing hostility toward AP, and although he relinquished to Courthope the writing of the life, which appears in vol. 5 (1889), his colleague was only a degree or two more charitable in his judgments. Even the volume on AP by **Sir Leslie Stephen** (*English Men of Letters*, 1880), though vigorously written and clearly argued, betrays some of the prejudices of the age regarding the poet's character and motives.

Twentieth-century lives begin with **George Paston**'s two-volume *Mr. Pope: His Life and Times* (1909), often using original findings but unreliable in detail. This was followed by a brilliant attempt to counter Victorian hostility, in the shape of *Alexander Pope* (1930) by **Edith Sitwell**. However, meticulous biographical research is not among the tools at the author's disposal. Much more solid and dependable, if less fun to read, is the study by **Robert Kilburn Root** (1938). By this time the first fully accurate biography had appeared, although it covers only the first half of AP's career: this is *The Early Career of Alexander Pope* (1934) by George Sherburn. As more advanced study of AP's work proceeded, with major advances in editorial and bibliographical sophistication, biography as such took something of a back seat. For example, the life history occupies a relatively minor role in such books as *Alexander Pope* (1951) by **Bonamy Dobrée**. With the appearance of Sherburn's edition of the *Correspondence* in 1956, and the definitive text of the *Anecdotes* prepared by **James Marshall Osborn** in 1966, fresh vistas were opened up. So far few biographies have been written to take advantage of these opportunities. The study by **Peter Quennell** (1968) is a graceful popular life, confined to the earlier phase; by contrast *Alexander Pope: A Literary Life* by Felicity Rosslyn (1990) offers a more searching and ambitious account of AP's career. A work in a category of its own is Reginald Berry's *A Pope Chronology* (1988), which has no connected narrative but lists the life records year by year.

All previous work in the field has been superseded by the magnum opus of AP's most distinguished student, **Maynard Mack**. His book *Alexander Pope: A Life* (1985) contains an unparalleled range of pertinent facts, a full appraisal of the meaning of these facts in relation to AP's work, and a brilliant contextualization of these data. It is likely to remain the standard biography for generations to come. Significant insights into AP's life are found in other books by Mack, notably *The Garden and the City* (1969) and *Collected in Himself* (1982).

Bird, Francis (1667–1731). Sculptor who studied in Rome. Regarded by some contemporaries as "the most famous Statuary, that this Nation ever bred." A director of the Academy of Painting set up under **Sir Godfrey Kneller**. Bird was noted for his statues of **Queen Anne**; the best known stood outside the west front of St.

Paul's Cathedral in London (1712) but had to be replaced in 1886 owing to atmospheric decay of the original. However, statues of the Queen attributed to Bird remain at Kingston, Surrey, and Taunton, Somerset (1719). He was responsible for a number of funeral monuments in Westminster Abbey, some to designs by **James Gibbs**, and sometimes in collaboration with other sculptors. He executed the monument for **William Congreve** (1729). AP negotiated with him in regard to the monument to **James Craggs junior**. Bird was also employed to carve the memorial to AP's parents in **Twickenham parish church**. AP was probably drawn into his orbit as Bird was a Catholic.

birth. AP was born at 6:45 on the evening of Monday, 21 May 1688, probably at the home of his parents in the city of London (see **Plough Court**). His mother, **Edith Pope**, was forty-four; his father, **Alexander Pope senior**, forty-two. AP recorded the time of his birth in a copy of **Virgil** (*EC* 1: 1), which is now lost.

Birthday poem to Martha Blount. Lines written to AP's closest female friend **Martha Blount**, originally for her birthday on 15 June 1723. AP composed what is probably the earliest version at **Twickenham** as a set of fourteen lines in couplets: this survives at **Mapledurham**. He later made several other surviving drafts of this version, which led at least one of the recipients, **Judith Cowper**, to believe that the poem was addressed to her—as AP quite likely intended (see *Corr* 2: 180). Six additional verses first appeared in a play by **James Moore Smythe** in 1727. These were incorporated into a version of twenty lines, which appeared in the *Miscellanies* in 1728. In the meantime, AP had drafted a further ten lines "On a Late Birth Day. 1724," which are found in the Portland papers. Six of these verses were included in the birthday poem when it appeared in the *Works* in 1738. Some of the versions also crept into print during these years in a number of journals and anthologies, under disparate titles. For the complex bibliographical history, see Ault 195–206 and *TE* 6: 244–47, as well as R.M. Schmitz, "Two New Holographs of

Pope's Birthday Lines to Martha Blount," *Review of English Studies*, 8 (1957), 234–40.

AP celebrates Martha in terms anticipating those he uses in the **Epistle to a Lady**. Indeed, the second version of this poem contains a passage (comprising the six additional lines) that was translated bodily to the *Epistle*, where they form part of the poet's devastating portrait of frustrated womanhood. This is one of several affecting poems that AP addressed to the Blount sisters.

Blackmore, Sir Richard (1650–1729). Physician and poet. Educated at Oxford. M.D., Padua; Fellow of the Royal College of Physicians, 1687. He served as physician to **William III** and **Queen Anne** and was knighted in 1697. His many works on medicine included books on spleen (melancholy), gout, smallpox, and bubonic plague. However, he was even better known for his epic poems, notably *Prince Arthur* (1695) and *Creation* (1712). His *Satyr against Wit* (1700) predictably provoked a chorus of opposition from the wits: see R.C. Boys, *Sir Richard Blackmore and the Wits* (Ann Arbor: University of Michigan Press, 1949). The elderly **Dryden** had been one of the first to poke fun at his poetry. Blackmore injudiciously revealed that much of his writing was done while he was traveling in his carriage from one appointment to the next. He also wrote on religion.

Originally he and AP seem to have been on good terms, although they met only twice, according to AP. Blackmore subscribed, indeed, to the *Iliad*. It was when he called **Swift** "an impious buffoon" in the first volume of his *Essays upon Several Subjects*, published by **Edmund Curll** in 1716, that a prolonged onslaught on him was mounted by the Scriblerian group. **John Gay** satirized him in *A Journey to Exeter* (1716); and AP added two mild references in his prose pamphlets against Curll. When Blackmore attacked **Three Hours after Marriage** and **A Roman Catholick Version of the First Psalm** in the second volume of his *Essays* in 1717, hostilities were raised to a higher pitch of bitterness. AP went assiduously about collecting choice examples of ba-

thos for his treatise **The Art of Sinking**, and the results are scattered about this work—hardly any of Blackmore's copious literary efforts escape without quotation. AP made fun especially of Blackmore's exercises in biblical paraphrase (see, for example *Prose* 2: 194–95). Blackmore emerges as "the Father of the Bathos, and indeed the Homer of it," a fact that may lend support to the attribution by **Norman Ault** of **Verses on England's Arch-Poet**. Swift also uses Blackmore as the acme of the "low sublime" in *On Poetry: A Rhapsody*.

Blackmore turns up, usually on account of his "rumbling" verse, in some of AP's **Imitations of Horace**. His style, "stately and yet dull," was likened by AP to the gait of a lumbering draft horse (*TE* 4: 279). The most damaging reference occurs in **The Dunciad**, where "sonorous Blackmore's strain" is heard resounding through the streets of London, until he is hailed as the noisiest of all the poets, "Who sings so loudly, and who sings so long" (2: 247–56). The note draws attention to Blackmore's "indefatigable Muse," which had produced "no less than six Epic poems: *Prince and King Arthur*, 20 Books; *Eliza*, 10," and so on (*TE* 5: 131–32). Since that day, the reputation of Blackmore has never fully recovered, even though **Samuel Johnson** found good things to say about *The Creation*. It is likely, as **James Sutherland** suggested, that AP used Blackmore as a stock example of literary ineptitude: "mere proximity to Blackmore was a form of ridicule" (*TE* 5: 429).

See A. Rosenberg, *Sir Richard Blackmore: A Poet and Physician of the Augustan Age* (Lincoln: University of Nebraska Press, 1953); and H.M. Solomon, *Sir Richard Blackmore* (Boston: Twayne, 1980).

Blast upon Bays, A. Prose pamphlet, subtitled *A New Lick at the Laureate* and promising "remarks on a late tatling performance, entitled, A Letter from Mr. Cibber to Mr. Pope." In 1742 **Colley Cibber** issued *A Letter from Mr. Cibber to Mr. Pope* as part of the exchanges that followed the dramatist's recent elevation to king of the dunces. (See edition for the Augustan Reprint Society, with introduction by H. Koon,

1973.) This contains a number of damaging stories concerning AP's earlier life and also makes allegations concerning the poet's attacks on Cibber (see *A Clue to the Comedy of the Nonjuror*). In the same year, the *Blast* appeared in reply, setting out AP's side of things. The pamphlet, published by T. Robbins, consists of twenty-six pages and is dated at the end "July 29, 1742." It is probable but not certain that AP was the author.

Blenheim Palace. Grand house in an imposing setting of parkland, situated at Woodstock, near **Oxford**. It was presented to the **Duke** and **Duchess of Marlborough** on behalf of the nation, as a reward for the Duke's victory at the battle of Blenheim in Bavaria in August 1704. Work began in 1705, but the house was not entirely completed when the Duke died in 1722. The Duchess continued to add embellishments, although she had long since dismissed the principal architect **Sir John Vanbrugh**. Others involved in this massive project were the architect Nicholas Hawksmoor, the painters Sir James Thornhill and **Louis Laguerre**, and the royal gardeners **Henry Wise** and **Charles Bridgeman**. The interior of the house was crammed with pictures, sculptures, wall hangings, and decorative designs, all celebrating the greatness of Marlborough's achievement. In the park stood numerous arches, columns, pavilions, and other ornaments expressing the same theme. The aim was to create not a private country house but a public monument, equivalent in its ideological content to Versailles, if not built on the same scale. After AP's time the most significant influence on the external landscape was that of Lancelot "Capability" Brown, in the middle of the eighteenth century. Much of his design remains intact today.

AP was skeptical regarding the "grandeur" of the palace and seemingly blind to its extraordinary qualities of imagination and daring. This was partly on political grounds—he regarded the Duke as a cruel instrument of the warmongering Whigs. He thought such a tribute to Marlborough as disproportionate and compared it unfavorably to the public-spirited creations of **Queen Anne** herself and of his friend the **Earl of Burlington**. It is not certain when he first visited the site, as he stayed in Oxfordshire on numerous occasions. A letter to an anonymous correspondent, possibly written around 1717, described the house as resembling its owners, with "no room for strangers," and as being disfigured by monstrous and inconvenient architectural features (*Corr* 1: 431–32). In a letter to **Martha Blount** of 6 August 1718, he refers to the palace as "the most proud & extravagant Heap of Towers in the nation" (*Corr* 1: 480).

In later years he was no less caustic, even though toward the end of his life he became friendly with the aged Duchess of Marlborough. A passage from *An Essay on Man* was adapted to form harsh lines on the Duke, with a stinging allusion to the "pompous Shade" in which the old general had lived out his last days (*TE* 6: 358–59). In the *Epistle to Burlington* his damning portrayal of **Timon's villa** seems to be based at least in part on the more grotesque features of Blenheim: he uses the expression "a labour'd Quarry above ground" (l. 110), and elsewhere tells us that this was how the **Duke of Shrewsbury** had described the house (see *TE* 3.ii: 148, 187). Partly on this basis, the famous **epigram** "Upon the Duke of Marlborough's House at Woodstock" has often been attributed to AP, since it makes a similar joke. However, it is not at all certain that AP wrote these lines on Vanbrugh, which were first published in 1714. Another candidate is **Abel Evans** (see *TE* 6: 412).

A leading authority on all matters relating to Blenheim is **David Green**, who wrote several books in this area. See in particular his study *Blenheim Palace* (London: Country Life, 1951); and his contribution to *Blenheim: Landscape for a Palace*, ed. J. Bond and K. Tiller (Stroud, Gloucestershire: Alan Sutton, 1987). For AP's links with the house, see *P&AGE* 309–17.

Blount, Edward (d. 1726). Friend of AP and distant relative of the Blounts of **Mapledurham**. A member of the Catholic gentry, he was the third son of Sir George Blount (d. 1667), of an old Worcestershire family. In 1686 he inherited his mother's seat at Blagdon, west of

Paignton in Devon, overlooking Torbay. He was married c. 1700 to Annabella Guise, sister of a Gloucestershire squire (see *Duke upon Duke*). Of his four daughters, Mary (1702–73) married Edward Howard, later ninth Duke of Norfolk, in 1727, while Elizabeth (d. 1788) married Hugh, third Baron Clifford in 1725, and Henrietta or Harriot (d. 1782) married the Duke's brother Philip Howard as his second wife in 1739. Henrietta's daughter Anne married the ninth Lord Petre, grandson of the **Baron** who stole the notorious lock in AP's poem. Blount's second cousin was the poet **William Walsh**. He assisted AP in mounting the subscription for the *Iliad*; he also subscribed to the *Odyssey* and to the poems of **Gay** and **Prior**. In 1716 and again in 1717 he lived abroad, at one time in Bruges. He tried to negotiate with the authorities about the taking of oaths of allegiance to **George I** by his fellow Catholics. As "*Ned Blount*" he is listed in *Mr. Pope's Welcome from Greece*. On at least one occasion he visited AP at the poet's **villa**, and his death in July 1726 caused AP deep sadness. Listed in the poet's obituaries as "the kindest of men" (*EC* 1: x). The family house was sold in 1727, pursuant to Blount's will (Public Record Office, PROB 11/610). His widow later lived in Antwerp. About a dozen of the poet's letters to Blount survive.

Blount, Martha (1690–1763). AP's closest female friend. Familiarly known as "Patty." She was the younger daughter of Lister Blount and his wife Martha, a member of the **Englefield family**. Goddaughter of **John Caryll senior**; this connection derived from one of many alliances between the Blounts and the old Catholic families of southern England. Educated at a Benedictine convent in Paris. She returned with her sister **Teresa Blount** to the Elizabethan mansion, **Mapledurham**, on the banks of the Thames upstream from Reading. AP probably made many visits to the house after he met the sisters around 1707. The girls were addicted to books and enjoyed quasi-romantic games of literary flirtation. At almost the same time that AP was forced to leave his home at **Binfield**, the sisters had to leave their home on the mar-

riage of their brother **Michael Blount** in 1715. They went to live with their mother in the West End of London, for some time in Bolton Street, off Piccadilly. Their means were fairly limited, and AP made repeated efforts to put Martha's finances on a more stable basis. He even invested on behalf of the Blounts in the South Sea Company, not altogether successfully (see **South Sea Bubble**). Later Martha spent many summers in the vicinity of **Richmond**, Kew, and Petersham, where she was within easy reach of AP. She was on intimate terms with many persons well known to AP, including **Hugh Bethel** and his sisters; **Lord Bathurst**; **Henrietta Howard, Countess of Suffolk**; and members of the **Scriblerus Club**. Listed as a subscriber to the *Odyssey* and to the poems of **John Gay**.

As time went on, AP became estranged from Teresa, but he never lost his admiration, respect, and affection for Martha. She was perhaps his most trusted confidante. Contemporary gossip suggested that a sexual relationship underlay their friendship, but there is no convincing evidence to prove or disprove this. Late in life AP was involved in an embarrassing quarrel at **Prior Park**, when he was staying together with Martha at the home of **Ralph Allen**. It seems that Allen was put out by Martha's use of his coach to go to Mass in **Bath**, while his wife was suspicious of early morning visits Martha made to AP's room. The resulting estrangement caused great pain to Martha, always a sensitive and shrinking individual. AP remained loyal and soon afterward began to make arrangements to buy the lease of a London town house that Martha was to occupy (see **Berkeley Street**). After the death of AP, she acquired the lease in 1746 and lived there for the rest of her life. In his **will** AP left her £1,000 outright, as well as a life interest in his residuary estate and most of his household goods and chattels. It is a striking testimony to his regard for Martha, although the bequest offended AP's half sister **Magdalen Rackett**. Thirty-six letters survive between the pair. They include some of AP's finest pieces of epistolary writing, both on topics of morality and personal life and on the romantic landscape scenery that Martha greatly loved. A number of anecdotes about AP were collected from her by **Joseph Spence**.

Martha has been described as a "touchy and indecisive woman" (Valerie Rumbold). This is perhaps a little harsh: she lacked confidence and was prone to depressive states then regarded as the effect of "sensibility," particularly in women. On the other hand, she was caring, self-abnegating, and loyal to her friends. She elicited some touching poetry from AP, including the **Birthday poem to Martha Blount**. Martha is the unnamed recipient of *An Epistle to a Lady* and serves as the embodiment of ideal womanhood. She displays the "sober light" of the moon, serene and modest, shows good temper as well as common sense, and remains "mistress of herself" amid the various trials of domestic life.

The best-informed and most intimate study of Martha will be found in *Women's Place*, esp. 251–94.

Blount, Michael (1693–1739). Younger brother of AP's friends **Teresa** and **Martha Blount** and grandson of Anthony Englefield (see **Englefield family**). On the death of his father Lister Blount in June 1710, he came into possession of **Mapledurham**, but the estate was already heavily encumbered with debt. Michael subscribed to the *Iliad*. His marriage to Mary Agnes Tichborne in 1715 forced the sisters to leave the house and move to London. Michael was dilatory in paying their allowances as stipulated by a legal settlement, and AP became irritated by what seemed to him Michael's lack of care for the family property, as well as his unkindness to his mother and sisters. He is said to have been addicted to the pleasures of the town, and once a companion was killed in a street brawl after a night out in London. In the year of his death Blount calculated that he had overspent his income by £2,500 over time; it would have been more, had his wife not consented to go without "Diament Earings." The impact of double taxation under the penal laws continued to ravage the family finances in the time of his son and successor, also Michael (1719–92).

Blount, Teresa (1688–1759). Member of a Catholic family with close ties to AP's circle and older sister of his closest woman friend **Martha Blount**. Probably born in Paris. Like her sister, she was educated in the English Benedictine convent at Paris. Despite her acknowledged beauty, the decline in the family's finances meant that she could expect no worthwhile dowry, and expectations of a glittering marriage withered away. She remained single. Unlike Martha, Teresa was attracted to the social life of the town and may have had an affair with a married man. Her relations with her sister were sometimes strained, although they never altogether broke down. In her later years she lived in London on a small income and often borrowed money from Martha.

AP met the sisters probably c. 1707 through his contacts with the Mapledurham family. Initially he seems to have been attracted to Teresa, but over time his affection (like those of most people who knew them) shifted to the quieter and less volatile "Patty." Both figure in *Mr. Pope's Welcome from Greece*. After about 1720 the poet had little to do with Teresa. According to **Magdalen Rackett**, AP's opinion came to be one summarized as, "*Patty Bl* the fair one, Mr. *Pope*'s, the other he did not love, call'd Bitch, Hoyden" ("New Anecdotes" 348). A portrait of the sisters by **Charles Jervas**, c. 1716, survives at Mapledurham. Musically inclined, Teresa was painted at the keyboard by **Kneller**.

Teresa is the possible recipient of AP's *Epistle to Miss Blount, with the Works of Voiture* and the likely addressee of *To Miss Blount, on her Leaving the Town, after the Coronation*. AP gave her a copy of his *Works* (**1717**), which also survives at Mapledurham with an autographed inscription, "Teresa Maria Blount given by the author." This would seem to be the volume referred to in AP's *Verses sent to Mrs T.B. with his Works*, where a tone of measured criticism is already apparent. Sixteen letters are preserved from AP to Teresa, none later than 1720.

See *Women's Place* for almost everything that is known about Teresa.

Blunt, Sir John (1667–1733). Projector, financier, and principal architect of the **South Sea Bubble**. The son of a shoemaker from Kent, he came from a Baptist family. According to AP, "He was a Dissenter of a most religious deportment, and profess'd to be a great believer" (*TE* 3.ii: 104). Blunt became a scrivener in the city of London and in 1703 secretary of the Sword Blade Company (an organization set up to mount elaborate credit schemes). It was he who persuaded the **first Earl of Oxford** to set up the South Sea Company and who drafted its charter. He was named as one of the original directors of the company. As South Sea stock climbed to dizzy heights, Blunt became a celebrity and was created a baronet in 1719. A year later, after the collapse of the bubble, he attracted intense public dislike. He was grilled by the committee of inquiry into the debacle and forced to reveal embarrassing facts, such as the gift of tranches of South Sea stock to the mistresses of **George I**. Branded as "the chief contriver and promoter of all the mischief," he was forced to sacrifice his huge estate, except for a tiny residue. He attempted to conceal £50,000 of his assets by means of a fraudulent conveyance to the forger **John Ward**. The scheme was detected, but Blunt was pardoned after revealing its nature. He continued to defend himself vigorously for the remainder of his life. He died at **Bath** on 23 January 1733.

AP may not have known Blunt personally, though many of his own acquaintances, such as **James Craggs junior**, certainly did. Blunt subscribed to the *Iliad*. The passage that AP wrote about the projector in his *Epistle to Bathurst* is richly complicated: although it clearly presents Blunt as a rogue on a massive scale, there is a measure of understanding and a sense that Blunt may have been a scapegoat used to protect the skin of others equally guilty. However, it would not have escaped AP's attention that Blunt was fined by the Court of Chivalry for illegally adopting the arms of the Blounts of Sodington—the family from which AP's beloved friend **Edward Blount** descended.

See *TE* 3.ii: 104–6 for AP's character sketch of Blunt. The most important account of his career and AP's response to him will be found in *Social Milieu* 166–203.

Boileau, Nicolas, called Despréaux (1636–1711). Poet. Sometimes known as "the legislator of Parnassus," he abandoned studies in theology and law to embark on a literary career. His friends included Jean Racine and Molière. Appointed historiographer royal with Racine in 1677. His early works were chiefly satires and epistles, expressing a combative element in his personality (he has been seen as a possible model for Molière's *Misanthrope*). In 1674 he brought out his *Art poétique*, an "art of poetry" based on **Horace** and in turn influencing AP's *Essay on Criticism*. This was one of the key documents of classicism. At the same time his translation of Longinus anticipated the cult of the sublime in England (see *The Art of Sinking*). A poem in six cantos, *Le lutrin* (The Lectern), published in 1674–83, developed **mock-heroic** to a new level of sophistication and technical skill, paving the way for AP's own *Rape of the Lock*, as well as lesser English examples headed by **Samuel Garth**'s *Dispensary*. Elected to the Académie Française in 1684, he became the leading light in the camp of the Ancients in the fierce contests between **Ancients and Moderns**. For a hundred years Boileau's reputation continued to shine brightly. During the nineteenth century he lost cachet and came to be regarded as a tedious apostle of literary conformity. More recently his stress on "correctness" has been reevaluated as pointing to much more than metrical smoothness and rhetorical decorum: it indicates a whole code of politeness and civilized discourse.

AP was certainly influenced by Boileau's work and by his projection of the role of the satirist as a "friend of the truth." He termed Boileau "the first poet of the French in the same manner as Virgil of all the Latin" (*Anecdotes* 1: 220). Some editions of the poet were preserved in AP's **library**. AP found little to praise in the translation of *Le lutrin* by **John Ozell**. A possible attribution is a version of a passage in Boileau's second epistle, printed in **Warburton**'s edition of the *Works* (see *TE* 6: 388). The nature and extent of AP's debt to Boileau needs to be fully explored in the light of modern criticism. See A.F.B. Clark, *Boileau and the French Classical Critics in England, 1660–1830* (Paris: Champion, 1925); E. Audra, *L'influence française dans l'oeuvre de Pope* (Paris: Champion, 1931); and G. Pocock, *Boileau and the Nature of Neo-Classicism* (Cambridge: Cambridge University Press, 1980).

Bolingbroke, Henry St. John, first Viscount (1678–1751). Statesman and author. One of the major figures in politics and culture during AP's lifetime and a close friend of the poet. He was an MP from 1701 and became Secretary at War from 1704 to 1708. During the period of the **Harley administration** he served as Secretary of State and took a leading share in the negotiations leading to the **Treaty of Utrecht**. Created a viscount, 1712. Gradually estranged from his chief, the **first Earl of Oxford**. After the death of **Queen Anne** and the fall of the ministry, his position grew exposed owing to his contacts with the Jacobite court. Fled the country in 1715 when under threat of impeachment for treason, and joined the court of the **Pretender**, accepting a Jacobite earldom. Broke with James Edward and was dismissed in 1716. Obtained a partial pardon and returned to England, 1723. Settled at **Dawley**, where he entertained AP, **Swift, Gay, Voltaire**, and others. Helped to launch the **opposition to Walpole** and to found its house organ, *The Craftsman*. Disillusioned by the failure of the effort to oust Walpole, he retired once more to France in 1735. He came back to England for a last time in 1743 and for a time renewed his attempts to form a "broad-bottomed" administration to supplant the durable Whig regime. Bolingbroke began to publish books on political, philosophical, and historical subjects, reflecting his classicizing, deistic, and reconstructed Tory attitudes. The most important of these works were *Remarks on the History of England* (1730–31); *A Dissertation upon Parties* (1733–34); *A Letter on the Spirit of Patriotism* (1736); *The Idea of a Patriot King* (1739); and *Letters on the Study and Use of History* (1752). Some of his writings were collected in 1748; after his death, his *Works* were edited in five volumes (1754) by **David Mallet**. They occasioned a great deal of controversy, partly on grounds of religious unorthodoxy but also because of his apparent disloyalty toward his former friend AP. His sternest critic was perhaps **William Warburton**.

Bolingbroke's relations with AP went through several stages across almost half a century. At the start of the poet's career, Henry St. John was one of those to support the young man's work ("New Anecdotes" 347): he was himself devoted to **Sir William Trumbull**, whom he addressed as "Dear Patron, Master and Friend." The estate of his first wife, Frances Winchcombe, lay in **Berkshire**, and during St. John's periods of retirement there, he was in easy reach of **Binfield**. When he entered government, he became a regular companion of Swift, and the two men were leading lights in the **Brothers Club**. At this stage AP was perhaps a more distant acquaintance. However, Bolingbroke subscribed for ten sets of the *Iliad*. After Bolingbroke returned from exile for the first time, the two became close friends and literary allies and often met at Dawley. Sometimes Bolingbroke would make the return journey of about seven miles and saunter in the garden at **Twickenham**. AP absorbed many ideas from Bolingbroke, and it has been thought (how reliably cannot now be said) that the philosophical structure of *An Essay on Man* was founded on his friend's views. The poem is certainly dedicated in fulsome terms to his "guide, philosopher, and friend" (*TE* 3.i: 166). Another work addressed to the peer is *The First Epistle of the First Book of Horace Imitated*. AP's admiration for Bolingbroke knew scarcely any bounds: he was "absolutely the best writer of the age"; he knew "more of Europe than perhaps all Europe put together at present"; and he was "something superior to anything I have seen in human nature. You know I don't deal in hyperboles. I quite think him what I say." More examples could be given (*Anecdotes* 1: 119–28). The two men renewed their intimacy when Bolingbroke finally came back to England, and the peer was present when

AP approached his **death**. According to one account, he leaned over AP's chair, crying like a child as the end came near (*Anecdotes* 1: 645). To the end AP kept a portrait of his friend by **Jonathan Richardson senior** in his house. In his **will** he made Bolingbroke the custodian of his manuscripts but not his books, which went to Warburton: an exception was a fine set of AP's own works bound in red morocco, bequeathed to the peer.

Unfortunately this harmony did not extend beyond the poet's grave. When Bolingbroke discovered that AP had arranged for a private printing of some of his work, he became violently angry and spent his remaining years in bitter recriminations. Warburton took on himself to act in defense of the dead poet, and bitter controversy ensued. It is an unedifying tale, which does not reflect great credit on any of the major participants. Bolingbroke's reputation had already begun to sink, and he has only been rehabilitated as a political thinker in the past thirty years.

See B. Hammond, *Pope and Bolingbroke: A Study of Friendship and Influence* (Columbia: University of Missouri Press, 1984). The best biography is H.T. Dickinson, *Bolingbroke* (London: Constable, 1970). A useful blow-by-blow account of the political infights during the Tory administration is S. Biddle, *Bolingbroke and Harley* (London: Allen & Unwin, 1975). A controversial statement of Bolingbroke's thought in relation to the evolution of a "new England" is I. Kramnick, *Bolingbroke and His Circle: The Politics of Nostalgia in the Age of Walpole* (Cambridge, MA: Harvard University Press, 1968; reprint Ithaca: Cornell University Press, 1992). See also *The Idea of a Patriot King*.

Bond, Donald Frederic (1898–1987). Scholar who taught at the University of Chicago. His many works on editorial and bibliographical topics are of great use to students of AP. He collaborated with **George Sherburn** on sections devoted to the Restoration and eighteenth century in *A Literary History of England* (1967). However, it is Bond's editions of *The Spectator*, 5 vols. (1965), and *The Tatler*, 3 vols. (1987), that have given indispensable aid to all scholars of the period. His essay on AP's letters is reprinted in *EA* 695–704: and see "Pope's Contributions to the *Spectator*," *Modern Language Quarterly*, 5 (1944), 69–78.

Bond, Richmond Pugh (1899–1979). Professor at the University of North Carolina, he did not write extensively on AP. However, his works on the early English periodical, including *The Tatler: The Making of a Literary Journal* (1971), hold considerable relevance, as do his study of *English Burlesque Poetry, 1700–1750* (1932) and his book on *Queen Anne's American Kings* (1952). See also *The Dress of Words: Essays on Restoration and Eighteenth Century Literature in Honor of Richmond P. Bond*, ed. R.B. White (1978).

Bononcini, Giovanni (1670–1747). Name often spelled "Buononcini." Italian composer who achieved early prominence in his native country and in Vienna. He met the **Earl of Burlington** in 1719, then worked in England from 1720 to 1732. *Astarto*, composed in 1720 to a libretto by **Paolo Antonio Rolli**, was published with a dedication to Burlington. At first Bononcini operated in association with **Handel** for the Royal Academy of Music, until party feuds over **opera** led to the two men being portrayed as rivals. Both men contributed to the triple-composed opera *Muzio Scevola* in April 1721, but Handel's portion was much the best received. Bononcini obtained some nonoperatic commissions, notably for an anthem at the funeral of the **Duke of Marlborough** in 1722. He also set to music some choruses intended for a version of *Julius Caesar*, written by the **Duke of Buckinghamshire**, which was performed privately in 1723: AP is thought to have written the words for these choruses. For text and annotation, see *TE* 6: 151–55. From 1725 to 1731 Bononcini was composer in residence for **Henrietta, Duchess of Marlborough**, daughter of the late Duke.

AP was drawn into his orbit when the operatic feuds were at their height. Bononcini went to live in **Twickenham** in the summer of 1721, where he was surrounded by well-wishers, including the **Earl of Peterborough** and his mistress **Anastasia Robinson**; the diplomat Giuseppe Riva; **Lady Mary Wortley Montagu**; and the **Duchess of Buckinghamshire**. Together this group promoted a campaign on behalf of their favorite. When Bononcini's *Cantate* were published in the same year, the subscription list was crammed with these cronies from Twickenham and surrounding areas. (Other local residents were Lord Radnor, **Thomas Stonor**, and Mrs. Vernon, wife of **Thomas Vernon**.) The key personages in the list were the Prince and Princess of Wales, later **George II** and **Queen Caroline**. The court was further represented by several attendants on the Princess, including **Mary Hervey** (plus her husband), **Henrietta Howard**, and Sophia Howe. The list also numbered in its coverage many of AP's own personal friends and allies at this juncture, including the **Dukes of Argyll, Chandos**, and **Queensberry**; the **Duchess of Hamilton**; the **second Earl of Oxford** and his wife; **Baron Digby**; **Sir Godfrey Kneller**; Lord Stanhope (later **Earl of Chesterfield**); **Viscountess Scudamore**; General **James Dormer** and his brother Robert; the printer **John Barber**; and **William Pulteney**. The poet's most intimate acquaintances represented include **Dr. John Arbuthnot, Charles Jervas**, and **Hugh Bethel**. All these facts strongly support the contention that AP took a leading share in pushing the subscription. He admitted as much, writing of the great esteem he had for Bononcini, "not only from his great Fame, but from a Personal Knowledge of his Character." AP also lamented the ill treatment the composer had received, probably on account of his Catholicism. It is anachronistic to speak of an "opposition" at this juncture, but the 220 subscribers contain an unmistakably high proportion of those who were well disposed toward the Prince of Wales. See *Corr* 2: 99.

For the background, see W. Dean and J.M. Knapp, *Handel's Operas* (Oxford: Clarendon, 1995).

Booth, Barton (1681–1733). Actor. He succeeded **Thomas Betterton** as the leading tragedian on the English stage in the first quarter of the eighteenth century, appearing first at the **Haymarket** and then at **Drury Lane Theatre**, where he served as joint manager with **Colley Cibber** and others. Mostly known for his Shakespearean roles, he achieved special prominence when he took the title role in **Joseph Addison**'s controversial hit *Cato* in 1713, an occasion at which AP was present. Famous for his mellifluous voice and articulate delivery, he seems to have offended AP, who devotes some double-edged lines to Booth in the **Epistle to Augustus**. Subscribed to the *Iliad*. He is one of the party greeting AP in *Mr. Pope's Welcome from Greece*, along with "Santlow fam'd for dance," that is, Hester Santlow (c. 1690–1773), whom Booth later married.

Borlase, William (1695–1772). Clergyman and antiquarian; Rector of Ludgvan, near Penzance in Cornwall, from 1722 until his death. FRS, 1750; LlD, 1766. He was the author of *Cornish Antiquities* (1754) and other works enlisting his special knowledge of mineralogy and geology, as well as routine antiquarian skills such as heraldry, genealogy, and classical learning. He was also a gardener. His cousin **Dr. William Oliver** wrote a letter of introduction to him for AP in 1740 and after this Borlase provided many rock specimens for the poet's **grotto**. He was an assiduous letter-writer, but unfortunately none of his correspondence to AP has turned up. Two letters from AP survive.

See B. Boyce, "Mr. Pope, in Bath, Improves the Design of his Grotto," in *Restoration and Eighteenth-Century Literature: Essays in Honor of Alan Dugald McKillop*, ed. C. Camden (Chicago: University of Chicago Press, 1963), 143–53.

Bounce, Lines on. A couplet included in AP's letter to his friend the **fifth Earl of Orrery**, written on 10 April 1744, only seven weeks before the poet died. It concerns the last of AP's **dogs** to be named Bounce, which had been given to Orrery at **Marston** two years earlier. Unhappily Bounce had been bitten by a rabid dog and had been put down; AP knew of his death but not the full story. He tells Orrery that he is sure Bounce was lamented, just as Arcite was in **Chaucer**'s *Knight's Tale*, and parodies a couplet in the tale: "Ah Bounce! Ah gentle Beast! Why wouldst thou dye, / When thou had'st Meat enough, and Orrery?" These tender lines by AP, comically echoing Chaucer's stress on "Emilye," were "probably the last he ever wrote" (see *Corr* 4: 517–18: *TE* 6: 405).

Bounce to Fop. In full, ***Bounce to Fop: An Heroic Epistle from a Dog at Twickenham to a Dog at Court***. A poem of ninety-four lines in octosyllabic couplets. It was first published by **Thomas Cooper** in London, falsely claiming to reprint a Dublin edition, about 4 May 1736. (A Dublin printing by **George Faulkner** is probably later in date [Foxon B326].) It was reprinted in the *Gentleman's Magazine* later that month. The London title page adds "by Dr. SW——T." One of the contemporary transcripts belonged to the **second Earl of Oxford**, who appended a gloss "much alterd by Mr Pope." The item entered the *Miscellanies* in 1736, omitting a final paragraph praising AP, and remained there in later issues of this series. Later in the eighteenth century it began to appear in collected editions of both **Swift** and **Gay**. Since 1950, influenced by the studies of **Norman Ault**, it has been reincorporated into the works of AP.

Gay is not really a serious candidate for authorship, and the only name that has been adduced, that of Henry Carey, seems wholly implausible. It is generally agreed that the original idea belonged to Swift, perhaps when he visited England in 1726 and 1727, and that AP played some part in revising the work. Disagreement focuses on the extent of this revision.

The verses are written in the voice of a dog named "Bounce": AP's **dogs** included several with this name, the best known of whom produced a puppy given to the **Prince of Wales** in 1736. It is addressed to "Fop," who may have belonged to **Henrietta Howard** (Ault's theory) or else to the ninth **Earl of Pembroke**. Internal examination suggests that the main lines of the poem were laid down by 1732 at the latest, although AP may have tinkered with the text after that. A very large range of parallels with Swift's known works, especially his satires in

octosyllabic verse, strongly suggest that his was the main hand in composition. AP's role was in all likelihood confined to preparing the manuscript for publication, perhaps in the Cooper edition and certainly the version in the *Miscellanies*.

The aim of the poem is to make playful fun of courtiers and court life. Reference is made to the Prince of Wales and also to leading aristocrats such as **Bathurst, Burlington, Cobham**, Oxford, and **Strafford**. The text as it appeared in Cooper's printing ends with eight lines celebrating "Master Pope."

For full discussion of these issues, see Ault 342–50; and P. Rogers, "The Authorship of 'Bounce to Fop': A Re-examination," *Bulletin of Research in the Humanities*, 85 (1982), 241–68.

Bowles, William Lisle (1762–1850). Clergyman and poet, best known for his sonnets, which influenced both S.T. Coleridge and Robert Southey. In 1806 Bowles published an undistinguished ten-volume edition of AP's works, in which he criticized AP as a man and as a poet. A controversy opened up in 1819 between Bowles, **Thomas Campbell**, Isaac D'Israeli, and others over these views. **Baron Byron** (Lord Byron) joined in the fray with his *Letter to [John Murray]* (1821). After Byron's death in 1824 the debate went on for some time, involving **William Roscoe**, among others.

The controversy has been extensively studied, as indicating the main tides in poetic tastes during this era. See J.J. Rennes, *Bowles, Byron and the Pope-Controversy* (Amsterdam: H.J. Paris, 1927).

Bowyer, William senior (1663–1737) **and William junior** (1699–1777). Printers, father and son. The elder Bowyer was a leading figure in the London book trade, apprenticed in 1679 and freed in 1686. He often worked with the publisher **Jacob Tonson senior**. The younger, who became a partner with his father in 1722, was known as "the learned printer." He was educated at **Cambridge** and was appointed printer to both houses of Parliament, as well as to the Royal Society and the Society of Antiquaries. He also wrote a number of books. His apprentice and successor was the well-known antiquarian John Nichols (1745–1826).

The father printed most of AP's main works c. 1714–25, including the *Iliad*, the *Works (1717)*, and *Poems on Several Occasions*, a volume AP almost certainly edited. He claimed rights in some items by **Jonathan Swift** that AP wished to reprint in the *Miscellanies*, a matter that caused a short-term breach between poet and printer. In his last years AP, seemingly dissatisfied with his protégé **John Wright**, adopted the younger Bowyer to print his works, including the so-called **deathbed edition**. The connection continued with the *Works* (1751), which **William Warburton** brought out after AP's death. Seven letters from AP to the son, all written late in life, are known to survive.

See J. Nichols, *Anecdotes Biographical and Literary of W. Bowyer, Printer* (London: Private printing, 1778), the germ of the well-known *Literary Anecdotes* of Nichols, which came out in 9 vols. (1812–15). For the conduct of the business, see a valuable compilation, *The Bowyer Ledgers: The Printing Accounts of William Bowyer, Father and Son*, reproduced on microfiche, together with *A Checklist of Bowyer Printing, 1699–1777*, ed. K. Maslen and J. Lancaster (London: Bibliographical Society, 1991). Further information is available in K.I.D. Maslen, *The Bowyer Ornament Stock* (Oxford: Oxford Bibliographical Society, 1973); and *An Early London Printing House at Work: Studies in the Bowyer Ledgers* (New York: Bibliographical Society of America, 1993).

Boyce, Benjamin (1903–97). Scholar who taught at Duke University. Wrote a number of studies of the "character" as a literary form, especially with regard to AP in his book *The Character-Sketches in Pope's Poems* (1962). Also responsible for a life of the comic writer **Thomas Brown** (1939). Later he developed a particular interest in AP's friend **Ralph Allen**: the outcome was *The Benevolent Man: A Life of Ralph Allen of Bath* (1967).

Bredvold, Louis Ignatius (1888–1977). Scholar at the University of Michigan, best known for his work on **Dryden**, Edmund Burke, and **Byron**. Together with **Robert Kilburn Root** and **George Sherburn**, he edited a selection of *Eighteenth-Century Prose* (1932), and with **Alan Dugald McKillop**, a widely used anthology of writing from the period (1939). His work on AP includes a selection of the poems (1926) and a much-debated essay, "The Gloom of the Tory Satirists," in *Pope and His Contemporaries*, ed. J.L. Clifford and L.A. Landa (Oxford: Clarendon Press, 1949), 1–19.

Breval, John Durant (c. 1680–1738). A former captain in the army of the **Duke of Marlborough** who became a regular author for **Edmund Curll** around 1716. His first success was *The Art of Dress* (1717). In the same year he produced a farcical satire on AP and his friends titled *The Confederates*. Often he wrote under the pseudonym "Joseph Gay," as with a volume of *Miscellanies* put out by Curll in 1719. AP alluded to this in *The Dunciad*: "Curl stretches after Gay, but Gay is gone, / He grasps an empty Joseph for a John!" (2: 119–20). A thorn in AP's flesh for several years.

Bridewell. A prison in London, situated in Whitefriars on the west bank of the **Fleet Ditch**, not far from its entrance into the Thames. It stood on the site of an ancient royal palace and had been given by Edward VI to the city of London in 1553 to provide a workplace for the poor and idle. In time this function was overtaken by its role as a house of correction for prostitutes, pickpockets, and vagrants. Prisoners were commonly given a whipping on their arrival and set to tasks such as spinning.

AP refers in *The Dunciad* to the moment when the troop of dunces reach Bridewell as "morning-pray'r and flagellation end." A note explains, "It is between eleven and twelve in the morning, after church service that the criminals are whipp'd in *Bridewell*" (*TE* 5: 133). The normal quota for prostitutes seems to have been twelve lashes. Spectators could witness this punishment from a special viewing gallery.

Bridgeman, Charles (c. 1690–1738). Name sometimes spelled "Bridgman." Landscape gardener, one of the most important figures in the transition from the formal French style to the "natural" English manner. Early in his career he worked under **Henry Wise** at **Blenheim** and afterward at Castle Howard. His two most important achievements were **Stowe** and **Rousham**; his major innovation was the use of the "haha" or sunken ditch. Other major gardens with which he was associated include **Amesbury, Chiswick**, Claremont, Cliveden, **Down Hall**, Houghton (for **Robert Walpole**), Hyde Park and Kensington Gardens (where he created the Serpentine and the Round Pond), **Marble Hill**, and **Wimpole**. From 1726 he was Royal Gardener along with Wise, and from 1728 to his death he held this post alone. He had a close collaboration with **Queen Caroline**, working for her at **Richmond** and elsewhere.

AP was on good terms with Bridgeman, who was employed by many of AP's own patrons, including **James Dormer**, the **second Earl of Oxford**, and **Viscount Bolingbroke**. The gardener often worked in collaboration with the architect **James Gibbs**. It is possible that Bridgeman played some role in the creation of **Pope's garden**, but the evidence is lost. The two men appear to have had some minor disagreements over landscaping matters: in the first printing of the *Epistle to Burlington*, AP had written a couplet, "The vast Parterre a thousand hands shall make, / Lo! *Bridgman* comes, and floats them with a Lake." Bridgeman regarded this as an insult, whereas AP claimed it was a compliment; but in later editions the gardener's name was replaced by that of **Viscount Cobham** (see *TE* 3.ii: 144).

See P. Willis, *Charles Bridgeman and the English Landscape Garden*, rev. ed. (Newcastle upon Tyne: Elysium, 2002). For AP's links, see *P&AGE* 163–70.

Bridges, Ralph (1679–1758). Clergyman. He was a nephew of **Sir William Trumbull**, as the son of Sir William's sister Elizabeth. His correspondence with his uncle gives us some of our fullest knowledge of AP's early years. He was educated at **Oxford** and became chaplain to the Bishop of London, Henry Compton. From this position he kept Trumbull informed on public affairs in London. In 1708 AP left with Bridges a draft of the **Episode of Sarpedon** from the *Iliad* and asked his friend to give his opinion of the translation. Bridges duly sent the verses back to Trumbull with detailed comments. Pope's response survives (see *TE* 1: 353–58; *Corr* 1: 43–45). The last known letter from Bridges to AP dates from 1715: however, he subscribed to the *Odyssey* a decade later. From 1713 to 1758 Bridges was Vicar of South Weald, near Brentwood in Essex. His brother John (1666–1724), a lawyer and antiquarian, also corresponded with Trumbull and subscribed to the *Iliad*.

See G. Sherburn, "Letters of Alexander Pope, Chiefly to Sir William Trumbull," *Review of English Studies*, 9 (1958), 388–406.

Brinsden, John (d. 1743). Secretary to **Viscount Bolingbroke**. AP wrote in March 1743 that Brinsden's death had "really grieved" him, as "he was the most faithfull Friend as well as Servant to his Lord, in the most trying Times, & has withstood all Temptations, as manfully as he supported all Pains" (*Corr* 4: 443). AP corresponded in a friendly fashion with Brinsden, whom he regarded as a candid and good-natured man, and to whom he once offered to lend his house (or possibly the adjoining cottage) while he was himself in Bath. John Brinsden subscribed to **John Gay**'s poems in 1720. A son, Charles Brinsden, became a clergyman and served as chaplain to the Duke of Chandos. Letters from AP to Charles survive, mostly relating to the health of the father.

Bristol. City and port in the west of England. In 1739 AP was advised to drink the waters at Clifton spa, overlooking the gorge of the Avon river. He traveled there after breaking his journey at **Bath** around 14 November. He stayed only a few days and was back at Bath on 22 November. In two letters written to **Martha Blount**, AP gave a detailed description of the spa and of the city of Bristol (*Corr* 4: 200–205). He stayed at Bath until 10 February and may have paid further visits to Bristol. While in the city AP made contact by letter with **Richard Savage**, who was then living there, but he did not see the poet. Savage had been due to seek a sheltered home at Swansea but continued to hang around Bristol.

In August 1743 AP made another visit of about a week to Bristol (*Corr* 4: 466–69), having traveled down the Avon with **George Arbuthnot**, "thro the most Romantic Scene I could desire."

Brooks, Cleanth (1906–94). Scholar and professor at Yale University from 1946. An important critic who together with Robert Penn Warren (1905–89) wrote influential studies of literary criticism, as well as a history of the discipline in conjunction with **William Kurtz Wimsatt**. He was responsible for a classic essay on *The Rape of the Lock*, "The Case of Miss Arabella Fermor: A Re-examination," first published in the *Sewanee Review* (1943), 505–24, reprinted in *EA* 247–65.

Broome, William (1689–1745). Clergyman and poet. Educated at Eton and **Cambridge**. Together with **John Ozell** and William Oldisworth, he produced a prose version of the *Iliad* (1712), which probably led to his employment by AP on the poet's own translation (Broome made extracts from the commentary of Eustathius, to be used in AP's notes). Rector of Stuston, on the border of Suffolk with Norfolk, from 1713. In 1728 he gained the crown living of nearby Pulham Market, Norfolk, and he also acquired benefices in the neighborhood at Eye and Oakley. He composed *Poems on Several Occasions*, published by **Bernard Lintot** in 1727, and two sermons.

After his work on the *Iliad*, Broome was employed by AP to translate eight books of the *Odyssey*. Later Broome came to feel that his work had not been recognized at its full worth, and a coolness developed between the two men. "He has used me ill, he is ungrateful," Broome told his fellow collaborator on the project, **Elijah Fenton**, in 1728 (*Corr* 2: 489). Broome actually figures in chapter 6 of *The Art of Sinking* (*Prose* 2: 197), and AP could not resist a thrust in *The Dunciad*: "Hibernian Politicks, O Swift, thy doom, / And Pope's, translating three whole years with Broome" (*TE* 5: 190–91). Af-

ter Broome naturally complained, AP took the reference out in 1736. The two seem to have been reconciled in later years but never again enjoyed a relationship of any warmth. About seventy letters from AP to Broome survive, dating between 1714 and 1736; many letters from Fenton to Broome are also preserved.

Brothers Club. More accurately "The Society." This was the popular name of a dining club that met weekly from the summer of 1711 and subsequently fortnightly from the end of 1712. The group broke up in the following spring. Its membership included politicians, courtiers, peers, men about town, and a few chosen solely for their wit and learning. Only one common factor united the members: their strong Tory proclivities. The original instigator was Henry St. John, later **Viscount Bolingbroke**, but its effective leader in terms of organization and effort was **Jonathan Swift**. Other members included **George Granville**; **Sir William Wyndham**; Edward Harley, later **second Earl of Oxford**; **Simon Harcourt**; the Earl of Arran, brother of the **Duke of Ormonde**; **Lord Bathurst**; **Matthew Prior**; **John Arbuthnot**; **Henry Disney**; Samuel Masham; and Dr. John Freind. The **first Earl of Oxford** was pointedly excluded. At first the club met at the Thatched House Tavern on St. James's Street; later it moved to the Star and Garter, Pall Mall.

AP was not a member and only came to know Swift during the course of the Society's existence. But some of the other members were already at least acquaintances, and several others became intimate friends of the poet in years to come.

Brower, Reuben Arthur (1908–75). Famous teacher at Amherst College and Harvard University. Known for his work on **William Shakespeare**, Jane Austen, and translation. His book titled *Alexander Pope: The Poetry of Allusion* (1959) is the outstanding study of AP in relation to classical models and exemplars.

Brown, Thomas (1663–1704). Generally known as "Tom Brown." Miscellaneous author, chiefly of comic works. One of the most visible figures in literature in AP's youth, he comes in for a slightly misplaced sideswipe in *The Art of Sinking*, chapter 12.

See B. Boyce, *Tom Brown of Facetious Memory: Grub Street in the Age of Dryden* (Cambridge, MA: Harvard University Press, 1939; reprint, New York: Johnson Reprint Corporation, 1968).

Browne, Sir George (d. 1719). An Oxfordshire gentleman, the original of **"Sir Plume"** in *The Rape of the Lock*. He was the fourth baronet, succeeding c. 1692. His family descended from the Brownes who held the title of Lord Montagu in Sussex. His first wife, Gertrude (d. 1720), was a sister of **John Morley**, who in turn was married to Browne's sister Elizabeth. His second wife was a sister of Sir George Thorold. It is possible that AP knew the baronet personally. Browne's uncle had married into the family of the Englefields in **Berkshire** (see **Englefield family**) and was the grandfather of **Arabella Fermor**, the original of Belinda in the poem. Moreover, Browne's grandmother was a member of the **Blount** family of **Mapledurham**. In 1714 Browne sold an estate in Berkshire to AP's mentor **Sir William Trumbull**.

There are signs that Browne may have been displeased by his portrayal in *The Rape*, as AP told **John Caryll junior** on 8 November 1712, "Sir Plume blusters." He may even have threatened reprisal against the author of the poem (see *Corr* 1: 151, 164). The character displayed was said to be "the very picture of the man" (*Anecdotes* 1: 44–45). For further details of Browne's life, see *TE* 2: 376–77.

Bruce, Charles, Baron (1682–1747), later third Earl of Ailesbury and fourth Earl of Elgin. A nobleman whose father, a **Jacobite**, lived most of his life abroad. One of the twelve peers created by the **first Earl of Oxford** at the end of 1711 to force through the peace process. His first wife was Anne Saville (d. 1717), sister of the **Countess of Burlington**; his second was Lady Juliana Boyle (d. 1739), sister of the **Earl of Burlington**; and his third was Caroline Campbell, daughter of **Mary Bellenden**. His

daughter Elizabeth (d. 1771) married the eldest son of **Lord Bathurst** in 1732; another daughter Mary (d. 1738) married the son of the **Duke of Chandos**. AP visited his seat at **Tottenham Park** in 1734. Lord Bruce appears among AP's friends in *Mr. Pope's Welcome from Greece*. He subscribed to the *Iliad*, and his second wife Lady Juliana to the poems of **John Gay**.

Brutus, **epic on.** Near the end of his life, in 1743, AP was planning to write an epic poem on "civil and ecclesiastical government." The hero was to be the legendary figure Brutus (not to be confused with Marcus Brutus, the hero of *Julius Caesar*), who was supposed to have been the grandson of Aeneas. According to a well-known myth, he had traveled from Troy to found the British nation. Although AP had a full scheme for the poem in his mind, he left only an outline together with the opening eight lines in blank verse, both of which survive in the British Library (*Anecdotes* 1: 153). An extensive summary was provided by **Owen Ruffhead** in his biography of 1769. For modern discussions, see E.G. Snyder, "Pope's Blank Verse Epic," *Journal of English and Germanic Philology*, 18 (1919), 580–83; F. Brie, "Pope's *Brutus*," *Anglia*, 63 (1939), 144–85; D.T. Torchiana, "Brutus: Pope's Last Hero," *Journal of English and Germanic Philology*, 61 (1962), 853–67; and H.-J. Zimmermann, "Bemerkungen zum Manuskript und Text von Popes *Brutus*," *Archiv für das Studium der neueren Sprachen*, 199 (1962), 100–106.

Brutus, Two Choruses to. AP wrote these two classically styled choruses to be performed between the acts of a tragedy entitled *Brutus* by his friend the **Duke of Buckinghamshire**. As part of an effort to improve **Shakespeare**, the Duke had divided *Julius Caesar* into two separate plays, named *Brutus* and *Julius Caesar*. AP's verses first appeared in his *Works* **(1717)**. Together with choruses by Buckinghamshire himself, the items were later set to music by **Giovanni Bononcini**. In this form they were performed by **Anastasia Robinson** and others at a concert hosted by the **Duchess of Buckinghamshire** for her son's birthday on 10 January 1723, held in the saloon at Buckingham House. AP included the choruses with the text of the play in his edition of *The Works of Buckingham*, issued in the same month as the concert. See *TE* 6: 151–55.

Buckingham, George Villiers, second Duke of (1628–87). Politician and writer. A member of the ruling "cabal" under Charles II. Author of the satirical play *The Rehearsal* (1671), in which he attacked **John Dryden**. The response was the portrait of "Zimri" in *Absalom and Achitophel*. Owned an estate at Helmsley, Yorkshire, to which AP refers in *The Second Satire of the Second Book of Horace*, ll. 177–78. The Duke died near Helmsley, reputedly at Buckingham House, Kirby Moorside, after falling from his horse. A more picturesque legend had it that he succumbed in a mean tavern in abject poverty. AP chose to follow the mythical version of events in his scathing characterization of Buckingham in the *Epistle to Bathurst*, ll. 299–314 (*TE* 3.ii: 117–19). In conversation AP rated the Duke as personally "an extreme bad man" and as a writer "superficial in everything, even in poetry, which was his forte" (*Anecdotes* 1: 199).

See J.H. Wilson, *A Rake and His Times: George Villiers, 2nd Duke of Buckingham* (New York: Farrar, Straus & Young, 1954).

Buckinghamshire, John Sheffield, first Duke of (1648–1721). (Sometimes named as "Buckingham.") Politician, author, and patron. As Earl of Mulgrave and Marquess of Normandy, he had wide experience in public life from the time of Charles II, both at court and in the armed services. He had served as one of the most important patrons to **John Dryden**, who dedicated his translation of the *Aeneid* to him. His reputation as poet and critic rested chiefly on his *Essay upon Poetry* (1682), which is a model for AP's own *Essay on Criticism*, and receives flattering mention there (ll. 723–24). He was a favorite of **Queen Anne**, and during her reign he came into his own as a politician, serving as Lord Privy Seal and Lord President of the Council. He lost this last office on the arrival of the Hanoverian regime, an event

obliquely noted in AP's *A Key to the Lock*. Created Duke, 1703. He built Buckingham House (1702–5) near St. James's Park, later converted into present-day Buckingham Palace. In 1706 he married as his third wife a natural daughter of James II, Katherine Darnley (see **Duchess of Buckinghamshire**). His poetry remained current long enough to earn him a place in *The Lives of the Poets* and a reasonably generous assessment by **Samuel Johnson**.

According to AP, he was one of the panel of notabilities who vetted the *Pastorals* for the young poet. He was happy, AP stated, to have been "honour'd very young with [the Duke's] friendship, and it continued till his death in all the circumstances of a familiar esteem" (*TE* 1: 324). Buckinghamshire subscribed for ten sets of the *Iliad*. His complimentary verses take pride of place at the head of AP's *Works* **(1717)**. In the same volume AP provided choruses for the Duke's two tragedies based on **Shakespeare**'s *Julius Caesar* (see *Two Choruses to Brutus*). He was among those greeting AP in *Mr. Pope's Welcome from Greece*. It was thanks to Buckingham that a monument to Dryden was erected in Westminster Abbey: AP originally wrote a couplet by way of epitaph but later substituted one in prose (*TE* 6: 237–38). After the Duke's death, AP was asked by the widow to edit the surviving *Works*, which he did in 1723 (see *Works of Buckingham*), in opposition to an unauthorized version by **Edmund Curll**. She also consulted the poet about the Duke's monument, for which **James Gibbs** proposed a flamboyant design; later the commission was given to **Peter Scheemakers** and others. His son, the second Duke, Edmund Sheffield died in 1735 aged nineteen: at his mother's request AP wrote an epitaph, but this was not used on the tomb in the Abbey (*TE* 6: 362–63). "Sheffield" is listed among AP's early supporters in the *Epistle to Arbuthnot*, l. 139. The entry in AP's **Memorial List** of his friends reads, "very friendly and gentle toward me" (*EC* 1: ix).

Buckinghamshire, Katherine Sheffield, Duchess of (c. 1681–1743). Daughter of James II by Catherine Sedley. In 1699 she married the fifth Earl of Anglesey (d. 1702). After his death, in 1706 she married as his third wife the **Duke of Buckinghamshire**, poet, politician, and friend of AP. Throughout her life she espoused the cause of her half brother, the **Pretender**, with a mixture of boldness and guile. It is not known when AP met her. He knew the Duke from his youth, so it is likely that he had been acquainted with the Duchess for many years before their first recorded contact, which related to her promotion of the operatic composer **Giovanni Bononcini** (see *Corr* 2: 99–100). Choruses that AP had written for the Duke's revision of *Julius Caesar* were performed at a concert in Buckingham House in January 1723 (see *Two Choruses to Brutus*). At this date AP was engaged in the task of bringing out the literary remains of her husband (see *Works of Buckingham*). The Duchess did not scruple to make difficulties for the poet in this matter. She subscribed for five sets of the *Odyssey*. AP was invited more than once to her country house **Leighs** in Essex. Her portrait hung at the poet's house.

Later the Duchess became embroiled in a lawsuit with the notorious **John Ward** and received help from AP and **Viscount Harcourt**. The poet bought an annuity from the Duchess around this time. By 1729 a quarrel had developed that was not healed for some years, but in 1735 the Duchess asked AP to write an **epitaph** for her son, who had died at the age of nineteen, and he complied. It seems that she had offered AP a bribe of £100 to perform some dishonorable act, but it is unknown what this was. As she aged Katherine Sheffield grew even more reckless, and she finally became insane. AP was dismayed to learn that at her death she had left all her letters to her executor, who was none other than Lord Hervey (see **John, Baron Hervey**). He naturally feared that compromising items in their correspondence would steal into print. Luckily, this did not happen. AP thought that this was disreputable conduct from someone who "seem'd once, a Woman of great honour & many generous Principles" (*Corr* 4: 446).

It is generally believed that the character of **Atossa** included in the *Epistle to a Lady* is modeled on the Duchess. Her imperious and unpredictable nature lends support to this view. For full discussion, see *TE* 3.ii: 159–70.

Buckley, Samuel (1673–1741). Printer, editor, and government official. Bred to the printing trade, he operated first in **Fleet Street** and later in Little Britain, near **Smithfield**. He first made his mark in 1702 as editor and publisher of the first regular daily newspaper in England, the *Daily Courant* (for most of its career a staid Whig organ). He printed the *Courant* until 1714. By that date he had also been responsible for printing *The Spectator* and another paper edited by **Richard Steele**, *The Englishman*. After the **Hanoverian accession**, in 1717, Buckley was assigned the grant for life of the post of official Gazetteer, formerly held by Steele. At the same time he worked in the office of the Secretary of State as a kind of press censor and watchdog over the information government services, taking part in the prosecution of offenders such as the printer Nathaniel Mist. He was also a Justice of the Peace for Westminster. An ally of **Addison** but a strong opponent of **Defoe**.

AP seems to have met him by 1717 at the latest. They remained on good terms for the next two decades: Buckley is listed as a subscriber to the *Odyssey*, although this may have been a gift by the poet, and to the **Shakespeare edition**. AP encouraged Buckley's important edition of the French historian Jacques-Auguste de Thou (Thuanus), which appeared in 1733. AP subscribed to this work, and in his **will** he left this copy to the **Earl of Marchmont**. Fourteen letters survive from AP to Buckley.

See H. Weinbrot, "Alexander Pope and Madame Dacier's *Homer*: Conjectures Concerning the Cardinal Dubois, Sir Luke Schaub, and Samuel Buckley," *Huntington Library Quarterly*, 62 (1999), 1–23.

Budgell, Eustace (1686–1737). Author, although his eccentric character and tangled life brought him as much notoriety as his writing. A second cousin of **Joseph Addison**, he wrote about thirty papers for *The Spectator*, more than anyone else apart from the two main writers. In 1714 he became Clerk of the Council in

Ireland; then in 1717, Accountant General of the Irish Revenue, at a time when his cousin was Secretary of State. However, he quarreled with the Lord Lieutenant's staff and was dismissed in 1718. He lost this post, according to **Swift**, "by great want of common Politicks" (*Corr* 2: 154). This led Budgell to engage in a bitter pamphlet war against the authorities, and together with heavy losses in the **South Sea Bubble** (perhaps as much as £20,000), he became increasingly unhinged. By 1733 he was heavily involved in litigation and was accused of forging the will of the deist Matthew Tindal. His final act of throwing himself into the Thames was sadly in character.

As a member of the Addison circle at **Button's**, Budgell was a natural target for AP. An early poem, *To Eustace Budgell, Esq.* (c. 1714), is relatively good humored. There are scornful references in some of the imitations of **Horace** and **Donne**, as well as in the *Epistle to Arbuthnot* (*TE* 4: 124). On top of this, Budgell earned a brief mention in the second book of *The Dunciad* (*TE* 5: 144). His principal offense may have been to accuse AP of slandering him in the *Grub-street Journal*, a paper from which AP wished so far as possible to dissociate himself.

Bufo. A satiric portrait of a patron in the *Epistle to Arbuthnot*, ll. 231–48. The name derives from the Latin word for "toad." Some of the features suggest the **Earl of Halifax**; rather more point to **George Bubb Dodington**, whose original family name Bubb makes him a likelier candidate. However, the lines are best read as a generic portrait of any self-satisfied Maecenas, proud to have second-rate authors vying for his attention in a toadying manner. See *TE* 4: 112–13.

burial. Following AP's **death** on 30 May 1744, he was buried at the nearby church of St. Mary the Virgin on 5 June. The churchwardens recorded the charge made by the parish as £1.0.0. See **Twickenham parish church**.

Burlington, Dorothy Boyle, Countess of (1699–1758). Daughter of William Savile, sec-

ond Marquess of Halifax. Married the **Earl of Burlington** in 1721. A lover of the arts, she was fond of drawing, especially caricatures, and followed the **theater** and music, especially **opera**. She was a great patron and a regular subscriber to artistic ventures. The Countess served as a lady in waiting to **Queen Caroline**. Among her favorites in the literary world was **John Gay**.

Her relations with AP also were particularly amicable. She drew a sketch of the poet in his **grotto** and took part in several playful exchanges, at times acting as his amanuensis. *A Master Key to Popery* survives in her hand at Chatsworth (in 1748 her younger daughter Charlotte married the fourth Duke of Devonshire, who owned the house). About 1732, AP composed an amusing set of verses, five quatrains of alternate rhymes, titled "On the Countess of B—— cutting Paper" (*TE* 6: 336–37). When the Duchess's elder daughter Dorothy died of smallpox in 1742 just before her eighteenth birthday, after a brief and deeply unhappy marriage to the Earl of Euston, AP shared with her parents a feeling of grief mixed with resentment at the brutal behavior of her husband. Thirteen letters from AP to Lady Burlington are preserved, mostly at Chatsworth.

See M. De Novellis, *Pallas Unveil'd: The Life and Art of Lady Dorothy Savile, Countess of Burlington, 1699–1758* (Twickenham, Middlesex: Orleans House, 1999).

Burlington, Richard Boyle, third Earl of (1695–1753). Patron and architect. Succeeded to the title in 1704 and inherited estates in England and Ireland, as well as a house in Piccadilly, London, and one at **Chiswick**. He was appointed to a number of public offices on the accession of **George I** but never obtained high political rank. FRS, 1722; Knight of the Garter, 1730; Grand Tour, 1714–15, 1719, spending most of his time in Italy. He sponsored the publication of major works on architecture by Palladio and Colen Campbell, the architect to whom he entrusted the rebuilding of Burlington House after initial work by **James Gibbs** (1715–20). The Earl was himself for the new villa, **Chiswick House** (1725–27), and he designed a number of important buildings elsewhere. He became the leading spirit in English **Palladianism**, recruiting architects and gardeners such as **William Kent, Charles Bridgeman**, and Isaac Ware to promote the movement. He also patronized painters and sculptors including **Michael Rysbrack** and Giovanni Battista Guelfi. Among those who lived on a regular basis at Burlington House were **George Frideric Handel** and **John Gay**. Burlington was a leading supporter of **opera** and one of the original directors of the Royal Academy of Music.

AP may well have met Burlington before he embarked on his first tour to Italy, although the earliest surviving letter dates from late 1716. Thereafter the two men maintained good relations for almost thirty years. In 1718 the Earl offered AP land on which to build a town house at the back of Burlington House, but AP decided against doing this. However, AP was a frequent visitor at Chiswick House and played some part in the planning of the gardens there. In addition, AP was on excellent terms with the Earl's wife, **Dorothy Boyle, Countess of Burlington**. He once visited the Earl at his estate near **York**, the furthest north he ever traveled. Burlington's circle of artistically minded Yorkshire cronies included some who would become friends of AP, notably **Hugh Bethel** and **James Moyser**. The poet's most effusive tribute to his valued patron comes in the *Epistle to Burlington* (1731), aptly devoted to the subject of "taste." About sixty letters are known to survive. Burlington subscribed for six copies of the *Iliad* and five of the *Odyssey*.

See *Earls of Creation* 103–69; T. Barnard and J. Clark, eds., *Lord Burlington: Architecture, Art and Life* (London: Hambledon, 1995); and J.M. Osborn, "Pope, the 'Apollo of the Arts,' and His Countess," in *England in the Restoration and Early Eighteenth Century*, ed. H.T. Swedenberg (Berkeley: University of California Press, 1972), 101–43.

Burlington House. House in Piccadilly, central London. Built by **Sir John Denham**, 1665–67, and owned by the Boyle family. AP's friend, the **third Earl of Burlington**, inherited the property and set about turning it into a monumental work of **Palladianism**. He first employed **James Gibbs**, who seems to have designed the stables and the long colonnade in the forecourt in 1716–17; but the remainder of the task was entrusted in 1717–20 to Colen Campbell, a more dependably orthodox architect. Here Burlington assembled a team of favorite artists, including **Handel, William Kent**, and **John Gay**, to work under his patronage. AP was probably at the house on a number of occasions in this period, and he did much to publicize Burlington's "academy": one result was that a graphic satire on the group called "Taste" (c. 1731) shows the poet as "a Plasterer whitewashing & Bespattering" Campbell's formal gateway of Burlington House. In any event, AP dined there as late as February 1744, not long before his death. In 1718 Burlington had offered AP a site on which to build a town house behind the mansion, to designs by Campbell, but after reflection, AP refused the offer with gratitude, as it would have been too expensive (see *Corr* 1: 516–17).

Burnet, Thomas (1694–1753). Lawyer and pamphleteer. A son of the famous Bishop of Salisbury, Gilbert Burnet (1643–1715). A Whig who emerged from **Addison**'s circle at **Button's** coffeehouse to launch a number of attacks on AP, some in collaboration with his friend **George Duckett**. A wild young man who grew respectable with age and became Justice of the Common Pleas, 1741; knighted, 1745.

His dealings with AP started with aggressive assaults in a pamphlet, *Homerides*, and a periodical called *The Grumbler*, both in 1715. A different attack, also entitled *Homerides*, followed the next year. His correspondence with Duckett shows that Addison and **Samuel Garth** were fully aware of these strikes against AP (see Guerinot 35–37). After this, things went quiet, apart from a passing reference in *Sandys's Ghost* (1717). Hostilities resumed when AP found a spot for Burnet and Duckett in Book 3 of *The Dunciad*, with a meticulously ordered indictment of the pair in the note (*TE* 5: 168–70). Mischievously AP implies that the "union" of these literary colleagues was in fact sexual in nature, and a "retraction" in the note deliberately makes matters worse. In later versions of *The Dunciad* AP toned down these references.

See *The Letters of Thomas Burnet to George Duckett 1712–1722*, ed. D.N. Smith (Oxford: Roxburghe Club, 1912).

Burton, Dr. Simon (c. 1690–1744). Physician in Savile Row, London, who served at St. George's Hospital and as a Royal Physician. He attended AP in the days before the poet's **death** in 1744. Burton himself died only twelve days later, on 11 June 1744.

Butt, John (1906–65). Scholar who was Regius Professor of Rhetoric and English Literature at the University of Edinburgh from 1959 and a Fellow of the British Academy from 1961. He served as editor of the *Review of English Studies* (1947–54). A leading authority on Dickens, he wrote an introductory survey on *The Augustan Age* (1950) and also coedited a bibliographical guide, *Augustans and Romantics* (1940). Other works include an introduction to Fielding and an edition of Richardson's *Clarissa*. He began the volume devoted to the age of Johnson in the *Oxford History of English Literature*: it was completed by G. Carnall and published in 1979. Edited Festschrift for **Bonamy Dobrée**, which includes **Butt's** essay "Pope: The Man and the Poet," reprinted in *PRE* 1–14. His work on AP includes essays on *Pope's Taste in Shakespeare* (1936); on "The Inspiration of Pope's Poetry," in *Essays on the Eighteenth Century Presented to David Nichol Smith* (1945); and on "Pope's Poetical Manuscripts," *Proceedings of the British Academy*, 40 (1954), 23–39, reprinted in *EA* 545–65. See also "Pope and the Opposition to Walpole's Government" in *Pope, Dickens and Others* (1969), 111–26. Butt was the first to publish AP's *Master Key to Popery* in 1949. He edited a volume of some 200 of AP's selected *Letters* in 1960. However, all other achievements are dwarfed by his role as general editor of the **Twickenham edition** of AP, for which he personally edited the volume on the *Imitations of*

Horace (1939, rev. ed. 1953) and coedited the volume of *Minor Poems* (1954) (see **minor poems**). He was also responsible for the one-volume epitome of this edition.

See a volume in tribute, *Imagined Worlds*, ed. **Maynard Mack** and Ian Gregor (London: Methuen, 1968).

Button's. A coffeehouse named after Daniel Button, its proprietor, who was a former servant of **Joseph Addison**. In 1712 Addison gained possession of a property on Russell Street, near Covent Garden, and set Button up in business. It served as a meeting place for the literary crowd, and it was also used as the office of **Steele**'s periodical, *The Guardian*. On the front door of the establishment the editors set up the head of a lion, which was used as a receptacle for contributions and also as a kind of house logo for the journal. Here Addison's "little senate" congregated, with the regular clientele including **Ambrose Philips**, **Thomas Tickell**, **Eustace Budgell**, Charles Johnson, **Samuel Garth**, and of course Addison and Steele themselves. AP sometimes visited the coffeehouse, as when in 1713 he attended lectures on astronomy by **William Whiston** there. But the tone of Button's circle was resolutely Whig, and AP gradually became estranged from most of its members. After the **Hanoverian accession** this distance grew. AP's scorn for the group at Button's can be seen in some of his minor poems, notably *Umbra* (c. 1715). The proprietor himself ended up on parish relief, indicating that the popularity of his shop did not last very long.

Byles, Mather (1707–88). American clergyman and poet, born in Boston. Well-known minister of the Hollis Street Congregational Church, Boston, from 1733. He was dismissed for his Tory sympathies after the British evacuation of Boston and condemned as an enemy to the country in 1777 (his sentence to imprisonment and exile was later commuted). From his uncle, Cotton Mather, he inherited a valuable library. His works include *Poems on Several Occasions* (1744). He corresponded with

AP, and sent the poet some of his own works. Byles was the principal booster of AP's reputation in colonial New England.

See A.W.H. Eaton, *The Famous Mather Byles: The Noted Boston Tory Preacher, Poet, and Wit, 1707–1788* (1914; reprint, New York: Irvington Publishers, 1991).

Byron, George Gordon, sixth Baron, known as **Lord Byron** (1788–1824). Poet. He first defended AP against the strictures of **William Lisle Bowles** in his satire *English Bards and Scotch Reviewers* (1809), where he advises Bowles, "Stick to thy sonnets, man!" In the first Canto of *Don Juan* (1818), he counseled, "Thou shalt believe in Milton, Dryden, Pope; / Thou shalt not set up Wordsworth, Coleridge, Southey." Later Byron plunged into the controversy that Bowles's edition had aroused with "Some Observations upon an Article in *Blackwood's Magazine*" (1820) and *A Letter to [John Murray]* (1821). In the *Letter* he answers the claim by Bowles that a walk in a forest is a more poetical subject than a game of cards, as in ***The Rape of the Lock***: "The *materials* are certainly not equal; but . . . 'the *artist*,' who has rendered the 'game of cards poetical,' is *by far the greater* of the two."

C

Caesar, Mary (1677–1741). She was the daughter of Ralph Freeman of Aspenden, Hertfordshire. In 1702 she married Charles Caesar (1673–1741) of nearby Benington. He was an MP who served as Treasurer of the Navy, 1711–14, but his undisguised Jacobite views meant that he afterward lost all prospect of political advancement. He helped to organize a plot with the Swedish ambassador in 1716–17, and after this he served as a quiet fund-raiser for the cause. Mary was equally active in this last capacity. Her correspondence with like-minded individuals survives at **Rousham**. In 1717 her friend Anne Oglethorpe gave her a portrait of the **Pretender**. Other allies of the Caesars were the **first Earl of Oxford**, the **Duchess of Buckinghamshire**, the **Earl of Strafford**, **Matthew Prior**, and **Judith Cowper**. They ruined the family fortunes in pursuit of the Stuart cause, and Charles was eventually arrested for debt. The couple died within three months of one another.

The Caesars were assiduous in subscribing to books by AP, Prior, **Swift**, **Mary Barber**, and others. Indeed, Mary was the most energetic and effective of all those promoting the campaign for the *Odyssey*. She obtained at least seventy subscribers for the list. Uniquely, her name was printed in capitals and augmented with a star in the printed list. AP referred to this as making "a Star of Mrs Caesar," in a letter from around April 1725 (*Corr* 2: 293). (In all, fourteen letters from AP to Mary survive, as well as one from her to AP.) It is difficult to avoid the conclusion that the *Iliad* campaign, at least as far as Mary was concerned, had links with efforts to drum up money for the upcoming **Atterbury plot** and indeed may have been a front for Jacobite fund-raising. AP dined with the couple in London and was invited at least once to Benington.

The most informative account of Mary Caesar will be found in *Women's Place* 231–50. Useful on her husband is L. Munby, "Charles Caesar of Benington, 1673–1741," *Hertfordshire's Past*, 39 (1995).

Cambridge. AP's only recorded visit occurred in late July 1727 (*Corr* 2: 441), in connection with a stay at nearby **Wimpole**, the seat of his friend the **second Earl of Oxford**. Although he had contacts with Cambridge men such as **Matthew Prior** and **Elijah Fenton**, he was not strongly linked to the university, with its Whiggish and strongly Hanoverian sympathies. The disparity with **Oxford** is apparent in the subscription lists to his **Homer** volumes: for example, four colleges in the latter subscribed to the *Iliad*, but none from its sister university, while the tally for the *Odyssey* was Oxford 13 and Cambridge 4. Only just over 30 individual Cambridge graduates can be identified on the *Iliad* list, as against 110 from Oxford. AP had little contact with the Duke of Somerset, the aloof Chancellor of Cambridge, 1689–1748, which cannot have aided his campaign to gain subscribers among members of the university.

Camden, William (1551–1623). Antiquarian and herald. Headmaster of Westminster School, 1593; among his pupils was **Ben Jonson**. Like all educated men and women of his time, AP knew Camden's great topographical survey *Britannia* either in its Latin original (1586) or in its augmented English translation, edited by Edmund Gibson (1695). The work was an important source for AP's poem *Windsor-Forest*. He seems to have used it almost as a substitute guidebook on occasions (see *Corr* 3: 430).

Campbell, Thomas (1777–1844). Scottish poet and critic. In 1819 he opposed the views of **William Lisle Bowles** and defended AP's ability to explore "human manners," which he contended was as poetical a task as the evocation of natural phenomena. Thus AP was affirmed to be "a genuine poet." Promptly Bowles registered his dissent and initiated a controversy that involved **Byron**, among others.

Cannons or Canons. Mansion near Edgware in Middlesex, about ten miles northwest of central London, and owned by James Brydges, created **Duke of Chandos** in 1719. It was a sumptuous building, erected from 1713 under the direction of several major architects, notably William Talman, John James, **John Vanbrugh**, **James Gibbs**, and Edward Shepherd. A whole army of decorators and designers were employed on the interior, among them **William Kent**, James Thornhill, and **Louis Laguerre**. "Its stately but mannered opulence, satirized by Pope, served as type and antitype for much building in the 1720s" (Christopher Hussey). Also in the employ of Chandos was **George Frideric Handel**, who wrote eleven "Chandos" anthems and a *Te Deum* in 1717–18. In addition, Handel's *Acis and Galatea* was probably first performed at Cannons in 1718: the libretto was almost certainly the joint work of **John Gay**, **John Hughes**, and AP. **John Arbuthnot** often dined at Cannons with Handel in this year; and it is possible that AP also saw the house.

AP and Chandos retained good relations for a number of years. However, the publication of the *Epistle to Burlington* in 1731 threatened to create a rift, after rumor-mongers alleged that the vulgar mansion described in the poem as **Timon's villa** was in fact a depiction of Cannons. AP denied the accusation, and Chandos seemingly accepted his word for it, but the episode precluded the growth of any real intimacy between the two men.

The fortunes of the family sank rapidly, and the Duke's legacy to his heirs was short-lived: Cannons was pulled down in 1747 and the contents auctioned off. North London Collegiate School for Girls now occupies part of the site, a portion survives as Canons Park, landscaped afresh in the nineteenth century by Alexander Blackwell.

Capon's Tale, The. An uncertain attribution. This poem of thirty lines, in octosyllabic couplets, first appeared in the *Miscellanies* in 1727. It was never acknowledged by AP, but a copy in his hand was found among the papers of **Lady Mary Wortley Montagu**, the obvious target of its satire. Moreover, the poem is marked in a volume owned by AP's friend the **second Earl of Oxford** as "By Mr. Pope." However, no certainty has been achieved on the authorship. The printed version substitutes a slightly sharper conclusion. The *Tale* attacks Lady Mary for foisting her own works on to others; yet there is no clear evidence that she ever did such a thing. The nearest case would seem to be *Court Poems*, but even here the situation is doubtful (and the episode, dating from 1716, was now old history). The poet appears to speak on behalf of *two* authors: if the attribution is correct, then this might refer to AP and **John Gay**. See Ault 243–47; and *TE* 6: 256–58.

caricatures. AP's opponents found it hard to match his skill when they tried to reply to him in the medium of words. An alternative strategy was to introduce his highly recognizable features into graphic satires. The best-known image depicted him as an ape, on the basis of a common form of reference "A. P-E." This was used as a frontispiece to *Pope Alexander's Supremacy and Infallibility Examin'd* (1729) (*Portraits* 7.11), and in a slightly different guise, it was sold separately as a print under the title "The Phiz and Character of an *Alexandrine* Hyper-critick & Comentator" (*Portraits* 7.10). It is not certain whether **William Hogarth** showed AP as the dwarfish figure in *The South Sea Scheme* (1724). On the other hand, it is probable that the figure spattering paint on a coach in the print *Taste* (sometimes called "Burlington Gate," *Portraits* 13.1) is meant for AP, as it was used in one of the **pamphlet at-**

tacks on the poet at the start of 1732 (*Portraits* 13.2). It is no longer believed that Hogarth was responsible for this print. Just occasionally AP appeared in a favorable light in one of these caricatures: see, for example, the frontispiece to *A Tryal of Skill between a Court Lord, and a Twickenham 'Squire* (1734), which shows AP confronting **John, Baron Hervey** in a duel.

For background, see H.M. Atherton, *Political Prints in the Age of Hogarth: A Study of the Ideographic Representation of Politics* (Oxford: Clarendon, 1974). For illustrations of the caricatures, see *Portraits* 7.10–11.

Carleton, Henry Boyle, Baron (1677–1725). Sometimes spelled "Carlton." Politician. A Whig MP who served as Chancellor of the Exchequer, Lord Treasurer of Ireland, and Secretary of State during the early part of the reign of **Queen Anne**. Squeezed out in 1710, but returned to favor after the **Hanoverian accession**, and granted a peerage in 1714. Lord President of the Council, 1721–25. Despite his high offices, he was for the most part a figure of the second rank, regarded as a moderate in party terms. The third volume of the collected *Spectator* papers was dedicated to him. He was a great-nephew of the scientist Robert Boyle and an uncle of AP's friend the **Earl of Burlington**. He built Carlton House, St. James's, which passed to his nephew.

AP singled him out in the *Epilogue to the Satires* because of his "calm sense" (*TE* 4: 317). In 1716 AP visited Carleton at his home, Middleton Park, near Bicester in Oxfordshire. Carleton was unmarried; the house passed to the Earls of Jersey on his death but was badly damaged by fire in 1753. The present structure was designed by Sir Edwin Lutyens, 1934–38, and is now converted into apartments. Without great intimacy the relations of Carleton and AP were obviously on a cordial basis. A subscriber to both of AP's **Homer** translations, he is listed prominently at the head of those under "C" in the *Odyssey* list, ahead of such luminaries as **Chandos**, **Carteret**, **Cobham**, and Lord Cowper, with a subscription for ten copies. He is included among the friends of AP in *Mr. Pope's Welcome from Greece*.

Caroline, Queen (1683–1737). Queen of England from 1727. She was a daughter of the Margrave of Ansbach and married the future **George II** in 1705. After becoming Princess of Wales in 1714, she sided with her husband in his quarrels with his father, **George I**. In these years AP became acquainted with her **maids of honor** and other members of the court. A firm supporter of **Sir Robert Walpole**, she played some part in ensuring that the Minister retained the confidence of her husband and thus held on to power. She took a special interest in ecclesiastical politics, helping to further the career of low churchmen, to the point that she was suspected of unitarian or even atheistic views. Another major obsession was landscape gardening, and she lavished particular attention on the grounds of her house at **Richmond** (see also **Merlin's Cave**).

It is reported by **Samuel Johnson**, perhaps unreliably, that the Queen once resolved to visit AP at **Twickenham** but that he decamped in order not to be at home when she arrived. His relations with Caroline were certainly involved, and they were further complicated by the attempts of his friend **Jonathan Swift** to win her over to his interests. AP regarded her intellectual pretensions as flimsy, but he admired aspects of her character, notably the fortitude with which she endured a painful death from a strangulated umbilical hernia. His poetry depicts her in various guises, including that of **Milton**'s Eve in the *Epistle to Arbuthnot*; the insipid "Carolina" flattered by poetasters in *The First Satire of the Second Book of Horace Imitated*: and the subject of a vicious epitaph, "Here lies wrapt up in forty thousand towels/The only proof that C*** had bowels" (*TE* 6: 390). She is allotted a central role in *The Dunciad* and indeed may contribute some of the lineaments of the tutelary figure in this poem, Queen Dulness. It is impossible to doubt that she was in AP's mind when the gardeners quarrel over the propagation of flowers in Book 4, since the prize bloom consumed by a butterfly is named "Caroline" by the florist who created it (see *TE* 5: 381–83).

See P. Quennell, *Caroline of England* (London: Collins, 1939). A new study is needed.

Carruthers, Robert (1799–1878). Scottish writer on miscellaneous topics. He produced an edition of AP's works in four volumes (1853–54), revised, 1857–58. The most notable part of the undertaking is the "Memoir," one of the fullest contributions to the subject that had then been attempted (see **biographies of Pope**). However, the researches of **Charles Wentworth Dilke** soon made the study by Carruthers obsolete in many areas of the poet's life.

Carteret, John, second Baron, later first Earl Granville (1690–1763). Politician and diplomat. Succeeded as baron, 1695. Educated at Westminster school and Christ Church, **Oxford**. Secretary of State in the ministry of **Robert Walpole**, 1721–24. Lord-Lieutenant of Ireland, 1724–30, where he managed to keep on reasonably good terms with the intractable **Jonathan Swift**. His secretary in this post was **Thomas Tickell**. Joined the **opposition to Walpole** in the 1730s, but along with **William Pulteney** he was suspected of attempting to carve out a niche for his own succession to power, rather than advancing the interest of the **Patriots**. His conduct after Walpole's fall, when he became Secretary of State again (1742–44), seemed to confirm this opinion. Succeeded to earldom, 1746, and was never able fully to regain his former influence. He is probably "C——t," mentioned in *One Thousand Seven Hundred and Forty*. A man of cultivation and lordly manner who lacked the skills of day-to-day political infighting, despite his wide knowledge of foreign affairs and diplomatic talents. In 1738 he sponsored an edition of *Don Quixote* with the first-ever life of Cervantes, issued by the firm of Tonson (see **Jacob Tonson senior**). It had been designed as a compliment to **Queen Caroline**, whose favor Carteret assiduously courted.

AP wrote to Carteret in connection with the *Works of Buckingham* in 1723 and two years later managed to obtain a grant of £200 in recognition of the *Odyssey* translation. He also entered his name for ten copies of this work and subscribed to other works by AP and his friends. They were not intimate friends.

B. Williams, *Carteret and Newcastle: A Study in Contrasts* (Cambridge: Cambridge University Press, 1943; reprint, London: Frank Cass, 1966), is now a little long in the tooth.

Caryll, John, Lord (c. 1626–1711). Jacobite courtier and poet. He served as secretary to Mary of Modena, Queen of James II from 1685. Followed his master into exile, 1689; Secretary of State to the former King, 1694. The family estates were forfeited in 1696 (see **Ladyholt**). Granted a Jacobite peerage as "Baron Caryll of Durford," 1699. Died in exile. His nephew and successor, **John Caryll senior**, became one of AP's closest friends, but it is improbable that the uncle and AP can ever have met. See *Social Milieu* 42–71.

An **epitaph** by AP was first printed by **Charles Wentworth Dilke** in 1854; the manuscript has been lost, and the date of composition is not known. AP used some of the phrasing in its opening lines again when he wrote an epitaph for **Sir William Trumbull** in 1717. See *TE* 6: 81–82.

See also H. Erskine-Hill, "John, First Lord Caryll of Durford, and the Caryll Papers," in *The Stuart Court in Exile and the Jacobites*, ed. E. Cruickshanks and E. Corp (London: Hambledon, 1993), 73–90.

Caryll, John junior (1687–1718). Eldest son of AP's close friend **John Caryll senior**. He was educated in France and returned to England in 1706. He was the heir of **John, Lord Caryll**, his father's uncle. On 12 July 1712 he married Lady Mary Mackenzie (1685–1740), daughter of the Earl of Seaforth, who had been imprisoned as a member of a strongly Jacobite family. Mary's own brother William, the fifth Earl (1681–1740), took part in the 1715 rising, raising 3,000 men for the **Pretender**, and was attainted. He ultimately made terms and was granted a limited pardon in 1726, although his titles were not restored. He was a subscriber to the *Iliad*, along with John Caryll junior.

AP had always been on excellent terms with young Caryll and his wife. He was shocked when John died of smallpox in April 1718, barely past the age of thirty. Lady Mary Caryll continued to maintain relations, showing kindness to the poet when she visited her mother at **Twickenham** (*Corr* 2: 140). Her name was accidentally omitted from the list of subscribers to the *Odyssey*. For about ten years she lived in Paris, while her children were educated there. After the death of John Caryll senior, she moved to **Ladyholt** with her son John Baptist, the heir to the family property.

Three letters from AP to John Caryll survive. They show AP as comically envious of the younger man's prowess in physical activities such as hunting.

Caryll, John senior (1667–1736). Country gentleman from an old Catholic family, based in Sussex but with numerous ties to **Berkshire**. Second Baron Caryll of Durford in the Jacobite peerage. His uncle, **John Lord Caryll**, was a leading figure at the exiled Stuart court. The nephew was educated in France and married Elizabeth Harrington in 1686. Ten years later he was implicated in a failed plot to assassinate **William III** and imprisoned for a time. In 1701 his father died, and he succeeded to the family estate, having regained **Ladyholt**, which had been sequestrated for a time following the assassination plot. After the death of Lord Caryll in 1711 he became the head of the extended family and for the rest of his life trod a delicate line between open rebellion against the Hanoverian regime and ostensible complicity. His family spent some time in France, but Caryll himself remained in England. He concerned himself with his responsibilities as, in effect, chief of a clan. For example, he acted as guardian to the young **Baron Petre**; it was in this way that he came to alert AP to the family's desire that the scandalous affair involving **Arabella Fermor** should somehow be smoothed over. AP's response, *The Rape of the Lock*, although dedicated to Caryll, cannot be said to have done this exactly. However, Caryll helped to arrange a marriage for **Michael Blount**; and he seems to have hoped that AP would wed Michael's sister, and his own goddaughter, **Martha Blount**. He also gave assistance to his poor cousin **Anne Cope**. In spite of his efforts the family assets were increasingly burdened by debts, and Caryll's grandson and successor

John Baptist was eventually forced to sell the estate.

AP may have known the Carylls by about 1704, almost certainly through the medium of the **Englefield family**. His first extant letter to Caryll dates from 1710. After this they remained close friends and correspondents until Caryll died on 18 April 1736, with only rare disagreements to mar their equable relations. The death of **John Caryll junior**, the eldest son and heir, in 1718 prompted a message of gentle grieving from AP (*Corr* 1: 474). About 140 letters from AP exist, although some were published in a revised form as though written to other correspondents. They are among the most simple and heartfelt in all AP's body of letters. It may have been the older man's reticence and his exposed position politically that ensured that AP never again addressed a major poem to his friend. The Caryll family took a leading part in promoting AP's subscription campaigns: John Caryll is listed as a subscriber to the *Iliad* and the *Odyssey*.

See *Social Milieu* 42–102. Some useful material is scattered through C.W. Dilke, *Papers of a Critic*, vol. 2 (London: Murray, 1875).

Case, Arthur Ellicott (1894–1946). Scholar who taught at Northwestern University from 1930. Best known as an expert on **Swift**, he published several important works on *Gulliver's Travels*; he was also a student of English drama. His *Bibliography of English Poetical Miscellanies 1521–1750* (1935) is a valuable resource for those working in the period. Case wrote a number of articles concerned with the canon of AP's work, including "New Attributions to Pope," *Modern Philology*, 34 (1937), 305–13; 35 (1937), 187–91: and a discussion of the card game in *The Rape of the Lock* in *Studies in English*, University of Texas (1945), 191–96 (see **ombre**). See *Studies in the Literature of the Augustan Age: Essays Collected in Honor of Arthur Ellicott Case*, ed. R.C. Boys (Ann Arbor, MI: Wahr, 1952; reprint, New York: Gordian, 1966).

Catholick Poet, The. Subtitled "Protestant Barnaby's Sorrowful Lamentation. An Excellent

New Ballad, to the Tune of, Which no body can deny." One of the earliest and most effective of the **pamphlet attacks** on AP. It appeared on 31 May 1716, with all the leading "trade publishers" of the day, including **James Roberts**, listed on the title page. Nevertheless, it is certain that the true instigator was **Edmund Curll**, who advertised the item as forthcoming on 7 April 1716. AP suggested in an appendix to *The Dunciad* that the item was written by **Susanna Centlivre** and others, but Curll later set him right, revealing that the author was in fact **John Oldmixon**.

The work is a folio of six pages, priced at threepence. In the main part, a ballad of thirteen three-line stanzas in triple rhythm, Pope and **Bernard Lintot** exchange speeches (Lintot's first name was Barnaby, hence the subtitle). The subject is "*Sawny*, The Poet of *Windsor*"—the name being a common perversion of Alexander used by AP's enemies. There follows the bookseller's "humble petition" in prose, which extends familiar charges. Throughout, AP is satirized for his crooked body, his papist religion, his unsuccessful efforts to translate from the Greek, and his bawdy verses. The writer amusingly apologizes for Lintot's profane language.

For a description of the contents, see Guerinot 38–40. The fullest account is P. Rogers, "*The Catholick Poet* (1716)," *Bodleian Library Record*, 8 (1971), 277–84.

Cato. A phenomenally successful tragedy by **Joseph Addison**, premiered on 14 April 1713. The first night was turned into a major political event by the vigorous and vocal support of both Whig and Tory members of the audience. AP is only one of many to report on the scenes at **Drury Lane Theatre**. Initially the Whigs seemed to be carrying the day, but a gesture by **Bolingbroke**, in presenting fifty guineas to **Barton Booth**, who had played the lead role, helped to equalize matters. In the following weeks a stream of pamphlets debated the issues. In AP's account, not only does the author receive the acclamations of the audience, but the "prologue-writer" too (the poet himself) is "clapped into a stanch Whig sore against his

will, at almost every two lines." See *Corr* 1: 174–76, in which AP tells **John Caryll senior** of the furor aroused by the play.

AP had read the manuscript of *Cato* earlier in the year, as he told Caryll. He described its affecting qualities and predicted that it would achieve great success if it reached the stage (*Corr* 1: 173). AP's prologue was delivered by the actor **Robert Wilks**: it consists of forty-six lines in heroic couplets. It appeared in *The Guardian* on 18 April and was appended to editions of the play that began to emerge on 27 April. AP included the item in his *Works* **(1717)**, and later borrowed lines from the text for other poems—most notably, twisting l. 23 of the prologue ("While *Cato* gives his little senate laws") against Addison, in a character sketch used in the *Epistle to Arbuthnot*. For the text, see *TE* 6: 96–98. AP also wrote a flippant poem *On a Lady who Pisst at the Tragedy of Cato*.

Posterity has not managed to share in the contemporary enthusiasm for *Cato*. It retained a kind of classic status into the nineteenth century, not often performed but providing a stock of familiar quotations (Bartlett's 1919 compendium still has eighteen citations from the play). However, five acts of high sentiments in blank verse have proved too much for modern taste. "To twentieth-century sensibilities the play now seems a vast echoing museum filled with plaster casts" (*Life* 219). This may be in part because the hero, Marcus Portius Cato (95–46 B.C.), leader of an opposition to the "tyrannical" Julius Caesar, resonates less in the mind today. His noble and philosophic death embodies a stoicism somewhat at odds with our own valuation of impulse and emotion at the expense of severe codes of principled behavior.

Cave of Spleen. A phantasmagoric section of *The Rape of the Lock* (4: 11–88). The gnome Umbriel travels down to the "central earth" to obtain a bag of passionate outbursts and a vial containing tears. Together they make up a dose of spleen, or what might be called essence of neurotic illness. This he subsequently pours over the heroine **Belinda** and thus produces a mixture of rage and self-pity that determines her response to the loss of her lock. The passage looks back to classical visits to Hades, but in its details it draws more fully on surreal transformations recalling **Ovid**. There is a good deal of localized satire on contemporary fine ladies, especially in regard to their sex life.

Spleen in the usage of the day referred to melancholia, depression, and moodiness. **Samuel Johnson** defines it both as "anger; spite; illhumour" and "melancholy; hypochondriacal vapours." According to the old doctrine of humors, the condition was related to secretions of black bile from a bodily organ, the spleen, but in AP's lines the root cause lies nearer the womb, the traditional seat of hypochondria. The herbal remedy was spleenwort, and Umbriel prudently carries a nosegay of this with him.

A background study is L. Babb, *The Elizabethan Malady* (East Lansing: Michigan State College Press, 1951). See also J.F. Sena, *A Bibliography of Melancholy, 1660–1800* (London: Nether Press, 1970).

Centlivre, Susanna (c. 1669–1723). Dramatist and poet. Born Susanna Freeman, either at Holbeach, Lincolnshire, or in County Tyrone, Ireland. Her early life is shrouded in mystery and myth, although it may have contained several relationships in addition to marriage to an army officer named Carroll, who was shortly afterward killed in a duel. She worked as a strolling player for some years. In 1707 she married a French chef named Joseph Centlivre, grandiloquently styled Yeoman of the Mouth and Cook of the Kitchen to **Queen Anne** and **George I** until his death in 1725. She had met her future husband while performing as Alexander in Nathaniel Lee's *Rival Queens* at Windsor. By this date she had already embarked on a career as a dramatist. Her comedies were among the most frequently performed of their time. Three particularly successful plays were *The Busy Body* (1709); *The Wonder! A Woman Keeps a Secret* (1714); and *A Bold Stroke for a Wife* (1718), which enjoyed hundreds of performances in the eighteenth century and held the stage until Victorian times. **William Hazlitt** delighted in the "provoking spirit and volatile salt" in the plays "which still preserves them from decay." Each of these plays was regularly reprinted.

As she was a Whig, Centlivre's sympathies lay with the Hanoverian dynasty, and she often attacked **Jacobites** and papists in her work. It is possible, but unlikely, that she is portrayed as Phoebe Clinket in the Scriblerian farce *Three Hours after Marriage*. AP gives her a brief cuff in *A Further Account* of the bookseller **Edmund Curll**; his reference to "the *Cook's Wife* in *Buckingham* Court" accurately places her residence near Charing Cross (*Prose* 1: 279). In *The Dunciad* AP treated her quite gently, with little more than a reference to her voice failing (2: 379): she may have had pretensions as a singer. In a note AP adds, "She also writ a Ballad against Mr. *Pope*'s *Homer* before he began it," a claim Curll showed to be false (see *The Catholick Poet*).

See J.W. Bowyer, *The Celebrated Mrs. Centlivre* (Durham, NC: Duke University Press, 1952). For a literary assessment, consult F.P. Lock, *Susanna Centlivre* (Boston: Twayne, 1979).

Chandos, James Brydges, first Duke of (1673–1744). A rich politician and patron who had amassed his money through graft as Paymaster to the Forces (1707–12). Under the Hanoverian regime he was created Earl of Carnarvon in 1714 and Duke of Chandos in 1719. He then acquired a reputation for profuse and even profligate ways. It was characteristic that he should enter his name for multiple copies of AP's **Homer** translations; he subscribed for fifty copies of the poems of **John Gay** in 1720. He was an acquisitive buyer of property in the West End of London and elsewhere, and he erected a huge mansion at **Cannons** outside the city.

AP seems to have been on good, though not intimate, terms with the Duke. This changed after the publication of the *Epistle to Burlington* in 1731, when the town echoed with rumors suggesting that the reference to **Timon's villa** was an ungrateful satire on Cannons by AP. This the poet denied, and he incorporated an unsubtle compliment to the Duke in his *Epistle to Cobham* (1733): "Thus gracious CHANDOS is belov'd at sight." But contact seems to have dropped away after the Timon episode.

See C.H. Collins Baker and M.I. Baker, *The Life and Circumstances of James Brydges First Duke of Chandos* (Oxford: Clarendon, 1949).

Charteris, Francis (c. 1675–1732). Name sometimes spelled "Charters" or "Chartres." Soldier but also rake, profligate, rapist, gambler, extortionist, duelist, usurer, pimp, and much else. Known as the "Rape Master-General of Great Britain." The archetypal Augustan villain, he was a Scottish landowner who had been dismissed from the army for various frauds but attained the rank of colonel in a cavalry regiment. On one occasion he was court-martialed after a complaint by a fellow officer, the **Duke of Argyll**. Acquired a large fortune by lending money to fellow gamesters and distraining their possessions when the loan was not repaid. He apparently drove away his wife by brutal treatment. A doughty Whig who made a not very heroic stand against the Jacobite army at Preston in 1715. Once he was brought to the bar of the House of Commons on his knees after an episode that involved taking bribes from army recruits. He is supposed to have made a fortune out of trading in stock at the time of the **South Sea Bubble**. In 1727 he spent £100 each day for a week trying to bribe electors in the constituency of Lancaster, but he failed to get into Parliament. In 1730 he was convicted of a rape and sentenced to death but was freed from Newgate prison within a month, supposedly through the influence of **Robert Walpole**; contemporary gossip had it that he was a "runner" (agent or spy) for Walpole. **Swift** alluded to the rape in his *Excellent New Ballad* (1730); as did **Fielding** in his play *Rape upon Rape* (1730); and **William Hogarth** depicted Charteris in the first plate of his *Harlot's Progress* (1732). Other references occur in the correspondence of Swift and **John Gay**.

AP mentioned the rake on several occasions in his *Imitations of Horace*, along with glancing references in the *Essay on Man*, *Epistle to a Lady*, and other poems. However, the most significant treatment comes in the *Epistle to Bathurst*, l. 4, where Charteris is named along with outstanding competitors in villainy, **Peter Walter** and **John Ward**. Even more damaging,

AP added a long note at this point, drawing attention to particular acts of cruelty and dissipation. He adds a long mock **epitaph** by **John Arbuthnot**, which further augments the history of the subject's criminal career (*TE* 3.ii: 85–86). It is likely that political prejudice caused some of his critics to heap opprobrium on Charteris, in order to identify him with that other "great man," Walpole: and some of the escapades credited to him in popular "rogues' tales" may not have been authentic. Nevertheless, it is beyond question that he was regarded in his day as one of the least savory members of the population. AP is unlikely to have had any personal encounters with him, although acquaintances like **John Barber** and **William Morice** were involved in his prosecution in 1730. A two-line epitaph by AP, which was also applied to **Thomas, Earl Coningsby**, sums up the poet's attitude. "Here *Francis Ch——s* lies—be civil! / The rest God knows—perhaps the Devil" (*TE* 6: 297).

There is no full-scale biography. E.B. Chancellor, *The Lives of the Rakes: Col. Charteris and the Duke of Wharton* (London: Philip Allan, 1927), 1–166, gives most of the gory details.

Chaucer, Geoffrey (c. 1343–1400). Poet. AP had doubtless known Chaucer's work from boyhood. However, it was the modernized versions of **John Dryden**, published in *Fables* (1700) that may have specially caught his attention. In this period Chaucer, though regarded as rough in his manner and clumsy in his handling of meter, was recognized as a major figure in early literature, and again Dryden's tribute to his skill in the preface to the *Fables* was a crucial document. There was enough interest to prompt John Urry to attempt a new edition of the poet in 1721, published by **Bernard Lintot**.

AP's own copy of Chaucer survives. It is a folio printed in black letter (1598), edited by Thomas Speght, and it contains a number of marginal markings by the poet. See *CIH* 179–94. "I read Chaucer still with as much pleasure as almost any of our poets," AP told **Spence** in 1730 (*Anecdotes* 1: 179). When he died, one of the pictures in his house was "a Chausor in a black frame" (*Garden and City* 255).

His earliest effort to copy Chaucer probably came with one of the youthful imitations of English poets, which may have been undertaken at any time from the age of about fourteen. The poem of twenty-six lines was first published as "A Tale of Chaucer" in 1727; see *TE* 6: 41–42. A more considerable attempt came with a version of "The Merchant's Tale," which appeared as "January and May" in **Tonson**'s *Miscellanies* in May 1709. This was the volume in which AP made his poetical debut with the *Pastorals*. AP reduces the scale from almost 1,200 to 820 lines, adding his own satiric observations and smoothing out Chaucer's notoriously "rude" effects. For the text and annotation, see *TE* 2: 14–54.

After this, AP moved on to an imitation of *The Wife of Bath's Prologue* (published in 1713) and a wholesale recasting of *The Hous of Fame* under the title of *The Temple of Fame* (1715). See separate entries for these poems.

Chelsea College. The old name for the Royal Hospital in Chelsea, so named from an older structure that the architect Sir Christopher Wren incorporated into his designs for the new buildings, erected between 1682 and 1692. The main buildings still survive. From the start the hospital was in fact what it remains, a retirement home for veterans of the British army, known as "Chelsea pensioners." AP's friend **William Cheselden** was resident surgeon from 1737, and AP visited him here for treatment at least twice in the last months of his life.

Cheselden, William (1688–1752). Surgeon. One of the most eminent practitioners in the field, he was famous both for his speed and dexterity in cutting for the stone by the "lateral" method and for his skill in cataract operations. Author of *The Anatomy of the Human Body* (1713) and *Osteographia* (1733), both standard texts for many years. FRS, 1712. Surgeon at St. Thomas's, St. George's, and Chelsea hospitals; surgeon to **Queen Caroline**, 1727. One of the teachers of the celebrated John Hunter (1728–93). Among his friends were **William Stukeley**

and **Dr. Richard Mead**. His portrait was painted by **Jonathan Richardson senior**, a neighbor in London. He was known to AP by 1722 and gave him help on the **Shakespeare edition**. Cheselden treated the poet for a urinary problem in 1740. Also attended AP in his final illness: AP went to visit the surgeon at **Chelsea College** in 1744 for this treatment. Cheselden remarked that he "could give a more particular account of [AP's] health than perhaps any man" (*Anecdotes* 1: 111). For AP's admiring comments to **Swift** on Cheselden as "the most noted, and the most deserving man, in the whole profession of Chirurgery," see *Corr* 4: 6.

See Z. Cope, *William Cheselden 1688–1752* (Edinburgh: Livingstone, 1953).

Chesterfield, Philip Dormer Stanhope, fourth Earl of (1694–1773). Politician, patron, and author. Today Lord Chesterfield is best known as a wit and as the writer of polished letters advocating a prudential approach to social life: his reputation has suffered above all from a contemptuous putdown by **Samuel Johnson**. He was caricatured by Charles Dickens as the epitome of a heartless eighteenth-century man of the world. In his own day he was regarded as a considerable statesman. He held positions in government and diplomacy before joining the **opposition to Walpole** as one of the **"Patriot"** Whigs. Opposed the theatrical licensing act passed in 1737. Later served as Lord-Lieutenant of Ireland and Secretary of State.

Chesterfield and AP had met by 1717, and they were on friendly terms in the last twenty years of the poet's life. They went on **rambles** together and hobnobbed at **Bath**. Once Chesterfield stayed at AP's home for a few days when he was taken ill, and he was one of those who made a point of greeting **Swift** when the Dean made a return visit to England in 1726. Later the peer would cultivate the acquaintance of **Voltaire**, one of the few who could outdo him in skeptical realism. He served as a pallbearer at the funeral of **John Gay** in 1732. AP paid Chesterfield a warm compliment in the *Epilogue to the Satires* and incorporated a reference to his patriotic stand against the licensing act in the last book of *The Dunciad* (4: 43–44 and note).

The standard account remains the "Life" in *The Letters of Philip Dormer Stanhope, 4th Earl of Chesterfield*, ed. B. Dobrée, vol. 1 (London: Eyre & Spottiswoode, 1932; reprint, New York: AMS Press, 1968). There is ample room for a new assessment.

Cheyne, George (1673–1743). Scottish physician and writer. An authority on gout and on nervous ailments such as melancholia, known for his views on diet and obesity (as befitted a man who once weighed 450 pounds). He settled in **Bath** in 1718 and ultimately acquired a good practice in this health-obsessed environment. Among his friends were individuals such as **John Arbuthnot**, the philosopher **David Hartley**, and the religious author William Law. Among his patients were the **Earl of Chesterfield** and **John, Baron Hervey**, as well as family members of **Robert Walpole** and the **Duke of Chandos**. AP knew most of these people, some intimately. As early as 1720 he figures as "Cheney, huge of size" in **Gay**'s poem *Mr. Pope's Welcome from Greece*.

Although AP generally used **William Oliver** as his physician in Bath, he did consult Cheyne on occasions and became an admirer of the doctor's dietary regime. He recommended Cheyne to friends and passed on good wishes through **Ralph Allen**. The physician was also a friend of Samuel Richardson, and in February 1741 he was able to tell the novelist about AP's estimate of his work: "Mr. Pope here charged me . . . to tell you that he had read Pamela with great Approbation and Pleasure, and wanted a Night's Rest in finishing it, and says it will do more good than many of the new Sermons." This must have been honey to Richardson's ears.

See A. Guerrini, *Obesity and Depression in the Enlightenment: The Life and Times of George Cheyne* (Norman: University of Oklahoma Press, 1999).

Chiswick. District of London, an outlying village in AP's day. The Pope family moved here from **Binfield** in the spring of 1716. Their home was in Mawson's New Buildings, on the corner of Chiswick Lane and Mawson Lane, standing near the spot where today the Great West Road is met by the Chertsey Road at the Hogarth Roundabout. It was no more than 200 yards from the Thames, and AP would often travel up and down the river on trips to the city. The location, only a mile from the Popes' earlier home at **Hammersmith**, was some six miles from central London. It may have been chosen for this reason, or because of the proximity of **Chiswick House**, where AP's friend and patron the **Earl of Burlington** was in the process of updating his house and gardens. AP's father died at home in 1717 and was buried in the nearby parish church. AP and his mother continued to live at Chiswick until moving to **Twickenham** around March 1719.

Chiswick House. Home of AP's patron the **Earl of Burlington**. He inherited a Jacobean house, but when he came of age in 1715, he began to remodel the property. After a fire in 1725, he decided to build a completely new "villa," in the form of a classical rotunda on the model of Palladio's Villa Capra outside Vicenza. It was finished by about 1728. There are two suites of rooms surrounding a central octagonal dome—a departure from Palladio's circular dome. Most of Burlington's favorite pictures, books, and furniture were eventually moved to the house. Work on the gardens had begun earlier and went on into the 1730s. Among those employed were **Charles Bridgeman** and **William Kent**; however, there is no doubt that AP had some input into the later stages of the garden's development. In 1732 he told Burlington that he considered Chiswick "the finest thing this glorious Sun has shin'd upon" (*Corr* 3: 313), and in his *Epistle to Burlington* he praised the Earl effusively as architect and landscape gardener.

For many years AP very often visited the house. He last dined there on 30 March 1744, only two months prior to his death.

See *Earls of Creation* 148–56; *Gardening World* 24–36; and T. Barnard and J. Clark, eds., *Lord Burlington: Architecture, Art and Life* (London: Hambledon, 1995).

Cibber, Colley (1671–1757). Dramatist, actor, theatrical manager, and author. Son of the German-born sculptor Caius Grabiel Cibber (1630–1700). Went on the stage, 1690, after a brief attempt at a military career. A specialist in performing comic roles, especially as the fop, he achieved fame as a playwright with *Love's Last Shift* (1696), *The Careless Husband* (1704), and *The Lady's Last Stake* (1707). His adaptation of **Shakespeare**'s *Richard III* (1700) continued to be played until well into the nineteenth century. Another work that created considerable interest was *The Non-Juror* (1717), a version of Molière's *Tartuffe* that featured a savage caricature of Jacobite plotters. *The Provok'd Husband, or A Journey to London* (1728) was a comedy begun by **Sir John Vanbrugh** and completed by Cibber after the playwright's death. Joint licensee of the **Haymarket Theatre** from 1710, and then at **Drury Lane Theatre** from 1712 to 1734, after which he continued to appear on the stage at intervals. Despite his minimal talent in poetry, he was appointed Poet Laureate in 1730, exasperating numerous writers who thought themselves better qualified and occasioning considerable mockery in AP and his friends. His candid and self-revelatory *Apology for the Life of Colley Cibber, Comedian* (1740) broke the accepted norms of literary decorum and prompted derision among the wits—not least **Henry Fielding**, whose *Apology for the Life of Mrs. Shamela Andrews* (1742) makes hilarious use of the actor's autobiography. Cibber's scapegrace son, Theophilus (1703–58), also an actor, earns a brief mention in *The Dunciad*; and his daughter Charlotte Charke (1713–60) wrote her own *Narrative* of her life and provoked almost as much scandalous attention as her father.

The exact date at which the prolonged hostilities between Cibber and AP began is not known. It may have been around 1715, when the actor is supposed to have played a practical joke on the poet at **Button's** coffeehouse. In 1717 Cibber withdrew the Scriblerian farce *Three Hours after Marriage* after a short run at Drury Lane; he also made some comic stage business out of the play at a royal command performance of an old comedy, *The Rehearsal*, attended by AP. Matters were scarcely improved when AP and his friends, by way of retaliation, brought out *A Clue to the Comedy of the Non-Juror* in 1718. However, only light blows were exchanged prior to the elevation of Cibber to the laureateship: indeed, he was allotted a fairly minor role in the first version of *The Dunciad* and gets away with a small appearance as "the most Undaunted Mr. Colly Cibber" in *The Art of Sinking* (*Prose* 2: 230). In 1728 Cibber refused *The Beggar's Opera* for Drury Lane, a decision he must later have regretted. Throughout the 1730s AP made regular use of Cibber's name in his satires, whenever it served his purposes. One of the most amusing concerns the elaborate coronation pageant that Cibber inserted into Shakespeare's *Henry VIII* in 1727, which AP describes with comic relish in the *Epistle to Augustus*, ll. 314–21. He also wrote some witty **epigrams** on Cibber (*TE* 6: 360–61, 397–98), and he is the most likely author of a ballad titled *An Ode for the New Year* (c.1733), which makes clever fun of Cibber's efforts.

It was only with the "new" *Dunciad* of 1742 that the quarrel flared up in full earnest. Cibber is now enthroned in the key role of King of the Dunces, and the material of the poem was reworked to inflict the most damage possible on him. AP was able to enlist a large amount of detail drawn from Cibber's life as an actor, a playwright, a manager, and a composer of inept laureate odes. One aim is to strike at the court through its appointed public bard. But AP also brings in the statuary work of the elder Cibber, who had created stone figures of mania and depression over the gates of **Bedlam**, near the spot where the dunces gather early in the poem. These allusions finally goaded Cibber into a serious act of retaliation, and he struck back with vigorous pamphlets, *A Letter from Mr. Cibber, To Mr. Pope* (1742), *A Second Letter from Mr. Cibber* (1743), and *Another Occasional Letter from Mr. Cibber to Mr. Pope* (1744), all making some effective points. See Guerinot 288–94, 310–11, 316–19. He may also have been involved with **John, Baron Hervey** in writing *The Difference Between Verbal and Practical Virtue* (1742), another attack on AP.

For the most part, AP treats Cibber with an amiable contempt rather than bitter personal hatred. Nor did Cibber lose control as completely as most the poet's adversaries. Their animosity began with political disagreements: Cibber was a loyal Whig and a strong supporter of the Hanoverian regime, who rewarded him amply. The *Apology* remains a live classic of theatrical history, in spite of its absurdities and garrulous anecdotes; and though Cibber's plays and adaptations are now very seldom performed, he stands as a colorful figure in Augustan culture, who was a big enough presence in the age to fit the major part he has to play in *The Dunciad*.

The best biography is R.H. Barker, *Mr Cibber of Drury Lane* (New York: Columbia University Press, 1939; reprint, New York: AMS Press, 1966). It focuses mainly on the subject's stage career but covers the quarrels with AP effectively. See also Ault 298–324. There is a critical edition of the *Apology for the Life of Mr. Colley Cibber* by J.M. Evans (New York: Garland, 1987); but no fully adequate annotated edition exists. *A Letter from Mr. Cibber to Mr. Pope* has been edited by H. Koon (Los Angeles: Augustan Reprint Society, 1973).

Cirencester. The house and park of the Bathurst family in Gloucestershire. Sir Benjamin Bathurst acquired the Oakley estate in 1695, together with an old-fashioned Jacobean mansion. It was his son Allen, AP's friend **Lord Bathurst**, who set about the improvement of the estate. He erected a large but plain house in 1715–18; the architect is unknown but could have been the owner himself. It is shielded from the adjoining town of Cirencester by a large yew hedge. The park was more ambitious. In 1716 Bathurst acquired a large portion of extra land to the west of his property, toward the village of Sapperton. He began extensive plantations that created a forest interspersed with rides and glades. This was perhaps the first attempt to implement the landscaping program that AP had set out in *The Guardian* in 1713. Bathurst may have employed the eminent gardener Stephen Switzer, but the dominant influence on the development of the park was undoubtedly AP.

It was in the summer of 1718 that AP first visited Cirencester. He sent its master an effusive account of his stay and of the attractions of "Oakley Wood," as it was still known. Included in the letter were verses on the plantation scheme (see *Corr* 1: 476–78; *TE* 6: 195–96). Thereafter AP was often at Cirencester, helping to create an oasis of elysian scenery that survives today. He was there in 1721, 1728, 1733, 1734, 1737, and 1743, and probably at other times. Various items of garden ornament were installed, including substantial structures such as the Wood House of 1721, transformed by 1732 into "Alfred's Hall," one of the earliest Gothic folly-type ruins. In addition, Bathurst constructed the Hexagon, at the junction of three rides; Ivy Lodge; and a Doric column, erected in honor of **Queen Anne** in 1741 near a newly created lake. There was also "Pope's Seat," a small classical temple, with a pediment and a niche on each side of the entrance, which stood near the far end of the park.

There are numerous references to the park in AP's poetry and correspondence. He sees himself as a "magician" appointed to guard "that enchanted Forest" (*Corr* 2: 115). The most striking use of Cirencester comes in his imitation of the second epistle of the second book, in the *Imitations of Horace*. Bathurst had considered a project to link the Severn to the west of his estate with the Thames, which rises just to the south. The two rivers were united by the Thames and Severn Canal, opened in 1789 not long after Bathurst's death in the midst of the canal boom. However, AP uses the scheme as a metaphor for unsustainable attempts to defeat the power of nature:

All vast Possessions (just the same the case
Whether you call them Villa, Park, or Chace)
Alas, my BATHURST! What will they avail?
Join *Cotswold* Hills to *Saperton*'s fair Dale,
Let rising Granaries and Temples here,
There mingled Farms and Pyramids appear,
Link Towns to Towns with Avenues of Oak,
Enclose whole Downs in walls, 'tis all a joke!
Inexorable Death shall level all,
And Trees, and Stones, and Farms, and Farmer
    fall. (*TE* 4: 183)

Cirencester park was organized around avenues of oak; while "mingled Farms and Pyramids" conveys the blend of rustic architecture to be found on the estate.

See *Earls of Creation* 33–56; and *Gardening World* 81–94.

Clarke, George (1661–1736). Architect, collector, antiquarian, and politician. A civilian lawyer who was a Fellow of All Souls College, Oxford, from 1680, and MP for Oxford University and other constituencies from 1685. A moderate Tory with Hanoverian loyalties, he was termed by the Jacobite **Thomas Hearne** "a pitiful proud sneaker" and defeated another highflyer, **Dr. William King**, in a parliamentary election. On the other hand, he was no friend to the **Duke of Marlborough**. Served in the Admiralty under Prince George, husband of **Queen Anne**. A student of architecture, especially **Palladianism**, he showed AP drawings by Inigo Jones when the poet stayed with him at Oxford in 1716. This is revealed in a letter (*Corr* 1: 376) from AP to **Charles Jervas**, who had been able to study painting in Italy, thanks to financial support from Clarke. AP was with Clarke again in Oxford during 1721. He was an assiduous book collector, and it is not surprising that he subscribed to all AP's ventures in this field: he subscribed to over twenty separate books by Hearne.

Cleland, William (c. 1673–1741). A member of an ancient Scottish family who had been a soldier and fought at the battle of Almanza in 1707. Enjoying the patronage of the Earls of Mar and Marchmont, he became a commissioner for the Scottish customs in 1713 and a commissioner for the land tax in 1723. He was the father of the novelist John Cleland, author of *Fanny Hill*. The origins of his friendship with AP are hard to trace: as a resident of St. James's Place, he was a near neighbor of AP's at **Cleveland Court**. His wife Lucy was well known to the circle of the Prince and Princess of Wales. A portrait by **Charles Jervas** of AP and **Martha Blount** was presented to him and survives today (*Portraits* 3.1).

The work that eventually became the *Epistle to Arbuthnot* derived from a poem of 260 lines which AP addressed to Cleland (see *L&GA* 419–23). In addition, Cleland lent his name to the "Letter to the Publisher," dated 22 December 1728, which is among the preliminaries to *The Dunciad*. He was perhaps used in this role as a front man because AP's enemies would not have found such an anonymous figure easy to attack. See *TE* 5: 11–19, where AP's tribute to his friend is cited.

See W.H. Epstein, *John Cleland: Images of a Life* (New York: Columbia University Press, 1974).

Cleveland Court. Here was located the house in St. James's of the painter **Charles Jervas**, which served as AP's London base for about a decade from 1713. It stood on the northern side of Cleveland Street, at the west end of Pall Mall, and gave easy access to Green Park. Next door lived Viscount Townshend and his wife Dorothy, the sister of **Robert Walpole**. Subscription copies for AP's translations of **Homer** were distributed from this address.

Cloe. A portrait of a heartless court lady. It was first published in the *Works* (1738) as "Cloe: A Character." Subsequently the twenty-four lines were transferred, with only very slight alteration, to *An Epistle to a Lady*, when this poem was included in the **deathbed edition**, printed but not published in 1744. It is uncertain whether the character formed part of the original design of the *Epistle*.

Discussion has centered on the identity of the real-life Cloe (if there was one). Early commentators, notably **Horace Walpole**, expressed the view that the woman in question was **Henrietta Howard, Countess of Suffolk**. However, many of the details do not appear to fit Lady Suffolk, and a convincing case was mounted by **Norman Ault** to discount this identification. It is possible that one or two traits of Lady Suffolk were utilized, but the character is probably a generalized picture of an excessively prudent woman. See *TE* 3.ii: 63–64; 6: 377; and Ault 266–75.

Clue to the Comedy of the Non-Juror, A. A pamphlet published on 15 February 1718 by **Edmund Curll** as an octavo in fours (Griffith 90a) at a price of sixpence. It relates to a play by **Colley Cibber**, first performed at **Drury Lane Theatre** on 6 December 1717 and published on 2 January following. A reprint appeared as *The Plot Discover'd* on 18 February. This time Curll advertised the work in the *Evening Post* with the words, "The manuscript of this Pamphlet was sent to me on Tuesday last, and I was this Morning given to understand, that this signal Favour was conferr'd on me by Mr. Pope, for which I hereby return my most grateful Acknowledgment for the same. E. Curll." A second edition of the *Plot* appeared on 18 March, with several alterations to the text (Griffith 90b). On the back of the half title Curll prints a quatrain urging AP to be "gen'rous" enough to admit responsibility for the work. In the event AP remained quiet, and the item only recently became established in the canon.

Cibber's comedy is an adaptation of Molière's *Tartuffe*. It came out in the aftermath of the **Jacobite rising** in 1715–16 and featured a Jesuit named Dr. Wolf who clearly represented the nonjuring clergymen involved in the rising. The play enjoyed great success, and Cibber was given £200 in return for his dedication to the King. At the same time it inevitably distressed Catholics who felt that the portrayal of Wolf as an evil conspirator reduced their faith. In a letter to **Robert Digby** on 31 March, AP wrote bitterly, "The Stage is the only place we seem alive at; there indeed we stare, and roar, and clap hands for K. *George* and the Government" (*Corr* 1: 473). Much later, after AP had installed Cibber as hero of the revised *Dunciad*, the dramatist accused AP of writing the *Clue* as an attempt to prove that it was "a closely couched Jacobite Libel against the Government." A reply was issued, titled *A Blast upon Bays*, which probably came from AP himself. In it he effectively admitted that this was the design of the *Clue* but added (what should have been obvious to any competent reader) that the work was a "Frolick." It is indeed a characteristic example of AP's humor, showing many close similarities to his slightly earlier *Key to*

the Lock. The absurd interpretations of Cibber's play are expressed in an excited, self-preening style: "So here is a *Prelate* and a *Jesuit* and his *Gang*, got into the Family of Sir *John*! Let us next see what they are to do there. Why, they contrive the *Ruin* of his Family."

The pamphlet, whether named as the *Clue* or the *Plot*, is couched in the form of a letter to **Nicholas Rowe**. Up to the time of Rowe's death on 6 December 1718 Rowe was one of AP's closest friends. A short section of an epilogue by Rowe is printed as a postscript to AP's pamphlet.

For attribution of the work to AP, see *Prose* 1: cxvii–cxxiv; for the text, 1: 305–14.

Cobham, Richard Temple, first Viscount (1675–1749). Soldier and politician. Succeeded his father as fourth baronet in 1697 and inherited the estate of **Stowe**. He served as a colonel of a regiment of foot in the army of the **Duke of Marlborough** and also sat as an MP for his local constituency of Buckingham. Joined fellow Whigs in the **Kit-Cat Club**, where he forged links with **Congreve, Vanbrugh**, and others. Lieutenant-General, 1710; created a baron in 1714 and a viscount in 1718. His greatest military success came with the capture of Vigo from the Spanish in 1719. From this time he devoted more of his time to improving the house and garden at Stowe. In 1733 he quarreled with the government over the Excise Scheme and became one of the leading figures in the **opposition to Walpole**. He was an uncle of AP's friend **Lord Lyttelton**, and William Pitt, the future Earl of Chatham, married his niece. These two men helped to form the group of "Cobham's Cubs," who constituted the nucleus of the **Patriot** opposition. When the Prime Minister ultimately fell in 1742, Cobham returned to favor and was made Field-Marshal, but he resigned his post on grounds of principle within little more than a year.

AP probably met Cobham around 1724. While he did not apparently take an active share in planning the garden at Stowe, he certainly exhibited a keen interest in what friends such as **James Gibbs** and **William Kent** were doing there, since he visited the house on an almost annual basis. On his own admission AP seldom wrote to Cobham, and only two letters survive from the peer. There are flattering references to him in the *Imitations of Horace*, but AP's most lasting tribute came in the form of the *Epistle to Cobham*, which the poet later put conspicuously at the head of his *Moral Essays*. In this work Cobham is singled out as a brave and disinterested patriot. More briefly, the *Epistle to Burlington* lauds him for his tasteful use of riches at Stowe.

Codrington, Elizabeth, Lady (1693–1761). Friend of AP, a sister of **Hugh** and **Slingsby Bethel**. In 1718 she married William Codrington (d. 1738), created first baronet 1721, an MP, and a subscriber to the *Odyssey*. Sir William was a first cousin of the famous sugar planter and philanthropist Sir Christopher Codrington and himself had large holdings in the West Indies. He owned Dodington House in Gloucestershire (converted into a large classical mansion around 1800 by James Wyatt). AP visited the house in 1728 and occasionally met the couple at nearby **Bath**, where he sometimes saw Elizabeth's sister Mary, Lady Cox (b. 1691), who had married Sir Richard Cox, MP (d. 1726), and lived in Queen Square. Later the poet often called on Lady Codrington at her London home. Like Mary, Elizabeth was on friendly terms with **Martha Blount**, for whom she attempted to obtain an annuity. Lady Cox and a third sister, Bridget (b. 1692), were among the earliest converts to Methodism and supported George Whitefield's mission to the new colony of Georgia in 1738.

For the family fortunes, see V.T. Harlow, *Christopher Codrington, 1668–1710* (Oxford: Clarendon, 1928).

Cole, Nathaniel (d. 1759). Lawyer. Clerk to the Stationers' Company from 1723. He regularly gave AP advice on piracy and copyright issues in the last years of the poet's life. He was involved with many of AP's associates in the book trade. See D. Nichol, "Pope, Warburton, Knapton, and Cole: A Longstanding Connection," *Notes & Queries*, 234 (1989), 54–56. Some letters from AP to Cole survive.

Comte de Gabalis, Le. Subtitled "colloquies on the secret sciences," this was a flippant exposition of the ideas of the Rosicrucians in the guise of erotic fantasy, published in Paris in 1670. Its author was Nicolas-Pierre-Henri de Montfaucon de Villars (c. 1638–73), a French priest whose sudden notoriety caused the Archdeacon of Paris to ban him from preaching in January 1671. He had already been in trouble with the authorities as a result of his libertine habits and incurred the opposition of the Jesuit leader Antoine Arnauld. According to some unreliable accounts, his death was connected with his book, as he was found shot by the roadside near Lyon—murdered by the **sylphs**, said **Voltaire**. The work itself was banned after enjoying great success on publication. A continuation by another hand appeared in 1718. As AP always admitted, the book provided the basis for the "machinery" in *The Rape of the Lock*.

The main part of the work consists of five dialogues on hermetic philosophy between Gabalis, a Rosicrucian initiate, and an anonymous narrator, who poses questions for his interlocutor to answer at length. The tone is light, but the work may be attempting to pass itself off as a semiserious treatment. *Gabalis* was translated into English by Philip Ayres and A. Lovell (both published in 1680). The more familiar version is that of Ayres (1638–1712), a friend of **Dryden**. In the wake of the interest excited by AP's poem, a new translation by **John Ozell** was issued by the resourceful **Edmund Curll**, this time in association with **Bernard Lintot**, in April 1714. It looks as if AP may have known something about this (see also *Corr* 1: 268). The English version was printed in a form "to bind up with Mr. Pope's Rape of the Lock"; and since Lintot was the publisher of the poem, it may have suited all concerned to have this translation available. AP's most immediate debt is to the description in the second discourse of the sylphs, gnomes, salamanders, and nymphs. Despite his grave endorsement of what Villars had written, in his prefatory letter to **Arabella Fermor**, there is little chance that AP was hoodwinked by this opportunistic and in some ways mischievous book.

There is no scholarly edition in English. The

fullest edition is *Le Comte de Gabalis: ou Entretiens sur les sciences secrètes*, ed. R. Laufer (Paris: Nizet, 1963).

Concanen, Matthew (1704–49). Irish miscellaneous writer who was born near Dublin, where he published a comedy and poetry. His *Poems upon Several Occasions* (1722) includes an amusing **mock-heroic** poem in three cantos on a football match between Lusk and Swords, villages to the north of Dublin. The volume also prints a number of attractive trifles. Moved to London in the 1720s. Joined the circle of literary friends including **William Warburton** and **Lewis Theobald** and attacked AP's **Shakespeare edition** in various places. He may have been disappointed not to gain entry to *The Art of Sinking*, for he wrote *A Supplement to the Profound* in 1728, ranging over several of AP's works (Guerinot 148–50). Duly incorporated in *The Dunciad*, where he aptly sinks lower than almost any of the mud-divers: "A cold, long-winded, native of the deep!" [2: 288]. **Swift** similarly wrote in *On Poetry: A Rhapsody* (1733), "Concanen, more aspiring bard, / Climbs downwards, deeper by a yard." AP added a note to *The Dunciad*, branding Concanen "an anonymous slanderer, and publisher of other men's slanders, particularly on Dr. *Swift* to whom he had many obligations and from he had received . . . no small assistance." Concanen denied this but could not dispute the fact that he had been allowed to print some of Swift's poems in a collection he published in 1724. Also included in the miscellany are works by **Thomas Parnell, Jonathan Smedley**, Thomas Sheridan, Patrick Delany, and others.

AP also noted that Concanen was "since a hired Scribler in the *Daily Courant*, where he pour'd forth much Billingsgate against the Lord Bolingbroke and others; after which he was surprizingly promoted to administer Justice and Law in Jamaica" (*TE* 5: 113–14). This is a reference to his appointment as Attorney-General of Jamaica in 1732. In that post he ran into trouble with the Governor, General Robert Hunter, who was known to AP and Swift. He was, or later became, a member of Sergeants Inn, the home of barristers in **Fleet Street**. AP's implication is that Concanen had been supported by the government of **Robert Walpole** all along. He was certainly a protégé of **Sir William Yonge**. It is believed that he was also the editor of *A Miscellany on Taste* (1732), which reprints the **Epistle to Burlington** "with jeering notes by Concanen(?)" (Griffith 266). The Jamaican post proved lucrative before Concanen returned to London in 1748. According to Warburton, he had married a rich widow while overseas. He died of consumption in the following year.

For the "Concanen Club" and other relations with the literary community, see R.F. Jones, *Lewis Theobald* (New York: Columbia University Press, 1919; reprint, New York: AMS Press, 1966).

concordances. The first attempt at a full concordance to the poems of AP was that of **Edwin Abbott** in 1875. This omitted the translations of **Homer** and other poets but otherwise served a useful function for nearly a century. It was supplanted in most respects by the more up-to-date methods of its successor, *A Concordance to the Poems of Alexander Pope*, ed. E.G. Bedford and R.J. Dilligan (1974), which used the **Twickenham edition** as its textual basis. There is no concordance to the prose.

Congreve, William (1670–1729). Dramatist and poet. Educated in Ireland with **Jonathan Swift**. Studied law at the Inner Temple. He became a favored member of the circle of **John Dryden** at **Will's** coffeehouse and elsewhere. He helped to negotiate publishing contracts for Dryden with **Jacob Tonson senior**. Congreve also wrote a short novel, *Incognita* (1691). After the success (to a greater or lesser degree) of his four famous comedies between 1693 and 1700, he effectively retired from regular authorship and lived off various government posts. One of his translations does appear, however, in the collective edition of the **Metamorphoses** brought out by Tonson in 1717. His first attachment was to the actress Anne Bracegirdle (1671–1748); later he transferred his affections to **Henrietta, Duchess of Marlborough**. In his will he left a bequest to Bracegirdle, but the bulk of his estate went to the Duchess. It is possible that Mary (1723–64), daughter of the Duchess and herself later Duchesss of Leeds, was fathered by the dramatist.

Congreve had already given up active work as a writer when he read AP's *Pastorals* and encouraged the young poet. AP once observed, "While Mr. *Congreve* likes my poetry, I can endure Dennis and a thousand like him" (*Corr* 1: 238). When he began his translation of the *Iliad*, he was proud to have the support of Congreve, and this is reflected in the fact that the work was ultimately dedicated to his friend, where it would have been usual to choose a powerful nobleman. AP writes of him as "one of the most valuable Men as well finest Writers, of my Age and Countrey" (*Prose* 1: 326). A further grateful reference occurs in the *Epistle to Arbuthnot*. Others such as **Voltaire** saw Congreve as worldly and idle; AP felt respect and affection for him. In January 1729 AP wrote to the **second Earl of Oxford**, "Mr Congreves death was to me sudden, & strook me through. You know the Value I bore him & a long 20 years friendship" (*Corr* 3: 10). "Aye, Mr Tonson," AP once exclaimed with a sigh, "he was Ultimus Romanorum!" Along with **Garth** and **Vanbrugh**, AP named Congreve as one of the "three most honest-hearted, real good men" of the **Kit-Cat Club** (*Anecdotes* 1: 50, 208). This was a tribute of friendship over politics, since throughout his career Congreve had been attached to Whigs such as **Addison**, **Halifax**, and **Somers**. "Friendly *Congreve*, unreproachfull man" is among the relatively few Whigs included in *Mr. Pope's Welcome from Greece*. In his list of departed friends, AP wrote, "a distinguished poet, a courteous and cultivated man, and extremely intimate with me" (*EC* 1: x). The dramatist was a subscriber to all three of AP's subscription ventures. A handful of letters between the two men survives.

See J.C. Hodges, *William Congreve the Man: A Biography from New Sources* (New York: Modern Language Association of America, 1941); as well as *William Congreve: Letters and Documents*, ed. J.C. Hodges (New York: Harcourt, Brace, 1964). Some helpful material

is found in K.M. Lynch, *A Congreve Gallery* (Cambridge, MA: Harvard University Press, 1951). A guide to secondary work is L. Bartlett, *William Congreve: A Reference Guide* (Boston: G.K. Hall, 1979).

Coningsby, Thomas, Earl (1656–1729). A Whig politician who had been accused of corruption in earlier posts and who helped to managed the impeachment of the **first Earl of Oxford** in Parliament. He inherited an old family grudge with the Harleys, who were neighbors in Herefordshire. Litigious and hotheaded, he became increasingly unbalanced. After wild accusations against the Lord Chancellor and capricious acts of revenge against his local enemies, he was removed from his offices by 1724. He exhibited a virulent dislike of Catholics. It is hard to think of an individual whose career more perfectly expresses the values against which AP fought. An unusual degree of personal hatred can be found in various references to Coningsby, at the end of the *Epistle to Bathurst* (*TE* 3.ii: 124), in lines addressed to **Lord Bathurst**, and in a scorching two-line epitaph on the peer (*TE* 6: 195, 297).

Cooke, Thomas (1703–56). Translator, dramatist, and miscellaneous author. Best known for his work in translating from the classics, especially his version of Hesiod (1728). AP gives a potted history of Cooke's career in a note to *The Dunciad*: "The man here specify'd was the son of a *Muggletonian*, who kept a kept a *Publick-house* at *Braintree* in *Essex*. He writ a thing call'd *The Battle of the Poets*, of which *Philips* and *Welsted* were the heroes, and wherein our author was attack'd in his moral character, in relation to his *Homer* and Shakespear." AP goes on to mention "some malevolent things" in newspapers, as well as other assaults on himself. "At the same time the honest Gentlemen wrote Letters to Mr. *P*. in the strongest terms his innocence.... His chief work was a translation of *Hesiod*, to which *Theobald* wrote notes, and half-notes" (*TE* 5: 112–13). For *The Battle of the Poets* (1725; revised with stronger abuse of AP, 1729), see Guerinot 91–93, 160–63. For Cooke's apologetic letters, see *Corr* 2: 509, 519–20). AP asked for but did not receive a public recantation (*Corr* 5: 7).

AP did not believe in the efforts Cooke made to exculpate himself. In *The Art of Sinking* he gave examples of the inane effects in Cooke's poems (*Prose* 2: 209, 215–16). In *The Dunciad* AP briefly mentioned Cooke as one of **Edmund Curll**'s authors (which he was), and as passing his work off as **Prior**'s (2: 130). In the *Epistle to Arbuthnot* AP lets go a single brief volley, linking Cooke with **Thomas Burnet** and **John Oldmixon** (*TE* 4: 106). There is no doubt that Cooke was one dunce who had given ample grounds for retaliation on AP's part. He possessed some ability, but his tough life in Grub Street caused him to stray beyond the bounds of sense and propriety.

Cooper, Samuel (1609–72). Painter. The greatest English miniaturist of the seventeenth century who enjoyed the patronage of both Oliver Cromwell and Charles II. Some of his portraits are believed to have hung at **Binfield** and to have become the poet's own property on the death of his aunt Elizabeth in 1710. Cooper had been married to another aunt, Christiana, who was AP's godmother; she died in 1693 (see **ancestry**: Christiana's will is printed by **Charles Wentworth Dilke** in his *Papers*). The family pictures were bequeathed by AP to his sister in his **will**.

See D. Foskett, *Samuel Cooper, 1609–1672* (London: Faber, 1974).

Cooper, Thomas (d. 1743). A "publisher," that is to say, a distributor and wholesaler who supplied hawkers and pamphlet shops and often acted as the title-page front for booksellers who held the actual copyright. His name often appears in the imprint of works by AP from the mid-1730s; however, he does not seem to have had any real share in ushering the works into print. The most important work by AP with which he is associated was *The New Dunciad* of 1742. After his death in February 1743, his widow Mary took over the business and carried out the same role for AP's later books.

Cope, Anne (d. 1728). A first cousin of AP's friend **John Caryll senior**. Her feckless brother Philip had not been able to provide for her before her marriage, and then she found herself joined to a bigamist, one Captain Cope, who had deserted her and taken a second wife in Minorca. Impressed by her qualities when he met her through John Caryll in 1711, AP tried to relieve her situation, in the hopes of getting her husband to provide for her. AP ultimately paid her an annuity of £20 per year. In her poverty she retired to Bar-sur-Aube in France, only to discover that she had cancer of the breast. She died on 10 May 1728, much regretted by AP. It is unlikely that her story contributed directly to the *Elegy to the Memory of an Unfortunate Lady*, but it is possible that AP's "Epitaph on Mrs. Corbet" was originally written for Mrs. Cope (see *TE* 6: 322–24). For the little that is known about her ill-starred life, see *Social Milieu* 74–77.

Copyright Act. The first significant legal measure to protect literary property. It was drafted in the age of **Queen Anne**, following a petition from leading London booksellers in 1709. A bill was introduced by the Whig MP Edward Wortley Montagu (soon to be husband of **Lady Mary Wortley Montagu**) in January 1710. After considerable revision during its parliamentary stages, the bill completed its passage and became law on 5 April. Its full title read "An Act for the Encouragement of Learning by Vesting the Copies of Printed Books in the Authors or Purchasers of such Copies, during the Times Therein Mentioned" (8 Anne, c.19). The provisions went into force on 10 April 1710. The act gave publishers a degree of copyright protection, although not the perpetual copyright they had been seeking, on condition that they entered their titles before publication in the Stationers' Register and sent nine copies of each book to Stationers' Hall to be forwarded to the nine so-called "copyright libraries." These were the royal library at St. James's Palace; **Oxford** and **Cambridge**; the four Scottish universities (Aberdeen, Edinburgh, Glasgow, St. Andrews); the Advocates Library in Edinburgh; and Sion College in London. The act made it legal for the first time for authors to claim copyright for fourteen years, with a further extension up to twenty-eight years if they were still living at the end of the original period. However, in the case of most books, authors sold their rights for a flat fee to booksellers (the royalty system had not yet evolved), and it was the publishing trade that stood most to benefit from the new provisions. Books already published were protected for twenty-one years.

Many booksellers were unhappy with the act in the form it was drafted, and they pressed for many years to hold on to a separate right to "perpetual" copyright under common law—a case they ultimately lost in the courts. The act was the basis of most subsequent copyright legislation around the world. AP was one of the few authors to grasp the potential gains to be made through strategic retention or sale of copyright. He defended his newly won rights in lawsuits against members of the trade, including **Edmund Curll**, who had infringed on the terms of the act.

For background, see *Book Trade*, esp. 237–51, as well as M. Rose, *Authors and Owners: The Invention of Copyright* (Cambridge, MA: Harvard University Press, 1993); and J. Feather, "The Book Trade in Politics: The Making of the Copyright Act of 1710," *Publishing History*, 8 (1980), 19–44.

Cornbury, Henry Hyde, Viscount (1710–53). Descended from the famous Earl of Clarendon, seventeenth-century politician and historian, and son of the fourth Earl. As MP for Oxford University, he was active in the **opposition to Walpole**, one of the "Boy Patriots" (see **Patriots**) who joined together under **Viscount Cobham** in the mid-1730s. AP was fond of the members of this group personally, as well as supporting many of their goals. Cornbury was a Tory and involved in **Jacobite** intrigues until he renounced the cause. He was on good terms with **John Gay**, who described him to **Swift** as "a young nobleman of learning & morals," and acted as a pallbearer at Gay's funeral in 1732. AP often stayed with him at his London house and at least once at the family home, **Cornbury**

Park. In 1738 Cornbury was one of a group of leading Opposition figures whom AP entertained at **Twickenham**. He wrote verses on the *Essay on Man*. He earned a complimentary reference from AP in the sixth epistle of the first book, in the *Imitations of Horace* (*TE* 4: 241).

Cornbury Park. Estate at Charlbury, Oxfordshire, in the Wychwood forest. A seventeenth-century house of two stories and eleven bays belonging to the Hyde family, where AP visited his friend **Viscount Cornbury** in 1743.

correspondence. An assiduous letter-writer, AP composed his messages on any paper to hand—hence the nickname bestowed on him by **Johnathan Swift**, "paper-sparing Pope." His habit of drafting sections of poems, notably his translation of Homer, on letters he had just received enables us to date these with more accuracy. It was **Edmund Curll** who first brought out some of AP's letters in 1726. However, the author himself was the earliest publisher of his own collected correspondence, after he had first tricked Curll into producing a "pirate" edition in 1735. From this time AP began to issue his collected letters systematically, issuing almost 300 in his lifetime. For a listing of early printings, see *Corr* 1: xix–xxv.

The standard edition of the *Correspondence*, occupying five volumes, contains over 2,100 letters. Of these about 1,600 are letters by AP, and the remainder are those addressed to him. Since that time over 50 more letters have been located and published, with a similar number for which better texts have emerged. In the standard edition over 1,400 letters were printed from manuscript, with the British Library furnishing over 550 items and substantial contributions from Harvard, Yale, and the Pierpont Morgan Library. Among private collections, the Portland papers at Longleat supplied nearly 250 letters, with more than 50 taken from the Mapledurham archives. Over 700 came from printed sources, including 186 which were taken from the **Elwin and Courthope edition**— a manuscript has turned up for a few of these more recently. Almost a hundred different correspondents are represented in the series. Among the largest surviving caches are letters to and from **Ralph Allen**, **William Broome**, **John Caryll senior**, **William Fortescue**, **John Gay**, the **Earl of Orrery**, the **second Earl of Oxford**, and Swift himself. Caryll and Oxford head the list in terms of the numbers of surviving letters they received from AP. The largest span of years covered is that of the letters to **Martha Blount** (1712–44).

Among AP's most important models were the letters of ancient authors such as Cicero and Pliny the Younger, as well as the Renaissance master of this form, Erasmus. More recent practitioners familiar to AP were the French writers Jean-Louis Guez de Balzac (1597–1654), famous for his harmonious prose and serious concerns, and Vincent Voiture (1598–1648), noted for a more spontaneous, witty, and gallant way of writing. AP's letters cover a very broad range of subjects, partly dependent on the identity of his addressee. His early correspondence is full of learned trifling, and attempts to portray himself in the guise of a rake. Later he wrote more seriously on religious and philosophic subjects (as those to **Francis Atterbury**), in addition to politics and literature (as to Swift). Others deal with connoisseurship or antiquarian matters. Several of his most highly wrought compositions were doubtless produced with a view to ultimate publication. Some of the finest concern his views on friendship, while another attractive group relate to gardening, landscape, and architecture, often revealing his attachment to "romantic" scenes and buildings.

See the standard edition, *The Correspondence of Alexander Pope*, ed. G. Sherburn, 5 vols. (Oxford: Clarendon, 1956). An excellent selection is *Alexander Pope: Selected Letters*, ed. H. Erskine-Hill (Oxford: Oxford University Press, 2000). The most complete analysis from a literary standpoint is J.A. Winn, *A Window in the Bosom: The Letters of Alexander Pope* (Hamden, CT: Archon, 1977). A briefer study is W.L. Jones, *Talking on Paper: Alexander Pope's Letters* (Victoria, BC: University of Victoria, 1990).

See also **epistles**; *Epistle to Miss Blount, with the Works of Voiture*.

"Cotta." Character sketch in AP's *Epistle to Bathurst*, ll. 176–218, incorporating the miserly father Old Cotta and the spendthrift son Young Cotta. It is likely that AP was referring to Sir John Cutler (c. 1608–93), a rich merchant in the city of London, and his son-in-law the second Earl of Radnor (1660–1723). Cutler was well known for his avarice and is actually named later in the poem (l. 315). Moreover, AP could have learned about the family from two sources: Radnor's nephew lived next door to AP at **Twickenham**, while Cutler bequeathed to his son-in-law **Wimpole**, which became the estate of AP's close friend the **second Earl of Oxford**. See *TE* 3.ii: 108–9.

Cotterell, Sir Clement (1685–1758). Courtier. He was Master of Ceremonies from 1710, succeeding his father. The post involved supervising protocol and ceremony in respect of diplomatic and state events. Knighted, 1710. His family had occupied this position since the time of Charles I, and his son followed in the reigns of **George II** and George III. Sir Clement took the name Cotterell-Dormer when he succeeded to the **Rousham** estate in 1741.

AP must have known him from an early age. One of his aunts was the first wife of **Sir William Trumbull**, and he later acted as adviser to the second Lady Trumbull after she was widowed. Another aunt was the mother of **James Dormer**. He was extensively occupied in family affairs and often in contact with AP over matters such as the *Odyssey* translation. Subscribed to all AP's undertakings, as also to volumes by **Gay**, **Prior**, and **Bononcini**. As a resident of **Twickenham** he was a neighbor of AP, and he also shared some antiquarian interests with the poet. He was left a small bequest in AP's **will**.

country house poem. A genre developed by poets such as **Ben Jonson** and Thomas Carew, which left its mark on much poetry in the seventeenth and eighteenth centuries and later even on the novel. Generally the writer celebrates beneficent landowners in contrast to those who oppress their tenants, allow their houses to fall down, and generally renege on their inheritance as custodians of the public weal.

See the pioneering essay by G.R. Hibberd, "The Country House Poem of the Seventeenth Century," *Journal of the Warburg and Courtauld Institutes*, 19 (1956), 156–74, reprinted in *EA* 401–37. For later developments, see V.C. Kenny, *The Country-House Ethos in English Literature, 1688–1750: Themes of Personal Retreat and National Expansion* (Brighton: Harvester, 1984); and M. Kelsall, *The Great Good Place: The Country House and English Literature* (New York: Columbia University Press, 1993).

Court Ballad, The. A satiric poem of eight six-line stanzas with a refrain, written to a well-known tune identified with the song "To All You Ladies Now at Land." It was issued as the work of AP on 31 January 1717, with Rebecca Burleigh named as publisher (Griffith 67; Foxon P762), price twopence. An almost identical version appeared under the imprint of "A. Smith" shortly afterward. Yet another came out in a small miscellany put out by **Edmund Curll** on 21 February. There were further printings (several in Curll's productions) during AP's lifetime, though he never openly acknowledged the item. A version appearing in 1735, this time with the authority of AP, was mysteriously entitled "The Challenge." It was first included in an edition of his works in 1757.

An autograph draft survives in the British Library. The poem is intensely topical and must have been composed only days prior to publication: it could hardly have been written before the death (16 January) and sumptuous funeral (19 January) of the Duchess of Argyll. Much of the poem hovers around the fortunes of her estranged husband, the **Duke of Argyll**, and his mistress Jane Warburton, a **maid of honor** to **Caroline**, Princess of Wales. AP was well acquainted with the maids of honor and refers in the poem to the doings of most of them. His particular favorites **Mary Bellenden** and Mary Lepell are among these. Some of the allusions

are obscure, but it is clear that the poem is making fun of the growing split at court between King **George I** and his son, the Prince of Wales (later **George II**), which also involved a power struggle between the Whig leaders. (**Walpole** and Lord Townshend were pitted against Sunderland and Stanhope.) During the course of this struggle, Argyll had been forced by the King from his position in the Prince's retinue. AP wittily and licentiously exploits the embarrassments, personal and political, that this situation prompted.

See *TE* 6: 180–84, as well as Ault 176–80. The fullest interpretation is that of P. Rogers, "Wit, Love, and Sin: Pope's *Court Ballad* Reconsidered," in *Eighteenth-Century Encounters* (Brighton: Harvester, 1985), pp. 56–74.

Court Eclogues. Six poems in the newly fashionable mode of "urban pastoral," pioneered by **Swift** and **Gay**. They were devoted to the days of the week from Monday to Saturday and satirize contemporary London high life. All are the work of **Lady Mary Wortley Montagu**, except "Friday," which is by Gay. Three of these poems, including the one by Gay, were published as *Court Poems* in March 1716 by **Edmund Curll**. The editor, later identified as **John Oldmixon**, suggested that they might be the work of "a lady of quality," or "Mr. Gay," or most likely "the judicious translator of **Homer**." Most people seemed to assume that AP was the guilty party, and the episode was one of the key events in the burgeoning quarrel between AP and Curll. The bookseller was still issuing *Court Poems* in 1726, garnished with various extraneous items.

Lady Mary made her own fair copy of the poems, but in addition AP transcribed them in 1717, "enclosed in a monument of red Turkey [leather], written in my fairest hand" (*Corr* 1: 441). The manuscript has been edited by R. Halsband (New York Public Library, 1977). The order of the poems as copied by AP is Monday, Tuesday, Thursday, Wednesday, Saturday. For the text based on Lady Mary's own copy, see her *Essays and Poems*, ed. R. Halsband and I. Grundy (Oxford: Oxford University Press, 1977), 182–204.

Courthope, William John (1842–1917). Poet and critic who served as a civil service commissioner. Wrote a history of English poetry in 6 vols. (1895–1910) as well as a life of **Addison** (1884). Professor of Poetry at Oxford, 1895–1900. Collaborated with **Whitwell Elwin** on the long standard **Elwin and Courthope edition** of AP.

Covent Garden Theatre. London playhouse built in 1732 by **John Rich** from the huge profits he had made on *The Beggar's Opera*. It stood between Covent Garden and Bow Street. Here a number of plays written by members of the **opposition to Walpole** were staged. A fire destroyed the original building in 1808. It has been the site of the Royal Opera House since 1858.

Cowley, Abraham (1618–67). Poet. One of the most influential writers in English in the century following his death. He was especially renowned for his lyric poems, but his epic works and prose essays also commanded great respect. AP may have been attracted to him partly because Cowley too was the son of a citizen of London and because of his Thames-side connections, especially his final home at Chertsey, not very far from **Windsor Forest**.

AP began to imitate Cowley at an early age (*Anecdotes* 1: 18). His early *Ode on Solitude* is modeled partly on the older poet's work; and other imitations survive in the shape of "Verses in Imitation of Cowley. By a Youth of Thirteen" (*TE* 6: 13–15) and "The Garden" (*TE* 6: 47–48). There are further echoes in AP's contributions to *The Spectator*. Reminiscences of the epic poems *The Civil War* (1679) and *Davideis* (1656) turn up in other poems, notably *The Rape of the Lock* and *The Temple of Fame*. However, AP's most sustained and heartfelt tribute to his predecessor comes in *Windsor-Forest*, where the poet invokes "the Shades where *Cowley* strung/ His living Harp" (ll. 279–80). He also recalls Cowley's early death and "the sad Pomp" of the ceremony by which his remains were floated down the river from Chertsey to London (ll. 272–76). The reference is apt for a number of reasons. Cowley

was a major figure in recent poetic history; he was an ardent Royalist; and he had spent his last years in close proximity to the court, the forest, and the river AP is celebrating. He was also the literary model for **George Granville**, whom AP is complimenting at this juncture.

A.H. Nethercot, *Abraham Cowley, The Muse's Hannibal* (London: Oxford University Press, 1931; reprint, New York: Russell & Russell, 1967), remains the most complete biography.

Cowper, Judith (later Madan) (1702–81). She was the daughter of Spencer Cowper (1669–1728), an MP and later Justice of the Common Pleas. Her uncle was the first Earl Cowper (1665–1723), Lord Chancellor and a major political figure in the early eighteenth century. She married Colonel Martin Madan (1700–56) in 1723; among her two daughters and seven sons were the controversialist Martin Madan and a bishop, Spencer Madan. Her brother, Rev. John Cowper, was the father of the poet William Cowper. Late in life she became a fervent Methodist.

AP may have met Judith Cowper when she sat for her portrait to **Charles Jervas**. However, the Cowpers were closely allied to another Hertfordshire family well known to AP, that of **Mary Caesar** and her husband Charles. Judith knew members of the retinue of the Princess of Wales (later **Queen Caroline**) with whom AP was in close touch. For a brief period in 1722–23 Judith and AP conducted a correspondence of chaste affection. He encouraged her to write poetry (aware, no doubt, that she was prone to bestow fulsome praise on him in her verse). He also used her as a counterpart to **Lady Mary Wortley Montagu** (who was falling from his favor), and he addressed her in lines that contrast the volatile Lady Mary with the milder Judith—later these lines were redirected to **Martha Blount**. She had already written a set of verses in imitation of *Eloisa to Abelard*, titled "Abelard to Eloisa," composed in 1720 and published in 1728. (Perhaps in response, Lady Mary wrote in Judith's voice an Ovidian complaint regarding her suitor, "Miss Cooper to ———," c. 1723). Another long poem by Cowper was "The Progress of Poetry" (c. 1721), published in 1731. Many other poems remain in manuscript.

The friendship with AP faded after Judith's marriage in December 1723, although she and her husband subscribed to the *Odyssey*. A drawing of Mrs. Madan was kept at the poet's house (*Garden and City* 254). Twelve letters to her from AP survive, first published as *Letters to a Lady* in 1769. There is no full biography. For her relations with AP, see *Women's Place* 145–50.

Cowper, Lady Sarah (c. 1708–58). Daughter of the first Earl Cowper (1665–1723). Along with her mother Mary (1685–1724) and her brother William (1709–64), she was listed among the subscribers to the *Odyssey*. So were her uncle Spencer and her cousin **Judith Cowper**. The explanation is that the family were close friends of **Mary Caesar**, who was organizing AP's subscription campaign and apparently trying to win the Earl over to the Jacobite cause. Lady Sarah called on AP at **Twickenham** in 1728 but found him away from home. AP wrote to her a kindly letter of excuse (*Corr* 2: 496–97).

Craftsman, The. A weekly journal that began on 5 December 1727 and continued in one form or another until the 1750s, running to over 1,000 issues. Also known as *The Country Journal, or the Craftsman*. Its original editor was Nicholas Amhurst (1697–1742), under the pseudonym of "Caleb D'Anvers," and its effectiveness, already reduced by 1737, diminished after his death. The paper was set up as an organ for the views of **Viscount Bolingbroke, William Pulteney**, and other members of the **opposition to Walpole**. It set out some of the broad themes of the opposition, such as resistance to the "corruption" of Walpole's ministry, and it mounted campaigns on topical issues, such as the Excise scheme of 1733. At this time its circulation has been estimated as 10,000 weekly, but this is probably too high. The printer was Richard Francklin, who was tried for seditious material in 1729 and 1731 (when he was imprisoned for a year). Many of

the items included were later reprinted in volume form. Contributors are believed to have included **Eustace Budgell** and **George Lyttelton**, as well as possibly **Henry Fielding**. Some of AP's work found its way into the pages of the journal, but it has never been satisfactorily shown that he wrote any original material for *The Craftsman*.

See *Lord Bolingbroke: Contributions to* The Craftsman, ed. S. Varey (Oxford: Clarendon, 1982); for a lively, if contentious, view of the background, see I. Kramnick, *Bolingbroke and His Circle: The Politics of Nostalgia in the Age of Walpole* (Cambridge, MA: Harvard University Press, 1968; reprint, Ithaca: Cornell University Press, 1992).

Craggs, Ann (c. 1697–1756). Friend of AP. She was a sister, and heiress, of **James Craggs junior**. Twice widowed and three times married, her husbands were John Newsham MP (1693–1724), **John Knight** MP (1686–1733), and **Robert Nugent** MP (1709–88). Mrs. Newsham, as she then was, spent a day at **Twickenham** with AP in 1724; the poet had befriended her young son James and recommended **David Mallet** to be his tutor. Ann and AP corresponded over a memorial to be set up in Westminster Abbey to her brother; it was finally erected in 1727, with an inscription by AP. She also commissioned a tomb jointly for her second husband and herself at **Gosfield**, and again AP supplied the inscription. According to a contemporary account, after Ann married for the third time in 1737 she ordered a screen to be placed over this monument when she attended the church. It is possible that AP refers obliquely to the third marriage in *The First Epistle of the First Book of Horace Imitated*, but both of the Nugents remained on good terms with the poet. She subscribed to the *Odyssey*.

Craggs, James junior (1686–1721). Politician, a Whig MP who served as Secretary of State from March 1718 until his sudden death from smallpox in February 1721. He was the son of James Craggs senior (1657–1721), Postmaster General, 1715–20, who died probably by suicide a month after his son. Both men had been heavily involved in the **South Sea Bubble**, and the younger Craggs had encouraged AP to invest in the company. The close relations enjoyed by politician and poet can be explained to some degree by the fact that they were neighbors in both **Chiswick** and **Twickenham**, where Craggs rented a house called the Grove. There were also visits to Craggs's home at Battersea. In 1720 AP arranged for **Elijah Fenton** to serve as Craggs's tutor, but this was forestalled by the politician's death. As early as 1715 AP wrote to Craggs of "that esteem and affection I have long born you" (*Corr* 1: 306). AP also knew James's sister **Ann Craggs**.

AP was deeply fond of Craggs, to whom he paid several tributes in verse. Among these is a short "Epistle to James Craggs, Esq; Secretary of State," written c. 1718, first published in 1735 (*TE* 6: 209–10). Six lines in praise of the statesman were included at the end of AP's epistle *To Mr. Addison* (1720); and slightly adapted, these verses appeared in an inscription that was placed on Craggs's tomb in Westminster Abbey, sculpted by Giovanni Battista Guelfi (*TE* 6: 204, 281–82). AP thought that the statue on the tomb "would make the finest figure" in the abbey (*Corr* 2: 457). As late as 1738, AP wrote in his *Epilogue to the Satires* that when visiting a country house belonging to the politician Henry Pelham, "I sit and dream I see my CRAGS anew!" (*TE* 6: 316). One of his warmest commendations comes in a letter to **John Caryll senior** soon after the death of his friend: "There never lived a more worthy nature, a more disinterested mind, a more open and friendly temper than Mr Craggs. A little time I doubt not will clear up a character which the world will learn to value and admire, when it has none such remaining in it" (*Corr* 2: 73). AP kept a portrait of Craggs in his house at Twickenham. Both father and son subscribed to the *Iliad*, but it is probably the son who appears as "bold, gen'rous *Craggs*" in *Mr. Pope's Welcome from Greece* (1720), since Craggs junior entered his name for ten copies of **Gay**'s *Poems* in that year. In his **Memorial List** of family and friends, AP recorded, "James Craggs, Secretary of State to the King of Great Britain, a man of liberal and upright character, a resolute friend, of fondest memory" (*EC* 1: ix).

Critical Specimen, The. A prose pamphlet of sixteen pages in octavo, stated simply to have been "Printed in the Year, 1711." No further details of publication have been discovered, and only a handful of copies are known to survive.

The work is an early blow in the battle between AP and **John Dennis**. Although AP never acknowledged the work, it is almost certain to be his composition. *An Essay on Criticism*, published on 15 May 1711, had contained a gleeful reference to Dennis as "Appius." On 29 June Dennis had replied with *Reflections Critical and Satyrical, upon a late Rhapsody, Call'd, An Essay upon Criticism*. This was one of the most virulent and unashamedly personal of all the **pamphlet attacks** on AP, accusing the poet of self-contradiction, plagiarism, and conceit as a critic; it also suggests that he is a Jacobite, and draws attention to his "squab, short" body (see Guerinot 1–11). AP changed some lines in the *Essay* as a result of the *Reflections*. A more direct response is found in the prose work, which sets out a specimen of a proposed work by "the Renown'd Rinaldo Furioso, Critick of the Woful Countenance." There follows a detailed list of the contents of each chapter in this work, to be entitled *The Mirror of Criticism*. The satire points unmistakably at an earlier production of Dennis, that is, *The Grounds of Criticism in Poetry* (1704). Like the *Grounds*, the *Specimen* announces a large critical work to be published by subscription; and like its model, the new pamphlet constitutes a proposal and outline of the longer work in progress. AP makes a number of ad hominem thrusts at Dennis, directed especially toward items such as his poem on the battle of Ramillies, along with incidental allusions to **Richard Bentley**, **Thomas Durfey**, **Colley Cibber**, **Robert Wilks**, **Barton Booth**, and the theatrical manager Christopher Rich (father of **John Rich**), among others. The penultimate chapter contains a reference to the quarrel of which this pamphlet forms part: "A Contention in Civility and good Breeding between the Critick and a little Gentleman of W[indso]r F[ores]t, in which the little Gentleman had some Advantage" (*Prose* 1: 16–17).

For text and background, see *Prose* 1: xi–xviii, 1–18. The work has never been fully annotated.

Croker, John Wilson (1780–1857). Irish-born politician, administrator and writer. Famous for a scathing review of John Keats, he often clashed with Thomas Babington Macaulay on historical issues. Edited James Boswell's *Life of Johnson*, as well as the correspondence of **Henrietta Howard** (1824), the letters of **Mary Hervey** (1821), and the *Memoirs* of her husband, **John, Baron Hervey** (1848). In 1831 he began the collection of materials for a new edition of the works of AP. This eventually formed the basis of the **Elwin and Courthope edition**.

Cromwell, Henry (1659–1728). Friend of AP. An elderly rake by the time that AP encountered him, probably through **William Wycherley** at **Will's** coffeehouse. He was a bachelor, a critic, a poetaster, and a man about town. Said to have been a first cousin once removed of Oliver Cromwell, with an estate in Lincolnshire. He and AP became friendly by 1708, but their intimacy lasted only until about 1712. He is still mentioned as "honest, hatless *Cromwell* with red breeches" among those to greet AP in **John Gay**'s poem *Mr. Pope's Welcome from Greece* (1720). However, Cromwell's good relations with **John Dennis** may have served to estrange him from AP. In addition, AP probably outgrew the boyish pose adopted by Cromwell, who was a dandy and an unthreatening flirt, given to frequenting fashionable resorts such as Epsom. Over forty letters surviving between the two men illustrate AP's early attitudes on literature and life. Cromwell later gave some of AP's letters to his mistress **Elizabeth Thomas**, who sold them to **Edmund Curll**.

Crook, Japhet (1662–1734). Also known as Sir Peter Stranger. A confidence man who became famous in his own days as the "hero" of a picaresque rogue's tale, titled *The Unparallel'd Impostor*, involving bigamy, bankruptcy, frauds, disguise, alleged complicity in the 1715 rising, and much else. In 1731, following earlier conviction for forgery in the Court of the King's Bench, he was sentenced to stand in the pillory at Charing Cross. He also was condemned to have his nose slit and his ears cut off. AP refers to the punishment in the *Epistle to Bathurst*, 1. 86, and takes the opportunity to supply a full run-down of Crook's crimes in his note (*TE* 3.ii: 95–96). He kept up the attack in the *Epilogue to the Satires*, linking this case to that of another forger, **John Ward**.

It should be noted that the modern use of "crook" for a swindler had not yet evolved, although the adjective "crooked" had long meant "deceitful." See P. Baines, *The House of Forgery in Eighteenth-Century Britain* (Aldershot: Ashgate, 1999), 65–80.

Crousaz, Jean-Pierre de (1663–1750). Swiss philosopher and miscellaneous writer. Taught at Lausanne and Gröningen. As a Calvinist he opposed the incipient liberalizing ideas of the Enlightenment represented by thinkers such as Leibniz. His *Examen de l'essai de M. Pope sur l'homme* (1737) and *Commentaire sur la traduction en vers de Mr. l'abbé du Resnel, de l'Essai de M. Pope sur l'homme* (1738) took issue with AP's *Essay on Man*, imputing a lack of logic and philosophic rigor to the poem. Crousaz made several effective points, although he was handicapped by his inability to read English (he worked from early French translations). There were soon English versions of both of the books by Crousaz, one published by **Edmund Curll** and another by his coadjutrix **Anne Dodd**. A translation of the *Commentary* with notes by **Samuel Johnson** was published in 1742.

See J.E. de La Harpe, *Jean-Pierre de Crousaz et le conflit des idées au siècle des lumières* (Berkeley: University of California Press, 1955).

Crux Easton. Estate in Hampshire, south of Newbury, belonging to the Lisle family, who had been settled in this area since the thirteenth century. It passed from Sir William Lisle to Edward Lisle (c. 1666–1722) and his wife Mary

(c. 1673–1749), who are said to have had twenty children. Two epigrams on their nine daughters were attributed to AP when first published in 1750, and the ascription has generally been accepted. A tentative date of composition is 1733. One story has it that the young ladies would "amuse themselves by standing on niches in the Grotto [at Crux Easton] as the nine Muses; Pope being placed in their midst, as Apollo." Both Lisle House and the grotto have disappeared. The site is marked by Grotto Copse. "Miss Lisle," together with her sisters Frances, Harriot, Mary, and Sophia, subscribed to a volume of poetry by Mary Leapor, published in 1748. Their brother Thomas, later Rector of Burghclere, wrote back letters in verse to his sisters when he traveled to the Middle East in 1734. These were printed in **Dodsley**'s *Miscellany*. For the text of AP's verses and commentary, see *TE* 6: 353–54.

Curliad, The. A pamphlet by **Edmund Curll**, published on 30 April 1729. Subtitled "A Hypercritic upon the Dunciad Variorum. With a farther Key to the New Characters," it carries on the battle Curll had waged with the earliest version of ***The Dunciad*** when it appeared in the previous year. One of the main purposes of the work is to correct AP's misattributions in his *Dunciad* notes, by pointing out the true author of the attacks on AP that the poet had singled out for attention. Curll knew who the dunces really were, if no one else did. For a description, see Guerinot 164–66.

Curll, Edmund (c. 1683–1747). Unscrupulous but resourceful bookseller, based around **Fleet Street** and the **Strand** in London, who brought new advertising skills and modes of self-publicity to the book trade. His specialties included scandalous memoirs, instant biographies of the famous dead, unauthorized editions of major writers, and obscene or risqué items, although he did publish serious works on antiquarian and legal topics. He was arrested more than once and in 1728 sentenced to stand in the pillory at Charing Cross.

By 1714 he had already tangled with **Jonathan Swift** and **Matthew Prior**. In that year he first offended AP by reprinting an obscene item titled ***Two or Three***, which AP had tried to suppress. Further liberties were taken with AP's work shortly afterward, and in 1716 Curll squeezed more illicit items into print, including some of the so-called *Court Poems* (see ***Court Eclogues***) and ***A Roman Catholick Version of the First Psalm***. It was he who brought into print items that AP may or may not have wanted to see enter the world, as in the case of ***Moore's Worms*** (1716). Curll also published one of the first full-blown attacks on AP, ***The Catholick Poet***. AP promptly retorted with pamphlets in prose, ***A Full and True Account*** and ***A Further Account***, setting out Curll's discomfiture when the poet took his revenge by administering an emetic. Sometime afterward AP added a third pamphlet, describing Curll's conversion to the Jewish religion (see ***A Strange but True Relation***). These works are not elevated in tone, but they are replies in kind to the publisher, and they offer an extremely funny picture of the workings of **Grub Street** at its seamiest. By 1717 the bookseller had assembled the offensive items, along with other productions that could be thought to be by AP (but were not), into a book titled *Pope's Miscellany in Two Parts*, nominally put out by Rebecca Burleigh. It was provocations like this that could be used to justify AP's decision to publish his own collected *Works*.

From this time on, Curll kept up a constant battle with AP. He produced a stream of responses to ***The Dunciad***, where he was allocated a prominent role in the "heroic" games of the literary underworld, with works such as *A Compleat Key to the Dunciad* (1728) and ***The Curliad*** (1729). Later AP tricked Curll into publishing a collection of his *Letters* in 1735. He also engineered Curll's appearance at the bar of the House of Lords on a charge of having issued matter reflecting on members of the house, but the bookseller characteristically turned the affair to his own advantage and escaped without punishment. The contest went on, both within the pages of literature and in the outside world: AP eventually brought an action in Chancery against Curll, regarding copyright in personal letters, and gained a qualified victory with Lord Hardwicke's judgment in June 1741. Even after the death of AP, Curll pursued his old antagonist with unrelenting energy. A hostile biography attributed to "**William Ayre**" (1745) was probably written by Curll himself.

The encounter between poet and bookseller symbolizes major forces at work in the cultural life of the time. Curll used AP as a source of highly salable material and as a means of attracting attention; but equally AP needed him as a gadfly, satiric catalyst, and convenient enemy at the heart of Grub Street (many of the "dunces" wrote regularly for Curll).

See R. Straus, *The Unspeakable Curll* (London: Chapman and Hall, 1927; reprint, New York: A.M. Kelley, 1970).

D

Dacier, Anne (1651–1720). French scholar, née Lefèvre. She published translations of many classical authors, including Sappho, Aristophanes, Plautus, and Terence. In 1683 she married the scholar André Dacier (1651–1722). AP had used with gratitude the commentary in her edition of the *Iliad* (1711) in preparing the notes for his own version. His own copy of volume 1, presented by **Simon Harcourt**, survives with AP's annotations (*CIH* 415–18). **Bernard Lintot** produced an English version of this edition, made by **John Ozell, William Broome**, and others, in 1712. However, matters changed in 1719 when Dacier brought out the second revised and augmented edition of her *Iliad*, "Avec quelques reflexions sur la préface angloise de M. Pope." Here it is argued that AP had underrated the symmetrical perfection of **Homer**'s epic and implied that AP's overweening confidence in his critical powers might lead to an ambition to reform politics as well. Naturally AP was dismayed to read these severe comments, placed at the end of her third volume, especially as they had been based on an inaccurate translation into French of AP's preface. A translation of Dacier's *Reflections* was published by **Edmund Curll** in 1724. In this the translator underlines claims by Dacier that AP had silently borrowed ideas from her work. For AP's response to the charges, see *Corr* 2: 157. A fuller reply was made in the Postscript to the *Odyssey*, where AP defends what he wrote and sets out his intention, *pace* Dacier, of preserving "the humble character of a faithful translator, and a quiet Subject" (*Prose* 2: 66).

See H. Weinbrot, "Alexander Pope and Madame Dacier's *Homer*: Conjectures Concerning the Cardinal Dubois, Sir Luke Schaub, and Samuel Buckley," *Huntington Library Quarterly*, 62 (1999), 1–23.

Dahl, Michael (c. 1659–1743). Swedish painter who settled in London in 1689. He was patronized by the husband of **Queen Anne**, Prince George of Denmark. A friend of **George Vertue**, he was also acquainted with many of AP's friends, including **James Gibbs, Charles Bridgeman**, and **William Kent**. He made two well-known portraits of **Matthew Prior** and also painted the **Earl of Peterborough**, **Addison**, and **John Gay**. One portrait of AP from the studio of Dahl was often reproduced: there are versions in the National Portrait Gallery and elsewhere. See **portraits** and *Portraits* 10. AP sent a version to **Jacob Tonson senior** in 1732 (*Corr* 3: 291). Dahl subscribed to the *Odyssey*.

Dancastle, John. Lord of the manor of **Binfield**, AP's home during his youth. The Dancastles (sometimes spelled Doncastle) were a Catholic family originally settled at Hampstead Norreys, on the Berkshire Downs. The manor of Binfield had been bought by an earlier John Dancastle about a century before AP lived there. In the seventeenth century the Dancastles intermarried with the **Englefield family**. Together with his younger brother Thomas (d. 1728), John was one of AP's most loyal friends, and the young man probably spent many hours at their residence, Binfield Manor, where a resident priest was installed. Thomas made a fair copy of the manuscript of the *Iliad* for the poet. (John subscribed for this work, his unique known book subscription.) The "two *Doncastles* in Berkshire known" figure in the party of AP's friends in *Mr. Pope's Welcome* *from Greece*. Only about a dozen letters survive between AP and the Dancastles, most likely because the brothers were always in close range when AP was in Binfield. He stayed at the manor house on a return visit in 1717 and possibly on other occasions. Subsequently the family sold the manor, and William Pitt the elder built a new mansion on the site c. 1754.

Dartiquenave, Charles (1664–1737). Man about town. Surveyor of the King's Gardens, and Paymaster of the Board of Works. He came from a Huguenot family. Member of the **Kit-Cat Club**, who contributed a small amount of material to *The Tatler*. The bookseller **Robert Dodsley** served as Dartiquenave's footman at the start of his career. Well known to **Jonathan Swift**, who mentions him as a friend on numerous occasions in the *Journal to Stella*: "Do not you know Darteneuf? That's the man that knows everything, and that everybody knows; and that knows where a knot of rabble are going on a holiday, and when they were there last" (*JTS* 1: 221). Swift emphasizes Dartiquenave's punning wit as well as his relish for eating. AP certainly knew him but probably less well. He mentions the fondness "Darty" had for his ham-pie in *The First Satire of the Second Book of Horace Imitated*, l. 46, and also alludes to "Dartineuf" as a gourmet in *The Second Epistle of the Second Book of Horace*, l. 87.

Davis, Herbert (John) (1893–1967). Scholar who was Reader in Bibliography at the University of Oxford. Fellow of the British Academy from 1954. He is best known as one of the leading scholars in the twentieth century on **Jonathan Swift**, whose *Prose Works* he edited in 14 volumes (1939–74), and as author of bibliographical studies on figures such as **William Bowyer**. He also produced a one-volume edition of AP's *Poetical Works* (1966; reprint 1978), which contains all the fully authenticated works apart from the **Homer** translations.

Dawley. Estate near Uxbridge in Middlesex, some fifteen miles from the center of London. It lay on the road from Hillingdon Heath to Harlington (now Dawley Road, A437), within seven miles of AP's home at **Twickenham**. His friend **Viscount Bolingbroke** bought the house in 1724, taking up residence by the summer of 1725. Known as Dawley Manor, it had been built by the first Baron Ossulton in the late seventeenth century and expanded by his son the second Baron (later Earl of Tankerville). When Bolingbroke acquired the property for about £22,000, it contained 400 acres of park as well as 20 acres of gardens around the house. He soon began to improve what he called "Dawley Farm," getting rid of some of the formal gardens and with the help of **Charles Bridgeman** creating a fashionable *ferme ornée* in most of the remaining park. The house was remodeled by **James Gibbs** (1725–28).

From the time that Bolingbroke acquired Dawley, AP often spent time there and addressed letters from this place. He regularly makes gentle fun of Bolingbroke's "agrarian" pursuits, especially when writing to **Swift**, who had visited Dawley in 1726 (see, for example, *Corr* 2: 525). When Bolingbroke returned to France in 1735, he decided to sell Dawley, but no buyer emerged, and he came to live with AP to arrange a sale. Soon he was reduced to offering it **Dr. Richard Mead** for a bargain-basement price of £6,000. AP tried to find another buyer after Mead dropped out and suggested to the **Earl of Orrery** that he should purchase the house at a similarly low price (*Corr* 4: 136). Finally in 1739 Bolingbroke managed to unload the property for £26,000, but even this sum would not have paid him back for all he had spent on Dawley. The house was all gone by 1800, and today the site is occupied by a factory.

A poem titled "Dawley Farm" (1731), praising Bolingbroke's works on the estate, was attributed to AP by **Norman Ault**, on the basis of internal evidence and external corroboration, for example, its appearance in a volume of AP's works published by **Curll**. However, the poem was not accepted into the canon by Ault's colleague **John Butt**: see *TE* 6: 452–55. It has also been suggested that Swift had a hand in the item.

See *Gardening World* 119–44.

Deane, Thomas (1651–1735). Schoolmaster. A former Fellow of University College, **Oxford**, who had converted to Catholicism in 1685 and served prison terms on account of "the Notion of his being in Popish Orders." He was also sentenced to the pillory. He had opened a private school at Marylebone, but it was scarcely thriving, and in 1696 it was broken up by the local magistrates. Later it moved to an open space near Hyde Park Corner, on the north side of Piccadilly. AP seems to have attended the school in both locations. He did not think he had learned much there (*Anecdotes* 1: 8–9). However, Deane fell on hard times in 1727, when he was again imprisoned for seditious writings; and AP agreed with some friends (possibly old schoolfellows), along with **John Caryll senior**, to come to his relief with a pension (*Corr* 2: 428). Most of what little is known of Deane is collected in *Life* 49–50, 829–30.

death. AP died quietly on the night of 30 May 1744, little more than a week after his fifty-sixth birthday. The event took place at home, and AP was buried at **Twickenham parish church** on 5 June (see **burial**).

The poet's last days were chronicled in detail by some of his friends, notably **Joseph Spence**. His **health** had gradually weakened over the previous year: it is likely that the condition of kyphoscoliosis, which caused his deformity, had come, as often, to affect the working of his heart and lungs. What his doctors termed "asthma" was the result of a shrinkage of the lung cavity. By 20 February 1744 he felt that together with his friend **Hugh Bethel** he was going "down the Hill." His medical attendants included the surgeon **William Cheselden** together with the physicians **Richard Mead** and **Simon Burton**. In the final weeks they were joined by an alternative practitioner, **Thomas Thompson**, whose diagnosis pointed to dropsy as the root of AP's asthma (probably wrongly). He recommended a more severe regimen, including regular doses of mineral waters. This proved to be too much for AP's weakened constitution, although it is likely that by the time Thompson started to treat him AP was beyond medical help.

Spence records a number of episodes in the final weeks of AP's life. He mentions visits by friends such as **George Lyttelton, Nathaniel Hooke, Anne Arbuthnot** (daughter of the doctor), **Viscount Bolingbroke**, and **Martha Blount**. AP gives out wise and pious statements, regulates his literary affairs (mainly in connection with the planned **deathbed edition**), and discusses his symptoms. His last consultation with Cheselden took place at **Chelsea College** on 7 May. We learn from Spence that about three weeks before his death AP complained of seeing everything in the room "as through a curtain." On 14 May he said that he could see "false colours on objects." The next day he was given cheering counsel by Thompson, and when Lyttelton came in, he remarked, "Here am I, dying of a hundred good symptoms." A visit by Martha Blount raised his spirits, and he continued to rise from his bed to take his dinner. Even up to the end he would not meekly lie down: according to Spence, AP "sat out with me in the garden for three hours in his sedan but two days before he died. He took an airing in Bushy Park the very day before he died." This refers to a royal park between Twickenham and **Hampton Court**, about a mile and a half south of AP's home. On the same day, at the prompting of Hooke, he was given the last sacraments by Edward Pigott, a Benedictine monk, who was the son of the lawyer **Nathaniel Pigott**. One version of this story, said to derive from Cheselden, has it that "such was the fervor of his devotion, that . . . he exerted all his strength to throw himself out of his bed, that he might receive the last sacraments kneeling on the floor." Another detailed account was sent by **David Mallet** to the **Earl of Orrery**.

The main facts about AP's last days, quoted here, can be found in *Corr* 4: 488–526; and *Anecdotes* 1: 258–70. The fullest medical analysis will be found in *This Long Disease* 73–81. See also *Life* 802–12.

deathbed edition. Late in life AP planned a definitive edition of all his works, but only the four *Moral Essays*, the *Essay on Man*, and the *Essay on Criticism* had been prepared at the time of his death. He had completed work on a revised version of the *Essays*, accompanied by a commentary from the hand of his literary executor **William Warburton**. The materials were printed by **William Bowyer junior** around March 1744; by early May AP had the first copies and was able to begin reading the proofs. An edition of 1,000 copies in quarto was intended. AP was observed by **Joseph Spence** assembling volumes to present to his friends. "Here am I, like Socrates," he told Spence, "distributing my morality among my friends, just as I am dying" (*Anecdotes* 1: 261). When AP died on 30 May, the survivors grew anxious about some of the contents of the poems, notably the scathing portrait of a great lady disguised as **Atossa**, which alarmed **Bolingbroke** in particular. The volume, which bore a title not previously used, *Epistles to Several Persons*, was ultimately suppressed. However, some copies must have escaped destruction and formed the basis of a work titled *Four Ethic Epistles* published by **John** and **Paul Knapton** in 1748. Characteristically, Warburton did not follow this source in his major edition of 1751 and instead supplied his own idiosyncratic text. The 1744 version was not properly reinstated until its use in the **Twickenham edition**. See *TE* 3.ii: ix–xvi. This "deathbed" volume is also notable for a long advertisement by AP and/or Warburton, in which the scheme of the *opus magnum* is set forth.

For the later history of the project in Warburton's hands, see *Book Trade* 144–52.

Defoe, Daniel (1660–1731). Author. To a modern eye Defoe is the most surprising inclusion among AP's gallery of dunces. It should be noted first that Defoe made his entry into *The Art of Sinking* on the basis of his work as a poet, which is one of the ways he would have been most familiar to contemporaries. "Who sees not," asks the writer of the satire, "that De Foe was the poetical son of Withers [George Wither]?" The use of the past tense is another deliberate slur. In chapter 6, "D.F." is placed among the group of "Ostriches," characterized

by their heaviness and inability to get off the ground (*Prose* 2: 197, 203). Second, it is apparent that Defoe earned a position in **The Dunciad** by reason of his troubled career as a writer. In particular, his doings in **Grub Street** had created a resemblance to the Puritan William Prynne, who had been pilloried and had his ears cut off for political writing: Queen Dulness sees "old Pryn in restless Daniel shine" (1: 101). The same logic applies to a reference in Book 2: "Earless on high, stood unabash'd Defoe" (2: 139). In reality, Defoe had been sentenced to the pillory in 1703 for having written *The Shortest Way with the Dissenters*, but his ears were left uncropped.

Today Defoe is best known as a novelist, even though he wrote hundreds of books in other genres, many of which were equally well known as his fiction in his own time. AP's comments to **Joseph Spence** were generous and perceptive in their time: "The first part of *Robinson Crusoe* [i.e., *The Life and Strange Surprizing Adventures*, the installment read today], good. DeFoe wrote a vast many things, and none bad, though none excellent. There's something good in all he has writ" (*Anecdotes* 1: 213). Many others would have expected Defoe to sink into oblivion as mutely as minnows such as Welsted, Gildon, or Roome.

Daniel's son Benjamin Norton Defoe did not escape the fate of obliteration by posterity. A struggling journalist and hack author, he figures briefly in Book 2 of *The Dunciad* as "Norton, from Daniel and Ostroea sprung" (2: 383), a reference to an unsubstantiated rumor that Norton was the outcome of an illicit relationship between Daniel and an oyster-woman. Norton is thought to have written a life of Alderman **John Barber** in 1741. Hardly anything is known about his career.

The fullest modern lives are P. Backscheider, *Daniel Defoe: His Life* (Baltimore: Johns Hopkins University Press, 1989); and M. Novak, *Daniel Defoe, Master of Fictions: His Life and Ideas* (New York: Oxford University Press, 2001). A handbook to secondary literature is S. Peterson, *Daniel Defoe: A Reference Guide, 1731–1924* (Boston: G.K. Hall, 1987).

Deloraine, Mary Howard, Countess of (1700–1744). In 1726 she married a courtier, Henry Scott, first Earl of Deloraine (1676–1730), a son of the Duke of Monmouth (illegitimate son of King Charles II). One of the **maids of honor** to the Princess of Wales, later **Queen Caroline**, 1721–26. Mistress of **George II** but not, as sometimes implausibly asserted, his wife. She was accused of attempting to poison another maid of honor, Mary Mackenzie: AP refers to the story in *The First Satire of the Second Book of Horace Imitated* (l. 81) and in the *Epilogue to the Satires* (2: 22).

Denham, Sir John (1615–69). Poet, born in Ireland of English stock. After **Oxford** he trained as a lawyer, then supported the Royalist cause in the Civil War, later escaping to Holland. Surveyor-General of the Works, 1660, with **Sir Christopher Wren** as his deputy; knighted, 1661. His later fame rests almost entirely on a single item among his many poetic works, *Cooper's Hill* (1642; substantially revised 1655, 1668). "Sir John Denham's Poems are very Unequal, extremely Good, and very Indifferent, so that his Detractors said, he was not the real Author of Coopers-Hill" (a note by **Swift**, included in *The Battle of the Books*). Generally he was considered one of those along with **Edmund Waller** who had introduced correctness to English poetry. *Cooper's Hill* exerted particular influence in the sphere of topographical poetry, where it inaugurated a native form of "loco-descriptive" verse. Cooper's Hill, a small eminence above the riverside meadows of Runnymede, stands close to the poet's family home in Egham, Surrey, known as Denham Place (demolished in the nineteenth century).

AP regarded Denham as one of the most "judicious" of poets in his kind, and bestowed some famous praise in *An Essay on Criticism*: "Where *Denham*'s Strength, and *Waller*'s Sweetness join" (l. 361). He possessed a copy of the 1709 edition of Denham's poems, and carried out a detailed analysis of changes in the text of *Cooper's Hill* between the first edition and this 1709 version (see *Anecdotes* 1: 194–

5). In many ways AP's *Windsor-Forest* was a deliberate replay of Denham's work, turning the earlier poem's concerns to new purposes without departing very widely from its ideology (Royalist), its manner (moral and political), its method (descriptive-cum-georgic), or even its locale (the Thames in the neighborhood of Windsor and London). AP pays tribute to his master, along with **Cowley**, in the most lyrical passage of the poem (ll. 259–76). See also AP's comment on the reflective quality of Denham's verse in a note to Book 12 of the *Iliad* (*TE* 8: 96). A famous quatrain from *Cooper's Hill* described the river in the words "Tho' deep, yet clear; tho' gentle, yet not dull." This was very often parodied, as it was by AP in *The Dunciad* (3: 163–66), at the expense of **Leonard Welsted**.

See *Expans'd Hieroglyphicks: A Critical Edition of Sir John Denham's* Cooper's Hill, ed. B. O Hehir (Berkeley: University of California Press, 1969); as well as B. O Hehir, *Harmony from Discords: A Life of Sir John Denham* (Berkeley: University of California Press, 1968). For the relation with AP, see E.R. Wasserman, *The Subtler Language* (Baltimore: John Hopkins University Press, 1959).

Dennis, John (1657–1734). Dramatist, poet, but especially critic. Sometimes regarded as the first "professional" literary critic in the English language. At the start of his career he was on good terms with figures such as **Dryden** and **Wycherley**. Three works published in 1704 illustrate his rising fortunes. His poem *Britannia Triumphans*, celebrating the battle of Blenheim and dedicated to **Queen Anne**, gained him the patronage of the **Duke of Marlborough**, while his patriotic tragedy *Liberty Asserted* caught the Francophobe mood of the day. His first major critical work, *The Grounds of Criticism of Poetry*, showed his powers and his ambition in this field. Unfortunately, he was already exhibiting a quarrelsome streak and a proclivity for the abuse of his opponents. In the next few years he engaged in acrimonious exchanges with **Addison**, **Steele**, and **Swift**, among others. Among other activities were his improvements on *The Merry Wives of Windsor* and *Coriolanus*, titled, respectively, *The Comical Gallant* (1702) and *The Invader of his Country* (1720).

It is his disputes with AP that have left the greatest mark. In 1707 AP was already joking at the expense of Dennis in his *Epistle to Henry Cromwell, Esq.*, although this poem was not published until many years later. Much more open was a thrust at "Appius" in the *Essay on Criticism*, ll. 585–87, a reference to the tragedy *Appius and Virginia* (1709); and Dennis replied with interest in his *Reflections Critical and Satyrical, upon a late Rhapsody* (1711). In turn, AP produced *The Critical Specimen* (1711), a merciless parody of Dennis's manner. More personal and more effective in its ridicule was *The Narrative of Dr. Robert Norris* (1713). Dennis duly came back with *A True Character of Mr. Pope, and his Writings* (1716), bringing together most of the familiar charges against AP (see Guerinot 40–45). *Remarks upon Mr. Pope's Translation of Homer* followed in 1717, also incorporating negative judgments on *Windsor-Forest* and *The Temple of Fame*. Dennis is given a role as the critic "Sir Tremendous" in the composite Scriblerian farce *Three Hours after Marriage* (1717).

Subsequently things went quiet for a number of years. However, the truce was a temporary one: There are several references to Dennis in *The Art of Sinking* (1728), including a cruel allusion to Dennis and **Charles Gildon** in 1720 as "the two greatest Critics and Reformers [of the stage] then living" (*Prose* 2: 231). This was naturally enough to provoke Dennis to issue his *Remarks on Pope's Rape of the Lock*, allegedly written many years before and held over AP's head *"in terrorem"* (as a threat). Dennis was given a comic-pathetic role in the first incarnation of *The Dunciad* (2: 271–78) later that year. After *The Dunciad Variorum* came out, Dennis responded this time with *Remarks upon Several Passages in the Preliminaries to the Dunciad* (1729). Late in life Dennis fell on hard times, and AP supported a benefit performance on his behalf at the **Haymarket Theatre** on 18 December 1733. For the occasion AP wrote a prologue in friendly if faintly amused accents (*TE* 6: 355–57: see also Ault 286–97). After the

old man's death, AP referred to him a few times, notably in the **Epistle to Arbuthnot**: "Yet then did *Dennis* rave in furious fret; / I never answer'd, I was not in debt" (ll. 153–54).

Ever since Dennis's own lifetime he has had some defenders, and his interest in the "sublime" has been seen as an important early signal that criticism was turning toward the affective aspect of literature emphasized by the Greek critic Longinus. He was also a passionate adherent of blank verse, who saw rhyme as a mere jingle. While AP may have been opposed to him on principle in such matters, the main basis of their protracted dispute was personal and opportunistic. To the Scriblerian group, Dennis seemed the living reincarnation of Zoilus, the "scourge of Homer," whose life **Thomas Parnell** had written (see *The Battle of the Frogs and Mice*). Dennis invited satire by his ludicrous assertions and naive xenophobic prejudice; as a result, AP never ceased to find amusement in his behavior. The best joke came when Dennis invented a new kind of theatrical thunder, seemingly operated by rattling a tin sheet backstage, for a scene in *Appius and Virginia*, and then found it was being used soon afterward in a performance of *Macbeth*. In all likelihood he did not actually cry out, "They have stolen my thunder," but the application was obvious, particularly as Dennis had already used thunder as an example of the truly sublime. In *The Critical Specimen*, AP writes of the critic's "Invention of a wonderful *Mustard Bowl* of a prodigious Size for the Players to make Thunder with" (*Prose* 1: 16). AP's long note to *The Dunciad* (*TE* 5: 72–75) expresses both his anger and his gratitude for the target that Dennis provided.

See *The Critical Works of John Dennis*, ed. E.N. Hooker, 2 vols. (Baltimore: Johns Hopkins University Press, 1939–43). The only full-length study is H.G. Paul, *John Dennis: His Life and Criticism* (New York: Columbia University Press, 1911; reprint, NewYork: AMS, 1966). Understandably this now seems very dated in its attitudes and partial in its approach.

De Quincey, Thomas (1785–1859). Essayist and man of letters. He professed himself a great admirer of AP and was chosen to write the entry on the poet in *Encyclopaedia Britannica*, 7th ed. (1842): See also a partly recycled version, based on **William Roscoe**'s edition, "The Works of Alexander Pope," *North British Review* (1848). He contributed three essays, "Lord Carlisle on Pope," to *Tait's Magazine* (1851). Mainly of note as providing a note of caution regarding Victorian misapprehensions of AP before such attitudes were fully in place. "It is a great calamity for an author such as Pope," De Quincey once wrote in an autobiographic piece, "that, generally speaking, it requires so much experience of life to enjoy his peculiar felicities as must argue an age likely to have impaired the general capacity for enjoyment."

Derwentwater, James Radcliffe, third Earl of (1689–1716). Member of an old Catholic family from Northumberland. His mother was a natural daughter of Charles II, and so he was a first cousin once removed of the **Pretender**, with whom he passed his boyhood at St. Germain. The Earl was beheaded on Tower Hill as one of the leaders in the **Jacobite rising**: before his trial he was given advice by the Catholic barristers **Nathaniel Pigott**, who came to be one of AP's most trusted counselors, and Henry Eyre (1676–1719), whose mother was a member of the Bedingfield family. In addition the Earl's wife, formerly Anna Maria Webb (1693–1723), was a relative of **John Caryll senior**. Her father subscribed to the *Iliad*, as did Henry Eyre. Much later AP reflected on the mutability of things when his carriage was drawn by a horse which had borne the Earl at the battle of Preston, an event that marked the end of the **Jacobites**' hopes (*Corr* 2: 513). James Radcliffe's brother Charles, who had been taken at Preston and condemned to death, managed to escape from Newgate prison to the Continent, but he was beheaded in 1746 on his return, a sign that memories were long. The Earl's son John (1713–31) died at an early age following an unsuccessful operation on a kidney stone by **William Cheselden**. Nathaniel Pigott acted as an executor of John's will. The Earl's daughter Anna Maria Barbara (1716–60) married Lord Petre, son of **Robert, seventh Baron Petre**, the original of the character of the Baron in *The Rape of the Lock*. Both of the couple were posthumous children.

Derwentwater had an affectionate relationship with **Lady Swinburne**, a family friend of AP. It is perhaps for this reason that his name was entered as a subscriber to the *Iliad*, which began to appear less than a year before he was beheaded on Tower Hill.

See R. Arnold, *Northern Lights: The Story of Lord Derwentwater* (London: Constable, 1959).

Digby, Robert (1692–1726). Friend of AP and one of his closest gardening allies. He was the son of the **fifth Baron Digby** and a first cousin of **Viscountess Scudamore**. He carried out work on the fine gardens at his family estate of **Sherborne**, which AP visited in 1724. In turn, Digby stayed with the poet at **Twickenham**. The two men had met by 1717. About twenty letters survive from their correspondence. Digby had long suffered from ill health, but his death on 21 April 1726 came as a considerable blow (*Corr* 2: 375–76). The great affection in which AP held the family is shown by the **epitaph** that AP wrote for Robert and his sister Mary, who died of smallpox in 1729, and that was placed in Sherborne Abbey by their father. These lines were first printed in 1730 (see *TE* 6: 313–16). Digby was a subscriber to the *Iliad* and *Odyssey*. In his brief obituaries, AP described Digby as "endowed with the ancient moral qualities of his father" (*EC* 1: x). There was a portrait of Digby in AP's house at Twickenham.

See *Social Milieu* 154–62.

Digby, William, fifth Baron (1662–1752). As an Irish peer he was able to serve as MP for Warwick and Deputy Lieutenant for Warwickshire (his base was in the town of Coleshill). However, his High Church principles and alliances (including friendship with Bishop Thomas Ken and the philanthropist Thomas Bray) pushed him toward the **nonjurors**, and he spent more time living a quiet country life at his seat, **Sherborne**. Two sons and a daughter died in young adulthood. One of these was **Robert Digby**, a friend of AP and pioneer in the landscape gardening movement. Lord Digby erected a monument to Robert and his sister at Sherborne, for which AP composed the memorial inscription: see AP's letter of September 1729 to Digby (*Corr* 3: 51–52). Another son, Edward (1693–1746), was known to AP and helped to distribute copies of *The Dunciad* in 1729. Like his father and brother Robert, he subscribed to the *Odyssey*. There is a warm reference to "good Digby" in the *Epilogue to the Satires* (*TE* 4: 326).

See *Social Milieu* 133–65 for a full account of Lord Digby's role in AP's life and work.

Dilke, Charles Wentworth (1789–1864). Critic. One of the most important figures historically in the study of AP's life (see **biographies of Pope**). Editor of *The Athenaeum*. Familiar with Keats, Shelley, Thomas Hood, Dickens, and other writers. His articles on AP, published between 1854 and 1860, were later brought together in his collected *Papers*. They prompted a major upheaval in Victorian attitudes toward the poet. "Dilke proved that Pope transferred letters from one correspondent to another, that he combined two or three letters into one, that he consequently misdated events intentionally or unintentionally, and that he changed the phraseology of letters when printing them" (*Early Career* 21). These revelations prompted some savage attacks on AP as duplicitous and devious and helped to condition the hostile presentation of his character in works such as the **Elwin and Courthope edition**, for which Dilke provided a large store of information. However, his own assessment of AP was more balanced. For example, he rejected ill-founded stories such as the tale that AP accepted a bribe of a thousand pounds from the **Duchess of Marlborough** to suppress his lines on **Atossa**. He had acquired the papers of the family of **John Caryll** (later bequeathed to the British Museum), and he was able to correct many pervasive errors and misunderstandings with regard to AP's life. He also made important discoveries in connection with AP's **ancestry**. Included in volume one of the *Papers*, along with the material concerning AP, are es-

says on **Swift** and **Lady Mary Wortley Montagu**.

Dilke adopts an overconfident tone at times and can be unduly combative. However, in terms of factual findings, he must be regarded as the most important student of AP's life prior to the twentieth century. See *The Papers of a Critic, Selected from the Writings of the late Charles Wentworth Dilke: with a Biographical Sketch by his Grandson, Sir Charles Wentworth Dilke*, 2 vols. (London: Murray, 1875).

Discourse on Pastoral Poetry. The name AP gave to an essay on the genre, which was set before his *Pastorals*, when they were reprinted in the *Works* (**1717**). He claimed that the original "Essay on Pastoral," like the poems themselves, were written in 1704, that is, at the age of sixteen. In the surviving manuscript the essay occupies nine pages; a further leaf is missing. The essay was revised for publication, with the addition of an introductory paragraph, but for the most part, the argument is left unaltered.

AP takes the side of René Rapin against Bernard de Fontenelle, in terms of a debate that formed a side skirmish to the battle of the **Ancients and Moderns**. The former had argued in *Dissertatio de carmine pastorali* (1659) that pastoral was a form imitative of the Golden Age, in which the poet should employ appropriately classical gestures and language. In his *Traité sur la nature de l'églogue* (1688) the latter claimed, with the backing of his English supporters **Ambrose Philips** and **Thomas Tickell**, that pastoral might copy simple "rusticity" and introduce a degree of realism. AP briefly considers the major writers in this form, that is, its founder Theocritus, **Virgil**, Torquato Tasso, and **Edmund Spenser**.

For the text, see *Prose* 1: 297–302. For the manuscript, see *L&GA* 24–32. The background is explored in J.E. Congleton, *Theories of Pastoral Poetry in England, 1684–1798* (Gainesville: University of Florida Press, 1952; reprint, New York: Haskell House, 1968).

Discovery, The. A poem in ballad stanzas, comprising eighty-eight lines. It was published on 20 December 1726 with a subtitle *The Squire*

Turn'd Ferret (Foxon P328). Later AP acknowledged the item as written by himself and **William Pulteney**; the likelihood is that AP took the leading part in its composition. The work did not appear in editions of the poet's works until recent times.

This ballad deals with the most newsworthy story of the moment, concerning the so-called rabbit woman, Mary Tofts (1703–63) of Godalming, near Guildford in Surrey. Mary had recently claimed to have delivered a succession of rabbits. For several weeks her case absorbed the British nation. Even after she confessed to the fraud on 7 December, and was sent to **Bridewell**, the episode dominated public attention. "London was inundated with diaries, public letters, depositions, factual accounts, facetious accounts that claimed to be factual, satiric poems, street ballads, mock suicide notes, false confessions, medical disquisitions, cartoons, engravings, pamphlets and squibs" (Dennis Todd). At **Drury Lane Theatre** the impresario **John Rich** put on a farcical drama on the subject. Medical opinion had been divided on the issue, and some of the physicians who had taken the side of authenticity were forced to defend their position.

The ballad may be seen as the only work of lasting literary interest to emerge from this flurry of activity. Its prime target is not Mary Tofts herself, a poor young countrywoman whose motives seem to have been simply to get money from her hoax. Instead, the poem makes fun of some of the key actors in the episode. These included the surgeon **Nathanael St. André**; **Samuel Molyneux**, astronomer and courtier; **James Douglas**, physician to **Queen Caroline**, later mentioned by AP in *The Dunciad*; and the diplomat and courtier Henry Davenant (1681–1739). Highly characteristic of AP's ballad vein is the conclusion to the poem, which disproves the proverbial line "Two heads are better than one."

For the text and annotation, see *TE* 6:259–64. For background to the Mary Tofts affair, see Dennis Todd, *Imagining Monsters: Miscreations of the Self in Eighteenth-Century England* (Chicago: University of Chicago Press, 1995).

Disney (Desaulnais), Henry (d. 1731). Generally known as "Duke" Disney. He joined the 1st Foot Guards in 1695 and became a colonel in 1710, selling his commission in 1715. He was a close friend of the members of the **Scriblerus Club**. **Swift** described him as "a fellow of abundance of humour, an old battered rake, but very honest" (*JTS* 2: 639). He figures in *Mr. Pope's Welcome from Greece* as "facetious Disney." Together with his colleague General **Henry Withers**, he is the first to greet AP in the poem. He later set up a monument to the general in Westminster Abbey, for which AP wrote memorial verses (*TE* 6: 320–21). A member of the **Brothers Club**, he subscribed to both the *Iliad* and the *Odyssey*. He died on 21 November 1731 and was buried in Westminster Abbey. On 1 December AP told Swift, "Poor Duke Disney is dead, and hath left what he had among his friends": among these legatees were **Viscount Bolingbroke** and the eldest son of **Sir William Wyndham** (*Corr* 3: 249). Not much is known about his personal life, except that he was a habitué of **Bath**. It seems probable (1) that he was of Huguenot origin, possibly with the family name of Desaulniers, and (2) that he was a bachelor.

Dobrée, Bonamy (1891–1974). Professor at the University of Leeds who wrote prolifically over a very wide range of subjects. His major works included a survey of the period 1700–1740 for the *Oxford History of English Literature* (1959), with two chapters on AP, as well as editions of **Chesterfield**, **Vanbrugh**, and many others. A collection that he edited, *From Anne to Victoria* (1937), contains a characteristic essay on AP by **W.H. Auden**. Dobrée wrote a short life of AP (1951) and edited the *Collected Poems* for the Everyman series (rev. ed., 1956). See a Festschrift, *Of Books and Humankind*, ed. J. Butt (London: Routledge, 1964), which contains material by **John Butt** on AP.

Dobson, (Henry) Austin (1840–1921). Civil servant, poet, and critic. It is a bizarre fact that Dobson never figures in bibliographies devoted to AP, since he made no *titular* contribution to the subject. Nevertheless, for the general reader at the turn of the twentieth century he was the most influential commentator on the world of AP. In fact, his extraordinarily profuse writings on the eighteenth century covered every corner of the field. He wrote lives of Frances Burney, Oliver Goldsmith, and **Henry Fielding**, as well as editing their works. Other studies were devoted to **Addison**, **Steele**, Samuel Richardson, and **Horace Walpole**. Hundreds of magazine articles were collected in a series of volumes with titles like *Eighteenth Century Vignettes*. They deal with subjects such as **John Gay**, **Matthew Prior**, the *Journal to Stella*, **Prior Park**, **Chesterfield**, **George Lyttelton**, **Aaron Hill**, and many of the authors just mentioned. He was the author of the entry for Gay in the *Dictionary of National Biography*. Naturally there are innumerable references to AP, who is usually treated with respect mingled with some condescension. Dobson also wrote "A Dialogue to the Memory of Mr Alexander Pope," reprinted in his *Collected Poems* (1897).

Dodd, Anne (c. 1685–1739). Née Barnes. Her name is sometimes spelled Dod. The widow of Nathaniel Dodd, whose business she seems to have inherited. Succeeded by her daughter, also named Anne. A "mercury" or distributor of books, pamphlets, and newspapers. She was named on the title page of several of AP's smaller works but can never have legally held copyrights. For some unexplained reason AP chose to have her name used on the title page of *The Dunciad*, a feint that cannot have deceived many. Her name also turns up in **pamphlet attacks** on AP, including some in which **Curll** may be presumed to have had a hand.

Dodington, George Bubb, first Baron Melcombe (1691–1762). Politician, patron, and minor author. A Whig MP who inherited a valuable estate in 1720 and added "Dodington" to his original name of Bubb. At first a loyal acolyte of **Robert Walpole**, he later went into opposition and served as an adviser to **Frederick, Prince of Wales**. After AP's death he held various government offices but was notorious in his day as a manager of corrupt electoral boroughs and as one willing to crawl at

any time in order to gain favor. AP portrays him in the *Epistle to Arbuthnot* as a self-satisfied patron, "full-blown *Bufo*, puff'd by ev'ry quill; / Fed with soft Dedication all day long" (*TE* 4: 112): see **Bufo**. He may also be the tasteless "Bubo" of the *Epistle to Burlington*; "Dorimant" in *A Letter to a Noble Lord*; and "sagacious *Bub*" in *One Thousand Seven Hundred and Forty*. See also a comment on Dodington's ignorance of architecture in a letter to the **Earl of Burlington** (*Corr* 3: 329). While the politician had his louche and comic sides, he gave generous support to **Thomson**, **Young**, and **Fielding**. AP seems to take undue pleasure in berating a man with some ability, for reasons that remain obscure.

See J. Carswell, *The Old Cause: Three Biographical Studies in Whiggism* (London: Cresset, 1954), 61–165.

Dodsley, Robert (1703–64). Author and bookseller. Began life as a footman to **Charles Dartiquenave**. His poem *Servitude* (1729) brought him to literary attention. *The Muse in Livery*, a collection of poems, followed in 1732. He then moved into the trade of bookselling, serving an unofficial apprenticeship with **Lawton Gilliver**. In April 1735 he set up his own shop at Tully's Head in Pall Mall, a fashionable quarter of London not well known for book trade connections. By this date he was also established as a dramatist, with a comic afterpiece called *The Toy-Shop* successfully put on by **John Rich**. This was followed by a "dramatick tale" titled *The King and Miller of Mansfield*, performed in 1737 at **Drury Lane Theatre**. When Dodsley issued **Samuel Johnson**'s *London* in 1738, he became identified with the **opposition to Walpole**, and after publishing *Manners* by Paul Whitehead in 1739, he was arrested and forced to apologize in the House of Lords.

In the next few years Dodsley embarked on several pioneering ventures that changed the face of the publishing world. He started a magazine, *The Publick Register*; founded the influential journal *The Museum*; and later set up *The Annual Register* (from 1758), in which Edmund Burke would find his first important outlet as a writer. Dodsley was the main initiator of Johnson's great *Dictionary* (1755). *The Oeconomy of Human Life* (1750) was a popular assemblage of moral maxims, often reprinted and translated. Above all, his *Select Collection of Old Plays* in 12 volumes (1744–45) greatly expanded the corpus of accessible drama, while his *Collection of Poems* in 6 volumes (1758) became the authorized standard of poetic taste for a generation to come. As a publisher Dodsley brought out other major works by Johnson, as well as books by Oliver Goldsmith, Thomas Gray, Mark Akenside, **Edward Young**, William Shenstone, and other notable authors. His own later creative work included a tragedy, *Cleone* (1758).

AP encouraged Dodsley from early on. In turn Dodsley addressed complimentary verses to the poet in *An Essay on Man* and composed works in imitation of his patron. Among works carrying Dodsley's imprint after AP split with Gilliver were some of the *Imitations of Horace, The Universal Prayer*, as well as editions of AP's *Works* and letters. In 1743 Dodsley reprinted AP's *Verses on the Grotto*, together with his own prophetic lines, "The Cave of Poetry," which set in train a process of mythologizing the poet. In his last days AP was visited by Dodsley, who reported a hallucination the dying man experienced (*Anecdotes* 1: 266).

See H.M. Solomon, *The Rise of Robert Dodsley: Creating the New Age of Print* (Carbondale: Southern Illinois University Press, 1996); and *The Correspondence of Robert Dodsley, 1733–1764*, ed. J.E. Tierney (Cambridge: Cambridge University Press, 1988).

dogs. There were dogs in the Pope household when the poet was growing up, but we do not know anything in detail about them. In an early letter to **Henry Cromwell**, AP wrote of the dog he currently owned and mentioned the fact that he remembered the "dam" of this animal, who lived to the age of twenty-two. There follows a comically learned "discourse" on dogs (*Corr* 1: 73–75). There are vague references in later letters, and throughout his life AP generally referred to dogs when pleading for a humane approach to animals.

Many of AP's dogs were named Bounce.

The first that can be identified was mentioned by **John Gay** in a letter of 1716. Around the time of *The Dunciad*, when violence threatened, AP had for his protection "a great, faithful Danish dog" (*Anecdotes* 1: 116). Another Great Dane of this name, a bitch, gave birth to puppies in 1736, and these were presented to friends including the **Earl of Strafford**, **Lord Bathurst**, the **Earl of Burlington**, and **Viscount Cobham**. These gifts are commemorated in the poem *Bounce to Fop*. Another found its way to **Frederick, Prince of Wales**, and gave rise to AP's famous *Epigram on the Collar of a Dog*. The last in the line, a male, was given to the **Earl of Orrery** and taken to **Marston** in Somerset. This Bounce was bitten by a mad dog and died in 1744, prompting AP's final poem, the *Lines on Bounce*. One of the series was depicted by **Jonathan Richardson senior** in a **portrait** of AP preserved at **Hagley**.

See Ault 337–50; and *Anecdotes* 2: 629–30.

Donne, John (1572–1631). Poet and divine. Although by no means totally forgotten, Donne was far from a fashionable poet in AP's day. The only book by the writer that is known to have been in AP's **library** was *The Pseudo-Martyr* (1610), a polemical tract. Donne does not figure in **Addison**'s versified history of English poetry, but then neither does **Shakespeare**. AP reflected some of the prejudices of the age when he wrote to **Wycherley** in 1708 that Donne "had infinitely more Wit than he wanted Versification" (*Corr* 1: 16) and when he told **Spence**, "Donne had no imagination, but as much wit I think as any writer can possibly have." Recognizing Donne's influence on the "metaphysical turn" of **Cowley**, AP commended Donne's "Progress of the Soul," epistles, and satires (*Anecdotes* 187–89).

It is indeed in the two modernized versions of Satyrs 2 and 4 that AP wrote that Donne's most direct impression is seen. Donne composed five verse satires between c. 1593 and 1597. They were not published in his lifetime but circulated widely in manuscript. They first appeared in print in 1633. AP had first attempted an imitation of the older poet around 1713, but his two published Donne poems date from 1733–35 and were later included in collected editions of the *Imitations of Horace*. See the *Fourth Satire of Dr. John Donne* and the *Second Satire of Dr. John Donne*.

For AP's general procedures in these works, see I. Jack, "Pope and the 'Weighty Bullion of Dr. Donne's Satires,'" *PMLA*, 66 (1951), 1009–22, reprinted in *EA* 420–38.

Dormer, James (1679–1741). General. Fought at Blenheim; commanded a brigade against the Jacobite forces in 1715 and was present at the battle of Preston. Colonel of the 6th Foot regiment, 1720; lieutenant-general, 1735, and colonel of the first troop of Grenadier Guards, 1737. He inherited the estate of **Rousham** in Oxfordshire from his brother Robert in 1737 and continued work on the famous garden there. Another brother was John Dormer (1679–1719), a member of the **Kit-Cat Club**. A noted book collector. He was a friend of **Viscount Cobham** and often stayed at **Stowe**, sometimes in company with AP. He and AP were good friends in the 1730s. It is possible that Dormer was the recipient of AP's *Second Epistle of the Second Book of Horace* (1737), although there are other candidates. Dormer was also on close terms with **John Gay** and acted as a pallbearer at Gay's funeral.

His elder brother, Colonel Robert Dormer (1676–1737), had come into possession of Rousham in 1719 and began the process of transforming the garden. AP visited him there at least as early as 1728, although their acquaintance began earlier. It is likely that the link was established through **Sir William Trumbull**, whose first wife was a sister of Anne Dormer, the mother of Robert and James. Both brothers, especially James, were allied to the circle of the **Earl of Burlington**.

Dorset, Charles Sackville, sixth Earl of (1643–1706). Poet in lyrical and satiric forms, as well as patron of **John Dryden** and **Matthew Prior**. "Like Dryden, Pope considered that [Dorset] was the most gifted poet among the titled wits of the Court of Charles II" (*Anecdotes* 1: 200). AP spoke highly of Dorset's abilities and communicated stories about the

Earl that had evidently been passed on to him by older friends. In his youth he also wrote some imitations of Dorset's style, published in the *Miscellanies* in 1728 (*TE* 6: 48–51). At the behest of the Earl's son, created first Duke of Dorset, AP composed an epitaph for the father around 1731. It was published in 1735 but never placed on the tomb (*TE* 6: 334–36). The Duke subscribed to the *Iliad* and the *Odyssey*.

See B. Harris, *Charles Sackville, Sixth Earl of Dorset, Patron and Poet of the Restoration* (Urbana: University of Illinois Press, 1940; reprint, New York: Lemma, 1972).

Douglas, Dr. James (1675–1742). Physician. FRS, 1706; M.D., Reims. Best known as an obstetrician. Wrote works on anatomy and contributed to books by his friend **William Cheselden**. He also gave an account of Cheselden's pioneering operation for the stone in *A History of the Lateral Operation* (1726). Physician to **Queen Caroline**. The famous surgeon William Hunter (1718–83) lived with Douglas for a time as his assistant and taught Douglas's son (also James). AP refers to the doctor in *The Dunciad* in a line of velvety implication: "And Douglas lends his soft obstetric hand" (4: 394). The note is kinder: "A Physician of great Learning and no less Taste." The catalog of Douglas's library of works by **Horace** had been published in 1739. Douglas had been involved in the exposure of the "rabbit woman," Mary Tofts (see *The Discovery*).

Down Hall. A house near Hatfield Broad Oak in Essex. It was found by **John Morley**, the land agent from nearby Halstead, for the use of **Matthew Prior** around 1719. Their first visit together to the property is described in Prior's amusing ballad "Down Hall," published in 1723. Half of the purchase price came from the success of Prior's subscription volume in 1718; the rest was supplied by his friend the **second Earl of Oxford**. An old timber and lath property, in pleasant wooded countryside, it provoked Prior to tell the Earl that he loved the place "more than Tully did his Tusculum, or Horace his Sabine Field." The house was to have been replaced by **James Gibbs** with an impressive three-storey mansion whose front contained nine bays. However, the patching up of the house proceeded slowly, and although Prior took up residence in 1721, his death in September of that year put an end to the project. The house reverted to Lord Oxford, who spent occasional vacations there.

AP spent some time there in January 1726 and shortly afterward asked leave from the Earl to use "my Garret at Downhall." He liked the house so much that he described himself as "utterly against Gibbs, & all his Adherents for Demolition" (*Corr* 1: 358, 364, 369). In the event, Oxford did not have the money to proceed with the new building, and his widow sold the property to a London merchant William Selwin in 1741. The house was rebuilt in the late eighteenth century. A large Victorian mansion was built on the estate in 1873; it is now a country house hotel of stunning dimensions. See *Earls of Creation* 197–204.

Drayton, Michael (1563–1631). English poet, noted for his sonnets, odes, and historical poems. A friend of **Ben Jonson** and, probably, **Shakespeare**. AP referred to Drayton as "a very mediocre Poet" who was "yet taken some notice of, because Selden writ a very few notes on one of his Poems" (*Corr* 4: 428); the allusion is to the commentary on *Poly Olbion* by John Selden (1584–1654), lawyer and antiquarian. However, the **mock-heroic** fairy story *Nymphidia* (1627) left traces in *The Rape of the Lock*, while *Englands Heroicall Epistles* (1597) was one of the English models for *Eloisa to Abelard*. Most obviously, *Poly Olbion* (1612–22) influenced AP in the composition of *Windsor-Forest*, Drayton's sections on the Forest of Arden in particular.

Drury Lane Theatre. The most famous of all London playhouses, it originally opened in 1663. After the building was destroyed by fire, a new theater designed by **Sir Christopher Wren** was built on the present site, off Russell Street, Covent Garden, in 1674. It stood until 1791 and saw many famous productions involving figures such as David Garrick, Richard Brinsley Sheridan, and Sarah Siddons. A fur-

ther fire took place in 1809, after which the present building was erected.

The theater enjoyed a period of great success in AP's day, under the management of **Colley Cibber**, **Barton Booth**, and **Robert Wilks**, among others. Other notable actors who worked here in this period were **Anne Oldfield** and James Quin. In 1714 **Richard Steele** was given a supervisory role as governor. Some of AP's work, including the collaborative farce *Three Hours after Marriage*, was presented at Drury Lane, but his relations with Cibber were generally bad. A strong suggestion was made in *The Dunciad* that the playhouse, under Cibber's watch, had become the home of tawdry sensationalist drama. See also the attack in the *Epistle to Augustus*, ll. 314–21, on an extravagant production at Drury Lane to mark the coronation in 1727.

See **theater**, as well as J. Loftis, *Steele at Drury Lane* (Berkeley: University of California Press, 1952).

Dryden, John (1631–1700). Poet, dramatist, and critic. AP's chief literary idol. He once caught a glimpse of his great predecessor, probably when taken to **Will's** coffeehouse at the age of about twelve—possibly younger (see *Anecdotes* 2: 611–12). Many of his earliest friends, notably **Thomas Betterton**, had been close friends of the writer. Afterward Dryden's poems "were never out of his hands," and they became his model for his own writings. "I learned versification wholly from Dryden's works," he told **Joseph Spence**, "who had improved it much beyond any of our former poets." AP particularly admired the older man's use of "proper language: lively, natural, and fitted to the subject." He respected Dryden's work as a dramatist at a time when the plays were going out of fashion (*Anecdotes* 1: 24–29). Even as a young man he kept a picture of Dryden, along with those of **Milton** and **Shakespeare**, in his room when he wrote. Later he owned a bust, and **Frederick, Prince of Wales** presented him with another bust around 1735. One or other of these (probably the latter) was in AP's **villa** at the time of his death and was bequeathed to **George Lyttelton**. A small summer house in his **garden** also contained a bust. It was AP who composed lines for Dryden's tomb in Westminster Abbey, erected by the **Duke of Buckinghamshire**; later he changed his plans and substituted a minimalist statement giving just the birth and death dates. The first name in AP's **Memorial List** of "departed relations and friends" is that of John Dryden, described as "the prince of poets, always deserving reverence" (*EC* 1: ix).

The influence of Dryden is so pervasive in AP's work that we can identify only the most obvious debts. *The Dunciad* builds directly on the earlier writer's *MacFlecknoe*. AP's imitations of **Chaucer** could not have been attempted without the example of Dryden's *Fables*; and his *Ode for Musick on St. Cecilia's Day* directly challenges the "Song for St. Cecilia's Day" his mentor had written in 1687. In addition, *Windsor-Forest* draws extensively on *Annus Mirabilis*; and his verse **epistles** bear the unmistakable stamp of Dryden's practice in this vein. Just as plainly, the values of Dryden's critical essays inform *An Essay on Criticism*, while the preface to the **Shakespeare edition** makes inconspicuous use of the same source. AP's *Epistle to Jervas* was attached to a work by the earlier master. Perhaps most important of all is the debt to the translation of **Virgil** that Dryden had undertaken at the end of his life. AP would not have embarked on his own version of **Homer**, had it not been for this powerful presence in the background; and he would never have decided to choose the vehicle of **subscription publishing** unless Dryden had given him the lead (see *Anecdotes* 1: 26–27). Dryden had himself undertaken a version of the first book of the *Iliad*.

There are scattered references to Dryden in AP's poetry, but few of them are truly revelatory. Possibly the most interesting occur in the *Epistle to Arbuthnot*, ll. 245–48, alluding to the poet's burial at the expense of the **Kit-Cat Club**; and ll. 267, describing the way in which "Dryden taught to join / The varying verse, the full resounding line, / The long majestic march, and energy divine." Books that survive from AP's **library** include copies of *Annus Mirabilis*; the *Fables*; the plays in two folio volumes,

published by **Jacob Tonson senior** in 1701; and the translation of Virgil (three volumes, 1709).

The fullest biography is J.A. Winn, *John Dryden and His World* (New Haven, CT: Yale University Press, 1987). Also useful is P. Hammond, *John Dryden: A Literary Life* (New York: St. Martin's Press, 1991). There is still no adequate account of the relations of the two greatest English poets of the Augustan era, Dryden and AP.

Duck, Stephen (1705–56). The "thresher poet." A farm laborer from Wiltshire who educated himself with the aid of a dictionary and books of verse. His poem "The Thresher's Labour" led to his being taken up by literati, including AP's friend **Joseph Spence** and the courtier-clergyman Alured Clarke, a protégé of **Queen Caroline**. His first volume, *Poems on Several Occasions* (1730), caused a stir and went through ten editions in the first year, despite its conventional modes and stiffly classical style. Spence supplied a life for later editions from 1736. However, it was the patronage of the Queen that ensured Duck's success. She gave him a pension and made him a Yeoman of the Guard in 1733, following his marriage to her housekeeper at Kew, Sarah Bigg (Duck's first wife had died in 1730). Then in 1735 she made him keeper of her remarkable contrivance, **Merlin's Cave**. After her death, Duck slipped into comparative oblivion. He later took orders, and in 1752 through the influence of Joseph Spence, he was presented to the living of Byfleet in Surrey. Four years later, he drowned himself in a fit of depression.

The Queen attempted to gain AP's support for her favored bard, which involved him in a certain amount of genteel equivocation (see *Anecdotes* 1: 215). Spence and others feared that AP would insert Duck into the gallery of dunces: the most that happened was that some glancing blows were aimed at Duck (but more at his patrons) in an appendix, "Of the Poet Laureate," added to *The Dunciad* in 1743 (*TE* 5: 413). It had been seriously suggested that Duck should become laureate, and Clarke stated that he was "a superior genius to Mr.

Pope" (see *Corr* 3: 132). AP contended himself with a wry observation to **John Gay** that people at court spoke of him "in the same breath with the Thresher" (*Corr* 3: 143). He seems to have thought Duck personally worthy but as a poet very limited. Privately he commented to Spence, "Duck no imagination, all imitation" (*Anecdotes* 1: 215).

Duck's fame rested more on his status as a natural phenomenon than on any supernal abilities as a writer. Some contemporary critics have rediscovered merit, or interest, in his works, although a more forthright riposte by Mary Collier, "The Woman's Labour: An Epistle to Stephen Duck" (1739), has attracted still greater notice. An amusing short poem by **Swift**, "On Stephen Duck, the Thresher, and Favourite Poet. A Quibbling Epigram, written in the Year, 1730," has no immediate personal feeling behind it.

The fullest account is still R.M. Davis, *Stephen Duck, the Thresher-Poet* (Orono: University of Maine Press, 1926).

Duckett, George (1684–1732). A minor politician who made his faint impress on history chiefly by attacking AP in some lighthearted squibs in collaboration with his friend **Thomas Burnet**. A Whig MP and Commissioner of Excise from 1722. Wrote first of his **pamphlet attacks** on AP, titled *Homerides*, in 1715 (Guerinot 20–24). AP thought that Duckett was involved in *Pope Alexander's Supremacy* (1729), where the frontispiece is marked, "Delin^t G.D.," but this may not be right. The pair certainly had a hostile attitude toward AP, as can be gleaned from *The Letters of Thomas Burnet to George Duckett 1712–1722*, ed. D.N. Smith (Oxford: Roxburghe Club, 1912). Duckett was a patron of a leading dunce, **John Oldmixon**. AP's revenge was to put Duckett into the group of secretive "didappers" in *The Art of Sinking*, chapter 6. A more damaging insinuation in Book 3 of *The Dunciad* was to link Duckett and Burnet not just as partners in literary crime but also as homosexual lovers (*TE* 5: 168–69). According to a later story, Duckett is said to have demanded satisfaction for the imputation; but it survived in later editions, after his death.

Duke upon Duke. Subtitled "An excellent new Ballad. To the Tune of *Chevy Chase*," this was first published anonymously in 1720. The earliest printing is perhaps an edition with music by "Mr Holdsworth," which was published by the nonexistent **A. Moore** (on this occasion "A. Moor") on 15 August of that year. See Foxon D502–7. Several other versions were issued up to 1738, and again after AP included it with several small revisions in the ***Miscellanies*** in 1742. According to **Spence**, a "good part" of the "ballad on Lechmere and Guise was written by Mr. Pope" (*Anecdotes* 1: 152). Although it was never directly attributed to AP until reprinted by **Norman Ault** in 1949, there is no doubt that it bears all the marks of his hand. Conjectural assignments that were once made to **Swift** and **Gay** have no basis of evidence to support them.

The poem consists of 148 lines in **ballad** stanza. It concerns an episode otherwise unknown to scholars, involving an aborted duel between the strident Whig lawyer and politician Nicholas Lechmere (1675–1728) and an obscure Gloucestershire knight of the shire, Sir John Guise (c. 1678–1732). He is styled a "Duke" from the title of a play by **Dryden**, *The Duke of Guise*. Lechmere had been Solicitor General and Attorney General and was still Chancellor of the Duchy of Lancaster (hence his naming in the poem as "Nic of Lancastere"). He had been one of the most ardent in bringing to book the Tories who had served in the **Harley administration**, following the change of regime in 1714. In 1721 he was rewarded with creation as Baron. The poem depicts him as passionate and capricious in his behavior, as he was known to be, and also suggests his cowardice in avoiding the duel with Guise. As for his opponent, less is known. Guise, a baronet, was an MP in the reign of **Queen Anne** and again in the 1720s. He was evidently a Tory but played no significant role in national politics. He emerges from the poem with less discredit than Lechmere but still cuts a rather foolish figure. His sister Anne was married to **Edward Blount**, a close friend of AP. The poet visited the Guises' family home at Rendcomb, north of **Cirencester**, in September 1721, and made brief reference to the quarrel when writing to Blount (*Corr* 2: 85–86). However, the allusion does nothing to clear up the mystery of what happened in real life to occasion the satiric narrative. AP takes advantage of the opportunity to utilize his familiar repertoire (in this form) of pun, proverb, and bawdy language, with witty innuendoes concerning the principals. An alternative title found in one of the early printings, "Pride will have a Fall," accurately describes the comic plot.

A. Moore also issued "An Answer" to the poem around 22 August 1720. In this AP is clearly identified as the author of the original ballad and indeed the main target of the reply. The usual charges are brought up against the poet, including his papist loyalties and his misshapen body. AP's contests with **Edmund Curll** are also mentioned. It is among the wittiest and most skillful of the **pamphlet attacks**. For a description, see Guerinot 79.

For the text and commentary, see *TE* 6: 217–24, supplementing the discussion in Ault 186–94.

Dulness. The tutelary figure of *The Dunciad*. The idea was taken up from previous writers and in particular from *MacFlecknoe*, by AP's mentor **John Dryden**. It was already a complex word. In the *Dictionary* of **Samuel Johnson**, the term is defined in a number of ways, with the major senses including "stupidity, slowness of apprehension," "drowsiness, inclination to sleep," and "sluggishness of motion." AP utilizes all these overtones of the expression.

Johnson defines *dunce* as "a dullard; a dolt; a thickskul; a stupid indocile animal." The dunces of AP's poem are both foolish and intractable. The king of the dunces has an appropriately royal station: He inherits the empire of his mother, Queen Dulness—who has some obvious affinities with **Queen Caroline**.

Dunciad, The. AP's great **mock-heroic** poem went through numerous revisions and recensions over the course of its creative lifetime (1728–44). This entry is divided into seven parts: (1) composition; (2) publication history; (3) literary sources and models; (4) analysis of the narrative; (5) targets of the satire; (6) contemporary response; and (7) critical history.

COMPOSITION

AP had been collecting materials to launch an attack on his enemies for many years, and the idea for a poem on "The Progress of Dulness" may well have its roots in the projects of the **Scriblerus Club** around 1714. However, *The Dunciad* seems to have taken shape only in the middle and late 1720s. Allegedly, "the first sketch of this poem was snatch'd from the fire by Dr. *Swift*, who persuaded his friend to proceed in it" (*TE* 5: 201). From time to time AP reported on a new satire, which is evidently the poem on Dulness: see, for example, AP's letter to **Swift** on 15 October 1722 (*Corr* 2: 332). One spur to action was the appearance of *Shakespeare Restored* by **Lewis Theobald** in March 1726, a work that led to Theobald's enthronement as the original king of the dunces. During Swift's visit to England in that year, the project seems to have gained momentum, with encouragement from AP's friend (see "New Anecdotes" 347). The poem took fuller shape in 1727, when the death of **George I** and succession of his son gave the satirist new opportunities. It was not until March 1728 that AP informed Swift that the poem titled "the Progress of Dulness" had now been rebaptized *The Dunciad* (see *Corr* 2: 480). After the publication of the earliest version, AP asked Swift for criticisms of his work and suggestions for the ancillary material that was to be added to ***The Dunciad Variorum*** (*Corr* 2: 503). At the start of Book 1, AP addresses Swift as the presiding spirit of the poem, referring to Cervantes and Rabelais—possible models for the work in a dispersed fashion. Even before publication, many in the literary world had gleaned some clues as to the work in progress. Thus, **Edward Young** had written to **Thomas Tickell** in February 1728 setting out the aims of the poem in some detail and stating that it was almost complete. He added that ***The Art of Sinking*** was also in the press but that he had not seen it—

which may indicate he had somehow gained a sight of *The Dunciad*.

AP continued to work on the poem for the rest of his life. After *The Dunciad Variorum* came out, he went on tinkering with the text in subsequent editions. Throughout the 1730s there were complicated publishing maneuvers and legal squabbles. The new fourth book probably drew on AP's planned *opus magnum*, which was to contain material on education and learning. It was mostly composed while AP was staying at **Prior Park** with **Ralph Allen** in the winter of 1741–42, and in this time AP proved suggestible to the ideas of **William Warburton**. There are few other clues to this later stage of composition. In November 1742 AP wrote to Warburton, nominating his friend as "in some measure the Editor" of *The Dunciad in Four Books* (*Corr* 4: 427). After the poet's death Warburton added further idiosyncratic notes and commentary.

"*The Dunciad*," AP stated in 1735, "cost me as much pains as anything I ever wrote" (*Anecdotes* 1: 147). Nor were his pains over at this date. An immense amount of labor went into assembling the materials, casting and recasting the verses, and preparing the ancillary materials. It was not entirely a joke when he ruefully declared to Swift: "It grieves me to the Soul that I cannot send you my Chef d'oeuvre, the Poem of Dulness, which after I am dead and gone, will be printed with a large Commentary, and letterd on the back, *Pope's Dulness*" (*Corr* 2: 468).

While no holograph manuscript exists for the poem, **Jonathan Richardson junior** transcribed AP's corrections into two copies of the poem, one the first edition of 1728 and the other an octavo reprint by **Lawton Gilliver** dated 1736. He drew on the "First Broglio" and "Second Broglio" manuscripts that AP wrote down at some stage of composition: both may be as early as 1728 and predate the earliest printing. The originals are lost. In a separate copy of the 1728 edition, Richardson collated for AP the changes that had been made since that original version up to the mid-1730s. The transcriptions are reproduced in *L&GA* 97–155. For a comprehensive review of these matters,

see D.L. Vander Meulen, *Pope's Dunciad of 1728: A History and Facsimile* (Charlottesville: University Press of Virginia, 1991).

PUBLICATION HISTORY

The bibliography of the poem is exceedingly complicated, and not all questions have yet been resolved. The summary that follows presents a brief outline of salient facts only.

The 1728 Version

AP abandoned an earlier plan to include the poem in his *Miscellanies* in March 1728. What is generally believed to be the first edition came out on 18 May 1728. It was a duodecimo of fifty-four pages. Another issue in octavo appeared at about the same time (Griffith 198–99: Foxon P764–65). In fact, part of the book was imposed in each format before the second portion was set up in type. There were further impressions from the same setting of type. The title page states that the volume was printed in London and reprinted in Dublin for **Anne Dodd**. Both statements are fictitious. The book was printed in London by **James Bettenham**, and the name of Mrs. Dodd, a pamphlet seller, was used simply as a convenience. The price was one shilling (5p). A piracy quickly made its way into the world, formerly attributed to **Edmund Curll** but now thought to be produced in Edinburgh.

In this form the work consists of three books amounting to 250, 384, and 286 lines, respectively, in heroic couplets. The only ancillary material is a preface entitled "The Publisher to the Reader." There were only a small handful of notes to the text.

On this version, see *TE* 5: 2–3, as well as Vander Meulen, 29–39. For a reprint of the text, see *Pope: Poetical Works*, ed. H. Davis (Oxford: Oxford University Press, 1980), 721–49.

The Dunciad Variorum

In advance of publication, AP assigned the copyright to three noble friends, **Lord Bathurst**, the **Earl of Burlington**, and the **second Earl of Oxford**. Later in 1729 the rights were assigned to Gilliver, but even if the bookseller took a share in the profits, the real control remained with AP. On 12 March 1729 an advance copy was presented to the King and Queen by none other than **Sir Robert Walpole**, a coup on AP's behalf that is still not easy to explain. **George II** is reported to have declared AP "a very honest man," which may indicate some lack of intellectual finesse on his part.

This was published on 10 April 1729, as *The Dunciad Variorum, With the Prolegomena of Scriblerus*, a quarto "printed for A. Dod" (Griffith 211; Foxon P711). It was printed by **John Wright**. The price had jumped to 6s.6d. (32.5p). Octavo editions said to be printed by Mrs. Dodd and by Lawton Gilliver followed in quick succession. A piracy "printed for A. Dob" was not long in appearing. A "second" edition had appeared by the end of the year, together with various issues and impressions, as well as a true Dublin edition.

The work consists of three books, running to 260, 396, and 358 lines. Added items are: an "Advertisement" or preface; A "Letter to the Publisher," signed by **William Cleland**; a series of "Testimonies of Authors"; a summary of the contents, titled "Martinus Scriblerus, Of the Poem"; and "Arguments" to each of the books. All of these precede the text, which is garnished with abundant footnotes throughout. At the end come corrections, jokingly written in the guise of Scriblerus, and appendices—namely, the preface from the 1728 version; a "list" of the abusive references to AP prior to the appearance of the poem; an extract from William Caxton; the parody of **Richard Bentley**'s methods, named *Virgilius Restauratus*; a reprint of the paper that had appeared in *The Guardian* in 1713, on the subject of pastoral; a "Parallel" between the characters of **Dryden** and AP; an incomplete "List of All our Author's Genuine Works"; and a maliciously detailed index.

On this version, see *TE* 5: 3–4. The same edition provides details of the changes AP made to his work in the course of the next few years, most significantly in the *Works* (1735).

The New Dunciad

The New Dunciad: As it was Found in the Year 1741 came out on 10 March 1742, as a quarto of forty-eight pages (Griffith 546; Foxon P787). The publisher is named as **Thomas Cooper**. Priced 1s.6d. (7.5p). Further issues and editions appeared in the same year.

This is the added fourth book of the poem, complete with notes, containing 618 lines. There is a note "To the Reader" and an "argument" to Book 4. On this version, see *TE* 5: 248.

The Dunciad, in Four Books

It was published on 29 October 1743 as a quarto of 260 pages (Griffith 578; Foxon P796). Full title: *The Dunciad, In Four Books, Printed According to the Complete Copy found in the Year 1742. With the Prologemana of Scriblerus, and Notes Variorum*. The publisher named was Mary Cooper, widow of Thomas. The volume was printed by **William Bowyer junior**, and the price was 7s.6d. (37.5p).

The four books contain 330, 428, 340, and 656 lines, respectively. The role of king of the dunces has been transferred from Theobald to **Colley Cibber**, and extensive revision has been made to the first three books. On top of this, there are changes to the fourth book, including the addition of the climactic passage describing the eclipse of light on earth by "Universal Darkness." Fresh elements include a new "Advertisement," signed "W.W." (Warburton) but doubtless written by AP; a mock declaration "By Authority"; another parody of Bentley's editorial manner, written by Warburton and titled "Ricardus Aristarchus of the Hero of the Poem"; a reprint of the prefatory note from 1742; and an appendix on the office of the Poet Laureate, taken from a piece in the *Grub-street Journal* in November 1730. Other supplementary items are retained from *The Dunciad Variorum*. On this version, see *TE* 5: 248–49.

The next major printing came in Warburton's edition of 1751.

LITERARY SOURCES AND MODELS

The most sustained level of allusion involves traditional epic. There are many passages replaying incidents and motifs from heroic poetry, from **Homer**, **Virgil**, **Milton**, and others. AP often recalls the translations of his predecessors, notably Dryden's version of the *Aeneid*, and occasionally looks back to his own Homeric renderings. Two models are most frequently drawn on. One is the *Aeneid*, pervasively present but seen most obviously, for example, in the "heroic" games (*A* Book 5; *D* Book 2) and in the journey to the underworld (*A* Book 6; *D* Book 3). The other is *Paradise Lost*, especially in the connections established between Satan and the principal dunce: for this motif, see the study of Aubrey Williams, listed at the end of this entry. Among other classical texts, the ***Metamorphoses*** of **Ovid** undergoes comical misapplication more than once.

Further passages refer back to the earlier exponents of mock-heroic, including Dryden, **Boileau**, and **Garth**. Naturally, AP does not forget the epic effusions of the writers whom he satirized in the poem: thus, there is evidence that he was familiar with the lengthy productions of **Sir Richard Blackmore**. More widely, AP remembers the dramatic productions of key dunces such as **Colley Cibber** and **Elkanah Settle**. Among other literary classics, echoes of **Shakespeare** and **Spenser** appear several times. There are many more references to the Bible than may be obvious to most modern readers, some of them close to blasphemous by the standards of the age. A wide range of scholarly writing, such as editorial work on the classics by **Richard Bentley** and others, underlies the text. Finally, AP revisited earlier poems of his own, such as *The Rape of the Lock* and *The Temple of Fame*, to import further ironies and deceits.

ANALYSIS OF THE NARRATIVE

This analysis refers to the shape of the poem as it emerged in its final form.

Book 1. After a formal invocation, and a dedication to Swift, the poet describes the origins of dulness. Its home or "college" is located close to **Bedlam**—this may be a reference to the historic **Grub Street**. Notionally the events take place on Lord Mayor's Day, when Sir George Thorold is installed in office (this was actually in October 1720, but the "George" in question is really George II, crowned in 1727). Queen Dulness reviews her favorite sons and chooses Bays (that is, Cibber) to carry out her purposes. The hero makes an altar of his library and starts to burn his own works on the pyre so formed. The goddess intervenes and quenches the flames. She transports Bays to her temple and anoints him as the chosen successor in the great line of dunces. He is carried to the royal court and proclaimed as the new king.

Book 2. The hero presides over his peers and acolytes. The Queen announces "high heroic Games" for her subjects. Poets, critics, patrons, and publishers assemble in the **Strand**, where the West End meets the city of London, and sports appropriate to their activity are prepared for them. Booksellers race for an empty humanoid decked out as a poet: Curll defeats **Lintot**, despite having to make a detour through the sewers around the **Fleet Ditch**. He is again the victor in a pissing contest, for which the prize is the person of **Eliza Haywood**. In the next competition, poets are required to tickle their patrons in order to extract money from their grasp. There follow games devoted to yelling and braying like animals (the loudest, Blackmore, wins) and to mud-diving. The latter, allotted to "profound, dark, and dirty partywriters," features an extended dive in the filthy ditch, in which the winner, a journalist named Arnall, is outdone by **Jonathan Smedley**, who plunges farther into the murk than anyone else. Finally, the critics are called on to stay awake while two "pond'rous books" are read in a monotonous voice. All those present succumb to the tedium and lull themselves into a drugged sleep.

Book 3. The goddess takes the king to her temple and allows him to sleep. He descends to the underworld amid visions of mad enthusiasts and projectors. On the banks of the Lethe, he encounters the shade of Settle, who carries him to a high point, from which the entire empire of dulness, past, present and future, is visible. The ghosts shows Bays how folly has progressed across the world and is now poised to occupy Britain, with some of the individuals who will bring this to pass. A sudden change takes place, parodying the transformation scenes popular in theatrical entertainments of the time. This confirms Settle's prophecy, that

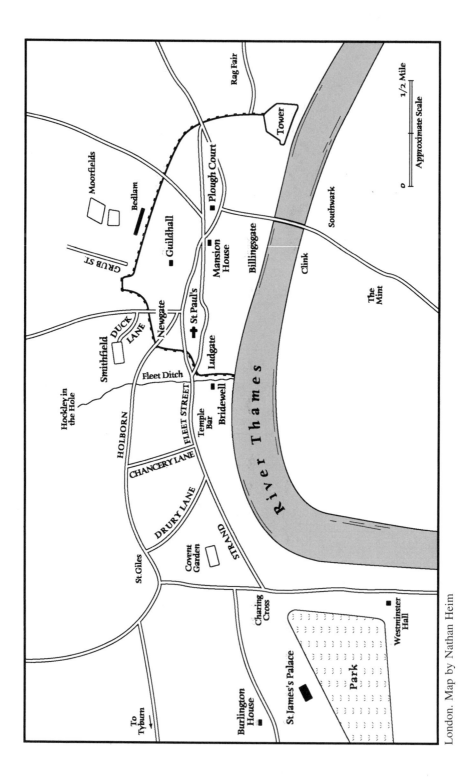

London. Map by Nathan Heim

the new reign will see dulness extend its perverse powers over the entire nation. Under this "Augustus" folly will be rewarded and merit thrown aside. The dream, or nightmare, comes to an end, and the king returns to his realm on earth.

Book 4. After a renewed invocation (another parody of epic decorum), the goddess mounts her throne and holds a levee or audience, at which assembled representatives of the arts and sciences congregate. A loyal address is presented to her by her subjects, beginning with members of schools and universities, who describe their blinkered view of education. These "pedants" are shoved aside by bright young gentlemen, just returned from the **Grand Tour**, whose representative boasts of their idle experiences in Europe. Other indolent persons are in attendance, for whom Dulness wishes to find a role. A pair of crooked **antiquarians** want these hapless individuals as their dupes. The next group of supplicants are a group of virtuosi, dedicated to pursuits such as growing tulips and catching butterflies: the goddess recommends that they should teach the lazy persons to collect shells and mosses. Next come shallow freethinkers and short-sighted scientists. The waiting young are allowed to taste a potion from the cup held out by a priest, in a ceremony uncomfortably close to the Mass. The Queen then hands out degrees and honors to the assembled company. She exhorts them in a speech that culminates in a vast imperial yawn. The whole nation falls into a state of torpor: all the institutions of government, law, education, and religion are overtaken with drowsiness. The reign of dulness comes into its own, as civilization and culture are blotted out. Chaos and anarchy are restored.

TARGETS OF THE SATIRE

The aims of the poem were always diverse, and they expanded as time went on and fresh incarnations emerged. Central from the start had been the assault on contemporary writing, embodied both in the hacks of Grub Street and the polite scholars whose methods AP satirizes in his notes and extratextual apparatus. Symbolizing these two groups are the king of the dunces, in turn Theobald and Cibber, and the "editor" Scriblerus, mainly pointing at Bentley. The figure of Dulness herself goes back to earlier depictions of folly, especially that of Erasmus in *Encomium Moriae*. However, she also has a political dimension and recalls **Queen Caroline** at certain moments. Politics is present from the opening of the work, with a contemptuous reference to the way in which "Dunce the second reigns like Dunce the first" (*TE* 5: 61). Later passages recall the coronation of the King and Queen in October 1727, as well as the associated ceremonials enacted at **Drury Lane Theatre**. Running beneath the surface is a current of allusion to the government of Robert Walpole.

Allied to the use of the coronation is a motif built around the pageantry of the installation of a new Lord Mayor. Just as the mayoral procession made its way from the city of London to the fashionable West End, so the dunces reenact this migration, with the suggestion that the commercial values of the city have invaded polite St. James's. An example of this is the way in which low **Smithfield** shows have transferred their debased energies to the theaters further west. Individual sections of the poem develop this motif in different ways: Book 3 focuses on the transplantation of drama, while Book 2 concentrates more on the sordid goings-on of venal journalists and squalid members of the book trade around **Fleet Street** and the Strand.

References to the Bible and *Paradise Lost* underlie a systematic portrayal of inverted spiritual values. This comes to a head in Book 4, which is by far the most extended in its satiric compass. Among the targets here are the educational system; the Grand Tour; antiquarians, collectors, and scientists; **opera**; freethinkers; and many other groups. In general, this portion of the satire is directed more openly against the great and good, in particular those who followed fashionable trends in social and intellectual life. However, all sections of society are enveloped in the final cataclysm, which brings the nation to its knees as dulness spreads its pestilence across the landscape.

CONTEMPORARY RESPONSE

As was only to be expected (and doubtless intended), the first edition of the poem immediately gave rise to a huge body of hostile replies. They appeared in newspapers, pamphlets, and books over the course of the next few years. For a representative sample of such items, see **pamphlet attacks**. The quickest off the mark seems to have been once more Edmund Curll, who produced *A Compleat Key to the Dunciad* within two weeks of the emergence of AP's work. Amusingly, his *Key* is said to be "Printed for A. Dodd," a deliberate effort by the bookseller to align his pamphlet with the poem and thus give it a kind of authenticity. In fact, Curll was extremely successful in filling in the blanks in the text and got many more names right than wrong. Other early ripostes were *A Popp upon Pope* and *The Progress of Dulness*, offering to give an "explanation" of *The Dunciad*. Soon afterward came *Sawney*, a poem "occasion'd" by AP's work, written by **James Ralph**; and *An Essay on The Dunciad: An Heroic Poem*. Efforts to reply to the poet in his coin were seldom effective, and **prose works** like Curll's *The Popiad* made greater inroads. In July 1728 **John Dennis** launched his first sally against *The Dunciad*, attached to an old critique of *The Rape of the Lock*. The next month *The Female Dunciad* contained lines by the obscure **Thomas Foxton**, but little else to the professed purpose. Another Curll production, *Codrus*, criticized the coarseness of AP's work in equivalently gross language. Late in the same year **Edward Ward** accused the poet of betraying his friends in writing his satire: Swift is alleged to have helped in composing the preliminary matter (a claim without any known warrant).

So it went on for some time to come. The appearance of the amplified poem in 1729 elicited the usual prompt response from Curll, this time *The Curliad: A Hypercritic upon The Dunciad Variorum*. An abusive piece of doggerel verse titled *Tom o' Bedlam's Dunciad: or, Pope, Alexander the Pig* may possibly be the work of the egregious **John Henley** (see Guerinot 170). Then came more detailed *Remarks*

on *The Dunciad* by John Dennis, in a letter to Theobald; and a pathetic attack on AP by an anonymous dunce, who claims to have lost his livelihood as an author because of his inclusion among the "Nameless Names" of the poem. Others such as **Leonard Welsted** and **James Moore Smythe** joined in the chorus of reprobation. Not until the appearance of the *Epistle to Burlington* did AP's critics find a new stick with which to beat him. Even then, they continued to dredge up *The Dunciad* and occasionally found some entertaining line of retort, as in *The Mirrour* (1733) by **Giles Jacob**. The publication of AP's letters in 1735 involved him in a lengthy brawl with Curll, who used the occasion to make fresh charges against AP's libels in the satire.

Full hostilities were resumed in 1742, when one of the dunces, **Bezaleel Morrice**, finally got around to responding to the original poem. The most prominent of the critics this time was Colley Cibber, who had found himself given a starring role in *The New Dunciad*, and composed *A Letter from Mr. Cibber, to Mr. Pope*. Another response linked **Richard Savage** with AP as an informant on Grub Street matters, while *The Blatant Beast* praises Cibber and derides AP. When the four-book version came out in 1743, there were fresh assaults by Cibber and others, but the sting had largely gone out of the exchanges. Even the trickle of pamphlets favorable to AP dried up.

CRITICAL HISTORY

Even though the immediate occasion of the poem grew more distant, critics in the eighteenth century continued to emphasize the personal nature of the satire. The first important discussion, that of **Samuel Johnson**, recognizes the merits of the work as a mock-heroic poem but still limits its scope to "the best specimen that has yet appeared of satire ludicrously pompous." Johnson took a realistic view in casting doubt on some of AP's professed motives of morality and located its true inspiration in the poet's desire to revenge himself on Theobald. Like other commentators, Johnson was put off by the offensiveness of AP's language and subject matter, an issue that loomed increasingly large as taste in these areas became more fastidious. On one occasion, Boswell reports, Johnson recited the concluding lines of the poem "in his forcible, melodious manner," adding "it was worth while being a dunce then." On the other hand, **Joseph Warton** declared that "the chief fault" of the poem was "the violence and vehemence of the satire, and the excessive height to which it is carried."

In the Romantic era the poem remained in fairly low esteem, although **Byron** made obvious use of it in works such as *English Bards and Scotch Reviewers* and *The Vision of Judgment*. For **William Hazlitt**, *The Dunciad* had "splendid passages, but in general it is dull, heavy, and mechanical." Hazlitt was not alone in preferring *MacFlecknoe* to it successor. Apart from a few favorable comments by **Thomas De Quincey**, little was said in a more positive way until in the middle of the nineteenth century **William Makepeace Thackeray** and **John Ruskin** produced unfashionably laudatory accounts of the poem, stressing the "consummate art" with which AP had composed his picture of dulness at work. A more representative view was that of **Mark Pattison**: even in his best-known satires, wrote Pattison, "because the incidents are trivial and the personages contemptible, Pope is not more than pretty in *The Rape of the Lock*, and forcible, where force is ludicrously misplaced, in *The Dunciad*." For other writers as late as **George Saintsbury**, one of the few "purple patches" where Pope was felt to have written above himself came in the conclusion of Book 4.

In the twentieth century attitudes began to change. What are often seen as the slightly woozy appreciative comments of **Edith Sitwell** included a precise refutation of the long-standing charge of monotony leveled against AP's verse. Sitwell wrote of the "enormous variations of height and depth, speed, and heavy consciously-dulled sloth." For the first time in two centuries, it was possible to read the poem as a poem, rather than merely as a polemic against AP's enemies, and to identify its technical attributes. It was on the grounds of its "strange murky and Tartarean beauty" that Sitwell felt able to pronounce *The Dunciad* to be

"one of the greatest poems in our language." Around the same time, the growth of academic criticism, both in the United Kingdom and the United States, led to more detailed analysis of local effects in the poem. Admiring accounts were given by **F.R. Leavis**, **Maynard Mack**, **William Kurtz Wimsatt**, Hugh Kenner, and many others. A landmark was the appearance in 1955 of the major study by Aubrey Williams, which showed a greater coherence and depth in the poem's workings than had ever been described before. By the 1960s *The Dunciad* was established as one of the poet's most intensely studied works. In recent works it has continued to hold this position, although new critical approaches have led to a shift in concerns: new discussions have often centered on matters such as the monstrous and grotesque, and AP's conflicted relations with the book trade have been explored. In the twenty-first century AP can no longer count on a sympathetic ride from his readers, any more than was possible in the Victorian era. However, the density of his poem, its thick description of material and corporeal existence, and its deep involvement in the politics of authorship ensure its survival as a living entity.

The standard edition, covering fully both the 1729 and 1743 versions, remains *TE* 5: but see also *The Dunciad in Four Books*, ed. V. Rumbold (Harlow, Essex: Longman, 1999). The most important study is A. Williams, *Pope's "Dunciad": A Study of Its Meaning* (London: Methuen, 1955). Other valuable items are: J.E. Sitter, *The Poetry of Pope's "Dunciad"* (Minneapolis: University of Minnesota Press, 1971); H. Erskine-Hill, *Pope: "The Dunciad"* (London: Arnold, 1972); D. Brooks-Davies, *Pope's "Dunciad" and the Queen of the Night: A Study of Emotional Jacobitism* (Manchester: Manchester University Press, 1985); and *More Solid Learning: New Perspectives on Alexander Pope's "Dunciad,"* ed. C. Ingrassia and C.N. Thomas (Lewisburg: Bucknell University Press, 2000).

Dunciad Variorum, The. The version of AP's poem first published in 1729. It consisted of three books with notes and an elaborate pseudoscholarly apparatus. See *The Dunciad*, "Publication History."

Durfey, Thomas (1653–1723). More often known as "Tom D'Urfey." Poet and songwriter. He wrote a large number of comedies from the 1680s onward and enjoyed great success with his editions of Henry Playford's anthology *Wit and Mirth: or Pills to Purge Melancholy: being a Collection of . . . Ballads and Songs*. His ditties were among the most popular of their day, but he had become a well-known butt of the wits since **Dryden**'s time. And it has been suggested that this was enough for AP to introduce him into Book 3 of *The Dunciad*, with a glancing and not-too-damaging blow. Equally, the brief attention Durfey receives among the "frogs" in chapter 6 of *The Art of Sinking* argues little by way of serious concern on AP's part; while the *Verses on Durfey* are witty persiflage rather than bitter satire. See *TE* 5: 439, as well as J. McVeagh, *Thomas Durfey and Restoration Drama: The Work of a Forgotten Writer* (Aldershot: Ashgate, 2000).

early imitations of English poets. Among AP's earlier works can be found a series of short poems in which he imitated the style and manner of English poets of the past. The main group consists of six items, devoted to **Chaucer, Spenser, Waller, Cowley**, and **Dorset** (two items), respectively. They were published at intervals between 1712 and 1736. AP claimed that they were written as early as his teens, but there is no independent evidence on the point. See *TE* 6: 41–51.

All these models were fashionable or influential. Their currency is further indicated by another group of verses in imitation of Waller and Cowley, also supposed to be teenage compositions, which were included in the collection *Poems on Several Occasions* (1717). See *TE* 6: 7–15. See also *On Silence*.

Easthampstead. Estate in **Berkshire**, in the hundred of Ripplesmere, near the center of **Windsor Forest**. It lay on the site of a medieval hunting lodge and had belonged to the Trumbull family since the early seventeenth century. However, the manor was bought by AP's patron **Sir William Trumbull** only in 1696, on his retirement from diplomacy and politics. Originally a royal hunting lodge, the property belonged in turn to William Trumbull I (d. 1635), to his son William II (d. 1668), and then to his grandson, AP's friend. In turn it passed to William IV (d. 1760). The house was surrounded by a park of some 250 acres. Sir William was a Verderer for Easthampstead Walk, an area of the forest extending beyond the parish and all except the park subject to royal jurisdiction. The population of the parish was about 200 in AP's day. It covered over 5,000 acres. The Jacobean house was demolished in 1860 and replaced by a Victorian mansion, situated a little to the north of the old building. This is now used as a conference center and school. Most of Easthampstead park has been swallowed up in the designated new town of Bracknell.

AP spent much of his youth at Sir William's residence, which was located less than three miles from his own home. He drew on his friend's well-stocked library and met some of the wide circle of friends that the diplomat had acquired. The church of St. Michael and St. Mary Magdalene dates from the twelfth century but was largely rebuilt in 1865–67. In the Lady Chapel are tombs of the Trumbull family, including Sir William's own. This tomb does not include the epitaph that AP had composed for him, possibly because of the political resentment simmering beneath its surface. However, AP's epitaph for **Elijah Fenton** is still to be seen in the north aisle of the church.

Eckersall, James (c. 1679–1753). Courtier, who began in a junior position under **William III** and held office for more than fifty years. Director of the African Company. He may be the father of "John Eckersall," who was gentleman usher to the future **Queen Caroline** when she was Princess of Wales and secretary to Caroline when she became Queen. He was a friend of **Charles Jervas**, who left him £1,000 in his will. At one period often in company with **Jonathan Swift**, who called him "honest Jemmy Eckershall" (*JTS* 2: 375). He and AP corresponded on business matters at the time of the **South Sea Bubble**; five letters survive. Eckersall subscribed to the *Iliad* and the *Odyssey*. He was one of those to greet AP in the poem *Mr. Pope's Welcome from Greece*.

education. AP was taught to read by "an old aunt," probably Elizabeth Turner (see **ancestry**). At the age of about eight he began to study under a priest, possibly named **Edward Taverner**, alias John Banister, for about a year. He then went to **Twyford** school, still under Banister's care. After that he went to a school at Marylebone, London, which soon moved to Hyde Park Corner, and was taught by **Thomas Deane**. Following this, AP reports, "when about twelve, I went with my father into the Forest and there learned for a few months under a fourth [*really* third?] priest. This was all the teaching I ever had, and, God knows, it extended a very little way" (*Anecdotes* 1: 8). The "fourth" priest is most likely to have been **William Mannock**. AP then began a serious program of self-education at **Binfield**, which lasted throughout his teenage years. The process involved learning Latin, French, and at least some Greek. A suggestion by **Edmund Curll** that AP studied at a school in Bloomsbury around the age of eleven is not substantiated (see *Anecdotes* 2: 609). As a Catholic, AP was of course debarred from attending universities, which required an oath of Anglican conformity.

Egmont, John Percival, first Earl of (1683–1748). Also spelled "Perceval." Irish politician, traveler, and diarist who was an MP; known as Lord Percival when he subscribed to the *Iliad* and *Odyssey*. Created Earl, 1733. Involved with **James Edward Oglethorpe** in the foundation of the colony of Georgia, as president of the original board of trustees. He must have been personally known to AP by 1717, when the poet visited him. They corresponded on business matters in the 1720s and had dealings in relation to the **opera**, another strong interest of Percival, who served at one time as a director of the Royal Academy of Music. See *Diary of Viscount Perceval, Afterwards Earl of Egmont*, 3 vols. (London: Historical Manuscripts Commission, 1920–23), which often illuminates events in AP's later career.

Ehrenpreis, Irvin (1920–85). Professor at the University of Virginia. Primarily known as a scholar of **Jonathan Swift** and as author of the standard three-volume biography of Swift (1962–83). He also wrote some important essays on AP and on the satiric world inhabited by the poet. See, for example, "Pope: Bipolar Implication," in *Acts of Implication* (Berkeley: University of California Press, 1980), 83–111; and "The Cistern and the Fountain: Art and Reality in Pope and Gray," in *Studies in Criticism and Aesthetics: Essays in Honor of Samuel Holt Monk*, ed. H. Anderson and J.S. Shea (1967), 156–75, reprinted in *PRE* 502–26. A Festschrift is *Augustan Studies: Essays in Honor of Irvin Ehrenpreis*, ed. D.L. Patey and T. Keegan (Newark: University of Delaware Press, 1985).

Elegy to the Memory of an Unfortunate Lady. Poem by AP that first appeared in his *Works* (**1717**) as *Verses to the Memory of an Unfortunate Lady*. This title was retained when it was published together with *Eloisa to Abelard* in a miscellaneous collection by **Bernard Lintot** in 1719. The title was altered when it was reprinted, with hardly any other revision, in the *Works* from 1736. It consists of eighty-two lines in heroic couplets.

The model is that of traditional elegy, whose conventions were modified by the genre of poems by abandoned women, of which the *Heroides* of **Ovid** were regarded as the primary example (see also *Eloisa to Abelard*). AP may also have been influenced by the pathetic "she-tragedies" of his friend **Nicholas Rowe**: it is one of his most dramatic performances in its bold verbal gestures and almost Gothic setting.

At the beginning the narrator meets the ghost of the "unfortunate" woman, who has stabbed herself in the breast rather than face either the dishonor of an unwanted marriage (perhaps imposed by a cruel guardian) or the consequences of an illicit love. She has gone to an anonymous grave, her humble grave adorned by "foreign hands." She now lies "without a stone, a name, / What once had beauty, title, wealth and fame" (ll. 69–70). With this studied **epitaph** the poem might be expected to conclude: but a short coda suggests that the poet himself will one day be in need of similar commemoration—an idea taken up in Thomas Gray's famous *Elegy*.

Several "real-life" cases have been proposed

as the basis of AP's poem, notably those of **Anne Cope** and **Elizabeth Weston**. Neither woman's life history really fits the circumstances, and AP attempted to deflect such speculations. It is more likely that AP was inspired by his correspondence with **Lady Mary Wortley Montagu**, who had told him of her dangerous travels in the Orient and a narrow escape from death. See especially her letter of 1 April 1717 (*Corr* 1: 396–401). For many links between Lady Mary and the text of the poem, see G. Tillotson, "Lady Mary Wortley Montagu and Pope's *Elegy to the Memory of an Unfortunate Lady*," *Review of English Studies*, 12 (1936), 401–12. An important article is I. Jack, "The Elegy as Exorcism: Pope's 'Verses to the Memory of an Unfortunate Lady,' " in *Augustan Worlds: Essays in Honour of A.R. Humphreys*, ed. J.C. Hilson et al. (Leicester: Leicester University Press, 1978), 69–83, reprinted in *PRE* 266–84. However, the most complete and informative account of the poem, together with the text, will be found in *TE* 2: 351–68.

Eloisa to Abelard. A poem of 366 lines in heroic couplets, first published in the **Works (1717)**, where it occupies the last place in the volume. In October 1719 a "second edition" appeared in a miscellaneous collection by **Bernard Lintot**, dated 1720, which also included the *Elegy to the Memory of an Unfortunate Lady*. The text was very little revised in subsequent reprints in AP's lifetime.

The exact date of composition has not been established with any certainty. AP once wrote to **Martha Blount**, "The Epistle of Eloise grows warm, and begins to have some Breathings of the Heart in it, which may make posterity think I was in love. I can scarce find it in my heart to leave out the conclusion I once intended for it" (*Corr* 1: 338). However, there is room for doubt whether the date assigned by editors, March 1716 is correct. **Geoffrey Tillotson** argued on the basis of an apparent reference in the text of a letter to **Lady Mary Wortley Montagu** that the conclusion to the poem could not have been written before Lady Mary left for Turkey in July 1716, and that the

letter to Martha must date from March 1717. If correct, this would indicate that the poem was still in the throes of composition only a few weeks prior to its publication in the *Works* on 3 June 1717, although probably begun some considerable time earlier. When he sent the poem to Lady Mary soon after publication, he slyly suggested that there was one passage "that I can't tell whether to wish you should understand, or not?" (*Corr* 1: 407). Equally, we cannot be sure if the tender concluding lines were a coded message to Martha, to Lady Mary, or to no one in particular.

AP's model was the set of twenty-one poems called *Heroides*, or "letters from heroines," written in elegiac couplets by **Ovid** at a date shortly before his exile in A.D. 8. They were immensely popular in Renaissance England and indeed spawned native versions in imitation such as **Michael Drayton**'s set of twenty-four poems, *Englands Heroicall Epistles* (1597). Individual poems in the series were translated by **John Dryden** and others. The original letters attributed to Abelard and Heloise, dating from c. 1117, had first been published in Latin in 1616. Their vogue grew in the seventeenth century and peaked in England with the appearance of the prose version by **John Hughes** (1713), itself based on a French paraphrase originally composed by Roger de Rabutin, comte de Bussy. See *Eloisa to Abelard: with the Letters of Heloise to Abelard in the Version by John Hughes (1713)*, ed. J.E. Wellington (Coral Gables: University of Miami Press, 1965). There were many imitations and replies to AP's poem, as well as translations into French, Italian, Portuguese, German, Swedish, Polish, and Latin.

AP's treatment is affected by his Roman Catholic faith, his interest in landscape and in "Gothick" properties, and possibly his own amatory experiences. Abelard's retreat at the abbey of the Paraclete, or Holy Spirit, was situated near Troyes: it became a favorite pilgrimage for Catholic travelers. The romantic aspects of the poem made it popular in earlier generations, and after a period of eclipse, it is again widely read and intensively discussed. The best account of its constituent elements will be found in *Life* 319–31. The relation of AP's poem to Hughes's rendering is discussed by R.P. Kalmey, "Pope's *Eloisa to Abelard* and 'Those Celebrated Letters,' " *Philological Quarterly*, 47 (1968), 164–78, reprinted in *PRE* 247–65. Another well-known article is M. Krieger, "*Eloisa to Abelard*: The Escape from Body or the Embrace of Body," *Eighteenth-Century Studies*, 3 (1969), 28–47.

For text and commentary, see *TE* 2: 317–49.

Elwin, Whitwell (1816–1900). An Anglican clergyman and men of letters who served as editor of the *Quarterly Review*. He was responsible for the first five volumes of the important **Elwin and Courthope edition** but was replaced after a hostile reaction in the press. The well-known **Oxford** scholar and polemicist **Mark Pattison** observed of these volumes, "We are made to feel from beginning to end that . . . Pope is a liar, a cheat, and a scoundrel, and his so-called poetry is ungrammatical, ill-rhymed, unmeaning trash." For a more favorable view of Elwin's proceedings, see a posthumous collection, *Some XVIII Century Men of Letters: Biographical Essays by the Rev. Whitwell Elwin . . . with a Memoir* (1902), edited by his son Warwick Elwin (London: Murray, 1902; reprinted Port Washington, NY: Kennikat Press, 1970).

Elwin and Courthope edition. This was the long-standard edition of AP. Entitled *The Works of Alexander Pope*, it appeared in 10 vols. (1871–89). The title page accurately stated that it included "several hundred unpublished letters, and other new materials," said to be "collected in part" by **John Wilson Croker**, who had originally designed the edition. The first four volumes were devoted to the poems; vol. 5 to a life; vols. 6–9 to the correspondence; and vol. 10 to correspondence and **prose works**. The publisher was John Murray in London. A reprint was published by the Gordian Press, New York, in 1967.

The first two volumes and vols. 6–8 (1871–72) were edited by **Whitwell Elwin**, who had taken over the project after the death of Croker. Disturbed by some caustic criticisms of his approach, Elwin then handed over the task to **Wil-liam John Courthope**, who wrote the life and edited the remaining volumes (1881–89). Inevitably the edition shows the limitations of its Victorian origins, in terms of what now seem to be religious bias, scholarly shortcomings, and literary incomprehension. Nevertheless it clearly marked a considerable advance on any previous attempt to collect AP's works. It made extensive use of previously unpublished materials, and it remains the only direct source for many items that have since disappeared from view. The editors provided many useful appendices and addenda, including AP's **Memorial List** of his friends and relations. Although the **Twickenham edition** and other modern collections of AP present a more reliable text and more complete bibliographical details, as well as fuller annotation of most works, Elwin and Courthope should not be totally overlooked, as they sometimes provide important information not otherwise available.

empire. When AP began to write, the British Empire was in its infancy and less widely extensive than those of Spain, Holland, and even Portugal. Its most important element was formed by eleven colonies in North America (the Carolinas were not yet divided, and Georgia had yet to be founded). In the Caribbean, the main British possession was Jamaica, with a few small islands including half of St. Kitts. The East India had a strong commercial hold in the subcontinent but no military or administrative presence. Otherwise there was nothing more than a handful of tiny trading posts, scattered across West Africa and South Asia. Britain (or England until 1707) was chiefly a European power, with no naval strategy on an oceanic scale.

One of the aims of the **War of the Spanish Succession** had been to resist the dominance of France and Spain in the world order. By the **Treaty of Utrecht** some significant gains were made: Britain acquired Newfoundland, Nova Scotia, and the Hudson Bay territory, but this left Canada largely in the hands of France, which also controlled the huge Louisiana territory stretching from the Mississippi delta to the Canadian border. Other acquisitions were

Minorca and Gibraltar, initially considered an expensive encumbrance. Although Britain forced France to cede the lucrative *asiento* contract for transporting slaves across the Atlantic, it failed to establish a footing in Spanish America, and the South Sea Company delivered on none of its promises regarding trade to the Western Hemisphere (see **South Sea Bubble**). In fact, it was not until the Peace of Paris in 1763 that the foundations of the later British Empire were properly laid.

AP's most fervent writing on the subject occurs in *Windsor-Forest*, a poem designed to celebrate the Utrecht settlement. At the end of the work, Father Thames envisions a global order opened up by voyages of trade and discovery. Peace will bring about a world where "Conquest [shall] cease, and Slav'ry be no more" (l. 408). Within the Spanish Empire, there will be a resurgence of the native civilizations of Peru and Mexico. This was not exactly the course imperial history would take in the next two centuries, but there is no call to doubt AP's sincerity.

See *The Oxford History of the British Empire: The Eighteenth Century*, ed. P.J. Marshall (Oxford: Oxford University Press, 1998).

Empson, William (1906–84). Famous both for his poetry and for his criticism, he was perhaps the most influential British critic of the twentieth century. Professor at the University of Sheffield from 1953 to 1971. Knighted, 1979; Fellow of the British Academy, 1976. His only formal study of AP came in an essay, "Wit in the *Essay on Criticism*," in *The Structure of Complex Words* (1951), reprinted in *EA* 208–26. However, there are many original insights into AP's use of words in *Seven Types of Ambiguity* (1930).

Englefield family. One of the most ancient Catholic families in **Berkshire**, they had been ejected from their large estates at Englefield in the reign of Elizabeth I for recusancy. They moved across the county to **Whiteknights** in 1606, and it was to this house that AP often came in his youth. They were relatives of the

Carylls, and AP possibly met his close friend **John Caryll senior** on a visit to Whiteknights.

The most important member of the family for AP was undoubtedly Anthony Englefield (1637–1712), one of a group of elderly men to whom the young poet looked up for advice and support. He succeeded his father at Whiteknights in 1667. When Anthony died in January 1712, AP recorded the event in his **Memorial List**, describing his friend as "an extremely witty man, the delight of my youth" (*EC* 1: ix). References in AP's correspondence indicate that he was regarded as a good-natured and ingenious man, with a taste for games and acrostics, and that he was liked by **William Wycherley** for his "waggish" ways ("New Letters" 393; *Corr* 1: 32). Anthony's daughter Martha (c. 1654–1743) married Lister Blount (c. 1650–1710), and became the mother of **Martha** and **Teresa Blount**.

Anthony's son Henry, who married Catherine Poole (1679–1758), left his widow and seven children financially embarrassed when he died of apoplexy in February 1720. He stuck loyally to his faith in 1715, when the authorities applied pressure on Catholics. His widow later married Edward Webb, a schoolfellow of AP. Anthony's daughter Helena became a nun in the Benedictine convent at Paris where the Blount sisters studied. Another daughter was **Mary, Lady Swinburne**, whose family was heavily involved in the **Jacobite rising**.

There was friction between AP and the younger generation of Englefields: hints of estrangement appeared as early as 1713, and specifically the poet quarreled with Henry and Catherine Englefield over a friend, **Elizabeth Weston**. Henry was succeeded in 1720 by his son, also named Henry (d. 1780), who inherited a baronetcy from his distant cousin Sir Charles Englefield. Sir Henry's brother Charles became a Franciscan priest and may have served discreetly at Whiteknights. The male line died out with Sir Henry Charles Englefield in 1822. The family intermarried with other recusant lines known to AP, such as the Dancastles (see **John Dancastle**), the Perkins of Ufton (where **Arabella Fermor** moved on her marriage to Francis Perkins), and the Brownes (see **Sir George Browne**).

Epigram on the Collar of a Dog. The full title is, *Epigram. Engraved on the Collar of a Dog which I gave to his Royal Highness*. One of the most famous of all AP's numerous **epigrams**, it was first published in the *Works* in 1739. The full text reads:

I am his Highness' Dog at *Kew*;
Pray tell me Sir, whose Dog are you?

The dog in question was one of the puppies of AP's own bitch Bounce and was presented to **Frederick, Prince of Wales**. The Prince, focus of the **opposition to Walpole** at this time, broke irreparably with his father the King after an explosive quarrel in July 1737. He had lived at Kew Park Lodge, later the White House, since about 1731 (see **Richmond**). For the epigram, see *TE* 6: 372.

epigrams. Depending on how strictly one defines this term, AP wrote something between twenty and forty such items that have survived. These are short poems turning on a point of wit or a satiric thrust, usually employing puns and ingenious rhymes. AP did not fully share the taste of his friend **Swift** for word-games, riddles, and puzzles. Instead, he worked in the tradition of Martial, lacing his commentary with sober reflections at times (see the "Imitation of Martial" [1716], *TE* 6: 166–68). Among the best known of the epigrams are those on **Colley Cibber**, on Richard Nash, and on the dog belonging to **Frederick, Prince of Wales** (see ***Epigram on the Collar of a Dog***). Other noteworthy examples are those on the **Kit-Cat Club**; the one written "in a Maid of Honour's Prayer-Book"; and the "Inscription upon a Punch-Bowl, in the South-Sea Year."

Epilogue to the Satires. Two poems originally published separately as a culmination of AP's *Imitations of Horace*. Both are couched in the form of "dialogues" between the satirist and a nameless interlocutor. The first appeared on 16 May 1738, a week before the poet's birthday.

It was a folio of sixteen pages, published by **Thomas Cooper** as *One Thousand Seven Hundred and Thirty Eight: A Dialogue Something like Horace* (Griffith 484; Foxon P932), price one shilling. There were further editions that year in London and Dublin by Cooper and **Faulkner**. The second part was published by **Robert Dodsley** on 18 July 1738 in the same format (Griffith 494). Both dialogues were printed by **John Wright**. AP entered both titles in the Stationers' Register and thus retained the copyright to himself. Around this time he assembled his *Imitations* for the first time, and in January 1739 the two dialogues were added. In 1740 he altered the title of these items to "Epilogue to the Satires. Written in 1738. Dialogue I [II]."

In the first poem, containing 172 lines in couplets, the writer's friend complains that AP has been too bold and rough, in contrast to his model, **Horace**, with "his sly, polite, insinuating stile." The poet defends his practice and points to the urgent need for a public scourge of contemporary morals. The work reaches a climax in a coruscating attack on "Vice," a code word in Opposition polemics for the government machine (see **opposition to Walpole**). In the second dialogue, which contains 255 lines, the exchange continues, with the satirist reviewing his career and again setting out the moral basis for his writing: "Ask you what Provocation I have had? / The strong Antipathy of Good to Bad." Both poems, especially the first, have generally been regarded as outstanding examples of AP's mature art. According to Dodsley, the manuscripts were worked over with great care and every line heavily revised. **Swift** told AP on 8 August 1738 that he thought the second dialogue "equal to almost any thing you ever writ," while **Aaron Hill** praised the way in which it united "the acrimony of *Juvenal*" with the "*Horatian* air of ease and serenity" (*Corr* 4: 112, 115).

In November 1739 a reply defending **Walpole**'s administration came out as *One Thousand Seven Hundred Thirty Nine. By way of Sequel to Seventeen Hundred Thirty Eight* [*sic*]: *By Mr. Pope*. It is written in rough-hewn heroic couplets and runs to seventy lines. For a description, see Guerinot 278–79.

For the political meaning of the passage on Vice, see J.M. Osborn, "Pope, the Byzantine Empress, and Walpole's Whore," *Review of English Studies*, 6 (1955), 372–82, reprinted in *EA* 577–90. For text and commentary, see *TE* 4: 311–27.

Episode of Sarpedon, The. A translation by AP of two sections from the twelfth and sixteenth books of the *Iliad*. The former part contains a famous speech by Sarpedon, son of Zeus and Laodameia, who was the leader of the Lycians (allies of the Trojans). AP contrived a delicious parody of this speech, put into the mouth of the virago Clarissa, in *The Rape of the Lock*, Canto 5. In the second episode Sarpedon is killed by the spear of Patroclus.

The translation, made with the encouragement of **Sir William Trumbull**, was included in the miscellanies of **Jacob Tonson senior** in 1709, part of AP's debut in print. It runs to 349 lines of heroic couplets. **Ralph Bridges** had made a number of comments on AP's draft in 1708, and the poet gave his response. AP was paid three guineas (£3.15) on 13 January 1709. Both passages were incorporated, with small revisions, in the full translation of the *Iliad*. For the text and commentary, see *TE* 1: 352–58; 447–62.

epistles. AP wrote a number of verse letters, which are entered under their individual names. For the versions of epistles and satires by **Horace**, see *Imitations of Horace*. For the so-called *Epistles to Several Persons*, see *Moral Essays*.

Epistle to a Lady, An. This was the last to be written and published among the four *Moral Essays* but normally appeared in the second place in the completed sequence. It appeared on 8 February 1735 as a folio of either sixteen or eighteen pages (depending on the presence or absence of a leaf carrying an advertisement). The publisher was **Lawton Gilliver**, and the printer **John Wright** (Griffith 360–61: Foxon P917). Gilliver paid AP £50 for the copyright. The full title reads: *Of the Characters of Women: An Epistle to a Lady*. Within three months the poem took its place in the group of "Ethic Epistles" in volume 2 of the *Works* (1735). Important changes were made in the **deathbed edition** printed in 1744. These include the addition of the characters of Philomede, possibly based on **Henrietta, Duchess of Marlborough**; of **Atossa**, an intensely debated passage; and of **Cloe**. These characters were apparently withdrawn from the 1735 text at the last minute. A section on **Queen Caroline** was also included in 1744. The work had evidently been extensively revised even prior to its first publication, and many small changes were made over the years. For the design of the work, see F. Brady, "The History and Structure of Pope's *To a Lady*," *Studies in English Literature 1500–1900*, 9 (1969), 439–62. Two autograph manuscripts that existed in the nineteenth century have been lost from view.

The major part of composition may have been undertaken in 1732. A letter from AP to **John Caryll senior** in January 1733 carries an oblique reference that suggests that the poem may already have been completed (*Corr* 3: 340). As it emerged at the end of AP's life, the poem consists of 292 lines in heroic couplets.

Although she is not named, the lady addressed by AP is undoubtedly **Martha Blount**. Her "mild" and "serene" presence at the end of the poem, as a model of feminine equanimity, makes a sharp contrast with the capricious and emotionally violent behavior of other women, whose "portraits" have been displayed in the tour of an imaginary gallery earlier on. The most vivid of these sketches include "Sappho" (a brief and brutal onslaught on **Lady Mary Wortley Montagu**); "Narcissa," possibly based originally on the **Duchess of Hamilton**; and the conflicted and contradictory "Atossa." These bitterly satiric depictions have prompted charges of misogyny against AP (see also **women**). The finest passage in the epistle is not purely satiric; rather, it is tinged with sympathy and a surreal radiance. Here AP incorporates an imaginative vision of aging women still in quest of pleasures as their youthful charms fade:

Asham'd to own they gave delight before,
Reduc'd to feign it, when they give no more:
As Hags hold Sabbaths, less for joy than spight,
So these their merry, miserable Night;
Still round and round the Ghosts of Beauty
  glide,
And haunt the places where their Honour dy'd.
  (*TE* 3.ii: 69)

For the text and commentary, see *TE* 3.ii: 46–74.

Epistle to Arbuthnot. The poem has a tangled history in terms of composition and publication. It first appeared as *An Epistle from Mr. Pope to Dr. Arbuthnot* on 2 January 1735. It was a folio of twenty-four pages, with the date "1734," and stated to be printed by **John Wright** for **Lawton Gilliver** (Griffith 352; Foxon P802). The title was entered in the Stationer's Register by Gilliver on the day of publication. The epistle appeared in the *Works* in the same year, in folio, quarto, and octavo editions, with a number of revisions. There was a Dublin edition and an Edinburgh piracy. In AP's lifetime the poem continued to form part of a disparate group of epistles, consisting chiefly of the *Moral Essays*, in successive editions of the *Works*. After AP died it came out in **Warburton**'s edition of 1751. Here it was placed at the head of the *Imitations of Horace* and retitled *Epistle to Dr. Arbuthnot, being the Prologue to the Satires*. In fact, the poem has no particular features of a "prologue" as such, and it has no basis in **Horace**. AP's initial impulse to group it with the *Moral Essays* has some logic to it.

The work was spliced together from existing fragments, some written many years before. The act of assemblage was carried out mainly in 1734. On 17 July of that year, AP's longtime friend **Dr. John Arbuthnot** wrote to disclose that he was suffering from a terminal illness. AP replied on 2 August, hinting that he intended to produce a new satiric onslaught. By 25 August the plan had become firmer, for AP told the doctor that he intended to address to his friend one of his epistles, "written by piece-meal many years, and which I have now made

haste to put together." On 3 September AP was able to assure Arbuthnot that the poem was completed and that it would serve "as the best Memorial I can leave, both of my Friendship to you, & of my own Character being such as you need not be ashamd of that Friendship" (*Corr* 3: 416–17, 423, 428, 431). Arbuthnot died on 27 February 1735, eight weeks after the poem was published.

Various manuscripts survive to indicate the "piece-meal" nature of the composition. The drafts comprise "an odd clutter of working papers, fair copies, verse fragments, and [Jonathan] Richardson [junior] collations" (*L&GA* 419). The most important of these materials is a poem of 260 lines addressed to another friend of AP, **William Cleland**. This was probably written in 1732. It contains much of the familiar *Epistle* as later published. However, the material is organized very differently, and the famous opening occurs at a point closer to the end than the beginning. Much of this draft concerns the furor stirred up by allegations that AP had attacked the **Duke of Chandos** in his satire on **Timon's villa**. Another fragment supplies a rough working draft, heavily corrected, of the famous lines on **Sporus**.

The earliest fragment to be used in the poem is the portrait of **Joseph Addison** under the name of **Atticus**. This goes back in its most basic form to a date around 1715: It first leaked out in a newspaper in 1723. A longer version appeared in the *Miscellanies* in 1728. Still more revision went on before the verses were sewn into the *Epistle to Arbuthnot*. See *TE* 6: 142–45, 283–86; and Ault 101–27.

The poem consists of 419 lines of heroic couplets in its canonical form. An "Advertisement" at the start described it as "a Sort of Bill of Complaint, begun many years since, and drawn up by snatches": a bill of complaint was the legal term for a plaintiff's submission to the court. It is AP's most directly autobiographical work, defending his practice as a satirist and taking aim at many of those who had attacked him over the years. Most of the leading Dunces are present, if only briefly. The work also celebrates friendship, in the person of Arbuthnot, singles out AP's early patrons for their kindness, and pays moving tribute to the author's own father. Among its character sketches, those of Atticus and of Sporus stand out for their differing modes of demolition. Addison is portrayed as a man of high talent, diminished by his fear and jealousy: the verse strikes a note of studied moderation, mimicking the reserve of its subject. Lord Hervey is seen as perverse, full of malice, and dangerous, yet almost absurd in the contradictory poses struck in his public and private life, something caught in the surreal brilliance of the writing (see **Hervey, John, Baron**). This is one of AP's most striking achievements, a work of authentic power, both tragic and comic, as well as great formal ingenuity, despite the near-chaos from which it emerged.

For the text and commentary, see *TE* 4: 91–127. For the manuscripts, see *L&GA* 419–54.

Epistle to Augustus. Popular name for the version of *The First Epistle of the Second Book of Horace Imitated*, which was subsequently included among AP's *Imitations of Horace*. In its standard form the poem contains 419 lines of heroic couplets (with one triplet). Written at **Bevis Mount** in 1736. It was first published by **Thomas Cooper** on 25 May 1737 as a folio of twenty-four pages (Griffith 458; Foxon P881), at a price of one shilling; the printer was Henry Woodfall. The poem was included in the *Works* in 1738. It is modeled on **Horace**'s famous survey of literature and patronage, addressed to the Emperor Augustus. AP gives a rapid and brilliant account of English literary history. Understandably he considered it among his best imitations (*Corr* 4: 491). One of AP's boldest satires, the poem contains a resounding tribute to **Swift** as a defender of Irish interests against the government. According to Alderman **John Barber**, the Privy Council had even contemplated arresting AP for this contumacious passage, but a technical sleight was used to avoid this potentially embarrassing step (see Swift *Corr* 5.50). AP's most risky maneuver was to replace the Roman emperor, with his immense standing and genuine interest in patronage, with the patently inadequate George Augustus, that is King **George II**. See also **Augustanism**.

For the text and commentary, see *TE* 4: 189–231. For a prophetic thread in the poem, see M. Schonhorn, "Pope's *Epistle to Augustus*: Notes toward a Mythology," *Tennessee Studies in Literature*, 16 (1971), 15–33, reprinted in *PRE* 546–64.

Epistle to Bathurst. The third of AP's *Moral Essays*, as generally published. It was in fact the second to appear, and it was probably written earlier than the "first" and "second" in the sequence, the *Epistle to Cobham* and the *Epistle to a Lady*. It was first published on 15 January 1733, although the title page was dated "1732." This was a folio of twenty-two pages, printed by **John Wright** for **Lawton Gilliver** (Griffith 280; Foxon P923), price, one shilling. It was registered by Gilliver for copyright at Stationers' Hall on 13 January. The full title ran: *Of the Use of Riches, an Epistle to the Right Honorable Allen Lord Bathurst. By Mr. Pope*. A second edition appeared in the same year, as well as what is apparently an Edinburgh piracy. Some revisions were made when the poem entered the *Works* in 1735 as one of the group of four **epistles**. More significant changes were introduced in the so-called **death-bed edition** of 1744 (suppressed), which had been prepared by **Warburton** in light of AP's late revisions in February of that year. A number of lines were transposed in this version. Modern editors regard this as the best source for AP's intentions with regard to the text at the end of his life, although Warburton also contributed his usual pennyworth. From 1751 the poem generally appeared as a dialogue between the poet and **Bathurst**, an alteration that Warburton had introduced without any evident authority from AP himself. It is recorded that Bathurst was displeased to find that this had been done, especially as it gave him a very lame role in the colloquy (see *TE* 3.ii: 79). The work in its standard form consists of 402 lines of heroic couplets. Two substantial working drafts survive in manuscript, which have been edited by **Earl Reeves Wasserman**.

The genesis of the work can be traced in the elaborate plans for AP's *opus magnum*, as these were relayed to **Joseph Spence** in May

1730. AP was intending to contrast prodigality with avarice: The former is anatomized in the *Epistle to Burlington*, the latter in the poem addressed to Bathurst. He was already contemplating using examples such as that of the **Man of Ross**, which duly figure in the epistle as finally drafted. We know from the same source that AP considered that " 'The Use of Riches' was as much laboured as any" of his works (*Anecdotes* 1: 131–32, 140–41, 139). He told his friend **John Caryll senior** that it was "the work of two years by intervals" and confirmed this information when he sent **Swift** a copy soon after publication: "I never took more care in my life of any poem" (*Corr* 1: 353, 348). AP regarded it as "not the worst" thing he had written, even though Swift worried that some of it might be obscure to readers in Dublin (*Corr* 1: 340, 362). The explanation for this is that AP had deliberately named names more insistently, in an effort to avoid the problems caused by the *Epistle to Burlington*. In that case, hostile critics had identified his satiric sketch of **Timon's villa** with the estate of an acquaintance of AP, the **Duke of Chandos**. At one point AP planned to make some amends to Chandos by incorporating a complimentary reference into the poem addressed to Bathurst, but he later confined the allusion to the **second Earl of Oxford**. After the debacle over Timon in 1731, he announced in an open letter it was his intention to "make use of *Real* Names and not of Fictitious Ones" in his next work (*TE* 3.ii: 132). At first AP had expected "much noise and calumny" to greet the epistle, but in the event its reception was reasonably good.

The work is a complex tessellation made up of diverse materials: moral, historical, political, and economic issues abound. There are vivid character sketches, culminating in the brilliant moral fable of **Sir Balaam**, which concludes the poem (ll. 339–402). A number of vicious and grasping misers are portrayed. Some are historic, like the Duke of Buckingham; some are topical like the infamous Colonel **Francis Charteris** and **Peter Walter**; and some are allegorical types like **"Cotta."** Another key figure in the design is **Sir John Blunt**, the chief architect of the **South Sea Bubble**: In fact, the epistle is AP's most direct poetic response to that national calamity. As a foil to this gallery of villains, comprising "the Fool, the Mad, the Vain, the Evil," AP offers the counterexample of The Man of Ross, otherwise **John Kyrle**, as a public-spirited and philanthropic individual who fed the poor and relieved the sick out of a modest personal income (ll. 250–84). Naturally the poet also exempts Bathurst from his criticism as a grandee "unspoil'd by wealth" (l. 226). For AP's dedicatee in this poem, see **Lord Bathurst**.

For text and commentary, see *TE* 3.ii: 75–125. The fullest analysis of the work will be found in E.R. Wasserman, *Pope's Epistle to Bathurst: A Critical Reading with an Edition of the Manuscripts* (Baltimore: Johns Hopkins University Press, 1960). For the relation of the *Epistle* to AP's planned philosophic masterwork, see M. Leranbaum, *Alexander Pope's "Opus Magnum"* (Oxford: Clarendon, 1977), 82–106.

Epistle to Burlington, An. The first to be written of AP's **Moral Essays**, normally placed fourth in the sequence when it was assembled. First published on 13 December 1731 by **Lawton Gilliver** as a folio of sixteen pages; the printer was **John Wright** (Griffith 259; Foxon P908). The full title read: *An Epistle to the Right Honourable Richard Earl of Burlington. Occasion'd by his Publishing Palladio's Designs of the Baths, Arches, Theatres, &c. of Ancient Rome.* The half-title read: *Of Taste. An Epistle To the Right Honourable Richard Earl of Burlington.* A second and a third edition appeared in January 1734, with the title in the latter altered to *Of False Taste.* There were also Irish editions and some piracies. The item went into the *Works* in 1735, when it was again renamed, this time as *Of the Use of Riches.* AP continued to tinker with the text in subsequent reprints, including the **deathbed edition** printed in 1744.

AP had long planned to address a work to his friend and patron the **Earl of Burlington**, and he also had it in mind to produce a "gardening poem." The bones of the poem seem to have been present when AP gave **Spence** his account of the work (*Anecdotes* 1: 138). Around 1730 these designs coalesced when Burlington produced the first of what was intended as a work in two volumes, *Fabriche antiche diseganta da Andrea Palladio Vicentio* (ancient buildings drawn by A.P. of Vicenza). The second volume never appeared. In time the project also merged with AP's wider plans for his *opus magnum* or grand philosophic scheme. This partly explains the adoption of titles that link the poem with the *Epistle to Bathurst*, otherwise "Of the Use of Riches."

On 4 April 1731 AP wrote to Burlington, enclosing a copy of the poem. A transcript was made for the Earl, which survives in the Chatsworth archives. AP makes it clear that he still intends to work on the poem (*Corr* 1: 187–88), and the existence of other manuscripts indicates that the text was put together from various fragments with considerable care. Alterations and expansions in the printed text show that the draft AP sent in April was far from the final version. The most important autograph draft surviving consists of sixty-four lines on two sides of a single leaf, now in the Pierpont Morgan Library. Other fragments copied out by another hand are preserved at **Mapledurham**. For all these manuscripts, see *L&GA* 156–67. As the poem now stands, it runs to 204 lines of heroic couplets.

The *Epistle* was one of the most contentious and most frequently reprinted items in the canon of AP's works. This was almost entirely because of a single long passage in the middle (ll. 99–176) describing a visit to the residence of a showy vulgarian (see **Timon's villa**). Very quickly Timon was identified with the **Duke of Chandos**, a story fomented by AP's enemies. Repeated denials by AP (including an open letter to Burlington in the third edition) failed to dispel rumors to this effect. A joking defense was also mounted in *A Master Key to Popery* (written c. 1732 but unpublished). The section on Timon is full of comic invention and surreal details, as on garden ornaments; "Here Amphitrite sails tho' myrtle bowers; / There Gladiators fight, or die, in flow'rs"(ll. 123–24). However, we should not be totally distracted from the precepts on landscape gardening earlier on, em-

phasizing the need to consult "the Genius of the Place," and holding out **Stowe** as a model. The poem ends with a sounding tribute to Burlington as architect, patron, and cultural entrepreneur. But in the last analysis the finest verses in the *Epistle* are perhaps those that describe the undoing of Timon's costly improvements:

Another age shall see the golden Ear
Imbrown the Slope, and nod on the Parterre,
Deep harvests bury all his Pride has plann'd,
And laughing Ceres re-assume the land. (ll. 173–
76)

For the text and commentary, see *TE* 3.ii: 127–56.

Epistle to Cobham, An. The third of AP's ***Moral Essays*** to be published, it was issued on 16 January 1734 by **Lawton Gilliver**. This was a folio of twenty pages, dated "1733," price, one shilling (Griffith 329; Foxon P920). The printer was **John Wright**. An alternative name is found on the half-title, *Of the Knowledge and Characters of Men: To Richard Lord Cobham*. There were a Dublin edition and an Edinburgh piracy in the same year. In 1735 the poem entered the *Works* as part of a group of **epistles**, where it was garnished with a prose "Argument" at its head. In this grouping the Cobham item was placed first among the *Moral Essays*, a position it has retained in printings right up to the present. There were significant revisions in this as well as in quarto and octavo editions of the *Works* between 1735 and 1740. The so-called **deathbed edition**, printed but not published in 1744, may have had AP's blessing, though it is almost certain that **William Warburton** was chiefly responsible for the form the poem now took. There were significant additions, as well as the cancellation of a short passage attacking the **Duke of Marlborough** (this was possibly at the instance of the Duke's widow, by now on friendly terms with AP). More widely, portions of the text were transferred from one point in the text to another, apparently on the basis of Warburton's belief that the poetic argument was confusingly laid out in the original. It was this rearranged version that was generally reprinted until recent years. Many anthologies of AP's work continue to present the poem in the form established in 1744. There is no decisive logic for preferring either version.

The date of composition is not known precisely. A conversation that AP had with **Joseph Spence** in 1730 shows that the guiding ideas of the poem were already in the poet's head (*Anecdotes* 1: 142). It was indeed assigned a place in the *opus magnum* or grand philosophical survey that AP was projecting around that time. On 23 October 1733 the work was evidently more or less complete, as AP told **John Caryll senior** of changes he meant to make in response to criticisms by Caryll. A few days later the addressee of the poem wrote to AP, thanking him for this "publick testimony of your esteem and friendship" and suggesting some minor alterations. On 8 November he wrote again, acknowledging the changes that the poet had agreed to introduce (*Corr* 3: 391–93). Just before publication, AP sent a copy to **Jonathan Swift**.

The poem, which consists of 265 lines in heroic couplets, seems today perhaps the least effective among the group of the four epistles to which it belongs. Its pervasive theme is that of the "ruling passion," a fairly blunt psychological category that is used to explain very disparate forms of human behavior. Here the poem may suffer artistically from the fact that it has been uprooted from its intended home in the philosophical master work. In literary terms, the most striking portrait is that of the dissolute **Duke of Wharton** (ll. 180–209). There is also a brilliant cameo of "Narcissa," who represents the actress **Anne Oldfield** (ll. 242–47). As is AP's normal habit in these epistles, he concludes with a warm tribute to his addressee, in whom the ultimate "ruling passion" turns out to be patriotism.

For Richard Temple, Viscount Cobham, AP's friend and patron, see **Cobham**. For the text of the poem and important commentary, see *TE* 3.ii: 3–38. A significant article on the work is J.E. Sitter, "The Argument of Pope's *Epistle to Cobham*," *Studies in English Literature 1500–1900*, 17 (1977), 435–49, reprinted in *PRE* 469–85.

Epistle to Henry Cromwell, Esq., An. A familiar letter in verse to AP's early friend **Henry Cromwell**, dated within the poem as 12 or 13 July [1707]. The manuscript printed by **Curll** in 1726 has since disappeared. AP did not reprint the verses. They contain 118 lines of octosyllabic couplets, with much fuller use of feminine endings than is normal with the poet. The style is gossipy and relaxed, with a great deal of references to persons of AP's acquaintance, including **Wycherley**, **Rowe**, and **William Whiston**, and what may be his earliest thrust at **John Dennis**. There is also mention of **Matthew Prior**, whose pacy and convivial manner seems to have influenced the writing. The text is available in *Corr* 1: 25–29; and *TE* 6: 24–29.

In the next year AP wrote another short verse epistle to Cromwell, this time dispersing its contents through a regular letter dated 25 April 1708. There are thirty lines in all, varied in rhythm and rhyme pattern. The manuscript survives in the Bodleian Library: the first printing by Curll (1726) follows this with surprising fidelity. AP never reprinted the item. See *Corr* 1: 46–48; *TE* 6: 39–40.

Epistle to Jervas. In full, *Epistle to Mr. Jervas, with Dryden's Translation of Fresnoy's Art of Painting*. First published in the second edition of **John Dryden**'s translation of *The Art of Painting; by C.A. Du Fresnoy*. This was issued by **Bernard Lintot** in March 1716, with an introduction and dedication by Richard Graham (d. 1741) to the **Earl of Burlington** (Griffith 46). The first edition had appeared in 1715. The original work was *De arte graphica* (1668), by Claude-Alphonse Dufresnoy (1611–65), which Dryden translated in 1695. AP's poem consists of seventy-eight lines in heroic couplets. What appears to be a first draft for the first half of the poem survives among the **Homer** manuscripts; its placing suggests that the draft was written in the autumn of 1715. This has been reproduced and transcribed in *L&GA* 91–96.

Small revisions were made when the poem appeared in the *Works* (1717).

In the poem AP celebrates his friendship with the painter **Charles Jervas** and at the same time hymns the union of the two men as expressed in their "love of Sister-arts." Reference is made to various beauties whom Jervas had painted, including daughters of the **Duke** and **Duchess of Marlborough**; **Lady Mary Wortley Montagu** (later suppressed); the sisters **Martha** and **Teresa Blount**; and "**Belinda**," that is, **Arabella Fermor**.

For the text and annotation, see *TE* 6: 156–60.

Epistle to Miss Blount, on her Leaving the Town, after the Coronation. The most brilliantly executed of all AP's shorter poems, this was probably written shortly after the event it obliquely celebrates, that is, the coronation of **George I** on 20 October 1714. It consists of fifty lines in couplets. First published in the *Works* (1717). The addressee is now thought to have been **Teresa Blount**, rather than her sister **Martha**, even though it is always printed in early editions next to the *Epistle to Miss Blount, with the Works of Voiture*, which may well have been directed to Martha. In the poem AP contrasts the vivid colors of life in town and at court with the dull routine of existence in a remote country setting, where a young lady absurdly named "Zephalinda" has been dragged to a world of "old-fashion'd halls, dull aunts, and croaking rooks" (l. 12). Understandably this has become one of the favorite poems by AP among modern readers, with its sly wit, delicate evocation of melancholy, and veiled romantic passion near the end. For the text and commentary, see *TE* 6: 124–27.

Sixteen lines allegedly "suppressed" by AP, forming the end of the poem, were noted by **Owen Ruffhead** and published in 1775. They may be by AP, but they do not make a wholly satisfactory conclusion to the poem as it stands. See *TE* 6: 232–33.

Epistle to Miss Blount, with the Works of Voiture. A poem of eighty lines in couplets, that first appeared in the miscellany AP edited for **Bernard Lintot** in 1712 (see *Miscellaneous Poems and Translations*). It was then headed "To a Young Lady," with no mention of an individual woman. AP reprinted it in his collected *Works* (1717) and grouped it with another item (see preceding entry) so as to suggest that one of the Blount sisters was the recipient. However, it was not until the poem appeared in the *Works* in 1735 that he inserted the name "Miss Blount."

The facts give rise to two interrelated questions. First, the date of composition. AP claimed that the **epistle** was written as early as 1705, but this is deeply unlikely to be true. It certainly existed in some form in December 1709, when **Henry Cromwell** praised the lines in a letter to AP (*Corr* 1: 109). If this is approximately accurate in fixing the date, then it is possible that AP had already met the sisters and intended the poem as a compliment to one or another. An alternative possibility, advanced by **Norman Ault**, is that the recipient was originally no more than an imaginary mistress. In either case, the second question as to the identity of the recipient remains unsolved, for we do not know which of the two sisters AP meant. The advice seems in many ways more suitable to the elder, **Teresa Blount**, and AP may have had her in mind when he placed the poem as he did in 1717. However, by 1735 it is sure that the younger, **Martha Blount**, must be intended as the "young lady" to whom the verses were once addressed. No certainty has yet been established on these points. The fullest discussion appears in Ault 49–59, 365–66. For the text and commentary, see *TE* 6: 62–65.

AP sets out his accustomed view of feminine virtue, contrasting the sense and good humor of an ideal woman with the excesses of "Pamela," a girl who chooses riches and status in marriage at the expense of emotional satisfaction: "She glares in *Balls, Front-boxes*, and the *Ring*, / A vain, unquiet, glitt'ring, wretched Thing!" The book presented long with the verses has not been recovered. It was evidently an edition of the letters of Vincent Voiture (1598–1648), French man of letters, possibly *Recueil des oeuvres de Monsieur de Voiture* (Amsterdam, 1709). Alternatively, AP might very likely choose an English translation such as *Select Letters of Voiture* (1696), the first of them rendered by **John Dryden** and the rest by **John Dennis**. Voiture was a polished and fashionable writer whose example may have encouraged the young AP to adopt certainly rakish poses. See J.A. Winn, "Pope Plays the Rake: His Letters to Ladies and the Making of the *Eloisa*," in *The Art of Alexander Pope*, ed. H. Erskine-Hill and A. Smith (London: Vision, 1979), 89–115; and E. Audra, *L'influence française dans l'oeuvre de Pope* (Paris: Champion, 1931), 315–46.

Epistle to Oxford. In full, *Epistle to Robert Earl of Oxford, and Earl Mortimer*. A poem of forty lines in couplets, dated 25 September 1721. It served as the dedication to Robert Harley, **first Earl of Oxford**, which AP appended to his edition of the ***Poems of Parnell*** (1722). Earlier, in 1719, **Swift** had suggested that AP should "bestow a few Verses on his friend Parnels memory" (Swift *Corr* 2: 288). On 21 October 1721 AP wrote from the home of the Earl's son in London, requesting permission from Oxford to make the dedication. In his reply from Herefordshire, dated 6 November, Oxford expressed his great pleasure in the proposed scheme and recalled with fondness the days he had spent with Parnell and other members of the **Scriblerus Club** in former times (*Corr* 2: 90–91). Both the poem and the letters are preserved among the Portland papers. There are small discrepancies between the manuscript and the printed version. AP included the item in his *Works* from 1735.

The poem begins with Parnell as Oxford's poet and incorporates a tribute to Swift before turning to its real subject: the grandeur of Oxford as a statesman, especially in the light of his fall from power and the persecution he had received from his political enemies. It rises to a sounding reflection on the closing stages of the Earl's life, now led in tranquil retirement, as the muse attends him to review his career and "dignify Disgrace."

For a full discussion, see G. Tillotson, "Pope's 'Epistle to Harley': An Introduction and Analysis," first published in *Pope and His Contemporaries*, ed. J.L. Clifford and L.A.

Landa (Oxford: Clarendon, 1949), 58–77, and reprinted in his *Augustan Studies* (London: Athlone, 1961), 162–83. For text and commentary, see *TE* 6: 238–42.

epitaphs. AP was in much demand as a writer of memorial inscriptions and composed about twenty-five that survive. Some were in verse, others in prose. Among the first to recognize AP's interest in this branch of literature was **Samuel Johnson**, who wrote an essay on the subject in 1756. This was later reprinted at the end of the study of AP in *The Lives of the Poets* (1779–81). Johnson analyzes thirteen items, all written in English and in verse, allocating praise and blame to the given poem according to his usual touchstones.

The most notable of AP's poetic epitaphs include those he wrote for the following: **Francis Atterbury**; **John, Lord Caryll**; Mrs. Elizabeth Corbett; **James Craggs junior**; **Robert Digby** and his sister Mary; the **Earl of Dorset**; **Elijah Fenton**; **John Gay**; **Simon Harcourt**; **Sir Godfrey Kneller**; **John Knight**; **Nicholas Rowe**; **Sir William Trumbull**; and General **Henry Withers**. Some were placed in Westminster Abbey, some in tiny country churches. Not all were used: those designed for **John Dryden** and **Sir Isaac Newton** were subsequently withdrawn. Three sets of verses on the **Stanton Harcourt lovers** were composed in differing styles and moods. In addition, AP wrote an "Epitaph for One who would not be buried in Westminster Abbey," first published in 1739. This has an obvious element of self-reference (see *TE* 6: 376); see also **Twickenham parish church**. A good example of a prose inscription is the one written for **Nathaniel Pigott** (*Corr* 4: 80).

Essay on Criticism, An. First published anonymously on 15 May 1711 as a quarto of forty-eight pages. The main publisher was William Lewis, and 1,000 copies were printed (Griffith 2). A second issue (identical apart from the title page) came out in January 1712. There was an octavo edition in November 1712 and two more in 1713. The work appeared in a miscellany published in 1714 by Lewis and **Bernard Lin-**

tot (see *Miscellaneous Poems and Transla-tions*), and subsequently in the *Works* (**1717**). Lintot bought the rights in July 1716 for £15. Revisions, mostly of a minor nature, took place throughout the poet's lifetime. In its standard form the poem consists of 744 lines in heroic couplets.

The date of composition has never been fixed with complete certainty. AP's own carefully prepared manuscript of the poem survives in the Bodleian Library, and it is headed "Written in the Year 1709." This was the formula he used in printed editions from 1717. In conversation with **Joseph Spence**, he confirmed the year (*Anecdotes* 1: 41–42). However, on another occasion he said that he showed the poem to **William Walsh** in 1706 (probably an error for 1707); and according to **Jonathan Richardson junior**, AP stated that the correct date was 1707 (*Anecdotes* 1: 31; *EC* 2: 10). It may be that the earliest drafts go back to the 1706 or 1707 but that the final version was not ready until 1709. For a full analysis of the issues, see *TE* 1: 197–202. We are on surer ground with respect to the method of composition, since AP himself observed, "I wrote the *Essay on Criticism* fast, for I had digested all the matter in prose before I began upon it in verse" (*Anecdotes* 1: 45). More than sixty lines in the manuscript were deleted prior to publication.

AP received criticisms from Catholic friends, possibly including members of the **Englefield family**. The charges concerned references to sects and schisms within the Church. He responded to this criticism in a letter to **John Caryll senior** on 19 July 1711 (*Corr* 1: 126–8). In addition, AP encountered one of the earliest sustained attacks on his work from the hand of **John Dennis**. This was provoked by a sneering reference to the critic as "Appius" at l. 585. The response was a pamphlet titled *Reflections Critical and Satyrical, upon a Late Rhapsody, call'd, An Essay on Criticism*, which appeared around 20 June 1711. AP took some note of Dennis's particular objections, but he could afford to brush off the indiscriminate abuse that was heaped on the *Essay* ("There is nothing more wrong, more low, or more incorrect than this Rhapsody upon Criticism").

Moreover, he soon had powerful backing, with a highly complimentary account in *The Spectator* on 20 December 1711. The work, declared **Joseph Addison**, was "a Master-piece in its kind." The observations followed one another like those in **Horace**'s *Art of Poetry*, but "without that methodical Regularity which would have been requisite in a Prose Author." The poem by Horace was undoubtedly an important model for AP, as were *L'art poétique* (1674) by **Boileau** and two English texts mentioned by Addison, that is, *An Essay on Translated Verse* (1684) by Wentworth Dillon, Earl of Roscommon, and *An Essay upon Poetry* (1682) by AP's friend the **Duke of Buckinghamshire**. Translations of AP's poem into French began to circulate within a few years: The first published version came out in 1717. There were translations into German, Italian, and Latin by the middle of the century; subsequently, Portuguese, Hungarian, and Swedish have added to the tally, the last as recently as 1970.

The *Essay* expresses for the most part orthodox neoclassic doctrine as this had evolved in France and England, but it performs this task with unparalleled brilliance and élan. AP's aim lay not so much in novelty of ideas as in the sparkle and compression of their embodiment in poetry. However, the very ease that attracted readers for 200 years has tended to work against the poem recently, since its epigrammatic manner, neat versification, and readiness to generalize have been uncongenial to modern taste, which often discounts aphoristic writing. Nevertheless, AP's treatment of topics such as **wit** has proved of lasting importance in the history and theory of criticism. We are also more attuned than formerly to the complex pattern of imagery through which the discourse develops. Apart from this, the organization of the poem is now seen to be subtle and less mechanical than once supposed. The table of contents that AP printed from 1736 suggests a rather schematic layout, with the work divided into three parts dealing, respectively, with "the study of the art of criticism" (ll. 1–200), "the causes of wrong judgment" (ll. 201–559), and "the morals of the critics" (ll. 560–744). Although a design along these lines can be discerned, it is unlikely that AP originally planned quite such a cohesive argument as the contents list (perhaps devised by Richardson) might indicate.

The standard edition, with a good introduction and full notes, is found in *TE* 1: 197–326. For AP's original version, see R.M. Schmitz, ed., *Pope's "Essay on Criticism," 1709: A Study of the Bodleian Manuscript Text with Facsimiles, Transcripts, and Variants* (St. Louis: Washington University Press, 1962). For some of the most influential articles on the poem, see under **Empson**; **Hooker**; and **Monk**. See also P.M. Spacks, "Imagery and Method in *An Essay on Criticism*," *PMLA*, 85 (1970), 97–106, reprinted in *PRE* 106–30; and D.B. Morris, "Civilized Reading: The Act of Judgment in *An Essay in Criticism*," in *The Art of Alexander Pope*, ed. H. Erskine-Hill and A. Smith (London: Vision, 1979), 15–39.

Essay on Man, An. An extensive work in four **epistles**, originally published separately. These appeared as follows:

Epistle 1. First published on 20 February 1733 as *An Essay on Man. Addressed to a Friend. Part I* (Griffith 294; Foxon P822). A folio of twenty pages. The publisher was listed as J. Wilford, and the piece was one shilling (5p). In later editions, this portion was subtitled "Of the Nature and State of Man, with respect to the Universe."

Epistle 2. First published on 29 March 1733 as *An Essay on Man. In Epistles to a Friend. Epistle II* (Griffith 300; Foxon P833). A folio of twenty pages, published by J. Wilford and priced one shilling. Later subtitled "Of the Nature and State of Man, with Respect to Himself, as an Individual."

Epistle 3. First published on 8 May 1733 as *An Essay On Man. Addressd to a Friend. In Epistles to a Friend. Epistle III* (Griffith 308; Foxon P840). A folio of twenty pages, published by J. Wilford and priced one shilling. Later subtitled "Of the Nature and State of Man, with Respect to Society."

Epistle 4. First published on 24 January 1734 as *An Essay on Man. In Epistles to a Friend. Epistle IV* (Griffith 331; Foxon P845). A folio of twenty-four pages, published by J. Wilford and priced one shilling. Later subtitled "Of the nature and State of Man, with Respect to Happiness."

The four items were first collected in April 1734 in a volume published by **Lawton Gilliver** and printed by **John Wright** (AP's handpicked representatives in the book trade). The quarto and large folio editions cost four shillings (20p), the small folio three shillings (15p). At the start was printed a summary called "The Design," while each epistle carried a subtitle and a detailed synopsis of contents, called an "Argument" at its head. Thereafter there were numerous reprints in various formats. Changes were introduced in most instances, notably in the quarto issued in February 1744 by Mary Cooper, widow of **Thomas Cooper**. This had been prepared by **William Warburton** under AP's direction. When the text became relatively stable in 1743, it consisted of 1,304 lines in heroic couplets.

The work was at first intended to form part of the prelude to a much larger survey of human experience. In the original scheme, this masterwork would have contained four main parts, of which the *Essay* would form the opening section. It is for this reason that the work came to be described as "the First Book of Ethic Epistles." See *opus magnum*. The exact sequence of composition is unknown. The first hints of the work appear in AP's correspondence in 1730. By 2 August 1731 **Viscount Bolingbroke** was able to report to **Jonathan Swift** that AP had completed the first three epistles and was at work on the fourth (*Corr* 3: 213–14). The peer also claimed that the poem had been undertaken "att my instigation." Two extensive manuscripts survive. One, in the Pierpont Morgan Library, contains drafts for all four epistles, while the other, at Harvard University, covers the first three only. Also preserved is a single leaf at Yale University, which shows that AP intended at one stage to include an attack on the **Duke of Marlborough** near the end of the fourth epistle. For a reproduction of all these manuscripts, see *L&GA* 190–418.

The epistles were all issued anonymously. This was a deliberate ploy by AP, who was able to enjoy the spectacle of widespread homage paid to the author of this noble and uplifting poem—often expressed most fervently by long-time enemies such as **Leonard Welsted**, in ignorance of the truth. AP did not reveal his hand until the poem went into the *Works* in 1735. But by then the authorship was an open secret, and **Voltaire**, a great admirer of the poem, was soon apprised of the truth. In addition, the "Friend" on the title page had now been identified as Bolingbroke. The opening address had begun, "Awake, my Laelius" (a cover name, taken from a Roman patron of **Horace**); this was subsequently replaced by "St. John," the family name of Bolingbroke.

From the outset the *Essay* achieved great success in Britain and abroad. Two French translations soon appeared, one in prose by Étienne de Silhouette (1736) and one in verse by the Abbé Jean-François du Bellay du Resnel in 1737. These were the first of many in all the major languages during the century to follow. A sign of the currency of the work is the appearance of a volume (Strasburg, 1762) containing the poem in five languages—English, French, German, Italian, and Latin. There were also versions in Danish, Dutch, Polish, Portuguese, Russian, Swedish, and other languages. Some were based on du Resnel rather than the English text. In 1743 the young Christopher Smart proposed a Latin version of the poem, but AP gently steered him in another direction (see *Corr* 4: 478, 483). Soon after the *Essay* came out, the animadversions of the Swiss theologian **Jean-Pierre de Crousaz** set off a debate over much of Europe on the orthodoxy of AP's religious and moral position. In this war of words it was Warburton who took the major role as champion of AP, although his efforts to portray the poem as a coherent, rigorous, and thoroughly Christian document have not been accepted by most subsequent scholars.

An equally fierce and latterly more vigorous controversy has surrounded the degree of AP's debt to the ideas of his mentor Bolingbroke. The claim that AP used a lost dissertation by Bolingbroke as the framework of his argument is now generally discounted. However, it is certain (at least for some sections of the poem) that AP employed a summary in prose that he later versified, and Bolingbroke may have contributed something to this. On these matters, see the discussion by **Maynard Mack** in *TE* 3.i: xxix–xxi; *Anecdotes* 1: 138–39, 2: 632–33. Commentators have detected a wide range of other influences, ranging from Plato to Leibniz and the Earl of Shaftesbury, but none seems to have been regularly enlisted as a controlling system of belief.

For the text, full annotation, and a comprehensive introduction, see *TE* 3.i. There are several useful full-length studies of the poem. Among recent works may be mentioned A.D. Nuttall, *Pope's "Essay on Man"* (London: Allen & Unwin, 1984); and H.M. Solomon, *The Rape of the Text: Reading and Misreading Pope's "Essay on Man"* (Tuscaloosa: University of Alabama Press, 1993).

Esther. Oratorio by **George Frideric Handel** in six scenes, written for the **Duke of Chandos** and first performed at **Cannons** around 1718. A revised version in three acts with additional words by Samuel Humphreys was performed at a number of venues from 1732 onward. Usually described as the first English oratorio. Contemporary sources, including the **Earl of Egmont**, attribute the original libretto to AP; others substitute the name of **Arbuthnot**. It is likely that both made some contribution. It survives in Handel's own manuscript score in the British Museum, though some portions are missing, as well as in a transcript: the title was then given as "Harman and Mordecai: A Masque." The plot is based loosely on Racine's *Esther* (1689), which had been translated by Thomas Brereton in 1715, as well as the book of Esther in the Old Testament. For details, see *TE* 6: 423–25. For the work as a whole, see W. Dean, *Handel's Dramatic Oratorios and Masques* (Oxford: Clarendon, 1990), 190–224; and D. Burrows, *Handel* (New York: Schirmer, 1994), 97–98. The fullest discussion of AP's possible involvement in *Esther* can be found in R. Smith, *Handel's Oratorios and Eighteenth-Century Thought* (Cambridge: Cambridge University Press, 1995), 276–87.

Eusden, Laurence (1688–1730). Poet and clergyman. His elevation to the post of Poet Laureate in 1718 caused outrage and astonishment, even though anticipations were not very high for those promoted to this office. He took clerical orders in 1714 and became Rector of Coningsby in Lincolnshire. Apart from this, his reputation was chiefly as a drunkard (see *Corr* 3: 143). In other respects he offered fewer handles to the satirist than his successor as laureate, **Colley Cibber**.

In the *Epistle to Arbuthnot* and *The Second Satire of the Second Book of Horace*, AP bestowed passing attention on Eusden. He receives more notice in *The Art of Sinking*, where he is placed in the category of "ostriches," whose motion is "between flying and walking" (*Prose* 2: 197). AP reserved his scorn mainly for *The Dunciad*, where Eusden is set afloat in both the text and the notes. According to AP, Eusden "was made *Laureate* for the same reason that Mr. *Tibbald* [**Lewis Theobald**] was made *Hero* of This Poem, because there was *no better to be had*" (*TE* 5: 187).

For some of his deathless poems, along with those of **Nahum Tate** and Colley Cibber, see *Selected Writings of the Laureate Dunces*, ed. P. Heaney (Lampeter: Mellen, 1999).

Eustace Budgell, Esq., To. The poem was addressed to **Budgell** "On his Translation of the Characters of Theophrastus" and consists of thirty lines of octosyllabic couplets. It relates to a translation of *The Moral Characters of Theophrastus*, published by **Jacob Tonson senior** in May 1714. AP's response survives in an autograph manuscript at Chatsworth. The poem remained unpublished until it was included in *TE* 6: 123–24. AP incorporates thrusts at other translators, that is, Abel Boyer, **Charles Gildon**, and **John Ozell**. However, his main target is the group of wits associated with **Button's** coffeehouse, headed by **Addison**, **Steele**, and **Ambrose Philips**, who are identified with some of the satiric "characters" in the work. This may explain why the poem was suppressed.

Evans, Abel (1679–1737). Clergyman and **Oxford** don, one of AP's best friends within the university (M.A., 1699; D.D., 1711). Chaplain of St. John's College. Well known as a poet and wit. AP may have stayed with him at Oxford, and he was one of AP's first guests at **Twickenham** in 1719. He helped to distribute the *Iliad* to subscribers at the university in 1717. In *Mr. Pope's Welcome from Greece* he is one of the party greeting the poet. Four letters to AP survive. Evans is mentioned in *The Dunciad* as one of the authors (along with **Swift** and **Edward Young**) whose works are fathered on to others by the unscrupulous **Edmund Curll** (*TE* 5: 109).

F

Fan, The. A poem in three books by **John Gay**, published in December 1713 (dated 1714). It is an extended treatment of feminine trinkets in **mock-heroic** idiom. AP encouraged Gay during its composition and probably made a number of revisions (*Corr* 1: 188, 195). Another adviser was Gay's friend from schooldays, **William Fortescue**. In the previous year AP had contributed a poem "On a Fan" to *The Spectator*, which may have given Gay his first inspiration. However, the principal influence was that of the original *Rape of the Locke* in two cantos. But on the day that Gay published *The Fan*, AP wrote to **Swift** that he had finished the augmented *Rape of the Lock* (*Corr* 1: 201), and it is possible that when he revised this poem prior to its publication in 1714, AP picked up some details from Gay's work.

Farewell to London, in the Year 1715, A. One of AP's most characteristic shorter pieces, this poem managed to escape publication until 1775, when it slipped into print and soon became a fixture in collections of his works—even though he never acknowledged authorship. Composition can be assigned with assurance to the summer of 1715, although early versions of the subtitle supply "1714." It probably took place when AP left London about the start of June, following a protracted spell in the capital. He spent most of the summer in **Binfield**, interspersing his stay with a visit to **Bath**. He returned to London no earlier than the end of October.

The poem is cast in the ballad stanza, with alternating rhymes, and runs to fifty-two lines. It contrasts the lively dissipations of town with the "sober, studious days" AP will pass in the country, working on his translation of **Homer**. The poet casts himself, a little wishfully perhaps, as living in the city as a "thinking Rake." There are references to his friends and patrons, while the concluding stanza pays a warm tribute to **John Gay**.

See text and notes in *TE* 6: 128–32.

Faulkner, George (1699–1755). Dublin bookseller and printer in Parliament Street who was the main outlet for the works of **Jonathan Swift** from the 1730s. He started the *Dublin Journal* in 1725. Often in trouble with the authorities in his early years, Faulkner ended up as an alderman of the city of Dublin. AP had to deal carefully with Faulkner when attempting to bring out his correspondence with Swift, since the publisher owned the rights to much of Swift's work. They dealt mostly at a distance, sometimes through intermediaries such as **Martha Whiteway** and the **Earl of Orrery**. However, Faulkner visited England on business in 1735 and seems to have called on AP with a letter of introduction from Swift. In addition, Faulkner brought out Dublin editions of AP's works, a touchy matter since the status of Irish republication of English books was a gray area legally. Two letters from AP to Faulkner survive.

See *Prince of Dublin Printers: The Letters of George Faulkner*, ed. R.E. Ward (Lexington: University Press of Kentucky, 1972).

Fazakerley, Nicholas (1682–1757). Lawyer and MP. He was a member of a Lancashire family who had long been Catholics, but he conformed and became a barrister at the Middle Temple. He acted on behalf of the **Earl of Burlington** and defended the printer of *The Craftsman* in court. He gave advice to AP at the time of *The Dunciad*, presumably with regard to potential libel cases. A Tory and very possibly a Jacobite, he subscribed to the *Odyssey*.

Fenton, Elijah (1683–1730). Poet. He was educated at **Cambridge** but was unable to proceed with his planned career in the church as he was unwilling to take the oaths of loyalty required for graduation (see **nonjurors**). He gained the notice of **Viscount Bolingbroke** and acted as secretary to the fourth Earl of Orrery, a Jacobite, and tutor to his young son, later the **fifth Earl of Orrery**. Master of Sevenoaks Grammar School. Partly through the offices of AP, Fenton was given the task of instructing **James Craggs** in polite literature in the summer of 1720; Craggs took a house at **Twickenham** close to AP's home for this purpose (*Corr* 2: 45). However, the bursting of the **South Sea Bubble** must have distracted the student, who was heavily involved in the scandal. After this Fenton became tutor to William, son of **Sir William Trumbull**, and remained at **Easthampstead** for the remainder of his life. His works included *Oxford and Cambridge Miscellany Poems* (edited for **Bernard Lintot**, 1708); *Poems on Several Occasions* (1717), also published by Lintot; *Mariamne*, a five-act tragedy in verse, successfully presented at **Lincoln's Inn Fields Theatre** in 1723; an edition of *Paradise Lost* by **Jacob Tonson junior** (1725), for which he wrote a life of **Milton**; and an edition of the poems of **Edmund Waller** (1729), again for Tonson.

He is best known for his collaboration with AP in the shape of four books that he contributed to the translation of the *Odyssey*. Unlike his fellow collaborator **William Broome**, he remained on good terms with AP after the nature of his work was uncovered. He also assisted AP in his **Shakespeare edition**. AP regularly spoke of him with a degree of affection: "Fenton is a right honest man. He is fat and indolent; a very good scholar: sits within and does nothing but read or compose" (*Anecdotes* 1: 213). **Samuel Johnson** related a story that he would "lie abed and be fed with a spoon." When Fenton died he was buried at Easthampstead, and AP wrote an **epitaph** that survives in the church

(see *TE* 6: 318–39). In his **Memorial List** of departed friends, AP noted, "Elijah Fenton, an honest man, and by no means a bad poet" (*EC* 1: x). Very few letters between the two men survive, but a larger number between Fenton and Broome have been preserved. Unconvincingly, Fenton is listed in the subscription list for the *Odyssey*; he also subscribed to the Shakespeare edition and to the poems of **Gay**.

See E. Harlan, *Elijah Fenton 1683–1730* (Philadelphia: University of Pennsylvania Press, 1937).

Fermor, Arabella (c. 1689–1738). The origin of **Belinda** in *The Rape of the Lock*, known as "Belle Fermor." She came from one of the most firmly established Catholic families in southern England. The name would be pronounced, and could be spelled, "Farmer." They acquired Somerton, Oxfordshire, on the banks of the Cherwell in the early seventeenth century, then moved to nearby Tusmore a generation later. In 1693 she was taken by her maternal grandmother Lady Browne (aunt of **Sir George Browne**, the basis of "**Sir Plume**" in the poem) to reside at the English Convent in Paris, where she stayed until 1704. Her father, Henry Fermor, had died in the previous year.

Arabella became one of the reigning toasts of London in her late teens. She figures in several poetic tributes published around this time. For example, she is numbered among "The Celebrated Beauties" in the *Miscellanies* of **Jacob Tonson senior** in 1709, the same volume in which AP made his debut as a poet. Arabella is described as modest and sweet, in addition to her other charms: "Fair without Art, and graceful without Pride." This is not quite the way she appears in AP's satire.

It was in 1711, most likely at Ingatestone Hall in Essex, that the notorious "rape" of a lock of her hair by the **seventh Baron Petre** took place. AP dedicated the expanded form of his poem to Arabella and also referred to her as Belinda in some shorter poems. Some time in 1714 she was married to a member of another old recusant family, Francis Perkins (1683–1736) of Ufton, **Berkshire**: AP wrote to **Martha Blount** around the end of November that he had only just heard of "Mrs Fermor's being Actually, directly, and consummatively, married" (*Corr* 1: 269). He also referred mysteriously to a guilty secret of the couple, shared by "their Accessories at Whiteknights," that is, the bride's relatives, the **Englefield family** who lived at Whiteknights. AP afterward printed a letter of compliment to Arabella on the occasion, but this may be a later invention. Her marriage portion was £4,500.

There is no evidence that Arabella and the poet enjoyed any later contacts, although she lived within easy range of his usual haunts, southwest of Reading. She had six children, a daughter, also Arabella (d. 1723), and five sons, who squandered away much of the family fortune. Following the death of the youngest son John in 1769, the Ufton estate passed to distant relatives and fell into ruin. Arabella herself maintained an unobtrusive way of life after her brief moment of fame. When her husband died, one of the trustees of his estate was Sir Henry Englefield of Whiteknights, showing how durably she was connected with the Berkshire gentry so well known to AP.

At some stage, perhaps even prior to her marriage, Arabella had her portrait painted, probably by W. Sikes, a little known artist; a version survives in the Bodleian Library, Oxford. The sitter is shown in a blue dress, wearing a cross round her neck, and the picture seems to allude to her status as Belinda in the poem. For a reproduction, see *TE* 2 (frontispiece).

For basic facts, see *TE* 2: 371–75.

Fielding, Henry (1707–54). Novelist and playwright. Although there were few firsthand contacts between the two men, Fielding's career at its outset overlapped with the end of AP's. They were both involved in the **opposition to Walpole** in the 1730s, and Fielding's targets were often identical with those of the older writer. He took over many of the forms and devices of **Augustan satire** and wrote in the guise of "Scriblerus Secundus." His portrayal of contemporary society in his plays owes much to AP, and his attack on **Grub Street** features some of the same cast of characters as

The Dunciad, including **Edmund Curll** and **Colley Cibber**. When Fielding emerged as a novelist, his procedures still mimicked many of the satirists' tricks. Finally, it was Fielding who succeeded AP in the favor of the notable patron **Ralph Allen**. Another of the novelist's leading patrons was the dedicatee of *Tom Jones*, **George Lyttelton**, himself a disciple of AP.

See M.C. Battestin with R.R. Battestin, *Henry Fielding: A Life* (London: Routledge, 1989).

finances. It is not possible to give an accurate statement of AP's finances, as no detailed accounts or bank records are known to survive. His father **Alexander Pope senior** had over 8,000 livres in French annuities: the exchange rate fluctuated, but this was worth something like £400 at a rate of three shillings to the écu. The modern purchasing power of this sum would be on the order of £30,000 or close to $50,000. The value of these annuities tended to drop after they were bought in the first decade of the eighteenth century. In 1710 AP's father lent **John Caryll senior** £200 at 5.5 percent; this loan was not repaid until 1727. It is thought that the poet received about £3,000 to £4,000 at his father's death in 1717. Subsequently he bought further annuities. When AP himself died in 1744, his estate is believed to have been worth up to £5,000 to £6,000. In his **will** he left £1,000 to **Martha Blount**, as well as legacies to the **Rackett family**, **John Serle**, and others, which came to about £1,280, including the remission of payment on a bond owing for £500. Martha also received income from the residue of his estate, which she calculated at no more than £2,000 (*Anecdotes* 1: 158). This may have been an underestimate.

We know something of AP's literary earnings in the first part of his career. For example, he obtained from **Jacob Tonson senior** payments of ten guineas (£10.50) for the *Pastorals* and three guineas (£3.15) for *The Episode of Sarpedon*, his earliest published works. This works out at rather more than two pence per line. He got £7 for the two-canto *Rape of the Locke* and £15 for the longer version (the latter was a much better deal for the publisher **Ber-**

nard Lintot). For *Windsor-Forest* AP was able to command £32.5.0, which is a rate of about 1s. 6d. (7.5p) per line, an exceptionally high figure at this date. A slightly longer poem in 1715, *The Temple of Fame*, earned the same sum. In 1716 Lintot had to pay £15 for the rights to *An Essay on Criticism*, although this may not all have gone to AP.

As is well known, it was the translations of **Homer** that brought AP into a quite different financial bracket. Estimates of his returns vary somewhat, but it is likely that he reaped a profit of at least £5,000 from the *Iliad* (more on the quarto than the folio), as well as a similar amount for the *Odyssey*. Less remunerative was the **Shakespeare edition**, which was mounted for the benefit of Tonson and made AP only £217. AP's exertions made it possible for him to refuse a pension of £300, apparently offered by **James Craggs junior**.

For the later career, it is hard to be as certain. AP took over more and more of the role of his own publisher, and we have less idea of what his earnings were. Sales figures are not generally available; and when AP employed men like **Lawton Gilliver** to distribute his works, we cannot say what commission or fee was paid to them. The continuing demand for items such as the collected *Works* and the *Letters* would suggest a steady, if not always spectacular, volume of sales. Obviously the author would have done best out of the individual poems that went into many editions, with *An Essay on Man* a sure-fire hit here.

Fineman, Daniel Abuhove (1915–91). Scholar who taught at Tel Aviv University. His works include *Leonard Welsted: Gentleman Poet of the Augustan Age* (1950), as well as essays on AP.

First Epistle of the First Book of Horace Imitated, The. One of AP's *Imitations of Horace*, written toward the end of the series. It was first "printed for" **Robert Dodsley** and "sold by" **Thomas Cooper** on 7 March 1738; however, the title page bears the date 1737. It was a folio of twenty-two pages, printed by **John Wright** (Griffith 480; Foxon P877), price, one shilling.

As usual, the Latin text was printed on facing pages. A corrected reprint followed, as well as an edition by **George Faulkner** in Dublin. Small revisions were made in subsequent printings, when the poem entered the *Works* later in 1738.

The original work introduced the first book of **Horace**'s epistles and was addressed to his patron Maecenas. It consists of 108 lines: AP omitted three lines from the middle of the Latin text in presenting his version of 188 lines in heroic couplets. Perhaps the most striking passage in the English poem is to be found in the concluding section, where AP personalizes the Roman poet's depiction of his own incongruities and inconsistencies. The role of Maecenas is allotted to AP's longtime friend **Viscount Bolingbroke**, and indeed the poem neatly recalls the phrase AP had used of the same man in the *Essay on Man*: "Is this my Guide, Philosopher, and Friend?" (l. 177). The imitation stays almost literally close to the host poem most of the way, but it brings in a few allusions to contemporaries such as Sir John Barnard and **Sir Richard Blackmore**. A vivid character sketch of "Sir Job" perhaps refers to **Sir Gregory Page**.

For text and commentary, see *TE* 4: 275–93.

First Epistle of the Second Book of Horace Imitated, The. See *Epistle to Augustus*.

First Ode of the Fourth Book of Horace, The. The only complete version of an ode to be found among AP's *Imitations of Horace*. It is a rendering of a poem addressed to Venus, where **Horace** at the age of fifty asks to be spared further invasions of his heart by love. The forty lines of the original Latin are expressed in forty-eight English verses. Horace had used quite an intricate lyrical scheme, with quatrains made up of alternating lines of eight and twelve syllables. AP substitutes an English metrical pattern of an octosyllabic followed by a pentameter line, with the addition of rhyme: "I am not now, alas! / As in the gentle Reign of My Queen *Anne*" (ll. 3–4). He replaces the Roman poet's young orator, Paulus Maximus, with the rising British barrister **William Mur-**

ray, later Lord Chancellor Mansfield. In the concluding lines, which describe a new love stealing up on the poet, AP mutes the homosexual implications of the original text. The earliest newspaper version includes the name "Patty," that is, **Martha Blount**, as the object of the poet's affection here, but the name is suppressed in the authorized text.

The *Ode* was first published in a newspaper on 1 March 1727 and reprinted in the *London Magazine*. An authorized version was issued by **James Roberts** around 9 March under the title *Horace His Ode to Venus,. Lib.IV. Ode I, Imitated by Mr. Pope*. It was a folio of eight pages, and as usual the Latin text was printed on facing pages (Griffith 443; Foxon P896): price, sixpence. The printer was **John Wright**. There is also an octavo of twenty-four pages, which may be an Edinburgh piracy. A manuscript copy in AP's own hands survives, as does a transcript by **Joseph Spence**. AP included the item in his *Works* in 1738.

For text and commentary, see *TE* 4: 148–53.

First Satire of the Second Book of Horace Imitated, The.

The first of AP's *Imitations of Horace*. It was probably written in late January 1733. AP had been confined to his room for several days with a fever, when **Viscount Bolingbroke** came to visit him. As the poet later told **Joseph Spence**, Bolingbroke picked up a copy of **Horace** and happened to open it at this particular satire. He remarked that it would fit AP's present state if he were to imitate it in English. "After he was gone, I read it over, translated it in a morning or two, and sent it to the press in a week or fortnight after. And this was the occasion of my imitating some other of the Satires and Epistles afterwards" (*Anecdotes* 1: 143). A manuscript survives in the New York Public Library, written partly in AP's hand and partly in that of an amanuensis. For a reproduction and transcript, see *L&GA* 168–89.

The poem was first issued as a folio of twenty pages on 15 February (Griffith 288; Foxon P886). Later printings give a price of one shilling. The title page states that the work was printed by L.G. (**Lawton Gilliver**) and

sold by the mercuries **Anne Dodd** and Elizabeth Nutt and by the booksellers of London and Westminster. In fact, the copyright was entered to Gilliver in the Stationers' Register on 14 February. The full title admits AP's authorship in a roundabout way: *The First Satire of the Second Book of Horace, Imitated in a Dialogue between Alexander Pope of Twickenham in Com. Midd. Esq; on the one Part, and his Learned Council on the other*. This wording parodies the formula used in a legal suit, with the plaintiff's address couched in Latin ("in the county of Middlesex"). Latin and English texts were placed on facing pages. There were several reprints in 1733, with only slight variants. In the following year the poem was reprinted along with a new imitation, *The Second Satire of the Second Book of Horace*. Both items were incorporated in the *Works* in 1735.

Horace's satire consists of 86 lines; AP's version is almost twice as long, at 156 lines of heroic couplets. Perversely, AP starts with what had been the last written among the satires of Horace. It is perhaps the most brilliant of all his imitations, showing a new colloquial freedom and a technical virtuosity scarcely apparent on this scale since *The Rape of the Lock*. Even the rendering of the same poem by **Ben Jonson** (1616) seems a little rough-hewn by comparison. Horace sets up a consultation between himself and a noted lawyer, C. Trebatius Tesca. The discussion centers on libel and other aspects of free speech. This gives AP a wonderful opportunity to play games with courtroom jargon, to pun and to dance around the terminology of the law. His interlocutor is **William Fortescue**, a brilliant and daring choice since Fortescue (though a distinguished barrister who later became a judge, and a personal friend) was actually a part of the establishment. He was an MP who loyally supported **Walpole** and Attorney-General to **Frederick, Prince of Wales**. Since the poem makes bold references to the government and royal family, this was an extraordinary move on AP's part. Even though he is not openly named, Fortescue must have seen the potential for trouble when AP wrote to him on 18 February about the poem (*Corr* 3: 351). The most immediate response came from **Lady Mary Wortley Montagu** and **John, Baron Hervey**; the former had been savagely lampooned by AP, the latter only lightly touched on. Lady Mary seems to have been chiefly responsible for *Verses Address'd to the Imitator of the First Satire of the Second Book of Horace*, published on 9 March (Guerinot 224). Although this lacks the finesse of the original, it is quite as vituperative as AP's satire and ranks as one of the most effective of the **pamphlet attacks** on him. Fortescue seems to have feared that there would be repercussions if AP replied to these *Verses*, and AP wrote to him promising to desist (*Corr* 3: 354–55). AP could claim at least a minor victory in that he was now able to present himself as having been "libell'd" by Lady Mary's hate, in the way that the imitation had predicted. There were other responses to the satire, at least one apparently from the fluent pen of **Edmund Curll** (Guerinot 222). In the course of the poem AP pays off some old scores, reverts to the imbroglio concerning **Timon's villa**, and nudges the Horatian text for his own purposes. AP made a point of building up a section near the end (ll. 105–32), as he indicated to **Swift** when a copy was sent to Ireland on 16 February (*Corr* 3: 348). As usual, there are tributes to friends such as the **Earl of Peterborough** and Bolingbroke.

For the text and commentary, see *TE* 4: 1–21.

Fleet Ditch. A filthy waterway running north-south through London. "The history of the Fleet River has been described as a decline from a river from a brook, from a brook to a ditch, and from a ditch to a drain" (Nicholas Barton). In fact, the river rises on Hampstead Heath and flows about six miles to join the Thames near modern Blackfriars Bridge. It is joined by a number of tributaries, some carrying down offal from **Smithfield** meat market are mentioned in the poem by **Swift**, "A Description of a City Shower." Its course runs through the Camden Town, King's Cross, and Clerkenwell districts. In Roman times it formed a tidal inlet, up to 600 feet wide at its mouth, but by AP's day it was a narrow, dark, and stinking channel, lined with squalid industrial and domestic buildings.

Most of the river is now underground, in places twenty-five feet below street level. Following the Great Fire of London in 1666, an attempt had been made by **Christopher Wren** and Robert Hooke to arrest its decline by creating a canal from Holborn to the Thames, along the last half mile of its course. The work proved difficult to carry out, and the hopes of creating an elegant waterway for trade were never realized. Part of the canal was bricked over in 1733 and a market erected on the site. In 1766 the stretch from the Fleet Bridge to the Thames was also covered. The market was taken down in 1829, and a new roadway, Faringdon Street, was built in its place.

AP was not alone in using the ditch as an emblem of urban pollution—the Fleet had been used as a sewer and refuse disposal site for many centuries. However, *The Dunciad* is unique in the way it makes the cloacal metaphor central to the plot and language of a sustained narrative. (AP may have gotten some hints from the second edition of the poem *Trivia* by his friend **John Gay** [1720], which relates the myth of Cloacina.) In Book II, the dunces make their way from **Bridewell** to the venue for their mud-diving games, "To where Fleet-ditch with disemboguing streams / Rolls the large tribute of dead dogs to Thames, / The King of Dykes! Than whom, no sluice of mud / With deeper sable blots the silver flood" (*TE* 5: 133). The combatants in this event plunge into the murky waters, even finding "a branch of Styx" that joins the Thames at the same point. An illustration for this sequence, designed by Francis Hayman and engraved by Charles Grignion, shows the games going forward in the shadow of the Fleet Bridge, with a participant diving from "a stranded lighter" (one of the coal barges that periodically got stuck in the mud). After this, the dunces make their escape to the nearby **Fleet Prison**, where debtors were confined: "While others timely, to the neighbouring Fleet / (Haunt of the Muses) made their safe retreat" (*TE* 5: 149).

See N. Barton, *The Lost Rivers of London* (London: Phoenix House, 1962).

Fleet Prison. A London jail dating from the twelfth century. It stood on the east side of the **Fleet Ditch**, on what is now Faringdon Street, south of Fleet Lane. Holborn Viaduct station adjoins the site. Rebuilt after it was destroyed in the Peasants' Revolt of 1381, again after the Great Fire in 1666, and once more after the Gordon Riots of 1780, it was finally demolished in 1846. In later times it was mainly used as a debtors' prison. Here many "Fleet marriages" were conducted, that is, clandestine and irregular ceremonies performed at the prison by clergymen confined for debt. The prison figures in *The Rake's Progress* by **William Hogarth** and also in *The Pickwick Papers* by Charles Dickens.

In *The Dunciad* AP consigns his victims to this apt location for penurious writers: "While others timely, to the neighbouring Fleet / (Haunt of the Muses) made their safe retreat" (2: 395–96). Elsewhere, in the *Epilogue to the Satires* AP refers to the warden of the prison, John Huggins (1655–1745), who had been accused of extortion and cruelty in his office. AP's note states that Huggins had "enriched himself by many exactions, for which he was tried and expelled" (*TE* 4: 298).

J. Ashton, *The Fleet: Its River, Prison, and Marriages* (London: Unwin, 1888), retains considerable interest.

Fleet Street. The main east-west route from the city of London to Westminster, running from Ludgate to the **Strand**. In AP's day it was not yet associated with the newspaper industry. However, many booksellers congregated in the area. At various times these included **Jacob Tonson senior**, **Bernard Lintot**, **Edmund Curll**, and **Lawton Gilliver**. AP is supposed to have administered his emetic to Curll at the Swan Tavern in Fleet Street, but this has not been confirmed. The premises of AP's banker **John Mead**, like those of the booksellers, was situated near the western end leading to Temple Bar. On the south side of the street lay two inns of court, the Inner Temple and Middle Temple.

The coach for **Twickenham** left the White Horse Inn in Fleet Street every day at 2 P.M. (*Corr* 4: 506). This inn stood on the north side of the street, about halfway along.

In *The Dunciad*, the dunces proceed down Fleet Street toward **Bridewell** and the **Fleet Ditch**. AP supplies a note that they move from the Strand "along *Fleetstreet* (places inhabited by Booksellers)" (*TE* 5: 133). In the later version of this poem, AP mentions the fact that the New Year odes of Poet Laureate **Colley Cibber** were generally rehearsed at the Devil Tavern in Fleet Street (*TE* 5: 294). This was a historic inn near Temple Bar where **Ben Jonson** had famously caroused; see also *TE* 6: 402. In his correspondence AP refers to "the garrets" of Fleet Street (*Corr* 2: 508).

Ford, Charles (1682–1741). Irishman educated at Eton and Trinity College, Dublin. Inherited the estate of Woodpark, County Meath, but spent most of his life in England. From the time of their meeting around 1707, he was one of the closest friends of **Jonathan Swift**; about seventy letters survive between the two men. A poem "To Charles Ford, Esq. on his Birthday" (1723) contains some of Swift's most biting satire on the Hanoverian regime. Thanks to the influence of Swift, Ford was appointed official government Gazetteer in 1712. Formerly a man of pleasure, he became a trusted agent in literary matters, especially in connection with the publication of *Gulliver's Travels*.

Ford was on good terms with AP by 1714, as he was with other members of the **Scriblerus Club**. He subscribed to the *Iliad* and the *Odyssey*, as well as the poems of **Gay** and **Prior**. He appears as "joyous *Ford*" in *Mr. Pope's Welcome from Greece*. Ford's lodging was in Pall Mall, and AP seems often to have visited him. The two were in contact as late as 1738 (*Corr* 4: 137). Nine letters between them are known to survive.

See *The Letters of Jonathan Swift to Charles Ford*, ed. D.N. Smith (Oxford: Clarendon, 1935).

foreign influence of Pope. For a century and more, AP was among the most widely read modern poets around the Western world. In all enlightened countries, *An Essay on Man* exercised considerable influence, although rather more as a work of moral philosophy than as a literary text. This was more obviously true in German-speaking countries. In France and Spain wider range of texts were known, while in Italy both *The Rape of the Lock* and *Eloisa to Abelard* enjoyed great popularity (see **Italian literature**). Translations were made into almost all the major European languages of at least some part of AP's work. Scholars have traced AP's reputation in Poland and Iceland. AP was of course very well known in colonial America (see also **Mather Byles**). There were many editions, of *An Essay on Man* especially, published in Boston, New York, and Philadelphia.

Fortescue, William (1687–1749). Lawyer. He came from a Devon family that numbered distinguished jurists in its history, and he was a schoolmate at Barnstaple of **John Gay**, whose elder sister Joanna married his brother. Barrister at the Inner Temple, 1715. Private secretary to **Robert Walpole**, to whom he introduced AP. Later MP, 1727–36, and Attorney-General to **Frederick, Prince of Wales**, 1730–36. His legal career saw him advanced from Baron of the Exchequer (a judge) in 1736 to Justice of the Common Pleas, 1738, and Master of the Rolls, a senior judge in the Court of Chancery, in 1741. Throughout this he remained a friend of AP and of Gay, despite his involvement with the court. Fortescue also retained his Devon links: he had estates at Buckland Filleigh, near Hatherleigh, held by his family since the fifteenth century, and Fallapit, near Totnes, an ancient mansion inherited through his wife Mary from his ancestor Sir Henry Fortescue. He had a house in the Vineyard, **Richmond**, which AP often visited. In addition, AP took an interest in the fortunes of Fortescue's only daughter Mary (d. 1752), who married a barrister, John Spooner, in 1736.

Over a hundred letters between AP and Fortescue survive. The earliest dates from 1720, but their friendship certainly dated back before that, to 1715 at the latest. Fortescue drew up the contract with **Lintot** for the *Odyssey* in 1723. The lawyer often gave AP professional advice, and this is cleverly utilized in the first of the poet's versions of **Horace**, that is, *The First Satire of the Second Book*, where Fortescue is made to argue for discretion and against satiric freedom. It is thought that Fortescue contributed legal material to the prose work *Stradling versus Styles*. In addition, he assisted **Martha Blount** in her financial dealings. Subscribed to the *Iliad, Odyssey*, and **Shakespeare edition**, as well as the poems of Gay. Among those described as greeting the poet in *Mr. Pope's Welcome from Greece*. Fortescue composed a warm commendation of AP in the form of a dream vision written for Gay (*Life* 185–86).

Fourth Satire of Dr. John Donne. In full, *The Fourth Satire of Dr. John Donne, Dean of St. Paul's, Versifyed*. Poem by AP, the first published of his two imitations of **John Donne**. Conceivably an early version dates from the time of the **Harley administration** (*TE* 4: 3), but if so, no trace of this remains.

The poem appeared on 5 November 1733 under the title of *The Impertinent, or A Visit to the Court* and ascribed only to "an Eminent Hand." This was a quarto of sixteen pages (Griffith 317; Foxon P898). The publisher was listed as "J. Wileord," which may be a deliberate misspelling of the name of John Wilford. In 1737 there were reprints, doubtless unauthorized, under this title. Meanwhile AP had admitted authorship by including the item in the *Works* in 1735, when he adopted the more neutral title given above and added a parallel text of Donne's satire. A number of small revisions were made to the text in this edition and in subsequent editions of the *Works*. As revised, the poem consists of 287 lines in heroic couplets, as against 244 lines of Donne's much more roughly constructed couplets. The poem bears an epigraph from **Horace**, emphasizing the complicated intertextual dealings of three writers. In fact, Donne's own work derived from one of Horace's most famous compositions, that is, the satire (Book 1, no. 9) describing a meeting with an importunate stranger. AP sticks quite closely to Donne, seeking to "refine" and Augustanize the verbal texture. For example, the vivid passage that deals with the entrance of the court ladies has a direct basis in the earlier poem (compare Donne, ll. 187–91, with AP, ll. 226–35); note, however, AP's more liberal use of dramatized dialogue. There are not quite so many topical references as in most of the imitations, although some of the poet's enemies—such as **John Woodward**—and several of the dunces—such as **Henley, Budgell**, and **Oldmixon**—receive a quick flick of scornful allusion, while **John, Baron Hervey** appears as "Fannius."

For text and commentary, see *TE* 4:23–49.

Foxon, David (Fairweather) (1923–2001). A leading bibliographical scholar who taught at the University of **Oxford**. Fellow of the British Academy from 1978. His major achievement was a monumental catalog of *English Verse, 1701–1750*, 2 vols. (1975), invaluable to those studying the history of publications in this era. More directly related to AP, and even more useful to specialists, is his magisterial survey of *Pope and the Early Eighteenth-Century Book Trade*, ed. J. McLaverty (1991).

Foxton, Thomas (1697–1769). Poet. Hardly anything is known about him except that he worked for **Edmund Curll**, sometimes as a translator. "Even among literary fleas he must be reckoned a small flea" (*TE* 5: 440). The only work with any later currency was *Moral Songs Composed for the Use of Children* (1728). He cannot have done very much to disoblige AP, but he was famous for about fifteen seconds when included in Book 3 of *The Dunciad Variorum*: "Lo Bond and Foxton, ev'ry nameless name" (*TE* 5: 164). A note explained: "Two inoffensive offenders against our poet; persons unknown, but by being mention'd by Mr. Curl." His hold on the interest of posterity was so feeble that he disappeared even as a name in the revised poem.

Frederick, Prince of Wales (1707–51). Son and heir of **George II** who never came to the throne owing to his early death. Immortalized as "Poor Fred, who was alive and is dead." He was long a thorn in the flesh of his father and served as a rallying point for more than one dissident group, starting with the **opposition to Walpole** from c. 1733. Problems came to a head in the summer of 1737 when the King and the Prince quarreled over the birth of a daughter. Some opposition rhetoric—by **George Lyttelton, Sir William Wyndham**, and **Viscount Bolingbroke**, as well as AP—urged the Prince to adopt the course of "virtue," that is, assist in getting rid of Walpole from the government. A patron of **James Thomson**, who dedicated the first part of his high-minded poem *Liberty* to the Prince in 1735. It was by command of the Prince and Princess that the first performance of the masque by Thomson and **David Mallet**, *Alfred*, took place in 1740. This featured the stirring lines of "Rule Britannia." The revised edition of Thomson's major work *The Seasons* (1744) was also dedicated to Frederick.

The Prince visited AP at **Twickenham** on 4 October 1735, a symbolic action noted in the press. Not long afterward AP presented his Royal Highness with a puppy from the litter of his dog Bounce. This ultimately produced the famous *Epigram on the Collar of a Dog*. In 1738 the Prince stayed at **Cirencester**, the home of **Lord Bathurst**, where Wyndham tried to enlist him in the cause of AP. The poet had previously dined with the Prince at Kew (see **Richmond**). In 1739 Frederick presented AP with some urns for his garden and busts of four great English poets. The busts, probably by **Scheemakers**, were bequeathed by AP to Lyttelton. There are several references to the Prince in the *Imitations of Horace*, mostly veiled. It is hard to assess the exact nature of AP's views on the Prince, but it seems clear that he could have exerted some influence if he had chosen.

No satisfactory biography of the Prince exists. For links with AP, see C. Gerrard, *The Patriot Opposition to Walpole* (Oxford: Clarendon, 1994).

freemasonry. AP was admitted to a lodge that met in the Haymarket, London, by 1730. His friend **John Arbuthnot** had joined another lodge a few years earlier. Others who became members in the first main burst of Masonic activity were the **Earl of Chesterfield**, **Frederick, Prince of Wales**, **William Hogarth**, **Richard Savage**, **James Thomson**, and the **Duke of Wharton**. It is possible that another initiate was the **Earl of Burlington**, whose architectural principles are thought by some to employ Masonic symbolism. At this date, freemasonry was particularly strong among Catholics and also **Jacobites**. The first Grand Lodge was formed in London in 1717, while the founding *Constitutions* were adopted in 1723. AP has a somewhat suspicious reference to the taciturnity of Masons in the later version of *The Dunciad* (4: 571–72). In 1738 Pope Clement XII had issued a bull *In eminenti apostolatus specula*, forbidding the faithful from joining the Masonic order, on pain of excommunication.

French influences. AP read widely in French sources, but few volumes survive from his **library** to document this fact. He had studied critics like Dominique Bouhours, René Le Bossu, and René Rapin. He was familiar with Bernard de Fontenelle on pastoral, and **Anne Dacier** on epic. The most important single influence was probably that of **Nicolas Boileau**, whose works were preserved in his library. Among older writers AP seems to have owed most to moralists such as Pierre Charron and, especially, Michel de Montaigne. Among religious writers he would have known Pascal and Fénelon, whose *Télémaque* (1699) was familiar to almost all readers at this time and served as the basis of *The Travels of Cyrus* (1727) by AP's acquaintance the Chevalier Ramsay.

Elsewhere, we can be sure that AP had a good knowledge of the tragedies of Pierre Corneille and Jean Racine, as well as the comedies of Molière. The character sketches in AP's poems, especially the *Essay on Man* and the *Moral Essays*, are drawn in some particulars from the *Caractères* (1688) of Jean de La Bruyère. His principal models in letter-writing included Balzac and Voiture (see **correspondence**). There are only a few references to François Rabelais, whose work made a more obvious im-

pression on the writing of **Swift**. Late in life AP exchanged letters with **Louis Racine** in the quest to defend *An Essay on Man* from charges of religious heterodoxy; he wrote in English.

See E. Audra, *L'influence française dans l'oeuvre de Pope* (Paris: Champion, 1931). Audra also compiled *Les traductions françaises de Pope (1717–1825): Étude de bibliographie* (Paris: Champion, 1931).

Frost, William (1917–88). Professor at the University of California, Santa Barbara. Best known as a student of **John Dryden**, he also wrote on AP. See, for example, a valuable article, "*The Rape of the Lock* and Pope's Homer," *Modern Language Quarterly*, 8 (1947), 342–54, reprinted in *EA* 266–83. One of the editors of the volumes devoted to AP's translation of **Homer** in the **Twickenham edition**.

Full and True Account, A. The first of three prose pamphlets by AP directed against the publisher **Edmund Curll**. The full title reads: *A Full and True Account of a Horrid and Barbarous Revenge by Poison, On the Body of Mr. Edmund Curll, Bookseller; with a Faithful Copy of his Last Will and Testament. Published by an Eye Witness.* It was published around 31 March 1716 as a folio of six pages, price, threepence (Griffith 52). Perhaps the item was reserved for an April Fool's joke on 1 April. The publishers are listed as **James Roberts**, John Morphew, Rebecca Burleigh, John Baker, and Sarah Popping. They were distributors who had often been named on the title page of works attacking AP, but they played no active role in the campaign against the poet. In fact, the entire piece simulates the productions of Curll, down to the inclusion of a comic "will" in the text of the pamphlet.

The events underlying this work began with the publication by Curll of an unauthorized volume of *Court Poems* (see **Court Eclogues**). According to the *Full and True Account*, this took place on 26 March. Supposedly on 28 March AP gained his revenge by inducing the publisher to take an emetic. If we can trust a later statement by Curll, the purging dose actually was administered in a glass of wine (see *Early*

Career 171). The narrative describes how Curll was tricked into meeting AP at the shop of **Bernard Lintot**, where they drank a glass of sack, and was then struck with acute stomach pains on returning home. He gathered together his associates, including Lintot, the bookseller John Pemberton, and the author **John Oldmixon**, who was suspected of taking a leading share in the appearance of the *Court Poems*. Curll makes a deathbed confession of his sins in the book trade and prepares for his end, only to be relieved suddenly by "a plentiful foetid Stool." It is one of AP's most inventive works in prose, gleefully displaying a close knowledge of the ins and outs of Curll's publishing career. A sequel came out later in the same year: See *A Further Account*. From 1732 the item was reprinted in the *Miscellanies*.

For the text and background, see *Prose* 1: xciv–xcviii, 257–72. No full annotated edition exists. Individuals and events in this pamphlet and *A Further Account* are identified in *The Oxford Authors: Alexander Pope*, ed. P. Rogers (Oxford: Oxford University Press, 1993), 615–19.

Further Account, A. The second of three pamphlets in prose by AP in which he attacked the rascally publisher **Curll**. The full title is *A Further Account of the most Deplorable Condition of Mr. Edmund Curll, Bookseller. Since his being found Poison'd on the 28th of March*. The title page adds, "to be publish'd weekly," a formula of **Grub Street** journalism. The imprint reads "London: Printed, and Sold by all the Publishers, Mercuries, and Hawkers, within the Bills of Mortality. 1716," the kind of phraseology associated with clandestine publications. It was an octavo of twenty-two pages (Griffith 56), price, sixpence. The exact date is uncertain. *Prose* 1: cvi suggests late November or early December 1716, but on balance August or September may be more likely. The item was reprinted in the *Miscellanies* from 1732.

The pamphlet forms a sequel to *A Full and True Account*, published earlier in the year. By now AP had further crimes to lay at Curll's door. The anonymous narrator distinguishes himself from the author of the former relation, drawing a line between "an undignify'd Scribler of a Sheet and half, and the Author of a Three-Penny stitcht Book, like my self." He describes Curll's frenzied behavior after he had taken the emetic and a summons that he issued to all his hack authors to come to his house. The assembled group plot measures to retaliate against AP, including abusive ballads and organized defamation of the poet in coffeehouses. The authors are about to leave, but the delirious Curll suddenly breaks out in a tirade against his books: "Are you not the beggarly Brood of fumbling *Journey-men*; born in *Garrets*, among *Lice* and *Cobwebs* . . ." The most exuberant of all AP's prose satires, it shows not for the only time an astonishingly intimate knowledge of what was going on in Grub Street.

For background and text, see *Prose* 1: xcviii–cvi, 273–85. There is no annotated edition.

G

garden, Pope's. AP's famous garden lay across the road (later known as Cross Deep) from his house. It occupied eight parallel strips of the old manorial field, stretching about 850 feet deep from the road to the line of what is now called Radnor Road. Its width was of the order of 260 feet. It incorporated three parcels of land, in different ownership but all leased or subleased to AP by **Thomas Vernon**, who had acquired the land only a year before AP took up residence in 1719 and began to rent the property by stages. A small parcel of land in the northeast corner belonged to the Heath Lane Lodge estate, belonging to Lady Ferrers (see **Lady Frances Shirley**). The southernmost strip of the garden was sold by Vernon's widow in 1729 to Bryan Hill. In all, the garden measured about five acres, which is exactly what AP claimed in one of his poems: See *The Second Satire of the Second Book of Horace*, l. 136 (*TE* 4: 65). The ground covered by the garden is essentially the area bounded today by Cross Deep to the east, Grotto Road to the north, Radnor Road to the south, and Popes Grove to the south.

On the other side of the road, beyond the house, there was a lawn stretching down to the river. It was linked to the main garden by a subterranean passageway, containing the **grotto**. This lawn measured perhaps 120 feet in length by 100 feet in width. AP did not devote the same attention to this part of his property as he did to the garden proper, although late in life he added two arched pavilions made of stone on the river bank. In 1743 he also planned an elaborate sculptural ornament, with two river gods, to be placed at the water's edge (*Anecdotes* 1: 257). It is not clear how much, if any, of this ornament was constructed before AP died in the following year.

It was the main garden that absorbed the poet's main energies for more than twenty years. He liked to joke about its Lilliputian dimensions but devoted an immense amount of time and effort to its improvement. As **Horace Walpole** observed, AP had somehow "twisted and twirled and rhymed and harmonized" the small patch of land, until lawns, groves, woods, and vistas appeared as on some grand country house estate. There was even a "Grand Walk" down the center and a vineyard on one side. AP divided the space into discrete parts: the grotto, three mounts, quincunxes (an arrangement like that of the spots on a five in dice), a wilderness (or a *relatively* informal and irregular portion of the garden), a bowling green, and a shell temple. These props could all be viewed as "symbols of aids to concentration" (Peter Martin). Near the villa stood stoves (hothouses), an orangery, a kitchen garden, and a garden house. The focus of the plan was found at the far end of the axis leading through the grotto and tunnel toward the river. This took the form of an obelisk erected in 1735 by AP to the memory of his mother, **Edith Pope**. It stood on a mound at the western end of the garden, sheltered by cypress trees. The tapering stone column, which may have been designed by **William Kent**, survives at Penn House, Buckinghamshire. Altogether, the garden was as an elaborate composition as any of AP's poems, and it drew on many of the same motifs to achieve its effect—literary and pictorial recollections, echoic effects, standard emblems, and coded personal references. There are many references in the poems, some in a vein of comic self-belittlement, as when he writes of his "five acres . . . of rented land" in *The Second Satire of the Second Book of Horace*: "Content with little I can piddle here, / On Broccoli and mutton, round the year" (*TE* 4: 65). In *The First Satire of the Second Book of Horace Imitated*, AP implausibly pictures his friend **Viscount Bolingbroke** as the one who "Now, forms my Quincunx, and now ranks my Vines" (*TE* 4: 17).

The garden has been much studied. Its physical layout has been most accurately plotted by A.B. Willson, *Mr Pope & Others* (Twickenham: For the author, 1996), 58–68. For a contemporary description by **John Serle**, AP's gardener, see *A Plan of Mr. Pope's Garden (1745)*, ed. M.R. Brownell (Los Angeles: Augustan Reprint Society, 1982). For the personal and emblematic meaning of the garden, see *Garden and City*, chapters 1–3. A useful survey will be found in *Gardening World* 39–61.

gardening. AP's interest in gardening was quite slow to develop, yet he became an amateur gardener of distinction. His own home at **Twickenham** provided him with a small canvas on which to work, but his design there was innovative and influential. Even more important was his activity as a consultant to friends in planning their own substantial estates.

AP's father had been a keen gardener at **Whitehill House**, although he had less than fifteen acres in his possession. The first concrete evidence that AP inherited this interest comes with his famous essay in *The Guardian* in 1713, which shows that he had absorbed many of his ideas from the description of the garden of Alcinous in Book 7 of the *Odyssey*. The stress laid in this essay on simplicity and nature gave an impetus to a burgeoning movement in English horticulture, which was reacting against the dominant formal styles modeled on Dutch and French gardens of the seventeenth century. AP's ideas of picturesque beauty were set out in the same year in the poem *Windsor-Forest*. As his friendship with **Martha Blount** grew, he began to give her accounts of romantic landscapes he encountered in his travels. He already

knew some impressive park scenery in his native county, and he sometimes met Martha at **Whiteknights**, a large estate belonging to her relatives, the Englefields. He would also have seen the work carried out at **Ladyholt** in Sussex by his friend **John Caryll senior**. However, it was when he had the opportunity to live on terms of intimacy with grandees such as **Lord Bathurst** and the **Earl of Burlington** that he came fully into contact with the theory and practice of "modern" landscape gardening.

From 1720 AP began to improve the small estate he had leased at Twickenham. The area was already celebrated as the scene of some of the most delicious garden in England: the poet's neighbor **James Johnston** owned a famous showplace a little way down the riverside. For the remainder of his life AP was busy building and remodeling his garden, drawing repeated plans and adding a variety of ornamental features. As well as his celebrated **grotto**, AP devised a series of groves, mounts, and lawns, cut across by walkways, which ultimately focused on an obelisk in memory of his mother situated at the top end. For details, see **garden**. The entire space set forth an elaborate coded message celebrating retirement, political and private independence, and the poetic vocation. This horticultural ideology is set forth in *Garden and City*, chapters 1–3.

Over the same period AP got to know many larger gardens, and in the case of his friends he was often invited to advise on the layout of their estates. Among the best-known examples are **Chiswick House** (probably the first in the sequence); **Cirencester**; **Riskins**; **Sherborne**; **Marble Hill**; **Dawley**; **Parson's Green**; **Bevis Mount**; **Prior Park**; **Rousham**; **Wimpole**; **Hagley**; and **Stowe**. In most instances a professional landscape designer was also employed, such as **Charles Bridgeman, Henry Wise**, or **William Kent**, but even here AP often seems to have exerted a decisive influence on at least some aspects of the design. Another large estate with which he had some familiarity was **Blenheim Palace**, but his response was negative. Indeed, Blenheim may be one of the models for the vulgar mansion described as **Ti-**

mon's villa. Other candidates are **Cannons** and the seat of **Robert Walpole**, Houghton. The satire on Timon comes in AP's most sustained discourse in verse on gardening theory and practice, the *Epistle to Burlington*. It was here that he set out most succinctly his ideas on the rule of taste in gardening, much of it constructed around the notion of the "Genius of the Place" (l. 57), that is, the physical character of the situation and the kind of horticultural features that will promote a sense of appropriate scale and mood. As early as 1712, in *Sapho to Phaon*, AP had anglicized the Latin phrase *genius loci* as "the Sylvan *Genius* of the Place" (*TE* 1: 401). References to gardening are found in AP's poems and letters from almost every period.

In his later years AP was in regular contact with **Joseph Spence**, who shared his interests in this area of life. Spence set down some of AP's views on the subject of gardens. Many have become classic statements of the ideology of landscape gardening in England during the eighteenth century (see *Anecdotes* 1: 249–57).

For AP's own activities, see *Gardening World* and *P&AGE*, chapters 3–9. For a general survey, see J.D. Hunt, *The Figure in the Landscape: Poetry, Painting, and Gardening during the Eighteenth Century* (Baltimore: Johns Hopkins University Press, 1976); and an anthology, *The Genius of the Place: The English Landscape Garden 1620–1820*, ed. J.D. Hunt and P. Willis (London: Elek, 1975; reprint, Cambridge, MA: MIT Press, 1988).

Garth, Sir Samuel (1661–1719). Physician and poet. M.D., 1691; FRS, 1706. Appointed Physician to **George I** and knighted, 1715. A member of the circle of **Dryden** at **Will's** coffeehouse. He came to literary prominence with his **mock-heroic** poem on a medical dispute, *The Dispensary* (1699), a major influence on *The Rape of the Lock*. A copy of this poem was in AP's **library**. Garth, "one of the best-natured men in the world," admired the *Rape* (*Anecdotes* 1: 44). Supported AP's early work on the *Pastorals*: "well-natur'd *Garth* inflam'd with early praise" (*Epistle to Arbuthnot*, l. 137). A Whig and member of the **Kit-Cat Club**, he

was excepted by AP from the run of the membership as "one of the real good men" in the club (*Anecdotes* 1: 50). A subscriber to the *Iliad*.

In 1717 AP contributed to the translation of the *Metamorphoses*, which Garth edited for **Jacob Tonson senior**, while Garth is represented in *Poems on Several Occasions*, published the same year, and probably edited by AP. Notoriously irreligious, Garth is said by AP to have undergone something of a deathbed conversion, but there is no other evidence for this. Some of the doctor's conflicting qualities are indicated in AP's lines: "*Garth*, the best good Christian he, / Altho' he knows it not" (*A Farewell to London*, ll. 15–16). In his private **Memorial List** of obituaries, AP described Garth as "an upright man and an elegant poet" (*EC* 1: x). A **portrait**, possibly a copy of one by **Kneller**, was in AP's house at his death. There is a modern study, J.F. Sena, *The Best-Natured Man: Samuel Garth, Physician and Poet* (New York: AMS, 1986).

Gay, John (1685–1732). Poet and dramatist. Born at Barnstaple, Devon, in modest circumstances, losing both parents at an early age, and educated in the town. At the age of eighteen, he went up to London and spent about three years as apprentice to a silk mercer, John Willet, in the **Strand**; but he was released from his articles and returned home for some months. Encouraged by **Aaron Hill**, he brought out an amusing mock-Miltonic poem, *Wine* (1708), written in the manner of **John Philips**. This indicates Whiggish sympathies, at least enough of them to flatter the current ministry. His essay *The Present State of Wit* (1711) shows less clear-cut political allegiance. In 1712 he became secretary to the Duchess of Monmouth, widow of the executed Protestant rebel. By now he was leagued with the other members of the **Scriblerus Club** and aided by the friendship of AP. *Rural Sports*, subtitled *A Georgic, Inscribed to Mr. Pope*, when it was published in January 1713, has some interesting parallels with *Windsor-Forest*, which came out at almost exactly the same moment. He published another **mock-heroic**, titled *The Fan*, in late 1713.

Equally, this shows obvious influence from the first version of *The Rape of the Locke*, which had come out together with some of Gay's early work in *Miscellaneous Poems and Translations* in the previous year.

Gay was taking sides more obviously at this juncture, as is evident from his dedication of *The Shepherd's Week* to **Viscount Bolingbroke** in April 1714. He had aligned himself with the Tory wits in their battle against **Addison, Ambrose Philips**, and the other habitués of **Button's** coffeehouse. His reward was an appointment in the suite of a mission to the court of Hanover in the following June. Sadly for Gay, the death of **Queen Anne** occurred too soon afterward for him to make any capital out of the post, although he made what could have been a valuable contact in the person of Caroline, the wife of the Electoral Prince, who was not long afterward to come to England as Princess of Wales. He came back to England, probably with the Prince and Princess, in September, with few prospects under the new regime, and turned to the stage. His first play, *The Mohocks*, had not achieved a performance in 1712, and his second, *The Wife of Bath*, had flopped in 1713, totally eclipsed by the hit of the season, *Cato*. More attention, by no means all of it favorable, was claimed by the farces *The What d'ye Call It* (1715) and *Three Hours after Marriage* (written in collaboration, 1717), by-products of his Scriblerian activity. However, his greatest success came with an ingenious adaptation of **georgic** to urban living, the poem *Trivia*, in 1716. Together with **Lady Mary Wortley Montagu**, he helped to develop another hybrid genre, the urban pastoral.

Gay's contacts now include the **Earl of Burlington**, whose patronage he celebrates in a witty *Epistle* written in 1716. He had doubtless met **George Frideric Handel** in the Earl's company, and he helped prepare the libretto for *Acis and Galatea* in 1718. He made a trip to the Continent with **William Pulteney** in 1717, and two years later went to Spa and Paris; but he was still far from finding a settled position in society. At first he appeared to have turned the corner with a major edition of his collected poems in 1720, jointly published by **Bernard Lintot** and **Jacob Tonson senior** (each held some of the rights). He is said to have earned several thousand pounds from the subscriptions, which had reached a total of 364 individuals, some for multiple copies—Burlington himself and the **Duke of Chandos** for no less than fifty. Unfortunately, he received his money just in time to invest and lose it in the **South Sea Bubble**. A full-length pastoral tragedy, *Dione*, failed to reach the stage in 1720, while another tragedy, *The Captives*, ran for seven nights at **Drury Lane Theatre** in 1724, netting the author a respectable profit. He continued to pass time with the Earl at **Burlington House** and **Chiswick House** but seemed to be drifting in his career.

Two works rescued him from this malaise. The first was the appearance of the first set of *Fables* in 1727. Gay had perhaps been stimulated by the visit of his old friend **Swift** to England in 1726 and had embarked on a series of beast-tales, lightly told but full of broad satire and unmissable political thrusts. A year later came *The Beggar's Opera*, which gave Gay a lasting place in the history of drama. His later attempts to follow up on these works with a second set of *Fables* (1738) and ballad operas like *Polly* (1729) did not achieve as much success—indeed, *Polly* fell foul of the government censors and caused Gay's patron the **Duchess of Queensberry** to be expelled from court. Gay's career ended with the unduly neglected political farce *The Rehearsal at Goatham* (written c.1731), a Cervantic episode with just a hint of *The Government Inspector* in it; and *Achilles*, another ballad opera that was a failure when posthumously produced in 1733. Gay died after a short illness, much regretted by his surviving colleagues, AP, **Dr. John Arbuthnot**, and Swift, and was buried in Westminster Abbey. A monument by **Michael Rysbrack** was erected with a verse inscription by AP (see *TE* 6: 349–52).

Soon after AP met Gay around 1711, the two men became firm friends, as they remained until Gay died. They were active in the Scriblerus Club and collaborated in stage plays and satiric squibs. They exchanged entertaining letters, of which about forty survive; Gay also conducted an extensive correspondence with Swift. They naturally subscribed to each other's works. Their network of friends included a large number of men and women equally attached to the pair of them, including **Henrietta Howard, Countess of Suffolk**; **Martha Blount**; Lord Burlington; **Charles Jervas**; Bolingbroke; and Pulteney. It was almost certainly Gay who introduced AP to **William Fortescue**, a close legal and personal associate. AP wrote engaging lines *To Mr. Gay* about 1720; at the same date, Gay composed his beautifully managed verses delivering *Mr. Pope's Welcome from Greece*. After his friend died, AP remembered him with affection, as at the start of *The Dunciad*: "Gay dies unpension'd with a hundred Friends" (*TE* 5: 189); and in the *Epistle to Arbuthnot*, ll. 256–60 (*TE* 4: 114). In fact, there were few ripples on the placid surface of their relationship. Some writers have thought that AP patronized Gay at times and presented him as more helpless in worldly affairs than was really the case; but no one can doubt the tenderness with which AP guarded the memory of his well-love colleague and coadjutor.

The most up-to-date and incisive biography is D. Nokes, *John Gay: A Profession of Friendship* (Oxford: Oxford University Press, 1995). For Gay's writings, see his *Poetry and Prose*, ed. V.A. Dearing and C.E. Beckwith, 2 vols. (Oxford: Clarendon, 1974); and *Dramatic Works*, ed. J. Fuller, 2 vols. (Oxford: Clarendon, 1983). See also *Letters*, ed. C.F. Burgess (Oxford: Clarendon, 1966). The stage background is studied by C. Wintoun, *John Gay and the London Theatre* (Lexington: University Press of Kentucky, 1993). For prologues and epitaphs by AP, see Ault 207–21.

George I (1660–1727). King of England from 1714. He succeeded as Elector of Hanover on the death of his mother a few weeks prior to the death of **Queen Anne** on 1 August and was crowned King on 20 October. AP commemorated this occasion in *An Epistle to Miss Blount, on her leaving the Town, after the Coronation*. Up to the very eve of the new King's arrival, there was intense anxiety about the possibility of an attempt to install the **Pre-**

tender in place of George. In the event, the **Jacobite rising** did not take place for another year. However, the Tory politicians who had been close to AP in the previous reign were all dismissed, and a number faced severe sanctions, as the Whigs took power on the **Hanoverian accession**.

AP had no close personal dealings with the King, although he did run him into him at **Hampton Court** on at least one occasion. In the divisive politics of this reign, AP identified more closely with the King's troublesome son, the Prince of Wales, later **George II**, and the Princess, later **Queen Caroline**. The King gave AP £200 as a subscription to the translation of **Homer**. References in the poetry are generally oblique, but there is nothing unintelligible about the verse "Still Dunce the second reigns like Dunce the first," which appeared at the start of *The Dunciad* only a year after George's death.

See R. Hatton, *George I* (New Haven, CT: Yale University Press, 2001).

George II (1683–1760). King of England from 1727. AP's explicit references to the King occur mainly in the *Imitations of Horace*, which contains some unflattering references, sometimes couched under a disguised name such as "Caesar." AP also calls him "Brunswick," alluding to his title as Duke of Brunswick and Lüneburg: this draws attention to what was regarded as the Hanoverians' primary loyalty, namely, their German possessions. The *Epistle to Augustus* is less ambiguous, thrusting George Augustus into embarrassing juxtaposition with the Emperor Augustus and opening with a nakedly ironic paean to George as "great Patron of Mankind." AP leaves the reader in little doubt that the monarch is no "Friend of LIBERTY" and ends with a declaration of his reluctance to bestow a panegyric on his sovereign (*TE* 4: 229). The ostensible reason is that "A vile Encomium doubly ridicules" (writer and subject alike). The true reason, obviously, is that the King does not merit such praise.

Equally, *The Dunciad* makes unmistakable fun of the King. The opening lines tell of the man who brings the low-life **Smithfield** muses "to the Ear of Kings" and remind us that "Still Dunce the second reigns like Dunce the first" (*TE* 5: 59–61). This could have only one meaning, a year after George II had succeeded George I. Additionally, there are many recollections in the action of the poem of the coronation of George and **Queen Caroline**, which had taken place in the previous October. This did not prevent the King from expressing interest in the poem and seeking a key to interpret it (see *Corr* 2: 502). On 22 March 1729 **Walpole** presented an advanced copy of *The Dunciad Variorum* to the King, who is said to have declared its author "a very honest man." It is inconceivable that he was blind to all the implications of the work, despite his lack of any taste for poetry and his relatively limited English. Another story suggests that the King asked, "Who is this Pope that I hear so much about? I cannot discover what is his merit. Why will not my subjects write in prose? I hear a great deal, too, of Shakespeare, but I cannot read him, he is such a bombast fellow." This is probably an apocryphal tale.

In earlier years AP had a great deal of contact with the alternative court that George had maintained at one period as Prince of Wales and especially with the **maids of honor** to Caroline. His own associations were mainly with the party of the Prince rather than that of his father, but he seems to have been content to exploit the dissentions at court for his satiric ends. See, for example, *The Court Ballad*.

georgic. A literary mode deriving from the four didactic poems on farming written by **Virgil**. The root sense goes back to Latin *georgicus*, itself from Greek *georgikos*, from *georgos*, farmer: ultimately *geo-*, geo- + *ergon*, work. The form entered English literature in the Elizabethan era, but its popularity spread with the translation of Virgil's poems by **John Dryden** (1697), preceded by an influential "Essay on Virgil's *Georgics*" by **Joseph Addison**. As time went on, the genre expanded, to embrace not just agricultural and horticultural pursuits but the life of the countryside generally, as well as covering instruction in practical activities such as those of the blacksmith. Among works with a strong element of the georgic are *The Seasons* (1726–30) by **James Thomson**; *Agriculture* (1753) by **Robert Dodsley**; *The Thresher's Labour* (1736) by **Stephen Duck**; *The Woman's Labour* (1739) by Mary Collier; and *The Fleece* (1757) by John Dyer.

For AP, the most important model other than Virgil and Dryden was the work of **John Philips**, especially *Cyder* (1708). He was probably also aware of some innovative works by William Diaper (1685–1717), whom **Swift** had patronized. His closest approach to formal georgic comes in *Windsor-Forest*, although residual elements appear in poems such as the *Epistle to Burlington* and *The Second Epistle of the Second Book of Horace*.

See J. Chalker, *The English Georgic: A Study of the Development of a Form* (London: Routledge, 1969). Contentious and stimulating background ideas are provided by R. Williams, *The Country and the City* (London: Chatto and Windus, 1973). The later fortunes of the form can be studied in two good books from different eras: D.L. Durling, *Georgic Tradition in English Poetry* (New York: Columbia University Ores, 1935); and J. Goodridge, *Rural Life in Eighteenth-Century English Poetry* (Cambridge: Cambridge University Press, 1995).

Gerrard, Samuel. Friend of **Jonathan Swift** who lived at Gibbstown, north of Navan in County Meath. In 1740 Gerrard visited London and **Bath**. He was given a clandestine packet containing a printed version of Swift's letters, including those to and from AP. These were then published by **George Faulkner** in 1741 (Griffith 533). Two letters from AP to Gerrard survive concerning the affair.

Gibbs, James (1682–1754). Scottish architect. After studying for the priesthood in Rome, he returned to Britain in 1708. Thanks to the patronage of the Earl of Mar and the **first Earl of Oxford**, he was appointed in 1713 as a surveyor to the Commission to build fifty new churches in London. Lost his post after the **Hanoverian accession** but was given work at **Cannons** by the **Duke of Chandos**. From this time his most loyal patron was the **second Earl**

of Oxford, who employed him in developing the Harley estates in London and at **Wimpole**, as well as at **Down Hall** for Gibbs's friend **Matthew Prior**. He also designed the monuments in Westminster Abbey for Prior, **James Craggs**, and **Dryden**. His best-known work includes St. Martin's in the Fields, the Senate House at Cambridge, and the Radcliffe Camera at **Oxford**. Other commissions were for **Dawley** and Sudbrook.

It was natural for AP to be drawn into the orbit of Gibbs. As a Tory, a Catholic, and a member of the Harley circle, he was congenial in outlook; as an architect, his personal version of the Baroque probably appealed to the poet more than the stiffer **Palladianism** that was coming into fashion. Gibbs subscribed to **Gay**'s poems in 1720. He worked several times at **Twickenham** for **James Johnston**, the **Earl of Islay**, and Barnaby Backwell. It is almost certain that he designed the alterations on AP's own nearby villa from 1720. Two letters from Gibbs to AP survive.

The fullest study is T. Friedman, *James Gibbs* (New Haven, CT: Yale University Press, 1984). See also B. Gibbs, *The Life and Works of James Gibbs 1682–1754* (London: Batsford, 1955). An informative recent essay is G. Balderston, "Rysbrack's Busts of James Gibbs and Alexander Pope from Henrietta Street," *Georgian Group Journal*, 11 (2001), 1–28.

Gildon, Charles (1665–1724). Critic, dramatist, and miscellaneous author. As usual, AP was well informed on the life histories of his victims. In a note to *The Dunciad* (*TE* 5: 92–93), he mentions the fact that Gildon, "a writer of criticisms and libels of the last age," had published the "blasphemous books against the Divinity of Christ" written by Charles Blount, an early proponent of Deism. Next, AP remarks that Gildon "signalized himself as a Critic, having written some very bad plays." The latter would include tragedies such as *The Patriot* (1703), although his biggest success was a version of *Measure for Measure*, subtitled *Beauty the Best Advocate* (1700), "and now very much alter'd; with additions of several entertainments of musick." Gildon's critical enterprises were

extremely varied. His essay on the history of the stage appeared in the seventh volume that **Edmund Curll** added to the edition of **Shakespeare** by **Nicholas Rowe** (1710). He also wrote *A Comparison between the two Stages* (1702); and *The Life and Strange Surprizing Adventures of Mr. D—— De F——, of London, Hosier, in a Dialogue between him, Robinson Crusoe, and his Man Friday* (1719), an amusing satire on **Defoe**. AP did not get round to mentioning Gildon's many anthologies of verse, such as *Miscellany Poems upon Several Occasions* (1692), which contains works by several major authors.

AP goes on to specify personal attacks by Gildon on himself. These include his depiction as "Sawny Dapper" in *A New Rehearsal, or Bays the Younger* (1714), a comic drama mainly directed against Rowe, as well as possible material for *A True Character of Mr. Pope* (1716), by **John Dennis**. In 1718 Gildon brought out *Memoirs of the Life of William Wycherley* (see **Wycherley**), another Curll production. In this there is a passage on "one *Pope*, a little diminuitive [*sic*] Creature, who had got a sort of Knack in smooth Vercification[*sic*], and with it was for setting up for a Wit and a Poet." AP is described as "this little *Aesopic* sort of an animal" (see Guerinot 71–72). Rather gentler is the treatment in *The Complete Art of Poetry* (1718), which assails the translation of the *Iliad* and expresses a clear preference for **Ambrose Philips** as a writer of pastoral. AP's only response at first seems to have been good-humored allusions to Gildon in minor poems and in the prose piece *A Further Account*. "Let *Gildon* and *Philips* rest in peace," he wrote to **Swift**, after the Dean had warned him that "Maevius [a Roman poetaster] is as well known as Virgil, and Gildon will be as well known as you if his name gets into your Verses" (*Corr* 2: 343, 347).

The comparatively early death of Gildon did not spare him from retribution in the end. He makes several entries into *The Art of Sinking* as theorist and practitioner. In chapter 6 he is (uniquely) picked out for his distinction in two branches of the "profound," that is, among the "flying fishes" and the "porpoises." He is also one of the promoters, with Dennis, of "A Project for the Advancement of the Stage" (*Prose* 2: 196–97, 230–32). In *The Dunciad* he makes two appearances, one of them cruelly drawing attention to a mysterious quarrel with a former ally: "Ah Dennis! Gildon ah! What ill-starr'd rage / Divides a friendship, long confirm'd by age" (3: 167–68). The best-known reference occurs in the *Epistle to Arbuthnot*: "Yet then did *Gildon* draw his venal quill; / I wish'd the man a dinner, and sate still" (ll. 151–52).

It would have been impossible for Gildon to compete on this plane, even had he survived. However, he was an able writer all round, who deserves more careful scholarly attention. A brief biography will be found in *Robinson Crusoe Examin'd and Criticis'd*, ed. P. Dottin (London: Dent, 1923).

Gilliver, Lawton (c. 1703–48). Bookseller. Apprenticed, 1721; freed, 1728. It was probably AP who set him up in business at the sign of Homer's Head, opposite St. Dunstan's Church in **Fleet Street**, London. He acquired the rights of **The Dunciad Variorum** from AP in 1729 for £100, but only after they were first assigned nominally to three peers. For the agreement, see R.W. Rogers, *The Major Satires of Alexander Pope* (Urbana: University of Illinois Press, 1955), 116–19. After this he became a leading shareholder and copublisher of the *Grub-street Journal* (1730–37). He issued many of AP's works in the next decade, generally working with the printer **John Wright**. Author and bookseller split up in 1737 after a quarrel over the rights in the *Works*. Gilliver was also involved with three of **Swift**'s later poems, though these items may have caused him more trouble than they were worth since they led to his brief arrest in 1734. Thanks to his links with AP, Gilliver was able to publish the works of writers friendly to AP, such as **Walter Harte** and **George Lyttelton**. After his break with AP, he concentrated on retail bookselling. However, his business failed to the point that his stock was sold in 1742, and he was made bankrupt later that year.

See J. McLaverty, "Lawton Gilliver: Pope's Bookseller," *Studies in Bibliography*, 32 (1979), 101–24.

God's Revenge against Punning. A short Scriblerian satire, probably the work of AP. It was published as a half-sheet folio, priced twopence, on 7 November 1716. The title page lists **James Roberts** in the imprint. Reprints followed in Edinburgh and Dublin in the same year. AP later included the item in the *Miscellanies* in 1732. A reference in the pamphlet can be connected to a small accident suffered by **John Gay**, which AP reported in a letter to **Teresa Blount** on 7 August 1716 (*Corr* 1: 350). The item was first included in the canon by **Norman Ault**, and while certainty has not been achieved, it is more likely to be by AP than anyone else, though Gay may have had some share. The pamphlet, though not the 1732 version, is signed at the end "J. Baker, *Knight*," a formula that AP used elsewhere. It refers to an eclipse of the sun in 1714 and the aurora borealis in 1716, both of which had engaged the attention of the Scriblerians (see **Scriblerus Club**).

A reply to *God's Revenge* was issued on 22 November 1716. This was also a folio half-sheet costing twopence, imitating the original even down to bibliographical details. The imprint lists John Baker and Thomas Warner, both trade publishers like Roberts. It is titled *A Letter from Sir J—— B—— to Mr. P——, upon Publishing of a Paper, intituled, God's Revenge against Punning; shewing the Miserable Fates of Persons addicted to this Crying Sin, in Court and Town. By J. Baker Kt.* Ault speculated that **Edmund Curll** perhaps lay behind this production. We cannot be sure of this either. The author certainly targets AP, as his title would indicate. For a description of the *Letter*, see Guerinot 46–47.

There was another sequel, *An Heroi-Comical Epistle from a certain Doctor to a certain Gentlewoman, in Defence of the most Ancient Art of Punning*, which was published on 27 November 1716. This is a rough-hewn ballad, sometimes attributed without very much hard evidence to **Dr. John Arbuthnot**.

Ault argues for the ascription to AP in *Prose 1*: cx–cxiv; for the text, see 1: 269–72.

Goode, Barnham (d. c. 1750). Journalist. He has previously been identified with Francis Goode (1674–1739), a Fellow of King's College, **Cambridge**, and teacher at Eton College from 1720 (second master by 1727). This may have been a brother. Barnham resided in Westminster and associated with fellow dunces such as **Theobald**, **Jacob**, **Dennis**, and **Cooke**. The translation of **Ovid**'s *Metamorphoses* published by **Edmund Curll** in 1716 was dedicated by **George Sewell** to Goode. He was also known to the Deist Anthony Collins. AP accused him of writing "many anonymous Libels in Newspapers for Hire." He is said to have been a schoolfellow of **Robert Walpole**, for whom he composed articles in the press. Curll told Walpole that Goode had interceded on his behalf to have "some provision" made for him. AP gives Goode a passing blow in *The Dunciad* (3: 147–48) and in *A Master Key to Popery*.

Gosfield. Estate near Halstead, Essex. The house was originally built in the mid-sixteenth century, from which some of the Tudor courtyard remains. Extensively altered in the eighteenth century by **Robert Nugent**, who also landscaped the park. During his exile in England Louis XVIII of France lived here from 1807 to 1809.

It was the home of AP's friends **John Knight** and his wife, formerly **Ann Craggs**. AP visited them in 1731 and 1733. After Knight's death AP composed an inscription for him, which he sent to his wife in 1736. It was placed on a funeral monument in Gosfield church, with a marble statue designed by **Michael Rysbrack**. By this time Ann had married Robert Nugent as her third husband. See *TE* 6: 364–65. AP's friend **Walter Harte** became rector of Gosfield in 1734.

Grand Tour. The customary initiation of British upper-class males into adulthood by means of a protracted tour of the Continent. Generally this included a spell in France and one in Italy; it might also include visits to Switzerland, the Austrian and German courts, and the Low Countries. It often lasted two or three years, with a long sojourn in major cities such as Paris, Venice, Florence, and Rome. In theory the aim was to inculcate French manners and Italian taste. While some young men of rank acquired a virtuoso's knowledge of antiquities and began a life of collecting, others learned more about gambling, drinking, and womanizing. There was no Grand Tour as such for women, although upper-class women such as **Lady Mary Wortley Montagu** managed by one means or another to visit France and Italy, usually at a slightly later stage in life. The formal tour gradually died out after the Napoleonic wars.

AP's health and lack of means precluded a tour of this kind, but many of his friends made one, including the **Earl of Burlington** and **George Lyttelton**. Others of AP's acquaintance served as a bear-leader or tour guide to a young man embarking on the tour: such was the experience of **Aaron Hill**, **David Mallet**, **Joseph Spence**, and **James Thomson**. AP wrote a brilliantly evocative portrait of a Grand Tour in *The Dunciad* (4: 293–330).

There is a large literature on the topic: W.E. Mead, *The Grand Tour in the Eighteenth Century* (Boston: Houghton Mifflin, 1914; reprint, New York: Blom, 1972), remains useful. A more up-to-date approach is J. Black, *The British Abroad: The Grand Tour in the Eighteenth Century* (Stroud, Gloucestershire: Sutton, 1992).

Granville, George, first Baron Lansdowne (1666–1735). Politician and author. Member of an important West Country family. A Tory MP with a considerable electoral interest in Cornwall. Secretary at War, 1710. Already well connected, he made a judicious marriage to a young and aristocratic heiress in 1711. Just weeks later he became a baron, as one of the twelve peers created to force through Parliament the peace negotiations designed to end the **War of the Spanish Succession**. Held offices at court, 1712–14. One of the leaders of the planned Western rising in 1715, he was arrested and accused of high treason. For two years he was imprisoned in the Tower but eventually freed in 1717. This did not deter him from further Jacobite activity. He was involved in the **Atterbury plot** and served as Secretary of State to the **Pretender**, who rewarded him with a meaningless title as Duke of Albemarle. Near the end of his life he made peace with the Hanoverian regime.

In his lifetime Granville was regarded as a writer of some significance. His poems appeared in various editions from 1712. One work, "An Essay on Unnatural Flights in Poetry," was separately reprinted in a number of collections. His plays included the tragedy *Heroic Love* (1698), which was commended by no less than **John Dryden;** the comedy *The Jew of Malta* (an adaptation of *The Merchant of Venice*, 1701); and an opera, *The British Enchanters* (1706). All of them retain a certain curiosity value at the least. His *Works* (2 vols., 1732; 3 vols., 1736) also print letters and historical tracts.

AP met Granville about 1706 through their common friend **William Wycherley**. Granville was so impressed that he wrote to a friend of "a young Poet, newly inspir'd," who "promised Miracles" (*Early Career* 52). When AP composed the first draft of his *Pastorals*, Granville was among the group of distinguished men who were allowed to offer their comments and "corrections," and indeed he may have been slightly more competent to adjudicate on such matters than most of those on the list. AP's poem *Windsor-Forest* was dedicated to Granville and manages to incorporate some tactful allusions to the dedicatee's verse. AP planned to stay with Lord Lansdowne, as he now was, in October 1714, at his palatial home, Longleat in Wiltshire; but it is not certain that this visit took place. However, the two men remained on good terms. The peer is listed among subscribers to the *Iliad* (ten copies) and the *Odyssey* and one of those in attendance in the poem *Mr. Pope's Welcome from Greece*. As late as 1732 Lansdowne was soliciting AP's advice concerning his plays. Lansdowne died on 29 January 1735, less than a month after AP celebrated his name in the *Epistle to Arbuthnot*. The poet refers to

him as "*Granville* the polite," one of those who had encouraged his early talent (*TE* 5: 105). Only three letters survive between the two men.

Posterity has not dealt kindly with Granville's reputation, and by the time **Samuel Johnson** came to write his *Lives of the Poets* (1779–81) he could safely be written off as a nonentity. However, AP was probably not insincere when he praised "*Granville*'s moving Lays" in the *Pastorals* (*TE* 1: 65), for a line of descent could be traced from **Waller** through to AP's own early works.

The fullest account is E. Handasyde, *Granville the Polite: The Life of George Granville Lord Lansdowne, 1666–1735* (London: Oxford University Press, 1933). This was well researched but now stands in some need of updating.

Green, David (Brontë) (1910–85). Writer who specialized on the family of the **Duke of Marlborough** and their connections, for example, in his book *The Churchills of Blenheim* (1984). He wrote the standard history of **Blenheim Palace**, as well as a biography of **Sarah, Duchess of Marlborough**; studies of the gardener **Henry Wise** and the wood carver Grinling Gibbons; and an account of the battle of Blenheim. Among his best-known works is a life of **Queen Anne**. His work illuminates the milieu in which AP operated, and some of it bears very directly on the poet.

Griffith, Anne (d. 1719). One of the **maids of honor** to **Caroline**, Princess of Wales, and thus well known to AP, **Gay**, and their circle. She was the daughter of Colonel Edward Griffith (d. 1711) and his wife Elizabeth, later Lady Mohun (d. 1725). Her sister, **Elizabeth Rich**, was also a maid of honor. AP was often in company with her around 1716–17 and refers to her in his letters as well as in his *Court Ballad*. He sometimes spells her name "Griffin." In 1718 she married William Stanhope, later first Earl of Harrington (1690–1756), but in December 1719 she died giving birth to twin sons, one of whom became the second Earl.

Griffith, Reginald Harvey (1873–1957). Scholar who spent most of his career at the University of Texas (1902–52), where he served as curator of the Wrenn Library. Best known for his essential work in **bibliography**, he wrote what remains the definitive work in its field, *Alexander Pope: A Bibliography*, 2 vols. (1922–27; reprint, University of Texas, 1962). Griffith compiled the entry on AP in *The Cambridge Bibliography of English Literature* (1940). He also wrote a number of significant articles on AP, including "Pope Editing Pope," *Studies in English* (University of Texas), 24 (1944), 5–108; and "The *Dunciad* of 1729," *Modern Philology*, 12 (1915), 1–18. See M.T. Osborne, ed., *The Great Torch Race: Essays in Honor of Reginald Harvey Griffith* (Austin: University of Texas Press, 1961).

grotto. Soon after he moved to **Twickenham**, AP began work on his grotto, "a piece of garden architecture whose fame has eclipsed the gardens" (Morris R. Brownell). Its origin lay in the fact that the **villa** faced toward the river and away from the road, Cross Deep, which divided the house from the main garden. A passageway was needed to from a connection, and it was in this space under the house that AP constructed his grotto. It was no more than part of the basement through which visitors could have access to the garden, with a view back toward the Thames opening up as they went.

In October 1720 AP was granted a license by the Manor Court to undertake the work. He worked on the tunnel and its growing assemblage of contents for the rest of his life. It was four feet wide and six feet six inches at the highest point. It extended for twenty-two feet from the rear of the house and culminated in a lobby of seven feet in length. (It was extended in later times to sixty-three feet.) When AP began his work the road under which the tunnel led was only twelve feet wide. The passageway rose about two and a half feet as it made its way up a slight natural gradient into the garden area. It was then prolonged by a path above ground that followed a steeper ascent for several yards. The structure was arched and constructed of smooth brickwork. There were lobbies at either end, with niches and seats, one light and open, the other (toward the garden) darker and rougher in its surfaces. As for the grotto itself, this occupied a space under the west (garden) side of the house, occupying an area of something like eight feet by seven. It was paved with pebbles, while the path outside was marked out in cockleshells, "in the natural Taste, agreeing not ill with . . . the Aquatic Idea of the whole Place." A crucial effect AP sought was that "when you shut the Doors of this Grotto, it becomes on the instant, from a luminous Room, a *Camera obscura*; on the Walls of which all the objects of the River, Hills, Woods, and Boats, are forming a moving Picture in their visible Relations" (*Corr* 2: 296). At some stage mirrors were set up in order to magnify these illusionist effects.

In 1733 AP constructed a portico at the east side of the house, and beneath it an undercroft that replaced the earlier porch at this end, with an archway leading out to the riverside lawn. In due course there was a water supply into the underground chamber, fed by a spring at the garden end. Further enlargement was carried out around 1740–41, when adjoining cellars were taken into the plan, and a "bagnio," presumably a cold bath, placed in one of these rooms. After AP's death considerable modifications were made. However, the grotto survives today (the only part of the entire house and garden to do so). Some of the original features, including arcades and columns, are still in place. Further work is needed if the grotto is to be restored to something like its original condition.

From the start AP saw his grotto as a place of retreat and reflection (he seems to have had table and chairs in place). The cave with its spring resembled some of the scenes in classical literature that the poet knew so well. Over the garden entrance was set a marble plaque, bearing the inscription "Secretum iter et fallentis semita vitae": the source is one of the epistles (1: 18) of **Horace**, with the sense, "a solitary journey down the path of a concealed life." Miscellaneous items were chosen to endow the location with a sense of privacy and to create emblems of retirement. There may have been statues along some of the walls, as well as busts and urns. To that extent the place had at first an element of the cabinet of "curiosities," that is, an assemblage of diverse natural phenomena and *objets d'art*. Around 1739 AP became passionately involved with geology and mineralogy, and the contents of the grotto took on a more specialized character. He acquired a large collection of marbles, crystals, ores, and other rocks. **Ralph Allen** donated stone from his quarries outside **Bath**, while the Cornish clergyman **William Borlase** provided a wide range of materials drawn from his own extensive collection. They sent major consignments with dozens of specimens, many of considerable bulk. Other donors included **George Lyttelton**; **Gilbert West**; **Joseph Spence**; **Sir Hans Sloane**; **John Brinsden**; the **fifth Earl of Orrery**; Philip Miller, the gardener; and many others.

AP's grotto was not as spectacular as some, and it did not celebrate the taste for the "grotesque" as openly as some later creations in this vein. Rather, it expressed his own identity, as a writer, a Catholic, a devotee of the classics, a lover of natural beauty, a gardener, a connoisseur of artistic and scientific objects, a refugee from the city, and a disciple of the past masters of "retirement" in its psychological and political senses. **Swift** was told of AP's work by their common friend **Charles Ford** and wrote to congratulate him on his "Subterranean Passage to your Garden whereby you turned a blunder into a beauty which is a Piece of Ars Poetica" (*Corr* 2: 325–26), a nicely turned compliment on the ingenious contrivances that went into the grotto. There are playful references to the "pensive Grott" in some of the *Imitations of Horace*, and the *Epistle to Arbuthnot* expresses AP's vulnerability to those who besiege him in his home: What Walls can guard me, or what Shades can hide? / They pierce my Thickets, thro' my Grot they glide" (*TE* 4: 96). See also *Verses on the Grotto*.

For an up-to-date account of the grotto in its physical surroundings, see A.B. Willson, *Alexander Pope's Grotto in Twickenham* (Twickenham: Garden History Society, 1998). For the contemporary account by **John Serle**, see also **garden**. For the emblematic meaning of the grotto, and its place in AP's life, see *Garden and City*, chapters 1–3. Useful historical information is provided by F. Bracher, "Pope's Grotto: The Maze of Fancy," *Huntington Library Quarterly*, 12 (1949), 141–62, reprinted in *EA* 97–121; and B. Boyce, "Mr. Pope, in Bath, Improves the Design of His Grotto," in *Restoration and Eighteenth-Century Literature: Essays in Honor of Alan Dugald McKillop*, ed. C. Camden (Chicago: University of Chicago Press, 1963), 143–53. A brief account by M.R. Brownell appears in *Alexander Pope's Villa* (London: Greater London Council, 1980), 5–17. For broader background, see N. Miller, *Heavenly Caves: Reflections on the Garden Grotto* (New York: Braziller, 1982). A later phase is intriguingly discussed by R.A. Aubin, "Grottoes, Geology and the Gothic Revival," *Studies in Philology*, 31 (1934), 408–16.

Grub Street. The most famous and pithy definition is that found in **Samuel Johnson**'s *Dictionary*: "GRUBSTREET: Originally the name of a street near Moorfields in London, much inhabited by writers of small histories, dictionaries, and temporary poems; whence any mean production is called *grubstreet*." There was a real street, running north and south for about a quarter of a mile, in the parish of St. Giles, Cripplegate, just north of the old walls of the city of London. It lay in what was a poor "suburb" within the jurisdiction of the city. By 1700 the term had acquired its metaphorical sense associated with the lower levels of the writing profession.

For AP, this expression came to operate as a major part of his symbolic capital. In an early draft of *The Dunciad*, the opening line read, "Books and the man, who first from Grub Street brings / The Smithfield muses to the ears of kings." The nerve center of Dulness, a hidden "Cell" of poverty and poetry, is located in the later version of the poem very close to the historic street; indeed, it may actually be identified with Grub Street itself. The term occurs several times in the course of the poem, as it does in other works by AP. Other Scriblerians developed the trope—notably **Swift** in *A Tale of a Tub* and poems such as *On Poetry: A Rhap-*

sody, and **Dr. John Arbuthnot** in *John Bull*. **Henry Fielding** composed *The Grub Street Opera* in 1731. Gradually the sense widened, and by the nineteenth century it had started to cover any sort of unrespectable writing, particularly yellow journalism. By this time the original thoroughfare had been renamed "Milton Street"; and in the late twentieth century most of its length disappeared under the Barbican development scheme.

Allies of AP (almost certainly with his own connivance) set up the **Grub-street Journal** in 1730. The editors claimed to be sending out the paper from the Flying Horse tavern, which stood on the east side of Grub Street.

Grub-street Journal. A weekly newspaper that ran for 418 numbers from 8 January 1730 to 29 December 1737. Its original editors were Richard Russel (b. c. 1686), a nonjuring clergyman, who served until 1735, and John Martyn (1699–1768), a botanist, who acted until 1731. The journal claimed to be issued from a tavern named the Flying Horse (a depraved Pegasus) in **Grub Street**, north of the city of London. It was distributed by **James Roberts**, **Lawton Gilliver**, and John Huggonson; the price was twopence per issue (Griffith 231). A sequel, *The Literary Courier of Grub Street*, ran for thirty issues from January to July 1738.

The principal targets of satire included **Colley Cibber**, **Lewis Theobald**, **Eustace Budgell**, **Stephen Duck**, and **Edmund Curll**, as well as the inept journalism to be found in other newspapers of the time. Butts of AP who figure in the *Journal* were **James Moore Smythe**, **John Henley**, **Richard Bentley**, **Matthew Concanen**, and **John, Baron Hervey**. Another frequent victim was **Henry Fielding**, then a rising young dramatist. AP's enemies claimed that he had a leading hand in the proceedings. It is not clear how much week-to-week contact he had with the journal (he scarcely ever mentions it in his extant letters), but its contents certainly reflected his own position with considerable accuracy. In fact, the journal operated as a kind of serialized *Dunciad*. The likelihood is that he contributed small items on a fairly regular basis, but they cannot be identified with assur-

ance. See *TE* 6: 324–33 for some suggested attributions.

Selections were published as *Faithful Memoirs of the Grubstreet Society* (1732); and *Memoirs of the Society of Grub-Street*, 2 vols. (1737). See J.T. Hillhouse, *The Grub Street Journal* (Durham, NC, 1928; reprint, New York: Blom, 1967); and B.A. Goldgar, "Pope and the *Grub-street Journal*," *Modern Philology*, 74 (1977), 366–80.

Guardian, The. A periodical paper appearing six days a week for 175 issues between 12 March and 1 October 1713. It was edited by **Richard Steele**, who was the major contributor of essays to its pages. **Joseph Addison** wrote about fifty papers, with **Eustace Budgell** another prominent contributor. Designed to capitalize on the success of *The Spectator*, the new journal found it harder to keep out of topical and political controversies, and it became identified as a Whig journal ranged in opposition to the Tory *Examiner*.

Initially Steele may have hoped that AP would take a major share in the enterprise. He wrote to AP on 12 November 1712, seeming to invite his friend (as AP still was) to send in material (*Corr* 1: 152). In the event AP wrote between seven and twelve papers; his increasing absorption with the planned translation of the *Iliad* and other works may have distracted him, but it is likely that he disapproved of the political tack that the journal had taken. The best known of these items occurs in issue no. 40 (27 April 1713), which provides a crushing attack on the feeble pastoral poems of **Ambrose Philips**. Equally sharp and amusing are nos. 91 and 92, dealing with a Club of Little Men; and a paper on **gardening** in no. 173 (29 September 1713), which opens with serious reflections and a translation of the garden of Alcinous in the *Odyssey*, before embarking on a hilarious account of contemporary excesses in the use of horticultural ornaments. It has been suggested by **Norman Ault** that AP wrote further items, but these remain unconfirmed (see *Prose* 1: lvi–lxxii).

The standard edition is *The Guardian*, ed.

J.C. Stephens (Lexington: University Press of Kentucky, 1982).

Gulliver's Travels. The famous satire by **Jonathan Swift** had its earliest roots in the activity of the **Scriblerus Club** from around 1714. AP noted that a portion of the *Memoirs of Martin Scriblerus* gave Swift his "first hints" (*Anecdotes* 1: 56). However, the actual composition does not seem to have been undertaken until several years after the author's return to Ireland, perhaps beginning c. 1721. Swift kept his friend **Charles Ford** abreast of his progress, and it may have been by this route that his English friends, including AP, learned of the existence of the *Travels*. There is no clear reference to the work in correspondence until AP and Swift both mention it in September 1725: Swift's account of his intentions is among his most famous pronouncements on *Gulliver* (*Corr* 2: 321, 325). When he visited England in 1726 Swift brought the manuscript with him, and the *Travels* were first published on 28 October. AP, who claimed not to have seen the book before its publication, wrote to Swift on 16 November with warm congratulations (*Corr* 2: 412). **John Gay** and **John Arbuthnot** also sent complimentary messages.

Around 17 February 1727 AP again wrote to Swift, mentioning some commendatory verses relating to *Gulliver*. In May, **Benjamin Motte** issued these verses as a small collection and immediately afterward included them at the head of the second edition of the *Travels* as a special insert. There are four poems in some copies, five in others (see Griffith 187–88, 190). Three of the items went into the *Miscellanies*. There is no doubt that AP wrote most of them, and probably he was responsible for all, though collaboration with Gay cannot be totally ruled out. They are playful comic verses, with a "Lilliputian ode" in lines of three syllables, and an Ovidian epistle from Mrs. Gulliver to welcome back her husband after his long years of absence. The most sophisticated in literary technique is the second, "the Lamentation of Glumdalclitch, for the Loss of Grildrig." This describes the sadness of the nine-year-old Brobdignagian girl who cared for Gulliver ("whom she called 'Grildrig' ") when he was carried away from her (see *Gulliver's Travels* 2: 8). It takes the form of a mock-pastoral elegy, but the text most insistently recalled is AP's own *Rape of the Lock*. The poem uses similar pathetic formulae ("Was it for this . . .") and creates a similar miniaturized world, where absurdity and lyrical beauty exist side by side. A transcript of an earlier version, preserved by the **second Earl of Oxford**, contains further recollections of the *Rape*.

For discussion of these poems, see Ault 231–42. For text and notes, see *TE* 6: 266–81.

Gyles, Fletcher (d. 1741). Bookseller who had acted for **William Warburton** and became involved with AP's affairs when the poet adopted Warburton as his editor in 1740. One letter from AP to Gyles survives from May 1741. His executor was Collet Mawhood, probably a relative of AP on the maternal side (Mawhood may have married Gyles's sister).

H

Hadrian, lines from. AP wrote two short poems based on a passage attributed to the Roman Emperor Hadrian (A.D. 76–138). The Emperor is supposed to have died repeating five lines beginning *Animucula, vagula, blandula*, a series of diminutives meaning "charming, wandering little soul." There were numerous renderings into English. AP wrote a short commentary on the poem, with a prose translation, in *The Spectator* on 10 November 1712. Then about a month later, in response to a request from **Richard Steele**, he sent a poetical version, expanding on the original, here listed as item B (*Corr* 1: 160). Next year he wrote to **John Caryll senior**, enclosing three separate verse translations and asking for his friend's opinion on their relative merits. These were a rendering by **Matthew Prior**; a new set of verses by AP, here listed as item A; and item B (*Corr* 1: 178–79). Both A and B were printed in a miscellaneous collection of poems issued in 1730, while each was separately included in AP's *Works* from the mid-1730s. However, the text of item B was heavily revised, with the second and third stanzas almost totally rewritten. Both poems have been subsequently accepted as the work of AP.

Item A consists of two quatrains in octosyllabics, with alternate rhymes. Item B consists in both versions of three six-line stanzas. It is generally headed "The Dying Christian to his Soul. Ode." The distinguishing feature of the revised version is heavier use of trochaic rhythm ("Steals my senses, shuts my sight"), although this was already apparent in the first stanza that is common to both versions ("Trembling, hoping, ling'ring, flying").

For the complex bibliographical history, see Ault 60–67. For the text and commentary, see *TE* 6: 91–95.

Hagley. Estate in Worcestershire, near Stourbridge, that had belonged to the Lyttelton family since the sixteenth century. In AP's day the master was Sir Thomas Lyttelton, an MP who was father of the politician **George Lyttelton**. The present Hagley Hall was built c. 1753–60 in a style of modified **Palladianism** to designs chiefly by Sanderson Miller. It replaced an old black and white timbered house, which **Horace Walpole** called "immeasurably old and bad." A decade earlier George Lyttelton had embarked on improvements to the wooded parkland. The seat was famous for its noble prospects and evocative landscaping, celebrated in a much-quoted passage by **James Thomson**, added to "Spring" (*The Seasons*). Among the features was Pope's Walk, including an urn on a pedestal, placed there apparently by AP around 1739. See *P&AGE* 220–22.

AP visited Lyttelton in 1743. In his **will** he bequeathed to Lyttelton four busts of great English writers, probably the work of **Peter Scheemakers**. These are still at Hagley, along with a famous **portrait** of AP by **Jonathan Richardson senior.**

Hales, Stephen (1677–1761). Biologist, inventor, and philanthropist. One of the leading figures in the history of plant physiology, especially in *Vegetable Staticks* (1727). His work on animal physiology, *Haemastatics*, in which he pioneered the technique for taking blood pressure, followed in 1733. Another area of interest was treatment for bladder stones (see also **Cheselden**). Fellow of the Royal Society,

1718. He was a clergyman (D.D. 1733) and a trustee for the new colony of Georgia. As perpetual curate of Teddington from 1709, a close neighbor of AP. One of the executors named in AP's **will**.

AP refers to "plain Parson Hale" in friendly terms in the *Epistle to a Lady* (*TE* 3.ii: 66), but otherwise there are few clues to what seems to have been an affable relationship. Hales called AP's constitution "very alkaline" and recommended that the poet drink Seville orange and lemon juice. It appears that AP was upset by Hales's experimental work, which involved animal vivisection. **Joseph Spence** asked if Hales cut up rats, to which AP replied with "emphasis and concern" that he did, "and dogs too" (*Anecdotes* 1: 259, 118). See D.G.C. Allan and R.E. Schofield, *Stephen Hales, Scientist and Philanthropist* (London: Scolar, 1980).

Halifax, Charles Montagu, first Earl of (1661–1715). Statesman and literary patron. A leading figure in national affairs under **William III**, he served as an MP, Chancellor of the Exchequer, and First Lord of the Treasury. A member of the Whig Junto, he was involved in the foundation of the Bank of England and in the recoinage. President of the Royal Society, 1695–98. Created a Baron, 1700; Earl, 1714. At the time of the **Hanoverian accession** he was again appointed to the head of the government but was too ill to take an active share in power. Halifax had been a supporter of **Matthew Prior**, his schoolmate, and also of **Joseph Addison**, his protégé; but his reputation suggested that he was sometimes a distant and condescending patron, even though he received an impressive barrage of tributes from aspiring authors. A minor poet in his own right, he earned a small niche in the *Lives of the Poets* by **Samuel Johnson**.

Halifax was one of the group of high-toned advisers who were allowed to see the *Pastorals* in advance of publication. When he returned to power in late 1714, Halifax apparently offered AP a pension, which the poet refused after due consideration (*Anecdotes* 1: 99; *Corr* 1: 271). He also offered assistance on the translation of the *Iliad*, with an important loan of the commentaries of Eustathius. AP gave him the first two books of his version to read around October 1714 (*Corr* 1: 263). In the preface to this work, AP acknowledged the support of Halifax, who was "one of the first to favour me" (*Prose* 1: 254). Before these words were in front of the public, Halifax had died. He subscribed for ten sets of the translation.

Despite these facts, AP's private references are sometimes equivocal. He told **Joseph Spence** that "the famous Lord Halifax was rather a pretender to taste than really possessed of it." As proof, he recounted the episode when Halifax asked him to read the early books of the *Iliad* at his house, with Addison, **Congreve**, and **Garth** in attendance. After asking for small changes, Halifax was delighted with the "revisions" shown to him, when AP brought the original text back a few weeks later (*Anecdotes* 1: 87–88). It is possible that "**Bufo**," the complacent patron of the *Epistle to Arbuthnot*, is based in part on Halifax. On the other hand the reference in the *Epilogue to the Satires* is a kind one, augmented by a note reading, "A peer, no less distinguished by his love of letters than his abilities in Parliament. He was disgraced in 1710, on the Change of Q. Anne's ministry" (*TE* 4: 317). See also the lines in *A Farewell to London*: "The Love of Arts lies cold and dead / In *Hallifax*'s Urn" (*TE* 6: 129).

Hall Grove. Estate at Windlesham, near Bagshot, lying just inside Surrey on the edge of **Windsor Forest**. The nearby road from London to Basingstoke was turnpiked from 1728 onward. It was acquired by AP's brother-in-law Charles Rackett (see **Rackett family**) from a "Mr Mountague" around 1698. AP often visited his sister and brother-in-law there, sometimes using it as a staging post on journeys between London and **Binfield**. After the Rackett family suffered financial reverses, the estate became heavily encumbered with mortgages and debts. It was decided to try to rent the property, but this proved difficult. After Charles died in 1728, it was leased in 1731 to a "Mr Butler," probably related to the Earl of Arran, who resided at nearby Bagshot Park. The widow **Magdalen Rackett** went to live with one of her sons. In 1739 AP advised Michael Rackett that he should sell the reversion of the property to a Protestant in order to avoid taxes (*Corr* 4: 160–61). There is no evidence that this was done before Magdalen died in 1749. Around 1770 a large new house was built, which was expanded in the Victorian era, but it fell into disrepair until restored in 1956 to be used as a preparatory school. Today Hall Grove School remains in operation on the site.

See M. Eedle, *A History of Bagshot and Windlesham* (Chichester: Phillimore, 1977).

Halsband, Robert (1914–89). Scholar who taught at the University of Illinois. He became the primary authority on **Lady Mary Wortley Montagu** by virtue of several notable publications: a *Life* of Montagu (1956), an edition of her *Letters*, 3 vols (1965–67), and with Isobel Grundy an edition of her *Essays* (1977). He also edited the town eclogues that Montagu wrote in 1716 and that AP transcribed (see *Court Eclogues*). A further biography is that devoted to AP's enemy **John, Baron Hervey** (1973). All these incorporate materials that are either new or substantially reordered. See also Halsband's book *The Rape of the Lock and Its Illustrations, 1714–1896* (Oxford: Clarendon, 1980).

Hamilton, Elizabeth, Duchess of (1682–1744). An imperious aristocrat who married in 1698 as his second wife the Scottish Jacobite leader James, fourth Duke of Hamilton. Her husband was killed in a famous duel with Lord Mohun in 1712. Thereafter she spent much of her life feuding with Mohun's widow. She was well known to **Jonathan Swift**, who helped to console her after the sudden death of the Duke. AP visited her more than once around 1717, and at this time both he and **Gay** corresponded with her. A legacy of this friendship is a portrait of the Duchess commissioned by AP, probably by **Charles Jervas**. This hung in the great parlor at AP's home at **Twickenham** (see *Garden and City* 252). The two were in fitful contact as late as 1724. The Duchess subscribed both

to the *Iliad* and to the *Odyssey*. She has been dubiously identified with the portrait of "Narcissa" in AP's *Epistle to a Lady*: see *TE* 3.ii: 54. However, she is probably "the cheerful Duchess" mentioned in *Mr. Pope's Welcome from Greece*. Aspects of her tempestuous character can be seen in V. Stater, *Duke Hamilton Is Dead!* (New York: Hill and Wang, 1999).

Hammersmith. Then an outlying village, about five miles west of the center of London, although it has long since been incorporated into the inner suburbs of the city. The Pope family moved here from **Plough Court** in 1692 and seem to have remained there until they moved to **Binfield** in or before 1700. They possibly chose this spot as it represented a gesture toward compliance with the anti-Catholic legislation, which required papists to remove themselves ten miles from Hyde Park Corner. In 1716 the family settled in **Chiswick**, closely adjacent to Hammersmith. No evidence has emerged of the life AP led at Hammersmith, from the age of four to about twelve.

Hampton Court. Royal palace on the banks of the Thames, a few miles upstream from AP's home at **Twickenham**. Built by Cardinal Wolsey and given to Henry VIII. The house and gardens were much improved by **William III** and his wife Mary. AP seems to have been there most often around 1717, at the time of his friendship with the **maids of honor** (see *Corr* 1: 427). He had formerly set the climactic event of *The Rape of the Lock* at the palace, during the reign of **Queen Anne**, though it is highly unlikely that the real-life "rape" took place there. It was not a favorite with the Queen, but this is unlikely to be (as suggested in *TE* 2: 399) because of an association with her last surviving child the Duke of Gloucester. The young Duke, who was the only hope for a peaceable Stuart succession, died in 1700 at Windsor, which remained Anne's most beloved palace.

Handel, George Frideric (1685–1759). Originally Georg Friedrich Händel. Composer of Saxon birth who settled in England in 1712 and obtained the patronage of **Queen Anne**. Kapellmeister to the Electorial Prince, later **George I**. AP seems to have come into contact with Handel when the latter was working at Burlington House for the **Earl of Burlington** around 1715–17. **John Gay** was also a house-guest of the Earl; like Gay and **Dr. John Arbuthnot**, AP continued to be in touch with the composer when his services were claimed in 1717 by James Brydges, Earl of Carnarvon, soon to be created **Duke of Chandos**. (Arbuthnot may well have been responsible both for Handel's introduction to the court of Anne and for his admission to the Burlington circle. The doctor dined with Chandos at least seventy times in 1717 and the first half of 1718.)

It is likely that AP contributed to *Acis and Galatea* along with Gay, and he quite probably wrote the original libretto for the oratorio *Esther*. During the struggles over **opera** in the following years, AP was led by personal and political considerations to side with the party of **Bononcini** against that of Handel. Nor did Handel's connections with the impresario **John James Heidegger** make it likely that AP would cling to his cause. However, he clearly recognized the merits of Handel's music, especially when the composer turned to oratorio. It is probably in this capacity that he is celebrated in the fourth book of *The Dunciad* as "Giant Handel" (*TE* 5: 65–70). There is also a reference to Handel's success in Dublin with *Messiah* (a subject that AP had of course had already treated), with the suggestion that the "opera" party had driven Handel out. Perhaps in gratitude, Handel incorporated lines from the *Pastorals* in his music drama *Semele*, first performed in February 1744. When AP asked Arbuthnot for his frank opinion of the composer, the doctor told him, "Conceive the highest that you can of his abilities, and they are much beyond anything you can conceive."

See G. Beeks, " 'A Club of Composers': Handel, Pepusch and Arbuthnot at Cannons," in *Handel Tercentenary Studies*, ed. S. Sadie and A. Hicks (Basingstoke: Macmillan, 1987), 209–21. Important general works are W. Dean, *Handel's Dramatic Oratorios and Masques* (Oxford: Clarendon, 1990); and D. Burrows, *Handel* (New York: Schirmer, 1994).

handwriting. AP's customary style of writing did not change much over the years. Although it grew a little less well formed as time went on, it remained elegant and instantly recognizable. The drafts of his poems show hasty corrections and interlineations; otherwise his poems and letters are wholly legible. His "paper-sparing" habits (as **Swift** called them) led him to compose verses on the back of old letters and covers; but his own correspondence was drafted quite carefully. In addition, AP had his own "print hand," a form of script resembling printed type. This can be seen in his fair copies of works such as the *Pastorals*, *An Essay on Criticism*, and *Windsor-Forest*. The largest sampling of handwritten items will be found reproduced in *L&GA*. See also **manuscripts**.

Hanoverian accession. In 1701 Parliament passed the Act of Settlement to ensure that a Protestant monarch would succeed **Queen Anne**. It named as the rightful successors the Electress Sophia of Hanover (technically the electorate of Brunswick-Lüneberg) and her heirs. Three months later the exiled James II died, whereupon Louis XIV of France recognized the former King's son, the **Pretender**, as "James III": It was precisely to exclude him that the act had been introduced. On the death of **William III**, Sophia became the immediate heir to the throne. However, she herself died in June 1714, two months before the Queen. Thus it was the Elector Georg Ludwig, her son, who came to the throne on 1 August 1714 as **George I**. He arrived in England in September and was crowned in October.

The advent of the Hanoverians led to a comprehensive overhaul of the entire political order. All those connected with the former **Harley administration** were ousted from their positions at court; the government was reshaped with Whigs replacing Tories at every level; and senior military officers under Anne found themselves out of favor, with supporters of the **Duke of Marlborough** reinstated. The beneficiaries in the literary world were figures such as **Addison** and **Steele;** the losers were Tory stalwarts such as **Swift** and **Dr. John Arbuthnot**. A general election in 1715 confirmed the dominance of the Whigs, which was to continue unchallenged for two generations. The failed rising of 1715–16 meant that Jacobitism became a proscribed cause, although risings in years to come (culminating in the rebellion of 1745–46) showed that it was not an altogether spent force ideologically, however inept its military forays.

AP's personal position was made much less comfortable, even though he was never implicated in **Jacobite** activities. As a Catholic he was subject to the reimplementation of severe antipapist laws, which caused his family to move from **Binfield** in 1716. He wrote bitter satires on both George I and **George II**, and although he accommodated himself to the regime (as most people did), he does not appear to have regarded the Hanoverians with any warmth.

Happy Life of a Country Parson, The. A brief poem by AP, first published in the *Miscellanies* in 1728. A manuscript in AP's hand survives. It consists of twenty-four lines in octosyllabic couplets, written in imitation of **Swift**. The poem was possibly written in the early days of the friendship of Swift and AP. See *TE* 6: 110–11.

Harcourt, Simon (1684–1720). Son of **Viscount Harcourt** and friend of AP. He was a Tory MP and unofficial secretary of the **Brothers Club** when he was on cordial terms with **Swift**. He was one of the main promoters of the subscription campaign for the *Iliad*. Both father and son figure in *Mr. Pope's Welcome from Greece*. There are many indications in AP's correspondence of his high esteem for the younger Harcourt, who extended hospitality to the poet at **Oxford** and **Stanton Harcourt**. After his death abroad in July 1720, he was buried at Stanton Harcourt, where an inscription by AP was set up on his memorial in 1724. For the text, see *TE* 6: 242–44.

Harcourt, Simon, first Viscount (c. 1661–1727). Tory MP and lawyer who served as Solicitor-General and Attorney-General under **Queen Anne**. One of the principal managers

for the defense of **Henry Sacheverell** in 1710. In the **Harley administration** he was appointed Lord Keeper (1710) and Lord Chancellor (1713–14). It was he who advised the dying Queen to appoint the **Duke of Shrewsbury** as Lord Treasurer. He was exempted from the general amnesty extended in 1717 to those with Jacobite links and took a leading part in freeing the **first Earl of Oxford** from custody. Later he was involved in the effort to permit his friend **Bolingbroke** to return to England. In his last years he was reconciled with the Hanoverian government. A friend of **Swift** in earlier times, he became close to AP in the early 1720s, when he gave legal advice and welcomed the poet to his homes in Oxfordshire. **Matthew Prior** is also thought to have visited Cokethorpe. In 1712 he acquired Nuneham Courtenay, which was later the chief seat of the Harcourt family. He seems to have coached AP for his appearance at the trial of **Atterbury**. When AP wrote an epitaph for his son **Simon Harcourt** (d. 1720) at **Stanton Harcourt**, the father was consulted on details of wording. Fifteen of AP's letters to him are known to survive. His third wife Elizabeth was a sister of AP's landlord **Thomas Vernon**. Harcourt subscribed for multiple copies of the *Iliad* and the *Odyssey*.

Harleian library. A splendid collection of books and manuscripts, which was begun by the first **Earl of Oxford** but was greatly augmented by his son the **second Earl of Oxford**. Ultimately it consisted of about 50,000 volumes, not counting 350,000 pamphlets, together with numerous prints and many thousands of manuscripts. It was under the direction of the eccentric **antiquarian** scholar **Humfrey Wanley**. AP was personally shown the collection by Wanley, and he donated materials to the second Earl. There seems also to have been a work on Roman architecture by AP among the manuscripts, but it has disappeared. The poet took a keen interest in the development of the collection, which he described as "one of the most noble Libraries in Europe" (*TE* 3.ii: 112).

Lord Oxford's reckless mania for collecting

finally reduced him to near penury. After he died, his widow got rid of the books and artifacts he had lovingly brought together. Miscellaneous bric-a-brac was disposed early in 1742. The books were bought for £13,000 in 1743 by Thomas Osborne, a leading figure in the trade. A sale catalog for the library was prepared in five volumes (1743–45) by William Oldys (1696–1761), who had latterly been curator of the collection, with a description of the contents by **Samuel Johnson**. A selection from the shorter work was published in eight volumes (1744–46), again edited by Oldys and Johnson. The manuscripts were acquired for the nation at a knockdown price of £10,000, and in 1753 they became the basis of the British Museum collection.

Harley, Robert. See the **first Earl of Oxford**.

Harley administration. The Tory government led by Robert Harley, first **Earl of Oxford**, in the last four years of **Queen Anne**'s reign. It lasted from 8 August 1710, when the Whig Lord Treasurer Sidney Godolphin (1645–1712) fell from power, until the eve of the Queen's death on 1 August 1714. Initially Harley operated as Chancellor of the Exchequer, but in May 1711 he was confirmed as effective leader of the government and appointed Lord Treasurer.

The Tories had come to power as a result of mounting differences between the Queen and her ministers, especially Godolphin and her former favorite the **Duke of Marlborough**. The botched prosecution of **Henry Sacheverell** earlier in the year had sealed the fate of the former leaders. At the general election in October the Tories won a comprehensive victory and were able to consolidate their position, ousting Whigs from their places in local and national politics. At first Harley had sought to take a moderate stance with a broad-based administration. However, as time went on, his principal lieutenant, the Secretary of State for the Northern Department, Henry St. John (from 1712 **Viscount Bolingbroke**), achieved greater sway as spokesman for the strong phalanx of root-and-branch Tories on the back benches,

some of whom were openly Jacobite in their sympathies. Harley continued to steer a middle course when he could, but Bolingbroke gained a central role in the negotiations leading up to the **Treaty of Utrecht**, and it grew increasingly hard to cover up cracks in the administration.

Prominent figures in the government included Simon Harcourt, later **Viscount Harcourt**, as Lord Keeper and then Lord Chancellor; the **Duke of Ormonde**, as Lord Lieutenant of Ireland, then Captain-General of the Forces; and the **Earl of Strafford**, as Lord High Admiral and peace negotiator. AP came to know all these men very well, as he did less important members of the ministry, such as the **Duke of Buckinghamshire** (Lord Steward); Lord Lansdowne (see **Granville**); and **Sir William Wyndham** (Lansdowne's successor and later Chancellor of Exchequer). AP had fewer dealings with the other individuals holding the post of Secretary of State, that is, Lord Dartmouth and William Bromley. His most intimate contacts were with Harley himself, as a fellow member of the **Scriblerus Club**, and with Bolingbroke, who joined **Swift** in the group known as the **Brothers Club**.

Nevertheless, events soon belied the hopeful prognostications of AP's poem *Windsor-Forest*, which lauded the Utrecht settlement and congratulated the ministry on its achievements in foiling the "war party" of Marlborough and his adherents. Divisions became more apparent as the troubling question of the succession proved impossible to solve, partly owing to the intransigence of the Old **Pretender**, James Francis Edward Stuart. Along with his friends, AP witnessed the gradual dissolution of the ministry, culminating in the removal of Harley from office on 27 July 1714. Within five days the Queen was dead, her Hanoverian successor poised to enter the country as **George I** and the Tories cast into the political wilderness for two generations to come. AP remained personally loyal to the friends he had made during the Harley years, but he must have known very soon that he would never again in his lifetime see a ministry of this political coloring govern the nation.

Harte, Rev. Walter (1709–74). Clergyman and poet. In 1727, while still an undergraduate at **Oxford**, he brought out *Poems on Several Occasions*, published by **Bernard Lintot**. These included complimentary verses to AP, and he may have corrected the entire volume (*Corr* 2: 430). AP subscribed to four copies. Harte became Rector of **Gosfield** in 1734, and AP tried to get him further promotion in the church. In 1737 he supported Harte's unsuccessful bid to become Professor of Poetry at Oxford. The highest dignity Harte ever achieved was as a Canon of Windsor from 1750.

Over the course of his career Harte wrote on a wide variety of topics. His *Essay on Satire, particularly on the Dunciad* (1730) was naturally laudatory toward his hero, and even AP seemed a little embarrassed: "There is also a poem upon satire writ by Mr. Harte of Oxford, a very valuable young man, but it compliments me too much," as he wrote to **John Caryll senior** (*Corr* 3: 173). In fact, **Lawton Gilliver** would never have published the item without AP's prior approval. Harte, who gave **Joseph Spence** several anecdotes concerning AP, was a friend of the ill-fated young poet William Pattison. His later works included *Essays on Husbandry* (1764), which was commended by **Samuel Johnson**. More generally, Johnson praised him as a scholar and "a man of the most companionable talents he had ever known," while acknowledging the streak of vanity in Harte.

See *An Essay on Satire*, with an introduction by T.B. Gilmore (Los Angeles: Augustan Reprint Society, 1968; New York: AMS Press, 1992).

Hartley, David (1705–57). Philosopher, best known today for his works on associational psychology. He worked as a physician and late in the poet's life met AP at **Bath**, where he was a member of the circle of **Ralph Allen**. In 1743 he prescribed medicines for AP, who wrote of him as "One I have a Sincere Esteem for" (*Corr* 4: 471).

Haymarket Theatre. A large playhouse built on the west side of the Haymarket, in a fashionable quarter of London, 1704–6, to the designs of **John Vanbrugh**. Known as the Queen's Theatre (King's from 1714). Sponsored by the Whig elite centered on the **Kit-Cat Club**, it was intended for the company of **Thomas Betterton** and initially operated under the direction of Vanbrugh and **William Congreve**. Used by the companies of **Colley Cibber** and others, it proved unwieldy for dramatic purposes, its echoing vaults swallowing up the voices of the actors. Later it became the main London home of **opera**. Under the management of **John James Heidegger**, it also served as a base for masquerades and lottery draws. The original building was destroyed by fire in 1790; today Her Majesty's theater stands on the site. AP refers to the playhouse on various occasions, and his prologue was delivered at a benefit concert for **John Dennis** that took place there in 1733.

See D. Nalbach, *The King's Theatre, 1704–1867: London's First Italian Opera House* (London: Society for Theatre Research, 1972).

Haywood, Eliza (c. 1693–1756). Née Fowler. Author and actress. She was a prolific writer in many forms, including fiction, drama, journalism, and conduct literature. A number of her works have provoked increasing interest over the last two decades, notably her periodical *The Female Spectator* (1744–46) and a fictional response to Samuel Richardson, *Anti-Pamela* (1741). Her most popular works in her own day were novels such as *Love in Excess* (1719–20), *Fantomina* (1724), and *The Masqueraders* (1724). Later successes included *The History of Miss Betsy Thoughtless* (1751), a work whose technique owes much to the new vein of **mock-heroic** fiction developed by **Henry Fielding**, and *The History of Jemmy and Jenny Jessamy* (1753). Haywood and her friend William Hatchett, a minor dramatist and translator, had earlier produced an adapted version of Fielding's play *Tom Thumb* (1733). A friend of **Lewis Theobald** and (at one time) of **Richard Savage**.

It was, however, a different branch of writing that attracted AP's attention to Haywood. Her book *Memoirs of a Certain Island Adjacent to* the Kingdom of Utopia (1724) takes the form of a *chronique scandaleuse*, relating the "secret history" of recent political events, including the **South Sea Bubble**. One section concerns a shameless and dissolute woman named "Marthalia." A key identifies her as "Mrs. Bl——t," and her lover, a necromancer Lucitario, as **James Craggs junior** (see *Early Career* 295–97). AP's horror at seeing his friend **Martha Blount** shown in this degrading way would have been sufficient to earn her a place in *The Dunciad*. Book 2 depicts her as the prize (complete with a china chamber-pot) to be awarded to the winners of a pissing contest in the duncely games. In a passage of cruel specificity, AP links Haywood with illegitimate progeny in literature and life ("Two babes of love close clinging to her waste"); with authorial vanity in producing *Works* in four volumes with "her picture . . . dress'd up" by the engraver; and as the new trophy mistress of **Edmund Curll** (2: 149–58). Haywood did in fact contribute to *The Female Dunciad*, issued by Curll in 1728, but not directly on AP. It has to be said that AP's reprisal was savage, even for the enormity of the offense against his friends Blount and Craggs; but Haywood's career in **Grub Street** had exactly fitted her for the role demanded of her in the action. As with **Defoe**, Haywood found that her talents did not compensate for the literary company she kept or the nature of the scandalous kinds in which she practiced.

Renewed interest in Haywood has led to reprints of many of her works, bibliographical studies, and extensive critical discussion. So far the pioneering biography, G.F. Whicher, *The Life and Romances of Mrs. Eliza Haywood* (New York: Columbia University Press, 1915), has not been fully replaced, though it is dated in approach and often inaccurate on details. A short study is M.A. Schofield, *Eliza Haywood* (Boston: Twayne, 1985).

Hazlitt, William (1778–1830). Essayist and critic. His scattered writings on AP represent some of the most articulate expressions of Romantic attitudes. In 1821 he wrote amusingly on the Bowles–Byron controversy (see **William Bowles**), and there are some references in *The English Comic Writers* (1819). His best-known discussion occurs in *Lectures on the English Poets* (1818), Lecture 4, "On Dryden and Pope." In a celebrated passage, he wrote of *The Rape of the Lock*, "It is the most exquisite specimen of *fillagree* work ever invented. It is admirable in proportion as it is made of nothing." In general, Hazlitt asserts, the "chief excellence" of AP lay "in describing pins and needles rather than the embattled spears of Greeks and Trojans." Elsewhere Hazlitt summarized the opinions of his age: "Pope is at the head of the second class of poets, *viz.* the describers of artificial life and manners. His works are a delightful, never-failing fund of good sense and refined taste. He had high invention and fancy of the comic kind. . . . He has no pretensions to sublimity."

health. AP spent his life as a semiinvalid. Apparently normal as an infant, he contracted tuberculosis of the bone as a boy and suffered protracted ill health between the ages of about twelve to sixteen. This left him dwarfish in stature, with a marked humpback and decreased mobility, as well as a range of painful side effects, some of which grew worse over time. He also suffered from a variety of other ailments in his later years.

A full "medical case-history" was compiled by **Marjorie Hope Nicolson** and G.S. Rousseau, supplanting all previous discussions of the topic. This has been used as the basis of the following summary.

1. **Pott's disease**. Spinal curvature, resulting from a tubercular condition of the bone and caused by infected milk. It produces uneven contraction of the spine, so that one side of the body is affected more noticeably. This is referred to as kyphoscoliosis (curvature in two different planes). AP was able to walk and ride in his youth but gradually became dependent on help for the most ordinary functions of everyday living. He needed to wear a corset in order to stand up. His height is generally stated to have been about four feet six inches, although there is no reliable evidence of the exact figure. The tubercular illness would help to explain the dangerous bouts of fever AP underwent as a young man, for example, in 1710

and 1712. His "languishing" ailment has been diagnosed as chronic rather than acute, immediately related to the symptoms of Pott's disease. Although he seems to have been relatively healthy in the period 1713–17, the term "relative" is central to this account. He continued to suffer pain and to resort to a variety of regimens to combat his illness. From 1728 he was advised by his doctors to visit **Bath** to take the mineral waters, and he made other trips to the resort in the 1730s, drawing on the expertise of medical men like **George Cheyne** and **William Oliver**. From about 1731 he adopted a diet of asses' milk, a universal panacea praised by **Dr. John Arbuthnot**, among others.

2. As a young man AP began to experience serious headaches. These may have been a form of migraine and may help to account for the tense muscles in his face noted by Sir Joshua Reynolds, when the painter met AP toward the end of the poet's life.

3. There could also be a link to persistent eye troubles, which grew worse as AP aged. By 1742 he was complaining that his sight grew ever "shorter and dimmer." Among the most noted ophthalmologists at the time was AP's friend **William Cheselden**; but it does not appear that AP underwent cataract surgery, as used to be thought.

4. Cheselden's aid was, however, required when AP found himself afflicted with a constriction of the uretha, quite likely as a result of a youthful bout of gonorrhea. An operation for urethral dilatation was performed by Cheselden in August 1740.

5. From about 1741 AP suffered from increasingly severe symptoms of an asthmatic condition. AP tried a number of remedies, including phlebotomy, and considered others. The unreliable **Dr. Thomas Thompson** regarded this complaint as dropsical and put AP on a course of mineral waters. This did nothing to arrest the patient's steady decline and his death soon afterward.

6. The immediate cause of death was probably a breakdown in cardiac and pulmonary functions, caused by the kyphoscoliosis. As the curvature of the spine proceeds, it finally induces problems in both cardiovascular and respiratory functions. It may be suspected that AP's "asthma" was itself a result of the underlying bone condition.

In the course of his life, AP met with the usual assortment of minor illnesses and also encountered some hazardous **accidents**.

AP refers wryly to his poor health in many of his poems, most notably in the **Epistle to Arbuthnot**, ll. 131–32: "The Muse but serv'd to ease some Friend, not Wife, / To help me thro' this long Disease, my Life" (*TE* 4: 105).

For a comprehensive survey, see *This Long Disease* 7–82. For the effects of AP's disabilities on his life and work, see "The Least Thing Like a Man in England," in *CIH* 372–92; as well as H. Deutsch, *Resemblance and Disgrace: Alexander Pope and the Deformation of Culture* (Cambridge, MA: Harvard University Press, 1996).

Hearne, Thomas (1678–1735). **Antiquarian** scholar, based in **Oxford**. Formerly an assistant keeper of the Bodleian Library, he lost his job because of his scruples as a **nonjuror** in 1716. His extreme political views and abrasive personality, as well as his own scruples, meant that he was never able to gain the recognition to which his learning and industry entitled him in the field of medieval scholarship. He produced a long series of editions of early texts, especially chronicles, some of which have still not been fully supplanted, even though they lack a modern critical apparatus. It is clear from the notes attributed to Martin Scriblerus in *The Dunciad* that AP had inspected some of these editions. Almost equally valuable to posterity has been his diary, an extensive and indiscreet record of Oxford life in the early eighteenth century.

Hearne grew up at White Waltham in **Berkshire**, just four miles from **Binfield**; his early patron was Francis Cherry (1665–1713) of nearby Shottesbrooke, where the local nonjuring community regularly congregated. After the death of **Humfrey Wanley**, Hearne had been lined up to succeed him as librarian to the **second Earl of Oxford**, but this fell through. The character of the uncouth pedant Wormius in Book 3 of *The Dunciad* is almost certainly based on Hearne, although AP stated in his note that the antiquarian "had in no way aggrieved our Poet, but on the contrary published many curious tracts which he [Scriblerus] hath to his great contentment perused" (*TE* 5: 171). There is another dismissive line in the **Epistle to Bur-**

lington, "Rare monkish Manuscripts for Hearne alone" (*TE* 3.ii: 135). It would have been unlike Hearne to accept criticism lying down. In his diary for 18 July 1729, he wrote: "This Alexander Pope, tho' he be an English Poet, yet he is but an indifferent scholar, mean at Latin & can hardly read Greek. He is a very ill-natured man, and covetous and excessively proud."

See T. Harmsen, *Antiquarianism in the Augustan Age: Thomas Hearne, 1686–1735* (Oxford: Peter Lang, 2000).

Heidegger, John James (originally Johann Jakob) (1666–1749). Swiss impresario. Born in Zürich of German ancestry. His father was the theologian Johann-Heinrich Heidegger (1633–98). Left his wife and children and moved to London in 1707, becoming manager at the **Haymarket Theatre** in 1713. For the next thirty years he remained at the head of affairs there. Among his enterprises were the Royal Academy of Music and other ventures involving **George Frideric Handel**. He also wrote operatic libretti. Heidegger started the fashionable craze for masquerades, held at the **theater** from c. 1717. Known, inaccurately, as "the Swiss Count." Master of the Revels to **George II**, Heidegger supervised the ceremonials at the coronation in 1727. Notorious for his ugliness, he was depicted by **William Hogarth** and **Jean-Baptiste Van Loo**, among others. He was a resident of **Richmond** and neighbor of several of AP's friends. Subscribed to the **Shakespeare edition** and to the poems of **John Gay**.

In *The Dunciad* AP turns the impresario into a kind of fabulous beast: "And lo! Her Bird (a monster of a fowl! / Something betwixt a H——r and Owl)," with the note, "A strange Bird from *Switzerland*" (1: 243–44). A poem satirizing Heidegger and his masquerades, found in Gay's handwriting, may be the work of either AP or Gay.

The only full treatment in any language is a fanciful work by J.L. Clerc, *L'enchanteur Carabosse. Le Zurichois John-James Heidegger, surintendant des plaisirs d'Angleterre* (Lausanne: L'Abbaye du Livre, 1942). For his role in the culture of the time, see P. Rogers, "Masquerades and Operas: Hogarth, Heidegger and Others," in *Literature and Popular Culture in Eighteenth Century England* (Brighton: Harvester, 1985), 40–70. A modern scholarly life is required.

Henley, John (1692–1756). A florid preacher, famed for his eccentric addresses and lessons in elocution, as well as for his self-publicizing and Whiggish journal, *The Hyp Doctor*, in which he often attacked AP. Other onslaughts came in *Tom o'Bedlam's Dunciad* (1729) and *Why How now, Gossip Pope?* (1743): see Guerinot 170–71, 314–15. He was one of the authors most annoyed to be cast in AP's gallery of dunces, where the "gilt tub" from which he preached in Newport Market is conspicuously mentioned (2: 2). Later in the poem he is also shown in full oratorical mode, "Tuning his voice, and balancing his hands." AP added a damaging note, referring to Henley's mountebank tricks and troubles with the law (*TE* 5: 174–75). There are further contemptuous references in the *Imitations of Horace*. Actually his public renown as "Orator" Henley left AP with little work to do in converting him into a figure of fun.

See G. Midgley, *The Life of Orator Henley* (Oxford: Clarendon, 1973).

heroic couplet. Two rhyming verses written in the "heroic" line, that is iambic pentameter (where the stressed syllables occur alternately, as ^/^/^/^/^/). There is generally a pause or "cesura" in the middle of each line, often after the fourth or sixth syllable. This may be a very marked break, emphasized by the syntax, as in "Forget her Pray'rs, | or miss a Masquerade" (*The Rape of the Lock*, 2: 166). Alternatively, the pause may be almost imperceptible, as in a verse like "Soon as thy letters trembling I unclose" *Eloisa to Abelard* 29), where the medial pause after "letters" is scarcely more pronounced than the momentary hesitation after "soon" and "trembling." AP uses an exceptional range of rhythmic and rhyming variations to utilize the full potential of the couplet form. See J.A. Jones, *Pope's Couplet Art* (Athens: University of Georgia Press, 1969).

An increasing distaste for the couplet is one

of the most marked features of the new fashions in poetry in the second half of the century and plays a major part in the diminished reputation of AP over this period.

Hervey, John, Baron (1696–1743). Name pronounced "Harvey." Politician, courtier, and writer. Son of the first Earl of Bristol. In 1720 he married the court beauty Molly Lepel, later **Mary Hervey**, one of the **maids of honor** who were well known to AP at this time. Succeeded to the courtesy title of Lord Hervey in 1723. MP from 1725; originally an adherent of **Frederick, Prince of Wales**, he switched his allegiance to **Sir Robert Walpole** and became Vice-Chamberlain in 1730. His quarrel with **William Pulteney** led to a duel in 1731. A key link between the Walpole government and the royal family, he was a close adviser of **Queen Caroline**. Lord Privy Seal from 1740 to 1742, when the fall of Walpole thrust him into opposition. Wrote pamphlets on behalf of the ministry and joined with his friend **Lady Mary Wortley Montagu** in attacks on AP. His *Memoirs of the Reign of George II* (first published by **John Wilson Croker** in 1848) are an important source for events at court in the 1730s. Polished and Tacitonian, they show political life as a game of intrigue and ambition.

As in the case of Lady Mary, Hervey and his wife had enjoyed good relations with AP in earlier years. They are jointly complimented in *Mr. Pope's Welcome from Greece*: "Now *Harvey* fair of face I mark full well / With Thee Youth's youngest Daughter, sweet *Lepell*." (Unless "Harvey" is an oblique reference to Mary's mother, Lady Bristol.) Both are listed in the subscribers to the *Odyssey*. Relations deteriorated, mainly perhaps because of Hervey's breach with Pulteney and switch to the side of Walpole. Together with Lady Mary, Hervey wrote a sharp riposte to AP, *Verses Address'd to the Imitator of the First Satire of the Second Book of Horace* (1733). This has been described as "the most famous of attacks on Pope and perhaps the only one where Pope has found worthy adversary" (Guerinot 225). Further counterblasts, generally less successful, were *An Epistle from a Nobleman to a Doctor of Divinity* (1733) and *A Letter to Mr. Cibber* (1742). He may also have had a hand together with **Colley Cibber** in *The Difference between Verbal and Practical Virtue* (1742).

It cannot be denied that the poet had given the peer ample cause for such retaliation. Again and again AP brought Hervey into his works, especially the *Imitations of Horace*, normally employing a transparent sobriquet such as "Lord Fanny" or "Fannius." *Sober Advice from Horace* contains some particularly brutal lines on Hervey and Lady Mary. The baron figures in several minor poems and was the object of a witty quatrain "To the Earl of Burlington, asking who writ the Libels against him" (*TE* 6: 355). He is targeted in *A Master Key to Popery* and the recipient of the coruscating *Letter to a Noble Lord*. In later editions of *The Art of Sinking* a niche was found for Hervey, while he makes a surreptitious entrance into the notes of *The Dunciad*. However, Hervey gained a secure hold on immortality when AP composed his blistering portrait of **Sporus** as the main set-piece in the *Epistle to Arbuthnot*. AP moves beyond the usual features employed in caricatures of Hervey—his epicene appearance and close relations with the Queen—to a depiction of evil incarnate in the modern world—Sporus becomes a Satan of the drawing room. Hervey and Lady Mary were AP's most formidable antagonists, and it is no coincidence that he assaults them with particular venom and satiric invention.

For a reliable life, see R. Halsband, *Lord Hervey: Eighteenth-Century Courtier* (Oxford: Clarendon, 1973). See also *Some Memorials towards Memoirs of the Reign of King George II*, ed. R. Sedgwick, 3 vols. (London: Eyre & Spottiswoode, 1931).

Hervey, Mary, Baroness (1700–1768). As a young court lady in the period 1715–20, known as beautiful Molly Lepell, she was well known to AP and friends such as **John Gay**, prior to her marriage to **John, Baron Hervey**. She appears as "Youth's youngest Daughter, sweet *Lepell*" in *Mr. Pope's Welcome from Greece*. She had in fact stayed with the poet and his mother in the weeks leading up to her wedding in October 1720. AP mentions her in his poems relating to the **maids of honor** of the Princess of Wales, notably *The Court Ballad*. She also figures in his correspondence. After her marriage, understandably, she had fewer dealings with the poet. Her portrait hung at **Twickenham**. Her letters, edited by **John Wilson Croker** in 1821, cast some light on the world of AP.

See D.M. Stuart, *Molly Lepel, Lady Hervey* (London: Harrap, 1936).

Hill, Aaron (1683–1750). Miscellaneous writer and projector. Hill's varied literary doings included work as a librettist for **George Frideric Handel** and as a theatrical director (see **opera**); as a playwright; as a poet; as essayist and editor of journals; and as translator. He "improved" **Shakespeare**'s *Henry V* and adapted the text of **Voltaire**'s tragedy *Mérope*. His specialty was orientalism and his particular hero Peter the Great, celebrated in *The Northern Star* (1718). Outside writing, his life was equally varied. As little more than a boy, he traveled to the Middle East and later went on a **Grand Tour** as a "bear-leader" or tutor. He took out a patent for manufacturing oil from beechnuts, for which he foresaw a large number of uses. Hill was one of the first to propose settling the colony that not long afterward became Georgia. He served as an agent of the dubious York Buildings Company, whose unwise financial ventures exemplified the speculative mania of the era of the **South Sea Bubble**, and introduced timber rafting to the Highlands of Scotland. One of his later schemes was to plant vineyards in Essex, around what is now the East End of London.

His contacts were equally wide. He was at school in Devon with **John Gay** and early in life gained the patronage of the **Earl of Peterborough**. As a manager at **Drury Lane Theatre**, he worked with actors such as **Barton Booth** and **Anne Oldfield**. He was familiar with many leading authors, including **John Dennis**, **Edward Young**, and **Eliza Haywood**. His closest alliance was with the group centering on **James Thomson** and **David Mallet**, with which **Richard Savage** was also associated. Late in life his main literary ally was the

novelist Samuel Richardson, who helped to put out an edition of Hill's *Works* in 1753 for the benefit of his daughters Urania, Astraea, and Minerva.

It is not surprising that Hill's relations with AP vacillated over time, so disparate was his career and so mercurial his approach to life. In bad moments their dealings were hostile: Hill targeted AP's **Shakespeare edition** in his journal *The Plain Dealer*, and AP allotted Hill a spot in *The Art of Sinking*. Hill's response was *The Progress of Wit* (1730), one of the numerous **pamphlet attacks** on the poet. There was also a reference in *The Dunciad* (2: 283) that Hill took, no doubt rightly, as directed against him. Periodically Hill attempted to mend fences, sent humble apologies, and included favorable references to AP in his works; but they never established a stable friendship. About sixty letters survive between the pair, fairly equally divided in terms of authorship.

An examination of Hill's career and his encounters with AP is D. Brewster, *Aaron Hill: Poet, Dramatist, Projector* (New York: Columbia University Press, 1913; reprint, New York: AMS Press, 1966). This has now been supplanted by C. Gerrard, *Aaron Hill: The Muses' Projector 1685–1750* (Oxford: Clarendon, 2003).

Hill, Richard (1655–1727). Diplomat, politician, and friend of **Sir William Trumbull**. Trumbull introduced Hill to AP in 1714 ("New Letters" 401–4). His London home from 1700 was very close to the house of **Charles Jervas** in **Cleveland Court** where AP frequently stayed. It was Hill who wrote to Trumbull and recommended his neighbor Jervas as a suitable artist to paint Trumbull's second wife. He also had a house at **Richmond**, besides developing the family estate in Shropshire. Hill had taken deacon's orders but went into public life, serving as a Lord of the Treasury and Lord of the Admiralty. However, it was his time as Deputy Paymaster under **William III** that permitted the "lucrative arithmetic" that laid the foundation of his wealth. Later he took priest's orders and became a Fellow of Eton College. Hill subscribed to the *Iliad*. Unmarried, he passed on his wealth to his nephew Samuel Hill, also a subscriber (*Corr* 1: 300).

Hillhouse, James Theodore (1890–1956). Scholar at the University of Michigan. Worked on **Fielding**, Scott, and other writers. Best known to students of AP as author of a study of the *Grub-street Journal*, published in 1928. He also wrote on **Martha** and **Teresa Blount**.

See *From Jane Austen to Joseph Conrad: Essays Collected in Memory of James T. Hillhouse*, ed. R.C. Rathburn and M. Steinmann, Jr. (Minneapolis: University of Minnesota Press, 1958).

Hoare, William (c. 1707–92). **Portrait** painter, specializing in pastels, who studied in Italy and settled at **Bath** in 1738. Among his early subjects was **Dr. William Oliver**. He owed much to the patronage of the benevolent **Ralph Allen**, and it may have been this connection that led to his painting AP while the poet was staying at **Prior Park** in 1739–40: see *Portraits* 63–64. Hoare often drew **William Warburton**.

Hogarth, William (1697–1764). Artist. In his early years Hogarth apparently had a dubious opinion of AP and may have introduced him into the print *The South Sea Scheme* (1721). In the 1730s the painter took on many of the themes and satiric targets of the Scriblerian group, although he seems to have had no personal contact with its members. There are often visual echoes of AP's work. *The Distressed Poet* (1737) is in many ways a graphic counterpart to *The Dunciad*: lines from the poem appear under the print. The central figure has even been identified as **Lewis Theobald**, although there is no evidence for this. The details of the scene are full of relevant material, including a copy of the *Grub-street Journal*. On the wall is a caricature of AP shown beating **Curll**. Hogarth's final work *Tail-Piece: or the Bathos* (1764) has several reminiscences of *The Art of Sinking*.

The most complete account is R. Paulson, *Hogarth*, 3 vols. (New Brunswick, NJ: Rutgers University Press, 1991). See also an excellent one-volume biography by J. Uglow, *Hogarth: A Life and a World* (London: Faber, 1997).

Homer. Greek epic poet who wrote probably in the eighth century B.C. AP first read his works at the age of about eight, in the English version by John Ogilby (1660, 1665). "Ogilby's translation of Homer was one of the first large poems that Mr. Pope read," according to **Joseph Spence**, "and he still spoke of the pleasure it gave him, with a sort of rapture only on reflecting on it." Despite imperfections in the translator's cumbrous language, "He saw the greatness of Homer's beauties through all the rags that were flung over him" (*Anecdotes* 1: 14). When he was about twelve he wrote a play to be performed by his schoolfellows, with speeches from the *Iliad* interspersed with verses of his own. AP's earliest poems included renditions of Homer: a translation of parts of Books 12 and 16 of the *Iliad* (see *Episode of Sarpedon*) and one from Book 13 of the *Odyssey*.

Although his knowledge of Greek was not very advanced, AP was able with the aid of translations and commentaries to grasp enough of the sense and mood of the original to produce his own versions of the two epics. He was helped by his collaborators, **Thomas Parnell** and **William Broome**, in particular. For several generations these were the most familiar dress of Homer in the English-speaking world. Dismissed in the nineteenth century as inauthentic and pompous, they have enjoyed a new currency in recent years. Their grand Augustan style now appears a noble attempt to reclaim epic as a literary property at a time when most developments—the rise of the realist novel, the growth of journalism, and the ubiquity of satire—were working against the form. There was a bust of Homer in AP's **villa**, and one was included in his design for his **garden**. In addition, the poet's seal bore the head of Homer. Several editions were found in AP's **library**, along with translations by George Chapman and Thomas Hobbes. See *Iliad*; and *Odyssey*, as well as *The Battle of the Frogs and Mice* and **Anne Dacier**.

Hooke, Nathaniel (c. 1690–1762). Historian and controversial writer. He came from a family of Catholics and **Jacobites** and may have studied with AP at a school in **Twyford**. No other links with AP are apparent for three decades, but in the later years of the poet's life Hooke was among his closest allies. Hooke's oddly secretive nature, combined with AP's own taste for clandestine dealings, has ensured that mystery still surrounds their activities.

Hooke was taken up by **Ralph Allen** by 1730. In that year Hooke issued his translation of the highly popular (and fictional) *Travels of Cyrus*, by Andrew Michael Ramsay (c. 1686–1743), a remarkable Scottish author and theologian. The book contains hints of Ramsay's fondness for the occult, which Hooke may have shared. The translation was carried out in **Bath**, at the home of **Dr. George Cheyne**. The impressive list of subscribers contains an extraordinary range of names, but one large block consists of personal friends and contacts of AP, such as the **second Earl of Oxford, Lord Bathurst**, and **Joseph Spence**, who was later friendly with Hooke and Ramsay, collecting their reminiscences (see *Anecdotes* 1: 441–76). Also present is "Mrs Blunt," probably **Martha Blount**. A surprising name is that of Sir Henry Englefield. The large Jacobite presence on the list includes the **Duchess of Buckinghamshire**, **George Granville** and his wife (Lord and Lady Lansdowne), **Mary Caesar** and her husband, **Dr. William King** (a friend of Hooke), and the **Earl of Strafford**. Either AP himself or someone very close to him was promoting the subscription, although there are signs that an underground Masonic network was also attracted by Ramsay's work.

Allen secretly supported the campaign for subscribers for Hooke's next book, the first installment of his *Roman History* in 1738 (the full work was not published until 1771). The first volume was dedicated to AP, who by this time was seeing a great deal of Hooke, both at Bath and at **Twickenham**. Their relations were generally very good, although the poet's quarrel with Allen over Martha Blount in 1743 made for some awkwardness. Hooke transcribed *The Universal Prayer* for Allen. He was present at the bedside as AP's **death** approached and passed on some details to Spence (*Anecdotes* 1: 265–69). He has been said to have supplied information on this subject to **Samuel Johnson** when the latter visited France in 1775, but this must have been a secondhand account by Hooke's son Luke Joseph (1716–96), a professor at the Sorbonne, since the father was long dead.

One of Hooke's best-known enterprises was his editing of the self-exculpatory memoirs of Sarah, **Duchess of Marlborough** in 1742. AP may well have played a part in securing this work for him. The story told by **Warburton** that Hooke tried to convert the elderly duchess to the Catholic faith has not been substantiated. AP left him £5 for a mourning ring in his **will**.

Hooker, Edward Niles (1902–57). Scholar who was Professor of English at the University of California, Los Angeles, from 1936 and helped to found the Augustan Reprint Society as well as the California edition of the works of **John Dryden**. His edition of *The Critical Works* of **John Dennis**, in 2 vols. (1939–43), is of considerable help to students of AP. See also his essay, "Pope on Wit: The *Essay on Criticism*," in *The Seventeenth Century: Studies in the History of English Thought and Literature by R.F. Jones and Others* (Stanford: Stanford University Press, 1951), 225–46; reprinted in *EA* 185–207.

Horace (Quintus Horatius Flaccus) (65–8 B.C.). Poet. Educated at Rome and Athens; fought in the army of Marcus Brutus during the Civil Wars. Acquired the patronage of the aristocrat Maecenas and later of the Emperor Augustus. Most of his works, including two books of satires, two books of epistles, epodes, and four books of odes, were widely read and studied in AP's lifetime. Individual poems such as *Carmen Saeculare* and the *Ars Poetica* also gained great currency. Numerous editions appeared, the most important one being that of **Richard Bentley** (1711), which introduced a large number of new readings (too many, AP probably thought). There were also many translations, building on a tradition established by writers such as **Ben Jonson**, **Abraham Cowley**, **John Dryden**, and the Earl of Rochester. Others along with AP attempted **imitation** rather than translation, most notably AP's friend **Jonathan Swift**. The standard version of the key works was for some generations that of Thomas Creech, *The Odes, Satyrs, and Epistles of Horace done into English* (1684), which left its mark on AP's work.

Although he did not have a conventional schooling, which would have exposed him to detailed study of Horace, AP became familiar with the poems at an early age. Tags from Horace are found in his correspondence from all periods. Much of his work reflects the influence of the Roman poet's themes and manner, especially the sly, insinuating wit of the satires and the graceful style of the odes. *An Essay on Criticism* reaches back to the founding work in this form, the *Ars Poetica*. However, AP's most direct use of his predecessor came in the series of *Imitations of Horace* published in the last decade of his life. AP used texts of Horace in a somewhat eclectic fashion. However, he seems to have employed most frequently the Elzevir edition prepared by Daniel Heinsius (Leiden, 1629). He also consulted the Bentley edition; the Delphin edition published by Guillaume Desprez in 1695; and a version by Alexander Cunningham (The Hague, 1721). All these apart from Bentley are known to have been in AP's **library**. See L. Bloom, "Pope as Textual Critic: A Bibliographical Study of His Horatian Text," *Journal of English and Germanic Philosophy*, 47 (1948), 150–55, reprinted in *EA* 533–44; and R. Steiger, *The English and Latin Texts of Pope's "Imitations of Horace"* (New York: Garland, 1988).

A venerable work, C. Goad, *Horace in the English Literature of the Eighteenth Century* (New Haven, CT: Yale University Press, 1918), remains an instructive book.

Horneck, Philip (d. 1728). Lawyer and journalist. He held the politically sensitive office of Solicitor to the Treasury from 1716 to 1728, a post that involved him in decisions regarding the prosecution of dissidents and critics of the government. He had earned this step up the lad-

der by his eccentric Whig polemic titled *The High-German Doctor* (1714–15), in which AP and his allies were regularly abused. The only known retaliation is a brief reference to Horneck as "a scurrilous Scribler" in the *Memoirs of Martin Scriblerus*, chapter 6, and a glancing reference together with **Edward Roome** in Book 3 of *The Dunciad*.

Howard, Henrietta, Countess of Suffolk (c. 1688–1767). The birthdate usually given, 1681, is inaccurate. Court lady. Née Hobart. Daughter of a Norfolk baronet. In 1706 she married an inconsequential and improvident figure, Charles Howard (1675–1733); he succeeded as ninth Earl of Suffolk in 1731, by which time the couple had long been estranged. Spent a period at the Hanoverian court, 1710–13. Her husband was appointed a Gentleman of the Bedchamber to the Prince of Wales, later **George II**, in 1714. She became Bedchamber Woman to the Princess, later **Queen Caroline**, and "official" mistress to the Prince. Retired from court, 1734, after the death of her husband in the previous year, and married **Hon. George Berkeley** in 1735. Following his death in 1746 she lived in retirement. A friend of **Swift**, to whom she was introduced by AP in 1726; many letters survive between Swift and Mrs. Howard. She was a strong supporter of **John Gay** and on good terms with other friends of AP such as **Martha Blount**, **John Arbuthnot**, and the **Earl of Peterborough**. She built a house, **Marble Hill**, designed by the **ninth Earl of Pembroke**, within easy reach of AP's own home at **Twickenham**, and had the poet's advice in planning the garden. Mrs. Howard appears in Swift's amusing "Pastoral Dialogue" (1727) and receives somewhat equivocal mention along with the Queen in *Verses on the Death of Dr. Swift*.

AP must have known her from the time of his fanciful dalliance with the **maids of honor** soon after the Hanoverians came to England. Gay names her among the poet's friends in *Mr. Pope's Welcome from Greece*. She subscribed to the *Odyssey*, as well as to the poems of Gay and **Prior**, and the cantatas of **Bononcini**. These acts imply a loyalty to the Prince and Princess of Wales against the King. Only three letters from AP to her survive. However, AP wrote a touchingly comic poem to Mrs. Howard, "On a Certain Lady at Court," almost in the vein of Swift's verses to Stella. This was published in the *Miscellanies* in 1732, with neither the author nor the subject of the poem acknowledged (see *TE* 6: 250–51). The epigrammatic close is based on her deafness, a handicap she seems to have been able to employ to her advantage in delicate situations at court. It used to be thought that Henrietta Howard may have served as the model for the character of **Cloe** in AP's *Epistle to a Lady*, but this is no longer believed to be the case (see Ault 266–75; *TE* 3.ii: 63).

Most modern work on Mrs. Howard goes back to an edition of her correspondence published by **John Wilson Croker** in two volumes, 1824. L. Melville, *Lady Suffolk and her Circle* (London: Hutchinson, 1924), is informative but sketchy. J. Bryant, *Mrs Howard: A Woman of Reason (1688–1767)* (London: English Heritage, 1988), is an excellent catalog for an exhibition at Marble Hill.

Howe, John Grubham (1657–1722). Tory MP and politician. He held minor office as Paymaster General under **Queen Anne** from 1703 to 1714 but became a carping backwoodsman in later years. **Swift**, in his Whiggish days, had mentioned Howe as a high Tory (see "A Digression concerning Madness," in *A Tale of a Tub*). The uncle of **Mary Howe**, he subscribed to the *Iliad*, as did his son John Howe, later first Baron Chedworth (1688–1742), to the *Odyssey*. In 1728 the son entertained AP at his home, Stowell, six miles northeast of **Cirencester**, when the poet found **Lord Bathurst** away from home.

Howe, Mary (d. 1749). One of the **maids of honor** to the Princess of Wales, later **Queen Caroline**, from 1723 to 1725. She was the daughter of the first Viscount Howe. In 1725 she married as his third wife Thomas Herbert, eighth Earl of Pembroke (1756–1733), a politician and collector, who subscribed to the *Iliad* and the *Odyssey*. AP mentions him in the *Epistle to Burlington*, l. 7. After his death she

married John Mordaunt (1709–67), brother of the fourth Earl of Peterborough, in 1735. She too subscribed to the *Odyssey*. Her close friend was **Judith Cowper**, and she is often mentioned in the correspondence between Cowper and AP. Lady Pembroke was a devotee of **opera** with a special fondness for the star singer Cuzzoni. In addition, she bestowed patronage on the librettist **Paolo Rolli**, who was without doubt known personally to AP. Mary's first cousin Sophia (d. 1726) was also one of the maids of honor from 1715 to 1717, and from 1720 to 1724; she figures briefly in AP's letters and minor verse.

Hughes, John (1677–1720). Poet and dramatist. Educated at a dissenting academy in London, along with the poet Isaac Watts. Appointed by Lord Chancellor Cowper secretary to the commission for naming justices of the peace, 1717. Hughes was attached to the Whig circle meeting at **Button's** coffeehouse and especially to **Joseph Addison**. His miscellaneous writing included contributions to *The Tatler*, *The Spectator*, and *The Guardian*. He had a strong interest in music and composed libretti for masques and cantatas. Some of his work, including a share in *Acis and Galatea*, was set to music by **Handel**. His reputation survived long enough to earn him an entry in the *Lives of the Poets* by **Samuel Johnson**.

He supported AP's campaign for subscriptions to the *Iliad* and is named in the list of subscribers, but this may reflect a gift on AP's part. Hughes edited the works of **Edmund Spenser** in 6 vols. (1715) and seems to have presented AP with a set (*CIH* 466). His version of the letters of Heloïse and Abelard (1713) provided an important basis for AP's own *Eloisa to Abelard*. When Hughes was preparing for the opening of his tragedy *The Siege of Damascus* in 1720, he asked AP to supply a prologue, but in the end AP declined, citing his poor health. The play was put on with great success on 17 February, but Hughes died of consumption the same day. AP wrote a letter of consolation to the dramatist's brother, Jabez Hughes (c. 1685–1731), also a writer, and soon after sent the last volumes of the *Iliad* (*Corr* 2:

28–29, 34, 46–47). Years later Swift inquired about Hughes, having noted that AP was listed as a subscriber to his posthumously published *Poems on Several Occasions* (1735). In reply AP agreed that Hughes was a poet of moderate ability, although "whatever he wanted as to genius he made up as an honest man" (*Corr* 3: 492, 508). The verdict expressed to **Joseph Spence** is a little fuller: "Hughes was a good, humble-spirited man, a great admirer of Mr. Addison, and but a poor writer, except his play [*The Siege of Damascus*]: that, very well" (*Anecdotes* 1: 211).

Humphreys, Arthur Raleigh (1911–88). Professor at the University of Leicester, 1947–76. Known for his work on **William Shakespeare**, as well as many important studies of the eighteenth century. These include his book *The Augustan World* (1954), as well as writings on **Addison, Steele**, and **Fielding**. He contributed to collections such as *Writers and their Background: Alexander Pope* (1972). An illuminating critic of AP and his setting. See a Festschrift, *Augustan Worlds: New Essays on Eighteenth-Century Literature*, ed. J.C. Hilson et al. (New York: Harper & Row, 1977), which contains items on AP.

Hymn Written in Windsor Forest, A. Poem of eight lines in alternating rhymes. In September 1717 AP made a sentimental journey to his old home at **Binfield**, which his family had quit in the previous year (see **Windsor Forest**). He reported in a letter to **Teresa** and **Martha Blount** that he had passed the day in the familiar woods where he had spent his boyhood and had made a "hymn" as he revisited these "groves." The verses that follow possibly relate to AP's feeling for one of the sisters as much as to the lost landscape of his youth. See *Corr* 1: 428–29; *TE* 6: 194.

Idea of a Patriot King, The. A polemical treatise written by **Viscount Bolingbroke** in the later part of 1738, intended as a guide to **Frederick, Prince of Wales** and his circle. It was probably completed when Bolingbroke was staying with AP during a stay in England, lasting from July 1738 to April 1739. The manuscript circulated among the Prince's friends, and AP was seemingly allowed by Bolingbroke to print a few copies for private distribution. In the event AP had **John Wright** print no less than 1,500 copies of a longer version, with some revisions of his own, and stored for future publication. When Bolingbroke found out what had happened after AP's death, he was enraged. Portions of the tract were published in 1749, and Bolingbroke had an authorized edition issued in the same year. By this time he had come to revile his former close friend AP.

For the text, see Bolingbroke's *Political Writings*, ed. D. Armitage (Cambridge: Cambridge University Press, 1997), 217–94. See also F.E. Ratchford, "Pope and the Patriot King," *Texas Studies in English*, 6 (1926), 157–77, supplemented by an important article by G. Barber, "Bolingbroke, Pope, and the *Patriot King*," *The Library*, 19 (1964), 67–89.

Iliad. With his early interest in **Homer**, it is not surprising that two of AP's most sustained creative enterprises were devoted to the two great epic poems of ancient Greece. As early as April 1708 **Sir William Trumbull** was urging him to undertake a translation, and short versions of selected passages survive from 1709. *The Episode of Sarpedon*, from the twelfth and sixteenth books of the *Iliad*, came out in **Tonson**'s *Miscellanies* in that year. A portion of Book 13 followed in a miscellany edited by **Richard** **Steele** in December 1713. The *Iliad* appeared between 1715 and 1720; the *Odyssey* in 1725–26. Both were published by subscription under the imprint of **Bernard Lintot**. The printer was **William Bowyer**.

AP gave notice of his intention to translate the *Iliad* in October 1713: no copy of the proposal is known to survive. An advertisement giving details of the work was included at the end of the third edition of *The Rape of the Lock* in 1714. On 21 October 1713 **George Granville**, now Lord Lansdowne, wrote to the poet expressing his pleasure at news of the venture (*Corr* 1: 194–95). In fact, AP did not begin serious work on the project until he was sure that the subscription would turn out successfully. Initially he thought that he might have a rival in the shape of a version by **Thomas Tickell**, but this rival translation quickly fizzled out. The contract with Lintot was signed on 23 March 1714, on terms that look remarkably favorable to AP. It was in June 1715 that the first installment appeared, and thereafter the volumes came out on a more or less annual basis. On 21 May 1720 **Robert Digby** sent a message that indicates that AP had completed the task, except for some of the ancillary material (*Corr* 2: 47).

During its gestation period of more than six years, the work caused AP immense labor and anxiety. He worked mainly in the summers, often in a rural location such as **Binfield**. He wrote fast, aiming to complete fifty lines each day, although there were naturally fallow periods. Much of the first draft was written on odd scraps of paper; it is for this reason that many incoming letters to AP survive among the Homer manuscripts in the British Library, since AP habitually used the back of letters for his

Homeric verses. A fair copy was subsequently made, sometimes by the hand of AP's neighbor Thomas Dancastle. AP strove to achieve certain qualities such as a graphic pictorial quality, while remaining as faithful as possible to the original text, and to preserve a dignity that he may have felt was absent from earlier English translations, such as those of George Chapman and Thomas Hobbes. There was, too, much intensive study of commentators such as Eustathius (d.c. 1194) and **Anne Dacier**. In compiling his notes he had some help from **William Broome** and **John Jortin**.

In the early stages of his work, AP was equally concerned by the need to rustle up sufficient subscribers. He had the help of **Jonathan Swift**, who was lobbying on his behalf by late 1713. By 19 November AP could inform Trumbull that "almost all the distinguished names of Quality or Learning have subscribed to it," though this was of course an exaggeration. Others who aided in the campaign were **John Caryll senior**, **John Gay**, and **Matthew Prior**. The deal for the buyers was that they should pay one guinea (£1.05) for each of the six volumes, with two guineas down at the start, and then a guinea each for the second, third, fourth, and fifth installments. In the end AP procured 575 subscribers, with multiple copies bringing the total up to 654 sets. Among these multiple subscribers were peers known to AP, such as **Bolingbroke**, **Buckinghamshire**, Carnarvon (later **Chandos**), **Halifax**, **Harcourt**, and George Granville. The list was large by the standards of the time, although not extraordinarily so. It was particularly distinguished in terms of the great names who were attracted: the most eminent individuals to appear on the list included **Sir Isaac Newton**, **Sir Christopher Wren**, and the **Duke of Marlborough**, to mention only the most Olympian figures. The average age was about 39; 8 percent were women (about the norm for such books), and the only member of the royal family present was the Princess of Wales, later **Queen Caroline**. Lintot paid AP 200 guineas (£210) for each of the volumes at dates between 23 March 1715 and 26 February 1720. In addition, AP had the proceeds of the subscription volumes,

and he cleared an estimated £5,000 to £6,000 overall. It was the turning point in his career financially, and it enabled him to move to **Twickenham**.

Subscribers received a handsome quarto volume (each containing the translation of four books). They went out as follows: Volume 1, 6 June 1715; Volume 2, 22 March 1716; Volume 3, 3 June 1717; Volume 4, 14 June 1718; and Volumes 5 and 6, 12 May 1716. Shortly after publication Lintot was entitled by the contract to bring out a separate printing for his own benefit. From 1720 he brought out a cheap edition in duodecimo. There were other editions in AP's lifetime up to 1743, many containing small revisions.

The first volume contains an important preface, as well as an "Essay on Homer," contributed by **Thomas Parnell**. Later AP said that this essay was "stiff" and prior to revision "was written much stiffer" (*Anecdotes* 1: 84). At the end of each book AP printed "Observations," that is, notes on matters of historical, doctrinal, or poetic interest. At the end of Volume 6 are various indexes. In the preface AP sets out his view of Homer's particular merits as the father of poetry, especially his unrivaled power of invention. Throughout the work, AP's aim was "to make sense of Homer as a poet" (Steven Shankman). The conclusion of this essay mentions those who had supported the translator in his endeavors, namely, **Addison**, Steele, Swift, **Garth**, **Congreve**, **Rowe**, and Parnell, along with patrons, the Duke of Buckinghamshire, the Earl of Halifax, Viscount Bolingbroke, George Granville, the Duke of Chandos, **James Stanhope**, and **Simon Harcourt**. Some of these were brave choices: Granville (now Lord Lansdowne) and, especially, Bolingbroke were in disgrace after the **Jacobite rising**. However, AP's most pointed gesture was to include a dedication to Congreve, dated 25 January 1720, at the end of the last volume. It was unusual to dedicate to a middle-class author, rather than to a member of the aristocracy or gentry. Even more unusual is the heartfelt expression of friendship it contains: AP never again wrote a dedication of such warmth.

The most complete account of the translation

will be found in the introduction to the volumes in the **Twickenham edition** devoted to the *Iliad*, that is *TE* 7 and 8. This contains material by **Maynard Mack**, Robert Fagles, Norman Callan, and Douglas M. Knight. Mack's contributions are reprinted in *CIH* 249–300. See also Knight's book *Pope and the Heroic Tradition: A Critical Study of His Iliad* (New Haven, CT: Yale University Press, 1951; reprint, Hamden, CT: Archon, 1969).

Another excellent edition of the translation is *The Iliad of Homer: Translated by Alexander Pope*, ed. S. Shankman (London: Penguin, 1996). See also Shankman's book *Pope's Iliad: Homer in the Age of Passion* (Princeton, NJ: Princeton University Press, 1983).

imitation. A mode of writing defined by **Samuel Johnson** in this way: "A method of translating looser than paraphrase, in which modern examples and illustrations are used for ancient, or domestick for foreign." Johnson then cites an example from **John Dryden**: "In the way of imitation, the translator not only varies from the words and sense, but forsakes them as he sees occasion; and, taking only some general hints from the original, runs division on the groundwork [i.e., plays variations on the theme]." In his preface to a version of **Ovid**'s *Epistles* (1680), Dryden had distinguished between three kinds of translation. These were *metaphrase* (word-for-word); *paraphrase* (free rendering); and *imitation* (a looser adaptation). Most commonly Augustan poets took classics of Greek and Roman literature and bent these works to their purpose by updating allusions and finding modern equivalents. The form was particularly well adapted to satire. On occasions more recent texts, such as the writings of **Chaucer**, or in AP's case, **Donne**, were subjected to the same procedure.

Imitation came to the fore in English literature in the Restoration period, with Dryden and the Earl of Rochester among the most notable practitioners. In France **Boileau** exercised comparable influence with his recensions of **Horace**. After AP's day, it was Johnson himself who achieved greatest success with his versions of Juvenal in the poems *London* and *The Vanity of Human Wishes*. However, AP developed the form in a more sustained way than any other English writer. His ***Imitations of Horace*** are to a large degree original poems, playing off the Latin text as a sort of "control" or "host." On this the English work is free to set up its own alternative system of ideas and implications. Thus, in the ***Epistle to Augustus*** AP uses the case of France as a contrast to England, just as Horace had used Greece as a counter example to Rome; but the subsequent analysis of cultural history takes off on its own almost surreal path, eliding some of the parallels in favor of a bitter attack on the arts under **George II**. Moreover, AP's naked contempt for the King differs from Horace's complicated but fundamentally respectful attitude toward the Roman Emperor.

See H. Weinbrot, *The Formal Strain: Studies in Augustan Imitation and Satire* (Chicago: University of Chicago Press, 1969).

Imitation of the Sixth Satire of the Second Book of Horace, An. A composite work. As the matter was stated on the title page in 1738, "The first Part done in the Year 1714, by Dr. Swift. The latter Part now first added, and never before printed." In fact, **Swift**'s portion was written at **Letcombe Bassett** in July–August 1714 and published in the ***Miscellanies*** in 1728 (also reprinted in Swift's *Works* in 1735). The full poem appeared on 1 March 1738, published by **Motte**, **Charles Bathurst**, and **Knapton** as a folio of twenty-eight pages, price, one shilling (Griffith 479). There is no doubt that the concluding passage (ll. 133–223 in the poem as we have it), is the work of AP. More disputable is the source of another short interpolation (ll. 9–28). These verses have been attributed to Swift, on the basis of comments he made in a letter to **Lord Bathurst** on 5 October 1737 on the "incorrect" state of the text (Swift *Corr* 5: 69). However, it is possible that these lines are also by AP. As he later told **Spence**, AP thought that in the imitation he had "hit [Swift's] style exactly, for it was familiar, lively, and with odd rhymes." But the doctor disagreed and did not consider it a good copy of his manner (*Anecdotes* 1: 59).

The satire by Horace is one of his most famous: it contrasts the peace of the author's Sabine farm with the tumult of the city. In their different ways both Swift and AP respond to this poetic stimulus. AP's task was a double one, as he had both to render the Latin original but also to copy Swift's idiosyncratic manner and vigorous octosyllabic couplets. The poem drives toward a fable of the town mouse and the country mouse—an episode more naturally suited to the talents of Swift but one brilliantly handled by AP. A major difference is that Swift's portion, dealing with life of the court and the city, uses a great deal of specific detail, with names like Harley (the **first Earl of Oxford**), **Bolingbroke**, **Parnell**, and **Gay** (not to mention "Pope") dropped freely. AP, dealing with life in retirement, has far fewer references of this kind, although there is friendly mention of **Matthew Prior**.

For text and commentary, see *TE* 4: 247–63.

Imitations of Horace. AP was slow to evolve as a writer in one of his most characteristic forms. He knew **Horace** from his youth and was familiar with the poetic **imitation** as this had come to prominence in the seventeenth century. In fact, he began imitating English poets such as **Chaucer** and **Cowley** at an early age. His friend **Swift** had produced some notable Horatian poems from about 1712 and 1716, which gave AP a lead in applying the text of the Roman author to the politics of the present day, especially as they concerned Swift's dealings with the **Harley administration**.

However, AP did not make any serious attempt in this genre until 1733. Even then the group took time to achieve a critical mass: in the *Works* of 1735 there are just two satires by Horace and two of the poems based on **John Donne**. Even when the epistles began to appear, they were not immediately grouped together with the satires in AP's collections. It was not until 1740 that a full-blown category of *Imitations* came into existence, in vol. 2, part 2 of the *Works* (Griffith 524). In AP's lifetime the group did not include the *Epistle to Arbuthnot*. Indeed, the responsibility for shifting that work into the Horatian group, and renaming it the "Prologue to the Satires," rests with

Warburton in his 1751 edition. We do not know if he had AP's approval for these changes. AP had reprinted *Sober Advice from Horace* in 1740, but the item was too scabrous for Warburton and still failed to gain admission to the **Elwin and Courthope edition**, more than a century later. The odes have generally been excluded from the category of "imitations" in the strict sense. A final anomaly concerns *One Thousand Seven Hundred and Forty*, which was left in a fragmentary state. It was first published by **Joseph Warton** in 1797, and although it closely resembles the other poems in this group as regards style and approach, it is not based on any Horatian text.

In 1735 AP explained the "Occasion" for publishing the first of these imitations, that is, the "Clamour" raised by such as works as the *Epistle to Burlington* (see *TE* 4: 3). For the inception of the scheme, see *Anecdotes* 1: 143; but it should be stressed that at this stage AP had no plans for an extended sequence, such as emerged in due course. He seems gradually to have realized that he could use the well-established form of "imitation" to mount a savage indictment of contemporary England. The poems attack individuals and institutions, blasting parties and causes. They betray consistent animus against **George II** and his principal minister, and they became an important organ for disseminating the ideas of the **opposition to Walpole**.

The following table summarizes the history of this sequence, in approximate order of publication. For more details, see the entries for individual poems.

There are several general studies of the imitations as a collectivity. See T. Maresca, *Pope's Horatian Poems* (Columbus: Ohio State University Press, 1966); P. Dixon, *The World of Pope's Satires: An Introduction to the "Epistles" and Imitations of Horace* (London: Methuen, 1968); J.M. Aden, *Something Like Horace* (Nashville: Vanderbilt University Press, 1969); F. Stack, *Pope and Horace: Studies in Imitation* (Cambridge: Cambridge University Press, 1985); J. Fuchs, *Reading Pope's Imitations of Horace* (Lewisburg: Bucknell University Press, 1989). For the background in earlier

Title	Date of Composition	First Publication	Griffith No.
Satire II.i	1733	February 1733	288
Donne *Satire IV*	[1713], 1733	1733	317
Satire II.ii	1733	July 1734	341
Sober Advice from Horace	1734	December 1734	347
Epistle to Arbuthnot	1731–34	January 1735	352
Donne *Satire II*	[1713], 1733	April 1735	370
Ode IV.i	?	March 1737	443
Epistle II.ii	1736	April 1737	447
Epistle II.i	1736	May 1737	458
Epistle I.vi	1737	January 1738	476
Satire II.vi (by Swift, completed by AP)	c. 1737	March 1738	479
Epistle I.i	1737	March 1738	480
Epilogue Dialogue I	1738	May 1738	484
Epilogue Dialogue 2	1738	July 1738	494
Epistle I.vii	1738	?May 1739	507
Ode IV.ix	?	1751	648
One Thousand Seven Hundred and Forty	c. 1740	1797	

satire, see H. Weinbrot, *Alexander Pope and the Traditions of Formal Verse Satire* (Princeton, NJ: Princeton University Press, 1982). See also R. Steiger, *The English and Latin Texts of Pope's Imitations of Horace* (New York: Garland, 1988).

Impromptu, to Lady Winchelsea. Poem by AP, with the subtitle "Occasion'd by four satyrical Verses on Women-Wits, in the RAPE of the LOCK." Written c. 1714 but not published until its anonymous appearance in 1741. Then included in the *Miscellanies* from 1742.

The full background to the poem is not known, but the main lines of what happened can be reconstructed. The **Countess of Winchilsea** took exception to some lines in the augmented *Rape of the Lock* (4: 59–62); she was objecting to an allusion to the "Poetic Fit" said to be incident to women in AP's description of the **Cave of Spleen**. She may well have considered that this maligned not just female writers in general but also herself (as author of a well-known poem on "The Spleen") in particular. Accordingly she defended women writers by appealing to "poetic Names of yore." In turn AP wrote this impromptu, to which Countess Winchilsea replied with good-tempered verses sent to AP (the manuscript survives in his working papers). Her reply was included in *Poems on Several Occasions* (1717), a miscellany that AP almost certainly edited.

For the text of the poem, which consists of twelve lines in couplets, together with commentary, see *TE* 6: 120–22.

Irving, William Henry (1891–1979). Scholar who taught at Duke University. His career was primarily devoted to **John Gay**, on whom he wrote *John Gay's London* (1928; reprint, 1968) and a biography, *John Gay Favorite of the Wits* (1940; reprint, 1962). He also wrote *The Providence of Wit in the English Letter Writers* (1955), which contains a chapter on AP's letters.

Islay, Archibald Campbell, first Earl of (1682–1761), later third Duke of Argyll. Sometimes spelled "Ilay." Soldier and politician. He had studied law, served under the **Duke of**

Marlborough, and helped to promote the Union with Scotland by the time he was created an Earl in 1708. Fought on the government side at the battle of Sheriffmuir in 1715; he was a doughty Hanoverian and managed Scottish politics in the Whig interest under **Robert Walpole**. Remained loyal to Walpole even when his brother, the **second Duke of Argyll**, defected; succeeded to the dukedom in 1743. A keen gardener, he built his own house at **Whitton** and assisted **Henrietta Howard, Countess of Suffolk** in acquiring nearby **Marble Hill**. He also rebuilt the family seat at Inveraray Castle.

AP was on good terms with his neighbor, their common interest in architecture and landscape gardening overcoming any political tensions that may have arisen. In 1735 Islay was "the agent in getting Curll brought before the House of Lords . . . for advertising that letters to or from peers (privileged) were included in the volume of Pope's Letters" (*Corr* 3: 478). Islay subscribed to the *Odyssey*.

Italian literature, Pope and. In the eighteenth century AP was widely read and translated across Europe (see **reputation**). However, his influence on poetic practice was probably greatest in Italy. There were several translations of *The Rape of the Lock*, *An Essay on Criticism*, *Eloisa to Abelard*, and *An Essay on Man*. Some of these were also the subject of **imitations**, such as a version of the last-named work by Pietro Chiari as *L'Uomo* (1758).

The most important conduit for transmitting AP's work was the priest Antonio Conti (1677–1749), who ran the Venetian intelligence system and spent several years in England. He became a close friend of **Lady Mary Wortley Montagu** and probably met AP during his sojourn, in the early Hanoverian years (Conti was elected FRS in 1715 and became a follower of **Newton**). His translation of *Eloisa to Abelard* into Italian with alternating rhymes was not published until 1760, but it was composed c. 1717. Around the same time Conti made a translation of *The Rape of the Lock*, which came out in his works in 1756. It was not the earliest version of the poem, as Andrea Bonducci had already produced one, published in Florence in 1739. However, Conti's work, if less verbally faithful, provides a more idiomatic rendering of what AP wrote. It influenced a number of Italian writers to produce their own "Popian" poems, that is, a rococo miniature infused with a sense of delicate artifice. The most important writer to draw on this vein was Giuseppe Parini (1729–99), whose four-part satire *Il giorno* ("The Day") was published between 1763 and 1801. It describes the life of a rich young aristocrat from morning to night, in the familiar Italian "endecasillabi" (verses of eleven syllables), unrhymed.

AP was admired by many other prominent figures in the Italian enlightenment, notably **Scipio Maffei** and Francesco Algarotti.

See A. Conti, *Versioni poetiche*, ed. G. Gronda (Bari: Laterza, 1966); and D. O'Grady, *Alexander Pope and Eighteenth-Century Italian Poetry* (Frankfurt: Peter Lang, 1986).

J

Jacob, Giles (1686–1744). Compiler and miscellaneous writer. Not much is known about his life except that he was born in Hampshire and apprenticed to an attorney. He worked as a steward to William Blathwayt of Dyrham Park, near **Bath**. His main career lay in the field of legal textbooks, especially those relating to land law. A representative title is *The Accomplished Conveyancer* (1714). Among his dozen or more books, the most popular included *Every Man his own Lawyer* (1736) and *A New Law-Dictionary* (1729), both of which went into many editions. For **Edmund Curll**, Jacob also composed memoirs of **Joseph Addison**, and he may have been responsible for a poor life of **William Congreve** in 1729.

He came into range of AP with *The Rape of the Smock* (1717), a "heroi-comical" poem with mild references to the poet. In 1718–20 Jacob brought out *The Poetical Register* in two volumes, containing "An Historical Account of the Lives and Writings of the most Considerable English Poets." AP was sent the proofs of his own entry, and according to Jacob he revised it to give a more positive slant to the material. This accusation probably has something in it. In *The Dunciad* AP immortalized the compiler in a single couplet: "Jacob, the Scourge of Grammar, mark with awe, / Nor less revere him, Blunderbuss of Law" (3: 149–50). The first line would appear to echo Jacob's popular title *A New Law Grammar*. But the first edition dates only from 1744. AP's note to the passage makes malicious capital from Jacob's own biography in the *Poetical Register*. Incensed because (as he claimed) AP had struck the first blow, Jacob gave **John Dennis** details of what had passed between AP and himself. He later retaliated with *The Mirror* (1733), containing

three letters aimed at AP. The most amusing passage concerns "the legal Tryal and Conviction of Mr. Alexander Pope of Dulness and Scandal." Bizarrely, the judges of AP in the court of Parnassus turn out to be Dennis, **Lewis Theobald**, and **Aaron Hill**. At the end AP is banished from the seat of the Muses (see Guerinot 229–32).

See J. McLaverty, "Pope and Giles Jacob's *Lives of the Poets*: The *Dunciad* as Alternative Literary History," *Modern Philology* 83 (1985), 22–32.

Jacobite rising. Ever since James II had been deposed in 1688, sympathizers had made various bids to reinstall the old King and then his son in the monarchy. After the first Hanoverian ruler, **George I**, acceded in 1714, supporters of the Stuart dynasty launched their most ambitious effort so far to place the **Pretender** on the throne. The main effort came in Scotland under the ineffective leadership of the Earl of Mar. Other campaigns were organized in the north of England and in the West Country. However, the progress of the Highlanders' army was arrested by the **Duke of Argyll** at Sheriffmuir on 13 November 1715, while another force was stalled and captured at Preston in Lancashire on the same day. A rising was planned for the West Country, which was to have been led by the **Duke of Ormonde**; **George Granville**, Lord Lansdowne; and **Sir William Wyndham**. Ormonde failed to reach Britain, while the other two leaders (good friends of AP) were arrested, so that the Western rising never took place. The Pretender belatedly arrived in Scotland on 22 December, but it was too late, and he was forced to slink back to France on 4 February 1716. Further risings were planned in the years to come, including the **Atterbury plot** of 1722, but none got fully off the ground. It was not until the year after AP's death that the next, and last, rising took place, led by the son of The Pretender, Charles Edward Stuart ("Bonnie Prince Charlie"). This was better executed but also ended in failure.

See B. Lenman, *The Jacobite Risings in Britain, 1689–1746* (London: Eyre Methuen, 1980; reprint Aberdeen: Scottish Cultural Press, 1995); J. Baynes, *The Jacobite Rising of 1715* (London: Cassell, 1970).

Jacobites. The adherents of the Stuart dynasty. (Their name derives from *Jacobus*, Latin form of "James.") They sought the restoration to the throne, first of James II, then of his son James Francis Edward, the **Pretender**, and (after AP's death) of his grandson Charles Edward, the Young Pretender. Their strength is hard to estimate. It consisted almost entirely of Tories, but probably a minority even in this group. Many Roman Catholics, but not all, supported the Stuart claimant. The **Jacobite rising** of 1715–16 was typical in that its success depended on volatile groups and individuals, based mainly in Scotland, the north of England, and the West Country. Like the failed rising in 1745, the rebellion was mounted after long planning but fell down on basic organizational skills. In the intervening years a number of plots were concerted, all eliciting strong support from devoted loyalists but never rousing sufficient public enthusiasm to overthrow the Hanoverian monarchy, unpopular as that often was.

AP's exact attitude toward this cause has never been satisfactorily established. He was not an open activist on behalf of the Pretender and may have found it embarrassing that so many of his friends and relatives were committed to the dynasty, leading to an imputed guilt by association. Several of his closest allies were deeply implicated in the 1715 rising; others helped to plan and fund the **Atterbury plot**, which drew the poet almost into the middle of the political crucible, when he was obliged to testify at the arraignment of his friend **Francis Atterbury**. As time went on AP seems to have distanced himself from the more extreme Jacobites, while some former adherents in his circle (such as **George Granville** and **Sir William Wyndham**) returned to the Hanoverian fold. But the most obdurate Jacobites of his acquaintance, including members of recusant families with whom AP had lifelong contacts, were to turn out yet again when Charles Edward led another rising, one year after the poet's death.

See D. Szechi, *The Jacobites: Britain and Europe, 1688–1788* (Manchester: Manchester University Press, 1994); and P.K. Monod, *Jacobitism and the English People, 1688–1788* (Cambridge: Cambridge University Press, 1989). Many sidelights on the world AP inhabited will be found in P.S. Fritz, *The English Ministers and Jacobitism between the Rebellions of 1715 and 1745* (Toronto: University of Toronto Press, 1975).

"Japhet." AP's name for a swindler variously known as Japhet Crook and Sir Peter Stranger (1662–1734). In 1729 he was convicted in the King's Bench for fraudulently making over a lease to himself. He was sentenced to life imprisonment and also to have his ears cut off and his nose slit. The latter part of the sentence was carried out at Charing Cross pillory on 10 June 1731, apparently the last occasion on which this was done. AP refers to the case and the punishment in a note to the **Epistle to Bathurst** (*TE* 3.ii: 95–96). There are several references to Japhet in AP's late satires, usually linking him to other well-known rogues such as **Francis Charteris**, **John Ward**, and Dennis Bond.

See P. Baines, *The House of Forgery in Eighteenth-Century Britain* (Aldershot: Ashgate, 1999), 61–80.

Jervas, Charles (c. 1675–1739). Pronounced "Jarvis." Irish painter who studied with **Sir Godfrey Kneller** and later spent some years in Italy. He settled in London around 1709 and achieved prominence thanks to a reference in an early *Tatler* paper. In the next few years he painted the four daughters of the **Duke** and **Duchess of Marlborough**, as well as the family of the **Earl of Strafford**. In 1723 he succeeded Kneller as Portrait Painter to the King but seems not to have pleased his royal patrons in this capacity. He was never again to regain his popularity fully. He made regular visits to Ireland and returned to Italy not long before he died in a vain search for relief from asthma.

Jervas's art has not gone down well with posterity. He is generally regarded as a feebler copy of Kneller, and his rather bland and prettified style has condemned him to a minor place in art history. However, many of the good and great in his day were happy to sit for Jervas, and friends and associates of AP like **Addison**, **Parnell**, **Prior**, and **Dr. John Arbuthnot** chose him for their portraits. A well-known dual portrait of **Martha** and **Teresa Blount** (1716) survives at **Mapledurham**: the painter described it as a "couplet," in which the contrasting looks and demeanor of the sisters are cleverly depicted. "They are Pope's favorites," he added, "& therefore . . . must have cost me more Pains than any Nymphs can be worth" (*Corr* 1: 332). Jervas also made famous paintings of **Swift**, with versions now at Knole, the Bodleian Library, and in the National Portrait Gallery.

Jervas played an important role in AP's life for several years, partly by reason of his suave manners and social skills. It was he who gave the poet instruction in painting in 1713–14 (see **painter, Pope as**). Around this time he painted AP at least twice, and one of these images in particular has enjoyed lasting currency (see **portraits**). The verse *Epistle to Jervas* (1716) is one of AP's most deeply felt shorter poems. He refers to the painter in other works, including *A Farewell to London* (1715) and *Sandys's Ghost* (1717), where the shared fate of the two men is adumbrated in the line "And *P-pe* translate with *Jervis*." Later Jervas undertook a translation of *Don Quixote*, published in 1742, but according to **Warburton**'s report AP said that he accomplished this "without a word of Spanish" (see *Anecdotes* 1: lxxxiii). Presumably it was rendered from a French version. Several letters between the pair survive, mostly from the same phase of AP's life. Jervas was a close friend of all the Scriblerians, and **Gay** mentioned him as "robust and debonair" in his greeting to the poet in *Mr. Pope's Welcome from Greece*. He was also on good terms with **Lady Mary Wortley Montagu**, whom he had once painted as a young shepherdess. AP used Jervas's London house in **Cleveland Court** as his London base for several years.

John Bull, The History of. Five prose pamphlets that were published between 6 March and 31 July 1712. They were often attributed to **Jonathan Swift**, but he denied this and told his friend Stella that they were in fact written by **Dr. John Arbuthnot** (*JTS* 2: 532). AP confirmed the fact that "Dr. Arbuthnot was the sole writer of *John Bull*" (*Anecdotes* 1: 57). The pamphlets carry individual titles, beginning with *Law is a Bottomless-Pit* and ending with *Lewis Baboon Turned Honest*. Each part went into several editions. The collective title was first used when the items were included in the *Miscellanies* in 1727: AP had asked the **second Earl of Oxford** for a copy of the work on 8 December 1726 (*Corr* 2: 421), and he was certainly responsible for its inclusion. A number of sequels and imitations followed the original five pamphlets, none of them now believed to be the work of Arbuthnot.

The *History* offers a satiric history of the **War of the Spanish Succession**. It draws on the tradition of beast fables to characterize the national foibles of European nations. For the first time, "John Bull" is employed to represent the stereotypical Englishman. For the most part the target are the Whigs, seen as wishing to prolong the war, with the encouragement of "an old cunning attorney," Humphry Hocus, otherwise the **Duke of Marlborough**. Though the work was written before the inception of the **Scriblerus Club**, it has some features of later Scriblerian satire, for example, in its play with the jargon of nations and professions.

See *The History of John Bull*, ed. A.W. Bower and R.A. Erickson (Oxford: Clarendon, 1976). The fullest account of the background to the satire remains L.M. Beattie, *John Arbuthnot: Mathematician and Scientist* (Cambridge, MA: Harvard University Press, 1935; reprint, New York: Russell & Russell, 1967), 33–189.

Johnson, Samuel (1709–84). Man of letters. AP played a significant role in Johnson's thinking about literature, and the study of AP in the *Lives of the Poets* (1779–81) constitutes one of the key documents in the history of the poet's reputation. The two men never met, although it is possible that Johnson visited the garden at **Twickenham** in AP's lifetime, in company with the learned Elizabeth Carter, but if so this was in the absence of the owner.

When Johnson began his literary career, with AP at the height of his influence, there was a symbolic moment when the torch was passed on from the dominant figure in English literature of one generation to his successor in the next. Johnson's first important work, *London: A Poem*, was published on 13 May 1738; the first dialogue of AP's *Epilogue to the Satires* appeared just three days later. Intrigued by the signs of the emergence of a major new satirist, AP asked **Jonathan Richardson junior** to find out the author's identity. He proclaimed that the author would soon be discovered and brought to attention. The poem is an exercise in **imitation**, closely modeled on AP's recent versions of **Horace**. Soon after AP tried to enlist the support of Lord Gower to aid Johnson, who was attempting to obtain posts as a schoolmaster and hoped to gain a degree from Dublin. AP wrote a short note to Richardson (*Corr* 4: 194). In addition he was a long-suffering patron of Johnson's close friend **Richard Savage**, as the former acknowledged in his *Life of Savage* (1744). Johnson responded instinctively to the superb literary skills of AP, whose matchless power of versification he commended to James Boswell. His conversation is scattered with allusions to AP's work, and he found AP among his most important predecessors as an editor of **Shakespeare**. The study of AP that Johnson prepared late in life was written "*con amore*," as Boswell remarks. It was the longest of the *Lives* and the last to be completed. Johnson was the first to make extensive use of the collections of **Joseph Spence**. It is by no means a wholly favorable account and deplores some aspects of AP's writings and character. However, there can be little doubt that AP was the English poet whose work Johnson had most thoroughly internalized, and his literary intuitions allowed him immediate access to the work of his great Augustan predecessor. All serious inquiry into AP must still take account of Johnson's *Life*.

See H. Kirkley, *A Biographer at Work: Samuel Johnson's Notes for the "Life of Pope"* (Lewisburg: Bucknell University Press, 2002).

Johnston, James (1655–1737). Scottish politician, son of the statesman Lord Warriston. He served as Secretary of State for Scotland from 1692 to 1696. In his retirement at **Twickenham**, from 1710, he built what is now known as **Orleans House** to a design by John James, adding the famous octagon by **James Gibbs** a decade later. He was best known for his exploits as a gardener, some of them based on the ideas on tree grafting propounded by Georg Andreas Agricola. AP does not seem to have admired Johnston's horticultural efforts, and in an imitation of **Spenser** he sneered at the garden decorations (*TE* 6: 44–45). Johnston may be the "Scotus" of the *Epistle to Cobham*, l. 158, and references in AP's correspondence are always hostile. The only reason that has been suggested for this dislike is Johnston's firm Whiggery. **Queen Caroline** held Johnston in higher esteem and visited the house in 1729.

Jones, Richard Foster (1886–1965). Professor at Stanford University. His many important works include *The Triumph of the English Language* (1953) and an edition of Bacon (1937). He also compiled an anthology of *Eighteenth Century Literature* (1929). Of particular interest to students of AP are his books on **Lewis Theobald** (1919) and on *The Background of the "Battle of the Books"* (1920), developed as *Ancients and Moderns* (1936; rev. ed., 1961). A collection *The Seventeenth Century: Studies in the History of English Thought and Literature from Bacon to Pope* (1951) contains essays by Jones and others writing in his honor. See also his essay in *Pope and His Contemporaries*, ed. J.L. Clifford and L.A. Landa (1949).

Jones, William Powell (1901–89). Professor at Case Western University. Author of studies of Thomas Gray and James Joyce, among others. His best-known book is *The Rhetoric of Science* (1966), relating eighteenth-century poetry (including *An Essay on Man*) to contemporary scientific ideas. He also wrote articles on AP and edited *Sawney and Colley (1742) and Other Pope Pamphlets* (1960). The items in question are **pamphlet attacks** relating to AP's quarrel with **Colley Cibber**: see Guerinot 298–99, 301–5.

Jonson, Ben (1572–1637). Poet and dramatist. A significant though largely unrecognized presence in the work of AP, who knew the plays, poems, and criticism. Jonson's version of **Horace** underlies much of *An Essay on Criticism*. His verses *To Penshurst* (c. 1612) inaugurated a line of the so-called **country house poem**, on which AP drew in his *Epistle to Burlington* (see G.R. Hibbard, "The Country House Poem of the Seventeenth Century," *Journal of the Warburg and Courtauld Institutes*, 19 [1956], 159–74, reprinted in *EA* 439–75). Equally, the pageantlike sections of *Windsor-Forest* draw on the tradition of masque, where Jonson and Inigo Jones were the leading figures in England. There are also several references to "old Ben" in the *Epistle to Augustus*: these are joking but not hostile. A judicious discussion of Jonson and **Shakespeare** is found in the Preface to AP's edition (*Prose* 2: 18–20). AP had in his

library a copy of Jonson's *Works* in the folio edition of 1692 with many annotations (*CIH* 420–22).

Jortin, John (1698–1770). Clergyman, classical scholar, and historian. As an undergraduate at Jesus College, **Cambridge**, he was recruited to help AP on the commentary to the *Iliad*. His job was to make "extracts" from the twelfth-century scholar Eustathius. He never met AP.

Journal to Stella. The name given to a series of letters written by **Jonathan Swift** to his friends in Dublin, that is, Esther Johnson ("Stella") and her poor relation Rebecca Dingley. Running from 2 September 1710 to 6 June 1713, they were composed in England and mostly directed from London or Windsor. First published in an unreliable form in 1766. Swift's earliest known reference to AP occurs in the entry for 9 March 1713: "Mr. Pope has published a fine poem, called Windsor Forest. Read it." The journal contains numerous references to individuals and events familiar to AP. The standard edition is that of H. Williams, 2 vols. (1948), reprinted as vols. 15–16 of *The Prose Writings of Jonathan Swift*, ed. H. Davis (Oxford: Blackwell, 1974).

K

Kempis, Thomas à (c. 1379–1471). Originally Thomas Haemerken. German religious writer, an Augustinian canon known chiefly for his Latin work *De imitatione Christi* (On the imitation of Christ), written c. 1420. AP wrote a "Paraphrase" of a section in the third book, on his reckoning at the age of twelve. It was first published in 1854. The poem is in six stanzas of six lines each, and besides warm religious (i.e., Catholic) feeling, it shows the formal influence of seventeenth-century devotional poets. See *TE* 6: 5–7. AP's **library** contained a copy of sermons by Thomas.

Kent, William (1685–1748). Architect, painter, designer, and landscape gardener. He studied in Rome with a view to becoming a painter. In Italy he met the influential young connoisseur, the **Earl of Burlington**, and returned to England with the Earl in 1719. He spent the rest of his life as a kind of house artist to Burlington and planning impresario. Much of his time was spent at Burlington House in Piccadilly, London, where he had many connections with figures such as **Handel** and also with AP, **John Gay**, and their circle. His other important patron was Thomas Coke, first Earl of Leicester (1697–1759): see *Earls of Creation* 221–63.

As time went on, Kent devoted less attention to painting. He became better known for his interior decorations, for his architecture, and for his landscape design. According to **Horace Walpole**, Kent "was a painter, an architect, and the father of modern gardening. In the first character he was below mediocrity; in the second, he was a restorer of the science; in the last, an original. . . . He leapt the fence, and saw that all nature was a garden." In addition, Kent achieved prominence in editing the designs of Inigo Jones and generally promoting the Palladian style of architecture (see **Palladianism**). He provided illustrations for Gay's *Fables* (1727) and **Thomson**'s *Seasons* (1730), as well as an end-piece to *An Essay on Man*.

AP's association with the Burlington coterie was close enough for a satiric print called "Taste" (1732) to adapt **Hogarth's** *Masquerades and Operas* (1724), allotting a role to the poet equivalent to that of Kent in the original. Some of Kent's drawings of AP, showing him in garden or **grotto**, have survived at Chatsworth. A portrait at **Chiswick House** is also attributed to Kent. See *Portraits* 14–18.

However, the connection between AP and Kent is most significant in the area of **gardening**. Here Kent's commissions included work for **Queen Caroline** in Richmond Park, outside London; at Chiswick; at **Rousham**, considered by many to be the masterpiece of eighteenth-century deign; at Esher and at **Stowe** (where AP figured among the great and good featured in Kent's Temple of British Worthies). In some instances, Kent may have been influenced by AP's ideas; in others, the reverse probably applied. Kent made some contributions of indeterminate nature to the ornamentation of AP's own **garden**.

AP and Kent maintained good personal relations, even though the bluff, convivial, and bibulous artist was very unlike the poet in character; nor was he particularly well educated or fastidious in his manners. The two men saw a lot of each other, and sometimes Kent may have acted as an intermediary between Burlington and AP. The friendship survived, despite the hostility of AP's patron, the **second Earl of Oxford**, to what he regarded as Kent's clumsy and overelaborate "decorative" work. AP refers briefly to Kent in the *Epilogue to the Satires* (*TE* 4: 316).

For a general overview, see M.I. Wilson, *William Kent: Architect, Designer, Painter, Gardener, 1685–1748* (London: Routledge, 1984). A more specialized treatment is J.D. Hunt, *William Kent: Landscape Garden Designer* (London: Zwemmer, 1987). For AP's connections with Kent, see *P&AGE* 171–83.

Kerby-Miller, Charles (1903–71). Scholar who taught at Wellesley College from 1938 to 1963. His main contribution to the study of AP was an outstanding edition of the *Memoirs of Martin Scriblerus* (1950; reprint, 1988).

Key to the Lock, A. Burlesque "interpretation" of *The Rape of the Lock*, subtitled "A Treatise proving, beyond all Contradiction, the dangerous Tendency of a late Poem, entituled, *The Rape of the Lock*." It was first published as an octavo pamphlet of thirty-two pages on 25 April 1715 (Griffith 37). The title page stated that it was "Printed for J. Roberts," but as usual **James Roberts** was acting on behalf of the real agents. In fact, it was **Bernard Lintot** who paid AP £10.15 for the work a few days after publication. A second edition appeared on 31 May, containing four absurd complimentary poems, attributed to Sir James Baker and others. There were further editions in 1718 and 1723.

The pamphlet is assigned on the title page to **Esdras Barnivelt**, described as "Apoth[e-cary]," a familiar Scriblerian pseudonym. However, there is no doubt that AP wrote the *Key*, and he later included it in his *Works* (1741). The date of composition was probably 1714; **Swift** appears to have seen the item before his return to Ireland, if we may judge from his letter to AP on 28 June 1715 (*Corr* 1: 302).

Barnivelt offers a detailed political reading of AP's poem, showing that it is an allegorical account of the **War of the Spanish Succession**, designed to promote popery. His ingenious demonstration of AP's secret message is only a shade exaggerated in comparison with the many serious onslaughts on the poet's loyalty and morality. The *Key* is one of AP's most successful comic works in prose.

For text, see *Prose* 1: 173–202. The poems appear in *TE* 6: 132–36. There is as yet no fully annotated edition of the pamphlet, although a selection of brief notes will be found in *Selected Prose of Alexander Pope*, ed. P. Hammond (Cambridge: Cambridge University Press, 1987), 308–9. Excerpts with annotation appear in *The Rape of the Lock*, ed. C. Wall (Boston: Bedford Books, 1998), 179–87.

King, Dr. William (1685–1763). Principal of St. Mary's Hall, **Oxford**, from 1717 to 1763. A High Tory and (until late in life) a fierce **Jacobite**. He should be distinguished from William King (1650–1729), Archbishop of Dublin and colleague of **Swift**; and William King (1663–1712), one of the Christ Church **wits** involved in the affair of the **Ancients and Moderns**.

He was one of those who continued the tradition of Scriblerian wit, in the manner of his friend Swift and of AP; but most of his work was written in Latin and has remained in obscurity. One exception is *The Toast* (1732), an elaborate mock-scholarly work composed partly in English heroic couplets. A prefatory letter is addressed to "Cadenus," that is, Swift. King was entrusted by Swift with *Verses on the Death of Dr. Swift* and *A History of the Four Last Years of the Queen*. The former he held onto for some time before publishing a truncated version in 1739, with probably some intervention by AP. The *History* was not published until 1758, without King's involvement.

Negotiations regarding the publication of items by Swift led to some extensive dealings between King and AP, often with the mediation of **Martha Whiteway**. Once, in 1743, AP visited King at Oxford and stayed in his lodging when he found King absent. The trip to Oxford was connected with an effort by King to obtain a D.D. degree for **William Warburton**, so that AP would agree to accept a degree of D.C.L. The attempt failed. In general, King seems to have had less warm personal relations with AP than he did with Swift, but he certainly held the poet in high regard. His own poem *Miltonis Epistola ad Pollionem* (1738) was dedicated to

AP. As AP's health declined in the last weeks of his life, their common friend the **Earl of Orrery** wrote to King, "When he is gone, farewell to English Poetry, & when you are gone, farewell to Latin poetry." King subscribed to the *Odyssey*. The posthumously published *Political and Literary Anecdotes of his Time* contain some interesting stories about AP and his circle.

See D. Greenwood, *William King: Tory and Jacobite* (Oxford: Clarendon, 1969).

Kingston, Evelyn Pierrepoint, first Duke of (c. 1665–1726). A Whig courtier, member of the **Kit-Cat Club**, and father of **Lady Mary Wortley Montagu**. Knight of the Garter, 1719. Kingston was well known to the authors who were members of the club, including **Addison**, **Steele**, **Congreve**, and **Garth**, but he does not seem to have been a very close acquaintance of AP, even though he was one of those asked to read the poet's *Pastorals* in manuscript. His name appears on all of the poet's subscription lists.

Kit-Cat Club. An informal political group formed by leading Whigs in the reign of **William III**, flourishing mainly in the time of **Queen Anne**. The name was taken from a kind of mutton pie supplied by Christopher Cat, who kept a tavern in Great Shire Lane, near Temple Bar in London. There were several venues for their meetings, but from 1703 the group commonly assembled at the villa of their secretary, **Jacob Tonson senior**, in Barn Elms, near the Thames in southwest London—the probable site was in what is now Elm Grove Road, Barnes. A former resident here was **Abraham Cowley**. The membership of the club ranged from wealthy aristocrats to men about town and figures in the dramatic and literary world. Among the most important personages were politicians from the group of Whig "Junto" lords, headed by AP's patrons **Somers** and **Halifax**. Other grandees included the Duke of Somerset and the Earl of Carlisle. The wilder hell-raising side of aristocratic life was embodied in the person of the rake and duellist Lord Mohun and the epicure **Charles Dartiquenave**. Younger men of affairs in the Kit-Cats were

Robert Walpole, **William Pulteney**, and **James Stanhope**. Literature was represented by **Samuel Garth**, **William Walsh**, **Joseph Addison**, and **Richard Steele**. On the cusp of writing and politics were **Arthur Maynwaring** and George Stepney. Drama supplied **Congreve** and **Vanbrugh**. As time went on, there were changes in the membership: The **Duke of Marlborough** was made an extraordinary member in 1709, and soon afterward **Matthew Prior** was expelled because of his new alliance with the Tories.

AP knew most of the individuals who have been named, several of them intimately. He remained on good terms with some of the Kit-Cats, such as the largely nonpolitical Congreve, while Tonson continued to publish his work. However, relations cooled with many other members, especially after the polarization that occurred at the **Hanoverian accession**. Paradoxically the club fell into abeyance not long after this juncture, since its principal objective of ensuring the Protestant succession had been achieved. In later years one of AP's few surviving contacts with the original group was with **Viscount Cobham**.

The club had no official business, though it sometimes attempted to concert political action, and no clear-cut artistic role. Members subscribed in bulk to the construction of the grand new **Haymarket Theatre** in 1705. Light verse was produced on special occasions, notably "toasts" in honor of reigning beauties such as the young **Lady Mary Wortley Montagu**, whose father the **Duke of Kingston** was a member. Probably the club's most durable impact on the arts was to be found in a series of **portraits** commissioned from **Sir Godfrey Kneller**, who painted members over a span of at least fifteen years (c. 1702–17). By adopting a larger size than usual (thirty-six inches by twenty-eight inches, henceforth known as the standard "Kit-Cat" dimensions), Kneller was able to include more of the sitter's upper body. The pictures were framed by the royal framemaker in 1733 and hung in a specially built gallery at the club's base in Barnes. Today more than forty survive, and they are on display at the National Portrait Gallery in London, with some at the subsidiary gallery at Beningborough Hall, Yorkshire. Thanks to etchings by John Faber (1735), they became some of the best-known images of the elite in early-eighteenth-century Britain. It scarcely needs to be said that the leading Tory politicians who figured in the **Harley administration** were absent from this assemblage, as were AP, **Swift, Gay**, and most of their close friends.

Nevertheless, AP remembered a good deal about the club and supplied **Joseph Spence** with many details on its membership (*Anecdotes* 1: 52). He also wrote an "Epigram on the Toasts of the Kit-Cat Club" in 1716 (*TE* 6: 177).

There is no full modern study of the club. On the portraits and the sitters, see M. Ransome, *The Portraits of Members of the Kit Cat Club, Painted during the Years 1700–1720 by Sir Godfrey Kneller for Jacob Tonson* (London: National Portrait Gallery, 1945).

Knapton, John (1696–1770) **and Paul** (1703–55). Booksellers in Ludgate Street, London. John was the major figure in the brothers' business, which had been started by their father James (d. 1736) in 1687. He was apprenticed in 1712 and freed in 1719. Works by AP began to appear under the Knapton imprint from 1737. After AP's death John had a leading share in the successive editions by **Warburton**, notably that of 1751. He was also a central figure in the group of booksellers who sponsored the *Dictionary* of **Samuel Johnson** in 1755.

See *Pope's Literary Legacy: The Book-Trade Correspondence of William Warburton and James Knapton, with Other Letters and Documents 1744–1780*, ed. D.W. Nichol (Oxford: Oxford Bibliographical Society, 1992).

Kneller, Sir Godfrey (1646–1723). Portrait painter of German origin, born in Lübeck, who studied in Amsterdam. He came to England c. 1675 and was soon one of the most popular artists in London. His success in gaining court patronage brought him the post of Principal Painter to the King in 1689, a knighthood in 1692, and a baronetcy in 1715. Kneller became Governor in 1711 of the new Academy of

Painting in London; he was also a Justice of the Peace and Deputy Lieutenant for Middlesex. He employed a large team of assistants in his studio, enabling him to turn out a succession of fashionable studies of the good and great. As well as his numerous portraits of royalty, he produced the famous series of members of the **Kit-Cat Club** in the first two decades of the century. Other sitters included **Dryden**, the **Duchess of Marlborough**, the **Earl of Burlington**, **Matthew Prior**, and John Locke.

Sir Godfrey's country house was at **Whitton**, adjoining **Twickenham**; its site is commemorated by Kneller Hall, although the present-day building preserves virtually nothing of the seventeenth-century house that the artist had renovated. By 1717 AP already regarded him as a neighbor, and the two men were in correspondence at this time—AP's earliest surviving letter dates from February 1718. The painter replies with lively if badly spelled letters. After the poet moved to Twickenham, their contacts grew more regular. Kneller rented a house to Edward and **Lady Mary Wortley Montagu**, who sat for him in 1720. (For AP's poem on this subject, see *TE* 6: 212–13.) AP engaged in cards and other social activities with Kneller, who also provided three large paintings of classical statues for the staircase in the poet's **villa**. AP told many stories about Kneller's robust and sometimes eccentric behavior and alludes to the way he dispensed justice from the bench in *The Second Epistle of the Second Book of Horace* (*TE* 4: 167).

Shortly before his death Sir Godfrey sent for AP and asked him if he would take down the monument to his father in **Twickenham parish church** (where Kneller was a churchwarden), as the painter wished to be buried there with a suitable tomb, designed by **Michael Rysbrack**, rather than "lie among the rascals" in Westminster Abbey (*Corr* 2: 306–9; *Anecdotes* 1: 49). AP reluctantly consented, but he then resisted efforts by Kneller's widow to have the memorial removed. In the end the Pope monument stayed, and Kneller was buried at Whitton. The monument by Rysbrack was erected in the Abbey, in 1729: the inscription is by AP, but he called these lines "the worst thing I ever wrote in my life" (*Anecdotes* 1: 49; *TE* 6: 312–13). Versions of paintings by Kneller commemorating several friends of the poet hung in his villa, although most were probably copies.

Kneller painted AP in 1716 and again in 1723. Both portraits were frequently copied and engraved as prints. In addition, there is a profile in crayon (1721), with the poet in a toga and a wreath of ivy round his brows. Each of these has become one of the most familiar images of AP. See *Portraits* 5–7; and **portraits**.

Knight, George Wilson (1897–1985). Scholar who taught at the University of Leeds. Best known for his influential studies of Shakespearean tragedy. He also wrote a book on AP, *Laureate of Peace: On the Genius of Alexander Pope* (1955), an idiosyncratic but often illuminating work.

Knight, John (1686–1733). An MP and Essex country gentleman whom AP visited at **Gosfield**. He was a subscriber to the *Odyssey*. In 1727 he married a widow, Mrs. Newsham (formerly **Ann Craggs**). For his tomb in the parish church, with a marble statue by **Rysbrack**, AP wrote an epitaph in verse (*TE* 6: 364–65). Several of AP's letters to Knight survive.

Kyrle, John (1637–1724). Philanthropist. Famous as "**The Man of Ross**," he is allotted a laudatory character sketch in AP's *Epistle to Bathurst*. Kyrle came from a modest background in the gentry and had no political sway. He lived most of his life in the Market Place of Ross-on-Wye, a small town in Herefordshire. He studied at **Oxford** and the Middle Temple but never practiced law. Indeed, he made it a mission in life to arbitrate in local quarrels in such a way as to avoid lawsuits. According to AP, his income was about £500 per year, and this does not seem to be far out. In his own time Kyrle became known for his good works, his charity to the poor, and his endowments to the parish church of St. Mary the Virgin (the spire was rebuilt in 1721 at Kyrle's expense, as AP reminds us in the poem). He lived modestly and was willing to work in the fields alongside his own men.

AP instances his career as that of a simple, pious, and generous figure who contrasts with the other characters in this *Epistle*, representing avarice or profligacy. While writing the poem, he wrote on 14 November 1731 to **Jacob Tonson senior**, now retired to nearby Ledbury, to find out details of Kyrle's career. He explained his motives in singling out Kyrle for such particular attention in a letter of 7 June 1732 (*Corr* 3: 244, 290). AP may also have had local information from his friend **Viscountess Scudamore**.

See *TE* 3.ii: 113–16; and *Social Milieu* 16–41.

L

Ladyholt. Estate at Harting in Sussex, near Petersfield, that had belonged to a leading Catholic family, the Carylls, since the end of the sixteenth century. It was used as Royalist garrison in the Civil War and sacked by the Parliamentary army. The Jacobite **John, Lord Caryll** built a new house there c. 1680, emparking what had previously been chalk downland. His estate was forfeited in 1696, but since it was entailed Lord Caryll possessed only a life interest, and this enabled his nephew, **John Caryll senior**, AP's friend, to redeem it in 1697. There are no reliable illustrations of the building, but a sketch suggests its main frontage had seven bays. Subsequently, owing to mounting debts, Caryll's grandson had to sell first the manor of West Harting in 1757 and then the house in 1767. It was demolished by 1770. The Caryll chapel at the parish church of St. Mary and St. Gabriel is now in ruins. The Carylls also possessed a house at West Grinstead, further east, which had been built in 1607 and acquired by 1667. This too was demolished in the early nineteenth century. St. George's parish church contains some memorials to members of the Caryll family.

AP visited the house on several occasions, but the only two dates that have been firmly established relate to the summer of 1712 (two months) and September 1733. Some other trips were planned but for various reasons deferred.

Laguerre, Louis (1663–1721). French decorative painter, a godson of Louis XIV who studied under Charles Lebrun. Moved to England c. 1684. Worked at first with Antonio Verrio (1630–1707), with whom AP links him in the *Epistle to Burlington* (l. 146). His commissions included work at Chatsworth, Burghley, **Hampton Court**, Buckingham House, **Cannons**, and St. Paul's Cathedral.

Landa, Louis A. (1901–89). Professor at Princeton University and one of the most distinguished scholars on **Swift**. His article "Pope's Belinda, the General Emporie of the World, and the Wondrous Worm," *South Atlantic Quarterly* 70 (1971), 215–35, reprinted in *PRE* 177–200, is a significant contribution to our understanding of *The Rape of the Lock*. See also "Of Silkworms and Farthingales and the Will of God," in *Studies in the Eighteenth Century II: Papers Presented at the Second David Nichol Smith Memorial Seminar, Canberra, 1970*, ed. R.F. Brissenden (1973), 259–77. Some other important studies are collected in *Essays in Eighteenth-Century English Literature* (1980). Together with James L. Clifford, Landa edited one of the most important scholarly works on AP, namely, *Pope and His Contemporaries: Essays Presented to George Sherburn* (1949). See *The Augustan Milieu: Essays Presented to Louis Landa*, ed. H.K. Miller, E. Rothstein, and G.S. Rousseau (Oxford: Clarendon, 1970).

Lansdowne, Baron. See **George Granville**.

Leavis, F[rank] R[aymond] (1895–1978). Famous literary critic, a Fellow of Downing College, **Cambridge**, 1936–62, and editor of the journal *Scrutiny*, 1932–53. He wrote an influential section on AP in his book *Revaluation* (1936), reprinted in *EA* 3–21, as well as essays on *The Dunciad* and on **Swift** in *The Common Pursuit* (1952).

Leighs (Lees). Estate near Braintree in Essex. On the site of a medieval monastery, dissolved in 1534, it was turned into a Tudor mansion by the Rich family. It was acquired c. 1723 by the **Duchess of Buckinghamshire**. She invited AP to visit her in 1724, but he does not seem to have gone until the following summer. Another planned visit in 1727 was aborted.

Lessing, Gottfried Ephraim (1729–81). German critic and dramatist, best known for his aesthetic work *Laokoon* (1766), as well as plays such as *Nathan der Weise* (1779). In 1755 he wrote a treatise *Pope, ein Metaphysiker* (Pope as a metaphysician) in collaboration with the philosopher Moses Mendelssohn (1729–1806). See P. Michelsen, "Ist alles gut? Pope, Mendelssohn und Lessing zur Schrift, 'Pope, ein Metaphysiker,' " in *Mendelssohn-Studien* 4 (Berlin: Duncker & Humblot 1979), 81–109.

Letcombe Bassett. Village in **Berkshire** (today in Oxfordshire), high up in the downs near Wantage. **Jonathan Swift** retired here in early June 1714, as the **Harley administration** collapsed in the last days of **Queen Anne**, to stay with his friend Rev. John Geree, the rector of the parish. He did not leave the village until 16 August, more than two weeks after the Queen's death, and never saw the **first Earl of Oxford** again. Here Swift began a version of **Horace** that AP later completed and published in the *Miscellanies* (1727). See ***The Sixth Epistle of the Second Book of Horace Imitated***. AP and **Thomas Parnell** made a trip of "thirty miles" (slightly more, in fact) from **Binfield** to Letcombe in the early part of July, staying with Swift for several days. See AP's account of the visit in a letter to **John Arbuthnot** (*Corr* 1: 234–35: Swift *Corr* 1: 646–48).

Letter to a Noble Lord, A. Prose pamphlet by AP, first published in 1751. It was provoked by a poem by his enemy Lord Hervey (see **Hervey, John, Baron**), which was titled *An Epistle from a Nobleman to a Doctor of Divinity* and published in November 1733. According to Hervey, AP quickly produced his response and showed it to a number of friends but held it back as it was "very low and poor." AP confirmed this in writing to **Swift** on 6 January 1734, observing, "There is a Woman's war declar'd against me by a certain Lord, his weapons are the same which women and children use, a pin to scratch, and a squirt to bespatter" (*Corr* 3: 201). AP takes the opportunity in his reply to deal additional blows against **Lady Mary Wortley Montagu**, who had recently been engaged with Hervey in attacks on AP. Many other pamphlets were published during the course of this episode, and it is possible AP had a hand in other items.

For the background, see R. Halsband, *Lord Hervey: Eighteenth-Century Courtier* (Oxford: Clarendon Press, 1973). For the text and commentary, see *Prose* 2: 433–83.

Lewis, Erasmus (1670–1754). Government official; son of a clergyman from Carmarthen in South Wales. A businesslike worker, long connected with Robert Harley, **first Earl of Oxford**, who called him "a punctual man." He was employed first as Harley's private secretary and then as an Under-Secretary of State from 1710 to 1713 during the **Harley administration**. MP, 1713–14. After the minister's fall he served as the Earl's steward. It was he who introduced **Swift** to Harley. One of Swift's most loyal friends in England, Lewis took part in the clandestine measures that were used in the publication of ***Gulliver's Travels***. He was on close terms with **Dr. John Arbuthnot, Gay, Prior, Lord Bathurst**, and other friends of AP. He also figures in ***Mr. Pope's Welcome from Greece***.

It was during the brief time when the **Scriblerus Club** met regularly that AP came into contact with Lewis, an ally of all the members. The two men remained amicable relations for the rest of the poet's life. As late as 1739 and 1740 he stayed at Lewis's house, which stood in Cork Street, near **Burlington House**: Dr. Arbuthnot had lived on the same street for many years. Lewis took part with AP in the plan to bring assistance to the destitute **Richard Savage** in 1741. There are many references to

Lewis in AP's correspondence but no surviving letters. By contrast, twenty-three letters from Lewis to Swift exist. He figures briefly in some of the poems. AP left him a small bequest in his **will**.

library. More than 150 books owned by AP are known to survive. They have been listed and briefly described by **Maynard Mack** in *CIH* 394–460. The subjects range from ancient and modern literature to history, religion, and philosophy. In some items there are extensive annotations in AP's hand. AP also bound together a number of **pamphlet attacks** on himself in four volumes. The books are widely scattered: the most important collection is probably that preserved at Hartlebury Castle, the historic palace of the Bishop of Worcester, which contains many of the books that passed into the ownership of **William Warburton**. They were placed there by Warburton's friend, Bishop Richard Hurd.

Lincoln's Inn Fields Theatre. Playhouse in London, on the north side of Portugal Street. First built as a tennis court in 1656 and used as a theatre from 1661. It was rebuilt in 1714 and operated by **John Rich**. Here the manager developed a specialty in spectacular entertainments, including harlequinades and pantomimes. These shows provided a considerable challenge to **Drury Lane Theatre**, which was forced to reply with its own brand of extravagant spectacle. AP satirizes this rivalry in *The Dunciad*: "Here shouts all Drury, there all Lincoln's-Inn: / Contending Theatres our empire raise, / Alike their labour, and alike their praise" (3: 266–68). Here *The Beggar's Opera* began its triumphant career in January 1728. The building ceased to operate as a theater in 1744 and was demolished in 1848.

See P. Sawyer, *The New Theatre at Lincoln's Inn Fields* (London: Society for Theatre Research, 1979).

Lintot, Barnaby Bernard (1675–1736). Bookseller. Apprenticed, 1690; freed, 1699. One of the main figures in the London book trade during AP's lifetime, he operated at the sign of the Cross Keys in **Fleet Street**, near Temple Bar. From the outset, one of his specialties was the poetic anthology, and he had issued collections edited by **Charles Gildon** and **Elijah Fenton** before his first dealings with AP. This came with *Miscellaneous Poems and Translations* (1712), which contained the two-canto work *The Rape of the Locke*. The project was designed as a counterblast to the famous *Miscellanies* of **Jacob Tonson senior**. Subsequently Lintot published *Poems on Several Occasions* (1717), a collective volume probably edited by AP. He was also the publisher of the *Works* (**1717**), AP's major retrospective assemblage of his early poems. Lintot had already been responsible for a number of AP's most important works, including *Windsor-Forest* and *The Temple of Fame*, not forgetting the five-canto version of *The Rape of the Lock* in 1714.

It was, however, the translations of **Homer** that brought poet and bookseller into the most prolonged contact. Lintot issued the *Iliad* on terms favorable to AP, and the profit he hoped to recoup from his own "trade" edition suffered from the appearance of pirate versions. There were tensions surrounding the *Odyssey* a decade later, and AP broke with Lintot from this time. In 1732 AP described him as "a Grand Chicanneur," who had been "a great Scoundrell to me" (*Corr* 3: 294). Less easily manipulated than most of his colleagues in the trade, he resisted some of the poet's plans and lost AP's patronage for good. However, Henry Lintot (1703–58), who inherited his father's business, retained the rights in several works and proved a thorn in AP's flesh. Henry had bought the rights of *The Dunciad Variorum* in 1740, and AP finally had to bring a Chancery suit against him to try to regain control of his literary property.

Lintot was associated with many leading writers of the age, including **John Gay**, **Richard Steele**, **Thomas Parnell**, **Nicholas Rowe**, **John Philips**, and others. His name crops up in poems by **Swift**, notably in the *Verses on the Death of Dr. Swift* and *On Poetry: A Rhapsody*, but it does not appear that the Dean had many firsthand contacts with the publisher. AP wrote an amusing account of his methods in describing a journey to **Oxford** in 1716 (*Corr* 1: 371–35). Lintot earns a brief mention in the *Epistle to Arbuthnot*, as well as a more prominent niche in *The Dunciad* (2: 49–70). The narrative has Lintot competing with **Curll** (as he did, to some extent, in real life) for rewards and honors in a footrace. In the couplet "With legs expanded Bernard urg'd the race, / And seem'd to emulate great Jacob's pace," AP makes play with the lasting rivalry between Tonson and Lintot, the two most significant literary publishers of the age.

Lounsbury, Thomas Raynesford (1838–1915). Pioneer of American and English studies in the American academy. A professor at Yale University from 1871, especially known for his work on **Chaucer**. He wrote *The First Editors of Shakespeare (Pope and Theobald)* (1906) as part of a sequence on the history of Shakespearean studies.

Lovejoy, Arthur Oncken (1873–1962). Historian of ideas. Professor of Philosophy at Johns Hopkins University, 1910–39. His famous book *The Great Chain of Being* (1936) provided an essential context for *An Essay on Man*. In addition, his *Essays in the History of Ideas* (1948) and other shorter writings offer many valuable perspectives on AP's works, particularly with regard to the poet's treatment of "nature."

Lowell, James Russell (1819–91). Poet and critic. Friend of Longfellow, Emerson, Oliver Wendell Holmes, and others. First editor of *The Atlantic Monthly*. Known for *The Bigelow Papers* (1848–67) and other books. Referred to AP in several poems and prose works. His essay on AP, reprinted in *My Study Windows* (1871), was once extremely well known, as was his study of **Dryden**.

Lyttelton, George, first Baron (1709–73). Politician and poet. An MP and one of the key figures in the **opposition to Walpole** in the 1730s. He had links both to **Frederick, Prince of Wales**, to whom he acted as secretary, 1737–44, and to the so-called Cobhamites, followers of **Viscount Cobham**, who was Lyttelton's uncle. He became leader of the "Boy Patriots" (see **Patriots**). The poet **Gilbert West**, who supported this group, was a first cousin. A patron of writers such as **James Thomson**, and the dedicatee of *Tom Jones* (1748) by **Henry Fielding**, a friend since schooldays. After the fall of Walpole he served as a Lord of the Treasury and Chancellor of the Exchequer and was made a Baron in 1756, but he never reached the pinnacle of power. Much admired in his lifetime as a poet but later treated with some scorn by **Samuel Johnson** in *Lives of the Poets*, which angered his remaining friends. Other works that enjoyed a high contemporary reputation were *Letters of a Persian in England to his Friend at Ispahan* (1735), a satirical survey of the political nation, and *Dialogues of the Dead* (1760).

Lyttelton was probably known to AP by the start of the 1730s: his father Sir Thomas Lyttelton (1686–1751), an MP and a loyal adherent of Walpole, was an old acquaintance. A verse epistle from Rome in 1730 was addressed to the poet. He visited **Twickenham** in 1735 and by this time had earned AP's warm admiration. The two men sometimes met at **Stowe** or **Bath**, where Lyttelton was familiar with individuals such as **Ralph Allen** and **George Cheyne**. AP was invited more than once to Lyttelton's seat at **Hagley**. AP described him to **Swift** in 1738 as "one of the worthiest of the rising generation" (*Corr* 4: 134), and in the poet's last years he was a particularly close ally. Lyttelton, who contributed materials to the famous **grotto**, visited AP only a few days before his **death** in 1744. He was bequeathed AP's busts of the great English poets in the poet's **will**.

The earliest of a dozen surviving letters between the two men dates from 1736, but their correspondence probably went back years earlier. AP paid his friend warm tributes in his later *Imitations of Horace*, notably in the *Epilogue to the Satires*. A footnote added later identified Lyttelton as "Secretary to the Prince of Wales, distinguished both for his writings and speeches in the spirit of Liberty" (*TE* 4: 301). It is possible that Lyttelton was the young man addressed in a fragment of "Lines to A Friend" (1731), subsequently adapted to form the conclusion of the ***Epistle to Arbuthnot*** (see *TE* 6: 333–34).

See R.M. Davis, *The Good Lord Lyttelton* (Bethlehem, PA: Times Publishing Co., 1939).

M

MacDonald, Wilbert Lorne (1879–1966). Professor at the University of British Columbia from 1919 and author of *Pope and His Critics* (1951).

MacFlecknoe. A poem by **John Dryden**, first published in 1682 and subtitled *A Satyr upon the True-Blew Protestant Poet, T.S.* It is written in heroic couplets and chiefly directed against the dramatist Thomas Shadwell (c. 1642–92), who would later succeed Dryden as Poet Laureate in a startling confirmation-by-negation of the poem's narrative. AP took over aspects of the plot in *The Dunciad*, notably the crowning of the new ruler of the dunces' preserves, and also adopted some features of Dryden's **mock-heroic** style.

Mack, Maynard (1909–2001). The greatest of all scholars of AP over the past three centuries. In range, learning, and critical power, he exceeds even **George Sherburn** and **John Butt**, the two other preeminent figures in modern Popian studies. Taught at Yale University from 1936 to 1978. President of the Modern Language Association, 1970; Corresponding Fellow of the British Academy, 1973. Wrote influential books on Shakespearean tragedy and edited widely used college anthologies as well as two series of critical guides on writers of all periods. He edited *Joseph Andrews* by **Henry Fielding** (1948) and coedited a Festschrift for Butt, *Imagined Worlds* (1968).

However, Mack is mainly known for his work on AP. In summary, this comprises:

1. Editorial work, centrally the volumes on the *Essay on Man* (vol. 3.i) and on the **Homer** trans-lations (vols. 7–10), as well as the index (vol. 11) for the **Twickenham edition**.

2. *Work on manuscripts*, including a number of shorter studies, as well as a full-length edition of surviving **manuscripts** for major poems, published as *The Last and Greatest Art* (1984).

3. *Bibliographical and textual studies*, especially those concerning AP's letters and *Works* in early printings.

4. *Scattered critical essays*, of which the most influential have been "On Reading Pope," *College English*, 7 (1946), 263–73; " 'Wit and Poetry and Pope,' " in *Pope and His Contemporaries*, ed. J.L. Clifford and L.A. Landa (1949), 20–40; and especially "The Muse of Satire," *Yale Review*, 41 (1951), 80–92.

5. *Collections of published criticism at large*, notably *Essential Articles for the Study of Alexander Pope* (1964; rev ed., 1968); and (ed. with J.A. Winn), *Pope: Recent Essays by Several Hands* (1980).

6. *Biographic studies*, including lectures titled "In Pursuit of Pope." The major item here is the full-scale work *Alexander Pope: A Life* (1985).

7. *Contextual and cultural interpretations*, especially *The Garden and the City: Retirement and Politics in the Later Poetry of Pope 1731–1743* (1969).

Note that shorter items in categories (2), (3), (4), and (6) are reprinted in *Collected in Himself* (1982), which also contains a study of AP's **library** and an important supplement to the **correspondence**. A final contribution came with the catalog for a bicentenary exhibition at Yale University, *The World of Alexander Pope* (1988).

Mack's impact on the entire subject has been huge. His biography of AP has been criticized on various grounds, but few students of the poet doubt that it is the fullest, most accurate, and most intellectually searching life that has ever appeared. In the same way, some younger scholars have questioned aspects of his critical method, which can be seen as lacking in theoretical rigor and unduly predisposed to see matters from AP's perspective; but such reservations hardly affect the scale of his achievement at the head of modern Popian study. See a Festschrift, *The Author in His Work*, ed. L.L. Martz and A.L. Williams (New Haven: Yale University Press, 1978).

Mackail, John William (1859–1945). Classical scholar and critic. Fellow of the British Academy, 1914; Order of Merit, 1935. Professor of Poetry at Oxford, 1906–11. His prolific works included translations of **Virgil**. His Leslie Stephen Lecture on AP at Cambridge University was published in 1919 and reprinted in his *Studies of English Poets* (1926).

Maffei, Francesco Scipione, Marchese di (1675–1755). Italian man of letters, scholar, and archaeologist. Originally best known as a poet and playwright, he became increasingly absorbed in historical and **antiquarian** studies relating to his native Verona. His tragedy *Merope* (1714) long set the standard for acceptable modern versions of classical drama and was used as the basis of **Voltaire**'s play (1743). In 1736 Maffei visited London and **Oxford**, where he was awarded a doctorate of laws. Among those he met in England were **Frederick, Prince of Wales**, **Lady Mary Wortley Montagu**, the **Earl of Burlington**, and **Dr. Richard Mead**. Maffei saw the collections of **Sir Hans Sloane** and the **second Earl of Oxford**. He also visited **Twickenham**, and AP is said to have stated that he wished to translate *Merope*. Nothing ever came of this project. However, AP somehow got wind of an encounter between Maffei and **Richard Bentley** at **Cambridge**, as emerges from a cryptic note to the last book of *The Dunciad* (4: 202).

maids of honor. Court ladies attending the Princess of Wales, later **Queen Caroline**, whom AP came to know well in the early years of the Hanoverian regime. AP gives a comic description of their life in a letter to **Martha Blount** in 1717 (*Corr* 1: 427). Among those familiar to AP were **Anne Griffith** and her sister **Elizabeth Rich; Mary Bellenden**; and Mary Lepell, later **Baroness Hervey**. In addition, they were involved in the imbroglio surrounding the Scriblerians' play *Three Hours after Marriage*. They figure in poems by AP such as *The Court Ballad* and "Epigrams Occasion'd by an Invitation to Court." In 1724–25 the Princess built a row of four brick houses on Richmond Green, adjoining the site of the old palace of **Richmond** and surviving today. AP may have encountered the ladies there as well as at **Hampton Court**. When Caroline became Queen, she was attended by a different group of ladies, with some of whom AP seems to have been acquainted: see *The Six Maidens*.

Mallet, David (c. 1705–65). Also spelled "Malloch." Scottish poet and dramatist who produced some popular ballads and a life of Francis Bacon. A friend of **James Thomson**, he came to the attention of the literary world with a Thomsonian poem *The Excursion* (1728). Later he was associated with members of the **opposition to Walpole**, including **Lyttelton** and **Aaron Hill**, and produced dramas along the approved lines. His best-known work is *Alfred* (1740), a masque cowritten with Thomson. In 1742 he was made Under-Secretary to **Frederick, Prince of Wales**, with a salary of £200 per annum. He had also gained the acquaintance of **Viscount Bolingbroke**, perhaps through AP's introduction. His part in editing the posthumous works of Bolingbroke excited some scornful remarks in **Samuel Johnson**'s *Lives of the Poets*. Mallet supported efforts to raise money in aid of **Richard Savage**, a friend from earlier times.

In 1733 Mallet published *Of Verbal Criticism: An Epistle to Mr. Pope*, which was issued by **Lawton Gilliver**. As Johnson says, this was written "to pay court to Pope." It achieved its object, although AP first requested the author to defer publication until after **Lewis Theobald** (who along with **Richard Bentley** was attacked in the poem) had enjoyed a benefit performance of a play then running (*Corr* 3: 357). AP helped to get Mallet the post of tutor in the family of **Ann Craggs**. The poet wrote to Mrs. Knight (as Ann now was) that Mallet was one "whom I love and esteem greatly" (*Corr* 3: 511). On his travels Mallet sent AP regular accounts of places visited. Eighteen letters from AP to Mallet survive. In his last days AP was visited by Mallet and an account sent to the **Earl of Orrery**, with whom Mallet had now ingratiated himself (see **death**).

There is no extensive modern work on Mallet. See a thesis by H. Gäumann, *The Excursion, mit einem Überblick über das dichterische Gesamtwerk* (Zürich: Juris-Verlag, 1977).

Man of Ross, The. An exemplary figure of pious charity whom AP introduced into the *Epistle to Bathurst*. The portrait was closely based on a real individual who had lived in Ross-on-Wye, Herefordshire, **John Kyrle**.

Mannock, William (1677–1749). Priest. He studied in the English College at Rome and became priest in the household of AP's brother-in-law Charles Rackett (see **Rackett family**) c. 1700. Charles's widow left Mannock some pictures in her will, made in 1746. He gave **Joseph Spence** details of the poet's early life. Mannock seems to have been a relative of John Weston, husband of **Elizabeth Weston**, and possibly of other Catholics known to AP. It has been claimed that he was a cousin of AP, but the connection has not been established.

manuscripts. Hundreds of holograph manuscripts by AP survive. They include a very large number of letters; abundant stores of drafts and working papers, covering more than fifty poems; and a handful of works in verse and prose that were carefully transcribed as printer's copy or as a permanent record. From a literary point of view, the most important surviving documents are fair copies of the *Pastorals*, *An Essay on Criticism*, and *Windsor-Forest*, together with a number of drafts and foul papers for other poems. The last group, which allows us to study AP's habits of revi-

sion, includes parts of the *Epistle to Bathurst*; of *The First Satire of the Second Book of Horace Imitated*; of *An Essay on Man* (two near-complete versions); and of the much-revised *Epistle to Arbuthnot*. Significant manuscripts in the hand of others include the transcriptions made by **Jonathan Richardson junior** of *The Dunciad*.

For a wide array of AP's manuscripts, see *L&GA*. A valuable study is J. Butt, "Pope's Poetical Manuscripts," *Proceedings of the British Academy*, 40 (1954), 23–39, reprinted in *EA* 545–65. As a study of AP's compositional habits, nothing to date has bettered G. Sherburn, "Pope at Work," *Essays on the Eighteenth Century Presented to David Nichol Smith* (Oxford: Clarendon, 1945), 49–64.

Mapledurham. House in Oxfordshire, on the Thames five miles upstream from Reading; the grounds lead down to the river, which separates the county from AP's own home shire, **Berkshire**. It was built by Sir Michael Blount at the end of the sixteenth century; he was an MP and Keeper of the Tower of London, where he guarded the martyr Robert Southwell. During the Civil War Mapledurham was sacked by the army under the Earl of Essex in 1643 and later sequestrated by Parliament. It passed to Lister Blount (1654–1710) from his cousin Walter in 1671. The Blounts remained committed Roman Catholics until the line died out in 1943; the property then descended to their cousins, the Eystons of nearby Hendred House, who retain it to the present day. It is a brick building in an H shape, with tall gables rising to four stories and a full complement of "priest's holes," where the recusant community could shield men of religion.

AP often visited the house after he became acquainted with **Teresa** and **Martha Blount**, the daughters of Lister, about 1707. His first recorded visit occurred in 1711, but it was probably not the earliest. It is possible that AP had something to do with the transformation of the gardens around this time into a more natural style. Here the young ladies engaged in literary fantasies, composing romantic missives under elaborate pseudonyms. In 1716, after their brother, **Michael Blount**, had married, the sisters were obliged to move to London. AP deplored the way they had been driven "out of house and home" (*Corr* 1: 336). It was a loss for them, but also for AP who shared the girls' tender feelings for their "old Monastery, Mapledurham" (*Life* 622). A number of important **manuscripts** and books connected with AP are preserved at the house.

Marble Hill. House on the north bank of the Thames, built in 1724–29 for **Henrietta Howard, Countess of Suffolk**. It stood less than a mile downstream from AP's home at **Twickenham**. Termed a "villa," like the neighboring house, it was a far more imposing structure with three stories, plus a garret, and five bays in width. There were extensive grounds on each side of the mansion, with an impressive front lawn sweeping 200 yards down to the river. The land was acquired for Mrs. Howard by the **Earl of Islay**; at first it consisted of only eleven and a half acres, later considerably extended to more than sixty acres.

The original design was made by the architect Colen Campbell in his favored style of **Palladianism**. Construction was carried through under the supervision of the **ninth Earl of Pembroke** by Roger Morris (1695–1749), who owned land in Twickenham adjoining AP's property. From 1723 AP was engaged on planning the garden. According to **Swift**, who wrote a "Pastoral Dialogue between Richmond-Lodge and Marble-Hill" (1727), "Mr. *Pope* was the Contriver of the Gardens, Lord *Herbert* the Architect, and the Dean of St. Patrick's chief Butler, and Keeper of the Ice House." The house was occupied from about 1724, and AP regularly visited in subsequent years. He even entertained Swift there in the absence of the house's owner in 1727.

After Lady Suffolk's death in 1767, it remained in the family, although the contents were dispersed. In the nineteenth century the property passed into other hands, and the last resident died in 1887. It was acquired for the nation in 1902 and opened to the public. A major restoration took place when the house reopened in 1966, since when many paintings and items of furniture have been put in place. It is now maintained by English Heritage.

See *Earls of Creation* 79–92; and J. Bryant, *Marble Hill House* (London: English Heritage, 1988).

Marchmont, Hugh Hume, third Earl of (1708–94). Scottish politician. Known as Lord Polwarth until he succeeded his father in the earldom in 1740. One of the Whig **"Patriots"** who took a leading share in the **opposition to Walpole** in the later 1730s. AP met him at this time and by 1739 was writing to **Swift** of him in terms of the highest regard (*Corr* 4: 178). The young man's ability and public spirit greatly impressed AP, who singled him out for praise in his *Verses on the Grotto* (1740) and also in the *Epilogue to the Satires* (1738). Marchmont came to stay with AP at **Twickenham** on occasions; at other times he lived at the home of **Viscount Bolingbroke** at **Battersea**, where AP paid visits late in life. He shared AP's interest in **gardening**.

It is difficult to avoid the conclusion that AP overrated the peer's talents and importance. "By 1740 Pope had become strangely infatuated with Marchmont (or what he thought he saw in him). . . . [He] focused on the 32-year-old Scot as an impossibly idealized political hero" (Christine Gerrard). Marchmont survived the poet by half a century but never achieved any great eminence, although he served for thirty-eight years in the House of Lords as a Scottish representative peer. He supplied **Samuel Johnson** with information on AP for *The Lives of the Poets*. He also served as an executor to AP's **will**, as he did for that of the **Duchess of Marlborough**. He was also left a gift by AP (see **Buckley**). About a dozen letters from AP to Marchmont are known to survive. See C. Gerrard, *The Patriot Opposition to Walpole: Politics, Poetry, and National Myth 1725–1742* (Oxford: Clarendon, 1994).

Marlborough, Henrietta Churchill, Duchess of (1681–1733). Eldest daughter of the **Duke** and **Duchess of Marlborough**. In 1698 she married Francis Godolphin, later second Earl of Godolphin, a courtier, minor politician, and member of the **Kit-Cat Club**. It was this marriage that cemented the political alliance of Marlborough and Godolphin. Her relations with her mother, the formidable Sarah, were often strained. She became the mistress of **William Congreve**, who may have been the father of her daughter. AP seems to have maintained good relations with the Duchess. It is unlikely that she is the model for the character of "Philomedé" in *An Epistle to a Lady*, as used to be thought (see *TE* 3.ii: 55–57). She subscribed to the *Iliad* and for five copies of the *Odyssey*; she also supported **John Gay**'s play *Polly* when it was under threat. Gay addressed *An Epistle* (1722) to the Duchess. A keen follower of **opera**, she patronized **Giovanni Bononcini**, who served as her house composer.

See K.M. Lynch, *A Congreve Gallery* (Cambridge, MA: Harvard University Press, 1951), 59–90.

Marlborough, John Churchill, first Duke of (1650–1722). Soldier and statesman. Son of a country gentleman, Sir Winston Churchill. Entered the Foot Guards, 1667. Married Sarah Jennings, 1678 (see **Sarah Churchill, Duchess of Marlborough**). Baron, 1682. Helped to crush the rising of the Duke of Monmouth in 1685. Long associated with James II, he went over to the side of the invading army of **William III** in 1688. Earl of Marlborough, 1689. Captain-General of the forces, 1702–11; Knight of the Garter and Duke of Marlborough, 1702. Achieved important victories at Blenheim (1702), Ramillies (1706), Oudenarde (1708), and Malplaquet (1709).

No one in his time doubted Marlborough's genius for warfare or his gifts in managing great affairs. Some factors that made him controversial, and prompted fierce criticism from his opponents, were the following: (1) His political alliance with Godolphin, c. 1704–10, brought Whigs to the head of affairs and angered Tories who had been displaced. (2) By extension, he attracted criticism from those who resented the influence that his wife exerted over **Queen Anne**. (3) There were suggestions that he had flirted with the **Jacobites**, confirming earlier stories of his disloyalty to James II. (4)

There was a widely held belief that he had deliberately prolonged the **War of the Spanish Succession** for reasons of personal aggrandizement. He was also felt to be cold and rapacious in dealing with defeated peoples. (5) There were charges of graft and corruption, which rested in turn on Marlborough's reputation for meanness in even the smallest monetary matters. (6) The scale of his mansion, **Blenheim Palace**, built at public expense, upset many. (7) Even after his death, the lavish and showy funeral organized by his widow was viewed as symbolic of his "princely" standing.

None of these criticisms was wholly just, but many people believed them. Tories were jealous of the power Marlborough achieved at court and happy to see his fall in 1711, since he had opposed men like the **first Earl of Oxford**. They resented the fervent acclamations he had received from writers great and small from the time of the battle of Blenheim in 1702. The series of honors he received at home and abroad fueled this hostility. With the **Hanoverian accession** in 1715, the Duke was completely rehabilitated, and nominally he took charge of the military operations to quash the **Jacobite rising** in the following year.

AP went along with most of these adverse judgments, perhaps influenced by the sublime hatred his friend **Jonathan Swift** expressed toward the Duke. However, AP recognized that Marlborough was an extraordinary figure. He once wrote that the "Great General . . . had meaner mixture [*sic*] with his great Qualities" and that his "real Merit" and "shining Virtues as a Public Man" had not been sufficiently transmitted to posterity (*Corr* 4: 36). He praised Marlborough's courage but deplored his parsimony, relating a number of stories on this theme (*Anecdotes* 1: 162–64). Most of the references in AP's poetry and correspondence are negative, though often veiled. His most direct assault on the Duke comes in a character sketch (c. 1731), originally written for *An Essay on Man*, Epistle 4, but omitted from the printed text. AP considered it "one of the best I have ever written" (*Anecdotes* 1: 162). It was published in the **Twickenham edition** from an autograph draft at Yale University. The lines refer to almost every one of the charges just listed and hint at Marlborough's adulteries, a topic that had not surfaced much since the time of his marriage to Sarah Jennings. See *TE* 3.i: 155; 6: 358–59. In fact, much of the critique was already in place at the time of the Duke's fall: though he is not mentioned in *Windsor-Forest*, the poem obliquely replays the familiar criticisms. The character sketch also points toward Marlborough's final years, when he lapsed into senile decay—a scene brilliantly evoked in another damning portrait, that of Swift's "Satirical Elegy on the Death of a Late Famous General." Swift's is the better-known poem today, but it is hard to say which is the more scathing or relentless portrayal of the Duke.

For the possibility that AP had Blenheim in mind in his description of **Timon's villa**, see the entry **Blenheim Palace**.

There is a huge literature on the Duke, with or without the Duchess. The fullest and most eloquent advocacy of his qualities can be found in Sir Winston Churchill's *Marlborough: His Life and Times*, 4 vols. (1933–38), reprinted in 2 vols. (Chicago: University of Chicago Press, 2002), even though it represents something of a Whig panegyric. A good introductory life is C. Barnett, *The First Churchill: Marlborough, Soldier and Statesman* (New York: Putnam, 1974). The nature of AP's opposition to Marlborough is made more intelligible by M. Foot, *The Pen & the Sword: A Year in the Life of Jonathan Swift* (London: MacGibbon & Kee, 1966). For contemporary items pro and con, see R.D. Horn, *Marlborough, A Survey: Panegyrics, Satires, and Biographical Writings, 1688–1788* (New York: Garland, 1975).

Marlborough, Sarah Churchill, Duchess of (1660–1744). Born Sarah Jennings, she was a **maid of honor** to the future **Queen Anne** as a girl. In 1678 she married John Churchill, later **first Duke of Marlborough**. Lady of the Bedchamber, 1683, and on the accession of Princess Anne to the throne in 1702 became mistress of the robes and keeper of the privy purse. Her hold on power gradually weakened as she alienated the Queen's affections, and she was forced to resign early in 1711, when her husband's fortunes were also on the wane. She was succeeded in her role as keeper by **Abigail Masham**, who was in fact a poor relation and a lowly servant at court. Underlying the intrigues that provoked Sarah's downfall were a number of tensions—relating to sex, family, and espionage. However, a major factor was the desire of the **first Earl of Oxford** (also a distant kinsman of Abigail) to sabotage the political power of the Churchills and to distance them from the Queen, so as to strengthen the Tories' influence at court. A press campaign was mounted to blacken the character of the Duchess, who was portrayed as arrogant, insolent, and ambitious. Unwisely she had incurred the dislike of **Jonathan Swift**, and some of the mud stuck.

Sarah was assuredly a volatile and capricious woman. She was fiercely loyal to her family but engaged in bitter quarrels with two of her four beautiful daughters. Intensely acquisitive, especially as regards property, she had little time for **Blenheim Palace**, the shrine bestowed on the Churchills by a grateful nation. Most people fell foul of her acid tongue, not least the main architect of Blenheim, **Sir John Vanbrugh**.

AP had little or no personal contact with the Duchess during her years in power or at the time of her sudden descent. He had followed what were in effect party lines in attacking the Duke on political and private grounds but showed no particular dislike for Sarah, as well as complimenting the daughters in his *Epistle to Jervas*. She subscribed to the *Odyssey*. According to one story, which cannot be confirmed, the Duchess offered AP "a very considerable sum" to insert a laudatory character of her husband in one of his works, but the poet is said to have refused (*Anecdotes* 1: 161). However, nothing that had happened would point to the friendship that sprang up between the long-widowed Sarah (at the age of almost eighty) and the middle-aged AP. "The Duchess of Marlborow makes great Court to me," AP wrote to Swift in 1739, "but I am too Old for her, Mind & body" (*Corr* 1: 178). The two corresponded for the rest of the poet's life; twenty of his letters survive. He also visited the Duchess at her home in **Windsor Forest**. He sent her pineapples, and she returned the favor with venison. An important intermediary was **Nathaniel Hooke**, a Catholic friend of AP who had been hired to assist in writing a defense of the Duchess's conduct in the days of Queen Anne. Eventually Sarah survived AP by just four months.

Controversy long surrounded the portrait of **Atossa** in AP's *Epistle to a Lady*. After the poet's death the lines were judged by his executors to refer to the Duchess, and they were suppressed. It is now thought that the **Duchess of Buckinghamshire** is the real model for this character, although AP may have drawn on an earlier satire on Sarah as "Orsini," now lost. See *TE* 3.ii: 159–70.

The most satisfactory biography is F. Harris, *A Passion for Government: The Life of Sarah, Duchess of Marlborough* (Oxford: Clarendon, 1991). Some aspects of her career relevant to AP are brought out by D. Green, *Sarah Duchess of Marlborough* (London: Collins, 1967).

Marriott, Mrs. Also spelled "Marriot." AP conducted a flippant and sometimes flirtatious correspondence with this lady and her daughter Betty around 1713–15. Three letters from AP survive. There was also a son known as Jack Marriott, who was later curate at **Easthampstead**. Nothing is known of the family except that they lived in the parish of Stuston, in Suffolk, where **William Broome** was rector from 1713. They may have been related to the Marriotts, prominent lawyers in nearby Stowmarket and Mendlesham.

Marston. Estate near Frome in Somerset, dating from c. 1600 and acquired by the Boyle family in 1641 with 800 acres of land. It remained in the family until 1905. The house was given a classical façade in the eighteenth century, and wings were added by Samuel Wyatt (1737–1807). It fell into decay in recent times but has been restored in the last two decades by the Yeoman family. The park was remodeled by Stephen Switzer in the 1720s and 1730s.

During AP's lifetime it was owned by John Boyle, **fifth Earl of Orrery**. AP visited the house with **Dr. William King** in 1739 (*Corr* 4: 180) and probably on other occasions. He sent his last dog Bounce to Marston in 1742, but she died some time afterward (see *Lines on Bounce*).

See M. McGarvie, *The Book of Marston Bigot: The Story of Marston House and the Earls of Cork and Orrery* (Buckingham: Barracuda, 1987).

Masham, Abigail (c. 1670–1734), later Baroness Masham. Née Hill. Confidante to **Queen Anne** who played an important role in politics during AP's early manhood. Sister of General John Hill, a soldier promoted through the influence of the Tory ministers. First cousin of **Sarah, Duchess of Marlborough**, who regarded her as a poor dependent; second cousin of the **first Earl of Oxford**. Bedchamber woman to Anne as Princess (1697) and Queen (1702). She gradually wheedled her way into the Queen's good graces, supplanting the Duchess as the principal backstairs favorite and becoming Keeper of the Privy Purse in 1711. Married Colonel Samuel Masham (1679–1758) in a secret ceremony in the lodgings of **Dr. John Arbuthnot**, 1707. He had served the Queen's husband, Prince George, and became an MP for Windsor. Samuel, a member of the **Brothers Club**, was granted a peerage by the **Harley administration** in 1712 as part of the political measures to secure a peace. Abigail provided Oxford with information regarding the Queen's attitudes toward current events, but near the end of the reign she became estranged from Oxford and sided with **Bolingbroke**. After the Queen's death she lived in retirement. She figures regularly in the *Journal to Stella*. A lasting friendship developed between **Swift** and Lady Masham, who pressed the Dean to visit her as late as 1733. After her death in the following year, Swift wrote to AP of "my constant friend in all changes of times" (*Corr* 5: 14). Few others had much good to say of her after her power at court had gone. AP mentions the Mashams only briefly. Both subscribed to the *Iliad* and the *Odyssey*.

Master Key to Popery, A. An ironic reply to AP's critics, amid the furor stirred up by the episode of **Timon's villa**, after the publication of the *Epistle to Burlington* in 1731. The work can be dated to the early part of 1732. It remained in manuscript at Chatsworth until published by **John Butt** in 1949. The copy is in the hand of the **Countess of Burlington**, a close friend and amanuensis of AP; her daughter married the fourth Duke of Devonshire in 1748 and thus came to live at Chatsworth. There is no serious doubt of AP's authorship, although the manuscript is unsigned. The writer amusingly accuses AP of displaying ingratitude and malice when he attacks patrons and great aristocrats, including the **Duke of Chandos**. For the text and commentary, see *TE* 3.ii: 175–88; *Prose* 2: 405–30.

Maynwaring, Arthur (1668–1712). Sometimes spelled "Mainwaring." Whig politician and author. Auditor of the Imprest. He was an MP and a member of the **Kit-Cat Club**. According to **Jacob Tonson senior**, "Maynwaring, whom we hear nothing of now, was the ruling man in all the conversations" of the club. AP added in 1730, "Indeed what he did write has very little merit in it" (*Anecdotes* 1: 51). This is a nakedly partisan verdict. Maynwaring was the most effective opponent of **Swift** during the battles that raged over issues such as the succession and the **Treaty of Utrecht** in the last years of **Queen Anne**. He edited a riposte to the Tory *Examiner* known as the *Medley*, together with **John Oldmixon**, and wrote a stream of pamphlets, as well as coordinating the Whig propaganda machine. His principal loyalties were to the Churchills, and he acted as a kind of political secretary to the **Duchess of Marlborough**. She was grief-stricken when he died of tuberculosis. He had a sexual liaison with **Anne Oldfield**, by whom he had a son. At his early death Maynwaring left the actress and her child half of his estate.

Maynwaring, whose early sympathies were Jacobite, had been one of the group of patrons to whom AP had submitted his *Pastorals* for advice (or rather as a means of gaining influential favor). Previously Maynwaring had performed the same function for the young **William Congreve**. He translated Book 5 of the *Metamorphoses* for the collective version edited by **Samuel Garth** (1717), to which AP also contributed.

See *Swift vs. Mainwaring: The Examiner and the Medley*, ed. F.H. Ellis (Oxford: Clarendon, 1985).

McKillop, Alan Dugald (1892–1974). An outstanding eighteenth-century scholar at Rice University who wrote only intermittently about AP and the Scriblerians. However, his work on **Thomson**, Samuel Richardson, Fielding, and others casts much light on the world they inhabited. Together with L.I. Bredvold he edited an influential anthology of poetry and prose from the period (1939). He wrote *English Literature from Dryden to Burns* (1948). See also a Festschrift, *Restoration and Eighteenth-Century Literature: Essays in Honor of Alan Dugald McKillop*, ed. C. Camden (Chicago: University of Chicago Press, 1963), which contains many important studies on AP.

Mead, John. Goldsmith in **Fleet Street**, London, who acted as AP's banker. He subscribed to the *Odyssey*. See *Corr* 2: 183.

Mead, Dr. Richard (1673–1754). Physician who established a lucrative practice, much of it inherited from **Dr. John Radcliffe**, and eventually earned a then astronomical income of £6,000 per year. He became one of the most noted book collectors of the age. Noted also for his classical learning. FRS, 1703. He was called to attend to **Queen Anne** shortly before her death. Physician to **George II**, 1727. Mead was consulted by many famous individuals, including **Sir Isaac Newton** and the painter Jean-Antoine Watteau. He was a longtime opponent of **Dr. John Woodward**, one of the principal butts of the Scriblerian group.

Toward the end of his own life, AP came under his care, and in the *First Epistle of the First Book of Horace Imitated* he asserted, "I'll do what MEAD and CHESLEDEN advise" (*TE* 4: 283), suggesting that he had taken medical advice earlier. In the *Epistle to Burlington*, he links Mead with **Sir Hans Sloane** as collectors of discrimination and humanity (*TE* 3.ii: 136). See also **Cheselden** and **Sloane**.

Mead and AP were on very good terms personally. It is not particularly significant that Mead was listed in all AP's subscription ventures, since he was a generous patron of literature who subscribed almost on a routine basis (over 200 examples can be traced). More indicative is the fact that he owned AP's *Works* in a large-paper gilt edition of nine volumes. Additionally, he hung up at his home in Great Ormond Street, London, a portrait of AP (alongside those of **Newton** and Edmond Halley) painted by his neighbor **Jonathan Richardson senior**. AP visited him at this house, which later became the site of the Hospital for Sick Children. The library here was designed by **James Gibbs**. He joined with AP and the **Earl of Burlington** to set up the **monument to Shakespeare** in Westminster Abbey. Mead himself has a monument with a bust by **Peter Scheemakers** in the Abbey. According to **Samuel Johnson**, "Dr. Mead lived more in the broad sunshine of life than almost any man."

Richard's brother Samuel Meade (1670–1733), a lawyer, also subscribed to the *Iliad* and the *Odyssey*.

The only full-length treatment is R.H. Meade, *In the Sunshine of Life: A Biography of Dr. Richard Mead 1673–1754* (Philadelphia: Dorrance, 1974). There is room for further work. For Mead's relations with AP, see *This Long Disease* 60–64.

Mein, Charles (d. 1735). Sometimes spelled, and doubtless pronounced, "Main." Irishman who worked at the Custom House in London as examiner of duty on wines. A close friend of **William Congreve**, who had taken a tour on the Continent with Mein and made a bequest to him. Mentioned several times by **Jonathan Swift** in the *Journal to Stella* and described there as "an honest goodnatured fellow, a thorough hearty laugher, mightily beloved by men of wit: his mistress is never above a cook-maid" (*JTS* 1: 49). His chief characteristic seems to have been a desire to live well, that is, eat and drink. Appears as "wondering *Maine*, with laughing eyes," in *Mr. Pope's Welcome from*

Greece. The following lines read: "(*Gay, Maine, & Cheyney*, boon companions dear, / *Gay* fat, *Maine* fatter, *Cheyney* huge of Size)." Subscribed to the *Odyssey*.

Melville, Lewis. Pseudonym for Lewis Saul Benjamin (1874–1932). A prolific miscellaneous writer, he was best known for his work on **Thackeray**, as well as on Regency beaux and beauties. However, he also wrote popular lives of writers such as **Horace Walpole**, William Beckford, Laurence Sterne, Tobias Smollett, and William Cobbett. His books on the eighteenth century include studies of the spas at **Bath** and Tunbridge Wells, an account of the **South Sea Bubble**, a survey of life *In the Days of Queen Anne*, and a biography of the **Duke of Wharton**. In addition, Melville wrote *Stage Favourites of the Eighteenth Century* (1928), covering performers such as **Anne Oldfield**. His books on **John Gay** (1913), **Lady Mary Wortley Montagu** (1725), and **George I** (1909) are now supplanted as reliable scholarly resources. However, judiciously used, they contain some valuable material on the age of AP, a comment that applies even more to still two more among Melville's many books, *Lady Suffolk and Her Circle* (1924) and *Maids of Honour* (1927).

Memoirs of Martin Scriblerus. The full title is *Memoirs of the Extraordinary Life, Works, and Discoveries of Martinus Scriblerus*. It first appeared in 1741, in *The Works of Mr. Alexander Pope, in Prose*, vol. 2 (1741) (Griffith 530). There were folio and quarto editions at the same time and, from 1742, an octavo edition. Later in 1741 **George Faulkner** issued a duodecimo edition in Dublin. In all these cases the work was attributed to AP and **Dr. John Arbuthnot**. Later printings were generally confined to collected works of AP, and usually they followed **Warburton**'s 1751 edition in omitting the risqué "Double Mistress" episode (see below). No satisfactory version came out until 1950.

The origins of the work go back much earlier and represent the most sustained outcome of the collaborative schemes begun in the reign of

Anne by members of the **Scriblerus Club**. The first idea was that of AP, who set out in ***The Spectator*** on 14 August 1712 a proposal for a monthly digest of "the Works of the Unlearned," and soon afterward the club took up the idea. We cannot be certain exactly what responsibility each member bore for the composition. According to **Swift**, writing to Arbuthnot in 1714: "To talk of Martin in any hands but yours, is a folly. You every day give better hints than all of us together could do in a twelvemonth; and to say the truth, Pope who first thought of the hint has no genius at all to it, to my mind. Gay is too young; Parnell has some ideas of it, but is idle; I could put together, and lard, strike out well enough, but all that relates to the sciences must be from you" (Swift *Corr* 2: 46). Despite what is said here, it seems that Swift took little part in the work after he went to Ireland in 1714; that neither Parnell, especially, nor Gay was ever a major contributor; and that it was Arbuthnot and AP who carried the enterprise through. The ground was laid in Scriblerian gatherings of 1713–14. Some advance was made in the following years, especially around 1716–18, with a number of short prose squibs drafted, which constitute pendants to the *Memoirs*. There was probably a further burst of activity when Swift visited England in 1726–27. Thereafter, it was left for AP to see matters to a conclusion. After the death of Arbuthnot in 1735, all the surviving materials appear to have fallen into his hands. He organized these into a coherent manuscript, and after various hesitations published the work in 1741.

The work belongs to a long line of satires on misapplied learning, sometimes referred to as "the tradition of learned wit." At the heart of the narrative is the foolish pedant Martin Scriblerus, a dabbler in a range of arts and sciences. The hero makes ill-judged forays into branches of the humanities, including logic, metaphysics, and rhetoric, but his particular obsessions lie in physiology and anatomy. A prime target here is the antiquarian **John Woodward**. Like his father Cornelius, Martin is prone to credulous antiquarian pursuits. His philosophic, biological, and legal interests come together when he

finds himself embroiled in the affair of "the Double Mistress," as a result of his marriage to Lindamira, one of a pair of Siamese twin sisters who are joined in the area of their genitals. Martin is impelled to bring an action in the spiritual court against the husband of the other sister, Indamora, for cohabitation with Lindamira. The lawsuit allows the Scriblerians abundant space for their favorite mode of intellectual farce, satirizing contemporary philosophical theories on the nature and site of personal identity. Owing to the freedom with which it uses deliberately bad taste to point up the absurdities of this situation, the episode incurred the hostility of moralistic editors and was excluded from all versions produced in the nineteenth and early twentieth centuries. However, it displays the recurrent Scriblerian infatuation with popular sights and freak shows and more narrowly AP's signature preoccupation with monstrous and grotesque conditions of the body.

A strange alternative version of the work appeared as *Memoirs of the Life of Scriblerus*, which was issued by the bogus publisher **A. Moore** in February 1723. It is a short pamphlet attributed to "D. S——t," although it is virtually certain that Swift had nothing to do with it. The story this time concerns Timothy Scriblerus, a hack author rather than a scholar. Hardly any of the details match those in the true *Memoirs*, but the spurious version borrows enough ideas (including the last name of the hero) to prompt questions about its origins. It is possible that the unknown author had somehow obtained copies of early Scriblerian fragments. There is one brief reference to AP as "*P——e.*" If any of the original group of satirists had any hand in the work, which is most unlikely, it could only be AP himself.

See the edition by C. Kerby-Miller (New Haven, CT: Yale University Press, 1950; reprint, New York: Oxford University Press, 1988), which contains an outstanding introduction as well as extensive notes.

Memoirs of P.P. Clerk of this Parish. A Scriblerian satire in prose on Bishop Burnet, written by AP probably with the assistance of **John Gay**. It first appeared in the ***Miscellanies*** in

1728 and later went into AP's *Works* (**1717**). The date of composition is uncertain. AP claimed that it was written "at the seat of Lord Harcourt in Oxfordshire" prior to Burnet's death in 1715 (*TE* 5: 34); but if the place is right here, the time is probably wrong. Possibly this was an early effusion of the Scriblerians, around 1714, and revised when AP and Gay were at Stanton Harcourt in 1718. An attempt by the hack writer **James Moore Smythe** to claim responsibility for the satire was easily dismissed by AP.

The work parodies the writings of Gilbert Burnet (1643–1715), Bishop of Salisbury from 1689. The satire is directed mainly against Burnet's busy, egocentric manner of narration, although the *History of his own Times* which most obviously fills AP's bill did not appear until 1724–34. In any case Burnet was a likely target on account of his vehement Whiggery, which had been manifested for half a century; his intervention in the affairs of his native Scotland against the Stuart monarchs; and the secular rather than spiritual emphasis of his career in the church. **Swift** wrote barbed comments on the *History* in his copy of the work. To cap everything, the bishop's son **Thomas Burnet** was an adversary of AP who earned a niche in *The Dunciad*.

The memoirs consist of prosy details regarding minor episodes in the life of a self-important parish clerk. In places an editor summarizes the course of the work: "Then follow full seventy Chapters containing an exact detail of the *Law-Suits of the Parson* and his *Parishioners*, concerning *Tythes*." The narrator is presented as a supporter of the High Church and of **Dr. Henry Sacheverell**, which is exactly the opposite of Burnet's position. Absurdly the clerk attributes the great events brought about in the period of the **Harley administration** to parish worthies named Amos Trainer, George Pilcocks, and so on.

For introduction, text and annotation, see *Prose* 2: 101–28.

Memorial List. At an unknown date AP wrote down "A Memorial List of Departed Friends and Relations" in a copy of an Elzevir Virgil.

It was transcribed at the head of the **Elwin and Courthope edition** (1: ix–x), but the volume has since disappeared. This must have been the edition by Daniel Heinsius (Leiden, 1636). The list extends to 1735, but it is not clear when it was begun: each of the entries is in Latin. The first entry is for **John Dryden** in 1700 and the last for the **Earl of Peterborough** in October 1735. All those named apart from Dryden were personally known to AP. They include his maternal aunt Elizabeth Turner (d. 1710). For the remainder, see entries in this volume for **William Walsh**, **Thomas Betterton**, Anthony Englefield (see **Englefield family**), **Thomas Parnell**, **William Wycherley**, **Sir William Trumbull**, **Alexander Pope senior**, **Simon Harcourt**, **James Craggs junior**, the **first Earl of Oxford**, the **Duke of Buckinghamshire**, **Mary Beach**, **Robert Digby**, **Edward Blount**, **William Congreve**, **Elijah Fenton**, **Francis Atterbury**, **John Gay**, **Edith Pope**, **Samuel Garth** (entered out of correct order), and **John Arbuthnot**. A brief descriptive phrase accompanies each entry ("my most faithful nurse" for Beach, "an honest man, and by no means a bad poet" for Fenton, and so on). English versions by the author of this volume.

Merlin's Cave. A kind of horticultural folly constructed in the gardens at **Richmond**, set up by **Queen Caroline** in 1735. It was not so much a cave as a thatched house with Gothic windows, designed by **William Kent**. There were several waxwork figures, accompanied by astronomical symbols and bookcases containing a small library of English works. The overall aim of the cave, an above-ground answer to AP's own **grotto**, was to connect the ruling Hanoverian house with earlier British monarchs and heroes. It borrowed the Arthurian motifs used earlier by Elizabeth I to suggest a dynastic continuity. **Stephen Duck** was appointed curator and his wife housekeeper: they were allowed to charge a fee to visitors. The cave was destroyed a generation later. AP refers to the cave in the *Epistle to Augustus*, with a dry note, "A Building in the Royal Gardens of Richmond, where is a small, but choice Collection of Books" (*TE* 4: 224).

See J. Colton, "Merlin's Cave and Queen Caroline: Garden Art as Political Propaganda," *Eighteenth-Century Studies*, 10 (1976), 1–20.

Messiah. A poem in heroic couplets, containing 108 lines, described as "A Sacred Eclogue, in Imitation of Virgil's Pollio." It first appeared anonymously in *The Spectator* on 14 May 1712 (Griffith 5). AP's authorship was revealed in the same journal on 12 November 1712. The poem was then collected in the *Works* **(1717)**, with an "advertisement" explaining the origins of the work, and went into several editions of the *Miscellanies* and other reprints of the *Works*. No separate edition is recorded before 1766, while a Greek translation by John Plumptre appeared in 1796 and a Latin version by C. Billinge in 1785. However, the most famous rendering is a Latin translation by **Samuel Johnson**, written as a college exercise and printed in an **Oxford** miscellany in 1731. AP is said to have admired Johnson's work, according to James Boswell.

The work is mentioned in AP's correspondence with **John Caryll senior** in May 1712 (*Corr* 1:142–44). **Richard Steele** thanked AP for his contribution, stating that he had compared it with its sources in the Book of Isaiah and found that the poet had "preserv'd the sublime heavenly spirit throughout the whole." Indeed, he told AP, "your Poem is already better than the *Pollio*" (*Corr* 1: 146). Steele was referring to various passages in Isaiah, including chapters 50 and 61; and to Virgil's fourth *Eclogue*, addressed to C. Asinius Pollio, a statesman and literary patron who was Consul in 40 B.C. The poem by Virgil, which depicts the reign of the Emperor Augustus as ushering in a Golden Age, had been interpreted by Christian scholiasts as foretelling the birth of a Savior. The passages from the Bible noted by AP are taken from the Authorized Version, but the text sometimes suggests rather the readings of the Douai Bible, used in Catholic homes like that of the Pope family. Although the poem enjoyed considerable currency for many years, it was often criticized for what **Joseph Warton** called "florid epithets, and useless circumlocutions," a reference to the luscious and highly stylized texture of the verse.

For the text and commentary, see *TE* 1: 99–122.

Metamorphoses. Some of AP's first poetic exercises were "imitations of the stories that pleased him most in Ovid." According to a report by **Walter Harte**, there was a version of "Pyramus and Thisbe" from Book 4 that AP showed to **John Dryden**, but if this existed it is lost. AP himself said that as a boy he translated "above a quarter" of the tales that make up the fifteen books of **Ovid**.

The surviving translations from the work are these:

1. **Joseph Spence** claimed to have in his possession the story of Acis and Galatea in the poet's hand, written at the age of fourteen (*Anecdotes* 1: 12). This was presumably "Polyphemus and Acis," from Book 13, first published in a magazine in 1749 (*TE* 1: 363–73).

2. "The Fable of Vertumnus and Pomona," from Book 14, first published in **Bernard Lintot**'s *Miscellaneous Poems and Translations* (1712). See *TE* 1: 375–82.

3. "The Fable of Dryope," in the sumptuous edition of the *Metamorphoses* published by **Jacob Tonson senior** in 1717 (see *TE* 1: 383–90). The editor was **Samuel Garth**, who himself translated Book 14. Others represented in the roll of translators were Dryden, **Joseph Addison**, **Laurence Eusden**, **Arthur Maynwaring**, **Nahum Tate**, **John Gay**, **William Congreve**, **John Ozell**, **Nicholas Rowe**, and **Leonard Welsted**. Tonson had already published several portions of the work in Dryden's translation, as well as individual pieces by Addison and others. He engaged Garth to find a team to cover the remainder of the entire series of poems. Each of the versions is cast in heroic couplets, an attempt to match the homogeneous quality of Ovid's hexameter. The prevailing note was set by Dryden, who had attempted to find a style that would convey something of the rapid shifts and witty modulations of the original. The volume is dedicated to the Princess of Wales, later **Queen Caroline**, and the excellent printing was the work of **John Watts**. Notwithstanding his own collaboration, AP had a little sport with the volume in *Sandys's Ghost*.

See a useful reprint of the Garth version, with an introduction by G. Tissol (Ware, Hertfordshire: Wordsworth, 1998).

Milton, John (1608–74). Poet. AP may have copied Milton's manner in his lost epic written in early youth, but otherwise he did not write any formal **imitations**. At the age of seventeen he lent the minor poems of Milton to **Sir William Trumbull**, who seems not to have been previously familiar with works such as *Lycidas* and *L'Allegro* (*Corr* 1: 10)—an indication of the emerging tastes of the time. AP regarded Milton's grand style as "exotic," something possible only because the poet was dealing with cosmic matter remote from ordinary earthly existence (*Anecdotes* 1: 197). The impress of *Paradise Lost* on his writing is most apparent in his **mock heroic** works. *The Rape of the Lock* uses **sylphs** to parody Milton's angels, while in *The Dunciad* there are many occasions where Satan is recalled in the portrayal of Dulness. See A. Williams, *Pope's Dunciad: A Study of Its Meaning* (London: Methuen, 1955).

AP kept a picture of Milton in his bedroom at **Binfield**. His **library** included copies of the older poet's works, including the 1707 edition of *Paradise Lost* published by **Jacob Tonson senior** (*CIH* 424–25).

minor poems. AP's shorter works in verse number more than a hundred. The count omits all the considerable poems, including the series of **epistles** to various friends. This leaves works in a wide variety of genres, including odes, character sketches, and presentation verses. The main categories are (1) about twenty **epitaphs**; (2) about twenty to thirty **epigrams**, depending on how this form is defined; (3) a small number of **ballads**; and (4) a handful of dramatic rologues and epilogues. Some fragments survive that cannot easily be allotted to any category. Necessarily more works of disputed authorship occur in this area than elsewhere in AP's corpus. The fullest collection of these items is to be found in the volume of *Minor Poems* in the **Twickenham edition**, vol. 6.

Miscellaneous Poems and Translations. An anthology published by **Bernard Lintot** on 20 May 1712 (Griffith 6). It contained seven poems by AP, all relatively minor items with the exception of *The Rape of the Locke*. This, the earliest two-canto version of AP's satire, occupies the last twenty-four pages of the text. Two gatherings, "Y" and "Z" (321–52), are missing from the volume at this point, and sheets with signatures "Aa" and "Bb" substituted. It is evident that some material was dropped at the last minute.

A second edition came out in December 1713, although dated 1714 (Griffith 32). This time the title page adds the information "particularly [various titles] by Mr. Pope." The name of William Lewis is included in the imprint. Much of the volume is simply a reissue of the original sheets from 1712. Newly included are *An Essay on Criticism*, at the end; and prior to that are *Windsor-Forest* and the *Ode for Musick on St. Cecilia's Day*. The two latter items occupy the gatherings signed "Y" and "Z," previously omitted. It has been shown that these pages have been set in a more crowded fashion. The explanation offered by **Norman Ault** was that AP had first intended to include the original shorter version of *Windsor-Forest*, together with *Ode*, in the 1712 volume. When the poem was revised and expanded, it would have occupied too much space for the pages available, and it was consequently reset in the more huddled form that appears in the 1714 printing.

Ault argued that AP was in effect the editor of this volume, at least until its fifth edition in 1725. New items by AP are added to later editions, which went into two volumes from 1720. See Ault 27–38.

Miscellanies. A series of volumes of composite authorship, often called the "Swift-Pope Miscellanies," which first appeared between 1727 and 1732. When **Jonathan Swift** visited England in 1726, he concerted with AP a plan to bring out some uncollected shorter works. Perhaps in response to the unauthorized volumes of *Miscellanea* issued by **Edmund Curll** in July of that year, the two men originally envisaged a two-volume set of prose and verse, later expanding the scheme to a set of three volumes. AP was to act as editor, and after Swift returned to Ireland he sent his friend some items for inclusion. The publisher was to be **Benjamin Motte**, who in the same year issued *Gulliver's Travels*: he agreed to pay £250 for the rights to the set.

In the event the series evolved into a group of four volumes, which appeared in a variety of formats and guises subsequently, with materials added and removed. The sequence of volumes, as they first appeared, runs as follows:

1. The first volume, published in June 1727. It contains a preface, signed by Swift and AP from **Twickenham** on 27 May 1717. AP wrote this preface; the rest of the volume is mainly by Swift. It was an octavo of 428 pages (Griffith 184).

2. The second volume. Published at the same time. This contained some new prose pieces by AP. It was an octavo of 372 pages (Griffith 185).

3. The so-called "Last Volume," published on 8 March 1728 (dated "1727"). It was an octavo of approximately 484 pages (Griffith 196); calculation is difficult because of several cancellations. The first section is taken up by the prose satire *The Art of Sinking*, here appearing for the first time. AP had originally intended to include *The Dunciad* later in the volume, but at a late stage this was removed and *Peri Bathous* substituted. Several other items in verse by AP were also printed for the first time.

4. The so-called "Third Volume," published in October 1732. This was an octavo of 390 pages (Griffith 276). Motte is named as publisher along with **Lawton Gilliver**, who had obtained the rights to this volume. Several new Scriblerian (see **Scriblerus Club**) items appear.

An ostensible continuation came out in 1735 as "Volume the Fifth," issued by Charles Davis. It contains material by Swift but nothing by AP.

Later reprints afford a complex bibliographical puzzle, with many confusing inclusions and exclusions. Unauthorized editions using the title "Miscellanies" reached a total of eleven volumes by 1746. Even in the legitimate editions the contents often vary in peculiar ways, and the authorship of individual items is seldom satisfactorily established. Some items in which

John Gay and **John Arbuthnot** almost certainly had a hand are also found in these editions. There were many difficulties over copyright, especially after AP quarreled with Motte around 1729: Curll and **Bernard Lintot** also claimed the rights in certain items. The most interesting version is perhaps the four-volume set of 1742, on which AP certainly gave editorial help to the publisher **Charles Bathurst** (son-in-law and successor to Motte). However, the series did nothing to enhance clarity as regards the genesis and composition of the works of the Scriblerian group.

mock-heroic. The essential trick of mock-heroic writing is to bestow the elevated style of epic (traditionally the "highest" kind of literature) on a trivial subject. It achieves satiric point at once by belittlement and aggrandizement. Epic action is scaled down, but footling events are accorded the dignity of inflated language. The opposite was the low burlesque or travesty, exemplified by Samuel Butler's *Hudibras* (1662–78), which dealt with high subjects in a debased linguistic manner.

The form has its roots in the comic epics of the ancient world, such as the Greek *Batrochomyomachia* (Battle of the Frogs and Mice), which was translated by **Thomas Parnell** in 1717 (see *The Battle of the Frogs and Mice*). However, it was most fully developed in the seventeenth and eighteenth centuries. The most influential early examples were *La Secchia rapita* (The Stolen Bucket) (1622), by **Alessandro Tassoni**, and *Le lutrin* (The Lectern) (1674–83), by **Nicolas Boileau**. Before AP, the most accomplished use of the form comes in the satires of **John Dryden**, in *Absalom and Achitophel* and, more directly, in *MacFlecknoe*. In AP's time the main exemplar of the form was *The Dispensary* (1699) by **Samuel Garth**. A particular dialect was evolved by **John Philips** in his mock-Miltonic blank verse poem *The Splendid Shilling* (1701), which was imitated by **John Gay** in *Wine* (1708). Later **Henry Fielding** converted the form to novelistic purposes with his "comic epic in prose," *Joseph Andrews* (1742). Mock-heroic continued to be practiced throughout the eighteenth century, with diminishing effect as epic itself lost some of its former caste. Remnants of mock-heroic can be detected in poems of **Byron**, including *Beppo* and some parts of *Don Juan*.

The two supreme masterpieces of mock-heroic in its strict form are AP's poems ***The Rape of the Lock*** and ***The Dunciad***. Both mimic the narrative, style, rhetoric, motifs, and other aspects of the standard epic. In particular, the *Rape* reduces the scale of an epic to the dimensions of a tiny domestic contretemps: it tells in epic fashion the story of a tempest in a teacup.

See U. Broich, *The Eighteenth-Century Mock-Heroic Poem*, trans. D.H. Wilson (Cambridge: Cambridge University Press, 1980); G.G. Colomb, *Designs on Truth: The Poetics of the Augustan Mock-Epic* (University Park: Pennsylvania University Press, 1992).

Molyneux, Samuel (1689–1728). Irish-born astronomer and courtier, son of the noted scientific writer William Molyneux (1656–98). FRS, 1712. MP from 1715 to his death and also Irish MP. Secretary to **George II** as Prince of Wales, 1715–27. A minor figure in politics, he carried out pioneering work with the reflecting telescope. He married Lady Elizabeth Capel, eldest daughter of the Earl of Essex, a member of a family with impeccable Whig connections. Through his wife, he acquired the White House at **Richmond**, where he built an observatory. After his death this became the property of **Frederick, Prince of Wales**.

Molyneux became involved with his friend **Nathanael St. André** in the Mary Tofts affair, which gave him a natural place in AP's ballad ***The Discovery***. It is less clear why he figures centrally in another satiric **ballad**, *Sandys's Ghost*. He subscribed to both the *Iliad* and the *Odyssey* and appears briefly in the poet's letters. In 1728 Molyneux died in mysterious circumstances, a few days after collapsing in the House of Commons. This gave rise to speculation that St. André had poisoned him, especially after his friend married Lady Elizabeth Molyneux in 1730 and inherited money.

Monk, Samuel Holt (1902–81). Scholar who taught at the University of Minnesota from 1947 to 1970. He is best known for his pioneering work on *The Sublime* (1935). In addition, he worked on **Dryden** and **Swift** and helped to edit the eighteenth-century section of the *Norton Anthology of English Literature*. His most important publication on AP is "A Grace beyond the Reach of Art," *Journal of the History of Ideas*, 5 (1944), 131–50, reprinted in *EA* 38–62. See *Studies in Criticism and Aesthetics, 1660–1800: Essays in Honor of Samuel Holt Monk*, ed. H. Anderson and J.S. Shea (Minneapolis: University of Minnesota Press, 1967).

Montagu, Lady Mary Wortley (1689–1762). Author. She was born Mary Pierrepoint, daughter of a Whig peer, later **Duke of Kingston**. He was a member of the **Kit-Cat Club**, and Mary is supposed to have been introduced as one of the club's "toasts," or favorite young women, at the age of eight. In 1712 Mary displeased her father by eloping with Edward Wortley Montagu (1681–1761), a wealthy MP and a close friend of **Addison**. Her husband did not progress as far in his political career as once seemed likely. However, in 1716 he was appointed ambassador to Turkey, which was then at war with the Austrian Empire. Mary accompanied her husband to Constantinople and wrote some famous letters home, which were published shortly after her death in 1763. In addition, she brought back the practice of inoculation for smallpox (a disease from which she had suffered in 1715): her energetic campaign in favor of this technique attracted the support of the Princess of Wales, later **Queen Caroline**, and exercised a deep influence on medical thinking.

The Wortley Montagus gradually became estranged, a natural development since he was closed up and parsimonious, while she was adventurous, witty, and outgoing. Eventually in 1739 Mary took herself abroad: She was at this time engaged in an affair with the cosmopolitan Italian intellectual Francesco Algarotti (1712–64), but he proved as unsatisfactory a lover as her husband. She lived in turn at Avignon, Brescia, and Venice. Finally, after Edward's death, she returned to England in January 1762, but after only a few months succumbed to breast cancer. All through her life her family relationships had been difficult: her sister Frances had married the Earl of Mar, leader of the **Jacobite rising** in 1715–16, and later suffered from depressive illness, while her son Edward Wortley Montagu junior (1713–76) was an unstable and prodigal creature who ended up as a Muslim convert. Her most satisfactory relative was her daughter Mary, who married the politician John Stuart, Earl of Bute, in 1736.

Lady Mary figures in AP's life history, first as a friend, then as a violent enemy. The two were known to each other by 1715, and AP made a careful transcript of the **Court Eclogues** that Lady Mary wrote in 1716. A correspondence was established when she went abroad, written on his side in a strain of self-mocking gallantry and on hers by a more realistic and observant mode of description. When she returned she became a neighbor of AP in **Twickenham**. For some unknown reason the pair quarreled bitterly within the next few years. One theory is that AP made romantic advances to Lady Mary, which she rejected with scorn. In any case, the upshot was a series of bitter exchanges in print. By 1727 the break had become irreparable. AP attacked his former friend in the **Miscellanies** that year, in a poem titled **The Capon's Tale**, and he added another thrust the next year in the first version of **The Dunciad**. He also accused Lady Mary of libeling him, although evidence is lacking for such an assault at this juncture. Thereafter AP brought her into poem after poem, especially in the **Imitations of Horace**. She sometimes figures as "Sappho," as in the cruelest couplet of all: "From furious *Sappho* scarce a milder Fate, / Pox'd by her Love, or libell'd by her Hate" (**The First Satire of the Second Book of Horace Imitated**, ll. 83–84). One of his regular accusations is that she was a slattern ("Linnen worthy Lady Mary," for example, in **The First Epistle of the First Book of Horace Imitated**, l. 164). Meanwhile, his adversary had not remained silent, and together with **John, Baron Hervey** she produced what is perhaps the most ferocious and effective attack on AP, *Verses Address'd to the Imitator of the First Satire of the Second Book of Horace* (1733). The

wounds never healed, and Lady Mary let loose some further salvos in conversation with **Joseph Spence** (*Anecdotes* 1: 304–7). Despite all this, AP kept a **portrait** of Lady Mary in his house: this was probably a picture by **Kneller** he had commissioned in 1719. About forty items survive in what was evidently once a more extensive correspondence.

See I. Grundy, *Lady Mary Wortley Montagu* (Oxford: Oxford University Press, 1999); and *The Complete Letters of Lady Mary Wortley Montagu*, ed. R. Halsband, 3 vols. (Oxford: Clarendon, 1965–67). A valuable addition is *Essays and Poems; and Simplicity: A Comedy, by Lady Mary Wortley Montagu*, ed. R. Halsband and I. Grundy (Oxford: Clarendon, 1977). The correspondence with AP is discusssed in C. Lowenthal, *Lady Mary Wortley Montagu and the Eighteenth-Century Familiar Letter* (Athens: University of Georgia Press, 1994). A relevant essay is I. Grundy, "Pope, Peterborough, and the Characters of Women," *Review of English Studies*, 20 (1969), 461–68.

monument to Shakespeare. AP was one of the chief promoters of the effort belatedly to honor Britain's greatest writer in the national shrine at Westminster Abbey. A public subscription was mounted. In December 1737 a notice in the press reported that proposals for the inscription should be sent to AP and that £300 raised by recent benefit performances in the London **theater** had been deposited in trust to the **Earl of Burlington**, **Dr. Richard Mead**, and AP (*Life* 920). These three together with Benjamin Martyn (1699–1763) seem to have been the leading figures in the campaign, though others assisted. The monument was erected in late 1740 with a lifesize effigy in white marble, designed by **William Kent** and executed by **Peter Scheemakers**. Above the bust was set an inscription, "Gulielmo Shakespear, Anno post Mortem CXXIV. Amor Publicus posuit" (public love placed [this] for William Shakespeare 124 years after his death," an implied reproach to artistic taste in the era of **Walpole**. A scroll was attached to a small column next to the dramatist. On it appeared lines from Prospero's speech in *The Tempest*, chosen after some debate. Two

epigrams possibly by AP can be found in *TE* 6: 395–96.

Moore, A. The pseudonymous form used to cloak the identity of clandestine publishers; most commonly identified as "A. Moore near St. Paul's Church." It is no surprise to find that many **pamphlet attacks** on AP came out under this bogus imprint, but it is also true that editions of some of his own works, for example, *Duke upon Duke*, bore this name on their title page. The spurious *Memoirs of the Life of Scriblerus* (1723) also carries this imprint.

Moore, Cecil Albert (1879–1968). Professor at the University of Minnesota from 1917 to 1947. He wrote several studies of literature and ideas in AP's time, including *Backgrounds of English Literature 1700–1760* (1953), which contains much with relevance to AP. In addition, he edited selections of eighteenth-century verse, prose, and drama, as well as one on Restoration literature.

Moore Smythe, James (1702–34). Miscellaneous writer and man about town. He was the son of the venal Tory politician Arthur Moore (1666–1730), a man of obscure origins who had acquired riches from contracting and public office. The son quarreled with AP over some lines in a play, *The Rival Modes* (1727), which he borrowed from the poet apparently with permission. This promptly earned Moore Smythe a minor role in *The Dunciad*, although AP may have simply found the vocable "More" a convenient and resonant-sounding name. Moore Smythe also managed to find a way into *The Art of Sinking*, where he figures in chapter 6 as one of the "frogs" who can "neither walk nor fly, but can *leap* and *bound* to admiration" (*Prose* 2: 197). Unwisely the young author attempted to reply and collaborated with **Leonard Welsted** on a poem titled *One Epistle to Mr. A. Pope*, published in April 1730. He was also active in the public prints. While Moore Smythe was not a serious threat, AP thought it worth responding with a number of **epigrams** on the puppyish hack writer, published in the *Grub-street Journal*; see *TE* 6: 324–30. The

references to him in the *Epistle to Arbuthnot*, following his early death, embody good-humored contempt rather than hatred.

Moore's Worms. A poem first published on 1 May 1716 as "To Mr. John Moore, Author of the Celebrated Worm-Powder"; it was advertised by its publisher, **Edmund Curll**, as "The Worms, a Satyr; written by Mr. Pope." This was a folio half-sheet, price, twopence (Griffith 53). Several other editions appeared in the next few years, and the item has been described as "probably the most popular poem (at least in his own day) that Pope is supposed to have written" (*TE* 6: 163). This is judging by the number of separate appearances in print. It was never acknowledged by AP himself.

The poem is written in **ballad** stanzas and contains forty lines. It takes off from the familiar press advertisements of John Moore (d. 1737), who sold worming powders from his shop in Abchurch Lane, off Lombard Street in the city of London. The fundamental method is that of finding verbal parallels and echoes relating to the word "worm," and the work concludes with a comically appropriate ending for the Whig literati at their fashionable coffeehouse: "Ev'n *Button*'s Wits to Worms shall turn, / Who Maggots were before." See *TE* 6: 161–64.

Moral Essays. The usual collective name for four **epistles** on contemporary themes addressed to friends of AP. The poet himself grouped them in his editions as "Epistles," and his modern editor has used the title *Epistles to Several Persons*, on the grounds that it was **Warburton** who was responsible for the label "Moral Essays" (see *TE* 3.ii.ix–xvi). The so-called **deathbed edition** that AP had printed shortly before he died in 1744, but was then suppressed, contains several new readings. The poems are also sometimes known as "Ethic Epistles." The situation is complicated, in view of the facts that (1) AP also included at various times other poems among the "Epistles," including poems addressed to the **first Earl of Oxford, Addison, Dr. John Arbuthnot, Jervas,** and **Teresa Blount**; (2) the four main epistles were originally designed to form part of the poet's grand ethical work, usually called his *opus magnum*; and (3) the individual items were written and published separately between 1730 and 1735. The order of composition (or at least completion), like that of publication, has the poem addressed to **Burlington** first, that to **Bathurst** second, then that to **Cobham**, and finally that to **Martha Blount**. However, the four were first issued collectively in the second volume of AP's *Works* (1735) (Griffith 370), in the order Cobham, Blount, Bathurst, and Burlington. This is the order they have traditionally followed, and the arrangement seems to be AP's own. It is true that Warburton had his own strong ideas on the shape of AP's oeuvre, but the conventional layout seems to have been authorial in origin.

For more detailed discussion, see individual entries for the *Epistle to Bathurst*, *Epistle to Burlington*, *Epistle to Cobham*, and *Epistle to a Lady*. The standard edition for all four is *TE* 3.ii. Monographs that devote particular attention to the poems as a group include R.W. Rogers, *The Major Satires of Alexander Pope* (Urbana: University of Illinois Press, 1955); and P. Dixon, *The World of Pope's Satires: An Introduction to the "Epistles" and Imitations of Horace* (London: Methuen, 1968).

Morice, William. A lawyer who became High Bailiff of Westminster, in which capacity he was heavily involved in the activities of his father-in-law **Francis Atterbury**, who was Dean of Westminster from 1713. He married Atterbury's daughter Mary (1698–1729) in 1715; she died at Toulouse while visiting her exiled father. This event prompted an emotionally charged exchange in letters between Atterbury and AP, besides an elegy by **Samuel Wesley junior**. Morice had been the main avenue through which Atterbury's English friends retained contact with him after his banishment. One letter from Morice to AP survives. Both husband and wife subscribed to the *Odyssey*.

Morley, John (1667–1732). A land jobber of Halstead, Essex, who acted as agent for the **second Earl of Oxford**, among others. He seems to have escaped AP's dislike for men of this profession, such as **Peter Walter**, because of the Harley connection and his friendship with **Matthew Prior**. The latter describes a visit to the site of his proposed home at **Down Hall** in company with Morley, who was fixing the purchase: See Prior's amusing ballad "Down Hall: A Poem" (1723). **Swift** thought less well of Morley, whom he called "a great land-jobber and knave," and accused him of helping to cause Lord Oxford's financial downfall (see *Corr* 1: 148).

Morley had certainly come up in the world. The son of a butcher, he followed this trade until he moved into the world of aristocratic business, serving, like Walter, as a marriage-broker at times. He helped to arrange the marriage in 1713 of Oxford, then Lord Harley, to the daughter of the immensely wealthy Duke of Newcastle. In return the **first Earl of Oxford** is said to have given him the huge sum of £10,000. In 1722 he applied for a grant of arms and chose the figure of a butcher for his crest. He was able to buy a Tudor mansion called Muchensies, east of Halstead; in the approved manner, he razed the building and erected a brick structure in its place, which he renamed Blue Bridge House. His daughter married the son of the Rector of Halstead in 1708. His wife was a sister of **Sir George Browne**, who married Morley's own sister: See also **Thalestris**. Two of AP's surviving letters to Morley show an easy and bantering relationship existed in the 1720s. Once AP attended him while he was laid up in bed after injuring his leg (*Corr* 1: 148, 359, 362). He figures as "hearty Morley" in *Mr. Pope's Welcome from Greece*. Morley was also a subscriber to the *Odyssey*, as he was to a wide range of books on historical, architectural, and antiquarian subjects. He left a handsome bequest to the town of Halstead and was buried in a fine tomb in St. Andrew's parish church.

Morrice, Bezaleel (c. 1675–1749). An energetic producer of verses, with titles like *The Amour of Cytherea* (1724). His life is otherwise largely lost to view. Nothing is so remarkable in his career as his admission to *The Dunciad*, where he figures in the triad of "Breval, Besaleel, Bond" (2: 118). AP seems to have found his name delicious enough to warrant inclusion, as a note to the line suggests that it was an implausible pseudonym: "As for *Besaleel*, it carries Forgery in the very name, nor is it, as the others are, a surname. Thou may'st depend on it no such authors ever lived: All phantoms!" (*TE* 5: 111). In reality he had earned his place by producing a number of attacks on AP, especially on the version of **Homer**, such as *Three Satires, Most Humbly Inscribed and Recommended to that Little Gentleman, of Great Vanity* (1719). See Guerinot 77–78, 82–83, 228–29, 286–88. He was still at it in 1738. Once he inadvertently wrote in praise of *An Essay on Man*, not having recognized the author.

Motte, Benjamin (1693–1738). Bookseller. Originally a printer, he succeeded to the business of Benjamin Tooke junior (1671–1723). Motte acted as the publisher in England for the later work of **Swift**, and it was he who brought out *Gulliver's Travels* in 1726. In March 1727 Motte contracted to publish the *Miscellanies*, but AP found him dilatory and perhaps too independent. There were problems when AP wished to reprint items from the *Miscellanies* in his own *Works*, and these had not been cleared up when Motte died in April 1738, leaving the business to be carried on by his partner **Charles Bathurst**. Seven letters from AP to Motte survive. There is also correspondence between Swift and Motte. The bookseller's brother Andrew Motte (d. 1730) translated the *Principia* of **Sir Isaac Newton**, published by Benjamin in 1729.

Motteux, Peter Anthony (1663–1718). Originally named Pierre-Antoine, he was a Huguenot from Rouen who went to England in 1685 after the revocation of the Edict of Nantes. He edited the *Gentleman's Journal* (1692–94), as well as translating *Don Quixote* into English (probably from the French) and Books 4–5 of Rabelais (1693–1708). However, his most notable contribution was to provide libretti for operas and masques, often set by John Eccles (1668–1735).

Motteux cannot have posed any serious threat to AP, even less so after his death from asphyxia during sexual activity in a London brothel. None the less, the poet gave him a passing swat in the *Fourth Satire of Dr. John Donne* and found him a small niche in *The Dunciad* (2: 380) and *The Art of Sinking*, chapter 6.

See R.N. Cunningham, *Peter Anthony Motteux, 1663–1718* (Oxford: Blackwell, 1933).

Moyser, James (c. 1693–1753). Friend of AP. Son of John Moyser, MP (c. 1660–1738). A resident of Beverley, Yorkshire, and member of the circle of **Hugh Bethel**, with whom he traveled to Italy in 1741. He was known as "the Colonel," as he had served in the First Regiment of Foot Guards (Captain in 1709). He was a brother-in-law of Colonel James Gee, also a member of Bethel's circle and familiar with AP. Like his father, he was an architect, who designed at least three houses in Yorkshire and seems to have collaborated with the **Earl of Burlington** on other projects. He also moved in **Bath** circles and was known to **Ralph Allen**. Only one letter from Moyser to AP survives, but he is often mentioned in the poet's correspondence with Bethel. AP regularly sent "hearty Compliments" to Moyser.

Mr. Pope's Welcome from Greece. A poem in eight-line stanzas by **John Gay**, written c. 1720, but not published until 1776, perhaps on account of its submerged satire on the King. **George I** had recently returned from one of his unpopular trips to Hanover; however, the details of the poem subtly recall the welcome extended to the King when he first arrived in England in September 1714. On the surface, the poem describes AP's "return" to England after "six years' toil" on the translation of the *Iliad*. Gay describes the party of friends greeting the poet as he sails up the Thames on his way back from Troy. Among those gathered to await AP's arrival are **maids of honor** and men about town. The numerous friends listed by name include Gay himself and **Dr. John Arbuthnot**, **Henry Disney**, **Prior**, **James Craggs**, **Robert Digby**, **William Fortescue**, members of the family of **John Caryll** "by dozens," **Congreve**, **Erasmus Lewis**, **George Cheyne**, **Edward Blount**, and his relatives **Martha** and **Teresa Blount**. Also present are **Viscountess Scudamore**, the **Countess of Winchilsea**, **Lady Mary Wortley Montagu**, and **Henrietta Howard**. The most interesting group consists of Tories who had been adversely affected by the **Hanoverian accession**: Some indeed had been imprisoned, exiled or attainted. The list includes peers such as **Bolingbroke**, **Bathurst**, **Bruce**, **Harcourt**, **Granville**, and the **Duke of Buckinghamshire**, the **second Earl of Oxford**, and **Francis Atterbury**. It is an impressive roll-call of acquaintances, although some on the list were closer to enemies than friends (such as **Tickell**, **Hervey**, and **Dennis**). The work can be seen as an oblique statement of anti-Hanoverian sentiments shared by AP and his friends in 1720, as the **South Sea Bubble** took its toll on the nation's confidence.

Murray, William, first Earl of Mansfield (1705–93). Scottish lawyer. One of the most famous jurists of the eighteenth century, he was a struggling young barrister when first acquainted with AP. Called to the bar, 1730; MP from 1742, when he gained a reputation as a parliamentary orator. Subsequently Solicitor-General and Attorney-General prior to becoming Lord Chief Justice of the King's Bench, 1756. Created Baron, 1756; Earl, 1776. Noted above all for his work in commercial law and on the law of evidence, he also delivered groundbreaking verdicts on libel, copyright, and slavery.

Murray knew AP by 1735 at the latest. In the following years AP often dined with Murray and his wife, formerly Lady Elizabeth Finch, whom he married in 1738. In turn Murray visited **Twickenham** on a number of occasions. He gave the poet advice on legal and family matters. He represented AP in his Chancery suit against **Edmund Curll** regarding the Pope-Swift letters in 1741. When the two first met, Murray had connections with the group known as "Cobham's Cubs," who took a leading share in the **opposition to Walpole**. However, before AP's death, he had allied himself solidly with the government. In addition, Murray acted for AP's friend **William Warburton**.

AP mentions Murray many times in his poetry and letters. However, his most lasting tribute came when he directed his poem *The Sixth Epistle of the First Book of Horace Imitated* to his friend in 1738. The young man is lauded as a future Cicero or Clarendon on account of his expressive "Pow'r of Words": There is an unconfirmed story that AP gave the barrister instruction in delivering his orations in court and Parliament. A striking passage describes Murray as "One whom Nature, learning, Birth, conspir'd / To form, not to admire, but be admir'd" (*TE* 4: 239), who yet finds himself rejected by a young lady in favor of some rich clodhopper. (It has been suggested that this refers to Lady Margaret Harley, daughter of the **second Earl of Oxford**, but the evidence is slender.) AP presented to Murray the portrait of the actor **Thomas Betterton** that he had painted and in his **will** left him busts of **Homer** and **Sir Isaac Newton**. Murray also acted as an executor.

The best biography remains C.H.S. Fifoot, *Lord Mansfield* (Oxford: Clarendon, 1936; reprint, Aalen, Germany: Scientia Verlag, 1977), although it has comparatively little on the early years.

N

Narrative of Dr. Robert Norris, The. A prose pamphlet satirizing the critic **John Dennis**, "containing the strange and deplorable frenzy of Mr. John Den—An Officer of the Customhouse." The title page continues, "Being an exact Account of all that past betwixt the said Patient and the Doctor till this present Day; and a full Vindication of himself and his Proceedings from the extravagant Reports of the said Mr. *John Denn*——." The item was published by John Morphew on 28 July 1713 as an octavo of twenty-four pages (Griffith 23). The price was threepence. Generally agreed to be the work of AP, though issued anonymously: It appeared in the *Miscellanies* in 1732. For the suggestion that he had a collaborator, see *Early Career* 104–13.

The work relates to AP's long quarrel with Dennis and seems to be an extension in some respects of an earlier pamphlet *The Critical Specimen*. However, more centrally it belongs to a debate about the talking point of the hour, the successful play *Cato*. The first night on 14 April 1713 had provoked an immense volume of comment. By 11 July Dennis had launched into the fray with his *Remarks upon Cato*, published by **Bernard Lintot**, in which he criticized **Addison** for not sufficiently observing the Aristotelian rules in the design of his drama.

AP constructs his good-humored retort around the publicity put out by a genuine quack doctor, Robert Norris, who practiced at Snow Hill in London, and frequently ran advertisements in the press at this date concerning his "Care of Lunaticks." In the *Narrative*, the doctor receives notice on 20 July of the raving condition into which Dennis has fallen since April. He rushes over to the writer's lodgings, near Charing Cross, where he finds Dennis together with Lintot and a mysterious stranger (whose identity is never revealed). In his Francophobe paranoia at the time of the **Treaty of Utrecht**, the patient takes Norris to be an agent of Louis XIV ("who cou'd have thought the Queen wou'd have deliver'd me up to *France* in this treaty?") A bizarre consultation begins, in which Dennis reveals that *Cato* is indeed the source of his mental problems, and in the end the doctor is forced to strap down the raging patient. However, the stranger, whom Norris has mistaken for an apothecary, helps the furious Dennis to escape and mete out revenge on the doctor and Lintot. As the bruised pair return home, Lintot tells the doctor of previous wild behavior on the part of Dennis. One occasion is when he came across *An Essay on Criticism* in the bookseller's shop and imputed two lines from the start of the poem to himself: "Some have at first for Wits, then Poet past, / Turn'd Criticks next, and prov'd plain Fools at last." Here, according to Lintot, "he flung down the Book in a terrible Fury, and cried out, *By G—— he means Me.*" The narrative is signed "Robert Norris, M.D. From my House in Snow-hill, July the 30th."

It is hard to believe that AP was not the perpetrator of this satiric hoax, taking advantage of the circumstances to advance his campaign against Dennis and also to make fun of the hullabaloo caused by *Cato*. Soon afterward, **Steele** wrote a letter to Lintot, in effect apologizing for the pamphlet and stating that Addison "wholly disapproved" of the way in which his adversary Dennis had been treated in the pamphlet. By now Addison and AP were beginning to find strains in their relationship.

For the background and the text, see *Prose* 1: xviii–xxviii, 155–68. For AP's distinctly unreliable version of events, see *Corr* 1: 183–84, 191. See also *Life* 222–25 for an appreciation of a pamphlet that is "high-spirited, funny, and . . . free of bitterness."

Newton, Sir Isaac (1642–1727). Scientist. Lucasian Professor of Mathematics at **Cambridge**, 1669. FRS, 1671; President of the Royal Society, 1703. Master of the Mint, 1699. Knighted, 1705. Works include *Philosophiae naturalis principia mathematica* (Mathematical Principles of Natural Philosophy), first published in Latin, 1687; and *Opticks* (1704).

Newton's influence was felt as strongly in the sphere of literature as it was elsewhere. AP's interest in Newtonianism developed at least as early as 1713, when he attended lectures by Newton's disciple **William Whiston**. When he came to write *An Essay on Man* two decades later, his mind was still pervaded by the Newtonian concept of the universe, even though his treatment is colored by other interpretations of the cosmos. There is one direct reference to Newton in the text of the *Essay* (2: 34), but he is present throughout the poem.

Soon after Newton's death in 1727, AP received a request from John Conduitt (1688–1737), who succeeded the former Master of the Mint, as well as marrying his niece. Conduitt sought AP's help in composing a dedication to **Queen Caroline** for Newton's *Chronology of Ancient Kingdoms Amended*, published in 1728. AP complied (*Corr* 2: 457–58). Newton subscribed to the *Iliad*.

The famous "Epitaph. Intended for Sir Isaac Newton, In Westminster-Abbey" was first published in June 1730, and reprinted in the *Grub-street Journal* soon afterward. It was included in the *Works* in 1735. There was a short Latin inscription, followed by the couplet:

Nature, and Nature's Laws lay hid in Night.
God said, *Let Newton be!* And All was *Light*.
(*TE* 6: 317–18).

AP had already parodied the biblical formula (Genesis 1:3) in *Windsor-Forest*, l. 327, and *The Rape of the Lock*, 3: 47. The epitaph, un-

derstandably, was not used in the Abbey. A bust of Newton by Giovanni Battista Guelfi was bequeathed by AP to **William Murray**.

For the broad impact of Newtonianism on literature, see M.H. Nicolson, *Newton Demands the Muse* (Princeton, NJ: Princeton University Press, 1946). For AP and Newtonian ideas, see *This Long Disease* 133–235.

Nicolson, Marjorie Hope (1894–1981). A major scholar who taught at Smith College and then became the first full-time woman member of the graduate faculty at Columbia University from 1940; W.P. Trent Professor Emeritus from 1961. Member of the Institute for Advanced Study at Princeton University. Her main area of interest concerned the links between science and literature, evident in such works as *Voyages to the Moon* (1948); *The Breaking of the Circle* (1960); *Mountain Gloom and Mountain Glory* (1959); *Newton Demands the Muse: Newton's Opticks and the Eighteenth Century Poets* (1946); and *Pepys' Diary and the New Science* (1965). She also wrote on the scientific background of *Gulliver's Travels*. Together with G.S. Rousseau, she was the author of the important study *"This Long Disease, My Life": Alexander Pope and the Sciences* (1968). See a collection of essays in her honor, *Reason and the Imagination: Studies in the History of Ideas, 1600–1800*, ed. J.A. Mazzeo (New York: Columbia University Press, 1962).

nonjurors. Those who refused the oath of allegiance to **William III** and Queen Mary after the Revolution in 1689. They included both churchmen and laypeople, who thereby disqualified themselves from public office. (As opposed to Catholics, who were ipso facto disqualified.) Most were High Church Tories who clung to the Anglican faith, as in the case of Heneage Finch, husband of the **Countess of Winchilsea**. In Scotland most Episcopalians, such as **John Arbuthnot**'s father, refused the oaths and were ejected. Others known to AP such as **Thomas Hearne** were nonjurors. So perhaps was **Samuel Johnson**, but the facts are not clear.

Nugent, Robert, first Earl (1702–88). Politician of Irish background who served **Frederick, Prince of Wales**. Starting out with a relatively small estate in rural Westmeath, he contrived to attain both wealth and power. He entered AP's orbit when, himself widowed, he married the rich widow **Ann Craggs** in 1737, garnering £100,000 as well as a parliamentary seat in Cornwall and an estate in Essex (see **Gosfield**). After the death of his second wife he married the dowager Countess of Berkeley in 1757 and acquired another fortune. Created Viscount in 1766. His only daughter Mary was married in 1775 to the future Marquis of Buckingham. In 1777, as a quid pro quo, Nugent was given an earldom, which the Marquis inherited. The term "Nugentize" was coined by **Horace Walpole** to refer to such marital careerism. In his time he was characterized as "a jovial and voluptuous Irishman who had left popery for the Protestant religion, money and widows."

It has been suggested that AP refers to the Craggs marriage in *The First Epistle of the First Book of Horace Imitated*, but there is no real evidence. In the last years of his life the poet was on very good terms with the Nugents, and in the five surviving letters from AP to the husband there is no hint of tension. Another visitor at Gosfield at this period was the **Earl of Chesterfield**.

O

Ode for Musick on St. Cecilia's Day. A Pindaric ode in seven stanzas of varying form and containing 134 lines in all. It was published on 16 July 1713 as a folio of twelve pages, issued by AP's usual publisher at this date, **Bernard Lintot** (Griffith 20; Foxon P904). AP was paid £15. Among later reprints was a version performed at **Cambridge** in 1730 to a setting by Maurice Greene (1696–1755), one of the most noted composers of the day. A Latin translation by Christopher Smart appeared in 1743.

Considerable doubt surrounds the composition of the work. AP later claimed that it was written in 1708, but if so, there is no surviving evidence. He also stated that the poem was written at the request of **Richard Steele**. This may relate to a letter from Steele on 26 July 1711, asking AP to supply words for a musical "interlude" to be written by another leading composer, Thomas Clayton (*Corr* 1: 131–32). In all probability AP gave the ode to Steele in the following winter (see *Corr* 1: 165). It is believed that the work would have first appeared in Lintot's *Miscellany* in May 1712 but was removed when a decision was taken to remove *Windsor-Forest*, as the *Ode* was also present in the sheets that were canceled.

AP maintained that "many people would like my ode on music better, if Dryden had never written on that subject" (*Anecdotes* 1: 28). He was referring to the famous "Song for St. Cecilia's Day" by **John Dryden** (1687). A number of other poets had written material for the celebrations that took place regularly on 22 November, the festival of St. Cecilia (patron saint of music). There is no sign that Clayton ever set AP's words. Like Dryden's "Song," the ode expresses the power of music in different situations. The contents range from bold dramatic effects and ardent patriotic fervor to moments of almost Tennysonian lyricism: "The Strains decay, / And melt away / In a dying, dying fall" (ll. 19–21). A passage near the end restates **Congreve**'s line, "Music has charms to soothe the savage breast."

See edition in *TE* 6: 29–36. The fullest discussion is by E.R. Wasserman, "Pope's *Ode for Musick*," *ELH: A Journal of English Literary History*, 28 (1961), 163–86, reprinted in *EA* 159–84.

Ode on Solitude. One of AP's first poems, perhaps the very earliest to survive. In July 1709 AP sent a copy to **Henry Cromwell**, claiming that he had just found the lines that were written "when I was not Twelve years old" (*Corr* 1: 68). This may or may not be true. It first appeared in the *Works* (**1717**): there were frequent reprints. Small differences exist between the printed text and the autograph version sent to Cromwell.

The *Ode* consists of five four-line stanzas, the last line of each containing just four syllables. It belongs to the Horatian *beatus ille* tradition, celebrating the joys of a virtuous private life led in retirement. Possible models have been found in the work of **Abraham Cowley**.

For the text and commentary, see *TE* 6: 3–5.

Odyssey. After the financial success of AP's translation of the *Iliad*, it was natural that he should contemplate a version of the other great epic by his lifelong master **Homer**. As early as August 1720 he seems to have borrowed a copy of the famous translation by George Chapman (*Corr* 2: 52), and he may have expected to make good progress. But there were obstacles and disincentives. He had been upset by the criticism of his *Iliad* by **Anne Dacier**; he was embroiled in the problems associated with his edition of the works of the **Duke of Buckinghamshire**; and he had been obliged, much against his instincts, to take a public stance after the discovery of the **Atterbury plot**. He had no lucrative publishing deal on offer. Moreover, he was now relatively well off, with a comfortable home at **Twickenham**. There were no longer such powerful urges to impel him to carry out such a protracted labor.

The answer he came up with has plagued his reputation ever since. He agreed to share the work with **Elijah Fenton** and **William Broome**, who had helped with the notes for the *Iliad*. In the end it was agreed that Fenton should be responsible for Books 1, 4, 19, and 20, while Broome would translate Books 2, 6, 8, 11, 12, 16, 18, and 23, with the remainder (half of the twenty-four books) left to AP himself. The collaborators may have started in 1722, AP not until a year later. Predictably rumors soon began to circulate about what was going on. A feeble attempt at damage limitation among subscribers was mounted, with Broome admitting to three of the eight books for which he had actually been responsible, and Fenton to just two out of four. Newspapers were quick to point out that this was to engage in the seamiest of **Grub Street** tactics. It was several years, and not until after Fenton's death, before AP grudgingly conceded the truth.

The original plan had been to issue proposals in 1722, but they were delayed until a press notice on 25 January 1725. By that time AP had recruited **Bernard Lintot** to act as publisher, having failed in his efforts to interest **Jacob Tonson senior**. Lintot drove a cagier bargain on this occasion, and he advertised his own separate edition of the translation in larger and smaller format on the very next day, 26 January. The contract between author and publisher survives (see *Early Career* 313–16), and it shows that AP would receive £315 in "copy money," in addition to what he would glean from subscription copies. In the end Broome received some £500 for his work on eight books, together with most of the notes; Fenton

obtained £200 for his four books. They were not altogether happy about the division of the receipts; but AP, who probably took away about £5,000, could reasonably claim that the initiative was his, the "name" that sold copies was his, the organization of the sales campaign was largely his, and the overall direction of the project was in his hands.

Once the proposals were issued at the beginning of 1725, efforts were made to top up the existing list of subscribers, for which **Mary Caesar** had been a particularly effective campaigner. Three guineas were to be put down immediately, then two more on the delivery of the first installment. This installment of three quarto volumes was available to subscribers at the house of **Charles Jervas** on 23 April 1725 (Griffith 151). The second installment, of two further volumes, came out in June 1726 (Griffith 166). At the end of the last volume appeared a critical "Postscript" to the translation, much of which is devoted to answering the charges of Mme. Dacier.

The original list of subscribers in 1725 contained 572 names, with 37 more added in 1726, making a total of 609 individuals and entities such as colleges. However, many of these entered multiple subscriptions, so that more than 1,050 copies were ordered. Among these generous patrons were the **second Earl of Oxford**, the **Duke of Chandos**, and **Viscount Harcourt**, who each took ten copies. (Chandos had had his wings clipped by the **South Sea Bubble**; he sometimes took more than ten.) The list is headed by members of the royal family, that is, **George I** and the Prince and Princess of Wales, later **George II** and **Queen Caroline**. No fewer than 120 subscribers, almost a fifth of the list, were sitting members of the House of Commons in 1725, an unusually high penetration into the citadel of power, in combination with about 130 members of the House of Lords. It was a less unambiguously Tory list than that for the *Iliad*, although there is still a strong Jacobite element. **Oxford** still outweighs Cambridge by a considerable margin, while the proportion of women (13 percent) is well above average for the period, which ran at about 9 percent for most kinds of books.

Like the *Iliad*, the new work excited some hostile criticism in the press, although there were fewer political innuendos. Some of the animus was seemingly deflected into comments on AP's attempt to hide the full contribution of Broome and Fenton. He was clear that the two epics were very different in nature, as had been asserted by the influential critic René Le Bossu, and he tried to reflect this in the style of the translations. The *Odyssey* was "the reverse of the Iliad, in *Moral, Subject, Manner,* and *Style.*" It embodied for AP a version of "the higher Comedy" (*Prose* 2: 51, 55), and with this in mind he sought to write in a plainer and more familiar manner than he had chosen for the "majesty of verse" appropriate to the *Iliad*.

The standard edition with full commentary will be found in *TE* 9 and 10. For an edited text of the Postscript, see *Prose* 2: 43–79.

Oglethorpe, James Edward (1696–1785). Founder of the colony of Georgia, soldier, MP, and prison reformer. His father, mother, brother, and four sisters were all actively committed to the Stuart cause, and most spent the greater part of their life on the Continent. His brother was given a barony by the **Pretender** in 1717 (with a reversion to James himself), and one sister made a countess in the Jacobite peerage in 1722. James Edward wavered: many were uncertain "whether he was a Whig or a Jacobite." In establishing Georgia, he was supported by his friend the **first Earl of Egmont**, and had the advice of **Rev. George Berkeley**. After an inglorious campaign as a general for the Hanoverian forces in the 1745 rebellion, he retired and lived long enough to become a friend of **Samuel Johnson**. A noted gardener. AP mentions him as exemplifying "strong Benevolence of Soul" in *The Second Epistle of the Second Book of Horace*, ll. 266–27. AP may have known him personally, but this has not been proved. **Swift** often mentions James's mother in the *Journal to Stella*; his sister Anne (1683–1756) was a legatee in the will of Alderman **John Barber**.

See A.A. Ettinger, *James Edward Oglethorpe: Imperial Idealist* (Oxford: Clarendon, 1936).

Oldfield, Anne (1683–1730). One of the leading actresses of the day. Famous for her skill on the stage but also (to some extent on dubious evidence) for her sexual exploits. Her first protector was **Arthur Maynwaring**, by whom she had a son, but her most lasting liaison was with Charles Churchill, brother of the **Duke of Marlborough**. In the **theater** she excelled in both tragedy and comedy and was long associated with **Colley Cibber**, starring in the role of Narcissa in *Love's Last Shift*. Another of her leading roles was in the popular tragedy *Cato*. AP wrote an epilogue for her to speak after **Rowe**'s *Jane Shore*, but it was not used. However, his references to her are usually barbed, for example, in *Sober Advice from Horace*: "Engaging *Oldfield!* Who, with Grace and Ease, / Could joyn the Arts, to ruin, and to please" (*TE* 4: 75). His unkindest cut can be found in the *Epistle to Cobham*, where the character "Narcissa" wishes to be made attractive prior to burial: "One would not, sure, be frightful when one's dead" (*TE* 3.ii: 36). (He may have used anecdotes in a recent biography published by **Edmund Curll**.) On the other hand, **Voltaire** contrasted her splendid funeral in 1730 at Westminster Abbey, where she was laid to rest alongside **Newton** and **Addison**, with the hole-and-corner ceremony reserved for the French actress Adrienne Lecouvreur later in the same year.

See J. Lafler, *The Celebrated Mrs. Oldfield: The Life and Art of an Augustan Actress* (Carbondale: Southern Illinois University Press, 1989).

Oldmixon, John (c. 1673–1742). Historian and miscellaneous writer. He started out as a creative writer, producing a number of plays and poems. However, his strong Whig sympathies were already in evidence, and they became even more pronounced when he moved into journalism, criticism, and historiography. He cowrote with **Arthur Maynwaring** the *Medley* (1710–11), a journal engaged in weekly battles with **Swift**'s paper the *Examiner*. He also opposed Swift's project for an English academy. In 1714 he inserted AP's obscene poem *Two or Three* into a collection that he edited. **Ed-**

mund **Curll** was probably behind this volume, although unnamed. In 1716 he edited the *Court Eclogues* as *Court Poems*, provoking confusion and embarrassment among AP's friends. Very shortly afterward he wrote *The Catholick Poet*, one of the most effective onslaughts on AP at this juncture.

From this point on he and AP were constantly at odds, especially when Curll revealed Oldmixon's responsibility for some of the **pamphlet attacks**. Oldmixon receives a brief flick in some of AP's **prose works**, notably *A Full and True Account*, and intermittently in his correspondence. Serious retribution was reserved for *The Art of Sinking*, where Oldmixon makes an appearance among the unwieldy "porpoises," and in *The Dunciad*. Here Oldmixon had his role augmented from 1735 onward, when he took over the position of oldest dunce from **Dennis**, having already figured in the duncely games from 1728. AP's cruel portrait of the superannuated writer striving to compete in the athletic events on the **Fleet Ditch** is backed up by a long and detailed note, drawing attention to the literary crimes Oldmixon had committed over his prolific career (*TE* 5: 125). By the later date, AP had many more offenses to read into the record. These included hostile references to AP in Oldmixon's literary works, notably *An Essay on Criticism* (1728). Worse, suggestions were made in *A History of England* (1729) and other tracts that the **Oxford** editors had tampered with the text of Clarendon's *History* (1702–4). This charge was deeply hurtful to Tories but more particularly to AP in view of his close relations with one of the editors, **Francis Atterbury**, who issued a riposte (see *Corr* 3: 245–28). One consequence was a further swipe at Oldmixon in the *Epistle to Arbuthnot*.

It is not surprising that Oldmixon and AP kept up such a prolonged warfare in words. Almost everything Oldmixon stood for marked him out as a prime candidate for the status of dunce. He wrote scandalous "secret histories"; he opposed the **Harley administration**, week in and week out, in newspaper articles and a lengthy stream of pamphlets; his works of history glorify Whig heroes such as Oliver Crom-

well; and his books on contemporary politics celebrate the Hanoverian regime. His criticism abounds in personal attacks on the Scriblerian group and holds up **Addison** as a shining light of modern literature. He compiled instant biographies of friends such as Maynwaring and the Earl of Wharton and probably did the same for enemies. All in all, his industrious, vehement, and ill-rewarded output could stand as an emblem of **Grub Street** productivity. *Memoirs of the Press* (1742) is a poignant record of this embittered life.

Oliver, Dr. William (1695–1764). A physician in **Bath**; nephew of another celebrated doctor, also William Oliver (1659–1716). Educated at **Cambridge** and Leiden. He settled in Bath in 1725: FRS, 1730. Inventor of the "Bath Oliver" biscuit. A patron of **Stephen Duck**. Friend of **Ralph Allen**, who introduced him to AP and **William Warburton**. AP first had contact with Oliver when he took the waters at Bath in late 1739, and they met regularly when AP stayed with Allen in the remaining years of his life, with Oliver often prescribing medicines for the poet. In addition, Oliver wrote a letter introducing AP to his cousin **William Borlase**, describing the poet as "the freest, humblest, most entertaining Creature you ever met with." Together with Borlase he helped AP to assemble materials for the **grotto**. In return for his aid Oliver was to be commemorated at **Twickenham** by a bath ("which is the Honour of a Physitian") alongside a spring marking Allen's friendship (*Corr* 4: 279). Ten letters from AP to Oliver survive.

ombre. Card game featured in Canto 3 of *The Rape of the Lock*. It was introduced into Britain from Spain in the seventeenth century and attained great popularity during the reign of **Queen Anne**. The name was pronounced "omber." The game is played with a deck of forty cards, omitting the 8s, 9s, and 10s from the pack. Each of the three players is dealt nine cards, and the object is to win a majority of the nine tricks. As "ombre" or principal player, **Belinda** declares trumps, in this case, spades. She wins the first four tricks but loses the next four to the Baron, who has a strong hand in diamonds. Consequently she needs to win the ninth trick in order to succeed. By playing the king of hearts, she trumps the Baron's ace and in this way triumphs. AP uses many technical terms from the game, including *matadors* (literally "killers"), the three highest-ranking cards (in this instance, the ace of spades, or *spadille*; the 2 of spades, or *manille*; and the ace of clubs, or *basto*); and *codille*, in effect, defeat for the ombre. In addition, AP describes the appearance of the individual court cards very accurately, as can be seen by examining decks of cards then in use. For some examples, see *The Rape Observ'd*, ed. C. Tracy (Toronto: University of Toronto Press, 1974), pp. 37–41. Attempts have been made, more or less seriously, to construe the course of the game as a political allegory.

The game as played by Belinda and her opponents has been reconstructed many times, first by William Pole. Later analyses of the play include E.G. Fletcher, "Belinda's Game of Ombre," *Texas Studies in English*, 15 (1935), 28–38; A.E. Case, "The Game of Ombre in *The Rape of the Lock*," *Studies in English* (University of Texas) (1945), 191–96; W.K. Wimsatt, "The Game of Ombre in *The Rape of the Lock*," *Review of English Studies*, 1 (1950), 136–43; and "Belinda Ludens: Strife and Play in *The Rape of the Lock*," *New Literary History*, 4 (1973), 357–74, reprinted in *PRE* 200–223. See also W. Kinsley, "Ombre Replayed," *English Studies in Canada*, 4 (1978), 255–63. However, the most useful general account remains that in *TE* 2: 357–74.

On a Lady who Pisst at the Tragedy of Cato.

This item of ten lines in heroic couplets first appeared in an anthology called *The Poetical Entertainer* in February 1714. It came out next in a collection of the poems of **Nicholas Rowe** issued in July 1714; but since this is an unauthorized publication by **Edmund Curll**, no faith can be placed in the ascription. A contemporary observer, **Thomas Burnet**, claimed that it was "written by Pope & Rowe both," but the balance of evidence suggests that AP is likely to have been the main instigator. He certainly

included the item in the **Miscellanies** in 1728; and copies from the library of the **second Earl of Oxford** bear the ascription "by Mr. Pope." The earliest version carries the title "Upon a Tory Lady who happen'd to open her Floodgates at the Tragedy of Cato." Other variants appear in early printings. It was the 1728 text that added a subtitle, "Occasion'd by an Epigram on a Lady who Wept at it." This points to the intention of the verses: they are intended to satirize the extreme responses to **Addison**'s tragedy, which had premiered to enormous publicity in the previous April (see *Cato*). The humor is very much in AP's usual manner: "Let others screw their Hypocritick Face,/She shews her Grief in a sincerer Place." The earlier **epigram** has not been identified. For background, see Ault 131–32, supplemented by commentary in *TE* 6: 99–100.

One Thousand Seven Hundred and Forty.

A fragmentary poem by AP, similar in some respects to the two dialogues known as the **Epilogue to the Satires**. Unpublished until it appeared in the edition of **Joseph Warton** in 1797, apparently from a rough draft in AP's hand. The scholar Edmond Malone also made a transcript of this manuscript, but neither the original nor any transcript survives. The work was probably composed in the second half of 1740. It has no specific model in **Horace**'s output.

There are ninety-eight lines of heroic couplets. A number of blanks are present, which may indicate that the draft was incomplete or that discretion prevailed. Many names are indicated by initial letters only and cannot be positively identified. AP writes in his late manner, that is, in a direct, challenging, and almost brutal style: "Can the light packhorse, or the heavy steer, / The sowzing Prelate, or the sweating Peer, / Drag out with all its dirt and all its weight, / The lumbr'ring carriage of thy broken State?"

For the text and commentary, see *TE* 4: 329–37.

On Lying in the Earl of Rochester's Bed at Atterbury.

Poem consisting of three quatrains of octosyllabics in alternating rhymes. First published in a magazine in August 1739 and soon attributed to AP. He never acknowledged the poem, but internal and external evidence supports the ascription. It concerns **Adderbury** in Oxfordshire, where the poet John Wilmot, Earl of Rochester (1647–80), had his country house, and owned in AP's day by the **Duke of Argyll**, to whom the poem pays a studied compliment. AP visited the seat in July 1739, as revealed in a letter to the Duke dated 11 July. The *Gentleman's Magazine* printed the item in September, with the information that AP used Rochester's bed on 9 July. It seems improbable that any other hand could be involved. See Ault 182–85; and *TE* 6: 380–82.

On Receiving from the Right Hon. the Lady Frances Shirley a Standish and Two Pens.

Poem, first published by **Warburton** in 1751. Never acknowledged by AP but certain to be his. It concerns a gift by **Lady Frances Shirley**, a neighbor of the poet in **Twickenham**. A "standish" was an inkstand. The work is in eight quatrains of alternately rhyming octosyllabics, a common form in AP's minor poems. Jokingly the lady advises the poet to stick to complimentary verse: its bromide quality will preclude the trouble associated with more plain-spoken political writing. The work may have been written in the late 1730s. See *TE* 6: 378–80.

On Silence.

A poem "in Imitation of the Earl of Rochester," first published in a miscellany in 1712 and reprinted in the *Works* **(1717)**. It was written at an age perhaps as early as fourteen. The model of the work is actually "Upon Nothing" (1679) by John Wilmot, Earl of Rochester. Like the original, the poem is composed in stanzas of three rhyming lines, ending with an Alexandrine. AP's poem consists of fourteen stanzas. An alternative version with sixteen stanzas, containing extensive variants, survives in AP's own hand: it is perhaps an early draft. See *TE* 6: 17–19, 463–64.

opera.

The London stage in AP's day was taken over by Italian *opera seria*, a form dependent on virtuoso arias interspersed with recitative. Attempts by composers such as Thomas Clayton and John Eccles to develop a native English style ended in failure, in spite of the support of **Joseph Addison**. After the arrival in England of **George Frideric Handel**, he dominated the London scene and managed to outdo rivals such as **Giovanni Bononcini**, a Catholic composer encouraged by AP and his friends. A number of attempts to make opera commercially viable were mounted, usually at the **Haymarket Theatre** under the management of **John James Heidegger**. Moreover, Handel regularly produced great works, and a cast of star Italian singers was always recruited. A profitable system remained elusive, even though there was a cadre of influential aristocrats behind these projects. In the end Handel shifted his main attention to oratorio, another form of Italian origin; among his first attempts in this direction was *Esther*, in which AP was probably involved. Meanwhile, popular opposition was aroused against opera by critics such as **John Dennis**, who deplored the "effeminacy" of the castrati, the public scandal of highly paid *prime donne* behaving badly, and the generally suspect quality of this un-English form.

AP's attitude is not easy to determine. Many of his friends, such as the **Earl of Burlington** and **Dr. John Arbuthnot**, were deeply involved in the presentation of operas. Among his later acquaintances was the singer **Anastasia Robinson**. His own work, and that of **Gay** and **Congreve**, was set by Handel. However, his championing of Bononcini may have been political as much as artistic. He seems to have been affected by the reigning prejudice against the elaborate stage effects sometimes employed, as well as the exaggerated gestures of *opera seria*. These are some of the things parodied in Gay's immensely popular *Beggar's Opera*. In the last book of *The Dunciad*, opera appears as a "harlot form," with "mincing step, small voice, and languid eye": the genre is coded feminine, foreign, and affected (4: 45–70). Handel is driven to Ireland, where his most famous oratorio *Messiah* was first presented in 1742, and the taste of the town is identified with shallow spectacle rather than with the moral and artistic seriousness of oratorio.

See R. Fiske, *English Theatre Music in the Eighteenth Century*, 2nd ed. (Oxford: Oxford University Press, 1986); and works listed under **Handel**. An informative study with many bearings on AP's circle is E. Gibson, *The Royal Academy of Music (1719–1728): The Institution and Its Directors* (New York: Garland, 1989).

opposition to Walpole. During the long ascendancy of **Sir Robert Walpole**, a number of diverse groups attempted to rally opposition to the ministry. These groups seldom managed to cohere for very long, and for more than a decade their efforts to unseat the Prime Minister were notably unsuccessful. Among the forces ranged against Walpole were the remnants of the Tory party, badly weakened after the squabble over the succession in the early years of the eighteenth century. There were also dissident Whigs who had broken with their former chief. Some independent members of Parliament hankered after a "country" party to oppose the interests of the court; but Walpole generally found ways of winning their support on key issues. He was threatened only at the time of the Excise Crisis of 1733, when the government proposed an unpopular scheme for levying inland duties to replace customs charges.

Just as diverse and ill coordinated were the leaders of this opposition movement: they included the formerly exiled **Viscount Bolingbroke**, the discontented Whig **William Pulteney**, the converted **Jacobite Sir William Wyndham**, and the cashiered general **Viscount Cobham**, whose group of "Cobham's Cubs" numbered in its ranks ambitious young politicians like William Pitt the Elder. Along with other leaders such as the **Earl of Chesterfield** and **George Lyttelton**, these individuals were known to AP and could count on his general support, but they achieved little until **Frederick, Prince of Wales** defected to their side in 1737 and gave them greater leverage in electoral contests. Another important accession to their ranks was the **Duke of Argyll**, who held comparable power in respect of Scottish constituencies. The death of **Queen Caroline** in 1737 was another setback for the Prime Minister. Finally, Walpole's reluctance to go to war with Spain irked some trading interests, a fact the opposition could exploit, and this contributed to his weakening hold on power. Ultimately Walpole fell in 1742, but in the long run his successors turned out to be the Pelham brothers, former acolytes of the Minister, rather than any of the vociferous opposition critics.

The groups sometimes tried to paper over their differences by adopting the label of "**Patriots**," a term implying disinterested and principle resistance to the government; but again this did not seem to sit easily with the conduct of the francophile Bolingbroke or the undisguised Jacobitism of men like **Viscount Cornbury**. Some inventive public relations campaigns were mounted in the effort to supplant Walpole, and a broad range of writers were recruited to the cause, notably **James Thomson**, Paul Whitehead, **Henry Fielding**, and the young **Samuel Johnson**. Landscape **gardening** was enlisted to support Patriot ideology, and AP was a habitué of such opposition gathering places as **Stowe** and **Hagley**. He also supported the theatrical endeavors of playwrights such as Henry Brooke; and if he did not contribute to the main party organ, *The Craftsman*, he certainly followed its broad lines in his own poetry, notably the *Imitations of Horace*. Yet AP was too sophisticated and too complex a writer to produce *agitprop* literature to order, and though he often assailed Walpole, he never subjugated the artistic needs of his work to propagandistic purposes.

See C. Gerrard, *The Patriot Opposition to Walpole: Politics, Poetry, and National Myth, 1725–1742* (Oxford: Clarendon, 1994); and B.A. Goldgar, *Walpole and the Wits* (Lincoln: University of Nebraska Press, 1976). AP's own relations to the cause are studied in *Garden and City* 116–231.

opus magnum. AP planned an elaborate series of poems intended to form a "system of Ethics in the Horatian way." He had begun this by 1731, and in 1734 referred to "my *Opus Magnum*" in a letter to **Swift** (*Corr* 3:401). The scheme included, but went far beyond, the works published as *An Essay on Man* and the *Moral Essays*. Portions of the scheme survive in the ***Imitations of Horace*** and perhaps in ***The Dunciad***. Somewhere in the design there was room for the **epic on *Brutus*** projected by the poet at the end of his life. AP did not formally abandon his plan, but it never came anywhere near completion. The outline of what was intended is set out in *TE* 3.ii: xvii–xxii.

For a thorough investigation, see M. Leranbaum, *Alexander Pope's "Opus Magnum," 1729–1744* (Oxford: Clarendon, 1977).

Origine of Sciences. In full, *An Essay of the Learned Martinus Scriblerus, Concerning the Origine of Sciences*. A prose satire, first published in the ***Miscellanies*** in 1732 and reprinted in subsequent editions. However, it is generally believed that the work derives from early sessions of the **Scriblerus Club**, and that its composition can be assigned to AP, **Dr. John Arbuthnot**, and **Parnell**.

The *Origine* satirizes the geologist **John Woodward**, taking aim principally at the habits of thought revealed in works such as *An Essay toward a Natural History of the Earth: and Terrestrial Bodies* (1695). The pedantic author tries to show that learning grew up not in ancient Egypt or Assyria but among a fierce race of pigmy warriors, otherwise known as *sylvestres homines*, or men of the forest. These creatures, resembling satyrs, dwell in close contact with wild beasts in Ethiopia and India and themselves possess apelike attributes. The author concludes by expressing a hope that "civilized" nations will send emissaries to these creatures in the hope of restoring a lost body of ancient learning.

For background, see *The Memoirs of the Extraordinary Life, Works, and Discoveries of Martinus Scriblerus*, ed. C. Kerby-Miller (New Haven, CT: Yale University Press, 1950). For an introduction, text, and explanatory notes, see *Prose* 2: 279–303.

Orleans House. Built to a design by John James, c. 1710, for **James Johnston**, who had acquired the property by 1702. It was a brick structure with a frontage of seven bays. The house lay downstream from the center of **Twickenham**, just above **Marble Hill**. Famous

for its gardens and for the octagonal garden pavilion designed by **James Gibbs**, c. 1720 (about the time Gibbs was remodeling AP's house), with elaborate decorations in stucco by Giuseppe Artari and Giovanni Bagutti. Here Johnston entertained **Queen Caroline** and her children in August 1729. It was occupied from 1815 to 1817 by the Duc d'Orléans, later King Louis-Philippe of France. The main house was demolished in 1926–27, but the octagon survives and now houses a notable gallery maintained by the Borough of Richmond on Thames. The gardens were praised by **Daniel Defoe** and admired by most people—but possibly not by AP.

Ormonde, James Butler, second Duke of (1665–1745). Irish soldier and **Jacobite** leader, a member of one of the great Anglo-Irish Protestant families. He had supported **William III** during the Revolution of 1688. Twice Lord Lieutenant of Ireland. Cast as the Tory "rival" to the **Duke of Marlborough** in the **War of the Spanish Succession**, although his military achievements scarcely warranted this. Succeeded Marlborough as commander in chief, 1712, but given restraining orders as part of the government policy to scale down the war. Lost his offices after the **Hanoverian accession**, when he became the hero of the High Church. Impeached for high treason in 1715 and fled to France, after which his estates were confiscated and all his honors extinguished. He was designated to take a leading part in **Jacobite risings** in 1715 and 1719 but never able to accomplish this. Also involved behind the scenes of the **Atterbury plot**. Lived in exile for the rest of his life, an unregenerate adherent of the Stuart line to the end.

A member of the **Brothers Club**, the Duke was well known to **Jonathan Swift** and other friends of AP connected with the Tory administration of 1710–14. However, Ormonde was apparently never close to AP. His brother the Earl of Arran (1671–1758) lived near the poet's sister **Magdalen Rackett** and maintained closer relations. His second wife, whom he married in 1685, was Mary Somerset (1665–1733), daughter of the Duke of Beaufort. She did not follow her husband into exile and remained in close touch with her loyal friend Swift. **Dryden** had dedicated his *Fables* (1700) to the Duke and added a verse epistle to the Duchess. Both Duke and Duchess subscribed to the *Iliad*.

See essays in *The Dukes of Ormonde, 1610–1745*, ed. T.C. Barnard and J. Fenlon (Woodbridge, Suffolk: Boydell, 2000).

Orrery, John Boyle, fifth Earl of Cork and (1707–62). A member of a distinguished Anglo-Irish family, he became a close friend of both AP and **Swift** from the early 1730s. He was the son of Charles Boyle, fourth Earl of Orrery (1674–1731), whose edition of Phalaris in 1695 sparked a controversy between the Christ Church **wits** and their adversaries, led by **Richard Bentley**. This was the most prominent episode in the long-running struggle of the **Ancients and Moderns**, satirized by Swift in *The Battle of the Books*. The fourth Earl was a Jacobite, implicated in the **Atterbury plot**. The fifth Earl was closely related to other distinguished figures. The scientist Robert Boyle was a brother of his great-grandfather Roger, the first Earl (a dramatist). The **third Earl of Burlington** was a third cousin, and **Baron Carleton** a third cousin once removed.

The fifth Earl was active in collecting Swift's manuscripts and together with his **Oxford** ally, **Dr. William King**, took an active part in their publication. Many items survive in the Orrery papers at Harvard University. The Earl's *Remarks on the Life and Writings of Dr. Jonathan Swift* (1751) constituted the first full biography of Swift, although the book generated disagreement and replies from the Dean's other friends. In his later years Orrery knew **Samuel Johnson**, who thought that his ambitions exceeded his powers as a writer.

AP's relations with the Earl were warm. Among Orrery's friends were the **Duke** and **Duchess of Buckinghamshire**. He rendered the poet many services and subsidized the publication of AP's letters in 1737. He also played a role in getting Swift to return letters that AP wished to put into print and negotiated with **George Faulkner** with regard to similar material. AP visited Orrery at his London home

and at his country estate, **Marston** in Somerset. Late in life AP gave the Earl his dog Bounce to care for (see *Lines to Bounce*). About eighty letters survive from the correspondence of the two men: Orrery's letters to Swift, King, and **Martha Whiteway** afford many insights into AP's life. After AP's death **David Mallet** sent Orrery a touching account of the poet's final hours (*Corr* 4: 522–24).

See *The Orrery Papers*, ed. Emily Charlotte, Countess of Cork and Orrery, 2 vols. (London: Duckworth, 1903).

Osborn, James Marshall (1906–76). Scholar who was long associated with Yale University as a research associate (1938–72) and founding curator of the important Osborn Collection at the Beinecke Library. He is known for his work on **John Dryden**, among others. His main contribution to the study of AP came with his edition, now standard, of the *Anecdotes* of AP, compiled by **Joseph Spence**, 2 vols. (1966). A major article by Osborn is "Pope, the Byzantine Empress, and Walpole's Whore," *Review of English Studies*, 6 (1955), 372–82, reprinted in *EA* 577–90.

See *Evidence in Literary Scholarship: Essays in Memory of James Marshall Osborn*, ed. R. Wellek and A. Ribeiro (Oxford: Clarendon, 1979).

Ovid (Publius Ovidius Naso) (43 B.C.–A.D. 17). Roman poet. He exercised a profound influence over Western poetry, especially from the Renaissance onward in England. His earlier works included the *Amores*, poems in elegiac verse addressed by legendary heroines to their lovers; and the *Ars amatoria*, or "Treatise on Love." From the middle of his career come the *Metamorphoses*, which cast the largest shadow over subsequent poetry, and the *Fasti*, a calendar of the Roman festive year. After his exile to the shores of the Black Sea in A.D. 8, he produced letters home in the form of *Epistulae ex Ponto*, and a series of laments from his remote outpost of Roman civilization, *Tristia*.

Like all educated readers of his day, AP was familiar with virtually all of Ovid's surviving work. **Joseph Spence** snootily argued that his early enthusiasm for the *Metamorphoses* showed a certain immaturity of taste (*Anecdotes* 1: 233), but in fact AP never outgrew his liking for the invention, charm, and daring of the Latin poet. His admiration for the *Heroides* is shown in his translation of **Sapho to Phaon** and also in his medieval (and semi-Gothic) version of this form in **Eloisa to Abelard**. The *Metamorphoses* are present more widely in AP's poetry, most pervasively in **Windsor-Forest** and **The Rape of the Lock**. This is apparent in AP's depiction of the **Cave of Spleen**, where "Unnumber'd throngs on ev'ry side are seen, / Of bodies chang'd to various forms by Spleen" (*TE* 4: 47–48). This is a close paraphrase of the opening of the *Metamorphoses*.

See R. Trickett, "The *Heroides* and the English Augustans," in *Ovid Renewed: Ovidian Influences on Literature and Art from the Middle Ages to the Twentieth Century*, ed. C. Martindale (Cambridge: Cambridge University Press, 1988), 191–204.

Oxford. It is natural that AP should have had more contacts with Oxford than with its sister university: The reasons are both cultural and geographic. Oxford was associated with religious orthodoxy and Tory sentiment and harbored noted **Jacobites** such as **Thomas Hearne**. Predictably, AP found Oxford "much forwarder" than **Cambridge** when it came to soliciting subscriptions for his translations of **Homer** (*Corr* 2: 271). Thus, ten Oxford colleges subscribed for the *Iliad* but none from Cambridge, while the respective figures for the *Odyssey* were thirteen and four. Only 5 percent of the individual *Iliad* subscribers have a Cambridge affiliation, as against almost 20 percent for Oxford. As for geography, it is plain that AP's roots lay in the Thames Valley, and he grew up in **Berkshire**, the adjoining county to Oxford. Many of his patrons and friends had a seat in the region: see, for example, **Adderbury**, **Cornbury Park**, **Rousham**, and **Stanton Harcourt**.

Within the university AP had a number of friends, including **George Clarke**, **Abel Evans**, and **Joseph Spence**. He paid visits on various occasions, including 1717, 1718, 1721, 1735, 1737, 1741, and 1743. Late in life a proposal was floated by **Dr. William King** to grant AP an honorary degree, but he refused to accept it unless one was bestowed also on **William Warburton**—and the university was unwilling to comply.

Oxford, Edward Harley, second Earl of (1689–1741). Friend and patron of AP. As the son of the **first Earl of Oxford**, he inherited some valuable property and notable art collections: These were augmented when a brilliant marriage was made for him in 1713, with the great heiress Lady Henrietta Cavendish Holles (1694–1755), partly through the services of **John Morley**. However, his political opportunities were limited by the fall of his father in 1714 and the subsequent demise of the Tory party. He sat in Parliament until he succeeded to his father's title in 1724, but by this time he had evidently settled for a quiet life of social mediocrity, preferring to devote his time to the splendid **Harleian library**, to architecture, and to desultory travel. He patronized the bibliographic scholar **Humfrey Wanley**, who managed the collection of books and manuscripts; the **antiquarian** George Vertue, who advised him on *objets d'art*, and a variety of artists. These included the painters **Michael Dahl** and John Wootton, the sculptor **Michael Rysbrack**, the architect **James Gibbs**, and the garden designer **Charles Bridgeman**. A sketch by Sir James Thornhill (c. 1721) shows Wanley, Gibbs, Dahl, Wootton, and **Matthew Prior** grouped together as Oxford's favorite virtuosi. Most of these men worked at Oxford's country house, **Wimpole**, and AP knew many of them well.

Oxford was also a generous literary patron and supported Prior and **Swift** (whom he had known from boyhood) as well as AP. In fact it was Oxford who inherited **Down Hall** when Prior died suddenly in 1721, and AP later visited his friend there. Lady Oxford (who was particularly close to **Lady Mary Wortley Montagu**) had no great fondness for AP but endured his company; with her daughter Margaret (1715–88), celebrated by Prior as "My noble, lovely, little Peggy," he seems to have enjoyed slightly better relations, at least during her youth. In 1734 Margaret married the second Duke of Portland, and it was through this agency that many of AP's **manuscripts** descended in the family collection.

AP may have met Lord Harley, as he then was, around 1713, when his father was a member of the **Scriblerus Club** and he himself one of the so-called **Brothers Club**. From 1715 he figured on AP's subscription lists, as he did for those of **Gay** and Prior, but it was only from around 1720 that he began to figure regularly in AP's life. Thereafter the two men enjoyed good relations, and Oxford preserved many of AP's works in manuscript. It is surprising that AP never addressed a major poem to Oxford, as he did to the first Earl. He did pay his friend a warm tribute in the *Epistle to Bathurst* (*TE* 3.ii: 112).

By 1740 Oxford's expensive way of life, fueling his habits as bibliophile and collector, had started to catch up with him, and he was forced to sell the estates his wife had brought him. "He sank into a decline of drink and apathy from which he could not even be roused to take one of his equestrian tours" (*Earls of Creation* 205). After his death, the Harleian library was split up; the printed books were sold at auction, with AP in attendance, and **Samuel Johnson** was given the task by a bookseller of cataloging the vast hoard. The manuscripts were later sold at a bargain price to the government and became the foundation of the celebrated Harleian collection in the British Museum in 1753.

See *Earls of Creation* 173–218.

Oxford, Robert Harley, first Earl of (1661–1724). Statesman. Member of an old Herefordshire family; brought up in the tradition of religious dissent. A moderate Tory, MP from 1689, Speaker of the House of Commons, 1701–5, and Secretary of State, 1704–8. In 1710 he came to power and set up the **Harley administration**, which lasted until the eve of the death of **Queen Anne** in 1714. Lord Treasurer and Earl of Oxford, 1711. Helped to create the South Sea Company in 1711. After the **Hanoverian accession**, he was accused of making a peace favorable to the **Pretender** and kept prisoner in the Tower of London from 1715 to 1717, when he was released and charges dropped. In his last years he retired to his country house and kept aloof from politics, although the **Jacobites** still hoped to gain at least his tacit support.

While in power Oxford liked to surround himself with men of letters, and he was allowed into meetings of the **Scriblerus Club**. His contributions to club activities seem to have been restricted mainly to short snatches of occasional verse (see *Corr* 1: 217). When the Club briefly reassembled in 1718, Oxford again took part. His closest links within the group were with **Jonathan Swift**. Although Swift had reservations about Oxford's political methods, particularly his obsessive secrecy, he wrote with deep affection of the minister. Over the years AP also came to value the Earl's courage and steadfast loyalty and paid ample tribute in the *Epistle to Oxford* (1722). In his conversations with **Joseph Spence**, he preserved a number of stories, which testify both to Oxford's confused management of the government and to his "great firmness of soul" (*Anecdotes* 1: 95–98).

He was the creator of the great **Harleian library**; this was later expanded by his son Edward, **second Earl of Oxford**, who was one of AP's closest friends in the 1720s and 1730s. Only a handful of letters survive between AP and the first Earl. Oxford was listed as a subscriber to the *Iliad* and (posthumously) to the *Odyssey*, as he was to the poems of **Matthew Prior** in 1718. The entry in AP's **Memorial List** of obituaries reads, "Robert Earl of Oxford, who was intimate and affable with me, died bravely in 1724" (*EC* 1: ix).

There are several biographies of Oxford. Perhaps the one with the closest bearing on AP's milieu is E. Hamilton, *The Backstairs Dragon: A Life of Robert Harley, Earl of Oxford* (London: Hamilton, 1969). See also J.A. Downie, *Robert Harley and the Press: Propaganda and Public Opinion in the Age of Swift and Defoe*

(Cambridge: Cambridge University Press, 1979), which explores the context of political writing at the time when AP met Harley.

Ozell, John (d. 1743). Translator. He became well known for his translations of such authors as **Boileau**, Voiture, **Tassoni**, and others for **Edmund Curll**. Versions of Molière, Perrault, and Cervantes were carried out for more respectable figures such as **Jacob Tonson senior** and **Bernard Lintot**. In addition, he produced a blank verse translation of the *Iliad*, done together with **William Broome** and William Oldisworth from the French of **Anne Dacier** (1712–22). This was actually issued by the publisher of AP's version, Lintot. Among his other works was a French-English dictionary (1717). Eventually Ozell tired of his former employer and in 1718 publicly repudiated Curll's methods.

AP first tangled with Ozell when he wrote an "Epigram, Occasion'd by Ozell's Translation of Boileau's Lutrin" (c.1708), which relates to a version of Boileau put out by Curll and his associates. For this epigram, see *TE* 6: 37–38. Suitably, it was first squeezed into print by Curll in 1726. There are brief references in other **minor poems** of this period, including *Sandys's Ghost*. Later Ozell was given a brief role in Book 1 of *The Dunciad*, which produced a furious response from the victim. See *TE* 5: 450–51.

P

Page, Sir Francis (c. 1661–1741). Judge. A former Whig MP. From 1718 held judicial office in turn in the courts of the Exchequer, the Common Pleas, and the King's Bench. Notorious as *the* "hanging judge," a remarkable distinction in an era when many might qualify for the title. Page figures in *Tom Jones* by **Henry Fielding**, where the servant Partridge describes his grisly jesting while delivering a death sentence (8: 11). In 1727 he sentenced **Richard Savage** to death for his part in a murderous brawl. Savage was granted a pardon and wrote a bitter "Character" of the judge.

AP mentions Page in his *First Satire of the Second Book of Horace Imitated*, warning the unwary to expect "Hard Words or Hanging, if your Judge be *Page*" (l. 82). In the *Epilogue to the Satires* further reference is made to Page pouring out "the Torrent of his Wit" (2: 159). He is briefly introduced into *The Dunciad*, with a scornful note about the judge "who before he hanged any person, loaded him with reproachful language" (*TE* 5: 343). It was Page who presided over the trial of the **Waltham Blacks** at Reading in 1723. AP may have met him at **Rousham** in 1739; the family home of the judge's wife, née Frances Wheate (1688–1730), was at nearby Glympton (*Corr* 4: 189–90).

Page, Sir Gregory (c. 1685–1775). Second baronet. The likely origin of the rich landowner "Sir Job" in AP's *First Epistle of the First Book of Horace Imitated*, ll. 138–47. In 1721 the estate of Writtlemarsh, covering some 270 acres at Blackheath, southeast of London, became available on the death of the widow of the former owner, Sir John Morden. It was bought by Page, who had come into a fortune of £800,000 when his father, a director of the

East India Company, died in 1720. He pulled down the old manor house and in 1723 embarked on erecting a new mansion, which was elaborately decorated, at a cost of £125,000. There was a fine collection of paintings. **Daniel Defoe** asserted that this was to be "a more magnificent Work than any Gentleman's Seat in this Part of *Great-Britain*." In turn this house was demolished by 1787 and the site used for residential construction. Two years before AP's poem appeared, Page had allegedly attempted suicide on two occasions, first by hanging and the next day by shooting himself. He was said by his neighbor the **Earl of Egmont** to have been overcome by the tedium of his well-heeled existence.

painter, Pope as. While still a boy AP is said to have amused himself with drawing, and in his teens he copied at least one portrait by **Sir Godfrey Kneller**. At the age of twenty-four, in February 1713, he described himself to his friend **John Caryll senior** as "a lover of painting"—no surprise, since his maternal aunt married the miniature painter **Samuel Cooper** and bequeathed the family pictures to her godson Alexander. Shortly afterward, he announced to Caryll, "I've been almost every day employed in following your advice in learning to paint, in which I am most particularly obliged to Mr Gervase, who gives me daily instructions and examples" (*Corr* 1: 174). Six weeks later, he told his friend that he was "in the close pursuit" of Caryll's advice, "painting at Mr Gervase's in Cleveland Court by St James's. I generally employ the morning this way" (*Corr* 1: 177). He kept up his studies with friend **Charles Jervas** for about twelve or eighteen months, concentrating like his tutor on portraiture. As a letter to Caryll on 31 August 1713 makes clear, he was dissatisfied with his progress: " 'Tis, however, some mercy that I see my faults; for I have been so out of conceit with my former performances, that I have thrown away three Dr Swifts, two Dutchesses of Montague, one Virgin Mary, the Queen of England, besides half a score earls and a Knight of the Garter. I will make essays upon such vulgar as these, before I grow so impudent as to attempt to draw Mr Caryll: tho' I find my hand most successful in draweing of friends and those I most esteem; insomuch that my masterpieces have been one of Dr Swift, and one of Mr Betterton" (*Corr* 1: 189). The only picture that has been positively identified as surviving is the portrait of Thomas Betterton, a copy of one by Kneller painted c. 1695. The original and the copy are reproduced in *Life* 90–91.

After his period of tutelage under Jervas, AP never resumed serious study of painting. However, his apprenticeship left its mark on his poetic descriptions and helped to inspire one considerable work, the *Epistle to Jervas* (1716). A few sketches of scenes such as garden designs are also preserved.

See Ault 68–100; *Portraits* 11–14.

Palladianism. Classical style of architecture based on the work of Andrea Palladio (1508–80). Especially influential were the houses he designed in the neighborhood of Vicenza, many disseminated through his widely read *Quattro Libri dell'Architettura* (1570). The movement first influenced British practice in the era of Inigo Jones (1573–1652), but the main revival of the style came in the first half of the eighteenth century, stimulated by works such as *Vitruvius Britannicus* (1715–25) by Colen Campbell and *The Architecture of A. Palladio* (1715–20) by Giacomo Leoni.

The high priest of the movement in Britain was the **Earl of Burlington**, whose contacts with AP began soon after he arrived back from Italy with his head full of new ideas. Burlington employed **William Kent** to put these ideas into practice, as well as designing buildings of his own, like **Chiswick House**. He published some unpublished drawings by Palladio (1730) and

sponsored an edition of *The Four Books* by Isaac Ware (1738). Although AP himself inherited traditional Vetruvian principles of architecture, on which Palladio's practice was founded, he may naturally have been drawn more to the modified Baroque manner of his friend **James Gibbs**. Initially Palladianism was associated chiefly with the Whig establishment, even though Houghton Hall, home of **Robert Walpole**, was constructed on slightly Baroque lines by **Thomas Ripley**, whom AP disliked. None the less, there were a few Palladian showplaces among many of the mansions AP visited when "rambling" (see **rambles**) between the seats of his aristocratic friends, including Sudbrook Park by Gibbs, **Burlington House**, and **Marble Hill**. See *P&AGE* 276–93. A plaster copy of a bust of Palladio was kept at AP's house.

pamphlet attacks. In his lifetime AP was assailed in every conceivable written medium, from books to newspapers. However, the most conspicuous of these attacks take the form of short pamphlets, which might consist of a single ill-printed sheet or a comparatively sophisticated satirical riposte to the poet. The first category is represented by anonymous broadsides such as *The Drury Lane Monster*, published by **James Roberts** in 1717, an onslaught provoked by the play *Three Hours after Marriage*. The second category is seen in *Verses Address'd to the Imitator of the First Satire of the Second Book of Horace* (1733), which was written by **Lady Mary Wortley Montagu** and **John, Baron Hervey**. This has been described by J.V. Guerinot as "the most famous of attacks on Pope and perhaps the only one where Pope has found a worthy adversary." Guerinot was able to find over 150 items of this kind: see his catalogue *Pamphlet Attacks on Alexander Pope 1711–1744* (London: Methuen, 1969). Among the other writers who contributed to the list were **John Dennis**, author of the first substantial attack in 1711; **Thomas Burnet; Colley Cibber; Matthew Concanen; Thomas Cooke; Charles Gildon; John Henley; Aaron Hill; Giles Jacob; Bezaleel Morrice; John Oldmixon; Jonathan Smedley; Lewis Theobald;**

Edward Ward; and **Leonard Welsted**. It will be immediately obvious that most of these figured in *The Dunciad*, some before and some after the time they assailed AP. Several of these items were published by **Curll**, who also wrote some himself.

Parker, E., Philomath. A pseudonym adopted by members of the Scriblerian group. Parker was named as the author of *Mr Joanidion Fielding His True And Faithful Account of the Strange and Miraculous Comet*, a six-page pamphlet (dated 1716) published by E. Berington at the end of 1716 or the start of 1717. This is an amusing squib containing New Year prophecies in the style of astrologers like **John Partridge**. Among those singled out for a curious fate of one kind or another are John Moore of worm-powder fame (see *Moore's Worms*), **John James Heidegger**, **Colley Cibber**, and **Edmund Curll**, while there are sidelong thrusts at **Ambrose Philips** and **Thomas Tickell**. Underlying the fun is a continuing interest in comets, stimulated chiefly by **William Whiston**, suggesting that AP is likely to have had the major role, though **Gay** and **Dr. John Arbuthnot** may also have been involved in the work.

Shortly afterward, on 2 February 1717, the name of Parker was borrowed by the unknown author of *A Complete Key to the New Farce, Call'd Three Hours after Marriage: With an Account of the Authors*, also sold by E. Berrington [*sic*]. This is one of the most bitter **pamphlet attacks** on the Scriblerian members, in which Curll seems to have had a hand. See Guerinot 49–51. For the text of the pamphlet, see edition of *Three Hours after Marriage* by R. Morton and W.M. Peterson (Painesville, OH: Lake Erie College Press, 1961).

Parkin, Rebecca Price (1918–78). Professor at the University of California, Sacramento. She was the author of the well-known study *The Poetic Workmanship of Alexander Pope* (1955). Among her articles are "Mythopoeic Activity in *The Rape of the Lock*," *ELH*, 21 (1954), 30–38; "Tension in Alexander Pope's Poetry," *University of Kansas City Review*, 19 (1953), 169–

73; and "The Role of Time in Alexander Pope's *Epistle to a Lady*," *ELH*, 32 (1965), 490–501, reprinted in *PRE* 486–501.

Parnell, Poems of. Following the death of his friend **Thomas Parnell** in 1718, AP started assembling materials for a posthumous edition (he may possibly have planned an edition in Parnell's lifetime). Around 1720 AP wrote to **Charles Jervas** that he had been thinking of recently deceased writers, including their common friend Parnell, "to whose Memory I am erecting the best Monument I can" (*Corr* 2: 24). AP selected items from the papers that Parnell had entrusted to him and subjected them to some unspecifiable degree of editorial emendation.

The outcome was *Poems on Several Occasions, Written by Dr. Thomas Parnell, late Arch-Deacon of Clogher: and Published by Mr. Pope*. It was an octavo of 222 pages, published by **Bernard Lintot** on 7 December 1721, although the title page is dated 1722 (Griffith 130). At the head of the volume comes AP's *Epistle to Oxford*, a dedicatory poem that includes a tribute to Parnell. See *Collected Poems of Thomas Parnell*, ed. C. Rawson and F.P. Lock (Newark: University of Delaware Press, 1989), 18–23, for the genesis and contents of this edition.

Parnell, Thomas (1679–1718). Irish poet and clergyman. He belonged to an Anglo-Irish family settled in County Laois. Educated at Trinity College, Dublin. Took priest's orders in the (Protestant) Church of Ireland, 1703. Archdeacon of Clogher, 1706. Married Anne Michin of Tipperary. Spent much time in England. A friend of **Jonathan Swift**, who introduced him to the **first Earl of Oxford** and **Viscount Bolingbroke**. It was Swift who persuaded Parnell to dedicate his *Essay on the Different Styles of Poetry* to Bolingbroke and even got the peer to suggest the improvements. The poem, published in March 1713 by Swift's bookseller Benjamin Tooke, was Parnell's first success. He made occasional contributions to *The Spectator* and *The Guardian*. D.D., Dublin, 1712. A member of the **Scriblerus Club**, he was enlisted by his colleague AP to help in the translation of the *Iliad*, for which he wrote the "Essay on Homer" included in the first volume. Returned to Ireland after the **Hanoverian accession** and appointed Vicar of Finglas, near Dublin, in 1716. The following year he published his translation of the pseudo-Homeric poem, together with a "Life of Zoilus." This satire had been planned by AP and Parnell as a retort to **John Dennis** (see *Battle of the Frogs and Mice*). Parnell came over to England in 1718 and joined his friends in inviting Lord Oxford to a renewal of Scriblerian activities. He saw AP on 11 September, but soon afterward he fell ill on his return journey to Ireland and died at Chester, where he was buried on 24 October, much regretted by his Scriblerian colleagues. He bequeathed his papers to AP "almost with his dying breath." In his register of departed friends and relatives (see **Memorial List**), AP wrote that Parnell was outstanding for the merit of his poetry and for his pleasant nature (*EC* 1: ix).

Parnell's subsequent reputation has been clouded by allegations of an addiction to drink, a notion not wholly dispelled in the fairly lukewarm treatment of his career in **Samuel Johnson**'s *Lives of the Poets*. There is probably something in the charge, though Parnell's tendency to depression was certainly made worse by the death of his wife in 1711. A fuller life had already been published by Johnson's friend Oliver Goldsmith in 1770. Several of Parnell's poems became favorite anthology pieces in the eighteenth and nineteenth centuries, notably "A Night-Piece on Death" and "The Hermit" (both published by AP in 1721).

From the days of the Scriblerus Club onward, AP seems to have been the most devoted of the group toward Parnell. The clergyman came down to **Binfield** in July 1714 and accompanied AP to **Bath** in the following September, helping on the Homer translation. When the first volume of the Homer appeared, Parnell was listed as a subscriber, despite his share in its production. Parnell contributed a poem of compliment to AP at the head of the *Works* (**1717**), as well as an item to *Poems on Several Occasions*, edited by AP in the same year. The latter was a translation into Latin of the description of the heroine at her dressing table in the first canto of *The Rape of the Lock*. After the death of his friend, AP began to collect materials for a posthumous edition, which eventually came out in December 1721 (see *Poems of Parnell*). In the dedicatory epistle to Lord Oxford, AP pays his most heartfelt tribute to Parnell: "With softest Manners, gentlest Arts, adorn'd! / Blest in each Science, blest in ev'ry Strain!" (*TE* 6: 238). A few other items appeared later in collections of Swift and AP. New material that came to light in the 1950s and 1960s has made it easier to distinguish some of Parnell's writings from those of his fellow Scriblerians, but he awaits full critical reassessment.

See *Collected Poems of Thomas Parnell*, ed. C. Rawson and F.P. Lock (Newark: University of Delaware Press, 1989). A useful introduction is T.M. Woodman, *Thomas Parnell* (Boston: Twayne, 1985).

Parson's Green. London home of AP's friend the **Earl of Peterborough**. It lay in Fulham at the end of what is now King's Road. Peterborough inherited it from his mother in 1679 and after his military career devoted his retirement to improving the celebrated gardens. **Swift** considered it the finest garden he had seen in London (*JTS* 1: 349; 2: 535). It was a brick house with gardens of ten acres. From about 1719 AP visited the house, as did his friends **Martha** and **Teresa Blount**, and he may have stayed there on occasions. For the little known of Peterborough's activity as a landscape gardener here, see *Gardening World* 178–80.

Part of the Ninth Ode of the Fourth Book of Horace. A poem first published in **Warburton**'s edition of 1751. The manuscript survives in the British Library. It is a rough draft, heavily corrected and interlined. The date of composition is unknown.

Horace's poem consists of thirteen Alcaic stanzas. AP renders the first three and the seventh, which contains the most famous passage in the poem: "Vixere fortes ante Agamemnona / multi" (many brave men lived before Agamemnon). He uses quatrains with alternating rhymes in octosyllabic verse; but he devotes just two quatrains to the first three stanzas in Horace and renders the seventh stanza in the remaining two quatrains. See *TE* 4: 155–59.

Partridge, John (1644–1715). Astrologer. One of the most famous practitioners in this field, he acquired further notoriety as a result of the hoax perpetrated by **Jonathan Swift**. In 1708–9 Swift wrote *Predictions for the Year 1708* under the guise of "Isaac Bickerstaff," pretending that Partridge was in fact dead. The victim indignantly denied this, but the joke was kept up in several subsequent pamphlets and poems, and he had difficulty in convincing the world to the contrary. Astrology was in case a regular target of the **wits** by this date. Partridge was the kind of "philomath" often satirized by the Scriblerians. Brought up as a shoemaker, Partridge issued his first almanac in 1678. However, what attracted AP's scorn was the violent Whiggery of his predictions, which unfailingly set out a bleak future for the pope and Catholics in general, as well as the High Church, Tories, Stuart monarchs, and all others of this kind. Late in life he made 1 August 1714, the date of the death of **Queen Anne**, a red-letter day to mark deliverance from "popery, French slavery and English traitors."

AP makes genial fun of Partridge at the end of *The Rape of the Lock*: "And hence th'Egregious Wizard shall foredoom / The Fate of *Louis*, and the Fall of *Rome*" (5: 139–40). The astrologer had been confidently prophesying these events for over thirty years. AP also portrays astrologers as a type of false prophet in *The Temple of Fame* (*TE* 2: 286): a reference to Partridge occurs in *A Key to the Lock* (*Prose* 1: 197). See B. Capp, *English Almanacs 1500–1800: Astrology and the Popular Press* (Ithaca: Cornell University Press, 1979).

Paston, George, pseudonym of Emily Morse Symonds (c. 1870–1936). Novelist, dramatist, and feminist author. She had a special interest in the eighteenth and nineteenth centuries, producing studies of social caricature (1903) and of **Lady Mary Wortley Montagu** (1907). Her work on AP is titled *Mr. Pope: His Life and Times* (2 vols., 1909). She was ahead of her time in digging out forgotten references and hidden evidence, and although her work is unavoidably dated in style and approach, it contains quite a few useful nuggets for readers of AP.

Pastorals. Four poems in the form of a traditional eclogue, which marked AP's first appearance as a published author. They were published on 2 May 1709, three weeks before AP's twenty-first birthday, at the end of a volume of *Poetical Miscellanies* issued by **Jacob Tonson senior**, starting on page 723 (Griffith 1). It is possible that AP's contribution was available separately as it carried its own title page. This volume also contained two poems by **Jonathan Swift**. In March 1708 Tonson had paid AP ten guineas (£10.50) for the work, together with a version of **Chaucer**. A second edition of Tonson's collection appeared in 1716, while the *Pastorals* were reprinted in the poet's own *Works* **(1717)**. Revisions were made and notes added in 1736 and 1751. AP placed his *Discourse on Pastoral Poetry* at the head of the series in the 1717 printing.

A manuscript survives, consisting of twenty leaves in the author's own careful printlike **handwriting**. On a cover sheet AP wrote that "this copy is that which passed through the hands of Mr Walsh, Mr Congreve, Mr Mainwaring [*sic*], Dr Garth, Mr Southern [*sic*], Sir H. Sheers, Sir W. Trumbull, Lord Halifax, Lord Wharton, Marquess of Dorchester, Duke of Buckinghamshire, etc. Only the 3rd Eclogue ["Autumn"] was written since some of these saw the other three, which were written as they here stand with the Essay, anno 1704—*Aetat. Meae*, 16" (*TE* 1: 38). For these individuals, see separate entries elsewhere. AP gives a slightly different list of his advisers in a note later added to first line of "Spring." The manuscript has been reproduced and transcribed by **Maynard Mack**: see *L&GA* 19–71.

The exact date of composition cannot be fixed with certainty. AP's claims are contradictory, and external evidence proves only that some portion of the work existed by 1705. It is likely that revision was going on well into 1707. The most important of AP's literary mentors was probably **William Walsh**, who died on 16 March 1708. Four pages survive in manuscript with queries by AP regarding the text and replies by Walsh. In "Winter" AP obliquely memorializes his friend.

Each poem is devoted to a single season, printed in the order spring, summer, autumn, winter. "Autumn" was the last to be written. The first three items are addressed, respectively, to AP's early mentor **Sir William Trumbull**; to **Samuel Garth**; and to **William Wycherley**. "Winter" is dedicated to the memory of Mrs. Henrietta Tempest. The dedicatory lines in the opening three eclogues are omitted in the surviving manuscript: with the exclusion of these verses, the entire work would run to 366 lines, a total with clear significance for a poem dealing with the course of the year. There are other minor differences between the readings of the manuscript and the text that AP printed in 1709. As well as the seasonal plan, AP follows a scheme relating to the times of day: "Spring" is set in the morning, "Summer" at high noon, "Autumn" at sunset, and "Winter" at midnight. These correspondences go back to traditional ways of defining time sequences in painting and literature.

The location of the poems is moved from the Sicilian countryside to the banks of the Thames, a deliberate anglicization of the pastoral genre that allowed AP to pay tribute to his native haunts in **Berkshire**. He also incorporated complimentary references to friends such as **George Granville**, as well as a topical allusion to the Great Storm that ravaged southern England in 1703. In his work and in the associated *Discourse*, AP proclaimed his status as an inheritor of the Ancients, as against the "modern" approach of **Ambrose Philips**, whose own eclogues stood in sharp contrast at the head of Tonson's volume.

Aesthetically, the work is characterized by symmetrical patterning, with heavy use of repetition, alternation, and reversal. This permits effects that approach those of lyric forms, even though the entire work is written in rhyming couplets. The best-known passage occurs in "Summer," lines 73–76, "Where-e'er you walk," which was incorporated into the second act of *Semele* (1744), set by **George Frideric Handel** to a libretto chiefly by **William Congreve**.

For the text and commentary, see *TE* 1: 37–95.

Patriots. The term *patriot* acquired a specialized meaning in AP's day. It was used as a cant term especially by the **opposition to Walpole**. In this usage, patriotism connoted "civic virtue, an ideal of selfless public activity which found its noblest embodiment in the classical republican hero Cato" (Christine Gerrard). The underlying ideology was developed in *The Craftsman* and in the works of writers such as **Viscount Bolingbroke**, who constructed a political creed around what he called *The Idea of a Patriot King* (written 1738, published 1749), a work that was given to AP in manuscript and caused a great deal of trouble. See also his *Letters on the Spirit of Patriotism* (1749). In fact, the term indicated less love of country in the broad sense than a particular view of history and of recent British politics.

In his work of the early and middle 1730s AP uses the expression in this way, with approval for the individuals labeled "Patriots" (see, for example, the *Epistle to Bathurst*, l. 150). As time went on, he came to apply the word more critically and even skeptically. A note added to the *Epilogue to the Satires*, 1: 24, reads, "This appelation was generally given to those in opposition to the Court. Though some of them (which our author hints at) had views too mean and interested to deserve that name" (*TE* 4: 299). Later in the same poem, AP links the signs of corruption "in Soldier, Churchman, Patriot, Man in Pow'r" (1: 161). Ultimately AP's brand of patriotism was too complex to fit the narrow propagandistic needs of the opposition campaign.

See C. Gerrard, *The Patriot Opposition to Walpole: Politics, Poetry, and National Myth, 1725–1742* (Oxford: Clarendon, 1994).

Pattison, Mark (1813–84). Rector of Lincoln College, Oxford. A formidable scholar sometimes thought to be the origin of Casaubon in George Eliot's *Middlemarch*. Famed for his *Memoirs* (1885). Perhaps the most representative Victorian critic of AP, he wrote widely on the eighteenth century, especially in his *Essays*, 2 vols. (1889), where he defended AP against **Whitwell Elwin**. Pattison wrote the section on AP in *The English Poets* (1880), a highly influential anthology. He edited *An Essay on Man* (1869) and AP's *Satires and Epistles* (1872).

Pembroke, Henry Herbert, ninth Earl of (1693–1751). Virtuoso and courtier, known as "the architect earl." His father, the eighth Earl, Thomas Herbert (1656–1733), was a noted collector who acquired the famous Arundel marbles for his house at Wilton, near Salisbury. The eighth Earl's third wife was **Mary Howe**, a friend of AP at court. The son attained a number of positions at court under the Prince of Wales, later **George II**. He had a lesser role in high politics than his father but compensated with a distinguished career in the world of the arts. He was a patron and friend of men like **William Stukeley** and **George Vertue**. His main accomplishments lay in the field of architecture, where he was a follower of **Palladianism**, and a competent practitioner on a level with all but the very best professionals. His work includes **Marble Hill**, the bridge at Wilton, and improvements for **Sarah, Duchess of Marlborough** at Wimbledon. He sponsored the construction of Westminster Bridge from 1739.

AP must have known him, but no direct sign of their contact has been traced. He subscribed to the *Odyssey* and to the poems of **Gay** and **Prior** (as did his father). He was also on good terms with **Swift**. The building of Marble Hill involved extensive collaboration with its owner **Henrietta Howard, Countess of Suffolk**, a close friend of AP. In his *Epistle to Burlington* AP refers dismissively to the father's habits as a collector: "He buys . . . / For Pembroke Statues, dirty Gods, and Coins" (*TE* 3.ii: 134). The eighth Earl may also be the acquisitive "Curio" of *To Mr. Addison* (*TE* 6: 204). However, when AP named "Pollio" in his satire of **antiquarians** in the fourth book of *The Dunciad*, he quite possibly had the son in mind.

See *Earls of Creation* 59–100 for Pembroke's many contacts with the Popian circle.

Peterborough, Charles Mordaunt, third Earl of (1658–1735). Soldier and diplomat. A mercurial personality who had taken a leading role in the successful incursion of **William III** in 1689. However, he achieved fame by his exploits in Spain during the **War of the Spanish Succession**. In September 1705 he mounted an attack on Barcelona and with less than a thousand foot soldiers took the key fort of Montjuic. Tories boosted this accomplishment, unrealistically, to the status of a victory equal to those of the **first Duke of Marlborough**. AP refers to this event in his tribute to Peterborough as "He, whose Lightning pierc'd the *Iberian* Lines" (*First Satire of the Second Book of Horace*, l. 129, *TE* 4: 17). After a campaign of less obvious success in Valencia, during which he quarreled with most of his colleagues, Peterborough was relieved and set off on a tour, "rushing round the capitals of Europe . . . boring or scandalizing each Commander-in-Chief in turn" (G.M. Trevelyan, *England under Queen Anne*). His freebooting diplomacy caused official displeasure, and he was recalled. With the change of regime in 1710, the Earl was back in favor, and he was voted a national hero by both houses of Parliament. He was made a Knight of the Garter in 1713 and sent on special embassies to Vienna and Italy. He again fell from grace on the **Hanoverian accession**. His final appointment as General of all the Marine Forces of Great Britain in 1722 was little more than a token appointment.

AP probably became familiar with this remarkable individual about 1718. Like many other writers and intellectuals, such as **Swift, Gay, Rev. George Berkeley, Dr. John Arbuthnot**, and **Voltaire**, he was captivated by the Earl's daring and imagination as a man of action who projected his own myth. Peterborough had a close alliance with **Henrietta Howard**, but his main liaison at this time of his life was with the singer **Anastasia Robinson**, with whom he contracted a secret marriage (see also **opera**). At first AP generally saw him at his town house (which became the poet's usual

London base) or his retreat outside the city at **Parson's Green**. After 1730, when the Earl acquired his villa outside Southampton, known as **Bevis Mount**, this became the setting for regular meetings. Here the two men could indulge their shared passion for **gardening**. On one occasion they made a naval "expedition" in a yacht belonging to Peterborough, culminating in a memorable visit to the ruins of Netley Abbey. The comic potential is enhanced by the Earl's title as General of the Marines. When, in 1735, Peterborough underwent a serious operation (probably for an enlarged prostate), AP made an emotional journey to see his friend, who was about to leave for Lisbon in a final unsuccessful bid for health (see *Corr* 3: 487–88). Peterborough bequeathed to the poet a watch presented to him by the King of Sicily. In subsequent years AP kept up contact with the widow, who was a devout Catholic.

In conversations with **Joseph Spence**, AP recalled a number of stories reflecting the Earl's talents and oddities. Remarkably, AP seems to have thought that Peterborough would have been the ideal person to lead the **Jacobite rising** in 1715–16 (*Anecdotes* 1: 112–16). Fifteen letters between the two men are known to survive. There is a portrait by **Michael Dahl**, as well as one by **Kneller**: it was possibly a copy of this last picture that AP had in his house at the time of his death (*Garden and City* 247). In his private register of departed friends (see **Memorial List**), AP listed Peterborough with the description: "a man of the most remarkable military prowess, and affability of manners" (*EC* 1: x).

A new biography is needed, to do justice to the Earl's political, military, and private lives. The standard source at present remains W. Stebbing, *Peterborough* (London: Macmillan, 1890).

Petre, Robert, seventh Baron (1690–1713). "The Baron" of *The Rape of the Lock*. His family had been settled at Ingatestone, near Chelmsford in Essex, since 1539. Much of the red brick Tudor mansion survives today. It was probably at Ingatestone that the real-life "rape"

took place, not at **Hampton Court** as in the poem.

AP had no personal knowledge of Petre, or at least he had none in 1711, immediately before the poem was written (*Corr* 1: 123). However, his friend **John Caryll senior** was related to the peer: Caryll's grandfather, another John, married Catherine, daughter of the second Lord Petre in 1625. Following the death of the sixth Baron, Caryll had acted as the young Robert Petre's guardian until he came of age in 1710. In addition, this was a leading Roman Catholic family who had intermarried for over a century with the recusant gentry, many of whose members were acquainted with AP. Both the Dowager Lady Petre (d. 1730) and her daughter-in-law subscribed to AP's *Iliad* in 1715. As for the Baron, his brief career took an anticlimactic turn subsequent to his dashing role in the *Rape*. He did not wed **Arabella Fermor**, and instead he was married on 1 March 1712 to a girl of fifteen, Catherine Walmsley (1697–1785). Just a year later, on 22 March 1713, he died of smallpox. His posthumous son, the eighth Baron, was born in June of that year. Some details of family history can be found in M.D.M. Petre, *The Ninth Lord Petre* (London: SPCK, 1928).

Pettit, Henry (1906–94). Scholar at the University of Colorado. Best known for his work on **Edward Young**, including a bibliography of Young's *Night Thoughts* (1954; reprinted 1978) and an edition of the *Correspondence* (1971). He also compiled *A Collection of English Prose, 1660–1800* (1962). His work on AP includes an essay, "Pope's *Eloisa to Abelard*: An Interpretation," *University of Colorado Studies: Series in Language and Literature*, 4 (1953), 69–74, reprinted in *EA* 320–32.

Philips, Ambrose (c. 1675–1749). Poet and dramatist. His unsophisticated pastorals were published along with AP's in 1709. **Thomas Tickell** praised these in *The Guardian* in 1713, to the exclusion of AP's works. In response, AP wrote his famous *Guardian* paper no. 40, ironically singling out Philips's most banal effects for commendation. Dismayed by this treatment,

Philips allegedly "hung a *Rod* over the Chimney at *Button's Coffee-House*, and declar'd he would take down our little Poet's breeches and whip him in Publick, the next Time he caught him there;—which obliged Pope to leave the House" (Guerinot 247). Philips was certainly a habitué of **Button's** and a member of the circle of **Joseph Addison**. A loyal party man, he was appointed to the staff of the British ambassador in Copenhagen and after his return served as secretary to the Hanover Club, a group of Whig politicians. AP believed that he had deliberately kept back subscriptions to the *Iliad*, paid by members of the club, which should have been forwarded to the translator (*Corr* 1: 229). Philips was later made a justice of the peace and a commissioner of lotteries. His tragedy *The Distrest Mother* (1712), a close adaptation of Racine's *Andromaque*, was his only successful play. Addison puffed this work, along with other items by Philips, in *The Spectator*, while the Scriblerians had some fun with the play in *The What d'ye Call It*.

In 1724 Hugh Boulter, who had written for Philips's journal *The Freethinker* in 1718–19, was appointed Archbishop of Armagh and Primate of Ireland. As a Lord Justice, Boulter held a key role in the English administration of the nation. Philips went with him as secretary and remained in Ireland for almost all of his remaining years. He became an MP in the Irish Parliament from 1727 and Registrar of the Prerogative Court from 1734. He had long been known to **Swift**, who had been on good terms with him when they were both courting the Whig establishment (see Swift *Corr* 1: 199–200). A few years later Swift termed Philips "party-mad," and they did not resume their friendship when Philips came to Ireland. In his poems Swift made occasional fun of his former ally.

After his early brush with Philips, AP lay low for some time, unless a reference to "a Pindarick Writer in red Stockings" (*Prose* 1: 278) refers to the other. A satiric portrait, "Macer," written c. 1715, was not published until 1728 (*TE* 6: 137–39). In *The Art of Sinking* extensive quotations are made from the poetry of Philips, who is ranked among the "tortoises" in chapter 6 and presented as the chief exemplar of the "infantine" style (see *Prose* 2: 214). By this time Philips had become known for his verses addressed to children, often written in very short trochaic lines. This had earned him the nickname of "Namby Pamby" from the poet Henry Carey. In *The Dunciad* AP predicts that, under the rule of Dulness, the world will see "Namby Pamby [be] prefer'd for Wit" (3: 322). In *An Epistle to Arbuthnot*, AP writes of "The Bard whom pilfer'd Pastorals renown, / Who turns a *Persian* Tale for half a crown," ll. 179–80. This is a reference to the *Persian Tales* that Philips had translated with the miscellaneous writer William King in 1714. Philips showed some prescience in his taste for oriental fantasy, as he did in his awareness of folk poetry. He was unlucky in that his more absurd moments were frozen for all time by the satirists.

See *The Poems of Ambrose Philips*, ed. M.G. Segar (Oxford: Blackwell, 1937), which contains the most complete biography.

Philips, John (1676–1709). Poet. His comic adaptation of the manner of **Milton**'s blank verse in *The Splendid Shilling* (1701) enlarged the compass of **mock-heroic** as a satiric device. *Cerealia* (1706), sometimes attributed to **Elijah Fenton**, is a joking version of **georgic** in Miltonic language, celebrating beer. Later Philips wrote *Cyder* (1708) in two books, on the topic of growing apples, a serious and worthwhile attempt to use Miltonic means to develop a form of English georgic. AP considered that "Philips, in his *Cyder*, has succeeded extremely well in his imitation of [Milton's style], but was quite wrong in endeavouring to imitate it on such a subject" (*Anecdotes* 1: 197). According to **Joseph Warton**, AP strongly disapproved of the deliberate archaisms in Philips's language. Nevertheless, AP's own *Windsor-Forest* shows some influence from this source.

Philips was a product of the High Church nursery at Christ Church, **Oxford**, and enjoyed the support of Tories such as **Viscount Harcourt**. After the triumphant publication of **Addison**'s Whiggish poem *The Campaign*, Philips was commissioned by the Tories to deliver a riposte in the shape of *Blenheim* (1705). He died young, just too soon to benefit from the ascent to power of his patrons the **first Earl of Oxford** and **Viscount Bolingbroke**. AP may have inherited some of the favor that Philips would have enjoyed. His life was written by **George Sewell** and later (very briefly) by **Samuel Johnson**.

Pigott, Nathaniel (1661–1737). Sometimes spelled "Pigot," "Piggot," or "Piggott." Barrister, a member of the Inner Temple, and friend of AP. He was the legal adviser to the **Earl of Derwentwater** in 1716, during the trial of the **Jacobite** lords. In 1715 he bought a house at **Whitton**, near **Twickenham**, and it was here that AP was carried after his coach was thrown into the river in 1726 (see **accidents**). He advised AP during a case in the ecclesiastical court with Lady Kneller regarding **Twickenham parish church**. Piggott was a Catholic and listed as a **nonjuror** in 1715 when he refused to take the oath of loyalty to the King. His daughter Catherine married Edward Caryll (1695–1766), son of AP's friend **John Caryll senior**, in 1730; previously Pigott had been involved in the father's legal affairs. AP wrote a short set of presentation verses to Pigott, dated 23 September 1726, in a copy of the translation of the *Odyssey*. They refer to "learn'd Pigot," as one who had twice saved AP in great distress, "Once in danger of Death, once in danger of Law" (*TE* 6: 255). Shortly after Pigott's death in July 1737 AP sent his son a prose **epitaph** for the barrister. Another son, a Benedictine father, gave AP the last rites shortly before his **death**. His monument in the parish church was designed by **Peter Scheemakers**.

Pilkington, Matthew (c. 1701–74) **and Laetitia**, née Van Lewen (c. 1708–50). An Irish clergyman and his wife, married in Dublin, 1725. They became known to the circle of **Jonathan Swift**, who unwisely took them under his wing. In 1732 Matthew traveled to London, after Swift had obtained for him the post of Chaplain to the Lord Mayor, Alderman **John Barber**. He was involved in negotiations to publish some of Swift's more combustible poems and possibly also to purloin Swift manu-

scripts from AP. Laetitia followed soon afterward, but relations between the couple deteriorated, and they returned separately to Dublin. Their behavior disappointed both Swift and AP: "He proved the falsest Rogue, and she the most profligate Whore in either Kingdom" (Swift *Corr* 5: 95). Matthew gained a divorce for adultery in 1738, and Laetitia settled in London once more. She wrote poems and drama but was reduced by poverty to the Marshalsea debtors' prison. Her friends in London included **Colley Cibber** and the novelist Samuel Richardson. Her tell-all *Memoirs* were published in three volumes (1748–54). Matthew remarried after her death and went on to write a *Dictionary of Painters* (1770).

The two surviving letters from AP to Matthew concern the rights in works to be printed in the *Miscellanies*. Both of the Pilkingtons soon outwore their welcome in AP's circle. See *Memoirs of Laetitia Pilkington*, ed. A.C. Elias, Jr., 2 vols. (Athens: University of Georgia Press, 1997); and *The Poetry of Laetitia Pilkington (1712–1750) and Constantia Grierson (1706–1733)*, ed. B. Tucker (Lampeter: Mellen, 1996).

Pitt, Christopher (1699–1748). Clergyman and poet. A distant relative of the imposing Pitt political connection. Educated at Winchester school and **Oxford**. Held a living in Dorset from 1722. A close friend of **Joseph Spence** and also of **Edward Young**. His chief works were verse translations, one of Vida's celebrated *Art of Poetry* (1725) and one of the *Aeneid*, published in 1740. A volume of miscellaneous verse was issued by **Bernard Lintot** in 1727. He contributed to the influential *Miscellanies* of **Robert Dodsley**. His works were often reprinted in collections of English poetry, especially the translations. This gave him a place in the *Lives of the Poets*, where **Samuel Johnson** deals kindly with him, even suggesting that Pitt's version of the *Aeneid* could bear comparison with that of **Dryden**.

It was no doubt with Spence's encouragement that Pitt wrote to AP in 1726 about his own work. The 1727 volume contained lines "To Mr. Pope on his Translations of Homer's

Odyssey." This does not stint in terms of flattery: "At a vast distance we of *Homer* heard, / Till you brought in, and nat'raliz'd the Bard." AP wrote a gracious reply on 23 July 1726 (*Corr* 2: 382–83), praising the translation of Vida in warm terms and later added a short note to one of Spence's letters to Pitt.

Plough Court. A small street in the heart of the city of London, running south off the east end of Lombard Street. Here AP was born and spent his early years, until his family moved to **Hammersmith** in 1692. The Popes' house was probably no. 2, standing at the foot of the street, with three stories and a garret and extending three bays in width. The property, which was located in the parish of St. Edmund's, Lombard Street, was rated in 1689 at a rate of twenty-one shillings and twopence (£1.06): this may represent a double imposition on AP's father as a Catholic. See *Life* 814–15.

Plowden, William (1666–1741). A member of the Catholic gentry in **Berkshire** and a Jacobite. His aunt Elizabeth married Walter Blount of **Mapledurham**, the first cousin once removed of **Martha Blount**. He commanded a regiment of foot for James II at the battle of the Boyne in 1690, then spent some years in France. In 1696 he married Mary Stonor (1676–1703), sister of AP's friend **Thomas Stonor**. His son William (d. 1754) married in 1726 Frances, daughter of the fifth Baron Dormer—another family known to AP. William the elder is mentioned in some of the poet's letters. His subscription to the *Iliad* was apparently obtained by **John Caryll senior**.

Poems on Several Occasions. A volume published by **Bernard Lintot** in 1717 and printed by **William Bowyer senior**. The full title continues: *by his Grace the Duke of Buckingham, Mr. Wycherly, Lady Winchelsea, Sir Samuel Garth, Bevil Higgons, and other Eminent Hands.* It is an octavo of 228 pages. AP may have contributed to the anthology at least twenty poems anonymously. According to the argument by **Norman Ault**, he had in fact edited the entire volume, and while this cannot be

regarded as quite certain, it is generally thought to be highly likely. Another contributor was **Thomas Parnell**.

See *Pope's Own Miscellany*, ed. N. Ault (London: Nonesuch Press, 1935).

Pope, Alexander senior (1646–1717). Father of the poet. A London merchant dealing in "Hollands," that is, Flemish lace. He was the posthumous child of a clergyman with livings in northern Hampshire, Alexander (d. 1646), and his wife Dorothy, née Pine (d. 1670). Alexander's sister Mary (1636–94) married another man of the church, Rev. Ambrose Stavely, rector of Pangbourne, **Berkshire**. For further details, see **ancestry**.

The poet's father went into business in London with his elder brother William, for which the two received £500 each from their father's estate in 1699. He established a considerable fortune of something like £10,000 and was able to retire in 1688. At this time he was living in **Plough Court** in the city, where his famous son was born in that year. The elder Pope had been married first to a woman named Magdalen, who died in August 1679. The couple had two children: **Magdalen Rackett** (d. 1749) and a boy who had also been named Alexander, who died as an infant in August 1682. The widower remarried at some date after June 1684. His bride was a member of the Turner family of York, who had hovered between Catholic and Protestant faiths for several generations: she was over forty by the time of her marriage (see **Edith Pope**). At some unknown time, Alexander had converted to Catholicism, and the couple brought up their son in this faith.

After the Revolution of 1688, papists endured a series of restrictive measures imposed by Parliament. Eventually the Popes made a token compliance with the Ten Mile Act and moved out from the city to **Hammersmith**, west of London. This was their home from the summer of 1692 until the end of the decade. In 1698 Mr. Pope acquired a house at **Binfield** in Berkshire from his son-in-law Charles Rackett. The family moved out to the country around 1700 and remained there until around April 1716, when they settled at **Chiswick**. Here the father died suddenly on 23 October 1717 after suffering a heart-attack. He was buried at Chiswick parish church on 26 October. An account of Mr. Pope's last hours was given by Magdalen Rackett (see *Life* 25). AP was deeply affected and wrote to his friends **Martha** and **Teresa Blount**, "My poor Father dyed last night. Believe, since I don't forget you this moment, I never shall" (*Corr* 1: 447). Afterward he erected a monument at **Twickenham parish church** on which both of his parents were commemorated. In his will, dated 9 February 1710 and proved 12 November 1717, he left most of his fortune to his son, who was also the executor. The poet probably inherited about £3,000 or £4,000 when his father died.

AP "used always to speak of his father as the best of men," according to Martha Blount *(Anecdotes* 1: 7). There is an extended tribute in *An Epistle to Arbuthnot*, ll. 388–405: "Unlearn'd, he knew no Schoolman's subtle Art, / No Language, but the Language of the Heart" (*TE* 4: 126). An even more heartfelt passage occurs in *The Second Epistle of the Second Book of Horace*, ll. 54–67: "For Right Hereditary tax'd and fin'd, / He stuck to Poverty with Peace of Mind" (*TE* 4: 169). In his brief obituaries, AP recorded the death of his father with the line: "endowed with all good moral qualities" (*EC* 1: ix).

For the essential facts, see *Early Career* 29–36.

Pope, Edith (or Editha) (1643–1733). Mother of AP. She came from a family long settled in York, as one of probably sixteen children, born to William Turner (1597–1665) and his wife Thomasine, née Newton (1604–81). She was christened at Worsborough, Yorkshire, on 18 June 1643. Her eldest sister Christiana married the miniature painter **Samuel Cooper**. None of her three brothers survived into AP's lifetime. For details, see **ancestry**.

Edith may have left York before her mother's death. At some date following June 1684 she had married the widower **Alexander Pope senior**. Her only child was the poet, born on 21 May 1688. Like many members of the Turner family, she adhered to the Catholic faith. After the death of her husband in 1718 she continued to live with her son and moved to **Twickenham** in 1719. By this time her own health was infirm, and she received the loving care of AP. She suffered from intermittent fevers and from jaundice. Sometimes in his absence she was attended by **Martha Blount**. From the later 1720s she was an almost permanent invalid. In October 1730, after a fall on to the fire at home, her clothes were set in flames, but luckily she escaped burns and made a slow recovery. During the course of the next year AP feared that she was on the point of death, but again her resilient constitution saw her through. She was, however, lapsing into a form of senile dementia.

Edith Pope died peacefully on 7 June 1733, around the date of her ninetieth birthday. On 11 June she was buried at **Twickenham parish church** after a plain service. AP had asked **Jonathan Richardson senior** to make a drawing of her prior to her burial: he had already drawn her from the life in extreme old age (see also *Portraits* 150). AP's correspondence reflects the deep grief he naturally felt but could not easily express. In the *Epistle to Arbuthnot* he paid her an affecting tribute, based on lines he had sent to **Aaron Hill** in 1731: these depict the poet maintaining a vigil at his mother's bedside and seeking "To rock the Cradle of reposing Age" (*TE* 4: 127). He added Mrs. Pope's name to the memorial in the church; and in 1735 he drew up plans for an obelisk, described as "a plain Stone Pillar resting upon a Pedestal," with a Latin inscription. This may be translated, "Ah Edith! Best of mothers, the most loving of mothers. Farewell." The obelisk, placed on a small mound, formed a visual focus at the end of the garden farthest from the house and the Thames. It survives at Penn House, Amersham, Buckinghamshire, in the ownership of Earl Howe, and has been restored since suffering storm damage in 1987. There was a portrait of his mother in the Great Parlour in the poet's villa, which was bequeathed to **Magdalen Rackett** in his **will**, along with other family pictures. In his list of obituaries, AP wrote,

"My dearest mother, the best and most pious woman, in her ninety-third [*sic*] year" (*EC* 1: x).

Maynard Mack has said of AP that "not only was he a very good son," but that "good sonship" occupied a crucial position in the "more or less edifying conception of the self" that the poet, like the rest of us, had constructed in order to survive (*Garden and City* 29). Certainly AP's lifelong devotion to both of his parents indicates a deep sense of filial gratitude and respect.

For the Turner family, see V. Rumbold, "Alexander Pope and the Religious Tradition of the Turners," *Recusant History*, 17 (1984), 17–37.

portraits. AP was painted more often than almost any previous British writer. Several of these formal studies became familiar in his own day as a result of engravings by **George Vertue**, John Faber, John Smith, and **Jonathan Richardson senior**, among others. This is in addition to a wide range of **caricatures** depicting the poet in various undignified poses.

The contemporary images of AP have been cataloged by **William Kurtz Wimsatt** in the standard work on this subject. The most important pictures are those listed below according to Wimsatt's classification. Copies were painted of many of them, sometimes as miniatures. Medium is oil unless otherwise stated.

Charles Jervas (1714). Bodleian Library, **Oxford** (*Portraits* 2.1).

(n.d.) with lady, perhaps **Martha Blount**: Elton Hall, Cambridgeshire (*Portraits* 3.1)

(n.d.) with lady, perhaps Martha Blount: National Portrait Gallery (*Portraits* 3.2)

Sir Godfrey Kneller (1716). Raby Castle, Durham (*Portraits* 5.1)

other versions: (n.d.) **Cirencester**, Gloucestershire (*Portraits* 5.2)

(n.d.) Balcarres, Fife (*Portraits* 5.3)

crayon drawing (c. 1721). British Museum (*Portraits* 6.1)

(1722). **Stanton Harcourt**, Oxfordshire (*Portraits* 7.1)

Jonathan Richardson senior (c. 1718). **Hagley**, Worcestershire (*Portraits* 9.1)

other version: (n.d.) Beinecke Library, Yale University (*Portraits* 9.2)

[attrib. Richardson] (n.d.) Petworth, Sussex (*Portraits* 49)

(n.d.) Patcham, Surrey (*Portraits* 50)

(n.d.) Museum of Fine Arts, Boston (*Portraits* 51)

(n.d.) Petworth, Sussex (*Portraits* 52.1)

(n.d.) Victoria and Albert Museum (*Portraits* 53.1)

(n.d.) National Portrait Gallery (*Portraits* 54)

(n.d.) Colstoun, Lothian (*Portraits* 55.1)

(1742) Fitzwilliam Museum, Cambridge (*Portraits* 55.2)

Michael Dahl (n.d.) Wilton, Salisbury (*Portraits* 10.1)

other versions: (n.d.) University of Reading (*Portraits* 10.2)

(n.d.) National Portrait Gallery (*Portraits* 10.3)

Michael Rysbrack marble bust (1730). Athenaeum Club, London (*Portraits* 11.2)

[attrib. Rysbrack] stone bust (n.d.) **Stowe**, Buckinghamshire (*Portraits* 19)

William Kent (c. 1735). **Chiswick House** (*Portraits* 18)

Louis-François Roubiliac terra cotta bust (n.d.). Elton Hall (*Portraits* 57.1)

marble bust from this (1738) Templenewsham, Leeds (*Portraits* 58)

marble bust (1740) Milton, Cambridgeshire (*Portraits* 59.1)

marble bust (1741) Shipley Art Gallery, Gateshead (*Portraits* 60.1)

marble bust (1741) Rosebery House, Lothian (*Portraits* 61.1)

See *Portraits* 248–66 for many variants of the basic Roubiliac type in numerous media.

William Hoare crayon (c. 1739) National Portrait Gallery (*Portraits* 63)

other version: (n.d.) New Haven, CT (*Portraits* 63.4)

crayon drawing (n.d.) National Portrait Gallery (*Portraits* 64)

Jean-Baptiste Van Loo (c. 1744). Scone, Tayside (*Portraits* 66.1)

other version: (n.d.) Farmington, CT (*Portraits* 66.2)

Wimsatt also lists many drawings by Richardson, **Lady Burlington**, Kent, and others.

The most familiar and influential renderings of AP include the following: Jervas (*Portraits* 3); Kneller (*Portraits* 5, 6, 7); Richardson (*Portraits* 9, 54); Roubiliac (*Portraits* 57; **Hoare** (*Portraits* 63); Van Loo (*Portraits* 66). For AP's own attempts at portraiture, see **Pope as painter**.

See W.K. Wimsatt, *The Portraits of Alexander Pope* (New Haven, CT: Yale University Press, 1965); and a "Supplement" by J. Riely and W.K. Wimsatt, in *Evidence in Literary Scholarship: Essays in Memory of James Marshall Osborn*, ed. R. Wellek and A. Ribeiro (Oxford: Clarendon, 1979), 123–64.

Pott's disease. Tuberculosis spondylitis, a rare form of bacterial tubercular disease affecting the spinal vertebrae. It causes shortening and curvature of the spine, as well as other side effects. The name comes from Percival Pott (1714–88), a prominent surgeon at St. Bartholomew's Hospital in London who taught the famous John Hunter and described the disease in a work published in 1779. AP believed, wrongly, that his condition was congenital; in fact, he probably contracted the ailment in infancy. At all events, it was Pott's disease that occasioned kyphotic deformity and was responsible for his short stature and distorted body shape. See *This Long Disease*, 7–82.

Praz, Mario (1896–1982). Critic and literary historian, perhaps the most distinguished Italian student of literature in English throughout the entire twentieth century. Among his well-known books that have been translated are *La carne, la morte e il diavolo nella letteratura romantica* (1930), translated as *The Romantic Agony* (1951); *La crisi del'eroe nel romanzo vittoriano* (1952), translated as *The Hero in Eclipse in Victorian Fiction* (1956); and *Mnemosyne* (1970). He also wrote a book on AP,

La poesia di Pope e la sua origine (1948), which deserves to be translated. See *Friendship's Garland: Essays Presented to Mario Praz on His Seventieth Birthday*, ed. V. Gabrieli, 2 vols. (Rome: Edizioni de Storia e Letteratura, 1966).

Preface to Shakespeare. See **Shakespeare edition**.

Pretender, The. In AP's day this meant James Francis Edward Stuart (1688–1766), otherwise known as the Old Pretender. After the death of his father, the deposed monarch James II, in 1701, he became the Stuart claimant to the monarchy. His reluctance to abjure the Catholic faith made his succession unappetizing even to his half sister **Queen Anne** and to many Tories. A number of attempts were made to seat him on the throne, notably in 1708, in the **Jacobite rising** of 1715–16, in 1718, and in the **Atterbury plot** of 1722. Ultimately he retired to Rome and in effect relinquished his claim to his son Charles, "Bonnie Prince Charlie," but the next rising in 1745–46 occurred after AP had died. There are overt references to the Pretender in AP's correspondence, but they are mostly facetious; and the few possible allusions in the poems are covert. Nevertheless, his shadow lay over the lives of everyone in AP's day, especially those of Catholics. See P. Miller, *James* (London: Allen and Unwin, 1971). A new biography is urgently needed.

Price, Ann (d. 1741). Daughter of Lord Arthur Somerset (d. 1743) and granddaughter of the first Duke of Beaufort. Her aunt Mary was married to the **Duke of Ormonde**. Ann's husband was Uvedale Price (1685–1764), of Foxley in Herefordshire, whom she married in 1714. She was a friend of **Martha Blount** and **Viscount Cornbury**. AP refers to her in his correspondence and wrote one surviving letter (*Corr* 4: 266).

printers. An increasingly specialized business in AP's day (see **publishers**). The most important representatives of the printing industry involved with AP's works were **John Barber**,

William Bowyer senior and **junior**, **John Watts**, and **John Wright**. See *Book Trade* for these connections.

Prior, Matthew (1664–1721). Poet and diplomat. Educated at Westminster school and **Cambridge**. Acquired the friendship and patronage of Charles Montagu, later **Earl of Halifax**. Diplomat at the Hague and in the negotiations of the Peace of Rijkswijk (1697). Elected as a pro-ministerial (Whig) MP in 1701, he transferred his allegiance to the Tories over the next few years. He published his collected poems in 1709, partly in order to outflank a piratical volume by **Edmund Curll**. Commissioner of Customs, 1711. Member of the **Brothers Club**. Took a leading share in the diplomatic preparations for the **Treaty of Utrecht** and, despite misgivings among some because of his low birth, acted as envoy to Paris. After the death of **Queen Anne**, he was recalled and grilled by a parliamentary committee inquiring into the behavior of the **Harley administration**. Imprisoned in the Tower, 1715, but released in 1717. Brought out a folio edition of his works, published by **Jacob Tonson senior**, which attracted not far short of 1,500 subscribers and is said to have earned Prior £4,000. Through this and the help of Edward Harley, later **second Earl of Oxford**, he was enabled to purchase a house known as **Down Hall** in Essex and planned a new home to be designed by **James Gibbs**. His premature death forestalled this intention.

Prior was the most accomplished and versatile English poet of his generation. He excelled in *vers de société* on everyday subjects but was also capable of more extensive works such as the semi-epic work in three cantos *Solomon: or the Vanity of the World* (1718), the most impressive didactic or philosophical poem in **heroic couplets** written in this period prior to *An Essay on Man* and a strong influence on **Samuel Johnson**. Prior was adept in bawdy Ovidian tales, in witty epigrams, in imitations of **Horace**, and in comic ballads—all forms AP attempted. Along with some brilliant miniatures, his masterpiece is the learned but jaunty poem in three cantos of octosyllabic verse, *Alma: or the Progress of the Mind* (1718). It is easy to see why he exercised so much influence on the poetry of **Swift**. His works were highly popular for a century or more but lost some currency in the wake of Victorian prudery.

AP, too, was well aware of Prior's qualities as a poet, although he rated the prose works less highly. However, he thought that Prior was morally "not a right good man," who used to "bury himself for whole days and nights together with a poor mean creature [probably Prior's mistress Ann Durham], and often drank hard" (*Anecdotes* 1: 94). It may well have been this consideration that led to Prior's exclusion from the **Scriblerus Club**, for his writing talents equipped him perfectly for the group, and he was on good terms with Swift and the **first Earl of Oxford**. Only one letter to Prior and one from him to AP survive. The two men never became fully intimate, and it is hard to avoid the conclusion that there was a measure of suspicion, if not outright jealousy, between them, even though their relations were outwardly cordial. Prior pays a warm tribute to "*Dan* Pope" in *Alma*. He subscribed to the *Iliad* and to the poems of **Gay**, as indeed did AP and Gay to his own volume.

See *The Literary Works of Matthew Prior*, ed. H.B. Wright and M.K. Spears, 2 vols., 2nd ed. (Oxford: Clarendon, 1971). The most complete biography is C.K. Eves, *Matthew Prior, Poet and Diplomatist* (New York: Columbia University Press, 1939; reprint, New York: Octagon Books, 1973).

Prior Park. Sumptuous Palladian mansion on the edge of **Bath**, the home of AP's friend **Ralph Allen**. It was built to a design by John Wood the elder (c. 1704–54) between 1735 and 1743. The warm golden stone was supplied from Allen's own quarries on nearby Combe Down. The house stands about 400 feet above the Avon below and commands extensive views northwards over the city of Bath. The main frontage of fifteen bays is about 150 feet in width, centered on a Corinthian portico, while arcades and outbuildings prolong the line for about 1,000 feet. The park slopes down steeply in front. Here AP was active when Allen landscaped the site, and he also gave advice on smaller features such as greenhouses on the top level. Among the more notable features of the estate as it evolved over time were a grotto, a Palladian bridge, and a sham bridge over a tiny rivulet. Later there was also a Gothic folly designed by Sanderson Miller (1718–80), known as the Sham Castle, set up on the adjoining slopes of Bathampton Down. Later still the gardens were remodeled by Lawrence "Capability" Brown. The main house is now a school. It was severely damaged by fire in 1984 but carefully renovated to bring it back to its former state. The grounds are in the care of the National Trust and open to the public.

After Allen took up residence in 1741, AP spent long periods at Prior Park. While staying there he was sketched by the painter **William Hoare** (see *Portraits* 64). In the summer of 1743 he was joined at the house by **Martha Blount**, but the visit ended in a quarrel that is obscure in its details but ended with AP leaving the house. Also present was **William Warburton**, who played his part in giving a cold shoulder to Martha (see *Corr* 4: 462). In 1746, at the age of forty-seven, Warburton married a girl of eighteen, Gertrude Tucker, who was the niece and in effect the adopted daughter of Ralph Allen. She had also been the only person in the house who had acted in a civil way to Martha in 1743. By this date Allen was also acquainted with **Henry Fielding**, who lived for some time in the vicinity of Prior Park and gave a disguised picture of the mansion at the start of *Tom Jones*. Fielding dined almost every day with Allen at one time.

See B. Boyce, *The Benevolent Man: A Life of Ralph Allen of Bath* (Cambridge, MA: Harvard University Press, 1967), 98–140. For AP's work at Prior Park, see *Gardening World* 207–26.

prose works. AP has always been best known as a poet. However, he wrote a considerable amount of prose, some of it collected in his own lifetime in editions of the *Works*. The main categories include (1) prose satires such as *A Master Key to Popery* and the various pamphlets satirizing **Edmund Curll**; (2) early contributions to journals such as *The Spectator* and *The Guardian*; (3) serious contributions to criticism, for example, the preface to AP's translation of the *Iliad* and to the **Shakespeare edition**; (4) collaborative works deriving from the joint efforts of members of the **Scriblerus Club**, such as the *Memoirs of Martin Scriblerus*. In addition, AP produced a rich and diverse body of **correspondence**.

See *The Prose Works of Alexander Pope*, which appeared in two volumes: Vol. 1, *The Earlier Works, 1711–1720*, ed. N. Ault (Oxford: Basil Blackwell, 1936); and Vol. 2, *The Major Works, 1725–1744*, ed. R. Cowler (Hamden, CT: Archon, 1986).

publishers. The London book trade in AP's lifetime was becoming more specialized, with a tendency for "publishers" in the modern sense to evolve. These were the members of the trade who commissioned books, arranged for them to be printed, advertised and promoted them, and arranged for their distribution. All these tasks had traditionally been the responsibility of the "bookseller," in addition to the actual business of selling. In this period the roles became more distinct, although most booksellers still had a retail outlet. Others continued to act as printers, and others were engaged in the wholesale trade. However, the dominant figures in the business operated chiefly in publishing, where the largest long-term profits accrued, especially after the passing of the **Copyright Act** in 1709. They left some of the other tasks to specialist printers; to distributors, generally known at the time as "publishers"; and to booksellers, pamphlet sellers, and hawkers throughout the land.

AP dealt with nearly all the important figures in the industry. Early on he was involved with **Jacob Tonson senior** and **Bernard Lintot**; later he worked with **Jacob Tonson junior** and **Robert Dodsley**. His works were also issued under the imprint of distributors such as **James Roberts** and **Thomas Cooper**, as well as "mercuries" such as **Anne Dodd**. He also engaged in a long battle with the principal exponent of opportunistic and unauthorized publishing, **Ed-**

mund Curll. In later years AP set up **Lawton Gilliver** in business to serve as his agent; but in effect he acted as his own publisher.

Another development in the period was a steady increase in the number of books issued by means of **subscription publishing**. In this area, too, AP was able to take advantage of the new opportunities to make a handsome profit.

The standard account is that of David Foxon in *Book Trade*. For background, see J. Feather, *A History of British Publishing* (London: Croom Helm, 1998).

Pulteney, William (1684–1764). Politician. A wealthy Whig MP from 1705 who had been educated at Westminster school and Christ Church, **Oxford**. He served as Secretary at War from 1714 to 1717, as an early supporter of **Robert Walpole**, but later quarreled with his former party chief. He helped to set up *The Craftsman* and became a leader of the **opposition to Walpole** in the 1730s. Party and personal enmities led him to fight a duel with **John, Baron Hervey** in 1731. After the fall of Walpole he unwisely accepted a peerage as Earl of Bath in 1742 and lost his former position of influence when failing to oust the reigning Pelham ministry in 1746. From this time on he devoted himself to literary pursuits.

Pulteney was known by 1717 to **John Gay**, who accompanied him on a trip to the Continent. Gay wrote an epistle to Pulteney, published in 1720, and describes him as "generous good and kind" in *Mr. Pope's Welcome from Greece*. AP was never quite such a close friend, but he collaborated with Pulteney on a ballad, *The Discovery*, and retained hopes for some years that the politician would lead a restoration after Walpole was dislodged. A compliment is paid in the *Epilogue to the Satires* (2: 317), but AP may already have begun to doubt Pulteney's commitment to the cause. **Swift** corresponded with Pulteney after his visits to England in 1726 and 1727 and wrote a poem on the other's expulsion from the Privy Council in 1731. Three fairly unrevealing letters from Pulteney to AP are all that survive.

A good study of Pulteney has never been written, despite his political importance for over thirty years. Accomplished, eloquent, and artistically learned, he failed to achieve as much as his powers would have allowed.

Q

Queensberry, Charles Douglas, Duke of (1698–1778), **and Catherine Douglas, Duchess of** (1701–77). The couple were married in 1720. The bride, formerly Catherine Hyde, was a sister of AP's friend **Viscount Cornbury**. She was a spirited and somewhat eccentric woman and a friend of **Henrietta Howard**. The Duke was an important figure in Scottish politics. They were the major patrons of **John Gay** and supported him after he ran into trouble with the government over his play *Polly*; consequently they were banished from court in 1729. In addition **Jonathan Swift** remained close friends with the Queensberry family. Although both of the pair subscribed to the *Odyssey*, it does not appear that they held AP in quite such strong affection, and the Duchess may have disliked some aspects of his character. Nonetheless he visited their seat at **Amesbury** and seems also to have spent time at their house at Ham, near **Richmond**, across the river from AP's home. AP mentions Queensberry in relation to Gay in the *Epistle to Arbuthnot*; he and his wife had paid for the monument to Gay in Westminster Abbey, carved by **Rysbrack**, for which AP wrote the inscription.

Quennell, Sir Peter (1905–93). Poet, critic, biographer, and autobiographer. Wrote over an immense range of topics, including **Byron** and **Ruskin**. Founding editor of the magazine *History Today* (1951–79). Works include a biography of **Queen Caroline** (1939). His book *Alexander Pope: The Education of Genius* (1968) is not a work of primary research, but it is a well-written and sane appraisal. Also edited *The Pleasures of Pope* (1949).

R

Racine, Louis (1692–1763). French poet. Son of the great dramatist Jean Racine and himself the author of pious verse of high technical polish. In 1742 he brought out *La religion*, which criticized the *Essay on Man* as a work of shallow skepticism, produced by "some abstract *raisonneur* in his Anglo-Saxon phlegm." An acquaintance of AP, the Chevalier Ramsay, had objected to this characterization of the poet and pointed out that AP's "optimism" did not exclude a belief in the real misery of human lives. Racine then wrote to AP enclosing a copy of his poem, and on 1 September 1742 AP replied in what Racine conceded were terms of "mildness and humility." Racine's own reply is dated 25 October. See *Corr* 4: 415–16; and E. Audra, *L'influence française dans l'oeuvre de Pope* (Paris: Champion, 1931), 98–104.

Rackett, Magdalen (c. 1679–1749). Half sister of AP, daughter of **Alexander Pope senior** and his first wife Magdalen. Her mother died while she was still an infant, and she was sent to live with her paternal aunt Mary Stavely at Pangbourne, **Berkshire**. The family may have been reunited after the elder Pope married for a second time, since Magdalen was familiar with AP's childhood (see *Anecdotes* 1: 3–4). She married Charles Rackett by 1694 and had her first child Mary (1695–96). Soon after, her husband bought the property at **Binfield**, which the Popes acquired in 1698. The Racketts moved to **Hall Grove**, not far away. Five sons were born to the couple and survived into adulthood (see **Rackett family**).

The relations of sister and brother were dutiful rather than truly heartfelt. Magdalen gave **Joseph Spence** several revealing glimpses into the poet's life, and after AP died she passed on further recollections. In fact, she was probably closer to her stepmother **Edith Pope**. Late in her life Magdalen left a detailed account of her father's death (*Life* 25).

After the arrest of her husband and son Michael in connection with the affair of the **Waltham Blacks** in 1723, Magdalen found herself in a totally new situation. Her finances were straitened, and she had difficulties in finding suitable careers for her sons, in the absence of her husband. AP became her main lifeline, helping her with monetary gifts, advising her on Charles's will, and trying to find a buyer for Hall Grove. Later she was entered into litigation involving one of her sons. Meanwhile AP had set up an annuity for Magdalen of £55 per annum. The signs are that AP often found his sister an irritation and only took the trouble he did (involving applications to friends such as **William Fortescue** and **John Caryll senior**) out of a sense of family obligation. For her part Magdalen felt aggrieved when she discovered the contents of AP's **will**. He left her £300 as well as £100 each to her sons Henry and Robert; and in addition a bond for £500 due to him from her son Michael. However, the main part of the estate went to **Martha Blount**, and only after Martha's death would Magdalen and the two sons receive a further £1,000. At one point Mrs. Rackett even contemplated legal action to have the terms of the will set aside. In the event Magdalen predeceased Martha, whom she looked on as far less saintly than her brother had.

According to Spence, AP never liked the company of his sister (*Anecdotes* 1:6). This may be exaggeration, but they were certainly signs of strain between the pair. They took, for example, different sides on the matter of **Eliz-**

abeth Weston. It is to the credit of both that they kept up a decent level of contact and mutual support. Five letters survive from AP to Magdalen.

The best summary will be found in *Women's Place* 29–34.

Rackett family. Apart from his parents, the only close kin AP had in adult years was the family of his half sister **Magdalen Rackett**. She married Charles Rackett, an apparently prosperous "gentleman" from **Hammersmith**. Rackett bought a property in **Binfield** that was subsequently sold to the Popes. If Charles was a Protestant, this may simply have been a legal fiction to enable **Alexander** and **Edith Pope** to acquire the house; but the Rackett children were brought up as Catholics, like their mother. The family moved to **Hall Grove**, near Bagshot; they were neighbors and friends of John Weston, whose disharmony with his wife **Elizabeth Weston** set up wider ripples in AP's world. In 1723 Charles and his eldest son Michael were caught up in the episode of the **Waltham Blacks**, and both appear to have fled the country. Charles died c. 1728, leaving his finances in turmoil, and AP spent much time and effort for the rest of his life in trying to sort out his sister's affairs.

An infant daughter died in 1696 and another small daughter in 1719 (see Magdalen's touching letter to AP's mother, *Corr* 2: 4). The couple's five surviving sons were: (1) Michael. After his sudden disappearance in 1723, Michael reemerged into AP's life in the 1730s, with his outlawry possibly purged. The poet offered him a loan of £150 to pay off debts and to enable Michael to purchase a commission in the (French?) army, but the outcome is not known (*Corr* 4: 160–61). (2) Bernard. Nothing is known. (3) Henry. He went into the law, but his status as a Catholic made it impossible for him to take the prescribed oaths as an attorney (see *Corr* 3: 150). One letter survives from AP to Henry, the closest of AP's cousins. Magdalen seems to have lived with him in North Street, Bloomsbury. (4) John. A sailor, he inherited the familial propensity for debt. AP had previously dubbed him "a very industrious so-

ber and well dispos'd lad" (*Corr* 2: 246). (5) Robert (d. 1780). Nothing known.

Radcliffe, Dr. John (1653–1714). Sometimes spelled "Ratcliffe." Prominent London physician who attended many members of royalty including **Queen Anne** and her family. The Queen came to distrust him, as did **Jonathan Swift**, who once referred to "that puppy Radcliffe" (*JTS* 1: 239). Nonetheless he took medicines prescribed by the doctor. Radcliffe acquired a large fortune, of around £140,000. Much of this he left to Oxford University, helping to endow a famous library, a hospital, and an observatory—all of which survive. Most of his lucrative practice went to **Dr. Richard Mead**. He served as an MP. A **Jacobite** at the center of a reputed "cabal," with close links to the **Duke of Ormonde** and the **third Earl of Derwentwater**, with whom he claimed a family relationship. Often satirized in *The Tatler* as "Æscapulius."

As a sickly boy AP was given advice by Radcliffe, to the effect that he should study less and ride every day, with beneficial effects to his health (see *Anecdotes* 1: 30). Just before he died Radcliffe treated **Martha Blount**; AP wrote to her that the doctor had left "an estate miserably unwieldy, and splendidly unuseful to him." He also quoted a well-known quip by **Samuel Garth**, that "for Ratcliffe to leave a Library was if an Eunuch should found a Seraglio" (*Corr* 1: 269). In fact, Radcliffe lived long enough to subscribe to the *Iliad*. AP refers to him briefly in the *Epistle to Augustus*, l. 183.

The only full-scale treatment is C.R. Hone, *The Life of Dr. John Radcliffe, 1652–1714, Benefactor of the University of Oxford* (London: Faber, 1950). A new study is needed.

Radnor, John Robartes, fourth Earl of (1686–1757). He first moved to his property in **Twickenham**, Radnor House, in 1722. This lay on the Thames to the south of AP's **villa**. In AP's day it was almost immediately adjacent to the villa, with perhaps two small properties intervening, before a house occupied by the painter Thomas Hudson was built in the late 1740s. Radnor House was constructed around

1673; after inheriting his title in 1741, the Earl set about improving the property, which he remodeled and finally thoroughly Gothicized. It had two stories, with an attic, and six bays in the time of AP. The gardens included land formerly owned by AP's landlord **Thomas Vernon**. **Horace Walpole** called the place "Mabland," presumably on account of its fantastic fairyland appearance. Some have suspected that Walpole disliked Radnor because the Earl had anticipated him in bringing a Gothic imagination to the Twickenham landscape. The house was remodeled in about 1847. Purchased by Twickenham Council in 1902, it was destroyed by bombing in September 1940, but the estate is commemorated by Radnor Road (formerly Worple Way), which marks the rear line of AP's garden. A cold bathhouse on the riverside, now resited in Radnor Gardens, survives from AP's time. The narrow strip of land next to the Thames attached to the property is also now part of Radnor Gardens.

In the garden here, in April 1740, AP first conversed with **William Warburton**. He also had conversations with **Joseph Spence** there. Radnor witnessed AP's **will**, while the poet countersigned a lease for his neighbor. Most of the evidence suggests that the two men were on goods terms for the twenty-two years during which they lived in close proximity.

See A.B. Willson, *Mr Pope & Others* (Twickenham: For the author, 1996), 24–36.

Ralph, James (c. 1700–1762). Miscellaneous writer. Born in Philadelphia, he served as clerk to a conveyancer before sailing to England in company with Benjamin Franklin in late 1724. His *Night: A Poem* (1728) came in for ridicule in *The Dunciad Variorum* (2: 159) but only after the hitherto unknown poet had made himself a target by assailing AP in a **mock-heroic** poem called *Sawney* (1728): see Guerinot 124–27. Ralph also edited a volume of miscellaneous poems in 1729, including works by **Swift, Garth, Thomson**, the **Duke of Wharton**, and others. He also composed plays and a survey of the capital called *A Critical View of the Publick Buildings in London and Westminster* (1734). At one time a schoolmaster in **Berk-** shire, he later wrote for **Robert Walpole**, criticized the apologia of the **Duchess of Marlborough**, and worked with **Fielding** on the *Champion*. He became a client of **George Bubb Dodington** and wrote on behalf of **Frederick, Prince of Wales**. His most interesting book dates from after AP's day, that is, *The Case of Authors by Profession or Trade* (1758).

There is little on Ralph beyond R.W. Kenny, "James Ralph: An Eighteenth-Century Philadelphian in Grub Street," *Pennsylvania Magazine of History and Biography*, 64 (1940), 218–42. See also *The Case of Authors by Profession or Trade, 1758. Together with The Champion, 1739–1740*, with an introduction by P. Stevick (Gainesville, FL: Scholars' Facsimiles & Reprints, 1966).

rambles. AP's own names for his regular tours into the country. They took place always within England, as AP was never able to travel abroad, and almost all in southern England. They were generally conducted in summer, when the roads were at least likely to be dry (if rutted and uncomfortable to negotiate). What induced him to make these trips were a number of factors. There was a connoisseur's interest in architecture and landscape, with a particular fondness for what later came to be thought of as romantic or picturesque scenery. There was an antiquarian taste for ruins and historical sites. There was the desire to keep up with friends, to meet new people occasionally, and at times a kind of fugue, which allowed the poet to get away from his usual self-imposed schedule of work and business. In addition, he was sometimes called in as a designer of pleasure parks, thanks to his acknowledged skill in **gardening**.

AP's first extended trip seems to have been in 1707, when he visited **Abberley** in Worcestershire. He would make regular journeys to **Ladyholt** in Sussex, to see his friend **John Caryll senior**; and once in 1714 he spent some time on the Berkshire Downs at **Letcombe Bassett** in pursuit of **Jonathan Swift**, who had fled the capital to write. **Oxford** lay on the axis of much of his traveling, and as the years went by he adopted a fairly regular itinerary that allowed him to visit some of the most choice locations, including **Cirencester**, **Tottenham Park**, and **Rousham**. Less frequent stopping places were **Adderbury**, **Cornbury Park**, and Middleton Park. On more or less the same route lay **Blenheim Palace**, which AP regarded less highly and where he did not stay. A long sojourn was passed at **Stanton Harcourt**, where AP was able at once to work and to relax in congenially "Gothic" surroundings. Further to the northeast, a full day's journey away by coach, was another great house, **Stowe**. Late in life AP began to spend time almost every year at **Prior Park** in the company of **Ralph Allen**; he had in fact visited nearby **Bath** much earlier. Bath and **Bristol** were on the list in part for a banal reason: that of taking the waters for reasons of health. On only one occasion does AP seem to have visited Bath's rival spa, at **Tunbridge Wells**. His contacts in the eastern counties were fewer, partly because he had fewer natural links with **Cambridge** than with Oxford and partly because the aristocracy found it harder to locate idyllic settings for their mansions in this corner of England. However, he did go to **Wimpole**, **Down Hall**, **Gosfield**, and **Leighs** in the East Anglian corridor. In Dorset, until his friend **Simon Harcourt** died, he had a congenial base at **Sherborne**. As for the coast, AP's main vacation home in the early 1730s became **Bevis Mount**, where he embarked on some of his more adventurous expeditions. A planned visit to Devon never took place. See also **Amesbury** and **Hagley**.

Restricted as AP was, by his health and moderate means, he was able to see a variety of different landscapes and buildings on his trips. He might have liked to be able to spend as much time on the road as his friend the **second Earl of Oxford**, and if that had been possible, he might have left us a major work of early touristic literature—but this was not to be.

Still valuable on the rise of travel for pleasure is E. Moir, *The Discovery of Britain: The English Tourists, 1540 to 1840* (London: Routledge, 1964).

Rape of the Lock, The. Mock-heroic poem, one of AP's most enduringly admired works. It was issued first in 1712 in a version of two cantos. The better-known version in five cantos first appeared in 1714. This entry is divided into seven parts: (1) the occasion; (2) publication history; (3) illustrations; (4) literary sources and models; (5) analysis of the narrative; (6) cast of characters and their supposed real-life originals, plus the locations; and (7) critical history.

OCCASION

In the summer of 1711 AP's friend **John Caryll senior** had been staying at Ingatestone, Essex, the presumed site of the action of the poem. His host was the **seventh Baron Petre**, for whom Caryll had acted as guardian during the peer's minority. It may have been here that Caryll learned of a quarrel that had recently broken out, after a rash act by the young Petre had offended another long-standing Catholic family. He had cut off a lock from the hair of a reigning beauty, **Arabella Fermor**, whose roots were in Oxfordshire and who was probably already known to AP. As the poet later recounted the episode, Caryll had asked him "to write a poem to make a jest of it, and laugh them [the feuding parties] together again." According to this story, told by AP to **Spence**, the work had its desired effect and the two families were reconciled (*Anecdotes* 1: 44–45). It was probably *The Rape* that AP sent to Caryll on 21 September 1711 as "a little Poetical Present" (*CIH* 461). In the usual way, copies of the poem began to circulate in the world, and AP decided to publish the poem in a miscellany of **Bernard Lintot** (see the next section of this entry). At this stage the poem consisted of only two cantos. In AP's lifetime, the dedicatory address to John Caryll was disguised by the form "C——l," although the poet told his friend as early as 1714 that he had wanted to print the name in full (*Corr* 1: 210). The opening line also contains a concealed allusion to a verse written by John's uncle, **John, Lord Caryll**.

After the appearance of this initial version, family attitudes hardened. The blustering **"Sir Plume,"** as **Sir George Browne** figured in the poem, made vague threats to the poet. Worse, Arabella herself, who had previously seemed well disposed, began to realize the full scandalous implications of the work, which may have been concealed from her by the elaborate compliments built into the verse. Possibly, the marriage of Lord Petre in March 1712, just before the poem first appeared, may have contributed to her vexed feelings. These developments, reported to Caryll's son on 8 November 1712 (*Corr* 1: 151) may have been part of the reason why AP embarked on a much expanded version of *The Rape*, which would enable him to equivocate more genteelly—that is, to surround the main plot with mythical and supernatural materials that would help to obfuscate the heroine's responsibility for any of the actions in this risqué narrative. Moreover, it gave AP the chance to write an introduction of some kind, which would help to make amends to the offended young lady. **Addison** is said to have tried to deter AP from meddling with the "delicious little thing" he had created; understandably, AP considered this ill judged, if not ill willed, and went ahead regardless. Others such as **Samuel Garth** had a much more positive attitude to the changes.

By the end of 1713, AP had completed the expanded work and decided to inscribe the new version to Miss Fermor by name. At one stage he had also contemplated a preface "which salv'd the Lady's honour, without affixing her name" but dropped this design. The dedication was used instead, after being written with great care and deliberation. AP claimed to have taken "the best advice in the kingdom, of the men of sense"—including even that of the Lord Treasurer, the **first Earl of Oxford**. The young lady herself, we are assured, approved of the dedication. In the event, this teasing address probably spread the scandal as much as it worked to silence gossip, and AP's claim that he had so "managed the dedication that it can neither hurt the lady, nor the author" cannot be taken altogether at face value (*Corr* 1: 207). For a separate poetic address to Arabella, see *To Belinda on the Rape of the Lock*.

PUBLICATION HISTORY

The first version of the poem appeared on 20 May 1712 in an anthology of *Miscellaneous Poems and Translations* (Griffith 6). For further details, see *The Rape of the Locke*.

The longer version came out as *The Rape of the Lock. An Heroi-Comical Poem. In Five Canto's. Written by Mr. Pope.* It was announced as forthcoming in a press notice on 28 January 1714. AP was paid £15 for the new poem on 22 February and sent advance copies to Caryll on 25 February. Finally, on 4 March, the poem was issued by Lintot as an octavo of forty-eight pages (Griffith 29; Foxon P941). A version also appeared in large paper. The deluxe edition on "a fine Royal Paper" cost 2s (10p). A second edition followed within days, a third in July. In October 1715 came a fourth edition, with small revisions. More important was the appearance of the poem in the **Works (1717)**, where the changes included the addition of the important speech by Clarissa in Canto 5. The last separately issued version of *The Rape* came out in 1723. Later editions continued to appear throughout AP's lifetime, but none contains revisions of substance or authority.

It should be noted that in early editions the epigraph to the poem was taken from **Ovid**: from 1717 onward, the epigraph came instead from Martial. In reality, the Ovidian quotation is perhaps more apt: it comes from the *Metamorphoses*, Book 8, and refers to the story of Nisus and Scylla (see below, under "Literary Sources and Models").

Sales were much healthier in the case of the revised version. It is natural to suppose that the work had gradually acquired a substantial reputation in the time since it had first been issued as a part of a miscellaneous volume. On 12 March 1714 AP told Caryll that *The Rape* had "in four days time sold to the number [of] three thousand, and is already reprinted tho' not in so fair a manner as the first impression" (*Corr* 1: 214). An ironic attack on the poem that appeared in 1715, written by AP himself, asserted that "above 6000" copies had been sold (see *A Key to the Lock*).

The history of the poem after AP's death largely overlaps with the narrative of successive editions of his work. Although there were separate editions of the poem, none has any striking importance in terms of text or commentary until the appearance of the second volume of the **Twickenham edition** in 1940. The only subsequent advance here has come with works providing supplementary information regarding the world of the poem, as in editions by **Clarence Tracy** and Cynthia Wall, and in a contextual volume by William Kinsley. There were fairly quickly translations of the poem into French, Italian, and German; later came Dutch, Czech, Estonian, Hungarian, Polish, and Swedish.

ILLUSTRATIONS

The 1714 printing was accompanied by six plates, comprising a frontispiece and one plate at the head of each canto. A small oval engraving is used to form a headpiece and an end piece. The plates were taken from designs by Louis Du Guernier (1687–1716), a French artist who had settled in London a few years earlier. The copperplate engravings were made by Claude du Bosc (1682–c. 1745), another French émigré artist. In the same year as *The Rape* appeared, the two men worked together on a set of engravings of the battles of the **Duke of Marlborough**. The frontispiece shows the **sylphs** assisting **Belinda** in her toilette, against the backdrop of an imposing edifice that has been identified as **Sir Christopher Wren**'s Park Front for **Hampton Court**, built in the 1690s. For the 1717 *Works*, Simon Gribelin (1661–1733) designed and engraved a headpiece, adapting the 1714 frontispiece inside an oval medallion. Gribelin was a Huguenot from Blois, who was among the most important book illustrators of the century.

The most famous of subsequent illustrations are those of Aubrey Beardsley, who ultimately provided eleven designs (1896–97). Individual depictions of particular scenes have been made by **William Hogarth**, Samuel Wale, Henry Fuseli, and Thomas Stothard (who produced several water-color scenes), among others. Nineteenth-century illustrators included Lady Georgina North, Charles Robert Leslie, and William Witherington.

For a full account, itself profusely illustrated, see R. Halsband, *The Rape of the Lock and Its Illustrations, 1714–1896* (Oxford: Clarendon, 1980).

LITERARY SOURCES AND MODELS

The Rape of the Lock stands as one of the most richly allusive works of literature in any language. Its texture is made up of a complex web of echoes, parodies, reminiscences, and other devices linking the poem to numerous genres and styles. Such references may be to the action, the form, or the language of the original. The most important models may be summarized in this way:

1. *Epic.* Serious epic, from ancient and Renaissance sources, is represented by some major works. They include **Homer**'s *Iliad*, pervasively; Virgil's *Aeneid*, especially in passages such as the **Cave of Spleen**; and **Milton**'s *Paradise Lost*, most obviously in Cantos 1 and 2. Such recollections aid principally in achieving mock-heroic effects; but they also supply a kind of traditional armature around which the story is organized.

2. *Mock-heroic.* Although the poem is itself one of the most innovative works in this genre, it draws on existing masterpieces in the form, notably *Le Lutrin* by **Boileau**; *MacFlecknoe* by **Dryden**; and *The Dispensary* by Samuel Garth. A consistent technique in the poem is to substitute the small, local, and feminine for the grand masculine properties of straight epic. Thus the plains of Ilium are reduced to the size of a young lady's boudoir. See also **mock-heroic**.

3. *Works of fantasy and transformation.* Here the key texts are **Ovid** (*Metamorphoses*, including the stories of Narcissus and Nisus); and **Shakespeare** (*A Midsummer Night's Dream*). AP also recalled the "faery" poetry of **Spenser** and **Drayton**. He seems to have recollected passages in the work of a minor poet called William Diaper (c. 1686–1717), namely, *Dryades*, published in December 1712. His mind may have been shifted in this direction by a paper written by Addison for ***The Spectator*** in July 1712, concerned with the "fairy way of writing."

4. *Periodical papers: Tatler and Spectator.* There are several other places where the influence of these immensely periodical papers may be felt. Examples are the inventory of the effects of a deceased beau (*Tatler* no. 113), foreshadowing the personal belongings of Sir Plume; and a section of *Spectator* no. 79, linking prayer books and paint much as Belinda's mind collapses the distinction between bibles and face paint.

5. *Restoration comedy.* Much of the intrigue resembles that found in plays by writers such as George Etherege, **William Wycherley**, and **William Congreve** (the latter two personal friends of AP). Moreover, the language sometimes mimics dialogue patterns in such plays, notably in the blusterings of Sir Plume, who has his roots in Etherege's character Sir Fopling Flutter.

6. There are sporadic references to a wide range of other works, ranging from the Bible (e.g., the blasphemous hint of the Annunciation in the opening scene of the poem) to the work of **Chaucer**, including some works not now regarded as canonical.

AP openly admitted in his prefatory letter that in creating the elemental spirits he drew his knowledge of the mythology of the Rosicrucians from a single text, that is, the playful philosophic work of the Abbé de Montfaucon de Villars: see *Le Comte de Gabalis*.

Sources and models can be found in *Contexts 2: The Rape of the Lock*, ed. W. Kinsley (Hamden, CT: Archon, 1979). Other valuable materials will be found in *The Rape of the Lock*, ed. C. Wall (Boston: Bedford, 1998).

NARRATIVE

Canto 1. The poem begins with an epic proposition of the theme and an invocation: in a poem that feminizes a martial genre, the muse is turned into a male figure, John Caryll. Then comes the start of the action, with Belinda belatedly waking at noon, then drifting back into sleep. Next comes the introduction of the machinery, that is, the elemental beings. Belinda's guardian spirit, the sylph Ariel, warns her in a dream of women's frailty in the face of male desires. Finally Belinda wakes, to prepare herself for the day by putting on makeup at her dressing table, as a hero would arm himself for battle.

Canto 2. Belinda makes a glamorous progress by boat up the Thames to Hampton Court. There is a close description of her beautiful appearance, especially her lustrous hair. **The Baron** is captivated by these charms and resolves to gain possession of Belinda. Having built an altar of love tokens, he makes a ritual offering by lighting them with "tender *Billet-doux*." Ariel grows alarmed at the prospect of disaster to his charge and summons his "denizens of air" to tighten her defenses. He orders them to their posts, with special care for the heroine's petticoat, equivalent to the shield of epic.

Canto 3. Belinda and the Baron have arrived at Hampton Court. They divert themselves with the card game **ombre**, corresponding to a battle scene in epic. After nine tricks, in which fortunes shift from one side to another, Belinda takes the final trick and so triumphs. Coffee is served, and at this moment comes Belinda's downfall. Clarissa draws out a pair of scissors and gives them to the Baron. He cuts off Belinda's lock as she is leaning over her coffee, as the sylphs are unable to intervene in time. Belinda's feeling of triumph is replaced by shame: she screams in horror at the "rape" she has undergone. Meanwhile the Baron vaunts himself on a proud victory.

Canto 4. The gnome Umbriel descends to the underworld in quest of the Cave of Spleen, to seek help in avenging the rape. Spleen and her minions are portrayed as strange transmogrified beings, living in a "sullen region" below the surface of the earth, symbolic of neurotic and repressed areas of the human personality. Umbriel is given a bag of sighs and a vial of tears that he takes back to the world above. There he encounters Belinda sunk in the arms of her friend **Thalestris** and empties the bag of sighs over her. Thalestris urges Belinda to avenge the rape and appeals for help to the beau, Sir Plume. He then raves at the Baron in slangy phrases and crude oaths, but the Baron rejects him without difficulty. At this point Umbriel empties the vial of tears over the heroine, and Belinda tearfully rues the day. She now recalls the warning Ariel had conveyed to her in her dream that morning.

Canto 5. At the start the prudish Clarissa gives Belinda sensible advice, in a speech that parodies one by Sarpedon in Book 12 of the *Iliad*. According to a note added later, this was designed "to open more clearly the MORAL of the Poem." Both combatants reject her platitudes with scorn and rush to combat. After a fierce contest Belinda eventually throws snuff in the Baron's nose and emerges as the vanquisher of the male. Flushed with triumph, she demands that he should restore the lock—but it has totally disappeared. Only the muse was quick enough to observe it rising into the heavens, now transformed into a star. Belinda has been immortalized as her lock shines out in the sky forever.

CAST OF CHARACTERS: LOCATIONS

The most important figure in the poem is the beautiful young socialite Belinda. She is broadly based on Arabella Fermor, a member of a Catholic family in Oxfordshire: AP may have known her, but if so, probably not very well.

Her antagonist is the Baron, who seems to have been closely modeled on Robert, seventh Baron Petre, with whom AP was not acquainted when he wrote the first version of the poem. He had been a ward of AP's friend John Caryll senior.

The affected beau Sir Plume was taken, it is certain, from Sir George Browne, also a relative of John Caryll.

The fierce virago Thalestris, who urges Belinda to revenge herself upon The Baron, may have her origin in Gertrude Morley, the wife of Sir George Browne.

The prude Clarissa, who gives Belinda sensible but unexciting advice on her conduct, has no known origin.

AP chooses Hampton Court as a setting for various reasons. As a royal palace, it allows some playful allusion to **Queen Anne**. By removing the events from their likely real-life venue, he distances the affair from the particular Catholic families involved and gives the narrative a jokingly "national" flavor. Moreover, the geographical placing of Hampton Court suggests a riverside location and makes room for the evocative description of the heroine's Cleopatra-like boat trip up the Thames. (It is a coincidence that a few years later AP at **Twickenham** would come to live on the bank of the river, only a short distance downstream from this very palace.) In fact, the description

of Hampton Court at the start of Canto 3 (especially the second line, "Where *Thames* with Pride surveys his rising Tow'rs") is a comic transposition of AP's solemn tribute to another royal palace on the river in **Windsor-Forest** (1713). Finally, there is a conscious pun (unstated) on the courting activities that go on around the game of cards: implicitly, the subject of Canto 3 is Hampton Courtship.

Other locations in London named in the poem are these:

The Ring (1: 44). Also named as Hyde Park Circus (4: 117), a fashionable carriage ride in Hyde Park, then outside the western edge of the city. Its site is now covered by the Serpentine, a lake created by **Charles Bridgeman** for **Queen Caroline** in the early 1730s, as a result of damming the Westbourne river.

The sound of Bow (4: 116). Within earshot of the bells of St. Mary le Bow in Cheapside, that is, in the commercial district of the city of London rather than aristocratic Westminster. Since the early seventeenth century, to be born within the sound of Bow bells had become the definition of a Cockney.

The Mall (5: 133). A tree-lined walk of about a quarter of a mile, running through St. James's Park past the front of the palace.

Rosamunda's Lake (5: 136). A fanciful designation for Rosamond's Pond, a narrow stretch of water at the west end of St. James's Park, close to where Buckingham House (now Palace) stood. It was a well-known trysting place for lovers and also "long consecrated to disastrous love, and *elegiac* poetry" (quoted in *TE* 2: 400).

CRITICAL HISTORY

When doubts were raised about AP's standing as a poet, in the second half of the eighteenth century, *The Rape of the Lock* was often exempted from general criticisms. Thus, **Joseph Warton**, in the first volume of his *Essay on AP* (1756), still found *The Rape* to be "the *best satire* extant," with "the truest and liveliest picture of modern life," and full of "exquisite poetry." For **Samuel Johnson**, the poem was "the most airy, the most ingenious, and the most delightful of all his compositions." He went even further than Warton in stating that "*The Rape of the Lock* stands forward, in all classes of literature, as the most exquisite example of ludicrous poetry. . . . He indeed never could afterwards produce anything of such unexampled excellence." Both Warton and Johnson see greater "invention" and imagination in this work than anywhere else in AP. In the Romantic era, **Byron** and **William Hazlitt**, though they took differing positions on AP's merits, concurred in finding especially delicate effects of poetic workmanship here: for Hazlitt, "The little is made great, and the great little. You hardly know whether to laugh or weep. It is the triumph of insignificance, the apotheosis of foppery and folly. It is the perfection of the mock-heroic!'

In the Victorian era the piece fared rather less well, not because it was depreciated but because it tended to get left out of the crucial discussion: the earnest touchstone of "high seriousness" applied by **Matthew Arnold** left little room for analysis of the mechanisms of this poem. Nor does *The Rape* figure centrally in the estimate of critics such as **Ruskin** and **Leslie Stephen**. Though it was admired by **William Makepeace Thackeray**, among others, it took something of an effort for AP's own editor **Whitwell Elwin** to acknowledge his high opinion of *The Rape*—which he rated above all the other poems, followed by *Eloisa to Abelard*.

Twentieth-century estimates have been much more generous, starting with critics such as W.P. Ker (1923), who restated Hazlitt's view in more unambiguously favorable terms: "the astral body of an heroic poem, pure form, an echo of divine music, how thin and clear!" As academic scholarship developed, space opened up for the poem: thus **William Empson** was able to expose the ambiguities hiding in the text, and New Critics like **Cleanth Brooks** and **William Kurtz Wimsatt** could find tension, irony, and esthetic distance. For half a century, indeed, Brooks's essay "The Case of Miss Arabella Fermor" (1943) was among the most influential studies of the poet. Subsequently Murray Krieger (1961) added metonymy to the rhetorical brew. The tide has naturally turned in recent years: a new emphasis has been placed on commerce, consumption, and commodity

(an approach pioneered by **Louis Landa** in 1971), while feminist approaches have directed attention to gender, sexual politics, courtship, psychology, and related matters. Interesting comparisons have been drawn between the poem and Swift's verses about women, example, by Ellen Pollak (1985). Collections of criticism have not yet caught up with this trend, for example *The Rape of the Lock: A Casebook*, ed. J.D. Hunt (London: Macmillan, 1968); *Twentieth Centenary Interpretations of "The Rape of the Lock,"* ed. G.S. Rousseau (Englewood Cliffs, NJ: Prentice-Hall, 1969); *Modern Critical Interpretations: "The Rape of the Lock,"* ed. H. Bloom (New York: Chelsea House, 1988). See, however, *The Rape of the Lock*, ed. C. Wall (Boston: Bedford Books, 1998). Useful background is provided by *The Rape Observed: An Edition of Alexander Pope's Poem "The Rape of the Lock,"* ed. C. Tracy (Toronto: University of Toronto Press, 1974); and *Contexts 2: The Rape of the Lock*, ed. W. Kinsley (Hamden, CT: Archon, 1979).

The standard edition remains that of **Geoffrey Tillotson**: see *TE* 2: 79–124 (introduction), 125–37 (text of earlier version), 139–212 (text of later version), 371–403 (appendices).

Rape of the Locke, The. The earliest version in two cantos of *The Rape of the Lock*: For fuller details of circumstances surrounding the origins of the poem, see the entry on the later version.

The first version is distinguished by an additional *e* in the last word of the title. It first appeared in a collection entitled *Miscellaneous Poems and Translations*, published by **Bernard Lintot** on 20 May 1712, which contained six other items by AP (Griffith 6). It occupied the last twenty pages of the volume. AP claimed to have written the poem in this initial form very fast—indeed, in less than two weeks (see *Anecdotes* 1: 45). If this is correct, then the likeliest period would be within the period August–October 1711. A few lines are taken over from a set of apparently impromptu verses that AP had sent to **Henry Cromwell** on 15 July 1711 (*Corr* 1: 125–26). It is just possible, though unlikely, that these represent a very early draft of what was to become *The Locke*. On 21 September 1711 AP wrote to **John Caryll senior** of "a little Poetical Present" he had to make his friend: it may well be that this was *The Locke* (*CIH* 461–62). AP received £7 from Lintot on 21 March 1714.

The poem undoubtedly circulated in manuscript and, according to AP, was well received by the families involved, who along with Caryll received advance copies of the printed text (*Anecdotes* 1: 44). However, there is evidence that **Arabella Fermor** herself began to feel some offense after publication took place, and this may be one of the reasons that AP embarked on the expansion of his work into the five-canto *Rape of the Lock*. AP made a joking statement to **Martha Blount**, in forwarding to her a copy of *The Locke*, that the poem contained "some things that may be dangerous to be lookd upon" (*Corr* 1: 143); but this remark cannot be regarded as material evidence, as in context it clearly has obscene overtones. Sales do not appear to have been particularly brisk, in spite of a generous commendation by **Addison** in a paper of 30 October 1712, in *Spectator* no. 523. The original version was reprinted once, in reissue of the *Miscellaneous Poems and Translations* in 1714 (Griffith 32), with the name of William Lewis added to that of Lintot on the title page. After that *The Locke* was effectively superseded by its more imposing successor.

The most obvious differences between earlier and later versions are these: (1) Expansion from two cantos (*Locke*) to five cantos (*Lock*); (2) addition of the "machinery" of elementals, including all the material concerning the **sylphs** in Cantos 1 and 2 of *The Lock*, as well as the gnomes and **Cave of Spleen** in Canto 4; (3) addition of passages such as **Belinda**'s toilette in Canto 1, her appearance on the barge in Canto 2, and the card game in Canto 3; (4) small verbal changes throughout, augmentations of detail and the like; (5) inclusion of prefatory letter to Arabella Fermor. No substantial passage in *The Locke* is dropped in the revised version. Broadly speaking, the corresponding sections are as follows: *Locke* Canto 1 = *Lock* Cantos 1–3 (all much expanded); *Locke* Canto 2 = *Lock* Cantos 4–5. More of Canto 5 derives from the original than

is the case with any other canto. In all, *The Locke* runs to 334 lines; *The Lock*, as it stands in the familiar form reached in 1717, consists of just under 800 lines. While the main lines of the poem remain as laid down in 1712, the expanded version is incomparably richer in the range of its allusion, the historical scope of its narrative, the complexity of its texture, and the wit of its language. AP especially prided himself on the way he had integrated the original material with the additions, considering this "one of the greatest proofs of judgement of anything I ever did" (*Anecdotes* 1: 45). A final touch was the addition of illustrations in the 1714 version.

See *TE* 2: 127–37 for the original text.

Receipt to make Soup, A. A poem of thirty lines, rhyming in an irregular pattern and based on verses of six or seven syllables with two stresses in each verse. It was written in September 1726, when AP entertained a party of friends at his home, with **Gay, William Pulteney**, and others in attendance. The special feature of the meal was a dish of stewed veal, cooked according to a recipe provided by Pulteney's cook Monsieur Devaux. The poem, which versifies a surviving recipe in ordinary prose, was included in a letter of composite authorship sent to **Swift** soon afterward. It forms the only surviving part of the letter, and it is written in Gay's hand. However, AP was temporarily disabled owing to a recent injury when his carriage was thrown into the river as he was returning home from **Dawley** (see **accidents**). It is known that Gay acted as his amanuensis during his recovery from this mishap, and most scholars believe that the poem was in fact written by AP. It contains some of his favorite riddling technique along with outrageous puns on "celary," "sorrell," and "tyme."

The first publication seems to have been contrived by **Edmund Curll**, as a "postscript" to one of his opportunistic collections titled *Atterburyana*, issued on 5 January 1727. There were other early editions without authority. Attributed to AP in Ault 225–31. For text and commentary, see *TE* 6: 253–55.

Receit to make an Epick Poem, A. A parody by AP of rule-based criticism of epic. It targets such proponents of high theory as **John Dennis**, as well as such would-be practitioners of lofty epic practice as **Sir Richard Blackmore**. Indirectly the parody undermines the increasingly fashionable doctrines of the ancient Greek critic Longinus, whom Dennis particularly admired, and the orthodox dogma of René Le Bossu (1631–80), expressed in his *Traité du poéme épique* (1675). The culinary "recipe" first appeared as a part of an essay in *The Guardian* no. 78 (10 June 1713). It was adapted to form chapter 15 of *The Art of Sinking* in 1727.

For text and notes, see *Prose* 2: 228–30, 271–73.

Reeves, James (1909–78). Poet and critic who compiled a number of widely used anthologies; known also for his children's verse. In his combative book *The Reputation and Writings of Alexander Pope* (1976) he sets his face against the twentieth-century revival of AP, arguing that the poet's personal failings have been overlooked and his talents as a writer overestimated. While few students of AP are likely to agree with Reeves's contentions to any marked extent, his arguments provide a worthwhile challenge to admirers.

Reichard, Hugo M. (1918–98). Professor at Purdue University, 1956–88. His articles on AP included "The Love Affair in *The Rape of the Lock*," *PMLA*, 69 (1954), 887–902; and "Pope's Social Satire: Belles-Lettres and Business," *PMLA*, 67 (1952), 420–34, reprinted in *EA* 747–67.

religion. AP was not a deeply religious man in the sense that he paid little attention to many of the forms and ceremonies of the Church. However, he was a devoutly loyal Catholic, rejecting opportunities to advance his worldly condition by defecting to Anglicanism. This was despite the fact that he suffered from major civil disabilities, in common with **Roman Catholics** at this date. He is sometimes called an Erasmian Catholic, that is, a liberal and tolerant adherent of the faith. AP certainly prided himself on the breadth of his acquaintance and on his refusal to take a bigoted position on matters where Christian denominations were at odds. There is abundant evidence from his poems and correspondence that he knew the Bible well, although he was not above treating the Scriptures flippantly on occasions (see, for example, *A Roman Catholick Version of the First Psalm*).

AP's fullest statement of his views on religious and moral questions can be found in *An Essay on Man*. He always insisted against critics like **Jean-Pierre de Crousaz** that this was a fundamentally orthodox document, untainted by the views of Leibniz, and to an extent the claim is fair. The poem sets out a view of the universe as created by a beneficent intelligence, in which human beings had been granted the freedom to act in accordance with or in opposition to the divine will. The poet sees humanity lodged a little below the angels in the great chain of being: brute creation is placed on a lower level, but clearly AP believes that humans owe some duty of care to the less advanced species. Essentially the work rests on the truce among contemporaries that allowed the cosmic vision of **Newton** and the traditional beliefs of the Church, as reflected in the work of thinkers such as Pascal, to cohabit without great stress. More easily than men and women a century later, AP was able to find a physicotheological account of the universe not just satisfactory but also imaginatively stimulating. Religion ought to be rational and free, spreading a spirit of gladness among believers rather than inducing gloom or promoting ill-will toward the rest of humanity. This was a creed which held little appeal for AP's Victorian critics, who thought that it reflected the complacence of the eighteenth century and lacked any sense of the transcendental and the mysterious. Modern commentators have been a little more sympathetic, recognizing a positive and generous quality in the religious outlook of the time.

The best short outline of AP's general position is to be found in A.R. Humphreys, "Pope, God, and Man," in *Writers and Their Background: Alexander Pope*, ed. P. Dixon (London: Bell, 1972), 60–100. A vigorous reading of AP's spiritual life is found in F.B. Thornton, *Alexander Pope: Catholic Poet* (New York: Pellegrini & Cudahy, 1952). The treatment is unequal, but the book deserves more attention than it has received.

reputation. This entry is divided into six sections: (1) contemporary, covering up to c. 1750; (2) later eighteenth century, c. 1750–1800; (3) Romantic era, c. 1800–1840; (4) Victorian, c. 1840–1900; (5) early twentieth century, c. 1900–1940; and (6) modern, from c. 1940.

CONTEMPORARY

There was little serious commentary on AP in his lifetime, although he was generally recognized to be the outstanding writer of his age in Britain. A few partial exceptions may be noted. First, the body of hostile observations enshrined in the numerous **pamphlet attacks** does occasionally lapse into sensible discussion. This applies most clearly in the case of **John Dennis**, for example, in his analysis of AP's translation of the *Iliad*. The best retorts, simply in terms of personal combat, are probably those of **Lady Mary Wortley Montagu** and **Colley Cibber**. AP was occasionally defended by able writers such as **Henry Fielding**. Second, the routine formulations in commendatory poems, like those attached to the *Works* **(1717)**, may just for a moment admit a ray of intelligence. Among the many poems addressed to AP, those of **Edward Young** rise a degree or two above the general level. Conventional panegyric is well bestowed by **Richard Savage**. The compliments **Jonathan Swift** paid to his friend are well known, as are those of **Joseph Addison**, but they do not amount to critical observation. Things began to improve with the *Essay on Pope's Odyssey* (1726–27) by **Joseph Spence**, which did at least attempt to describe aspects of AP's writing in detail and to make discriminations. Third, the most searching account of AP in his literary and social context is probably that of **Voltaire** in his *Lettres philosophiques* (1733). The debate set off by **Jean-Pierre de Crousaz** set off an important European debate concerning the theological

standing of *An Essay on Man*, even though this did not reckon in any worthwhile manner with the poetry itself.

After AP died, the mantle passed for some time to biographers and editors, notably **William Warburton** (who had his own agenda to execute), **William Ayre**, and **Owen Ruffhead**. See **biographies of Pope**.

LATER EIGHTEENTH CENTURY

The dominant figures in this period were **Joseph Warton** and **Samuel Johnson**, fellow members of the Literary Club and longtime acquaintances if not intimate friends. Warton represented the growing feeling that poetry should be gauged by the standards applicable to **Shakespeare** and **Milton**. In spite of his admiration for *The Rape of the Lock* and *Eloisa to Abelard*, Warton concluded that AP belonged in the second class of poets, along with figures such as **Cowley, Dryden, Addison, Prior, Gay**, and **Parnell**. (However, Swift made only the third class, like **Donne**.) For Warton, AP lacks the transcendental qualities of the sublime and the pathetic. His work chimed in with the opinions of other readers who found AP deficient in some essential poetic quality: William Cowper wrote in "Table Talk" that he had "made poetry a mere mechanic art." In a letter Cowper had remarked that "there is hardly a thing in the world of which Pope was so entirely destitute, as a taste for Homer." The learned lady Catherine Talbot deplored AP's use of scriptural phrases in "much too ludicrous a way." She was irritated, too, by his letters expressing benevolence and affection but wrongly supposed that a recipient of letters in this vein, **Edward Blount**, was the father of AP's friend **Martha Blount**. The novelist Samuel Richardson was another to state strong reservations, contending that AP would not have shone as a writer of blank verse and that he always required "the assistance of rhyme, of jingle"—a sign of the growing reaction against the dominance of the **heroic couplet**. For Richardson's friend Edward Young, AP relied too much on imitation and (as in his religion) looked back to revered models from the past, who have been "canonized for ages," instead of seeking out fresh inspiration.

On the other hand, Johnson stood for those who considered AP one of the great masters in English literature. He turned Warton's doubting remarks back on the critic: "It is surely, superfluous to ask that has once been asked, whether Pope was a poet, by asking, in return, if Pope be not a poet, where is poetry to be found?" Johnson's study of AP in *The Lives of the Poets* remains one of the most searching and intelligent that has ever been written. In the short term the tide was with those like Warton who wished to relegate AP to a lower position on Parnassus, but Johnson's appreciation of AP's extraordinary skills has had more resonance in the past eighty years. He was supported by his friend Oliver Goldsmith, who asserted that AP "carried the language to its highest perfection, and those who have attempted still farther to improve it, instead of ornament have only caught finery." Another admirer was Arthur Murphy (1727–1805), dramatist and biographer of Fielding, Johnson, and David Garrick: he recognized the deep originality of *The Dunciad*, when this was beyond the capacity of most critics.

For lives of the poet by W.H. Dilworth and Owen Ruffhead, see **biographies of Pope**.

ROMANTIC ERA

AP's reputation had thus already undergone serious challenge by the time that the Romantic poets used his work as a touchstone of a corrupt and passé style that needed to be supplanted. **William Wordsworth**, Samuel Taylor Coleridge, and Robert Southey were all keen readers of AP's work and made some complimentary noises at times, as when Coleridge drew attention to "the almost faultless position and choice of words in Mr. Pope's *original* compositions" (*Biographia Literaria*, 1817). It was the translation of Homer that these writers regarded as vicious in its influence on subsequent English poetry. Contemporaries such as **William Hazlitt**, Leigh Hunt, and **Thomas De Quincey** admired some facets of AP's work but generally concurred in the view that AP's "mechanical" verse and primarily social material limited his

stature in comparison with the greatest figures in literature. In a famous conversation, reported by Hazlitt, Charles Lamb asserted that AP's compliments were the finest "ever paid by the wit of man. Each of them is worth an estate for life—nay it is an immortality." When **William Lisle Bowles** set off the heated controversy concerning AP's standing, around 1820, it was **Byron** and **Thomas Campbell** who most ardently took the poet's side. But these two were exceptional in their insistence on AP's virtues of clarity and precision as a healthy counterbalance to the prevailing vagueness and effusiveness of much Romantic verse.

For the ways in which the Romantics wrestled with AP, see R.J. Griffin, *Wordsworth's Pope: A Study in Literary Historiography* (Cambridge: Cambridge University Press, 1995).

VICTORIAN

By 1850 AP no longer stood as an unquestioned master in the line of English poets, but his verse was still widely quoted and familiar to educated readers. His popular standing was enhanced by the appreciative treatment he received from writers such as **William Makepeace Thackeray** and **John Ruskin**. On the other hand, the assertive Thomas Babington Macaulay had little sympathy with AP, all of whose poems outside the narrow sphere of wit and satire he pronounced to be "failures." Similarly, the limiting judgments of **Matthew Arnold** served to reinforce the view that Dryden and AP were no more than "classics of our prose," while Alfred, Lord Tennyson found the "regular da da, da da" of AP's heroic meter monotonous—even though Algernon Charles Swinburne and **James Russell Lowell** offered a more positive view. An almost equally damaging blow was struck by **Whitwell Elwin**, who used his opportunities given him in his work on the important **Elwin and Courthope edition** to criticize AP's human failings and his limitations as an artist. The more balanced writings of **Sir Leslie Stephen** and **Mark Pattison** were not altogether able to stem the tide of hostile commentary.

In the field of biography the most important

contributions were made by **Robert Carruthers** and **Charles Wentworth Dilke**. Even though Dilke's work was first enlisted by critics such as Elwin to display the pettiness and moral deviance of AP, his findings have had a more lasting value in the exploration of the poet's relations with family and friends. Dilke indeed may be regarded as the first real Popian scholar.

EARLY TWENTIETH CENTURY

Around 1900, as Victorianism itself began to grow passé, the atmosphere became more propitious for a more understanding approach to AP. A popular critic such as **George Saintsbury** could discuss the poet's use of the heroic couplet and make distinctions between its more and less successful features, without finding it necessary to assail AP's character. The taste of the time is perhaps best reflected in the abundant writings of **Austin Dobson**: even though Dobson composed no full account of AP, he helped to inculcate an idea of the Augustan age as one of charming persiflage, rather than one of corruption and skepticism. Little progress was made at first on the biographic front, although the work of **George Paston** contains some fresh material. Gradually more rigorous scholarship began to emerge in the United States especially, with pioneers in the field such as **Thomas Raynesford Lounsbury** and **Robert Kilburn Root**. The outstanding figure, and the founding father of modern Popian studies, was **Reginald Harvey Griffith**, best known for a **bibliography** that has still not been supplanted after eighty years.

Griffith was followed by **George Sherburn**, who took biographic study to a new level with his account of AP's early career (1934) and later his edition of the **correspondence**. Sherburn was also a critic of considerable acuity, whose interpretation of AP's habits of composition has not been improved upon. He has had a lasting effect on the course of Popian studies, even though in the short term it was the more impressionistic writing of **Lytton Strachey** and **Edith Sitwell** that gave AP a more favorable image in the reading public at large. Poets such as T.S. Eliot and **W.H. Auden** also expressed admiration and from time to time slipped in covert **imitations** of AP's style.

By the 1940s academic study had taken on a highly professionalized cast. It was advanced by the work of scholars such as Sherburn, **Maynard Mack**, Robert K. Root, and **Austin Warren** in the United States. Meanwhile in Britain the leading figures were **John Butt**, **James Sutherland**, and **Geoffrey Tillotson**, all of whom were involved in the monumental **Twickenham edition** of AP's entire body of poetry, including the translations, which began in the 1930s. A start was made on editing the **prose works** by **Norman Ault**, whose various attempts to clear up questions of the canon were collected in a volume, *New Light on Pope*, in 1949.

MODERN

From the mid-century there was a further scholarly expansion, and AP had become the subject of intense academic research. The most important outcome was the completion of the Twickenham edition in the 1950s and 1960s. At the same time there came an almost equally significant contribution to the subject, that is, the edition of AP's **correspondence** compiled by George Sherburn in 1956. Understanding of biographic issues was further enhanced by the appearance of Spence's *Anecdotes* in a full edition (1966) and by the most comprehensive life of the poet ever to have been published, that of Maynard Mack (1985).

Mack is unquestionably the most influential of all students of AP, and his work dominated the field for most of the period. His critical position, which drew on the tenets of the New Criticism, was generally close to that of other major scholars, especially **William Kurtz Wimsatt** and **Cleanth Brooks**. AP was now thoroughly rehabilitated, and critics of different persuasions, including **F.R. Leavis** and **William Empson**, treated him with a high degree of respect. AP's stature in the academic community rose to such a pitch that a poet, **James Reeves**, was led in 1976 to issue a counterblast, reviving many of the Victorian objections against AP's perceived flaws—his mechanical versification, lack of feeling for nature, philosophical shallowness. Despite this, scholarship continued to find new ways of locating interest and point in the works. **Reuben A. Brower**, for example, brought out AP's complex relations to the classical tradition; Ian Jack and **Irvin Ehrenpreis** related his mock-heroic works to a broader corpus of satire, while **Earl R. Wasserman** investigated his links to seventeenth-century ideas, and Patricia Meyer Spacks gave detailed attention to his use of imagery.

In the last twenty-five years a challenge has been mounted to the humanist approach adopted by Mack and his followers. AP's stature has been called into question on several grounds, as a misogynist, as a shortsighted imperialist, and as a traitor to the hardpressed community of professional authors. In particular, feminists like Ellen Pollak and Carole Fabricant have questioned AP's credentials on matters of gender (see **women**); new historicists and neo-Marxists like Laura Brown have raised doubts about his attitudes toward **empire** and toward the capitalist marketplace; and others have increasingly sought the man within, disdaining the former "objective" scrutiny of the poet in favor of a more psychological analysis seeking to trace AP's sense of his own identity as man and poet. In addition, an increasing body of work has examined AP in relation to the fortunes of the **Jacobites** and their cause. No final adjudication, naturally, can be made on any of these issues. They serve to remind us that AP continues to absorb the best critical minds, regardless of the particular flavor of the year or decade.

Among living scholars, the individuals who have built up the largest body of critical achievement are Aubrey Williams (b. 1922), Howard Erskine-Hill (b. 1936), and Howard Weinbrot (b. 1936), all of whom have published distinguished work on several aspects of the subject. Apart from those mentioned in the previous paragraphs, the following might be seen as a fair selection of some other critics who have made a special mark in the past quarter of a century: Douglas Brooks-Davies, Morris Brownell, J.S. Cunningham, Peter Dixon, David Fairer, Dustin Griffin, Isobel Grundy, Brean Hammond, Peter Martin, James Mc-

Laverty, David B. Morris, Felicity Rosslyn, G.S. Rousseau, and Valerie Rumbold. (Many more could be named.) Several younger writers have produced exciting work in the last decade that carries the story of Popian scholarship into a new millennium.

The eighteenth century is fully covered in *Pope: The Critical Heritage*, ed. J. Barnard (London: Routledge, 1973). This phase is also discussed by W.L. MacDonald, *Pope and His Critics: A Study in Eighteenth Century Personalities* (London: Dent, 1951). Useful general collections of criticism include *Discussions of Alexander Pope*, ed. R.A. Blanshard (Boston: Heath, 1960); *Critics on Pope*, ed. J. O'Neill (London: Allen & Unwin, 1968); and *Alexander Pope: A Critical Anthology*, ed. F.W. Bateson and N.A. Joukovsky (Harmondsworth: Penguin, 1971). Modern scholarship is assembled in *Essential Articles for the Study of Alexander Pope*, ed. M. Mack (Hamden, CT: Archon, 1968); and *Pope: Recent Essays*, ed. M. Mack and J.A. Winn (Hamden, CT: Archon, 1980). For a selection of work from the most recent phase, see *Pope*, ed. B. Hammond (Harlow, Essex: Longman, 1996).

Rich, John (1692–1761). Theatrical manager and performer. He was the son of Christopher Rich (1657–1714), from whom he took over the new **Lincoln's Inn Fields Theatre**. His main specialty for many years was playing the role of Harlequin in pantomimes, a form he helped to naturalize in England with a series of successful farces blending commedia dell'arte, slapstick, music, and dance. He enjoyed his greatest triumph when he put on *The Beggar's Opera* in 1728. The profits were enough to enable him to build a new **Covent Garden Theatre**, on the site of the modern opera house. This opened with a performance of *The Way of the World*, by **William Congreve**, in December 1732. In 1735 **Handel** moved his center of operations to Covent Garden, and thereafter many of his oratorios were first heard there. At his death the composer bequeathed to Rich the great organ used at these performances.

AP mentioned Rich briefly in the *Epilogue to the Satires* (*TE* 4: 306). A fairly soft target, the manager came in for much more extensive satire in Book 3 of *The Dunciad*, where he appears as "Immortal Rich." AP gives a bravura description of the spectacular shows put on by Rich at Lincoln's Inn Fields (3: 249–68). He is depicted as the pioneer of an empty new brand of theatrical display, substituting special effects for serious dramaturgy. It did not help Rich's cause that his main librettist for the harlequinades he produced in the 1720s was **Lewis Theobald**, doomed to be elevated as the first king of the dunces. In fact, Theobald would dedicate to Rich his *Shakespeare Restored* (1726), a riposte to AP's **Shakespeare edition**.

Rich, Lady (Elizabeth Rich) (1692–1773). High society belle. At one time a close friend of **Lady Mary Wortley Montagu**, who later tired of her "flighty, clueless manner" and made fun of the "decayed beauty." She was the daughter of Edward Griffith and his wife Elizabeth, later Lady Mohun; her husband Robert was an army officer who ended up as a Field-Marshal but who earlier inhabited a circle surrounding Lord Mohun noted for their rowdy and ruffianly behavior. AP had a number of contacts with her around 1716, partly through his association with her sister **Anne Griffith**, and she figures in his *Court Ballad* in this year. See I. Grundy, *Lady Mary Wortley Montagu* (Oxford: Oxford University Press, 1999).

Richardson, Jonathan junior (1694–1771). Painter and friend of AP. See **Jonathan Richardson senior**.

Richardson, Jonathan senior (1665–1745). Portrait painter and writer on art. Built up a flourishing practice in the early years of the eighteenth century: member of the Academy of Painting founded in 1711 with **Kneller** as director. He wrote *An Essay on the Theory of Painting* (1715), which influenced Joshua Reynolds, as well as *Two Discourses* (1719). Among his well-known works are portraits of **Lady Mary Wortley Montagu**, **Richard Steele**, **John Vanbrugh**, **William Cheselden**, the **first Earl of Oxford**, the **Earl of Burlington**, and the **Duke of Buckinghamshire**. At his death AP

possessed a portrait of **Bolingbroke** by Richardson. The artist was a friend of **Matthew Prior**. His son Jonathan Richardson junior (1694–1771) was also a painter and collaborated with his father on literary projects, including a pioneering work on **Milton** (1734). The younger Richardson took a keen interest in the **manuscripts** of AP's poems and collated revisions of *The Dunciad*.

The elder Richardson seems to have been a family friend of the Popes and made a drawing of AP's mother perhaps as early as 1703. The first among many studies of AP himself dates from 1718, the last from 1742. Probably the best known of several images is one with a **dog** and a profile of AP with a crown of laurel (see *Portraits* 9, 54; and **portraits**). Richardson left a wider array of striking pictures of AP than any other artist. He also engraved AP's head for reproduction in editions of his works. His critical essays contain admiring references to the poet. Over fifty letters from AP to the Richardsons (mostly to the father) survive, dating between c. 1721 and 1744. The elder Richardson was evidently a congenial friend with whom AP maintained close relations. In 1730 AP dictated biographical notes to his friend (*Anecdotes* 2: 617). One factor linking the two men was that each suffered from a painful pulmonary condition diagnosed as "asthma" (see **health**).

Richmond. Historic settlement on the Thames, on the opposite bank from **Twickenham** and just downstream. The great palace here was created by Henry VII on the site of the royal manor of Shene, while nearby Richmond Park was enclosed by Charles I in 1637. Today only small portions of the palace remain near Richmond Green. The village grew fashionable as a result of its riverside setting, sweeping open spaces, and fine vantage point of Richmond Hill, beloved of eighteenth-century artists such as **Joseph Mallard William Turner**.

AP had many friends and contacts in the area. Close to the river stood Richmond Lodge, originally a royal hunting lodge. It was occupied by the **Duke of Ormonde** as Ranger of the Park until his enforced exile, then in 1719 acquired by the Prince and Princess of Wales (later **George II** and **Queen Caroline**), who spent the summers there. The grounds there were developed for the Princess by **Charles Bridgeman** by 1723: in the early stages the Queen seems to have consulted AP as a friend and ally. Later buildings designed by **William Kent** were erected, to proclaim political and cultural values that AP and his allies found risible (*Gardening World* 147–53). See also **Merlin's Cave**; and "A Pastoral Dialogue between Richmond Lodge and **Marble Hill**" (1727) by **Swift**. The house was demolished in 1772. However, White Lodge, a house in the park built by Roger Morris for the new King and Queen after their accession in 1727, survives today, and since 1955 it has been part of the Royal Ballet School. Another resident in the park was **Robert Walpole**, whose son became Ranger in 1727 and had a home at Old Lodge in the park. Just outside the boundary of the park **James Gibbs** designed a house at Sudbrook (1726–28) for the **second Duke of Argyll**. AP probably knew most of these houses at firsthand.

On Richmond Green stood the houses occupied by the **maids of honor** to the Princess, who were close friends of the poet. The sisters **Martha** and **Teresa Blount** had a home in Ham, on the southern side of Richmond, and Martha on occasions made a retreat to a house owned by **William Fortescue** in the Vineyard, not far from the Green. From 1736 the writer **James Thomson** was settled in Kew Foot Lane, which ran north from the center of the village, and from this date his friendship with AP became more intimate. Kew itself was the home of **Frederick, Prince of Wales**, titular head of the **opposition to Walpole**: his residence, the White House, was remodeled by William Kent from a building formerly occupied by Samuel Molyneux, the amateur astronomer ridiculed in AP's poem *The Discovery*. AP dined there at least once. At New Park in Petersham he visited Lady Rochester in 1717. Nearby were Ham House and Douglas House: the latter was a residence of the **Duke** and **Duchess of Queensberry**, the patrons of **John Gay**. Here traditionally *The Beggar's Opera*

was, at least in part, composed. It is all but certain AP also knew the house, just a short ferry trip across from Twickenham.

After the publication of *The Dunciad* had provoked a hostile response, AP in a fit of bravado took to walking regularly between his home and Fortescue's house in Richmond, despite threats of retribution. Accompanied by his faithful dog Bounce, he would cross the river by ferry and cover the rest of the two-mile journey on foot. See *Anecdotes* 116–17.

For an overview of the history of the locality, see J. Cloake, *Richmond Past* (London: Historical Publications, 1991). For a splendid visual record, see B. Gascoigne, *Images of Richmond* (Richmond: Saint Helena Press, 1978).

Ripley, Thomas (1683–1758). Architect. He became the royal Master Carpenter in 1721, then Comptroller of the Works in 1726 in succession to **Vanbrugh**. His most important patron was **Robert Walpole**, who used him to supervise the construction of Houghton Hall, Norfolk (1722–25). It is quite likely that AP had Ripley's work at Houghton in mind when he wrote his satire on **Timon's villa** in the *Epistle to Burlington*. Elsewhere in the same poem AP refers contemptuously to "Ripley with a Rule," adding the note, "This man was a carpenter, employ'd by a first Minister, who rais'd him to an Architect without any genius in the art; and after some wretched proofs of his insufficiency on public buildings, made him Comptroller of the Board of works" (*TE* 3.ii: 137). There is a brief uncomplimentary reference in the *Epistle to Augustus*. Politics entered into these judgments.

Riskins, or Richings. Estate of AP's friend the **Earl of Bathurst**, situated in Buckinghamshire south of Iver. It lay across the Thames from AP's childhood home in **Berkshire** and only about ten miles from **Twickenham**. It came to the Bathurst family by marriage with the Apsley family, who had acquired it in 1678. Now the site of Richings Park, a residential estate; the house was destroyed in World War II, and the gardens have disappeared. Bathurst carried out modernization of the house after he inherited the estate in 1704, but his main efforts went into the garden, on which Stephen Switzer was the main influence, with many varied elements including a canal. In 1735 Bathurst passed the estate on to his son, but in 1739 he was obliged to sell the property to the Earl and Countess of Hertford, who rechristened it "Percy Lodge" and carried out further improvements of the garden.

Swift and **John Gay** paid several visits to Riskins, but it was AP who was most often there. Bathurst invited him to the house in 1723, 1725, 1727, and 1730 and probably again in later years. The poet's visits "normally were frequent and brief" (*Corr* 2: 302). When Lady Hertford came into possession, she wrote that the estate was what AP called Bathurst's "*extravagant bergerie*" and added that the surroundings "come nearer to my idea of a scene in Arcadia, than any place I ever saw." It felt as though one were a hundred miles from London (rather than barely twenty). She also penned some verses on the literary associations of the seat:

> By Bathurst planted, first these shades arose;
> Prior and Pope have sung beneath these boughs:
> Here Addison his moral theme pursu'd,
> And social Gay has cheer'd the solitude.

See *Earls of Creation* 21–33; *Gardening World* 66–78. See also **Cirencester**.

Roberts, James (c. 1670–1754). One of the most important figures in the London book trade in the first half of the eighteenth century. For many years he was the leading "publisher," that is, a distributor and wholesaler holding stocks of books and pamphlets for the booksellers who actually instigated publication and who owned the copyright. Roberts came to the fore in 1713 on the death of his mother-in-law, Abigail Baldwin, and remained at the head of his profession for the next few decades, serving as Master of the Stationers Company for four years (1729–33), a rare distinction. Trained as a printer, he worked from the Oxford Arms in Warwick Lane. His name appears on several of

AP's works and equally often on the title page of **pamphlet attacks** on the poet, including some items for which **Edmund Curll** was certainly responsible. There is no indication that the two men had any personal contact. Roberts is also listed in the imprint of books by **Swift**, **Gay**, **Defoe**, and others.

Robinson, Anastasia, later Countess of Peterborough (c. 1692–1755). English singer, born in Italy, the daughter of a portrait painter. She started out as a soprano and joined the **opera** at the **Haymarket Theatre** in 1714. Later she sang for the Royal Academy of Music, now as a contralto, when she earned the remarkable salary of £1,000. She retired two years after making a secret marriage in 1722 with the **Earl of Peterborough**. The couple did not live together, and from 1723 she continued to live near to the Earl's house at **Parson's Green**, Fulham, with her mother and sister. The sister, Margaret, was married in 1728 to George Arbuthnot, half brother of **Dr. John Arbuthnot**, but she died in 1729. **Lady Mary Wortley Montagu** unkindly said that Anastasia was at once "a prude and a kept mistress."

AP was told around 1722 that "Mrs Robn haunts Bononcini" (*Corr* 2: 123). In fact she was closely associated with the group of devotees supporting **Giovanni Bononcini**. Many of this group were based near **Twickenham**; some had Italian connections and several were Roman Catholics—as was Anastasia. She was instrumental in gaining a pension for Bononcini from **Henrietta, Duchess of Marlborough**. AP had probably known her for some time before her marriage. She subscribed to the poems of **John Gay** in 1720 and later to the *Odyssey*. Shortly before the death of Lord Peterborough in 1735, the marriage was finally acknowledged. AP continued to visit the widow at **Bevis Mount** and met her at **Bath**. She was perhaps the most devout Catholic among his acquaintances.

Rogers, Robert Wentworth (1914–92). Scholar and educator, associated with the University of Illinois from 1948. His work includes a book, *The Major Satires of Alexander Pope*

(1955), together with articles on the *Essay on Man*.

Rolli, Paolo Antonio (1687–1765). Italian author and librettist. Born in Rome, he worked in England from 1716 to 1744. He wrote books on many subjects and produced numerous translations, including a version of *Paradise Lost* in Italian (1735), dedicated to **Frederick, Prince of Wales**. He taught the Italian language to Frederick's sisters, daughters of the future **George II** and **Queen Caroline**: the girls' music master was **George Frideric Handel**. His *Rime* (1717) went through many editions. However, his main sphere of activity was in **opera**, and he served as librettist both to the Royal Academy of Music and to the Opera of the Nobility. He moved in the circle of the Modenese diplomat Giuseppe Riva (c. 1685–c. 1737), whose efforts to promote opera brought him into contact with several of AP's friends and patrons. Rolli's words were set by Handel and **Giovanni Bononcini**, among others. FRS, 1729. AP allots him an unflattering reference in *The Dunciad*, together with a scornful note, which mentions that Rolli "taught Italian to some fine Gentlemen who affected to direct the Opera's" (*TE* 5: 124). In fact, Rolli was on good terms with several of AP's friends, including the **Earl** and **Countess of Burlington**, and **Mary Howe**. The first edition of the *Rime* is dedicated to **Lord Bathurst**. However, Rolli's somewhat abrasive personality jarred on many people, and this may help to account for AP's seeming antipathy toward him. After returning to his homeland, Rolli settled at Todi in Umbria.

See a thorough study by G.E. Doris, *Paolo Rolli and the Italian Circle in London 1715–1744* (The Hague: Mouton, 1967). Still useful is T. Vallese, *Paolo Rolli in Inghilterra* (Milan: Società anonima editrice Dante Alighieri, 1938).

Rollinson, William (c. 1678–1774). Sometimes spelled "Rawlinson." A former wine merchant who became a friend of AP, **Swift**, and **Bolingbroke**. His first wife died in 1730, regretted by AP (*Corr* 3: 132). He later married

Sarah Finch (d. 1735), widow of Charles, third Earl of Winchilsea (d. 1712), whose uncle the fourth Earl was the husband of the poet **Anne, Countess of Winchilsea**. Rollinson subscribed to the *Iliad* and the *Odyssey*, and he was one of those to greet AP in *Mr. Pope's Welcome from Greece*. AP left him a small bequest in his **will**.

Roman Catholick Version of the First Psalm, A. First published as intended "for the Use of a Young Lady, by Mr. Pope" on a single sheet (Griffith 58; Foxon P953), price twopence, and advertised on 30 June 1716. The imprint was that of Rebecca Burleigh, but she was a "trade publisher," and responsibility has always been allotted to **Edmund Curll**. There were reprints in many of Curll's collections over the years to come. AP never acknowledged the poem and indeed sought to distance himself from the production.

This item lay at the heart of the burgeoning quarrel between AP and Curll. Its appearance caused a furor, deliberately fomented by a Whig journal, *The Flying Post*. On 14 July 1716 the paper ran an inflammatory story quoting the poem in full and printing a response titled "The Eccho to Pope's Drury Lane Ballad." On 31 July AP inserted an advertisement in the Tory paper *The Post Man*, attempting to clear himself of any knowledge concerning the "publication" of this piece, without explicitly denying authorship. His guilty feelings emerged in a letter to **Teresa Blount** on 7 August: "If you have seen a late Advertisement, you will know that I have not told a lye (which we both abhominate) but equivocated pretty genteely" (*Corr* 1: 350). The effort at damage control proved unavailing, and many of the **pamphlet attacks** that rained down on AP made reference to the affair (see, for example, Guerinot 55, 63, 84, 143). AP's miscalculation plagued him as late as 1728, when Curll raked over the history of this "profane Version of the *First Psalm*," and even into 1735 when the charges were laid again (Guerinot 112, 259).

The poem consists of five four-line stanzas in alternate rhyme. This form is significant, since AP was parodying not the biblical version of Psalm 1 but a metrical paraphrase by Thomas Sternhold and John Hopkins. These versions of the Scriptures had first appeared in Elizabethan times and were widely used in the Protestant church, though not of course by Roman Catholics. AP follows his model quite closely and neatly misapplies its wording: Thus, in the original the godly man "doth exercise / himself both day and night" in the service of the Lord, whereas in the parody the young lady's husband "in her Love shall Exercise / Himself both day and Night."

A poem that could be regarded as both blasphemous and obscene was bound to hurt AP's reputation. He never fully rid himself of the scandal: the poem gave his most entrenched opponents, like **John Dennis** and **Sir Richard Blackmore**, ample scope for their venomous retorts.

For the background, see Ault 156–62; for the text and commentary, see *TE* 6: 164–66.

Roman Catholics. As a Catholic, AP belonged to a small minority of the British people, who numbered perhaps 60,000 in a population approaching 6 million. The penal laws went back to Tudor times, and they were specifically designed to place a stranglehold on the religious, educational, and civic expression of those who remained loyal to the old faith. More recent legislation had limited their political rights, along with those of the dissenters. The Corporation Act (1661) and more especially the Test Acts (1673, 1678) excluded Catholics from offices in the army and the state; they were already banned in effect from universities, which were Anglican institutions.

Although penal laws were suspended under James II, the climate was less favorable for papists under **William III** and Queen Mary. The provisions of the Toleration Act (1689) benefited dissent more directly than Catholicism. By a measure of the same year, anyone declared by the justices to be a "Popish Recusant Convict" could be ordered to retire to a distance of ten miles from London and Westminster. It is probably for this reason that the Pope family moved to **Hammersmith** and then to **Binfield**. In 1692 recusants (those who refused to attend Church

of England services) were subjected to double land taxation; while in 1700 they were debarred from inheriting or purchasing land, a matter that directly affected **Alexander Pope senior** and his family (see **Whitehill House**). By the same act Catholics were forbidden to keep a school or take upon themselves the education of children. AP's formal schooling, whether by private tutors, at a mysterious establishment near Hyde Park, or at **Twyford**, was thus technically illegal (see **education**).

After a period of benign neglect under **Queen Anne**, the Catholic community had to endure renewed scrutiny under the Hanoverian monarchs. The threat posed by the **Jacobite rising** caused the government to reactivate some of the penal laws that had lain dormant since the 1690s. The rules were tightened on entry to professions such as the bar: this would handicap AP's nephew Henry Rackett in years to come. In 1715 a statute was enacted that appointed commissioners to "inquire of the estates of certain traitors," which actually meant that Catholics had to register their estates to make heavier taxation more convenient to introduce. This was what happened as a result of a measure in 1723, brought in at the height of the scare over the **Atterbury plot**. AP's own Catholic relatives, the **Rackett family**, were implicated in criminal activity at this juncture and perhaps made outlaws. AP greeted these successive bouts of anti-Catholic legislation with stoical resolve, although they imposed burdens financially.

People of the Roman faith had for a long time been associated with the **Jacobites**. In fact, only a minority of Catholics actively supported the cause of the **Pretender**. Their numbers were scattered through the nation, with little of the dense concentration in urban areas that followed waves of Irish immigration starting later in the century. Catholicism was strong in the North of England, especially Lancashire, and in other parts of the country remote from London. Recusancy around **Berkshire** and Oxfordshire, AP's home district, centered on a few ancient papist families, almost all of them known to the poet personally. Prominent in his acquaintances from youth were members of the Blount, Englefield, Dancastle, Plowden, Talbot, Browne, Fermor, Webb, and Stonor families. Further afield, he came into regular contact with Carylls, Petres, Swinburnes, and very many others. They were nearly all related to one another, through repeated intermarriage. One of this group, John Talbot Stonor, brother of AP's friend **Thomas Stonor**, became Vicar-Apostolic for the Midland district in 1716, with responsibility also for the Thames Valley region. It was he who urged in 1719 that the Catholics should break with the Stuart cause and make a declaration of loyalty to the Hanoverians, but though this made it easier for Stonor to exercise his mission and travel freely between Catholic houses, it did not destroy all the old loyalties.

AP prided himself on his liberal attitudes in religion and the ecumenical range of his friendship. Nevertheless, it is apparent that many of his deepest allegiances lay with coreligionists, such as **Martha Blount, John Caryll senior**, and **Edward Blount**.

See J. Bossy, *The English Catholic Community 1570–1850* (New York: Oxford University Press, 1976). Some of AP's local connections can be traced in T. Hadland, *Thames Valley Papists: From Reformation to Emancipation* (N.p.: Privately printed, 1992).

Roome, Edward (d. 1729). Lawyer and minor author. He succeeded **Philip Horneck** as Solicitor-General in 1729, probably as a reward for journalistic services to the government of **Robert Walpole**. In a paper called *Pasquin* in 1723, he had alleged that AP was implicated in the **Atterbury plot**. He was the probable author of *Dean Jonathan's Parody of the 4th Chap. of Genesis* (1729), a travesty of the biblical story in which AP is cast as Cain and **Theobald** as Abel. In fact, Roome was a close friend of Theobald and **Concanen**, as indicated in *An Author to be Lett*. AP said all he needed to say in a single line of *The Dunciad*, "Lo Horneck's fierce, and Roome's funereal face," with a damagingly explicit note on these "virulent Partywriters" (*TE* 5: 162–63).

Root, Robert Kilburn (1877–1950). Professor at Princeton University, 1916–46. Primarily a

medievalist, he was also active in eighteenth-century studies. He wrote a widely used biography, *The Poetical Career of Alexander Pope* (1938), and edited *The Dunciad Variorum* (1929).

Roscoe, William (1753–1831). A remarkable individual, beginning as an attorney, banker, and MP in Liverpool. He eventually went bankrupt. However, he had turned himself into a historian of the Italian Renaissance, poet, translator, children's author, art collector, political sage, and much else. His edition of AP's works in 10 volumes, with a life (1824), has some interest in the wake of the controversy that had been waged between **Byron** and **Bowles**. There was another edition in 1847. See **biographies of Pope**.

Roubiliac, Louis-François (c. 1705–62). French sculptor. After training in Saxony and Paris, he settled in London in the early 1730s. It was in 1738 that he came to the fore with his statue of **Handel** for Vauxhall Gardens (now in the Victoria and Albert Museum). Later successes included a statue of **Newton** (1755) and many tombs in Westminster Abbey, notably the **Duke of Argyll** (1749). His other subjects included **Colley Cibber**, David Garrick, **Sir Hans Sloane**, and **Robert Walpole**.

Four marble busts of AP survive, dated between 1738 and 1742. There are also many models and replicas: Roubiliac's image of the poet became one of the best known, appearing in many guises. For example, Angelica Kauffmann designed a picture titled "The Muses Crowning the Bust of Pope," which was engraved in 1783. See *Portraits* 57–61; and **portraits**. For wider surveys, see K.A. Esdaile, *The Life and Works of Louis François Roubiliac* (London: Oxford University Press, 1928); and D. Bindman and M. Baker, *Roubiliac and the Eighteenth-Century Monument: Sculpture as Theatre* (New Haven, CT: Yale University Press, 1995).

Rousham. House and famous twenty-acre garden belonging to AP's friends, the brothers Robert and **James Dormer**. It lay north of **Ox-**

ford, near Steeple Aston, on the banks of the Cherwell. The house was built for Sir Robert Dormer in 1635 and came to Colonel Robert Dormer from his brother in 1719. On Robert's death in 1737 it passed to his brother, General James Dormer. In the 1730s **William Kent** added wings and a stable block and altered the interior. From about 1738 he also transformed the garden as it had been laid out by **Charles Bridgeman** in the 1720s, and it is generally considered the most perfect example of naturalistic eighteenth-century **gardening** surviving today. Kent disperses informal groups of trees, statues, and temples amid winding paths: there is an "eye-catcher" or folly on the skyline. AP knew Rousham in its earlier state but may have contributed something to Kent's remodeling, specifically with regard to a feature known as "Venus's Vale." He stayed at the estate on numerous occasions between 1728 and 1743: Rousham "attracted him like a magnet year after year during his **rambles**" (Peter Martin). As he described it to **Martha Blount**, this was "the prettiest place for water-falls, jetts [cascades], ponds inclosed with beautiful scenes of green and hanging wood, that I ever saw" (*Corr* 2: 513). After the death of James Dormer in 1741 the estate passed to his cousin **Sir Clement Cotterell**, also well known to AP. The Cotterell-Dormer family remains in occupation and has preserved the gardens in virtually their pristine state. Some memorabilia associated with AP are still kept at the house.

For AP's interest in the garden, see *Gardening World* 17–18, 26.

Rowe, Nicholas (1674–1718). Dramatist and poet. Educated at Westminster school, he studied law at the Middle Temple, but he did not practice after he was called to the bar in 1696. He was the most successful writer of tragedy between the Restoration and the nineteenth century. His plays *Tamerlane* (1702), *The Fair Penitent* (1703), *Jane Shore* (1714), and *Lady Jane Gray* (1715) enjoyed great success. His *Works of Shakespear* (6 vols., 1709) was in effect the first independent attempt to produce a critical edition, although Rowe's editorial skills were limited. His life of **Shakespeare** provided

the basis for most biographic accounts for a century of more (AP would use it in his own **Shakespeare edition**). He received a number of small posts from the government, and in 1715 he was appointed Poet Laureate, partly as a result of his solid Whig credentials. His last major work was a translation of Lucan's *Pharsalia* (1718), which went through many editions.

AP spoke highly of his affectionate and cheerful nature. They probably met by 1708, and by 1713 they were exchanging visits to each other's homes: Rowe spent a week at **Binfield** in September of that year. Together they engaged in minor literary enterprises, some concerned with the famous play *Cato*. At the height of their friendship AP wrote an epilogue for *Jane Shore*, seemingly rejected by the actress who took the heroine's role, **Anne Oldfield** (*TE* 6: 113–51). He may also have composed a prologue for *Lady Jane Gray*. When Rowe died at the age of forty-four, AP wrote a short **epitaph**. However, this was not used when the dramatist was buried in Westminster Abbey. It was not until 1743 that a monument was erected to Rowe, and for this AP adapted his earlier lines to provide the inscription now in place. The verses now refer also to Rowe's daughter Charlotte (1717–39), who had married Hon. Henry Fane in 1735 (*TE* 6: 208–9, 400–401). AP was a witness to Rowe's will.

Rowe's friendship with AP caused him to bear the brunt of some hostile criticism by writers in the pay of **Edmund Curll**, notably **Charles Gildon**. AP both admired and liked him, as is evident from his presence in *A Farewell to London* and *Sandys's Ghost*. Rowe subscribed to the *Iliad*. In defining Rowe's special field in drama as "the Passions," as he does in the *Epistle to Augustus* (*TE* 5: 201), AP was following received opinion.

For AP's relations with Rowe, see Ault 128–55. There is a short modern study, A. Jenkins, *Nicholas Rowe* (Boston: Twayne, 1977). *Three Plays by Nicholas Rowe*, ed. J.R. Sutherland (London: Scholartis, 1929), contains some material of lasting interest.

Ruffhead, Owen (1723–69). Barrister, journalist, and legal compiler. His *Life of Alexander Pope* (1769) was the most important of the **biographies of Pope** that had appeared to that date. It was promoted by **William Warburton** in order to set forth the views of AP's literary executor, in opposition to those of **Joseph Warton** in particular. Ruffhead prints some new materials with regard to AP's interest in antiquarianism but made no major advance on Warburton's published editions with respect to most features of AP's career.

Rural Sports. A poem in two cantos by **John Gay**, published on 13 January 1713. It is subtitled, "A *GEORGIC*: Inscribed to Mr. *POPE*." The work opens with a dedicatory paragraph to AP, somewhat unrealistically portrayed as living "undisturbed" and at ease in "*Windsor* groves." The pastoral poet, surrounded by nymphs and river gods in his idyllic Thames-side retreat, provides a sharp contrast to Gay, who depicts himself as careworn and immured in the "noisie town." Formally Gay's tribute must allude to AP's *Pastorals*, but there is little doubt that he is also thinking of *Windsor-Forest*, which must have circulated in the preceding months among AP's circle. Like AP, although much more obliquely, Gay relates the activities of the countryside, traditionally described in **georgic** poetry, to the state of peace that was anticipated with the imminent closure of the **Treaty of Utrecht**.

Ruskin, John (1819–1900). Writer. Ruskin several times recorded a profound debt to the work of AP. This started with childhood readings by his father and continued with his own study of the Homeric translations as a boy. In his *Lectures on Art* he stated that, putting **Shakespeare** aside, he held AP to be "the most perfect representation we have, since Chaucer, of the true English mind; and I think the *Dunciad* is the most absolutely chiselled and monumental work 'executed' in our time." Indeed, there is no mind "in its range, so perfect." In *Modern Painters* Ruskin claimed that AP was the greatest man "who ever fell strongly" under the influence of "the classical spirit." The *Pastorals* showed him cold-hearted, but after this phase, "his errors were those of his time, his wisdom was his own." In manuscript notes for his lectures, delivered in 1853, he wrote, "A greater man in many respects never lived, but he lived at the most unnatural period." Such hyperbolic praise of AP often goes with denunciation of the age as a whole. Nevertheless, few Victorians would have easily swallowed this estimate of the poet. Ruskin once thought of writing a study of AP to rescue him "from the hands of his present scavenger biographer" (**Whitwell Elwin**), but nothing came of this.

Rysbrack, Michael (1694–1770). Flemish sculptor who worked in London from about 1720. A versatile and prolific artist who after initial success promoted by the **second Earl of Oxford** and the **Earl of Burlington** lost popularity in favor of **Scheemakers** and **Roubiliac**. He was employed on commissions by **William Kent** and **James Gibbs**. Among his best-known works is the funeral monument to **Sir Isaac Newton** in Westminster Abbey. In the Abbey he was also responsible for the monument to **John Gay**, for which AP supplied the inscription, while he carved the figures for Gibbs's monument to **Matthew Prior**. See also **Gosfield** and **William Benson**.

For Rysbrack's bust of AP, made in the later 1720s through the agency of Gibbs, see **portraits** and *Portraits* 11. AP wrote an epigram on the subject, following scurrilous comments in the press that the sculptor had maliciously presented him as a hideous monster. The epigram was incorporated into a note in *The Dunciad*, Book 2. See *TE* 5: 115–16; 6: 302–5; and *Corr* 2: 298; 3: 100. It is possible that Rysbrack sculpted the bust of AP included among the Temple of Worthies at **Stowe**, designed by Kent; see *Portraits* 19.

See K. Eustace, *Michael Rysbrack, Sculptor 1694–1770* (Bristol: City of Bristol Museum and Art Gallery, 1982); and G. Balderston, "Rysbrack's Busts of James Gibbs and Alexander Pope from Henrietta Street," *Georgian Group Journal*, 11 (2001), 1–28.

S

Sacheverell, Dr. Henry (c. 1678–1724). Clergyman. Educated at Magdalen College, **Oxford**, where he was a friend of **Joseph Addison**. D.D., 1708. His high-flying attitudes on church and state culminated in the delivery of two incendiary sermons in 1709. His prosecution on four counts by the House of Lords in the following year divided the nation. The show trial was held in Westminster Hall and provided the biggest public spectacle in the reign of **Queen Anne**. Sacheverell was accused basically of promoting resistance to the Revolution of 1688 and of supporting the charge that "the church was in danger" under the Whig government. It was this episode that did most to polarize political opinions in this era and to bring about the inception of the **Harley administration**. By narrow margins, Sacheverell was found guilty. However, the lenient sentence passed (three year's suspension from preaching) was widely regarded as tantamount to acquittal. Sacheverell made a tour of the nation and was greeted as a martyr for the church. After his triumph he slipped gradually into obscurity. **Swift** met him in 1712 and found him "not very deep" (*JTS* 2: 516). Like others, he was glad at the turn of events the doctor had precipitated but had little regard for the man.

AP refers to the episode in the *Memoirs of P.P. Clerk of this Parish*. In his joking "interpretation" of his own poem *A Key to the Lock*, AP pretends that the lapdog Shock, who awakes **Belinda** in the first canto, represents the doctor (*Prose* 1: 192). All the peers with whom AP then or later enjoyed close relations voted for Sacheverell at his trial. The main speech made by the accused in his own defense was probably drafted by **Francis Atterbury**. He was a subscriber to the *Iliad*.

See G. Holmes, *The Trial of Doctor Sacheverell* (London: Eyre Methuen, 1973), which supplants all other works on the subject.

Saintsbury, George (1845–1933). Literary historian and critic. Regius Professor of Rhetoric and English Literature at Edinburgh, 1895–1915. Fellow of the British Academy, 1921. He wrote on a huge range of topics connected with English and French literature across the centuries. Best known in his time for comprehensive works of literary history (as well as books on wine). His "connoisseur" model of criticism is now deeply out of fashion, and his appreciation of AP in the once influential work *The Peace of the Augustans* (1916) seems perfunctory today. However, Saintsbury's *History of English Prosody*, 3 vols. (1906–8), remains not just the fullest treatment of the subject but one of the most observant and intelligent. It is instructive on AP's use of the couplet and demonstrates that along with more cerebral qualities an essential attribute of any critic of AP is a good ear.

Sandys's Ghost. A poem subtitled "A Proper New Ballad on the New Ovid's Metamorphosis: As it was Intended to be Translated by Persons of Quality." First published in the **Miscellanies** in 1727 without attribution. However, a manuscript in AP's hand in the Portland papers makes it almost certain that he was the author. The date of composition has not been fixed but seems certain to be around 1716–17. (Some anachronistic references suggest a later revision.) The form is ballad stanzas, and the poem contains seventy-six lines.

It is possible to fix the occasion of the lines, though not very much more. A major translation of the *Metamorphoses* was edited by **Samuel Garth** and published by **Jacob Tonson senior** in July 1717. The contributors included **Dryden, Addison, Eusden, Gay, Congreve, Rowe, Welsted,** and Temple Stanyan, as well as AP himself (see **Ovid**). The project was on a grander scale than a rival translation brought out by **Curll** a few months earlier, to which AP had also contributed. See the edition of the Garth version, with introduction by G. Tissol (1998).

This is among the less decipherable of AP's shorter satires. It targets among others the astronomer **Samuel Molyneux,** but the grounds for singling out this figure, who is not listed among Garth's contributors, remains obscure. Molyneux had a place at court, and it seems that the poem is an offshoot of AP's friendly dealings with the **maids of honor** and other retainers. Among those mentioned in the ballad are **Tickell,** Addison, **Jervas,** and **Lady Mary Wortley Montagu.** The title refers to George Sandys (1578–1644), author of a highly popular translation of the *Metamorphoses* (1621–26), whose ghost appears to Molyneux as he desperately searches for poetic inspiration.

For the text and commentary, see *TE* 6: 170–76.

Sapho to Phaon. A translation of the fifteenth of the *Heroides* of **Ovid,** first published in the collection of **Jacob Tonson senior** known as *Ovid's Epistles,* eighth edition, which came out in March 1712 (Griffith 4). A revised version was printed in the **Works (1717)** and later editions. The poem consists of 259 lines in **heroic couplets** (one triplet).

A holograph **manuscript** survives at the Pierpont Morgan Library, New York. It was most likely written out in 1711, although work on the poem could have begun as early as 1707. The fair copy is interspersed with corrections and AP's response to suggestions by an unknown commentator, who has been tentatively identified as AP's early friend **Henry Cromwell.** For a reproduction of this manuscript, see *L&GA* 72–90.

The poem reflects a current interest in the figure of the abandoned woman and a strong vogue for such Ovidian confessions. The historic poet Sappho, who flourished in the sixth century B.C. on the Aegean island of Lesbos, had already acquired a legendary status. Her supposed death by flinging herself from a high cliff, following rejection by the boatman Phaon, had become a commonplace poetic theme.

See *TE* 1: 393–44 for the text and annotation and 1: 339–46 for a valuable introduction.

Savage, Richard (c. 1698–1743). Poet. He claimed to be the illegitimate child of the fourth Earl Rivers and the Countess of Macclesfield. According to Savage, he was disowned at birth by his mother, who subsequently married Colonel Henry Brett. The truth of this allegation has never been established, although it was given wide currency by **Giles Jacob** in his *Lives of the Poets* (1719). It was then given an immortal standing in literary history by *An Account of the Life of Mr. Richard Savage, Son of the Earl of Rivers* (1744), one of the first great biographies, written by Savage's close friend and ally in poverty, **Samuel Johnson.** Savage lived a dissolute and feckless life. An early scrape, when he was arrested for his participation in the **Jacobite rising** of 1715, did not lead him into a safer course of conduct. His *Miscellaneous Poems* were published by subscription in 1726. In fact, his poetry, including *The Wanderer* (1729), was accomplished enough to bring him some well-heeled patrons, but he generally spurned their aid. In 1723 he played without great success the title role in his tragedy *Sir Thomas Overbury.*

Things took an even worse turn in 1727, when Savage was accused together with James Gregory of killing a man named Sinclair in a tavern brawl near Charing Cross, London, and on conviction at the Old Bailey was sentenced to death by the notorious judge **Francis Page.** Early in 1728 he received a royal pardon from **Queen Caroline.** He began to write a series of annual poems in tribute to the Queen, titled *The Volunteer Laureate,* and received a pension of £50 per year from her. Despite this aid, Savage continued his feckless ways, and after the Queen's death in 1737 grew even more disturbed in his behavior. A subscription was set up to allow him to retire to a quiet haven in Wales, but he inevitably quarreled with his benefactors. He died in a debtors' jail in **Bristol**.

Savage seems to have served as AP's man in **Grub Street**. He had an unparalleled range of contacts in the literary and theatrical worlds. His friends and benefactors included **Aaron Hill**, **Eliza Haywood**, **Anne Oldfield**, **Robert Wilks**, **David Mallet**, and others far too numerous to mention. When *The Dunciad Variorum* appeared, AP's victims were quick to accuse Savage of having acted as the poet's informant, and they were undoubtedly right (see *TE* 5: xxv–xxvi). It was largely on AP's behalf that Savage wrote his cutting satire *An Author to be Lett* in 1729. After Savage's drift into terminal decline, AP did as much as anyone to support him. The poet and his friend **Ralph Allen** each donated £10 quarterly toward his assistance, but finally Savage's truculence and ingratitude wore out AP's patience. In addition, Savage had been the middle-man through whom AP had helped the young Samuel Johnson. Three letters from AP survive.

See C. Tracy, *The Artificial Bastard: A Biography of Richard Savage* (Toronto: University of Toronto Press, 1953); and R. Holmes, *Dr Johnson and Mr Savage* (London: Hodder and Stoughton, 1993). Also useful is Johnson's *Life of Savage*, ed. C. Tracy (Oxford: Clarendon, 1971).

Scheemakers, Peter (1691–1781). Flemish sculptor from Antwerp who settled in London c. 1720. He carved the **monument to Shakespeare** that was placed in Westminster Abbey (1740–41) to a design by **William Kent**. AP had been one of the main promoters of the scheme to erect a monument. Scheemakers also provided the bust for a monument to **Dryden** in the Abbey: AP was again involved in this project. He worked with **James Gibbs** on other monuments, including that for the **Duke of Buckinghamshire**. At **Stowe**, together with **Michael Rysbrack**, Scheemakers supplied busts of the leading members of the **opposition to Walpole**. It is likely that the busts of four great English poets that AP bequeathed to

George Lyttelton also came from Scheemakers's hand.

Schmitz, Robert Morell (1900–1985). Professor at Washington University, St. Louis. Known for his edited transcriptions of AP's works, namely, *Windsor Forest, 1712: A Study of the Washington University Holograph* (1952); and *Essay on Criticism, 1709: A Study of the Bodleian Manuscript Text with Facsimiles, Transcripts, and Variants* (1962). Among his bibliographical essays on AP is "The 'Arsenal' Proof Sheets of Pope's *Iliad*," *Modern Language Notes*, 74 (1959), 486–89, reprinted in *EA* 664–67.

Scriblerus Club. An informal group of like-minded friends who collaborated on a number of satiric projects. The club met regularly only for a few months in 1713–14, before the course of events separated its members after the death of **Queen Anne**. However, some of the Scriblerians continued to work on literary schemes in the following years, and something of a revival occurred briefly in 1715–18. The visits of **Jonathan Swift** to England in 1726–27 prompted another resurgence of interest in the old projects.

The members along with Swift and AP were **Dr. John Arbuthnot**, **John Gay**, **Thomas Parnell**, and the **first Earl of Oxford**. Meetings seem usually to have been held on Saturdays, commonly at the lodgings of Arbuthnot in St. James's Palace. Gay is supposed to have acted as secretary, perhaps because of his junior status (only AP was younger than he was within the group). Part of the inspiration for the club may have come from a proposal AP had floated in *The Spectator* on 14 August 1712, in which he announced his plan to publish every month "*An Account of the Works of the Unlearned*" (*Prose* 1: 62). Apart from a few trifles in verse, such as rhymed invitations to dinner, nothing is known to survive from this original phase of activity; but it is certain that a start was made on a number of satiric works that appeared in later years, notably the *Memoirs of Martin Scriblerus*. With the death of the Queen and the fall of Oxford's ministry, Arbuthnot lost his place at court, while Swift was condemned to exile in Ireland (where Parnell soon followed). Even Gay found his hopes disappointed after he returned from a diplomatic mission to Hanover. Oddly, it was AP who was least directly affected by the sudden turn in events, in part because his religion and his health had precluded official advancement. Thus it was he who became the guardian of the club's conscience, as well as its archives.

Parts of the Scriblerian enterprise first reached the outside world with items such as the collaborative drama *Three Hours after Marriage* (1716) and a number of short squibs in prose. Later full-length works such as *Gulliver's Travels* (1726), *The Art of Sinking* (1728), and *The Dunciad* (1728) had significant roots in the club's early project. In addition, the publication of the *Miscellanies* of AP and his friends from 1727 allowed several of the smaller items to appear in print, usually some years after their composition. As time took its toll on members of the group, AP was left by 1735 as the only active and competent individual surviving. It was he who superintended release of materials in successive editions of the *Miscellanies*; and he who contrived to see the *Memoirs of Martin Scriblerus* finally come before the world in 1741. Most of these items appeared anonymously, and few of the shorter works can be attributed with certainty to any one member of the club. Overall, AP was the leading presence in later years, and it is likely that he edited the works of his colleagues with some freedom before they appeared in print.

Scriblerian satire belongs to a tradition of learned wit. It satirizes pompous and pretentious writing, bogus scholarship, trifling and word-chopping criticism, and other kinds of *déformation professionelle* in the world of letters. Its inspiration comes from older writers such as Erasmus, Rabelais, and Cervantes, although Swift's own *Tale of a Tub* qualifies as a pre-Scriblerian example of Scriblerus humor.

Scudamore, Frances, Viscountess (1685–1729). She was the daughter of the fourth Lord Digby and a first cousin of AP's close friend **Robert Digby**. In 1706 she married James, third Viscount Scudamore (c. 1684–1716) and went to live at Holme Lacy, a large seventeenth-century mansion southeast of Hereford. She seems to have been on bad terms with a neighbor, Thomas Coningsby, later **Earl Coningsby**. AP is thought to have stayed at Holme Lacy more than once, though definitive proof is lacking. He certainly knew both Lady Scudamore and her daughter, also Frances (1711–50), who married the third Duke of Beaufort in 1729. This marriage ended in scandal and divorce in 1743, a fact that pained AP and his friends (see *Corr* 4: 266). Lady Scudamore subscribed to the *Iliad* and *Odyssey*, as well as to collections by **Gay**, **Prior**, and **Addison** and musical works by **Bononcini**. She figures as "decent Scudamore" in the poem *Mr. Pope's Welcome from Greece*.

Second Epistle of the Second Book of Horace, The. One of AP's *Imitations of Horace*, it was probably composed not long before its first publication on 28 April 1737. It was a folio of twenty pages, issued by **Robert Dodsley** (Griffith 447; Foxon P955). The poem consists of 327 lines in **heroic couplets**. The Latin original, of 216 lines, was printed in full, opposite the English text, only when the item entered the *Works*.

Horace addressed his verse letter to Julius Florus, a courtier. AP directs his poem to an unnamed "colonel," who has been identified as either Anthony Browne of **Abscourt** or App's Court, Surrey, or less plausibly Colonel Cotterell, a member of the **Rousham** family. The former is evidently the Hon. Colonel Browne, who subscribed to many books in this period, including the *Poems* of **Matthew Prior** in 1718. The second belonged to the family of **Sir Clement Cotterell**. The two men, Browne and Cotterell, were in fact distantly related through marriages in earlier generations. It may be that the reference should be to **James Dormer**, who owned Rousham (he was a first cousin of Sir Clement). AP sticks remarkably close to the original, bending its text in small ways with pointed allusions. Two striking passages are drawn directly from Horace, with a highly personalized effect achieved by minimal changes on AP's part. The first concerns AP's upbringing as a member of a persecuted minority, the Catholics, especially under the unsympathetic rule of **William III**, with the family "depriv'd . . . of our Paternal Cell" (ll. 58–68). The second might be described as inspired translation rather than **imitation** (ll. 246–64): AP follows Horace in the line "Heir urges Heir, like Wave impelling Wave," then brilliantly modulates into a reflection on mutability, as suggested by the estate of his friend **Lord Bathurst** (see verses quoted in **Cirencester**). This is one of AP's most distinguished renderings of Horace, in terms of applying the literal sense of the Latin to contemporary themes.

For text and commentary, see *TE* 4: 161–87. One of the fullest readings of the poem is that of A.L. Williams, "Pope and Horace: *The Second Epistle of the Second Book*," in *Restoration and Eighteenth-Century Literature: Essays in Honor of Alan Dugald McKillop*, ed. C. Camden (Chicago: University of Chicago Press, 1963), 309–21.

Second Satire of Dr. John Donne . . . Versifyed. A poem by AP, first published in the *Works* in 1735. It consists of 128 lines in **heroic couplets**. One of two satires by **Donne** that were modernized, that is, Augustanized, by AP. It is perhaps the more effective of the two, especially in a sustained attack on lawyers. Among those introduced into the satire are **Francis Charteris** and **Peter Walter**.

Long before AP had written another version of the same poem. This was probably carried out during the years of the **Harley administration**, around 1711 to 1714. It was then, according to AP, that he began to "versify" Donne's satires, at the instance of the **first Earl of Oxford** and the **Duke of Shrewsbury** (*TE* 4: 3). The manuscript of the second satire passed into the hands of the Lord Treasurer's son, the **second Earl of Oxford**, who mentioned it to AP in 1726 (*Corr* 2: 371). It remained unpublished until it was included in the **Twickenham edition** in 1939. This earlier version consists of 134 verses.

For the text of both versions, and commentary, see *TE* 4: 129–45.

Second Satire of the First Book of Horace, The. See *Sober Advice from Horace*.

Second Satire of the Second Book of Horace, The. One of AP's *Imitations of Horace*, written around March–April 1733. In fact, the poem was said to be "paraphrased," rather than "imitated," as in most cases, when it first appeared on 4 July 1734. It was issued along with the second edition of *The First Satire of the Second Book of Horace Imitated*, which had originally come out in 1733. The two poems together made a quarto of forty-two pages, "printed for L.G. [**Lawton Gilliver**]" and sold at a price of two shillings by **Anne Dodd** with Elizabeth Nutt, together with "the booksellers of London and Westminster" (Griffith 341; Foxon P961). In fact, the printer was **John Wright**. The names of the two women "mercuries" were merely a blind: Gilliver in reality no longer had the copyright for the first satire, since he had bought it for a year only, and so the rights belonged to AP himself. There was also a folio edition of thirty-eight pages. The work appeared separately in October 1734 (dated 1735), as "printed by J. Wright for L. Gilliver." Minor revisions were made when the poem went into the collected *Works* in 1735, 1739, and 1740.

AP's paraphrase consists of 180 lines of **heroic couplets**. Alongside the English text AP printed selections from the Latin original, amounting to 116 out of the full 136 lines. Horace had put the "sermon" in the voice of Ofellus, a shrewd country neighbor. In the adaptation, AP allots this eulogy of the simple life to his own sturdy friend **Hugh Bethel**. Minor adjustments were needed: Horace claims to have known Ofellus from boyhood, a touch AP omits as it was not true in respect of Bethel. The best-known passage in AP's work occurs when he describes his own brand of plain living, on his "five acres . . . of rented land." Content with little, he can "piddle" on broccoli and mutton: although he has no fancy fish on which to dine, still there are "gudgeons, flounders, what my Thames affords." In verses that struck **Matthew Arnold** as exemplifying the strengths and weaknesses of AP's style, the poet maps out the imaginative viewpoint he has attainted at **Twickenham**: "To Hounslow-heath I point, and Bansted-down, / Thence comes your mutton, and these chicks my own." The work ends with a vigorous examination of the way in which property shifts from hand to hand and concludes that it is more important to live well than to take pride in owning showy estates. In fact, AP lived a less than frugal life and did not confine his fare to local produce. He also spent freely what resources he had on the ornamentation of his house and garden. However, the satire does not profess to be a work of strict biographical accuracy.

For the text and commentary, see *TE* 4: 51–69.

Serle, John (d. 1746). Sometimes spelled "Searle or "Searl." AP's gardener. If we may trust **Edmund Curll** (usually a hazardous step), Serle had been in AP's employment "above eleven years" in 1735. He was probably a local man. After AP's death he was employed briefly by **Ralph Allen** on the gardens at **Prior Park**. He was buried at **Twickenham** on 21 February 1746, leaving a widow Sarah (d. 1783?), who may have acted as AP's housekeeper. He had three daughters, born between 1730 and 1739.

AP placed heavy reliance on Serle's horticultural skills, especially his ability in growing the newly fashionable pineapple plant. Serle may have acted as a general manservant: He is certainly "good John" who is asked to repel boarders from **Pope's villa** at the start of the *Epistle to Arbuthnot*. The high esteem in which he was held is evident from the poet's **will**: AP's bequest runs, "To my Servant, *John Searle*, who as faithfully and ably served me many Years, I give, and devise the Sum of One hundred Pounds over and above a Year's Wages to himself, and his Wife; and to the poor of the Parish of *Twickenham*, Twenty Pounds to be divided among them by the said *John Searl*; and it is my Will, if the said *John Searl*, die before me, that the same Sum go to his Wife or Children" (*Garden and City* 264–65).

In addition, AP stipulated that after the death of his residuary legatee, **Martha Blount**, a further £100 should go to Serle if he were still living. In the event, Martha Blount outlived him by many years.

Serle is named as having drawn the plans of AP's garden and **grotto**, which were published in a pamphlet titled *A Plan of Mr. Pope's Garden*, published by **Robert Dodsley** in 1745. See the edition of this work by M.R. Brownell (Los Angeles: Augustan Reprint Society, 1982). For the little that is known of Serle, see A. Beckles Willson, *Mr Pope & Others* (Twickenham: For the author, 1996), 134–35.

Settle, Elkanah (1648–1724). Poet and dramatist. Settle became City Poet in 1691; AP explains that "his office was to compose panegyricks upon the Lord Mayors, and Verses to be spoken in the Pageants: But that part of the shows being by the frugality of some Lord Mayors at length abolished, the employment of City Poet ceased; so that upon *Settle*'s demise, there was no successor to that place" (*TE* 5: 69). In the same note, AP gives a detailed account of Settle's career, from the time of his ripostes to **Dryden** a generation earlier. In a further note, AP remarks that at the time of the Popish Plot, Settle "had managed the Ceremony of a famous Pope-burning on *Nov*. 17, 1680." He continues, "After the Revolution he kept a Booth at *Bartlemew-fair*, where in his Droll call'd *St. George for England*, he acted in his old age in a Dragon of green leather of his own invention. He was at last taken into the Charterhouse, and there dyed" (*TE* 5: 183). With typical frugality, AP utilizes almost all this information in the text of *The Dunciad*.

In fact, AP had first treated Settle in a satiric tone in one of his earliest poems, *To the Author of a Poem, intituled, Successio*, which may have been written in 1702 and was published anonymously in 1712 (see *TE* 6: 15–17). There are occasional references to the elderly poet in later works. However, it was not until *The Dunciad* was written that AP found a major role for Settle to play. Here he is cast as a "Sage," corresponding to Anchises in Book 6 of the *Aeneid*, who foresees the coming triumph of

Dulness. Most of the third book of AP's poem (3: 35–356) is taken up by this prophetic vision.

Settle exactly suited AP's needs in a number of ways. (1) As an elderly man who had recently died, he corresponds to Anchises in **Virgil**'s poem and could be depicted as father of the present king of the dunces. (2) Since Dryden's day, Settle had often been treated as a figure of fun, on account of his obsequious hunt for patrons and his extreme bitterness against Catholics. (3) His work as a fairground dramatist, producing spectacles for Bartholomew Fair, aptly fitted AP's design to explore the muse of **Smithfield**. These works prefigured the tawdry farces that, AP claims, have taken over the legitimate London **theater**. (4) Settle's position as manager of the Lord Mayor Show pageants places him centrally in the action of the poem and adds to its carnivalesque dimension. (5) Settle had actually produced an elaborate "opera" on the fall of Troy, first at **Drury Lane Theatre** in 1701 and later at the fairground in 1707. **John Gay** witnessed a performance of the latter in 1726, possibly in the form of a puppet show, and described it to the **Countess of Burlington**. It is likely that either Gay or his companion at the droll, **William Kent**, told AP about this "improvement" of Virgil, as it would underpin one of the main themes of *The Dunciad*. Settle was the godfather of Alderman **John Barber**.

F.C. Brown, *Elkanah Settle: His Life and Works* (Chicago: University of Chicago Press, 1910), remains unsupplanted despite its age. For Settle's role in *The Dunciad*, see P. Rogers, "Pope, Settle and the Fall of Troy," in his *Literature and Popular Culture in Eighteenth Century England* (Brighton: Harvester, 1985), 87–101.

Seventh Epistle of the First Book of Horace, Imitated in the Manner of Dr. Swift, The. One of AP's *Imitations of Horace*, unusual in that the poet mimics **Swift**'s characteristic style throughout. It first appeared in the octavo *Works* (Griffith 507): the volume was dated "1738" but in fact not published until 1 May 1739. Revisions were made in a later reprint of this series. The date of composition is unknown.

The poem by **Horace** is a good-humored and quite short work, consisting of ninety-eight verses. AP imitates only the first forty-odd lines. The reason is that Swift had already produced his own distinctive version of the second half of the epistle, in an imitation addressed to the **first Earl of Oxford** in 1713. AP refers to the poem by Swift at the end of *his* version and gives this as a reason why he need not continue. AP mimics Swift's favorite octosyllabic couplets and takes over some authentically Swiftian feminine rhymes, such as *debtor/better*. There are comparatively few topical references in the poem, which occupies eighty-four lines. Horace had addressed his poem to Maecenas; it has been suggested that AP had **Viscount Bolingbroke** in mind, but there is no real evidence to this effect. However, there does seem to be a recollection of youthful escapades in company with the addressee, in the old days when "Belinda rais'd my Strain" (l. 50).

For text and commentary, see *TE* 4: 265–73.

Sewell, George (c. 1690–1726). Miscellaneous writer who originally practiced as a doctor in London and Hampstead. He had studied at Leiden and taken an M.D. at Edinburgh. Wrote poems, plays, translations, and pamphlets, many of them for **Edmund Curll**; others for **Bernard Lintot**. For Curll he provided a life of the poet **John Philips** (1713), frequently reprinted. It was Sewell whom Curll again employed to edit a collective translation of the **Metamorphoses** (see **Sandys's Ghost**). Produced *Observations* on **Cato** (1713) and a satiric life of AP's adversary **Thomas Burnet** (1715). Sewell edited an additional volume of poems to go with AP's **Shakespeare edition** in 1725. Altogether he was one of the abler hack writers to earn a niche in *The Art of Sinking*. AP had mentioned him in an early draft for what became the *Epistle to Arbuthnot* but took this out. It is also significant that Sewell is an absentee from *The Dunciad*. Sewell's political convictions, when the need to make money by his pen was not paramount, seem to have been Tory, but he ended up writing for **Walpole**.

Shakespeare, William (1564–1616). Shakespeare was one of the authors who presided over AP's apprenticeship as a writer, and he remained a lifelong favorite. In youth, AP had enjoyed the friendship of **Thomas Betterton**, a great Shakespearean actor who had worked in a company led by Sir William Davenant, allegedly a godson (natural son, some even said) of the bard. A few years later, AP kept a picture of Shakespeare as one of those watching over his labors in his writing room (*Corr* 1: 120); and around 1735 **Frederick, Prince of Wales** presented him with marble busts of **Spenser**, **Milton**, and **Dryden** along with one of the national poet. The inventory of the contents of **Pope's villa** after his death shows that a picture and the bust were still there. AP bequeathed the busts in his **will** to his friend **George Lyttelton**, and they are preserved at **Hagley**. They may be the work of **Peter Scheemakers**, who was responsible for the effigy in Westminster Abbey that a small group including AP caused to be set up in 1740 (see **monument to Shakespeare**). At this juncture the **opposition to Walpole** was attempting to hijack Shakespeare as a patriot and scourge of corrupt government: see M. Dobson, *The Making of a National Poet: Shakespeare, Adaptation and Authorship 1660–1789* (Oxford: Clarendon, 1992).

One of AP's friends as young man was **Nicholas Rowe** who performed two relevant functions: he wrote tragedies in imitation of Elizabethan or Jacobean playwrights, and he produced the first attempt at a critical edition of Shakespeare in 1709. AP used the second edition of Rowe's work as the basis of the text he himself prepared and took over his friend's life of the dramatist. It is likely that AP, as a regular theater-goer, saw a number of productions of Shakespeare, including adaptations and burlesques, but this cannot be fully documented. Certainly he made great play with the spectacular performances of *Henry VIII* that **Colley Cibber** and **Barton Booth** mounted at **Drury Lane Theatre** in 1727 (see *TE* 4: 223).

AP claimed to have owned a copy of the First Folio of 1623 (which he misdated 1621), but this has disappeared. The only known to survive from his **library** is a late edition of *Othello*. He sought out early quartos when he was preparing his **Shakespeare edition** and made some halfhearted efforts to collate early texts. However, it could never have been as a textual editor that AP was likely to shine: his prejudices against minute editorial adjustments were too strong, as his battle with **Lewis Theobald** showed all too clearly. Nor does his habit of relegating "low" passages to the status of footnotes accord well with modern attitudes toward scholarship in this field. However, his preface shows a warm and genuine appreciation of the plays and has earned him a creditable place in the history of Shakespeare criticism.

It is harder to gauge the degree and nature of the influence on AP's own writing. There are many quotations from Shakespeare in his letters and several stories dealing with the dramatist, especially his relations with **Ben Jonson**, in the ***Anecdotes*** collected by his friend **Joseph Spence**. However, direct allusions in the poetry are scattered quite sparsely. The most indicative occur in the ***Epistle to Augustus***, where AP uses Shakespeare as the embodiment of "the Tragic spirit" and wrote two couplets that sum up the Augustan response to the Elizabethan climate for literature:

> Shakespear, (whom you and ev'ry Play-house bill
> Style the divine, the matchless, what you will)
> For gain, not glory, wing'd his roving flight,
> And grew Immortal in his own despight. (*TE* 4: 199)

A characteristic touch of wit is used to inflect the subtitle of *Twelfth Night*, "what you will." Nevertheless, few careful readers of AP will doubt that Shakespeare remained a pervasive presence. There are subtle recollections of *A Midsummer Night's Dream* in ***The Rape of the Lock*** and ***The Dunciad***; glancing allusions to *Hamlet* in several poems, notably the ***Elegy to the Memory of an Unfortunate Lady***; and repeated signs of a deep intimacy with the plays in ***An Essay on Man***—see, for example, the refashioning of Jaques's famous speech from *As You Like It* in Epistle 2, ll. 275–82 (*TE* 3.i: 88). For that matter, the ruminations of Duke senior in the last-named play seems to have informed the portrait of the hermit-philosopher in *Windsor-Forest*, modeled in part on **Sir William Trumbull**. Close study of the poems suggests that Shakespeare was seldom very far removed from AP's imagination.

Shakespeare edition. AP's edition appeared in six quarto volumes on 12 March 1725 as *The Works of Shakespear... Collated and corrected by the former Editions, By Mr. Pope*. The publisher was **Jacob Tonson senior**, and the price to subscribers five guineas (£5.25) for an unbound set (Griffith 149). A seventh volume, containing the nondramatic works, was issued at the same time: It was edited by **George Sewell**, and AP had no hand in this part of the undertaking. A reprint with a small subscription list was published in Dublin in 1726. There were various reprints from 1728 onward.

From an early age AP had taken a great interest in **Shakespeare**. He embarked on the edition around 1721. On 21 October of that year he placed an advertisement in the *Evening Post*, requesting that anyone with "old Editions" would get in touch with Tonson. On 18 November Mist's *Weekly Journal* carried a statement that "The celebrated Mr. Pope is preparing a correct Edition of Shakespear's Works; that of the late Mr. Rowe being very faulty." AP's friend **Nicholas Rowe** had produced his edition in 1709. This had been the first independent effort to produce a critical text and contained the fullest biography of Shakespeare up to that date.

It is clear from AP's correspondence that he set out with the intention of producing a scholarly performance. He consulted his friends, sought out the advice of interested persons such as **William Cheselden**, and reclaimed an early copy (perhaps the third folio of 1663–64) he had lent to **Francis Atterbury**. However, he had other irons in the fire, notably his translation of the *Odyssey* and an edition of the works of the **Duke of Buckinghamshire**. He found "the dull duty of an editor" a restricting task and sought help from others. His friend **John Gay** and his collaborator on the **Homer** translation, **Elijah Fenton**, were both paid sizable

sums by Tonson for their aid; while an unknown "man or two here at Oxford" was recruited to "ease [AP] of part of the drudgery of Shakespear" and paid £35 (*Corr* 2: 81). By 31 October AP could report to **William Broome** that "Shakespeare is finished. I have just written the preface," and he anticipated speedy publication (*Corr* 2: 270)—but there were more delays.

There is another reason why AP displayed less energy for this task than for most of the others he embarked on. It lies in the fact that the entire operation was conducted for the benefit of Tonson. AP himself received £217 12s. (£217.60), a sum that fell far short of the amount he cleared for the Homer translations. The subscription was announced in November 1724, with a cutoff date given as 16 December. A list of the subscribers already committed was printed, but the results were disappointing enough for Tonson to place a further advertisement on 18 January 1725. The ultimate tally of 411 names was moderate in size, but it was far lower in social distinction than the lists for the Homer translations, as well as one third smaller in number. There were also fewer multiple subscriptions entered by individuals. Among other things, this reflects AP's unwillingness to mount the intense personal campaign that he had waged on behalf of his own subscription ventures.

Some of the defects of AP's editing were pointed out by a better Shakespearean scholar, **Lewis Theobald**, in a book titled *Shakespeare Restored: Or, A Specimen of the Many Errors, as well Committed, as Unamended, by Mr. Pope in his Late Edition of this Poet*, published in March 1726. Theobald knew more of the background in Elizabethan drama than did AP and was more accurate in his references. In fact, AP set out the duties of an editor reasonably well in his preface; unfortunately, he was more capricious in his handling of textual matters than his claims would suggest. Moreover, he had little to add to Rowe on the biography. AP was forced to acknowledge the justice of some of Theobald's points, and without much grace he adopted some of the improvements into a second edition, which came out in 1728. But he had a more effective way of humiliating his critics. It was in the same year that the first version of *The Dunciad* appeared, with "Tibbald" enthroned as the principal laureate of dulness. Even though Theobald brought out his own, rather better, edition of Shakespeare in 1733, much of the damage had been done, and it has taken him almost three centuries to regain some of his reputation.

AP's taste was essentially that of his contemporaries, and he looked for the things in Shakespeare that Augustans admired: eloquent moralistic speeches, touches of pathos, high rhetorical gloss. He showed some independence in raising plays that were then unpopular, but he offended readers of later generations by his habit of signalizing "the most shining passages" with marginal stars. The most lasting achievement of the edition is to be found in AP's preface, a warm tribute to the dramatist's originality, humanity, and emotional power. It remains one of the essential documents in the history of Shakespeare's reputation.

There is no critical edition of AP's undertaking. The preface has been edited on several occasions, most adequately in *Prose* 2: 3–40. Important critical studies are J. Butt, *Pope's Taste in Shakespeare* (London: Shakespeare Association, 1935); J.R. Sutherland, "The Dull Duty of an Editor," *Review of English Studies*, 21 (1845), 202–15, reprinted in *EA* 675–94; P. Dixon, "Pope's Shakespeare," *Journal of English and Germanic Philology*, 63 (1964), 191–203; and J.A. Hart, "Pope as Scholar-Editor," *Studies in Bibliography*, 23 (1970), 45–59.

Shepherd's Week, The. A sequence of six pastoral poems by **John Gay**, published in April 1714. They were dedicated in a verse prologue to **Viscount Bolingbroke**, which contains references to the **Treaty of Utrecht** and (in advance of its occurrence) the death of **Queen Anne**. According to AP, it was to the conduct of **Ambrose Philips** that "the world owes" *The Shepherd's Week* (*Corr* 1: 229). In fact, this work extends the satire on Philips that AP had initiated with his essay on pastoral in an issue of *The Guardian* in April 1713. Gay brings pastoral down to earth by exaggeration of the naïveté of Philips's poems, pushing their "realism" into awkward bucolic language and scenes.

Sherborne. Estate in Dorset. Built by Sir Walter Ralegh in 1594, not far from a Norman house known as "Old" Sherborne Castle. Bought by the Digby family in 1617 and still owned by their descendants. In the 1620s wings were added to Ralegh's rectangular building. During the Civil War the old castle was reduced to a ruin by the Parliamentary troops. The medieval deer park was developed in the seventeenth century in the area between "old" and "new" castles. In AP's day the castle was owned by the **fifth Baron Digby**. His son **Robert Digby** carried out extensive modifications with the advice of AP, then Lancelot "Capability" Brown redesigned much of the park in the 1770s.

AP and Digby had many contacts before the poet visited Sherborne in June 1724, having planned (but probably not made) a visit in 1722. In a letter to **Martha Blount** on 22 June he gave his most detailed description of any garden. He responded to the charm of the natural setting with its hills and woods, the "romantic" quality of the ruins, the proximity of the historic town of Sherborne with its impressive abbey, and most of all the sense of unity amid all the irregularities of the site. One feature is a rustic arbor now known as Pope's Seat. AP obviously gave his friend some ideas for further improvements, and work proceeded until Digby's early death in 1726. This event "spelled the premature end of a potentially influential partnership with Pope in the landscape movement" (Peter Martin).

See *Gardening World* 95–118.

Sherburn, George (Wiley) (1884–1962). Professor at Chicago, Columbia, and Harvard Universities. One of the most important figures in the history of Popian scholarship. Among his major contributions was *The Early Career of Alexander Pope* (Oxford, 1934; reprint, New York: Russell and Russell, 1963), a detailed and astute account that supplanted all earlier works on this subject. It carries the story of

AP's life as far as 1726 and contains an important introductory study of earlier biographers of AP. Even more significant in the development of Popian studies was his edition of *The Correspondence of Alexander Pope*, 5 vols. (Oxford: Clarendon, 1956). This was supplemented by an article, "Letters of Alexander Pope, Chiefly to Sir William Trumbull," *Review of English Studies*, 9 (1958), 388–406. It remains the first port of call for any student of AP's life, gathering together by far the most complete and fully edited collection of the letters that has ever been undertaken. He edited *the Best of Pope* (New York: Nelson, 1929). Sherburn also wrote several important articles on AP that deserve to be collected. A classic example is "Pope at Work," in *Essays on the Eighteenth Century Presented to David Nichol Smith* (Oxford: Clarendon, 1945), 49–64. See also his essay on "The *Dunciad*, Book IV," *Texas Studies in Literature and Language*, 24 (1944), 174–90, reprinted in *EA* 730–46. He was the author of studies of Samuel Richardson, **Fielding**, **Swift** and **Johnson** and a well-known survey of the literary history of the eighteenth century. He is commemorated in a notable Festschrift titled *Pope and His Contemporaries*, ed. J.L. Clifford and L.A. Landa (Oxford: Clarendon, 1949), which contains several major items on AP and his circle.

Shirley, Lady Frances (c. 1706–78). She was one of ten children of the first Earl Ferrers (1650–1718) and his second wife Selina Finch (c. 1681–1762): by his first wife Ferrers had fathered seventeen children. The Earl acquired the Heath Lane Lodge estate in **Twickenham** in 1714, along with an adjoining meadow leading down to the river two years later. This meadow remained open, and no building occurred there until long after AP's death. During her widowhood the Dowager Countess lived at the Lodge, a short distance north of the Cross Deep neighborhood where **Pope's villa** stood. She built c. 1718–20 a grand domed summer house of brick, with stone dressings, near the southern edge of the estate, which bordered the poet's own garden. It is possible that this building was based on designs by **James Gibbs**. The Lodge itself was demolished c. 1781.

Lady Fanny continued to live at the Lodge until her own death. She had a close liaison with the **Earl of Chesterfield**, whose brother occupied the villa after AP died, and she was a friend of **Martha Blount**. AP certainly knew her well. She figures in the poem *On Receiving from the Right Hon. the Lady Frances Shirley a Standish and Two Pens*.

For the Shirley family in Twickenham, see A. Beckles Willson, *Mr Pope & Others* (Twickenham: For the author, 1996).

Shrewsbury, Charles Talbot, first Duke of (1660–1718). Statesman. Shrewsbury is an enigmatic figure, and little is known about his dealings with AP, although they may have been quite extensive.

Generally regarded as a lukewarm Whig, Shrewsbury held both court and political offices under **William III** and **Queen Anne**. In 1709 he became Lord Chamberlain, and in that role he did nothing to resist the Tory coup of 1710. In 1712 he was involved in the negotiations for the **Treaty of Utrecht** as ambassador to France; and in 1713 he served as Lord Lieutenant of Ireland. Just before the death of the Queen, he was appointed Lord Treasurer (the last holder of this historic post) and helped to usher in the **Hanoverian accession**. After this he went back into retirement. His family was divided between Protestant and Catholic loyalties, while his own second wife Adelhida (d. 1726) was at once Italian, Catholic, volatile, and politically engaged. She was a Lady of the Bedchamber to the Princess of Wales, later **Queen Caroline**.

AP may first have met Shrewsbury through **William Walsh**. Certainly he was "soon introduc'd" into the Duke's acquaintance (*Anecdotes* 2: 616). Around 1716 AP sent his friend a copy of *The Universal Prayer*. The Duke asked AP to write his versions of **John Donne** (*TE* 4: 3). The only recorded visit by AP occurred in 1717; this was probably at a small riverside house at Isleworth (now demolished), which was later remodeled by **James Gibbs** for the Duke's successor. The new owner, George Talbot, "fourteenth" Earl (d. 1733), assumed the title in place of his elder brother Gilbert (d. 1743), who was a Catholic priest. AP almost certainly knew the fourteenth Earl, a relatively close neighbor.

Almost the only surviving evidence of the relations between the two men comes in AP's poetry. In the *Epistle to Arbuthnot*, he refers to the encouragement he received as a young writer from a group of aristocrats including "the Courtly *Talbot*." In the *Epilogue to the Satires*, AP mentions his friend as an example of principled retirement from public life: "I study'd SHREWSBURY, the wise and great" (*TE* 4: 105, 317). A portrait was hung in AP's house (*Garden and City* 245).

See D.H. Somerville, *The King of Heart: Charles Talbot, Duke of Shrewsbury* (London: Allen and Unwin, 1962).

"Sir Plume." Character in *The Rape of the Lock*. See **Sir George Browne**.

Sitwell, Dame Edith (1887–1964). Poet. Her prose works included a novel about **Jonathan Swift** titled *I Live Under a Black Sun* (1937). Her biography *Alexander Pope* (1930) was an effort to rehabilitate AP from belated Victorian attitudes and contains much sympathetic and evocative writing. It makes no pretense to scholarship.

Six Maidens, The. A short poem in quatrains, rhyming AABB. The autograph **manuscript**, untitled, was discovered by **Norman Ault** in the Portland papers and first printed in *New Light* 276–80. The title supplied by the editor refers to Windsor Castle. The subject is **Frederick, Prince of Wales** and his flirtations with six **maids of honor** in the retinue of **Queen Caroline**. They include the notorious Anne Vane (1705–36). A plausible dating is around 1732. AP has his usual fun with puns, proverbs, and biblical allusions. See *TE* 6: 341–43.

Sixth Epistle of the First Book of Horace Imitated, The. One of the series of *Imitations of Horace*, it was first published by **Lawton Gilliver** around 24 January 1738. It was a folio of twenty pages, dated "1737" on the title page

(Griffith 476; Foxon P965), price one shilling. The printer was **John Wright**. Minor changes were made in the version included in a quarto volume of the Horatian poems published later in 1738. The poem contains 133 lines of **heroic couplets**, compared with 68 lines in the Latin original.

The poem is addressed to **William Murray**, the great lawyer who later became Lord Chancellor Mansfield. (Nothing much is known about the addressee of **Horace**'s epistle, Numicius.) AP fills out the ancient poet's admonition to his friend—"wonder at nothing"—and reformulates his warning that even a wise man may be seen as crazy if he pursues virtue with excessive zeal: "The worst of Madmen is a Saint run mad." Death lies in store, and even one as eminent as Murray (as AP prophetically describes him) will one day be interred as Cicero and Clarendon have been. There is a submerged compliment here, since Murray had modeled his own oratorical style on Cicero. The most striking passages in the poem relate to the temptations afforded by wealth, gluttony, and lust—where AP is more explicit than his model, and introduces the notorious figure of the rapist **Francis Charteris**. A concluding tribute recalls **Swift**'s motto "Vive la bagatelle"(long live fun!)

For text and annotation, see *TE* 4: 235–46.

Sloane, Sir Hans (1660–1753). Doctor, naturalist, and collector. President of the Royal Society, 1717–41; President of the Royal College of Physicians, 1719–35. Created baronet, 1716. Physician to **Queen Anne** and to **George II**. He amassed a huge collection of curiosities and specimens, especially of plants, as well as a huge library. His collections went to form the basis of the British Museum in 1759; others made up part of the founding collection of the Natural History Museum in 1881.

AP mentions Sloane briefly in his work. In the *Fourth Satire of Dr. John Donne*, there is a reference to all that "*Sloane, or Woodward's* wondrous Shelves contain" (*TE* 4: 29). See also **John Woodward**. In the *Epistle to Burlington*, we learn that the miser buys to impress experts rather than his own taste, in particular "Books for Mead, and Butterflies for Sloane." AP's note reads, "Two eminent physicians; the one had an excellent Library, the other the finest collection in Europe of natural curiosities; both men of great learning and humanity"(*TE* 3.ii: 136): see also **Dr. Richard Mead**. In 1732 Sloane gave AP two stones from the Giant's Causeway, a spectacular basalt formation in Northern Ireland, for the poet's **grotto**. AP thanked him for the gift and for an invitation to undertake a "Review" of Sloane's famous collection at Chelsea (*Corr* 4: 391, 397). The tone of these letters does not suggest any intimacy. Sloane was a subscriber both to the *Iliad* and to the *Odyssey*.

E. Brooks, *Sir Hans Sloane: The Great Collector and His Circle* (London: Batchworth, 1954), is informative but cumbrous in organization. A. MacGregor, ed., *Sir Hans Sloane: Collector, Scientist, Antiquary, Founding Father of the British Museum* (London: British Museum, 1994), presents various facets of Sloane's career.

Smedley, Jonathan (1671–1729). Irish clergyman and author. Dean of Killala, 1718, and of Clogher, 1724. A virulent critic first of **Swift** and later of AP. He eventually left for India but died on the voyage. Smedley was a strong Whig who owed his preferment to Viscount Townshend. Swift responded to the taunts of "that rascal Smedley" in a number of poems, including *A Letter from Dean Swift to Dean Smedley* (1725). As regards AP, Smedley began his assaults in 1721, but it was his savage imitation of the *Miscellanies*, titled *Gulliveriana* (1728), that occasioned AP's desire for a riposte (see Guerinot 144–48; and *Corr* 2: 523). The result was an extended role in *The Dunciad*, in the mud-diving games that occupy much of Book 2. Smedley eventually emerges from the slime beneath the Thames and describes how he encountered dunces of the past among the poisonous vapors of the London sewers running along channels like the **Fleet Ditch**.

Smith, David Nichol (1875–1962). Scholar who taught at Oxford University. He is chiefly known for his books and editions involving **Swift** and **Johnson** as well as the *Oxford Book of Eighteenth-Century Verse*, which he edited in 1926. However, he discussed AP in works like *Some Observations on Eighteenth Century Poetry* (1937); and *Shakespeare in the Eighteenth Century* (1928). AP's "preface" to the **Shakespeare edition** is reprinted in *Eighteenth Century Essays on Shakespeare*, ed. Smith (1903; rev. ed., 1963). An item of great use to students of AP is the collection of letters from **Thomas Burnet** to **George Duckett**, which Smith edited in 1914. See *Essays on the Eighteenth Century Presented to David Nichol Smith* (Oxford: Clarendon, 1945; reprinted, New York: Russell & Russell, 1963), which contains some excellent pieces on AP and his contemporaries.

Smithfield. The area known as West Smithfield, north of the historic city of London, contained a large open space used for tournaments and markets. From 1123 to 1855, Bartholomew's Fair was held here on St. Bartholomew's Day (24 August). It was originally a cloth fair, but in the sixteenth century it became a pleasure fair lasting two weeks. The area was also the main horse and cattle market from 1150 until 1855. Finally, it was a place of execution for 400 years, with both Catholic and Protestant martyrs hanged or burned there.

AP mentions the "Smithfield muses" at the start of *The Dunciad*, referring to the low fairground "drolls" performed annually at the show. A note describes the process by which "Shews, Machines, and Dramatical Entertainments, formerly agreeable only to the Rabble" had recently been transferred to the "polite" West End stage (*TE* 5: 60). In Book 3 of the poem, a leading role is given to **Elkanah Settle**, who specialized in Smithfield shows such as "St George for England" (*TE* 5: 183). He lived in the Charterhouse, almost adjoining the fairground.

Jonathan Swift had also made free use of the associations of Smithfield. His *Description of a City Shower* culminates in a flood sweeping down through Smithfield and carrying along with it "sweepings from Butchers Stalls, Dung, Guts and Blood."

A venerable work by H. Morley, *Memoirs of Bartholomew Fair* (London: Warne, 1859; reprint, Detroit: Singing Tree Press, 1968), supplies abundant background to AP's use of the area.

Sober Advice from Horace. This was the name given to one of the *Imitations of Horace*, when it first appeared on 21 December 1734 (Griffith 347; Foxon P968). It was a folio of twenty-four pages, price one shilling: Latin and English verses face each other on opposite pages, with each of the two pages numbered alike. The title read in full: *Sober Advice from Horace, to the Young Gentlemen about Town. As Deliver'd in his Second Sermon. Imitated in the Manner of Mr. Pope.* Yet more followed: "Together with the Original Text, as Restored by the Revd. R. Bentley, Doctor of Divinity. And some Remarks on the Version." The work was anonymous and undated, with the publisher listed as T. Boreman, one of four booksellers who acquired the copyright, allegedly for the sum of £60. An unsigned dedication was addressed to AP himself. Another edition appeared, perhaps in 1735. The poem was reissued in 1738 by **Thomas Cooper** as *A Sermon against Adultery*. In May 1739 it went into the *Works*, with some revisions and the spoof scholarship directed against Bentley removed. The title was altered to *The Second Satire of the First Book of Horace. Imitated in the Manner of Mr. Pope.* On account of its scabrous contents, the item was left out of eighteenth- and nineteenth-century editions of AP.

Composition is usually assigned to the summer of 1734, though it may have been started earlier. On 27 June **Bolingbroke** reported to **Swift** that AP had sent him a copy of the work, in which the poet chose "rather to weaken the images than to hurt chaste ears overmuch." Duplicitously AP told friends such as **John Caryll senior** that the item should not be taken as his, since it would seem "a very indecent Sermon" in the wake of the *Essay on Man* (*Corr* 3: 413–14, 447). AP took a calculated risk in modeling his work on one of **Horace**'s most openly erotic satires. The English version runs to 178 lines in **heroic couplets**. The Latin text printed alongside consists of 134 lines. Unusually AP actually used Bentley's edition of Horace (1711), perhaps in order to give added plausibility to his takeoff of the great scholar's manner.

A marked feature of the original is an abundance of proper names, and AP displays considerable ingenuity in finding local equivalents. Thus, at the start, he replaces the Roman example (a singer called Tigellius) with the celebrated actress **Anne Oldfield**: an obtuse note by "Bentley" is inserted drawing attention to this change of gender. Similarly the grasping Fufidius becomes "Fufidia," a cover for the identity of **Lady Mary Wortley Montagu**. Overall it is a boisterous and high-spirited performance, full of double entendre and racy allusion, closer to Rochester's poetry than is most of AP's satire.

For text and commentary, see *TE* 4: 71–89. See also L. Moskovit, "Pope's Purposes in *Sober Advice*," *Philological Quarterly*, 44 (1965), 195–99.

Somers, John, Baron (1651–1716). Lawyer and politician. A member of the Whig Junto. A successful barrister who was made Solicitor-General and knighted in 1689, after taking a prominent role in the ousting of James II in favor of **William III**. Lord Keeper, 1693; Lord Chancellor, 1697–1700. Lost power during the reign of **Queen Anne** but returned as Lord President of the Council in 1708–10.

He was a considerable figure in the culture of the age and one of the original members of the **Kit-Cat Club**. President of the Royal Society, 1698–1703. He was a noted patron of literature, with a large collection of books. **Jonathan Swift** dedicated *A Tale of a Tub* (1704) to Somers, one of many such addresses he received. He also supported **Joseph Addison** and **William Congreve**. Not long before his death he subscribed to the *Iliad*. He was one of those who, AP claims, saw the poet's *Pastorals* in **manuscript** and gave advice (*TE* 1: 59). AP refers gratefully to this encouragement both in the *Epistle to Arbuthnot*, l. 139, and in the *Epilogue to the Satires*, 2: 77. It does not appear that he knew Somers as intimately as did some of the other writers mentioned, but he evidently remained proud of the connection.

See W.L. Sachse, *Lord Somers: A Political Portrait* (Manchester: Manchester University Press, 1975).

Southcott, Thomas (1671–1748). Also spelled "Southcote." Benedictine father. He was the son of Sir John Southcott and educated at Douai. His sister married **John Stafford-Howard**. Sent on a mission to England, he began to collect funds for the Stuart cause around the time of the **Jacobite rising** of 1715–16. President-General in the General Chapter at Douai, 1721–41.

A friend and adviser to young AP, he came to the aid of the teenage poet when a breakdown was threatened by excess of study and lack of exercise. Southcott persuaded the famous physician **Dr. John Radcliffe** to review AP's symptoms and returned to **Binfield** with detailed instructions. AP was soon restored to health. In return, he was able to help in 1728 when Southcott, who had long been settled in France, sought to become head of the Abbey of St. André, at Villeneuve-lès-Avignon. AP intervened with **Robert Walpole**, and the appointment was approved (see *Anecdotes* 2: 615). This was surprising since Southcott had long been an embarrassment to the English government, because of his activities on behalf of the **Pretender**. Southcott held the abbot's post in absentia and lived at Cambrai in Flanders. He had again been one of the principal agents raising money for the **Jacobites** in the years leading up to the **Atterbury plot**. It is natural that Southcott was a supporter of the subscription campaign for AP's translations of **Homer** since the two fund-raising exercises seem to have overlapped at times. Southcott had also come to the assistance of **John Caryll senior** when AP's friend was attacked in the press.

See Abbot Geoffrey, "Thomas Southcott 1671–1748," *English Benedictine History Commission*, Symposium 2002, 1–5.

Southerne, Thomas (1660–1746). Dramatist who emerged in the early 1680s and was still active half a century later. His best-known work was probably *Oroonoko* (1696), a commercially successful dramatization of Aphra Behn's novel that long held the stage. He was a friend of both **Dryden** and **Congreve**. One of the early supporters of AP, he was named among the group of mentors who advised the young poet on the composition of his *Pastorals*. It was Southerne who named the budding writer "the little nightingale." It is probable that he came into AP's orbit through his connections with **Sir William Trumbull**. He receives a brief mention in the *Epistle to Augustus*. Though **William Broome** told AP in 1725 that Southerne's laurels "were withered with extreme age" and that "his fire is abated" (*Corr* 2: 358), AP continued to recall his help with gratitude. Two poems reflecting AP's interest are an epigram "In Behalf of Mr. Southerne," addressed to the **Duke of Argyll** in 1719 (*TE* 6: 214–15), and verses on "Tom Southerne's Birthday Dinner at Lord Orrery's," commemorating the old man's eighty-second birthday in February 1742 (*TE* 6: 398–99). AP can hardly have suspected that Southerne would outlive him by two years.

J.W. Dodds, *Thomas Southerne, Dramatist* (New Haven, CT: Yale University Press, 1933), is now a little antiquated.

South Sea Bubble. A major financial crisis in Britain brought about by the giddy inflation of stock prices and then their collapse over the summer of 1720. Prices had risen to 1,050 on 24 June but rapidly plummeted in September and October, falling below 200 by the end of the year. Thousands of investors, as well as annuitants and creditors, lost heavily in the process. A rescue operation was belatedly mounted, with an example made of a few obviously guilty directors who lacked political shelter in the storm; but others escaped, and **Robert Walpole** was able to take advantage of the confusion to achieve unchallenged power.

The South Sea Company had been formed in 1711 with Robert Harley, **first Earl of Oxford**, as its chief promoter and governor. It had been designed as a Tory counterforce to the Whig

Bank of England: It was not able to engage at any serious level in trade in Spanish America, as had been confidently proclaimed at the outset, and it became in effect a stock-jobbing operation. After the collapse, it became apparent that corruption had existed at the top of the company (with the King himself now serving as governor) and that many leading politicians had bought and sold stock in return for favors or influence. **Swift** was an early investor in the company and seems to have emerged without serious loss, although he railed bitterly against the course that the company had pursued under the Hanoverian regime. By contrast, **John Gay** lost most of the profit of £1,000 he had just gained by his subscription volume of *Poems*. AP himself had bought shares valued at £500 when the price stood at £113 in August 1719. He is thought to have sold a large tranche of shares in July 1720, in time to reap the benefits of the price offered at the top of the market; but he evidently went into the market again later and lost money. His judgment was probably affected by close friendship with **James Craggs junior**, one of the senior politicians most deeply implicated in the affair.

AP alludes obliquely to the episode in several of his poems. The most direct treatment occurs in the *Epistle to Bathurst*, which contains a full-scale assault on the prime architect of the bubble, **Sir John Blunt**. "An Inscription upon a Punch-Bowl" (1720) is a witty **epigram** on South Sea investment, probably but not certainly by AP (*TE* 6: 224–25).

See J. Carswell, *The South Sea Bubble*, rev. ed. (Stroud: Sutton, 2001). For AP's involvement, financial and literary, see H. Erskine-Hill, "Pope and the Financial Revolution," in *Writers and Their Background: Alexander Pope*, ed. P. Dixon (London: Bell, 1972), 200–229; and C. Nicholson, *Writing and the Rise of Finance: Capital Satires of the Early Eighteenth Century* (Cambridge: Cambridge University Press, 1994).

Spectator, The. Perhaps the most influential periodical paper in English literature, it ran for 555 issues on six days a week from 1 March 1711 until 6 December 1712. There was a brief and less successful revival in 1714. It focused less on news than on the manners and social concerns of the day. Most issues were written by either **Joseph Addison** or **Richard Steele**. The contributions of Addison are now the most highly regarded, especially his pioneering essays in literary criticism, dealing with topics such as *Paradise Lost*, popular ballad poetry, and the role of the imagination in responses to works of art. At this time Addison and AP were on good terms, and the paper included on 20 December 1711 a warm commendation of the recently published *Essay on Criticism*. AP acknowledged this in a letter to Addison dated 10 October 1714 (*Corr* 1: 263–64).

Two contributions have long been recognized as coming from the pen of AP. These are the poem ***Messiah***, which appeared anonymously in issue no. 378 on 14 May 1712; and a letter to Steele, also anonymous, which came out in issue no. 532 on 10 November 1712. Other certain attributions are an unsigned letter to Steele, included in no. 406 (16 June 1712); and a poem in imitation of **Edmund Waller**, titled "On a Fan," which was printed in no. 527 (4 November 1712). A further nine pieces were attributed to AP by **Norman Ault**: see *Prose* 1: xxxiii–lv. These remain conjectural.

See *The Spectator*, ed. D.F. Bond, 5 vols. (Oxford: Clarendon, 1965).

Spence, Joseph (1699–1768). Author, clergyman, friend of AP, and collector of literary anecdotes. Educated at Winchester school and Oxford. Ordained, 1726. Published an *Essay on Pope's Odyssey* in two parts (1726–27). Professor of Poetry at Oxford, 1728–38. Traveled with the Earl of Middlesex on a **Grand Tour** of Europe. Obtained the undemanding Regius Professorship of Modern History at Oxford, 1742. Prebendary of Durham, 1758. His most important books were *Polymetis* (1747), an investigation of classical mythology, and *Crito: A Dialogue on Beauty* (1761). He took under his wing some peasant poets, most notably **Stephen Duck**, whose life he wrote in 1731 and whom he set up in the living of Byfleet, near Spence's own home. His massive collections were used by some of AP's early biographers, including **Samuel Johnson**, but the famous *Anecdotes* did not really take shape until 1820.

When Spence wrote his work on the *Odyssey* translation, he had not yet met AP. It consisted of five dialogues, with a careful mixture of fulsome praise and judicious criticism. AP was interested by the first installment and mentioned it to **William Broome** on 10 June 1726 (*Corr* 2: 379). After this AP made inquiries regarding the author, and Spence wrote to him, with the result that they met and AP helped to revise the second installment. Spence told his friend **Christopher Pitt** that AP had shown great magnanimity in responding to the criticism. In addition, Spence's correspondence with Pitt, which was preserved by **Joseph Warton**, makes it clear that he was soon invited to **Twickenham**, and AP seems to have supported his appointment as Professor of Poetry. Thereafter, the two men spent time with each other on a regular basis, often for several days at a stretch. Among their shared preoccupations was **gardening**. Regrettably, only a handful of letters has been preserved. All the while, Spence was busy assembling his stock of Popian lore, with the ultimate aim of producing a life of the poet. It is a matter of general regret that he did not carry out this plan and instead passed on materials to **William Warburton**, who himself would relinquish the task in favor of a lesser writer (see **biographies of Pope**). Nevertheless, the collection embodies the most important single archive relating to AP, outside of the poet's own writings, and constitutes the most fully documented personal record of any major English writer, especially in his intimate moments, prior to Boswell's work on Johnson.

The only full-length biography is A. Wright, *Joseph Spence: A Critical Biography* (Chicago: University of Chicago Press, 1950). See also *Joseph Spence: Letters from the Grand Tour*, ed. S. Klima (Montreal: McGill–Queen's University Press, 1975).

Spenser, Edmund (1552–99). Poet. Spenser was an early favorite of AP, who read the *Faerie Queene* at the age of about twelve. Even at the end of his life he confirmed that he continued to read the poem with undiminished pleasure. The great "landmarks" in English poetry were easily identified as **Chaucer**, Spenser, **Milton**, and **Dryden** (*Anecdotes* 1: 19, 178, 419). A bust of the poet was placed alongside those of the two last-named, as well as **Homer**, **Newton**, and **Shakespeare**, at AP's house. In his **library** was a copy of the *Faerie Queene* (1611 edition).

Among AP's first poetic attempts were **imitations** of Spenser. One that survives is "The Alley," published in 1727 (see **early imitations of English poets**). In writing his *Pastorals*, AP took account of the *Shepheardes Calender*, and in his prefatory *Discourse on Pastoral Poetry* he allots the work measured praise (*Prose* 1: 301–2). There are further echoes of the *Faerie Queene* in **The Rape of the Lock** and in **Windsor-Forest**. However, it is perhaps in **The Dunciad** that the lasting impress of Spenser is most clearly observable. AP had originally intended to use a stanza from the opening canto of the Elizabethan epic as an epigraph to his own mock-epic, and although he abandoned this plan, there are several points in the poem where he echoes, transmutes, or parodies Spenserian effects.

See K. Williams, "The Moralized Song: Some Renaissance Themes in Pope," *ELH*, 41 (1974), 578–601.

Sporus. The name AP used for his enemy **John, Baron Hervey** in the *Epistle to Arbuthnot*, ll. 305–33, one of the most devastating passages in all satire. AP was taking the opportunity to reply to some of the attacks that Hervey and **Lady Mary Wortley Montagu** had launched against him. The name "Sporus" is borrowed from the boy whom the Emperor Nero loved and "married" in a mock-wedding (see Suetonius, *Lives of the Caesars*, "Nero," §28). The transparent allusion is to Hervey's perceived effeminacy and suspected bisexual inclinations. See *TE* 4: 117–20.

Stafford-Howard, Hon. John (d. 1714). A friend of AP who was a member of the Catholic aristocracy and connected with many families close to the poet. His father, William Howard, Viscount Stafford (1614–80), was one of the lords arrested during the Popish Plot and subsequently beheaded at Tower Hill, a martyrdom that seems to have been recalled with bitterness by **John, Lord Caryll**. William Howard was beatified in 1929. John's brother, Henry Stafford-Howard (1658–1719), was created Earl of Stafford in 1688; while his sons William (c. 1690–1734) and John Paul (1700–1762) succeeded in the earldom. His daughter Mary (d. 1765) married in 1699 Francis Plowden (d. 1712), an official in the household of James II and uncle of **William Plowden**. However, AP had "little or no acquaintance" with the second Earl (*Corr* 3: 346), probably because he lived mainly in France.

John Stafford-Howard was married first in 1682 to Mary, sister of the Benedictine father **Thomas Southcott**: she died in 1700 at St. Germain en Laye, apparently in giving birth to John-Paul. His second marriage in 1707 was to Theresia Strickland, a member of an ancient Catholic family, some of whom followed James II into exile. John's ancestral line was closely allied to that of the Dukes of Norfolk: his father was the son of the connoisseur and collector the Earl of Arundel (1585–1646), who also held the title of Earl of Norfolk.

John served as controller of the household in the court of the exiled James II to Louis XIV and later as Vice-Chamberlain to James's widow, Mary of Modena. In 1695–96 he acted as ambassador to Louis XIV, an indication of his high standing in Stuart circles. He died in Paris on 11 November 1714, but he had already been listed in the subscribers to the *Iliad*. AP, who had "obligations" toward him, told **John Caryll junior** in 1712 that he would like to make the acquaintance of his son, presumably William (*Corr* 1: 164). It seems likely that the two young men had been educated together at St. Omers College (the Jesuit academy near Calais).

St. André, Nathanael (1680–1776). Swiss-born surgeon. He came to England as a young man and possibly worked as a dancing master. He studied under a London surgeon, although he never became a member of the Company of Barber-Surgeons. Lectured on anatomy and appointed Surgeon and Anatomist to the royal household in 1723. However, he lost credibility as a result of some well-publicized misadventures. The most prominent of these was the affair of the "rabbit woman," Mary Tofts, in 1726, about which AP wrote his ballad *The Discovery* in conjunction with **William Pulteney**. St. André was considered to have been either credulous or deceptive in this episode. Also implicated in the Tofts imbroglio was his friend **Samuel Molyneux**, an MP and astronomer, who collapsed in the House of Commons in 1728 and died a few days later despite St. André's care. Two years later, the surgeon eloped with Molyneux's widow, which prompted accusations that he had poisoned his friend by administering opium with the connivance of Lady Anne Molyneux. Although St. André was able to dispel this charge in a libel suit, he could never regain favor at court or with the public.

St. André treated AP after the poet had suffered a hand injury when his coach overturned in 1726 (he may have been conveniently on hand at **Richmond**, where Molyneux lived). He ministered to the health of the **Earl of Peterborough**, a neighbor in Southampton, and seems to have socialized with AP occasionally, even after his disgrace.

Stanhope, James, first Earl (1673–1721). Soldier and statesman. A distant relative of the **Earl of Chesterfield**. Member of the **Kit-Cat Club**. One of the managers of the trial of **Dr. Henry Sacheverell** in 1710. AP writes of Stanhope's "noble Flame" in the *Epilogue to the Satires* and in a note describes him as "a Nobleman of equal courage, spirit, and learning. General in Spain [during the **War of the Spanish Succession**], and Secretary of state" (*TE* 4: 317). He was a Whig and allied to some of AP's enemies but evidently encouraged the translation of the *Iliad*, to which he subscribed.

See B. Williams, *Stanhope: A Study in Eighteenth-Century War and Diplomacy* (Oxford, Clarendon, 1932).

Stanton Harcourt. Manor house in Oxfordshire, situated not far from the Thames near

Witney, some eight miles west of the city of **Oxford**. The home of the Harcourt family since it was built in the fifteenth century. It was vacated by Lady Harcourt after the death of her husband Sir Philip in 1688, and her son (later **Viscount Harcourt**) spent most of his time at nearby Cokethorpe. The property was almost abandoned when AP came to stay in the summer and autumn of 1718, in order to work on his translation of Book 5 of the *Iliad*. In later years much of the house and outbuildings were demolished. A process of restoration began in the nineteenth century, and the house is now occupied by the family once more. There are also notable gardens of some twelve acres with a large fish pond; most of the estate was disposed of in the early twentieth century. The surviving buildings include the fifteenth-century chapel, with a tower that has come to be known as "Pope's Tower" above it, as well as the kitchen on the west side of the courtyard, and the sixteenth-century gatehouse. AP worked in one of the three rooms in the tower. It is possible that there was an earlier visit, as AP knew **Simon Harcourt** (son of the peer) at least as early as 1714. After Simon's premature death in 1720, AP wrote an **epitaph** for his tomb, which survives at the adjoining Norman parish church of St. Michael's (in the Harcourt chapel, to the south of the chancel).

AP gave a vivid if highly colored account of his surroundings at Stanton Harcourt to friends, most notably in a letter to **Lady Mary Wortley Montagu** written about September 1718 (*Corr* 1: 505–9). This is perhaps the finest comic set piece in all his correspondence. During his stay there occurred the touching episode of the **Stanton Harcourt lovers**, which afforded AP material both for letters and for brief **epigrams** in verse.

For the history of the manor, see George, third Earl Harcourt, *An Account of the Church and Remains of the Manor House of Stanton Harcourt in the County of Oxford* (Oxford: Collingwood, 1808).

Stanton Harcourt lovers. Two young people, Sarah Drew and John Hewet, engaged to be married, who were killed on 31 July 1718 while AP was staying at the home of **Viscount Harcourt**. They were sheltering in the shade of a haystack when lightning struck them in the course of one of the worst thunderstorms experienced in the area for many years. AP gave a number of accounts of the event, including a letter to **Martha Blount** on 6–9 August following, with adaptations in other letters in the following weeks, one attributed to **John Gay**: see *Corr* 1: 479–99. The most elaborately worked of these descriptions is in a letter to **Lady Mary Wortley Montagu**, dated 1 September, which contains two sets of short verses. The first was included in the *Works* from 1737. The second, designed as an **epitaph**, was first printed in a newspaper on 23 September. Originally consisting of twelve lines, it was reduced to ten by the omission of a couplet on the advice of **Francis Atterbury**. It was duly placed on the wall of the parish church at Stanton Harcourt, where it still survives, and was used in collections by **Curll** and others. It was omitted from the *Works* until 1751.

Lady Mary replied caustically to AP's message, supplying some more down-to-earth verses on the subject (*Corr* 1: 523). AP himself wrote a bawdy couplet about the lovers that survives at **Mapledurham**. Another poet to refer to the episode was **James Thomson**, in his "Summer," from *The Seasons* (1727). The story contains many of the features associated with sentimental romance: The lovers died in each other's arms, they were due to be married a week later, they were at work in the harvest fields, and so on.

For the background, see Ault 329–33; for the text and commentary, see *TE* 6: 197–201.

Stanyan, Abraham (c. 1669–1732). Diplomat and author. A cousin of **Viscount Cobham**, Whig MP and member of the **Kit-Cat Club**. Like his younger brother Temple (c. 1677–1752), he was friendly with AP; his first diplomatic post was secretary of the embassy to **Sir William Trumbull** in Constantinople. One of the brothers (probably Abraham) is mentioned in *A Farewell to London*. Abraham was a particularly close friend of **Joseph Addison**. Temple was the author of *The Grecian History*

(1707–39) and contributed to the collective translation of the *Metamorphoses* edited by **Samuel Garth**. Both subscribed to works by AP, Abraham to the *Iliad* and Temple to the **Shakespeare edition**.

Statius, The First Book of. This appeared at the head of a volume of *Miscellaneous Poems and Translations*, issued by **Bernard Lintot** on 12 May 1712 (Griffith 6). It was entitled "The First Book of Statius His Thebais." There was a second edition in 1714 and later editions subsequently. AP made some revisions when he reprinted the poem in the *Works* **(1717)**. Minor changes were introduced in later printings during AP's lifetime.

AP claimed in the "Argument" that the translation was performed "almost in his Childhood" (*TE* 1: 408). In 1717 he glossed the poem "Translated in 1703"; and on another occasion, he claimed that it was written when he was "but 14 Years old." AP sent a **manuscript** to **Henry Cromwell** for criticism, at some date around 1708 (*Corr* 1: 36). About the same time **Sir William Trumbull** was attempting to obtain for AP a copy of a French translation of the work by the scholar Claude Saumaise (Salmasius), but he was not able to do so ("New Anecdotes" 344). The reason appears to be that no such translation exists. AP may have had suggestions offered by **William Walsh**.

The poem consists of 864 lines in **heroic couplets**, in a style mainly derived from that of **John Dryden**'s later manner. It describes the journey from Thebes to Argos made by Polynices, son of Oedipus, prior to his assault on his brother Eteocles to regain the city with the seven champions of Thebes. The Latin epic was written in twelve books by Publius Papinius Statius (A.D. c. 45–c. 96) and published in A.D. 90–91. AP encountered the work of Statius at any early age and to the end of his life regarded him as "the best of all the Latin epic poets after **Virgil**" (*Anecdotes* 1: 232). AP's own copy of the works of Statius survives (*CIH* 442). It is an octavo of more than 880 pages, which was published in Leiden in 1671.

For introduction, text, and commentary, see *TE* 1: 346–52, 405–46.

St. Aubyn, Sir John (c. 1702–44). Cornish baronet. A High Tory who was MP for Cornwall, 1722–44, and may have been involved in plans prior to the **Atterbury plot**. He later joined the **opposition to Walpole**; in 1739 the **Pretender** was informed that he could raise 8,000 to 10,000 Cornishmen to take arms in a rising against the Hanoverians. A friend of **William Borlase**, **Ralph Allen**, and **William Oliver**. He visited AP's home in 1741 and dined there with the **second Earl of Oxford** near the end of the poet's life: Indeed, he thought that AP was on the point of expiring from his dropsy during the meal. There was a picture in the Great Parlour at **Pope's villa** of St. Aubyn's seat, which lay at Crowan, near Helston.

Steele, Sir Richard (1672–1729). Writer and politician. Educated at Charterhouse school and Oxford, alongside his friend and collaborator **Joseph Addison**. Served in the army and ultimately became a captain in the foot guards. First acquired a literary reputation for his stage comedies, beginning with *The Funeral* (1701). Gained favor among influential Whigs and became a member of the **Kit-Cat Club**. Appointed editor of the official *Gazette*, 1707. Initiated the hugely popular *Tatler* in 1709 and two years later with Addison started the even more influential *Spectator*. At this time he came to know AP, probably through **John Caryll senior**, and it was most likely Steele who introduced Addison to AP. After a period of good relations, AP became estranged from the Whig writers, especially when Steele's work took on a more political coloring. His periodicals *The Guardian* (1713) and *The Englishman* (1713–14), as well as pamphlets such as *The Crisis* (1714), were strongly critical of the Tory ministry, and especially of AP's friend **Jonathan Swift**. He helped to publicize the story of Alexander Selkirk's stay on the island of Juan Fernández. By this date Steele had been elected as a Whig MP, although he was briefly expelled because of his political writing.

With the **Hanoverian accession** came a dramatic revival in Steele's fortunes. He was returned to Parliament, gained a number of small posts and sinecures, and became governor of

Drury Lane Theatre. In 1715 he received a knighthood. This was the pinnacle of his achievements. Within a few years he had quarreled with Addison over the Peerage Bill of 1718; he backed what was for a time the losing faction in the Whig party; he had the Drury Lane patent withdrawn; and his long-suffering wife died. A vigorous critic of the **South Sea Bubble**. His last comedy, *The Conscious Lovers*, came out in 1722. Two years later he was forced to make a composition with his creditors, which meant that he retired to the Welsh estate of his late wife. His health was declining, and he took no further part in public life.

While the brief window of their friendship remained open, AP and Steele collaborated more than once. For example, AP wrote papers for *The Spectator* and *The Guardian*: he also contributed four items to the *Poetical Miscellanies* that Steele edited for **Jacob Tonson senior** in December 1713. It was Steele who asked AP to compose the *Ode for Musick on St. Cecilia's Day*. At this juncture AP regarded Steele as a useful ally and tried out some of his works in progress on his friend, including *The Temple of Fame*. In turn, Steele sought AP's help on some of his own projects, including a strange venture called the Censorium in rooms off the **Strand**. This was one of a number of bizarre enterprises Steele attempted to launch. After the two men had been divided by "the curse of party," there are few places in which AP mentions Steele. Like almost everyone else, he liked Steele for his ready good humor and sense of fun, while being distressed by the other's partisan zeal. See AP's letter to Caryll, 19 March 1714 (*Corr* 1: 215).

Improvident, reckless, and headstrong, he made some enemies and more friends. It is hard not to regret the circumstances that caused a rift between two men who were in most respects highly congenial. The statement recorded by **Joseph Spence**, describing Addison and Steele as "a couple of H——s" may or may not reflect a view on AP's part they were "hermaphrodites," that is, homosexual (*Anecdotes* 1: 80). The few references in AP's poetry are mostly noncommittal. Thirteen letters survive from their correspondence, all dating from 1711 and 1712. Steele was a subscriber to the *Iliad*.

The standard modern biography by C. Winton was published in two volumes: *Captain Steele: The Early Career of Richard Steele* (Baltimore: Johns Hopkins University Press, 1964); and *Sir Richard Steele M.P.: The Later Career* (Baltimore: Johns Hopkins University Press, 1970). Useful for the understanding of events that led to the split between AP and Steele is B.A. Goldgar, *The Curse of Party: Swift's Relations with Addison and Steele* (Lincoln: University of Nebraska Press, 1961). A convenient bibliographical source is C.A. Knight, *Joseph Addison and Richard Steele: A Reference Guide 1730–1991* (New York: G.K. Hall, 1994).

Steeves, Edna Leake (1909–95). Scholar who was a professor at the University of Rhode Island from 1967. She prepared a valuable edition of *The Art of Sinking in Poetry* (1952; reprint, New York, 1968): see **The Art of Sinking**. This also contains a bibliographical appendix on the *Miscellanies* written by Steeves in conjunction with **Reginald Harvey Griffith**.

Stephen, Sir Leslie (1832–1904). Critic and biographer; his first wife was a daughter of **William Makepeace Thackeray**, and by his second wife Julia he became father of the novelist Virginia Woolf and the artist Vanessa Bell. Edited the *Cornhill Magazine* from 1871 to 1882. Founder editor of *The Dictionary of National Biography* (*DNB*) from 1882; he wrote the entry on AP for this work. His studies in the age of AP began with *A History of English Thought in the Eighteenth Century*, 2 vols. (1876), and culminated in *English Literature and Society in the Eighteenth Century* (1904). In between came many entries in the *DNB* and a volume on AP for the English Men of Letters series (1880). See also "Pope as a Moralist," in *Hours in a Library*, lst series (1874). Stephen was certainly knowledgeable about the period. One difficulty with his *History*, it has been noted, was that he conceived it purely as a study of ideas: this meant that "the Pope of the *Dunciad*, *The Prologue to the Satires* and *The*

Rape of the Lock never appeared on the stage and the poet made his entry solely as the didactic author of the *Essay on Man*" (Noel Annan). In addition, Stephen was greatly affected by the discoveries of **Charles Wentworth Dilke**, concerning the poet's manipulation of his career, and came to regard him as a treacherous and insincere man. Despite this, he made great efforts to be fair to AP the author, whom he recognized as a preeminent figure in the literature of an age Stephen had made his own. "He has the courage," wrote an early critic of Stephen, "to aver that he reads the *Dunciad* with pleasure"—an admission "we notice to be rare these days."

See N. Annan, *Leslie Stephen: The Godless Victorian* (London: Weidenfeld and Nicolson, 1984).

stock quotations. Many of AP's lines have entered the language as familiar quotations, and he is the author of numerous stock phrases. He has become in fact among the most quoted poets in English. The following list provides a brief indication of some of the more familiar examples. Texts are normalized.

Where'er you walk, cool glades shall fan the glade,
Trees, where you sit, shall crowd into a shade.
(*Pastorals*, "Summer," ll. 73–74)

First follow nature, and your judgment frame,
By her just standard, which is still the same.
(*Essay on Criticism*, ll. 68–69)

A little learning is a dangerous thing,
Drink deep, or taste not the Pierian spring.
(*Essay on Criticism*, ll. 215–16)

Th' increasing prospect tires our wandering eyes,
Hills peep o'er hills, and Alps on Alps arise!
(*Essay on Criticism*, ll. 231–32)

A perfect judge will read each work of wit
With the same spirit that the author writ.
(*Essay on Criticism*, ll. 233–34)

True wit is nature to advantage dressed,
What oft was thought, but ne'er so well expressed.
(*Essay on Criticism*, ll. 297–98)

True ease in writing comes from art, not chance,
As those move easiest who have learned to dance.
(*Essay on Criticism*, ll. 363–64)

To err is human, to forgive, divine.
(*Essay on Criticism*, l. 525)

For fools rush in where angels fear to tread.
(*Essay on Criticism*, l. 625)

Where order in variety we see,
And where, though all things differ, all agree.
(*Windsor-Forest*, ll. 15–16)

And peace and plenty tell, a Stuart reigns.
(*Windsor-Forest*, l. 42)

What dire offence from am'rous causes springs,
What mighty contests rise from trivial things.
(*Rape of the Lock*, 1: 1–2)

They shift the moving toyshop of their heart.
(*Rape of the Lock*, 1: 100)

Puffs, powders, patches, bibles, billet-doux.
(*Rape of the Lock*, 1: 138)

On her white breast a sparkling cross she wore,
Which Jews might kiss, and Infidels adore.
(*Rape of the Lock*, 2: 7–8)

Belinda smiled, and all the world was gay.
(*Rape of the Lock*, 2: 52)

Whether the nymph shall break Diana's law,
Or some frail China jar receive a flaw,
Or stain her honour, or her new brocade,
Forget her prayers, or miss a masquerade,
Or lose her heart, or necklace, at a ball.
(*Rape of the Lock*, 2: 105–9)

Here thou, great Anna! Whom three realms obey,
Dost sometimes counsel take—and sometimes tea.
(*Rape of the Lock*, 3: 7–8)

The hungry judges soon the sentence sign,
And wretches hang, that jurymen may dine.
(*Rape of the Lock*, 3: 21–22)

Not louder shrieks to pitying heav'n are cast,
When husbands or when lapdogs breathe their last.
(*Rape of the Lock*, 3: 157–58)

O hadst thou, cruel! been content to seize
Hairs less in sight, or any hairs but these!
(*Rape of the Lock*, 4: 175–76)

Is it, in heav'n, a crime to love too well?
(*Elegy to Unfortunate Lady*, l. 6)

Most souls, 'tis true, but peep out once an age,
Dull sullen pris'ners in the body's cage.
(*Elegy to Unfortunate Lady*, ll. 17–18)

I will conclude by saying of Shakespeare, that with all his faults, and with all the irregularities of his drama, one may look upon his works, in comparison of those that are more finished and regular, as upon an ancient majestic piece of Gothic architecture, compar'd with a neat modern building: the latter is more elegant and glaring, but the former is more strong and more solemn.
(Preface to *Shakespeare*)

Nature, and nature's laws, lay hid in night,
God said, "Let Newton be," and all was light.
(*Epitaph on Newton*)

Consult the genius of the place in all.
(*Epistle to Burlington*, l. 57)

Another age shall see the golden ear
Imbrown the slope, and nod on the parterre,
Deep harvests bury all his pride has planned,
And laughing Ceres re-assume the land.
(*Epistle to Burlington*, ll. 173–76)

Who shall decide, when doctors disagree?
(*Epistle to Bathurst*, l. 1)

Search then the Ruling Passion: there, alone,
The wild are constant, and the cunning known.
(*Epistle to Cobham*, ll. 174–75)

Woman's at best a contradiction still.
(*Epistle to a Lady*, l. 270)

A mighty maze, but not without a plan.
(*Essay on Man*, 1: 6)

Hope springs eternal in the human breast.
(*Essay on Man*, 1: 95)

Lo! The poor Indian, whose untutor'd mind
Sees Gods in clouds, or hears them in the wind.
(*Essay on Man*, 1: 99–100)

Why has not man a microscopic eye?
For this plain reason, man is not a fly.
(*Essay on Man*, 1: 193–94)

Or quick effluvia darting through the brain,
Die of a rose in aromatic pain.
(*Essay on Man*, 1: 199–200)

The spider's touch, how exquisitely fine!
Feels at each thread, and lives along the line.
(*Essay on Man*, 1: 217–18)

One truth is clear, "Whatever is, is right."
(*Essay on Man*, 1: 294)

Know then thyself, presume not God to scan;
The proper study of mankind is man.
(*Essay on Man*, 2: 1–2)

The glory, jest, and riddle of the world!
(*Essay on Man*, 2: 18)

For forms of government, lets fools contest;
Whate'er is best administer'd is best.
(*Essay on Man*, 3: 303–4)

A wit's a feather, and a chief a rod;
An honest man's the noblest work of God.
(*Essay on Man*, 4: 247–48)

Mark by what wretched steps their glory grows,
From dirt and sea-weed as proud Venice rose.
(*Essay on Man*, 4: 291–92)

Say, shall my little bark attendant sail,
Pursue the triumph, and partake the gale?
(*Essay on Man*, 4: 385–86)

Thou wert my guide, philosopher, and friend.
(*Essay on Man*, 4: 390)

As yet a child, nor yet a fool to fame,
I lisp'd in numbers, for the numbers came.
(*Epistle to Arbuthnot*, ll. 127–28)

To help me through this long disease, my life.
(*Epistle to Arbuthnot*, l. 132)

Damn with faint praise, assent with civil leer,
And without sneering, teach the rest to sneer.
Willing to wound, and yet afraid to strike,
Just hint a fault, and hesitate dislike.
(*Epistle to Arbuthnot*, ll. 201–4)

Who breaks a butterfly upon a wheel?
(*Epistle to Arbuthnot*, l. 308)

Yet let me flap this bug with gilded wings,
This painted child of dirt, that stinks and stings.
(*Epistle to Arbuthnot*, ll. 309–10)

And he himself one vile antithesis.
(*Epistle to Arbuthnot*, l. 325)

Ask you what provocation I have had?
The strong antipathy of good to bad.
(*Epilogue to the Satires*, 2: 197–98)

Yes, I am proud; I must be proud to see
Men not afraid of God, afraid of me.

(*Epilogue to the Satires*, 2: 208–9)

Where Bentley late tempestuous wont to sport,
In troubled waters, but now sleeps in port.

(*Dunciad*, 4: 201–2)

To happy convents, bosomed deep in vines,
Where slumber abbots, purple as their wines.

(*Dunciad*, 4: 301–2)

Lo! Thy dread empire, Chaos, is restored;
Light dies before thy uncreating word:
Thy hand, great Anarch! Lets the curtain fall,
And universal darkness buries all.

(*Dunciad*, 4: 653–56)

I am his Highness' dog at Kew;
Pray tell me, sir, whose dog are you?

(*Epigram on the Collar of a Dog*)

Stonor, Thomas (1677–1724). Member of an ancient Catholic family who owned both Stonor and Watlington Park in Oxfordshire. His mother Lady Mary Stonor was a sister of the **Duke of Shrewsbury**. His second wife Winifred (d. 1722), whom he married in 1705, was descended from the Browne family of Sussex and was a granddaughter of Viscount Montague (see **Sir George Browne**). Both husband and wife were fined as recusants at **Oxford** in 1707: two years earlier each of their main properties was searched for arms in a clamp-down on Catholics. Thomas's brother John Talbot Stonor (1678–1756) became a priest, bishop, and Vicar Apostolic. His sister Mary was married to **William Plowden**. His daughter Winifrede (1706–31) married Philip Howard, son of the sixth Duke of Norfolk, in 1725; after her death, Philip married Harriot, daughter of AP's close friend **Edward Blount**.

AP must have known Thomas Stonor before he moved to **Twickenham**, when the two men came into further contact as fellow residents. However, he had not visited the family home at Stonor before he made an atmospheric visit in 1716. Stonor subscribed to the *Iliad* and to the **Shakespeare edition**, as well as to the collected poems of **Prior** and **Gay**. He was among those to greet AP on his "return" in *Mr. Pope's*

Welcome from Greece. The poet wrote with regret to Catholic friends of the death of both Winifred Stonor in 1722 and then her husband in 1724, when AP termed him "a very easy, human, and gentlemanly Neighbour" (*Corr* 1: 117, 253). In 1765 his grandson Charles married Mary Blount, of the **Mapledurham** family.

Stopford, Rev. James (c. 1697–1759). Irish clergyman and friend of **Jonathan Swift**. Fellow of Trinity College, Dublin, 1717–27. Obtained a number of preferments in the Church: Vicar of Finglas, near Dublin, 1727, in the parish formerly served by **Thomas Parnell**. He became Bishop of Cloyne in 1753, in succession to **Rev. George Berkeley**. A great favorite with Swift, who called him "in all regards the most valuable Young Man of this Kingdom" and addressed him as "Jim" in some of the twelve surviving letters: see Swift *Corr* 2: 509. In 1725 he went on a continental tour as tutor to a young man named William Graham, and Swift instructed him to call on **Charles Ford** in London to make the acquaintance of AP, **Gay**, and **Arbuthnot**. At the same time Swift wrote to AP, "requiring" his friend to introduce Stopford to the other Scriblerians (*Corr* 2: 310–11). After his travels Stopford came back to England in late 1726 and made a very good impression on AP. He returned to Ireland in February 1727, carrying with him letters to Swift from AP, Gay, and **Bolingbroke** (*Corr* 2: 425). AP wrote to Stopford on 20 November 1728, but after this, the paths of the two men appear not to have crossed.

Stowe (or Stow). Mansion with famous gardens, four miles northwest of Buckingham, belonging to **Viscount Cobham**. The house was originally built by his father, Sir Richard Temple, 1678–83. He inherited the property in 1697 and began to develop the grounds around 1711. The major reconstruction work on the house began c. 1719. Among those employed on house and garden were **Sir John Vanbrugh, Charles Bridgeman, James Gibbs, William Kent**, and later, from 1741, Lancelot "Capability" Brown. Before long, Cobham had transformed the previously regular Dutch-style garden into a show-place of the new naturalistic taste: "Bridgman began the process of blending the landscape with the garden, and Gibbs, Vanbrugh, and Kent dotted temples, columns, and arches about" (*TE* 3.ii: 143). The grounds were very extensive and included 250 acres within the circuit of the famous ha-ha, as well as a much greater area of parkland surrounding.

The entire site was designed to make cultural and political points, which were more and more aimed against the government of **Robert Walpole**. Among the most celebrated features of the landscape Cobham created here were the Elysian Fields; the Temple of British Worthies (containing busts with inscriptions by **George Lyttelton** and perhaps AP: after his death the poet himself was added to the gallery); and the Temple of Ancient Worthies. Almost as renowned were the Palladian Bridge; a statue of **Queen Caroline**, possibly designed by **Rysbrack**; the Temple of Venus; the Temple of Friendship; and the monument to **William Congreve**. There were also a Doric Arch, a Chinese House, a Gothic Temple, a Hermitage, a Grotto, and a Shell Bridge. After AP's death Brown continued to improve the gardens, and new features added by Cobham or his nephew and successor Earl Temple included the Temple of Concord and Victory, as well as Lord Cobham's Pillar. Most of these survive in good condition. Features that have disappeared include the Temple of Modern Virtue (constructed as a ruin, with deliberate ironic intent); the Temple of Bacchus; statues of Saxon deities; and the Temple of Contemplation.

AP visited Stowe many times, perhaps first in 1724, and then more or less annually, certainly as late as 1739. He was attracted there not only by his architectural and gardening tastes but also as an adherent of the **opposition to Walpole**, whose members sometimes gathered at Stowe to forge ineffective plots to bring down the Prime Minister. It is generally believed that AP "helped articulate the governing iconography" of the landscape (*Gardening World* 14); and he may even have chosen the site of some features in the garden as deliberate allusions to the *Aeneid*. While staying at the house in 1731 he wrote to a friend, "If any thing under Paradise could set me beyond all Earthly Cogitations; Stowe might do it" (*Corr* 3: 217). AP's major poetic tribute occurs in the *Epistle to Burlington*, ll. 65–74 (*TE* 3.ii: 143–44). Many other poets wrote in praise of the setting, most notably **James Thomson**.

Since 1923 the house has been occupied by Stowe School, an independent boarding school. The grounds belong to the National Trust and are open to the public at set times.

For a general overview, see G. Clarke and M. Gibbon, "A History of Stowe, 1–26," *The Stoic* (1966–77); and M. Bevington, *Stowe: The Garden and the Park* (Stowe: Capability Books, 1996). For AP's relations with Stowe, see *Gardening World* 11–15.

Strachey, (Giles) Lytton (1880–1932). Biographer and critic, famous for his work *Eminent Victorians* (1918). His Leslie Stephen lecture delivered at the University of Cambridge in 1925 has been seen as the beginning of a reaction against Victorian attitudes to AP, initiating a more sympathetic and less moralistic approach to the man and his work. See the reprint of the 1926 edition (Folcroft, PA: Folcroft, 1976). He also wrote on AP, **Swift**, **Addison**, **Steele**, **Lady Mary Wortley Montagu**, and **Chesterfield** as letter writers in *Characters and Commentaries* (1933). Other relevant items are reprinted in *Spectatorial Essays* (1964).

Stradling versus Stiles. A short Scriblerian work in prose, satirizing legal mumbo jumbo. It was first published in the second volume of *Miscellanies* in June 1727 (Griffith 185). It was probably written around 1716, when AP was at work on a similar law case described in the *Memoirs of Martin Scriblerus*. Later AP admitted authorship but at the same time acknowledged the help of a lawyer, almost certainly **William Fortescue** (see *Anecdotes* 1: 57). The absurd case relates to six piebald horses and is presented in Anglo-French jargon of the courtroom. Even the report uses this language: "Le reste del Argument jeo ne pouvois oyer, car jeo fui disturb en mon place." For text and commentary, see *Prose* 2: 131–42.

Strafford, Thomas Wentworth, third Earl of (1672–1739). A former soldier and ambassador who became a Tory politician and served in the **Harley administration**. Created Earl in 1711, he was one of the negotiators for the **Treaty of Utrecht** in 1711–13. Impeached by Parliament on suspicion of treasonable activities, 1715, but eventually proceedings were dropped. Undeterred, he was involved in the plans for a **Jacobite** rising at the time of the **Atterbury plot**. Strafford was a cousin of AP's close ally **Lord Bathurst** and a friend of Charles and **Mary Caesar**. He had a house at Mount Lebanon in **Twickenham**, on the bank of the Thames not far from **Marble Hill**, and a pew in **Twickenham parish church**—hence his interest in the affair concerning Lady Kneller in 1725. His mother Isabella, Lady Wentworth (c.1653–1733), an aunt of Lord Bathurst, occupied the house from 1692 until her death. Lebanon House, a symmetrical Palladian building of seven bays, renovated c.1702, was demolished in 1794. The Earl subscribed to both the *Iliad* and the *Odyssey*; a few letters survive from what might have been a more extensive correspondence with AP but for the close proximity of their houses. AP seems to have given the Earl one of the puppies of his dog Bounce; there is a brief reference in the poem *Bounce to Fop*.

Strand, The. One of the leading commercial streets in London, leading east-west from **Fleet Street** and the city to the polite West End at Charing Cross. It terminated at Temple Bar, where the two jurisdictions of London and Westminster met. Noted for its inns of court and other legal institutions. It was also the home of fashionable markets and one of the main centers of the book trade. Publishers as different as **Jacob Tonson senior** and **Edmund Curll** had their shops here. Appropriately, in *The Dunciad*, the hoard of dunces proceed along the street and gather at the church of St. Mary le Strand, a building erected by **James Gibbs** as ordained by "ANNE and Piety" (2:

25). This was one of the new foundations recently established and known as the **Queen Anne** churches. Here the booksellers conduct their less-than-heroic games.

Strange but True Relation, A. A prose pamphlet by AP, narrating "How *Edmund Curll*, of Fleetstreet, Stationer, Out of an extraordinary Desire of Lucre, went into *Change Alley*, and was converted from the Christian Religion by certain Eminent *Jews*: And how he was circumcis'd and initiated into their Mysteries." It survives only by its inclusion in the *Miscellanies* in 1732. However, **Norman Ault** was able to establish from a variety of internal and external evidence that the pamphlet must indeed have appeared soon after it was written, that is, around the beginning of April 1720 (see *Prose* 1: cvii–cix).

The attack follows on AP's earlier satires on **Edmund Curll**. It may have been provoked by Curll's erroneous ascription to AP of some lines on **Lady Mary Wortley Montagu**, which he was advertising in February and March 1720, sometimes listing these verses as "The Second Eve." In fact, the poem is not by AP at all (see *TE* 6: 423). Despite this, the work belongs in some respects to the abundance of literature concerned with the speculative fervor of the South Sea year (see **South Sea Bubble**). Exchange Alley, off Cornhill, was the epicenter from which this mania spread over the entire nation; and it lay only sixty yards from AP's birthplace at **Plough Court**. According to the narrative, Curll was driven by desire for riches to leave "the Business in which he was educated, but thriv'd little, and resolv'd to quit his Shop, for *Change Alley*." He met a number of Jews at their "club" in Cornhill and was gradually persuaded to sell out his Christian convictions in return for various advantageous bargains. Returning on 17 March, he was obliged to undergo circumcision, when as a result of "an unfortunate Jerk" he suffered more serious bodily losses in the operation than intended. As a result he was rejected by the Jews and forced to return to the lamentations of his wife, "for the barbarous Jews still keep, and expose at *Jonathan*'s and *Garraway*'s [coffeehouses where stockjobbing went on] the Memorial of her Loss, and her Husband's Indignity."

For the text, see *Prose Works* 1: 317–22. No proper annotated edition yet exists.

Straus, Ralph (1882–1950). Novelist and miscellaneous writer. Among his works are a biography of **Robert Dodsley** (1910; reprint, 1968) and a collection of eighteenth-century pamphlets *Tricks of the Town* (1927). He also wrote an introduction to *The London Spy* by **Edward Ward** (1924). He is best known to students of AP for his book *The Unspeakable Curll* (1927; reprint, 1970). This life of the scandalous publisher **Edmund Curll** lacks many of the features expected of a modern scholarly biography. However, it has many virtues: apart from its valuable checklist of Curll's publications, it provides a racy and amusing account of the battles between AP and his old adversary. All serious inquiries into this aspect of AP's career still have to take account of the work of Straus.

Stukeley, William (1687–1765). Physician, clergyman, **antiquarian**, and pioneer archeologist. FRS, 1718. In his later days he became known for his wild fantasies concerning the Druids, but he had done much to lay the foundations of archeology. His scientific background was as a follower of **Isaac Newton**. The books he based on his travels helped to develop the genre of touristic writing and in odd cases might have influenced AP's work.

AP did not have an intimate relationship with Stukeley. However, they ran into each other in a number of contexts. Both AP and **John Gay** were introduced by the lawyer Maurice Johnson (1688–1755) to the Gentleman's Club of Spalding, a group of antiquarians founded by Johnson along with his close friend Stukeley. Like AP, Stukeley was drawn into **freemasonry**. Shared interests of the two men included gardening and grottifying; collecting curiosities; early British history; numismatics; and architecture. Common friends and acquaintances included **Richard Mead** (who taught Stukeley); **Hans Sloane**; **William Warburton** (though he and Stukeley later quarreled); **Humfrey Wanley**; **John Anstis**; and many more. AP may have had Stukeley in mind for some of the excesses parodied in Book 4 of *The Dunciad*, but this was precisely because Stukeley represented the kind of man AP could easily have become, given slightly different circumstances.

See S. Piggott, *William Stukeley: An Eighteenth-Century Antiquarian* (London: Thames and Hudson, 1985).

subscriber, Pope as. AP is recorded as entering over forty book subscriptions. The first is for an edition of **Spenser** in 1715; the last, posthumously, is for *Polymetis* by his friend **Joseph Spence** in 1747. A wide range of topics are covered in the books concerned, with **gardening**, medicine, and history among the fields represented: books on materia medica botanica, on navigation, and on the Arundel marbles are found. However, poetry forms the largest single group of items. At the time of the disputes over **opera** in the 1720s, there are subscriptions to cantatas by **Bononcini** and Ariosti. AP's friends and colleagues are naturally well represented, with volumes by **Prior**, **Gay**, **Rowe**, **Addison**, **Hughes**, and **Thomson**. However, he also entered his name for the ventures of those who he did not know or with whom he had less cordial relations: these included **John Dennis**, **Stephen Duck**, William Pattison (an author from **Curll**'s stable), Joseph Mitchell (a client of **Robert Walpole**), Allan Ramsay, and Robert Luck. He encouraged two women poets who were then little known, namely, **Mary Barber** (entering also a subscription for his mother) and Sarah Dixon of Canterbury. The Barber subscriptions were prompted by **Swift**. Other writers on the list are **Milton**, Montaigne, and Bacon. There is an edition of **Horace** by John Pine and the life of Cicero by Conyers Middleton. At the end of his life AP supported the first volume of the important *Select Collection of Old Plays* brought out by **Robert Dodsley**. Among his more generous subscriptions was one to *The Grove* (1721), reprinting works by his early mentor **William Walsh**: AP ordered four leather-bound copies. Oddly, very few of these books are numbered among the surviving items from his **library**.

By the standards of his day, AP was not an extraordinarily prolific subscriber. Many aristocrats reached a much higher score, and among professional men **Dr. Richard Mead** entered over 200 subscriptions, many for multiple copies of the book. Nevertheless, AP outscores Swift and **Arbuthnot** and far exceeds most other writers in this period. Gay has only about a dozen, **Defoe** about nine. **Congreve**'s five are confined to works by **Dryden**, AP, Rowe, Prior, and Gay.

subscription publishing. The system of publication by subscription evolved in the later seventeenth century. In essence, the method consisting of circulating a prospectus for a new book and inviting buyers to put down money in advance, to help defray the costs of production. Sometimes the full price of the volume or volumes was required; on the other occasions, one half or some other fraction was called for, the rest to be paid on publication. The profits on such a venture might go to the publisher; alternatively, the bookseller might deduct his or her expenses, leaving the rest of the receipts to go to the author.

The first important such undertaking in English literature was *The Works of Virgil*, translated by **John Dryden** and published by **Jacob Tonson senior** in 1697. This attracted about 350 subscribers, of whom 100 paid five guineas to have their names and coats of arms printed along with plates. Among this number were several of AP's own later patrons, notably **Sir William Trumbull**. Throughout the following decades subscription was regularly used to launch books in almost very field. Major editions in AP's lifetime included collections of the works of **John Gay, Matthew Prior**, and **Joseph Addison**. Some volumes attracted as few as 50 or an even lower number of subscribers; others reached totals as high as 1,000 or more. Prior's volume (1718) achieved 1,440, while the little-known Mary Masters in 1733

and **Mary Barber** in 1734 reached several hundred names. Robert Burns's *Poems, Chiefly in the Scottish Dialect* attained over 1,500 in 1787. Some individuals would subscribe day in and day out to all kinds of books: thus **Dr. Richard Mead** appears on well over 200 lists. Institutions such as colleges and societies also subscribed. Certain authors had a particular fondness for subscription publishing, including **Thomas Hearne**, who used this method more than thirty times. The method continued into the nineteenth century, when it was used by authors such as Mark Twain, and even into more recent times.

AP's three ventures into this method can be divided into those for the *Iliad* and *Odyssey*, both highly successful and financially advantageous to the poet; and that for the **Shakespeare edition**, a less popular campaign mounted for the benefit of the publisher Tonson. In terms of sheer numbers, his lists for the **Homer** translations were not outstandingly large. However, they were notable for the range of their appeal and the broad inroads he made into the cultural and political establishment—thus his *Iliad* list contains **Sir Isaac Newton**, **Sir Hans Sloane**, and **Sir Christopher Wren**, as well as aristocrats, political leaders, churchmen, lawyers, soldiers, artists, and writers.

Sutherland, Sir James (Runcieman) (1900–1996). A scholar with a broad range of interests who taught at London University from 1936; he was Lord Northcliffe Professor of English Literature at University College from 1951 to 1967. A Fellow of the British Academy from 1953, he served as editor of the *Review of English Studies* (1940–47). Knighted in 1993. Among his published works are important studies of Restoration literature and of **Dryden**, as well as general works on satire and English prose. He wrote a much admired biography of **Defoe** (1937) and a valuable *Background for Queen Anne* (1939). *A Preface to Eighteenth-Century Poetry* (1948) was long one of the most widely read surveys of the topic. His work on AP includes an essay on the **Shakespeare edition**, "The Dull Duty of an Editor," *Review* of *English Studies*, 21 (1945), 202–15, reprinted in *EA* 630–49; and a British Academy lecture, *Wordsworth and Pope* (1944). His main contribution to the field is a major edition of ***The Dunciad***, which he compiled for the **Twickenham edition** (1943; rev. ed., 1963).

Swift, Jonathan (1667–1745). Writer. Born in Dublin, of primarily English ancestry. His father Jonathan Swift senior (1640–67) died before his birth; his mother Abigail Erick (c. 1640–1710) survived her husband by more than forty years and returned to England. Her son was educated at Kilkenny school and Trinity College, Dublin, as was his near-contemporary **William Congreve**. After graduating from Trinity in 1686 he stayed a further period at the college, before moving to England. From 1689 to 1694 he was secretary to Sir William Temple (1628–99), a retired diplomat and author, at his seat Moor Park in Surrey. Took an M.A. degree at Oxford as a step toward ordination, 1692; ordained priest in the Church of Ireland at Dublin, 1695. Spent an unhappy year in a poor parish near Belfast, in the north of Ireland. Returned to Moor Park and began work on *A Tale of a Tub*. He had already written his earliest surviving poems, six rhapsodic odes. In 1699 Temple died and Swift traveled to Dublin as chaplain to the Earl of Berkeley, Lord Justice of Ireland. Soon afterward Swift obtained the living at Laracor, near Trim, a town situated on the Boyne river about thirty miles northwest of Dublin. In 1701 his friend Esther Johnson ("Stella"), whom he had met at Moor Park, came to Dublin. Awarded D.D. by Trinity College in 1702.

For the next few years Swift's residence alternated between Ireland and England. In 1701 he had written a tract in the Whig interest, and when he returned to London as an emissary of the Irish church, his first contacts were with supporters of the government, including **Addison** and **Steele**. In 1704 he brought out a volume of original satires, including the *Tale* and ***The Battle of the Books***, which provoked in readers a variety of responses, from amazement to laughter, and from bafflement to resentful anger. His English contacts led to his induction into the London literary scene, marked by works such as the *Bickerstaff Papers* (1707) and contributions to ***The Tatler*** (1709–11). From 1710 to 1714 Swift passed most of his time in England, now working on behalf of the **Harley administration**. This phase is charted in his brilliant series of letters back to Dublin known as the ***Journal to Stella***. He gained the friendship of its leaders the **first Earl of Oxford** and **Viscount Bolingbroke**, became a habitué of the court, and produced some of the most influential of all political writings on behalf of the Tories. His weekly journal *The Examiner* laid the groundwork, and it was followed by pamphlets such as *The Conduct of the Allies* (1711), attacking the war strategy of the **Duke of Marlborough**. In addition, his first authorized collection, *Miscellanies in Prose and Verse*, came out in 1711. His political and literary interest fused in his membership of the **Brothers Club** and the **Scriblerus Club**, in which he fraternized with leading writers. At the same time as he grew closer to **Dr. John Arbuthnot**, **Gay**, **Parnell**, and AP, Swift's friendship with Addison and Steele was rapidly cooling, mainly for political reasons. He seemed to have reached a pinnacle of influence in the life of the nation. However, he had made important enemies, and he was regarded with deep distrust by **Queen Anne**. As a result, he was unable to obtain the plum appointment in the English church he coveted, and in 1713 he had to accept a less glamorous and remunerative position as Dean of St. Patrick's cathedral in Dublin. The fall of Oxford's ministry and the death of the Queen confirmed his relegation to a minor role in what he regarded as permanent exile.

It took several years for Swift to regain full buoyancy, as a man and a writer. His relations with two women, Stella and "Vanessa" (Esther Vanhomrigh), complicated his life. But he also had to adjust to a different world, in which he was separated from his closest colleagues in the writing profession and where his former patrons were in jail or in exile, some following the increasingly hopeless cause of the **Pretender**. Gradually he became more active again and started to write on Irish politics. His forthright denunciation of the Anglo-Irish establishment in *The Drapier's Letters* (1724–25) brought him a new prominence and a cult status among the people of Dublin. By this time he had begun work on *Gulliver's Travels*. When he finally made a return visit to England in 1726, he brought the manuscript with him, and the book appeared to great *éclat* in October of that year. Swift made his final trip to England in the following year. On both occasions he spent much of his time in the company of old friends like Gay, Arbuthnot, and Bolingbroke, and he stayed at **Twickenham** with AP. He also had contacts with the court through **Henrietta Howard, Countess of Suffolk**. Though Swift and **Robert Walpole** were able to observe the proprieties when they dined together in 1726, each was aware that he was in the presence of a mighty adversary.

He was back in Ireland in time to witness the death of Stella on 28 January 1728, a deeply traumatic event for him. Despite this, he produced a further masterpiece in prose, *A Modest Proposal* (1729), and opened up a new vein of biting satiric poetry. Among his works of the 1730s are the so-called "excremental poems," such as *The Lady's Dressing Room*; the *Verses on the Death of Dr. Swift*; and *On Poetry: A Rhapsody*. Several of these utilize the methods of AP, and some draw on the cast of villains AP had created, such as **Charteris**, **Cibber**, **Concanen**, **Curll**, **Moore Smythe**, and **Welsted**. Few of these had given Swift any personal affront. Other striking poems are addressed to friends such as Gay and Dr. Patrick Delany. A major collection of his works was published by **George Faulkner** in 1735. By this time Swift's health had started to decline, and his spirits were depressed by the loss of friends such as Gay and Arbuthnot. Increasing dementia took its toll, and in 1742 he was judged legally incapable. He died in October 1745 and was buried alongside Stella in St. Patrick's cathedral.

Swift was already well established before AP began to write seriously. Nonetheless, from the start of their relationship, they operated as equals. Swift admired *Windsor-Forest* on its appearance, just after the pair had met, and ad-

vised Stella to read it. They remained close literary allies ever afterward. Even though Swift grew suspicious of AP's publishing schemes in the 1730s, and resented some of his friend's manipulative habits, he never ceased to express his huge respect for the poetry. About ninety letters survive from their correspondence, dating between 1713 and 1741, and these contain some of the most heartfelt written by either man. They discuss their literary projects with a frankness not usually seen elsewhere, and Swift sets out to AP a number of his most fundamental views on literature. See, for instance, his message of 20 September 1723 (*Corr* 2: 198–200). AP awaited *Gulliver* with as much impatience as Swift looked forward to *The Dunciad*, and their exchanges tell us a lot about their differing approaches to writing. It was a matter of considerable regret to them that their meetings were so rare. Each wished the other to make a journey across the Irish Sea. Many letters were written jointly to or from the wider circle of their friends, including Bolingbroke, Gay, Arbuthnot, Henrietta Howard, and the **second Earl of Oxford**.

It is hard to fix the precise degree of influence Swift exerted on AP, and vice versa. From the time of their collaboration in the **Scriblerus Club**, they worked together on composite satires, imitated one another's style (see *An Imitation of the Sixth Satire of the Second Book of Horace*), and generally supported one another's activities. Swift helped to get Irish subscribers to the *Iliad* and subscribed also to the *Odyssey*. The famous couplet in Swift's *Verses*, "In Pope, I cannot read a line, / But with a sigh, I wish it mine," might have been repeated in mirror fashion by AP. *The Dunciad* is appropriately dedicated to Swift, in his various guises as "Dean, Drapier, Bickerstaff, or Gulliver," and as the author who had inherited the mantle of Cervantes and Rabelais (1: 17–20). There are also warm commendations of Swift in the *Imitations of Horace*. It is a testimony to the strength of character in both men that their friendship survived almost unscathed for so long, in the face of separation and conflicting ambitions. They must have been aware of a potential rivalry, and some members of their extended acquaintance would have been glad to drive a wedge between them. Swift's lack of jealousy toward his younger colleague is remarkable and can best be explained less by pure magnanimity (a quality he did not always display) than by genuine love and respect for AP.

The standard biography is I. Ehrenpreis, *Swift: The Man, His Works, the Age*, 3 vols. (London: Methuen, 1962–83). For the *Poems* see the edition by H. Williams, 3 vols. (Oxford: Clarendon, 1958). At present the most complete edition of the *Correspondence* is by H. Williams, 5 vols. (Oxford: Clarendon, 1963–65, with corrections 1972). However, this in the process of being superseded by a new edition by D. Woolley, 4 vols (Frankfurt: Peter Leang, 1999–), 2 vols. so far published. See also *Journal to Stella*.

Swinburne, Mary, Lady (d. 1724). She was the daughter of Anthony Englefield, one of AP's early mentors (see **Englefield family**), and thus the aunt of **Martha** and **Teresa Blount**. In 1697 she married Sir William Swinburne (c. 1670–1716), second baronet, a member of a prominent Northumberland family of recusants. Her son John (1698–1745), third baronet, was married in 1721 to Mary Bedingfield (d. 1761), daughter of AP's friend Edward Bedingfield. Her husband was taken into custody prior to the **Jacobite rising** in 1715: both her brothers-in-law were captured at the battle of Preston and condemned to death. Edward (1685–1716) died in prison, while James (d. 1728) pleaded insanity and escaped from custody. Two Miss Swinburnes, probably sisters of Sir William, acted as couriers for the **Jacobites** during the rising. AP was well aware of the family circumstances (see *Corr* 1: 327). Mary was particularly close to the **third Earl of Derwentwater**, a relative of the Swinburnes. AP spoke to Sir John, the third baronet, in 1743 (*Corr* 4: 464). The poet Algernon Charles Swinburne was a descendant, as a grandson of the sixth baronet.

A letter written by AP to Lady Swinburne in 1709 has quite recently turned up, showing the extent of the contacts between the Pope family and the Swinburnes. Such findings swell the growing body of information that shows that AP had many private links with those most centrally involved in the Jacobite movement, whatever his opinion of the rising may have been. See H. Erskine-Hill, "A New Pope Letter," *Notes & Queries*, 218 (1973), 207–9. For the background, see L. Gooch, *The Desperate Faction? The Jacobites of North-East England 1688–1715* (Hull: University of Hull Press, 1995).

sylphs. One of the four groups of elemental spirits added as part of the "machinery" in the second version of *The Rape of the Lock*. The basic idea is taken from the Rosicrucian mythology found in a work called *Le Comte de Gabalis*, as AP told **Arabella Fermor** in his prefatory address. However, AP's creatures have their own mythic identity, drawing on a wide range of sources and models—the angels and demons of *Paradise Lost*; the fairies of **Shakespeare**, **Spenser**, and **Michael Drayton**, and an array of old English folk traditions, mostly pagan in origin, which collectively embodied the fairy lore of the nation.

In terms of the standard grouping of "elements," the sylphs correspond to the air. However, a series of associations radiated out from this basic correspondence. Thus, within the poem, AP links the sylphs to morning, to youth, and ultimately to levity in behavior. It is significant that they are described in the greatest detail and put to work most fully as part of the narrative action, in the aubade that comprises Canto 1. By contrast the gnomes are connected to the element of earth; they relate to evening, to mature years, and to prudery. Naturally they enter the poem most directly in Canto 4, where their attributes are mirrored in the **Cave of Spleen**. The sylphs are sanguine in complexion, if we invoke the old psychology of "humors," whereas the gnomes are melancholy. On one level the poem operates as a struggle between these competing forces for the soul of **Belinda**, as they urge her toward either coquettishness or chastity, sexual expression or repression. Ariel and Umbriel represent the two antagonistic powers. The salamanders (fire/noon/the prime of life/choleric humor) have much less importance in the working out of the action, even though **Thalestris** seems to belong to this group; and so do the nymphs (water/midnight/old age/phlegmatic humor).

For further background, see *TE* 2: 378–83.

T

Tale of a Tub, A. Prose satire by **Jonathan Swift**, written 1696–97 and published anonymously in 1704. It is constructed around two blocks of material, (1) a narrative of the history of the church, told in allegorical form, which is regularly interrupted by (2) a series of essays on the corruptions of modern learning. This second portion, especially, exercised great influence on the course of **Augustan satire**. Swift satirizes the incompetence of writers of his day, foreshadowing AP's works such as the *Epistle to Arbuthnot* and *The Dunciad*. His mockery of "scholarly' " procedures anticipates books by AP and his friends, including the *Memoirs of Martin Scriblerus*. Equally, Swift recognizes a "Corporation of Poets" who band together with booksellers to unloose a tide of unwanted literature, much in the way of AP's later "dunces." At the same time Swift follows the example of **Dryden** and creates a line of hereditary poetasters. He identifies a group of "Profound Writers," specialists in low matter and bathetic manner, thus providing a basis for *The Art of Sinking*. Where AP dramatizes the collapse of culture under the onslaughts of dulness, Swift embodies the follies he anatomizes in the person of his narrator, a conceited sciolist unaware of his own limitations.

See *A Tale of a Tub*, ed. A.C. Guthkelch and D.N. Smith, 2nd ed. (Oxford: Clarendon, 1958). A work that brings out some themes relevant to AP is M.K. Starkman, *Swift's Satire on Learning in A Tale of a Tub* (Princeton, NJ: Princeton University Press, 1950; reprint, New York: Octagon, 1968).

Tassoni, Alessandro (1565–1635). Italian poet, born at Modena into a family of the nobility. Studied at Bologna and Ferrara; spent his life in the service of prelates and aristocrats. His best-known poem, *La Secchia rapita*, or *The Stolen Bucket* (1622), was among the first and greatest works in the vein of **mock-heroic**. It satirizes petty quarrels between the city–states of Bologna and Modena and comprises twelve cantos in ottava rima. AP certainly knew the poem and borrowed certain effects in *The Rape of the Lock*. Tassoni's characters sometimes lapse from heroic diction into pure Modenan dialect, and AP has the Baron spouting contemporary slang. He also capitalizes on an ambiguity in the Italian title: "rapita" can mean stolen/kidnapped or ravished. In the original Tassoni uses the word in the former sense: AP deliberately brings in the sense of sexual assault. **John Ozell** had translated the poem as *The Trophy Bucket* in 1710: seeing his opportunity, **Edmund Curll** reprinted this item in June 1713 after the success of AP's work.

Tate, Nahum (1652–1715). Irish poet and dramatist. Educated at Trinity College, Dublin. Poet Laureate, 1692; even more inappropriately, Historiographer Royal, 1702. Best known on three accounts: first, his version of *King Lear* (1681) with a happy ending, which held the stage for over a century; second, his metrical version of the Psalms with Nicholas Brady (1696); third, his libretto for Henry Purcell's *Dido and Aeneas* (1689). He added a second part to **Dryden**'s *Absalom and Achitophel* (1682) and contributed to a joint translation of Juvenal and Persius that Dryden mounted (1693). Brady (1659–1726), also an Irishman, was vicar of **Richmond** and master of a charity school there; he was also chaplain to successive sovereigns and to the Princess of Wales, later **Queen Caroline**.

By the time that AP came to maturity, Tate had sunk into oblivion—he died in the Mint, Southwark, escaping from his creditors. He appears in AP's work simply as one in a line of bad poets: see a joke in *The Art of Sinking*, chapter 9 (*Prose* 2: 203), and the reference to poetasters, "nine such Poets made a *Tate*" in the *Epistle to Arbuthnot*, l. 190 (*TE* 5: 109). Tate figures in a number of places in *The Dunciad* but always in terms of friendly contempt toward "our Father Tate" (the formulation evokes singsong repetition of liturgical formulas, as in the metrical Psalms). AP liked to have fun with these familiar verses, which would have been known to all Anglican churchgoers. A few of the versions survive as the words of hymns, including "As pants the hart," "While shepherds watched," and "Through all the changing scenes of life."

See C. Spencer, *Nahum Tate* (New York: Twayne, 1972).

Tatler, The. A highly innovative journal, the forerunner to *The Spectator*. It was started by **Richard Steele** on 12 April 1709, running three days a week for 271 numbers until 2 January 1711. Steele and **Joseph Addison** were the main contributors throughout, although others including **Jonathan Swift** occasionally wrote for the journal. The paper claimed to present the "lucubrations" of one Isaac Bickerstaff, a name borrowed from Swift's hoaxes against the astrologer **John Partridge**.

While AP arrived too late on the London literary scene to become a contributor, he undoubtedly read *The Tatler* along with almost everyone else. There are obvious links between the paper and AP's early work, especially *The Rape of the Lock*. On almost very page of the standard edition of this poem, the text is glossed by reference to quotations from *The Tatler*. A good example of the close similarity between aspects of the two works can be seen if the description of **"Sir Plume"** in the poem is compared with *Tatler* no. 113, which draws up an inventory of the effects of a deceased beau.

See *The Tatler*, ed. D.F. Bond, 3 vols. (Oxford: Clarendon, 1987).

Taverner, Edward, alias John Banister (d. 1745). The Popes' family priest by 1692, who lived with them in **Plough Court** and **Hammersmith**. He gave AP he first rudiments of his education (*Anecdotes* 1: 8–9).

Temple of Fame, The. A version of a dream poem by **Chaucer**, which AP wrote c. 1711. On 10 November 1712 **Richard Steele** reported in *Spectator* no. 532 that AP had sent him "an admirable Poem" that he hoped would shortly see the light. Two days later he wrote a personal letter to AP, stating that he found in the poem "a thousand thousand beauties" (*Corr* 1: 152). However, the journal soon ceased its run and the poem remained unpublished. On 30 December **John Gay** told a friend that AP intended to publish *The Temple of Fame* "as soon as he comes to Town." In the event it appeared on 1 February 1715 as an octavo of fifty-six pages, under the title *The Temple of Fame: A Vision. By Mr. Pope* (Griffith 36). The price was one shilling. On the same day the publisher, **Bernard Lintot**, paid AP £32.5.0 (£30.25) for the rights. A second edition appeared later in the same year. A number of revisions were made when the poem was included in the *Works* (**1717**) and a few further changes in 1736.

AP departs widely from his source text. Chaucer's poem *The Hous of Fame* (c. 1379) was left unfinished; it consists of three books and about 2,150 lines of octosyllabic verse. The **imitation** drops virtually all of the first book, most of the second, and even makes cuts in the third. Most of the surviving materials are rearranged in some way, and there are few sustained passages closely following the original. In 1736 AP indicated some lines in his poem with a direct basis in Chaucer: Even these are loosely paraphrased. As a result the imitation is contained within 524 lines in **heroic couplets**. In general, AP's aim is to produce a more refined and tightly organized poem than the original. As **Geoffrey Tillotson** expressed it, "For Chaucer's cinematographic speed and lightness there is Pope's Handelian tempo and harmony, for Chaucer's narrative, Pope's scene" (*TE* 2: 222). Indeed, AP uses a characteristic Augustan mode, the "prospect" piece, and he is happy to leave out the almost surreal narrative of an airborne journey that occupies the second book of Chaucer's poem.

"Fame" in earlier times could mean either "rumor" or "reputation, renown," and AP enlists both senses in describing the palace of fame. He invokes a number of heroic exemplars who are carved in effigy at the center of the palace: they are, significantly, all writers from the classical age, suggesting that the work is casting its weight behind the Ancients against the Moderns (see **Ancients and Moderns**). The four faces of the structure also carry sculptured representations of celebrated figures; thus, the western wall displays gods and heroes of Greece, the eastern wall those of Persia and Assyria, the southern those of Egypt, and the northern those of Nordic legend. Each face is given an architectural design in line with its allegorical character—on the west, a classical facade, on the east an oriental tableau, on the south a scene with obelisks and hieroglyphs, and on the north a set of Gothic columns. After a blast of the trumpet summons petitioners to the court of the goddess of Fame, a more satiric note enters the poem, with a strong foretaste of the last book of *The Dunciad*. The contemporary world is imaged in terms of gossip and backbiting, rather than the noble quest for an honored name that had activated the great figures of the past.

See *TE* 2: 215–89, which provides, along with the text, what is still the most informative commentary on the poem.

Thackeray, William Makepeace (1811–63). Novelist and critic. He was deeply immersed in the eighteenth century, which forms the background for much of his fiction, including *Barry Lyndon* (1844); *The Newcomes* (1853–55), and *The Virginians* (1857–59). AP and his circle make a cameo appearance in *Henry Esmond* (1852). Thackeray published lectures on *The Eighteenth-Century Humourists* [*sic*] in 1853 and on *The Four Georges* in 1860. The former contains an essay on "Prior, Gay, and Pope." Here the author sets out the highest estimate of AP to be expressed in the entire nineteenth cen-

tury, singling out *The Rape of the Lock* and *The Dunciad* as supreme masterpieces in their genre. Thackeray's praise of the "consummate art" revealed in AP's poetry was eccentric in its own day and would not be echoed in quite such terms for almost another hundred years. Equally ahead of its time was the critic's claim that "[i]t was Pope, and Swift to aid him, who established among us the Grub Street tradition"—although Thackeray felt that "the profession of letters was ruined by that libel of *The Dunciad*."

Thalestris. Character in *The Rape of the Lock*. A fierce virago named for the Queen of the Amazons who seeks the return of **Belinda**'s lock and urges the heroine to action against **the Baron**. She has been tentatively identified with a "Mrs Morley," who might be Elizabeth Morley, sister of **Sir George Browne** and wife of **John Morley**; or more likely, Gertrude Morley (d. 1720), first wife of Sir George. See *TE* 2: 376.

theater. AP's contacts with the stage were extensive, although he wrote no full-length play unaided. In collaboration with his Scriblerian colleagues he was responsible for the farce *Three Hours after Marriage* (1717). It is possible that he had a small hand in other works for the stage. The only certain attributions that can be made include prologues and epilogues, of which the most notable is that for the smash-hit *Cato* (1713). He supplied extra choruses to a version of *Julius Caesar* (see *Two Choruses to Brutus*); and he seems to have contributed to libretti for **Handel**, most notably in the case of *Acis and Galatea*.

Nonetheless, it is apparent that AP took a keen interest in drama, and he probably made some juvenile experiments in writing stage works. He had many personal friends involved with the theater, from his early contact with the actor **Thomas Betterton** and the dramatist **William Wycherley** to his prolonged relations with **Congreve** and **Rowe**. In the years following the **Hanoverian accession** he enjoyed a playful association with actresses like the sisters **Margaret Bicknell** and Elizabeth Younger. This link was facilitated by his intimacy with **John Gay**, who had a long record in the theater even before he produced his most famous work, *The Beggar's Opera*, in 1728.

From quite early in his career AP had given support to playwrights such as **John Hughes** and **Elijah Fenton**. During the 1730s AP was often consulted by members of the **opposition to Walpole** who were using drama as a vehicle of political protest. In particular, the writers **James Thomson**, **David Mallet**, and **Aaron Hill** sought his advice on plays they intended to put on in London. A good example is Thomson's *Agamemnon* (1738), where AP took an active part in the efforts made to promote this fiercely anti-Walpole drama. He also encouraged **Robert Dodsley**'s ventures into the theater and exercised a strong influence on the daring young playwright **Henry Fielding**. AP attended the premiere of George Lillo's popular domestic tragedy *The London Merchant* in June 1731 and went backstage to commend the author and the performers.

Apart from this, AP was drawn into theatrical affairs by his battles with the Dunces. Both of the two men who served in turn as king dunce, **Lewis Theobald** and **Colley Cibber**, had an extensive involvement with the London stage. This choice of an epic "hero" testifies to the significance of drama in the action of *The Dunciad*, in all its various guises. Malcolm Goldstein has rightly indicated the "persistent concern" displayed in the poem for the theater. Other leading characters in AP's satire such as **John Rich** and **Elkanah Settle** were equally prominent figures in this world. Several minor episodes in the action involve authors of stage plays, among them **Susanna Centlivre**, **Eliza Haywood**, Charles Johnson, and **James Moore Smythe**. Elsewhere in his satires AP aims blows at stage favorites such as **Anne Oldfield**; and in *The Art of Sinking* he makes a wider survey of the absurdities of the theater in a "Project for the Advancement of the Stage" (*Prose* 2: 230–33). Among the targets here are the critics **John Dennis** and **Charles Gildon**.

In one more way AP impacted on the course of theatrical history. His **Shakespeare edition** was sloppy and eccentric by modern standards,

and Theobald gained a central role in *The Dunciad* largely as a result of his temerity in pointing out some of these failings. However, the edition represented an advance on that of his predecessor Rowe in its use of early quartos, while its preface represented some of the most adult commentary on Shakespeare's plays to appear before the work of **Samuel Johnson**. His partisanship lay at the heart of a growing cult of **Shakespeare**. It is revelatory, first, that AP played a big part in setting up a **monument to Shakespeare** in Westminster Abbey and, second, that he was able before his death to see David Garrick perform as Richard III. Thus at the end of his life AP could welcome the next great interpreter of Shakespeare and hail the actor/producer who would do most to convert the dramatist into a national icon over the next few decades.

See M. Goldstein, *Pope and the Augustan Stage* (Stanford: Stanford University Press, 1958).

Theobald, Lewis (1688–1744). Editor, poet, and dramatist. Started life as an attorney in London. By 1713 he was working for **Bernard Lintot**, chiefly as a translator from Greek. In 1714 he contracted to translate the *Odyssey*, but the plan fell through, no doubt because the publisher was heavily engaged in the expensive project of AP's *Iliad*. A few original works in verse made little impact, with the minor exception of *The Cave of Poverty* (1715). In the same year he produced a tragedy, *The Perfidious Brother*, that was later alleged to be plagiarized. By this date Theobald was working for **Edmund Curll**, and he had also started to antagonize AP. He probably had a hand in an attack on the farce by **John Gay** and others, *The What d'ye Call It*, in April 1715. The suppressed edition of the works of the **Duke of Buckinghamshire** that Curll projected in 1722 carried a life of the Duke by Theobald. After this Theobald reinvented himself as a writer of "pantomimes" for the stage, that is, entertainments put on at **Lincoln's Inn Fields Theatre** by the impresario **John Rich**. He had some success with efforts like *Harlequin Sorcerer* (1725) and *The Rape of Properpine* (1725).

The major clash with AP was instituted by the appearance in March 1726 of Theobald's work *Shakespeare Restored: Or a Specimen of the Many Errors, as well Committed, as Unamended, by Mr. Pope in his Late Edition of this Poet*, dedicated to Rich. AP was not slow to reply, casting ridicule in *The Art of Sinking* on lines from Theobald's play *The Double Falshood* (1727) and ranging him among the "obscure" but "nimble" eels (*Prose* 2: 197–99). The drama had allegedly been based on a lost original by **Shakespeare**, but scholarship has never been able to confirm this line of descent. Soon after, Theobald was cast as the king of the dunces in the first version of *The Dunciad*. The affronted scholar defended himself with a number of letters and articles in the press. His friends included **Matthew Concanen** and **William Warburton**, at this early stage an opponent of AP. An edition of the posthumous works of **William Wycherley** in 1728 gave more ammunition to AP. A more effective blow in the contest between the two writers was Theobald's major edition of Shakespeare, which came out in eight volumes in January 1734. The reception disappointed him, and it was put about that AP had somehow damaged the sales. In the pages of the *Grub-street Journal* over the next few years, Theobald attracted regular satiric attention. Theobald continued to work for the rest of the decade, bringing out more plays and pantomimic shows, as well as embarking on an edition of Beaumont and Fletcher, completed by others and published in 1750. In 1730 Theobald had been disappointed in his bid for the post of Poet Laureate, which went to **Colley Cibber**; in 1742 AP ironically reasserted this preference when he removed his former king and gave the role to Cibber.

Unquestionably Theobald had higher competence as an editor of Shakespeare than his rival. He knew much more about the Elizabethan and Jacobean stage and had made a more thorough trawl of early editions. Besides this, he was more attentive to verbal nuances and had a stronger historical grasp of the language. Many of his objections to AP's text were valid, as is shown by the adoption of many readings in AP's second edition. Theobald had learned something from the practice of **Richard Bentley** in the editing of classical texts, though not all of it was to prove useful to his task. The 1734 edition supplies some valuable new literary analogues, as well as some famous conjectural emendations. AP must have known that he had come off second best in terms of scholarly accuracy and assiduity. His response was to construct a composite dunce who performs microsurgery on texts while missing the true meaning of the work; who produces vulgar spectacles for the London stage; and who attributes his feeble play to the matchless Shakespeare (see *TE* 5: 180–82). "Tibbald," as the construct is called, emerges as a barren pedant, a tasteless pretender to polite literature, and a coadjutor of the lowest **Grub Street** hacks. All these criticisms have a measure of truth to them, in spite of Theobald's real claims in the narrow sphere of editing.

See R.F. Jones, *Lewis Theobald: His Contribution to English Scholarship with Some Unpublished Letters* (New York: Columbia University Press, 1919; reprint, New York: AMS Press, 1966). This makes a strong case for Theobald's merits as a scholar and preposterously denigrates almost everything about AP. A more balanced but still sympathetic approach will be found in P. Seary, *Lewis Theobald and the Editing of Shakespeare* (Oxford: Clarendon, 1990).

Theocritus. Greek poet of the third century B.C. who wrote a series of *Idylls* describing the lives of Sicilian shepherds and reapers in a stylized "Doric" dialect. He has always been recognized as the founder of bucolic poetry. At the start of his *Pastorals*, AP invokes the "*Sicilian* Muses," those presiding over this mode of poetry. AP remarked in his *Discourse on Pastoral Poetry* that "*Theocritus* excels all others in nature and simplicity" but found fault with aspects of the poetry (*TE* 1: 29–30). The poem "Winter" in AP's *Pastorals* is based in part on the first of the idylls of Theocritus, and the eleventh idyll recounts the story of *Acis and Galatea*.

Thomas, Elizabeth (1675–1731). Poet. Raised as a gentlewoman in London, she attracted the interest of **John Dryden** for her early poems. He gave her the sobriquet "Corinna," as well as considerable advice. Thomas wrote some eloquent verses to the memory of Dryden in 1700. Her friends included Mary Astell and Lady Mary Chudleigh. Later she became acquainted with **Henry Cromwell** and possibly his mistress. He endowed her with another nickname, "Sappho." Around 1714 Cromwell gave her the early letters his friend AP had written to him, and she was led by her poverty to sell these for ten guineas (£10.50) to **Edmund Curll**, who published them in 1726. Predictably this led to the incarceration of Thomas in *The Dunciad*, where the speeding bookseller slips on a "lake" that "Curl's Corinna chanc'd that morn to make" (2: 66). In response, Thomas joined with Curll to produce a stinging mock-biography of AP in *Codrus: or, The Dunciad Dissected* (1728), one of the many **pamphlet attacks** on the poet flung about at this time (Guerinot 153–56). Pope added a note to *The Dunciad*, pretending to exculpate Thomas, as "he has been inform'd she is a decent woman and in misfortune" (*TE* 5: 106), but really making matters worse for her. Thomas had been imprisoned in the Fleet debtors' jail since about 1727.

Among Thomas's works are *Miscellany Poems on Several Subjects* (1722), containing some lively early verse; and *The Metamorphosis of the Town: or, A View of the Present Fashions. A Tale: after the Manner of Fontaine. To which is added, The Journal of a Modern Lady ... By Dr. Swift* (1730). Later editions are titled *The Metamorphoses of the Town*. She supplied some highly colored and far-fetched stories about Dryden in a biography of **William Congreve**, published in 1729. The best of her witty and sometimes passionate writing can be found in *Pylades and Corinna*, a posthumous work published by Curll in two volumes in 1731 and dramatizing her long-term relationship with a lawyer named Richard Gwinnet (1675–1717).

Thompson, E[dward] P[almer] (1924–93). Social historian and radical activist. His many influential books include *The Making of the English Working Class* (1963). A brilliant study of the episode of the **Waltham Blacks**, titled *Whigs and Hunters: The Origins of the Black Act* (1975), contains a great deal of material relating to AP, his family, and his milieu in **Windsor Forest**.

Thompson, Dr. Thomas (d. 1756). Physician. A practitioner of fringe medicine, widely regarded as a quack, though his eccentric habits and alleged connection with the satanic "Monks" of Medmenham Abbey did not help his reputation. He treated **Henry Fielding** for gout and received a warm tribute in *Amelia*. Among his other patients were **Frederick, Prince of Wales** and **George Bubb Dodington**, for whom he acted as house physician.

Thompson was recommended to AP by **Hugh Bethel**, who reported on the successful treatment of Sir John Eyles. This was in March 1744, two months before the **death** of AP. In the following weeks Thompson began to treat AP for his asthma, putting his patient (against the advice of his other doctors) on doses of mineral waters. Thompson regarded AP's complaint as dropsical, but his severe regimen evidently did nothing to arrest the course of the illness. However, it may be unfair to accept at face value the comments of the **Earl of Orrery**, that Thompson "is said to have hastened [AP's] death," and of **David Mallet** that the doses of physic "evacuated him into absolute inanition" (*Corr* 4: 521–53). It is unlikely that any practitioner of the day could have saved the poet. See also *Anecdotes* 1: 261; and *This Long Disease* 73–81, 297–305.

Thomson, James (1700–1748). Scottish poet and dramatist. He achieved success early, with his four-part discursive poem in blank verse, *The Seasons* (1726–30). Later works included *Liberty* (1735–36); *Alfred: A Masque* (1740), cowritten with his friend **David Mallet** and containing "Rule, Britannia"; and the Spenserian **imitation** *The Castle of Indolence* (1748). His plays were mostly set in classical or medieval times, but they bore directly on contemporary politics as expressions of the ideology of the **opposition to Walpole**. Thomson's patrons included **George Bubb Dodington**, the

Countess of Hertford, and **George Lyttelton**. Another close ally was the writer **Aaron Hill**.

AP must have known him by 1730, when he wrote a prologue for Thomson's first play *Sophonisba*, which had a successful run at **Drury Lane Theatre** early in that year. Mallet may have written the last portion of this prologue (see *TE* 6: 310–11). Shortly afterward AP subscribed for three copies of the collected *Seasons*. Others on the subscription list included **Martha Blount** and **Richard Savage**, who was to prove an ungrateful friend to Thomson, as to so many others. According to **Samuel Johnson**, AP wrote an epistle to Thomson when the younger poet was on the **Grand Tour** as tutor to the son of a prominent lawyer, Lord Talbot; however, no trace of this remains. The two men continued on affable terms for the rest of AP's life, even though Thomson's rather metaphysical brand of Whiggery may not have been wholly to AP's taste. In 1736 Thomson moved quite close to AP's home when he took up residence in **Richmond**, but their meetings seem to have been infrequent.

See J. Sambrook, *James Thomson 1700–1748: A Life* (Oxford: Clarendon, 1991); and *James Thomson (1700–1748): Letters and Documents*, ed. A.D. McKillop (Lawrence: University of Kansas Press, 1958). For Thomson's political writing, see works listed under **opposition to Walpole**.

Thoughts on Various Subjects. A collection of aphorisms and observations, in the manner of La Rochefoucauld. **Swift** had made his own anthology of maxims, and these were included in the first volume of *Miscellanies* (1727). Those by AP appeared in the second volume. Alterations were made for a reprint in the *Works* of AP in 1741. They are characteristic maxims of the age, dealing with general moral topics and reflections on literary matters ("Get your Enemies to read your works, in order to mend them, for your friend is so much your second-self, that he will judge too like you"). See *Prose* 2: 145–70.

Three Hours after Marriage. A farce in three acts, written mainly by **John Gay** with the collaboration of **Dr. John Arbuthnot** and AP. Opening at **Drury Lane Theatre** on 16 January 1717, it ran for seven performances in the face of lively audience participation, some friendly and some hostile. A campaign was waged against the play in the playhouse and in the press: "Broadsides, newspapers, and pamphlets all expressed loud disapproval of the play and especially of its authors" (*Early Career* 195). Originally it was rumored that Pope was the author, a fact that did nothing to stem the flow of criticism. At least nine replies and "keys" are known to have been produced in the immediate aftermath of the performances. Among its critics were **John Durant Breval**, Charles Johnson, and **Leonard Welsted**. One source alleges that two principal actresses refused to go on stage after the noisy reception they had faced on the opening night and that three of the **maids of honor** to the Prince of Wales had rescued the show with a gift of 400 guineas (£420). This story is now generally discounted, but it may have some kernel of truth.

The work was published by **Bernard Lintot** on 21 January in an octavo of eighty pages (Griffith 66); there was a Dublin reprint by George Risk in the same year. In the preliminary matter Gay acknowledges his own share in the work but mentions also assistance from "two of my friends," that is, AP and Arbuthnot. It is generally thought that AP had some share at least in the prologue: for these verses, see *TE* 6: 178–80. The only substantially different text appears in a Dublin edition of *A Supplement to the Works of Alexander Pope, Esq.* (1758), which supplies a version in five acts, together with material in an appendix concerning the original reception of the play. This version has been edited by J.H. Smith (Los Angeles: Augustan Reprint Society), 1961. The presumed obscenity of the text ensured that no edition appeared after 1807 for a century and a half.

Some of the characters are obvious caricatures of real persons: thus the credulous **antiquarian** Dr. Fossile certainly represents **John Woodward**, while the bumptious critic Sir Tremendous is taken from **John Dennis**. Doubt surrounds other figures, notably the demented writer Phoebe Clinket, who has been variously identified. The most daring move was to cast **Colley Cibber** in the role of a playwright named Plotwell, who can suggest no one other than Cibber himself. One story has it that Cibber was fooled into guying himself in this part, then took revenge by introducing hostile references to the Scriblerian farce when he revived Buckingham's old favorite, *The Rehearsal*, early in February. As Cibber himself reports it, AP grew passionately angry and confronted Cibber backstage: this was one of the earliest episodes in the long-standing quarrel between the two men, which culminated in the enthronement of Cibber as king of the dunces in the revised *Dunciad* of 1743.

The play contains some knockabout episodes but works chiefly by ridiculing the speech and ideas of pretentious figures in the world of literature and science. It has occasionally been revived in recent times, notably at the Swan Theatre, Stratford upon Avon, in 1996 (Royal Shakespeare Company, dir. Richard Cottrell).

For the text, see John Gay, *Dramatic Works*, ed. J. Fuller (Oxford: Clarendon, 1983), 1: 207–63; and the edition by J.H. Smith (Los Angeles: Augustan Reprint Society, 1961). For explanation of the background, see G. Sherburn, "The Fortunes and Misfortunes of *Three Hours after Marriage*," *Modern Philology*, 24 (1926), 91–109; and D. Nokes, *John Gay: A Profession of Friendship* (Oxford: Oxford University Press, 1995), 233–49.

Tickell, Thomas (1685–1740). Poet. His first work *Oxford* (1707) celebrated his alma mater as "the bless'd abode of every Muse" and praised his mentor **Joseph Addison**, among others. He gave lectures as Professor of Poetry in the university, 1711. His poem *On the Prospect of Peace* (1712) earned AP's admiration even though it threatened to forestall his own poem on the subject, **Windsor-Forest** (see *Corr* 1: 157). Tickell contributed to *The Spectator*, and he was given a post as assistant to Addison when the latter served as secretary to the Lord Lieutenant of Ireland in 1714; however, he did not leave England at this time. His translation of the first book of the *Iliad* appeared in 1715.

Addison became Secretary of State in 1717 and appointed Tickell as one of his undersecretaries. Following Addison's death, Tickell brought out the works of his old friend (1721), with AP's epistle *To Mr. Addison* printed in volume 1. Three years later Tickell was made secretary to the Lord Justices of Ireland and spent almost all the rest of his life in Dublin. He became a close friend of **Swift** and was reconciled to AP. He subscribed to the *Odyssey* and the **Shakespeare edition**.

Tickell was a reliable Whig and a decent poet of the second rank, but his determination to single out Addison for commendation in almost everything he wrote is apt to grow wearisome. His "Fragment of a Poem on Hunting" (1714) employs a **georgic** mode and makes obvious use of passages in *Windsor-Forest*, which is also the source for key ideas in his *Ode Inscribed to the Earl of Sunderland at Windsor* (1720). A poem long included among Tickell's works, "Thersites," is actually the second part of Swift's verses on "Traulus" (1730).

The coolness that developed between AP and Addison was partly occasioned by what Tickell did, or what AP thought that he did. Five essays on pastoral that Tickell wrote in *The Guardian* in April 1713 prompted AP to launch into an attack on **Ambrose Philips**, but there is no sign that the poet held special animus toward Tickell. It was the suspicion that Addison had engaged Tickell to produce a version of **Homer** to rival AP's own translation of the *Iliad* which caused all the trouble—and even more since AP took in into his head to believe that Addison himself had written this version under the cloak of Tickell's name. Indeed, AP later claimed, "Tickell himself, who is a very fair, worthy man, has since in a manner as good as owned it to me" (*Anecdotes* 1: 69). The story is not true, however. AP slyly alludes to this canard in his poem *Sandys's Ghost*: "[Let] Tickell and Addison combine"(*TE* 6:173). The proposed translation did not get any further than the opening book of the epic, and **John Gay** made playful fun of this in *Mr. Pope's Welcome from Greece*: "Tickell whose skiff (in partnership they say) / Set forth for Greece but foundered on the way."

The fullest account is R.E. Tickell, *Thomas Tickell and the Eighteenth Century Poets (1685–1740)* (London: Constable, 1931). A new treatment is urgently needed.

Tillotson, Geoffrey (1905–69). Professor of English at Birkbeck College, University of London, and Fellow of the British Academy from 1967. A major critic of eighteenth- and nineteenth-century literature, who often worked in collaboration with his wife Kathleen Tillotson (1906–2001). His work on AP includes books *On the Poetry of Pope* (1938) and *Pope and Human Nature* (1958). A portion of his *Essays in Criticism and Research* (1942) deals with AP. Included in the essays collected in *Augustan Studies* (1961) are studies of the *Epistle to Oxford*, AP's letters, and the **minor poems**. However, Tillotson's most lasting contribution to the field has been his outstandingly helpful edition of *The Rape of the Lock* and other early poems, which he compiled for the **Twickenham edition** (1940; rev. ed., 1962).

Timon's villa. The seat of a rich but vulgar landowner in AP's *Epistle to Burlington*, ll. 99–176. The passage immediately aroused contention, with regard to the supposed real-life model of Timon, that is, the **Duke of Chandos**. More recently, debate has focused on the possible basis of the architectural and **gardening** satire. The prime candidate has been **Cannons**, the princely estate of Chandos, which was located at Stanmore in Middlesex, northwest of central London. Another site proposed is Houghton Hall in Norfolk, the seat of **Robert Walpole** (see *Garden and City* 272–78). A third possibility is **Blenheim Palace**, home of the **Duke** and **Duchess of Marlborough**, a house certainly known to AP. Finally, there are some features that strongly suggest Chatsworth, Derbyshire, created by the first Duke of Devonshire. It was here that Charlotte, daughter of AP's friends the **Earl of Burlington** and his wife, lived after the poet's death, and ironically here was preserved the **manuscript** of his satiric treatment of the Timon episode, titled *A Master Key to Popery* (c. 1732).

See G. Sherburn, " 'Timon's Villa' and Cannons," *Huntington Library Quarterly*, 8 (1935), 131–52; *P&AGE* 381–83; and *TE* 3.ii: 170–88.

To Belinda on the Rape of the Lock. A poem of 30 lines in heroic couplets. It was first published anonymously in *Poems on Several Occasions* in 1717. Another version was printed by **Owen Ruffhead**, in his *Life of Alexander Pope* (1769), pp. 131–33. Almost certainly these lines were written soon after the expanded version of *The Rape of the Lock*, in 1714, and they may represent a form of joking apology to the young woman whose reputation had been put in jeopardy, that is, **Arabella Fermor**. In his accustomed manner AP mixes genuine tenderness and delicate compliment with some risqué implications. For the text and annotation, see *TE* 6:107–10.

Tobin, James Edward (1905–68). Scholar at Queens College, New York. He prepared a bibliography of eighteenth-century English literature (1939) and, together with **Louis Landa**, a bibliography of critical studies on **Jonathan Swift**. He is known to students of the **bibliography** of AP by reason of his compilation *Alexander Pope: A List of Critical Studies Published from 1895 to 1944* (1945).

To Mr. Addison, Occasioned by his Dialogue on Medals. This poem first appeared in some copies of an unauthorized collection, *The Works of Alexander Pope*, issued in 1720 (Griffith 126). However, AP may well have sanctioned the inclusion of this item. It had always been intended as a preface to a work by **Joseph Addison**, titled *Dialogues upon the Usefulness of Ancient Medals*. These dialogues had been started as far back as 1702, and Addison planned to publish them around 1713, the year in which he contributed a short essay on medals to *The Guardian*. They set out a rationale for the study of coins in illuminating history and enriching the understanding of the arts of the ancient world. It was not until the posthumous edition of Addison's *Works* by **Thomas Tickell** in 1721 that the dialogues first appeared in print, with AP's poem attached.

According to AP, his verses were written in

1715. This might be the case, since Addison's *Guardian* essay was reprinted by **Edmund Curll** that year in a book called *The Knowledge of Medals*, which AP seems to have consulted in writing his poem. However, his relations with Addison had started to decline by this time, and it may be that composition actually took place c. 1713. Near the end AP quotes a tribute to his friend **James Craggs junior**, later used as the inscription to the memorial to Craggs in Westminster Abbey. The **epistle** was reprinted a number of times, and in 1726 AP added four lines near the start. As it subsequently evolved, the poem consists of seventy-two lines in **heroic couplets**. From 1735 it was set alongside AP's major epistles, and in 1751 **William Warburton** gave it the status of the fifth of the *Moral Essays*, an inappropriate placing because of its comparative shortness and singleness of purpose. Nevertheless, it is certainly one of AP's most accomplished exercises in the poetic epistle and also serves to illustrate AP's knowledge of *virtù*, that is, what has recently been called "taste and the antique."

The text and commentary will be found in *TE* 6: 202–7. For background, see Ault 120–24. For an important analysis, see H. Erskine-Hill, "The Medal against Time: A Study of Pope's Epistle *To Mr Addison*," *Journal of the Warburg and Courtauld Institutes*, 28 (1965), 274–98, reprinted in *PRE* 285–314.

To Mr. Gay. In full, "To Mr. Gay, Who wrote him a congratulatory Letter upon the finishing his House." A poem of fourteen lines in couplets, written c. 1720. It surfaces for the first time when quoted in a letter from **Lady Mary Wortley Montagu** written in that year, in which she refers to AP's continued work to "embellish" his new house at **Twickenham** (where Lady Mary was then a neighbor). The poem contains a compliment to her on her fine eyes and constitutes a kind of displaced love letter, although it is nominally addressed to **John Gay** and refers mainly to the writer's house and garden. Soon afterward she quarreled with AP, and the poem did not appear in full until it was included in an edition of her correspondence in 1803. However, the last eight lines crept into print via a letter published in a newspaper in 1737. Meanwhile, AP had himself written a slightly different version of these eight lines in a letter to **Judith Cowper** dated 5 November 1722 (*Corr* 2: 141). For the text and annotation, see *TE* 6: 225–27.

Tonson, Jacob junior (1682–1735). Publisher. His father Richard (1653–90) had been in the book trade, as had his mother Mary Draper Tonson. He took over the business of his famous uncle, **Jacob Tonson senior**, c. 1718, and lived in the older man's home at Barn Elms, where he built a special room for the **Kit-Cat Club** portraits. The nephew had already been part of the family firm over a period of at least fifteen years and indeed signed an agreement with AP in 1713 (see *Corr* 1: 191–92). He seems to have specialized in the lucrative government contract work that underlay the prosperity of the business.

His relations with AP were generally good, as they were jointly involved in projects such as the *Works* **(1717)**, the **Shakespeare edition**, and the edition of the works of the **Duke of Buckinghamshire**. AP invited Tonson to **Twickenham** and corresponded with him in a free and friendly style. More than twenty of the letters that passed between them survive. Tonson also published the *Poems* of **John Gay** in 1720. Late in life he and AP moved further apart. He died at Barnes on 25 November 1735, predeceasing his uncle, an event marked by AP (*Corr* 3: 512). His estate was worth the huge sum of £100,000.

Tonson, Jacob senior (1655–1737). Publisher. Apprenticed, 1670; admitted as a freeman of the Stationers' Company, 1678. Sometimes worked in the trade with his brother Richard, who had an independent business. One of the greatest of all British publishers, he played a key role in the literary culture of his day. His decision to acquire the copyright of *Paradise Lost*, resulting in the fourth edition of 1688, brought **Milton** more squarely to the center of attention than ever before. His firm produced the first attempt at a critical edition of **Shakespeare**, that is, the work of **Nicholas Rowe**

(1709). Later Tonson's nephew and successor brought out AP's own **Shakespeare edition** and that of his rival **Lewis Theobald** (1733). In 1715 he issued a beautiful edition of **Spenser** in six volumes, prepared by **John Hughes**. There were other deluxe productions, including a sumptuous volume devoted to the *Metamorphoses* (1717).

His dealings with living writers were equally crucial in the formation of taste. Above all, he issued many of the most important works that **John Dryden** produced in the last two decades of his life. He also originated the series of "Dryden's *Miscellanies*," collections that exercised immense influence and allowed AP his first entrance into print in 1709. Tonson was the great pioneer in the field of publishing by **subscription**. He supported a wide range of contemporary authors, of whom a brief list suffices: **Addison**, **Steele**, **Garth**, **Congreve**, **Gay**, and **Prior**. Perhaps his most intimate friend was **Sir John Vanbrugh**. Most of these writers were members of the **Kit-Cat Club**, for which Tonson acted as secretary. This group represented not just the cultural elite of the nation but also a milieu in which (despite its Whiggish tone) AP could flourish as a young man.

When AP began his career with the *Pastorals*, he was told by **William Wycherley** that the young poet would be able to "make *Jacob's Ladder* raise you to immortality" (*Corr* 1: 63). With his eye for talent, Tonson had in effect headhunted AP. There were occasional hitches in the course of their relationship, as when Tonson encouraged **Thomas Tickell**'s abortive translation of **Homer**. For the most part, however, Tonson gave AP fair treatment, as he managed to do with authors in general, despite a keen sense of business. The connection went on well enough when the older Jacob gave way to his nephew **Jacob Tonson junior** around 1718, at least initially. The firm now had an interest chiefly in AP's earlier poems, as reprinted in the *Works* (**1717**), and in the later part of his career AP had less need of the giants of the book trade, such was the degree of independence he had achieved. Nevertheless, AP kept in contact with old Jacob, who had retired to Herefordshire, sickly and almost totally deaf.

The last of their surviving letters dates from December 1735, no more than three months before the old man died. By creative accounting his estate was assessed at £40,000, almost certainly a severe underestimation.

Some of the gossip that Tonson exchanged with AP in later years has been preserved in the *Anecdotes* of **Joseph Spence**. There are some double-edged references to "genial Jacob" and "left-legg'd Jacob" in *The Dunciad* (*TE* 5: 66, 299). But a large measure of underlying respect is apparent in what AP wrote to the **second Earl of Oxford** in 1731: "I will show you . . . a Phaenomenon worth seeing & hearing, Old Jacob Tonson, who is the perfect Image & Likeness of Bayle's Dictionary; so full of Matter, Secret History, & Wit & Spirit; att almost fourscore" (*Corr* 3: 176).

The most generally useful biography is K.M. Lynch, *Jacob Tonson: Kit-Cat Publisher* (Knoxville: University of Tennessee Press, 1971).

Tottenham Park. House in the Savernake Forest, near Marlborough, Wiltshire. Designed in a modified style of **Palladianism** by the **Earl of Burlington** for his brother-in-law **Charles, Baron Bruce** and built under the supervision of Henry Flitcroft, 1721–24. Later the gardens were remodeled by Lancelot "Capability" Brown. The house was rebuilt in the nineteenth century. AP visited Lord Bruce here in August 1734.

Tracy, Clarence (1908–93). Professor at the University of Saskatchewan. He wrote a biography of **Richard Savage**, *The Artificial Bastard* (1953); edited Savage's *Poetical Works* (1962); and edited **Samuel Johnson**'s *Life of Savage* (1971). In addition, he published *The Rape Observ'd* (1974), an edition of *The Rape of the Lock* augmented by numerous illustrations of the objects, places, and persons mentioned in the text.

Trivia. A poem in three books by **John Gay**, subtitled "The Art of Walking the Streets of London" and published by **Bernard Lintot** in January 1716. The printer was **William Bow-**

yer senior. AP had been following the composition of the work since 1714 and announced its imminent publication to **John Caryll senior** on 10 January (*Corr* 1: 327). It draws on various literary forms, most notably the didactic element in the *Georgics* of **Virgil**, which coalesced with the ancient "Ars" or how-to-do-it poem. In his portrayal of the seamier side of urban existence, Gay recalls the town eclogues of **Swift**; but he also looks forward to *The Dunciad*, for which *Trivia* is an important model. Compare the story of Cloacina, goddess of the sewers, which Gay added to Book 1 in 1720, with the episode of Lutetia in *The Dunciad*, Book 2 (*TE* 5: 139–40). Gay incorporates a tribute to his friend **William Fortescue** and singles out a few centers of civilization amid the surrounding blight: one such is **Burlington House**, where the music of **Handel** "transports the Soul, and thrills thro' ev'ry Vein" (2: 498). The poet also alludes to Lintot. In the closing lines there is an ironic reference to "W* and G**, mighty Names," which anticipates the use made of **Edward Ward** and **Charles Gildon** in *The Dunciad*.

Trumbull, Sir William (1639–1716). Diplomat and politician, AP's most important early patron. A civil lawyer educated at Oxford, where he became a Fellow of All Souls in 1657. Knighted, 1684. Engaged on a number of missions, including a spell as ambassador to Turkey, 1686–91. MP and from 1695 Secretary of State. He was forced out of office in 1697 and retired to his seat at **Easthampstead**, which lay a very short distance from AP's boyhood home. There Trumbull served as a Verderer (local supervising officer) of **Windsor Forest**. His first wife Katherine Cotterell (b. c. 1630), whom he married in 1670, died in 1704. Two years later he married Lady Judith Alexander (1681–1743), daughter of the fourth Earl of Stirling. His son and successor was William Trumbull IV (1708–60), to whom **Elijah Fenton** acted as tutor and whose granddaughter married the second Marquis of Downshire and inherited Easthampstead.

Sir William had been a patron of **John Dryden** and knew other writers such as **William Wycherley**. Having discovered the talented young poet in his neighborhood, he devoted much of his remaining years to promoting the fortunes of his protégé. AP himself gave this account: "It was while I lived in the Forest that I got so well acquainted with Sir William Trumbull, who loved very much to read and talk of the classics in his retirement. We used to take a ride together three or four days in the week, and at last almost very day" (*Anecdotes* 1: 31). AP dedicated "Spring," the first of his *Pastorals*, to Trumbull, who read the complete sequence before publication, and it was he who urged Pope to translate **Homer**. The pair continued in regular contact until the old man died in December 1716. Formerly an ardent Whig, Trumbull seems to have acquired different political opinions as he aged, ending up as something close to a committed Tory, like his nephew **Ralph Bridges**. It is possible that AP had Trumbull in mind in his portrait of the hermit-philosopher in *Windsor-Forest*. He certainly wrote that this noble retirement was the one embraced by Scipio, Atticus, and "Trumbal" (ll. 257–58), and elsewhere he claimed that he had celebrated Sir William's retirement to the groves of Windsor in that poem (see *Corr* 1: 328). According to Sir William, he had "long since put" AP on the subject of the Forest and even given him "severall hints" for it. In the last year of Trumbull's life, AP addressed him in the guise of "some Superior Being, that has been once among Men, and now sits above, at distance, not only to observe their actions, and weigh them with Truth and justice, but some times charitably to influence and direct them." He wrote a fully pondered **epitaph** on his old friend in 1717 (*TE* 6: 169–70). About twenty letters survive between the two men.

See G. Sherburn, "Letters of Alexander Pope, Chiefly to Sir William Trumbull," *Review of English Studies*, 9 (1958), 388–406; and "New Anecdotes" 343–49. A useful addition is C. Jones, "Party, Rage, and Fiction: The View from Fulham, Scotland Yard, and the Temple," *British Library Journal*, 19 (1993), 148–80. The best short survey of Trumbull's relations with AP is found in *Life* 104–9.

Tunbridge Wells. Fashionable spa town in Kent, thirty miles southeast of London, that was greatly developed in AP's lifetime. He seems to have visited the town only once, when he went in company with the **Duke of Buckinghamshire**, probably in the summer of 1720. **John Gay** and other friends were at Tunbridge on other occasions; while **Edmund Curll** had a shop there from 1712, as AP well knew (see *Prose* 1: 285).

Turner, Joseph Mallard William (1775–1851). The artist lived at various times in several villages adjoining the Thames, including Brentford, Isleworth, **Hammersmith**, **Twickenham**, and Chelsea. It is natural that he composed many landscapes based on the famously picturesque stretch of the river which is also connected with AP. Turner had a great reverence for the cultural associations of the district and in particular held AP and **James Thomson** in high regard as the poets of this favored spot. Two pictures that enshrine this interest are *View of Pope's Villa at Twickenham, during its Dilapidation* (1808) and *Thomson's Aeolian Harp* (1809). The former expresses Turner's outrage at Lady Howe's desecration of **Pope's villa**. In addition, Turner planned to write a poem "On the Demolition of Pope-House at Twickenham," of which drafts survive in his *Verse Book*. Other lines on the subject are found in the sketchbook that Turner used at this time and that contains a preparatory drawing for the painted *View*.

See A. Wilton, *Painting and Poetry: Turner's "Verse Book" and His Work of 1804–12* (London: Tate Gallery, 1990).

Turner family. The maternal line of AP's **ancestry**, who had long been settled in **York** and who had hovered between Catholic and Protestant faith.

Twickenham. The historic settlement grew up on a small rise near the medieval church, where the Middlesex bank of the Thames takes a pronounced curve to the right as the river flows down toward **Richmond**. The village stands on a low gravel shelf. **Pope's villa** was located a short way to the south of the center of the village, along the road to Teddington and **Hampton Court**. At this date Twickenham stretched no further than Cross Deep, the bounds of which were marked by a stream running into the Thames just above AP's home and which gave its name to the surrounding area. (The name Cross Deep refers to the stream, a crossing, the road, the district, and a house.) South of this stream, from 1747, **Horace Walpole** created his fanciful dwelling, Strawberry Hill, on the site of what was once known as "Chopped Straw Hall." This was a small house built in 1698, once occupied by **Colley Cibber**. Downstream the village extended in the direction of **Marble Hill**. Other important mansions stood near the river bank, including **Orleans House**, Lebanon House, and Radnor House. Nearer at hand, where Cross Deep approached the center of the village, the pioneer in psychiatric medicine Dr. William Battie built a house; previously, this site was occupied by a house owned by the Earl of Denbigh. The earlier house was destroyed by fire, in June 1734, causing AP to return home in haste (*Corr* 3: 409).

The chief road leading westward from the center of the village to the Common was Heath Lane, which branched off from King Street at its junction with the Hampton road (later known here as Cross Deep). Among those whose homes stood near Heath Lane were Lady Ferrers and her daughter **Lady Frances Shirley**; and **Lady Mary Wortley Montagu**. On the corner of Cross Deep and Heath Lane was the Grove, rented in turn by **James Craggs junior** and the **Duke of Wharton**. East of the church, in the direction of Orleans House, lay Mount Lebanon, where the **Earl of Strafford** had a house. In the years following AP's death the village expanded as it grew more fashionable, and among those who came to live in the vicinity were the painters Thomas Hudson and Samuel Scott, as well as the authors Paul Whitehead and **Henry Fielding**. Their homes were relatively modest, and of course there were many humble dwellings occupied by ordinary people.

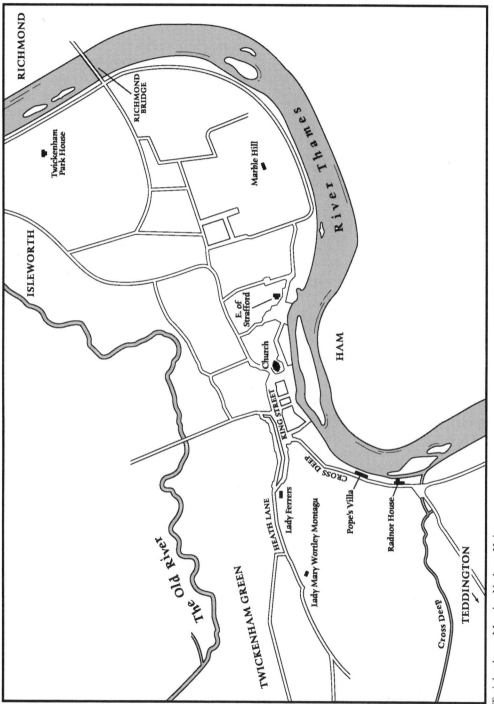

Twickenham. Map by Natham Heim

Much of the life of the village revolved around the river. The Thames provided a beautiful setting (especially with the picturesque islets or aits and the attractive Hamwalks on the Surrey bank) about which AP often rhapsodized. It also afforded a transportation link and a commercial artery. AP would regularly travel to and from London by boat; his boatman was one Bowry. A ferry had existed from the middle of the seventeenth century, crossing the river below Eel Pie Island (then known as Twickenham ait); AP would have used this regularly to get to Richmond and other places.

In nearby villages such as **Whitton** lived many other individuals known to AP. A small riverside house at Isleworth that was inherited by the Earl of Shrewsbury in 1718 was later remodeled by **James Gibbs**: this is almost certainly the house at which AP had visited the **Duke of Shrewsbury** in 1717. The minister in the adjoining parish of Teddington was **Stephen Hales**.

The most thorough account of the village will be found in Susan Reynolds, "Twickenham," in *The History of the County of Middlesex*, ed. S. Reynolds (London: Oxford University Press, 1962), 139–66. For the visual record, see B. Gascoigne and J. Ditchburn, *Images of Twickenham, with Hampton and Teddington* (Richmond: Saint Helena Press, 1981). The topography of the area is now best studied in works by A. Beckles Willson, including *Strawberry Hill: A History of the Neighbourhood*, 2nd ed. (Richmond, Surrey: Strawberry Hill Residents Association, 1995) and, especially for AP's links, *Mr Pope & Others at Cross Deep, Twickenham in the 18th Century* (Twickenham: For the author, 1996).

Twickenham edition. The standard version in modern times of AP's poems. Enititled *The Twickenham Edition of the Poems of Alexander Pope*, it appeared in eleven volumes between 1938 and 1968 (London: Methuen; New Haven, CT: Yale University Press): volume 3 was divided into two parts. For the first seven volumes, devoted to the poet's "original" works, **John Butt** acted as general editor. For the last

four volumes, devoted to the translations of **Homer**, the general editor was **Maynard Mack**. Individual volumes cover the following:

1. Pastoral Poetry and *An Essay on Criticism*
2. *The Rape of the Lock* and shorter translations
3.i. *An Essay on Man*
3.ii. *Moral Essays*
4. *Imitations of Horace*
5. *The Dunciad*
6. Minor Poems
7–8. *The Iliad*
9–10. *The Odyssey*

Distinguished scholars involved in the enterprise, along with the general editors, included Émile Audra, **Norman Ault**, **Frederick Wilse Bateson**, **Sir James Sutherland**, **Geoffrey Tillotson**, and Aubrey Williams.

Twickenham parish church. The church of St. Mary the Virgin, Twickenham. Here AP set up a monument to his parents, and the poet himself was buried there on 5 June 1744.

The main fabric of the church collapsed on 9 April 1713, with only the tower spared. This was probably caused by the digging of vaults underneath, undermining the foundations, but the weakness of the rag stone construction may have been a factor. Unavailing efforts had been made to stabilize the structure. A new red brick nave, very different in style from the medieval original, was built by the prominent architect John James (c. 1673–1746) in 1714–15, paid for by local subscriptions. A faculty for this purpose was issued by the Bishop of London on 30 April 1714. As churchwardens **Sir Godfrey Kneller** and **Thomas Vernon** took a leading part in the rebuilding project.

Alexander Pope senior was buried in **Chiswick** on 26 October 1717, but **Edith Pope** was laid to rest at Twickenham parish church on 11 June 1733. At some date around 1720 AP placed at the end of the north gallery of the church a monument to his father, with room for his mother's name to be added later. The work, to be made of white marble, was entrusted to **Francis Bird** (see *Corr* 2: 26–27). It is referred to in a note to the *Epistle to Arbuthnot* (see *TE* 4: 125). The Latin inscription may be translated: "It is given to all to die. For Alexander Pope, an honest and pious man, who lived 75 years and died in 1717; and his blameless and most pious wife Edith, who lived 93 years, and died in 1733; this monument was erected by their son for his parents and for himself." (AP was mistaken with regard to his father's age.) In his **will** AP requested that details of his own death should be briefly added to the tablet, as was done by adding the words "et sibi." He had told **Joseph Spence** much the same in December 1743 (*Anecdotes* 1: 259). The burial place is marked by a stone marked "P" next to a brass plate near the chancel steps. A memorial was set there in 1962 by three members of the Faculty of English of Yale University. It carries a Latin tag from *The Art of Poetry* by **Horace**, which may be rendered, "One who never exerted his powers in vain" (Horace was thinking of **Homer**). On the north wall of the north gallery of the church, considering the original too plain, **William Warburton** in 1761 placed a large pyramidical monument, with a medallion showing the poet's profile by Prince Hoare. With a hint of absurdity, Warburton added an inscription containing a four-line "Epitaph, For one who would not be buried in Westminster Abbey," which AP had written a few years earlier (*TE* 6: 376).

After the death of the Popes' faithful servant **Mary Beach**, in November 1725, AP placed a monument to her on the wall of the church. The short inscription, in English, pays tribute to thirty-eight years of faithful service to the poet and his family.

Around June 1725 AP became embroiled in an unfortunate dispute concerning a monument to Kneller, who had died in October 1723. Lady Kneller wished to erect "a vast three-hundred-pound Pyle," with effigies of her husband and herself, near the pew of the **Earl of Strafford** in the church. As AP told the Earl, this would result in great inconvenience, "overshadowing my Lady Strafford with the immense Draperies

& Stone Petticoats of Lady Kneller, & perhaps crushing to pieces your Lordships Posterity." Worse, it meant dismantling the wall tablet AP had erected to his father. AP resisted this measure in the ecclesiastical court, enlisting the support of "some of the chief gentleman of this Parish" in opposition. The Chancellor of the Court, Dr. Humphrey Henchman, visited the church in August, and the monument was not built. Kneller's tomb was placed instead in Westminster Abbey. AP had promised Kneller to write an **epitaph**. This he did, but he privately added a companion piece for Lady Kneller:

> One day I mean to Fill Sir Godfry's tomb,
> If for my body all this Church has room.
> Down with more Monuments! More room! (she
>   cryd)
> For I am very large, and very wide. (*TE* 6: 249)

For what is known of the episode, see *Corr* 2: 300–329; and Ault 325–27. Also buried in the church with an epitaph by AP was his friend **Nathaniel Pigott**.

See Anthony Beckles Willson, *The Church of St. Mary the Virgin Twickenham* (Twickenham: St. Mary's Parish Church, 2000).

Two or Three. Alternatively "A Receipt to make a Cuckold," this seven-line squib caused AP a good deal of trouble on account of its mildly salacious quality. It first appeared as "Epigram upon Two or Three" in the second edition of **Lintot**'s *Miscellany*, a volume that was probably edited in effect by AP, on 3 December 1713. Although the item was anonymous, it was unwise of AP to allow publication. In any case the resourceful **Edmund Curll** managed to get hold of a copy of the poem, and it was printed under the alternative title by **John Oldmixon** in a collection appearing on 6 April 1714, with a sly dig in the preface. As has been pointed out, "There can be very little doubt that this offence against Pope stands near, if not at, the very beginning of his life-long quarrel with Curll and of his persistent animosity to Oldmixon" (*TE* 6: 104). Following the illicit reprint, AP wrote to his friend **John Caryll senior** on 19 November 1714, "The thing they have been pleased to call a Receipt to make a Cuckold, is only six lines which were stolen from me," then proceeded to quote the full text of seven lines (*Corr* 1: 267–68). This clearly settles any questions of authorship. Later AP allowed the item to appear in the *Miscellanies*, but he never openly acknowledged his own responsibility.

For background, see Guerinot 15. For text and commentary, see *TE* 6: 104–5.

Twyford. Village three miles south of Winchester in Hampshire. Here AP attended a Catholic boarding school from the age of about eight. Here he learned basic grammar (chiefly Latin) but stayed for only a year. According to his sister **Magdalen Rackett**, the young boy was "whipped and ill-used . . . for his satire on his master, and taken from thence on that account." AP himself acknowledged writing the satire (*Anecdotes* 1: 9–10). The building then occupied by the school survives in Segars Lane, on the west side of the village.

⇒ U ⇐

Universal Prayer, The. Poem of fifty-two lines, in quatrains with alternating rhymes. Much reprinted and anthologized. It was first published by **Robert Dodsley** on 22 June 1738 in a folio of eight pages (Griffith 492; Foxon P492), price sixpence. However, the poem had originally been written in 1715, and a draft was sent to AP's friend, the **Duke of Shrewsbury**. A copy was forwarded to **Ralph Allen** in 1736, and **Lady Mary Wortley Montagu** also possessed a transcript. **Warburton** considered it a pendant to the *Essay on Man*, and in his editions the *Prayer* was regularly attached to AP's philosophic work. However, the poem is now more generally seen as an expression of a moderate and tolerant Christianity.

There is a setting in the form of a cantata by Andrzej Panufnik (1968–69) for soprano, contralto, tenor, and bass, with a mixed chorus, three harps, and organ. This was premiered under Leopold Stokowski in New York (1970). It was afterward performed at St. Mary's Church, **Twickenham**, where AP is buried. Panufnik was a local resident, and his own funeral took place there in November 1991.

See R.W. Rogers, "Alexander Pope's *Universal Prayer*," *Journal of English and Germanic Philology*, 54 (1955), 613–24, reprinted in *EA* 375–91. For text and commentary, see *TE* 6: 145–50.

Utrecht, Treaty of. The main peace agreement that brought the **War of Spanish Succession** to an end, following protracted negotiations initiated in 1711. It was signed at the culmination of a peace conference that had been taking place in the Dutch city of Utrecht since January 1712. The agreement on 31 March 1713 was signed by the British, the Dutch, the French, and the Spanish. A separate peace between France and the Holy Roman Empire was delayed until 1714. On 13 July 1713 a treaty was signed between Britain and Spain, which made territorial concessions to Britain, and transferred the "Asiento" to the South Sea Company. This was the Asiento de Negros, a grant allowing the exclusive right to export slaves to the New World. Other commercial clauses affected international trade between the combatants. Among those involved in the negotiations was the poet and diplomat **Matthew Prior**; its chief architect on the British side was **Viscount Bolingbroke**.

For the most part the treaty, negotiated by representatives of the **Harley administration**, was welcomed by Tories in Britain. The Whigs opposed its terms, especially those provisions that seemed to favor the "defeated" party, France. AP deals in a serious way with the treaty in *Windsor-Forest* and handles it comically in *A Key to the Lock*.

V

Vanbrugh, Sir John (1664–1726). Architect and dramatist. After a brief military career, he came to the fore as a playwright with *The Relapse* (1696) and *The Provok'd Wife* (1697). Soon afterward he gained renown as an architect after designing Castle Howard, **Blenheim Palace**, the **Haymarket Theatre**, and other buildings. He held official positions in the government Board of Works and in the management of the playhouse. Appointed Clarenceux King of Arms, 1703, even though he was not well versed in heraldic matters. Knighted, 1714. As a director of the Royal Academy of Music, he was a colleague of friends of AP like the **Earl of Burlington**, General **James Dormer**, and **Dr. John Arbuthnot**, and a member of the **Kit-Cat Club**.

AP did not know him well, and there are no surviving letters. A dismissive reference to Vanbrugh's plays occurs in the *Epistle to Augustus*: "How Van wants grace, who never wanted wit!" (l. 289). This is despite the fact that he apologized in the preface to the *Miscellanies* (1728) for raillery on "two Persons only," that is, **Addison** and Vanbrugh (*Prose* 2: 91). The satires here had in fact been written by **Swift**, whose cheerfully malicious lines on "Vanbrug's House" were included in the work. Elsewhere, AP told **Joseph Spence** that Vanbrugh ranked among the finest English comic writers in respect of their free and easy (i.e., civilized, unaffected) manner and that he could serve as a model for aspirant dramatists in his "familiar dialogue." AP also singled him out along with **Samuel Garth** and **Congreve** as "the three most honest-hearted, real good men of the poetical members of the Kit-Cat Club" (*Anecdotes* 1: 50, 170, 207). Nor were Vanbrugh's ventures into landscape architecture at **Stowe** and elsewhere uncongenial to AP's taste.

The explanation for this apparent contradiction may lie in Vanbrugh's political allegiances. His friends and patrons were almost all Whigs, and they promoted his architectural work even though the Tories preferred **James Gibbs**'s lighter and often more imaginative version of the Baroque style, quite apart from the supreme achievements of **Sir Christopher Wren**. Vanbrugh had been chiefly responsible for the building of Blenheim, which AP did not admire and which was regarded by many as an excessive reward for the **Duke of Marlborough**. Moreover, having lost his government post at the time of the **Harley administration**, he prospered once more under the Hanoverian regime, when AP's allies were mostly suffering a reversal in fortune. He managed to keep a much more learned armorial figure, **John Anstis**, from the office of Garter King of Arms: AP knew and cared enough about heraldry to resent this slight on a loyal Tory. It looks as if AP had no strong animus against Vanbrugh, but they were kept apart personally by their different cultural alliances.

See K. Downes, *Sir John Vanbrugh: A Biography* (London: Sidgwick & Jackson, 1987).

Van Loo, Jean-Baptiste (1684–1745). Flemish painter who after an itinerant career reached London in 1737, having lost a fortune at Paris in the Mississippi bubble. Not long afterward he painted AP's friend **James Dormer** and began to achieve considerable popularity among English sitters, including the royal family and Prime Minister **Robert Walpole**. He painted AP around 1744: see **portraits** and *Portraits*

66 for one of the most frequently reproduced images of the poet.

Vernon, Thomas (c. 1670–1726). AP's landlord. A Turkey merchant, army contractor, and MP. Son of the East India Company director Sir Thomas Vernon (d. 1711). A director of the South Sea Company, 1711–15. He moved to Twickenham Park in 1702 and lived there until his death. During this period he bought up a large number of estates in **Twickenham**, including about fifteen in the Cross Deep area. Two of these constituted the land where AP's home was located. He seems to have helped AP to install himself in the new residence and may have built a cottage for his tenant near the main dwelling. Vernon was a churchwarden of **Twickenham parish church**. He left his property to his wife Jane, née Stiles; at her death, in 1741, when two surviving daughters Annabella (c. 1706–77) and Matilda (d. 1766) inherited the family holdings in the village, these amounted to more than 100 items. At this date AP was given the opportunity to buy the house and garden but declined (see **Pope's villa**).

Verses on Durfey. In full, *Verses Occasion'd by an &c. at the End of Mr D'Urfy's Name in the Title of one of his Plays.* A poem of eighty-three lines in octosyllabic couplets, this minor *jeu d'esprit* enjoyed some popularity. Before **Curll** released it into print in 1726, with an attribution to AP, the item was evidently already circulating in manuscript, and transcripts survive in the papers of the **second Earl of Oxford**. AP responded to Curll's action by including the poem in the *Miscellanies* in 1728. No reliable evidence exists concerning the date of composition, though it seems likely to have been an early work. The poem is built around some witty wordplay involving letters of the alphabet, typographic signs such as + and &, and learned references. No real malice is shown toward **Thomas Durfey**, the author of popular song lyrics. See *TE* 6: 85–90.

Verses on England's Arch-Poet. A poem satirizing **Sir Richard Blackmore**, first published in the *Miscellanies* in 1732, with the full title *Verses to be placed under the Picture of England's Arch-Poet: Containing a compleat Catalogue of his Works.* It consists of thirty-four lines of octosyllabic couplets. Once assigned to **John Gay**, the work has been attributed to AP with some show of plausibility. The main target is found in Blackmore's notoriously long-winded epics. See Ault 248–58. For text and commentary, see *TE* 6: 290–93.

Verses on the Death of Dr. Swift. Perhaps the most famous poem by **Jonathan Swift**. Its writing goes back to the early 1730s, and an abbreviated version titled *The Life and Genuine Character of Dr. Swift* was published in 1733. Some have thought that AP was responsible for the truncated text, but an alternative view proposed is that Swift himself was directing a joke against AP's editorial methods in the *Miscellanies*. The first publication of the *Verses* by that name occurred in 1739, under the imprint of **Charles Bathurst**; by this time Swift had entrusted the manuscript to **Dr. William King**. The text was still bowdlerized and infected by the *Life and Character*. It is likely that AP and perhaps the **Earl of Orrery** had some hand in this editorial process. A more authoritative text was then published by **George Faulkner** in Dublin, also in 1739.

The Dean's satiric view of his career incorporates references to many of those close to the Scriblerian circle, as well as a famous couplet foreseeing reactions to his death: "Poor Pope will grieve a month; and Gay / A week; and Arbuthnot a day." Among those mentioned are **Bolingbroke**; **Ormonde**; the **first Earl of Oxford**; **Henrietta Howard, Countess of Suffolk**; and **William Pulteney**. Swift takes over a number of AP's targets such as **Walpole** and **Francis Charteris**; he also includes figures from **Grub Street** such as **Curll, Theobald, Cibber**, and **Moore Smythe**—with many of whom Swift had no personal contact. A warm tribute to the writer's old friend is often quoted: "In Pope, I cannot read a line, / But with a sigh, I wish it mine."

Verses on the Grotto. In full, *Verses on a Grotto by the River Thames at Twickenham, composed of Marbles, Spars, and Minerals*. A short poem (fourteen lines of **heroic couplets**, in most versions), perhaps notionally intended as one of the inscriptions in AP's garden at **Twickenham**. It presents the famous **grotto** as a cave of prophetic knowledge and pays tribute to his friends **Bolingbroke**, **Marchmont**, and **Wyndham**—the last of whom was recently dead when AP wrote the verses, probably in the second half of 1740. He sent one draft to Bolingbroke in September (*Corr* 4: 262). There are several early transcripts. The first publication was in the *Gentleman's Magazine* in 1741. See *TE* 6: 382–85; and *Garden and City* 69–72.

Verses sent to Mrs. T.B. with his Works. Subtitled "By an Author." A short poem of twenty-two lines in octosyllabic couplets. It first appeared in an anthology called *The Grove* (1721), perhaps edited by **Lewis Theobald**. AP subscribed for four large-paper copies of this volume. A manuscript in the Harley collection transcribes the six last lines with minor variants, as "wrote in Mr. Gay's works." However, the bulk of the evidence points directly to AP. The verses carry his usual bantering manner when writing to **Teresa Blount**; and the strictures implied in the poem (that the recipient, like most women, is unduly impressed by surface appearances and does not read books) are exactly those AP brought against Teresa. Moreover, we know that AP gave the Blount sisters a copy of his sumptuous *Works* **(1717)**. The book survives at **Mapledurham**, bound in red morocco with gold tooling—the colors specified in this poem as earning the lady's admiration. Finally, there are digs against **Charles Gildon** and **Giles Jacob**, habitual butts of AP.

On these grounds **Norman Ault** assigned the poem to AP: see Ault 163–71. It is not beyond the bounds of possibility that the volume was really by **Gay**: but his collection in 1720, to which Teresa and her sister **Martha Blount** subscribed, was titled *Poems on Several Occasions*, rather than "Works." Even if the book itself were Gay's, AP was perfectly capable of

writing in his voice as "an Author." For the text and commentary, see *TE* 6: 189–92.

Verses to be prefix'd before Bernard Lintot's New Miscellany. A poem of thirty lines in octosyllabic couplets. It amounts to an in-joke on AP's part, since it makes fun of the very anthology in which it first appeared: namely, a volume of *Miscellaneous Poems and Translations*, published by **Bernard Lintot** on 20 May 1712. AP seems to have conceived the idea for this item in December 1711, after reading a poem by his friend **John Gay** intended for the same miscellany (see *Corr* 1: 138–39). AP revised the poem subsequently and included it in the *Miscellanies* in 1728, not, however, before **Edmund Curll** had managed to purloin a copy and print it (as he had already done with the original 1712 version). AP contrasts Lintot's productions with the old editions of classics produced by famous printers such as Elzevir and Aldus Manutius. The modern volumes are preferable, he concludes, because they are less read and therefore in mint condition. Moreover, they possess an advantage in that their utility is not confined to scholars: "*Lintot's* for gen'ral Use are fit; / For some Folks read, but all Folks sh——."

For text and commentary, see *TE* 6: 82–85.

Vertue, George (1684–1756). **Antiquarian** and engraver. He served as engraver to the Society of Antiquaries from 1717 to 1756 and was a member of the circle of the **second Earl of Oxford**. Vertue engraved portraits of **Swift** and AP by **Charles Jervas**, as well as a number of pictures by **Sir Godfrey Kneller** and **Jonathan Richardson senior**, among others. However, he is best known for his voluminous collections in the field of art history, which formed the basis of *Anecdotes of Painting in England* (1762–71) by **Horace Walpole**. There are occasional references to AP in Vertue's notebooks and mention of Vertue in AP's correspondence. Vertue also engraved the bust of **Homer** for AP's *Iliad*, as well as the portrait of **Shakespeare** and the Stratford monument for the first volume of AP's **Shakespeare edition**.

villa, Pope's. Some time in 1718 AP leased a plot of land at **Twickenham**. It was located on the road from London to **Hampton Court** in the Cross Deep hamlet south of the main village. The house was built on two strips of land, one freehold and one copyhold, and each containing a cottage when AP acquired the lease. The plot and adjoining land had been acquired not long before by **Thomas Vernon**. Separately, on the side of the road furthest from the river, lay the **garden**, containing barely five acres in all. In the following year, perhaps as early as April or May, he moved into the property with his mother and nurse. One of the two existing cottages was demolished or totally transformed in the reconstruction. The other may have stood in some form, probably on the southern side of the villa, and could be used as a guest annex. AP's landlord seems to have provided a separate freestanding cottage. It is just possible that AP's mother lived in this.

Soon after his arrival AP began to remodel the house with the help of the architect **James Gibbs**, and he was able to report progress to friends by the summer of 1720. In the following year he described it as "quite finished" (*Corr* 2: 77). What emerged was a symmetrical structure of three stories, with a basement standing above ground on the river frontage and containing the entrance to AP's famous **grotto**. The design conformed to the fashionable style of **Palladianism**. There may have been a side bay with a pediment over it on the north side of the house. At first there were two simple staircases leading up either side of the main doorway. In March–April 1733 a portico was added to the riverside front, after consultations with the **Earl of Burlington** and **William Kent**. A balcony with a balustrade was added at second-floor level. Since the frontage consisted of only three central bays plus a single bay on each wing, it was little more than a cut-down version of the mansions AP had seen at the home of his aristocratic friends, and it represents a typical piece of Popian miniaturization. A lawn sloped down to the Thames in front of the house: the formal garden lay on the other side and was reached by a subterranean passage. In the basement were small chambers whose use is not totally

certain; one may have served as a wash-house. The first floor probably contained a hall, together with rooms fronting the river: the great parlor, the small parlor, and a private retiring room for AP. In the back may have been some offices such as the kitchen. On the second floor were three major rooms overlooking the river and, it is likely, Pope's **library** behind. The garret floor was confined to the central block and contained three rooms, probably bedrooms. There were cottages and outhouses of indeterminate character near to the villa. A boathouse rented by AP stood a short way further upstream, beyond the estate of **the fourth Earl of Radnor**.

Among the immediate neighbors were Lord Radnor upstream and Lady Ferrers, mother of **Lady Frances Shirley**, downstream. AP's landlord was a merchant and MP named Thomas Vernon. The property and some adjoining cottages were offered for sale to AP in 1743, at a price of approximately £1,000, but he decided not to go ahead with the purchase, chiefly on grounds of expense (see *Corr* 4: 446; *TE* 4: 391). After AP's death the property was bought by Sir William Stanhope (1702–72), brother of the **Earl of Chesterfield**; he removed the loggia and made considerable additions, including two wings, from 1756. Stanhope's daughter Elizabeth was married in 1747 to the politician Welbore Ellis, later first Baron Mendip (1713–1802), who inherited the property. A near neighbor, **Horace Walpole**, deplored these changes in 1760, although he considered that the house was "small and bad" and needed remodeling. He wrote that Stanhope had "hacked and hewed" the garden, on the advice of Ellis. He had cut down "the sacred groves" once created by AP, who had "twisted and twirled and rhymed and harmonized" the grounds.

After Ellis died, the Stanhope family sold it in 1804 to Sir John Briscoe, from whom two years later it passed to Charlotte Sophia, Baroness Howe (1762–1835). She demolished the house in 1807, provoking a chorus of criticism in years to come. Lady Howe was dubbed "the Queen of the Goths" after she also laid waste to the garden and stripped the grotto. The villa had long been a favorite subject for topographic painters, and **Turner** painted an evocative view of its sad state during the process of demolition. In 1840 the new house Lady Howe had built to a Gothic design, about a hundred yards from the old villa, was advertised for sale as "highly worthy the attention of the nobility, capitalists, the gentry and others." The structure was divided into two: one half survives as Ryan House, while the other part was demolished after war damage in 1944 and now forms part of Radnor Gardens. Most of the site of AP's home, on both sides of Cross Deep, is now occupied by St. Catherine's Convent School, which moved to this location in 1919.

See M. Brownell, *Alexander Pope's Villa*, the catalog of an exhibition held at Marble Hill House in 1980 (London: Greater London Council, 1980); as well as *Garden and City* 3–40.

Virgil (Publius Virgilius Maro) (70–19 B.C.). Roman poet. His main patrons were the Emperor Augustus and the aristocrat Maecenas, who helped him regain his family estate near Mantua, which had been expropriated. His works formed part of the staple reading of all educated persons in AP's time. There were numerous editions and translations, several of which were drawn on by **John Dryden** in his momentous version of *The Works of Virgil in English* (1697), a key document in the formation of English literature in the eighteenth century. A set of this work was in the **library** of AP, who termed Dryden's *Aeneid* "the most noble and spirited Translation that I know in any Language" (*Prose* 1: 251). See the edition of Dryden's *Aeneid* by F.M. Keener (London: Penguin, 1997).

Just as Virgil had modeled his own works on those of his Greek predecessors, so AP tried to replicate the shape of Virgil's career in his own writing. The *Pastorals* correspond to Virgil's *Eclogues; Windsor-Forest* to the *Georgics*; and in its starkly "modern" way *The Dunciad* represents in part a recomposition of the *Aeneid*. More generally, AP was influenced by the Latin poet's attitude toward nature and the landscape, and hardly any of his longer works were without some trace of the master. Many of his ideas on **gardening** draw on recollections of Virgil's

poetry; and plans for his own **garden** included a bust of his idol. Tags from the works are dotted through AP's writing in prose and verse. He possessed an edition of 1636 by the Dutch classical scholar Daniel Heinsius. Some interesting comments by AP are reported by **Joseph Spence**, including, "The *Aeneid* was evidently a party piece, as much as *Absalom and Achitophel*," and " 'Tis difficult to find any fault in Virgil's *Eclogues or Georgics*. He could not bear to have any appear in his *Aeneid*, and therefore ordered it to be burned" (*Anecdotes* 1: 229–30).

Virgilius Restauratus. That is, "Virgil Restored," a parody of the scholarly methods of **Richard Bentley** as applied to the text of **Virgil**. It first appeared as an appendix to *The Dunciad* in 1729, attributed to the pedantic critic "Martinus Scriblerus" and presented as a specimen of a work in progress. It offered comically ingenious (but wildly wrong) emendations of Virgil's text. The appendix was removed from later editions of *The Dunciad* and included in the *Miscellanies* (1732). Most authorities suggest that the author of this satire was **John Arbuthnot**, but no real evidence has been adduced. It is possible that AP had a large share in the production of the work. See *TE* 5: 217–21.

Voltaire (François-Marie Arouet) (1694–1778). French author. He met the exiled **Viscount Bolingbroke**, and through this agency AP was asked in 1724 to read his epic poem on King Henri IV, *La Ligue* (*Corr* 2: 228–29). Voltaire spent the years 1726–29 in England. During this time he met AP and **Swift** and renewed his acquaintance with Bolingbroke. Voltaire drew a vivid contrast between the poet's appearance, deformed and wasted, and his conversation, fluent and charming (see *Life* 447). He saw AP as "the best poet of England, and at present of all the world." In turn AP described Voltaire as "the first of the French poets" (*Anecdotes* 1: 222–23). A section of *Lettres philosophiques* (first published in English, 1733) is devoted to "Mr. Pope and some other

Famous Poets." This contains a free, but in its way idiomatic, translation into French of a passage on the **Cave of Spleen** from *The Rape of the Lock*. AP is termed "the most elegant, the most correct Poet; and at the same Time the most harmonious . . . that *England* ever gave birth to." In September 1726 Voltaire wrote AP a note of sympathy, in his stiff yet accurate English (*Corr* 2: 399), following a mishap AP had suffered when returning from **Dawley** (see **accidents**).

When *La Ligue* was published in England in 1728, under the title *La Henriade*, Bolingbroke headed the list of subscribers with a call for twenty copies. Others to subscribe were **John Barber**; **Lord Bathurst**; **Rev. George Berkeley**; **Baron Bruce**; **Colley Cibber**; the Duchesses of **Buckinghamshire**, **Marlborough**, and **Queensberry**; the **Dukes of Argyll** and **Chandos**; the **Earls of Chesterfield**, **Islay**, and **Peterborough**; Lord and Lady **Hervey**; **Erasmus Lewis**; **Samuel Molyneux**; **Lady Mary Wortley Montagu**; **Dr. Richard Mead**; **William Pulteney**; **William Rollinson**; Swift; **Thomas Tickell**; **Sir Robert Walpole**; **Sir William Wyndham**; and many others well known to AP. The poet himself was not among the subscribers.

In 1756 Voltaire added a section to the *Lettres*, reiterating his view that the *Essay on Man* was "the most beautiful didactic poem and the most useful and sublime that has ever been written in any language."

Voltaire's marginalia on the *Essay on Man* survive. See G.R. Havens, "Voltaire and Alexander Pope," in *Essays on Diderot and the Enlightenment in Honor of Otis Fellows*, ed. J. Pappas (Geneva: Droz, 1974), 124–50.

W

Waller, Edmund (1606–87). Poet. His vacillating conduct during the Civil War led to his exile in France but ultimately helped him to regain favor after the return of Charles II. In his time he was known less for the lyric poems that preserve his fame today than for his panegyrics and works on public themes. He was especially admired for the emollient ease of his couplet verse. AP's colleague **Elijah Fenton** produced an edition of the poet in 1729.

It is clear that AP shared in the general estimate of his poetry: "Waller was smooth; but Dryden taught to join / The varying verse, the full resounding line" (*Epistle to Augustus*, ll. 267–68). The orthodox view was that Waller had helped to introduce "correctness" into the nation by following French models. He was often linked with **Sir John Denham** as one who had elevated the prosody of English writers: in *An Essay on Criticism* AP commended "the *Easie Vigor* of a Line, / Where *Denham*'s Strength, and *Waller*'s Sweetness join" (ll. 360–61). As a boy AP placed Waller along with **Spenser** and Dryden among his favorite authors. But even late in life he still included the poet among the limited group of writers who "might serve as authorities for poetical language," in the company of Spenser, **Shakespeare**, **Milton**, Dryden, **Prior**, and **Swift**. He enjoyed the sonorous effects of poems such as "The Battle of the Summer Islands." See *Anecdotes* 1: 19, 170, 196–97.

Some of AP's earliest surviving works are the six sets of "Verses in Imitation of Waller," allegedly written "by a Youth of thirteen." These were first published in *Poems on Several Occasions* (1717). Another imitation, "On a Fan," appeared in *The Spectator* in 1712. See *TE* 6: 7–11, 45–47. There are several echoes of Waller in earlier poems such as *Windsor-Forest*.

Walpole, Horace, fourth Earl of Orford (1717–97). Writer, connoisseur, and collector. Son of **Sir Robert Walpole**. In 1747 he moved to what became Strawberry Hill, on a site just south of AP's home at **Twickenham**. Although AP had died three years earlier, Walpole interested himself in the poet. He resented criticisms of his father by AP and also the targeting in *The Dunciad* of the classical scholar **Richard Bentley** (father of his own friend Richard Bentley junior). Walpole held a low opinion of the **Pope's villa**, which he called "small and bad." However, he recognized the merits of AP's **garden**, prior to its effective destruction, observing that "it was a singular effort of art and taste to impress so much variety and scenery on a spot of five acres." Walpole assembled prints of the neighborhood, some of them showing AP's villa; and his collection of pictures may have included items once owned by AP, as well as **portraits** of the poet. A "little pocket Homer" much used by AP later came into the possession of Walpole, and it is now preserved in the Walpole Library at Farmington, Connecticut. There is no evidence that the two men were personally acquainted; but Walpole certainly did know a number of people who had been familiar with AP, including local residents like **Lady Frances Shirley**, as well as many other individuals including **Joseph Spence**.

See *Notes on the Poems of Alexander Pope, by Horatio Earl of Orford*, ed. W.A. Fraser (London: Chiswick Press, 1871).

Walpole, Sir Robert, first Earl of Orford (1676–1742). Britain's first Prime Minister as generally recognized and the longest-serving occupant of this position (1721–42). A Whig MP from 1701 who came to prominence as Secretary at War, 1708–10. Member of the **Kit-Cat Club**. After the death of **Queen Anne**, he took a leading part in the political disgrace of members of the **Harley administration** and in the punishment of those involved in the rising of 1715–16. Later he was behind the arraignment of one of AP's friends when the **Atterbury plot** was uncovered. It was the collapse of the **South Sea Bubble** that allowed Walpole to assume almost total control of government for the next two decades. Knight of the Bath, 1725; Knight of the Garter, 1726. Despite occasional reverses he was able to retain the confidence of the first two Hanoverian Kings and was not ousted until early 1742, when he was created Earl of Orford. Father of **Horace Walpole**.

AP perhaps came to know Walpole through his contacts with the court of the Prince of Wales in the early years of **George I**. The two men were on good terms personally: AP attended some of Walpole's Sunday receptions, and the Minister did the poet some unknown favor in 1725, probably related to AP's family or friends. He seems to have visited AP at **Twickenham** at least once. A more generous patron of literature than he is often supposed to be, Walpole entered his name for ten copies in the **subscription** list for the *Odyssey*. It was even contrived that Walpole should present a copy of *The Dunciad* to the King and Queen in March 1729, though the poem is fairly open in its satire on both the royal pair and the Minister. The main factor cementing this relationship seems to have been the presence of **William Fortescue**, Walpole's private secretary, among AP's own circle of advisers. But there may have been a degree of mutual respect, as well as a social congeniality fostered by Walpole's skill in human relations and his easygoing and thick-skinned nature.

From about 1730 the two men drifted further apart, especially as AP identified himself more and more with the **opposition to Walpole**, where fundamental differences in outlook became more evident. Although there are some complimentary references in the poems to Walpole as a private man, most of AP's work in the 1730s echoes the views of critics of the Minister in his public capacity. The critics exaggerated Walpole's corruption and cynicism and ignored his success in achieving peace and prosperity over a number of years. Whenever possible, AP seems to have distinguished between the leader of the government and the instruments of his power: "Sure, if I spare the Minister, no rules / Of Honour bind me, not to maul his Tools" (*TE* 4: 321). Despite this, AP and Walpole have come to seem in retrospect "mighty opposites," symbols of differing values—in Walpole's case, profuse living (his home at Houghton may be a model for **Timon's villa**) and coarse manners, in AP's case, a moderate way of life and fastidious concerns in the sphere of morality and taste. Most of the *Imitations of Horace* are relevant to these issues.

A concise modern appraisal of Walpole's career will be found in J. Black, *Robert Walpole and the Nature of Politics in Early Eighteenth-Century Britain* (New York: St. Martin's, 1990). See also J. Black, *Walpole in Power* (Stroud, Gloucestershire: Sutton, 2001); and J. Black, ed., *Britain in the Age of Walpole* (London: Macmillan, 1984). For the relations of AP and Walpole, see *Garden and City* 116–231.

Walsh, William (1663–1708). Poet and critic. He was a Whig MP and also gentleman of the horse (a minor court position) to Queen Anne from 1702 to 1708. A relative of AP's friend **Edward Blount**. His sister Octavia Walsh (1677–1706) also left a number of poems at her early death. According to **Samuel Johnson**, who gives him brief treatment in the *Lives of the Poets*, Walsh was "known more by his familiarity with greater men, than anything done or written by himself," and it is certainly true that his connections with his mentor **John Dryden**, as well as **Addison** and his fellows in the **Kit-Cat Club**, have preserved his name more than the poetry he contributed to collections such as the *Miscellanies* of **Jacob Tonson senior**. Dryden's description of him as "the best critic of out nation" certainly flatters Walsh.

Nevertheless, AP thought highly of him and always recalled the assistance Walsh gave him when he was starting out as a poet with works such as the *Pastorals*. There is a commendation of "knowing Walsh" in the *Epistle to Arbuthnot* and a warm tribute in the concluding lines of *An Essay on Criticism*: "the Muse's Judge and Friend, / Who justly knew to blame or to commend" (*TE* 1: 325). In his **Memorial List** of obituaries, AP recorded the death of Walsh with an entry: "a wise critic, friend and good man" (*EC* 1: ix). A portrait hung at AP's house.

Walter, Peter (c. 1664–1746). One of the archetypal villains of **Augustan satire**. He was a moneylender, estate manager, steward, marriage broker, attorney, and finally a landowner in Dorset. In addition, Walter was MP for Bridport, a borough where elections were conducted with less than clean hands, during the reign of **George I**. As a result of his skill in buying up estates, he grew on intimate terms with many of the largest aristocratic families. He acted for the Duke of Newcastle and in this capacity took a central role in the arrangements for the marriage of the Duke to Henrietta Godolphin, granddaughter of the **Duke** and **Duchess of Marlborough** and daughter of **Henrietta, Duchess of Marlborough**. In this transaction Walter "appears producer, stage-manager and prompter all in one" (Howard Erskine-Hill). These events also brought him into the orbit of **William Congreve**, who left Walter a bequest of £20.

AP was the first major writer to fix on Walter's depredations on the public: there are many cutting references in the *Imitations of Horace*. (Usually AP calls him "Peter" or "Waters," a device to avoid retaliation from the legally adroit Walter.) **Swift** inherited this hatred at a distance; while **Henry Fielding**'s satire on "Peter Pounce" in *Joseph Andrews* can be explained by firsthand knowledge of Walter's depredations in the neighborhood of Shaftesbury. The fullest assault is mounted in the text and notes to the *Epistle to Bathurst*, where AP's view of this "dextrous attorney" are made fully apparent (*TE* 3.ii: 86, 102), and where he is linked with **Francis Charteris** and **John**

Ward. On top of everything else, Walter was notorious for parsimony in his private life.

See *Social Milieu* 103–31.

Waltham Blacks. A group of "wicked and evil-disposed persons going armed in disguise," as they were named in the Black Act of 1723 (9 Geo. I, c. 22). This act was a measure of great severity, designed to curtail the depredations of the so-called Blacks; it survived on the statute books for a century. The Blacks were men who conducted a campaign against the authorities in certain royal forests, often blacking their faces and adopting other disguises. They took deer and attacked the property of local landowners. Their name comes from Waltham Forest in Hampshire. However, their most important sphere of operations was in **Berkshire**, AP's home county, and parallel activities went on in the New Forest and Enfield Chase. Serious trouble emerged around 1720, but it was in 1722 and 1723 that matters came to a head.

National politics had some bearing on the episode, even though at a local level the main cause of disaffection was the existence of harsh forest laws dating from medieval times. Some of those involved may have lost money in the **South Sea Bubble**. Others were possibly **Jacobites** and using the occasion to strike at the Hanoverian establishment. Prime Minister **Robert Walpole** began an energetic exercise to crush the Blacks, allowing the impression to get about that they were linked with the **Atterbury plot**. Eventually some prosecutions were mounted, although only a few convictions were obtained, and sporadic outbursts of Blacking broke out in the forests for years to come.

Since the epicenter of the troubles lay in **Windsor Forest**, AP would naturally have had some awareness of these events. However, his personal connections were more extensive. First, his brother-in-law Charles Rackett and his nephew Michael Rackett (see **Rackett family**) were heavily implicated in the affair, and both were arrested in May 1723. Each escaped punishment, although Michael went abroad and for some unknown reason suffered outlawry. Second, AP's mentor **Sir William Trumbull** had served for many years as a Verderer, helping to administer forest law. Some of the major activity took place within close range of **Easthampstead**, where Sir William was lord of the manor. Although Trumbull was dead by 1722–23, his family remained. Third, AP's patron **Viscount Cobham** held the office of Constable of Windsor Castle, and as such he stood at the head of the administration of law within the forest. Fourth, an *agent provocateur* used by the government in Berkshire was Rev. Thomas Power, the curate of Easthampstead and son of the absentee vicar. In 1725 he was given a living in Ireland, to get him out of the way, and there he fell foul of **Jonathan Swift** (Swift *Corr* 3: 116). Lady Trumbull, the widow of AP's patron, was embarrassed by the activities of Power. Fifth, Philip Caryll, the first cousin of AP's close friend **John Caryll senior**, was mixed up in the grubby relations of Jacobite conspiracy and Blacking, emerging as a government informer in 1723. Sixth, AP had contacts with many of those who lived in the neighborhood, including some who were the victims of Blacking. He referred disparagingly to some of the Whig grandees affected (notably Lord Cadogan) and also officials seeking to enforce Walpole's measures. It is likely that there were other undiscovered links between AP and the principal actors in the affair of the Waltham Blacks. The episode casts retrospective light on the forest as AP had portrayed it in the time of **Queen Anne** (see *Windsor-Forest*).

The most important study is E.P. Thompson, *Whigs and Hunters: The Origin of the Black Act* (London: Allen Lane, 1975; reprint, Harmondsworth: Penguin, 1977). For AP's involvement, see Thompson, "Alexander Pope and the Blacks," in *Whigs and Hunters*, 278–94; and P. Rogers, "Blacks and Poetry and Pope," in *Essays on Pope* (Cambridge: Cambridge University Press, 1993), 168–83.

Wanley, Humfrey (1672–1726). Antiquarian scholar. He worked for the Bodleian Library from 1696, then from 1700 to 1708 for the Society for the Propagation of the Gospel. He made his name as a paleographer through work on Anglo-Saxon manuscripts. He began cataloging the **Harleian library** in 1708 and

thereafter acted as librarian to the **first Earl of Oxford**, as well as the latter's son and successor. His pedantic speech and fusty ways amused the Scriblerian group; however, he also excited their liking, and **Matthew Prior** wrote of Wanley with great affection. AP often saw him during the time of the second Earl, visiting the library, for example, on 4 August 1725, but only two letters survive between the two men.

See *Earls of Creation* 175–85; *The Diary of Humfrey Wanley, 1715–1726*, ed. C.E. Wright and R.C. Wright (London: Bibliographical Society, 1966); and *Letters of Humfrey Wanley: Palaeographer, Anglo-Saxonist, Librarian, 1672–1726*, ed. P.L. Heyworth (Oxford: Clarendon, 1989).

Warburton, William (1698–1779). Churchman and author. Originally an attorney, he was ordained in 1723 and obtained a living near Lincoln. He became known for his controversial writings before producing widely read works in theology, *The Alliance between Church and State* (1736) and *The Divine Legation of Moses* (1737–41), a learned and crotchety attack on deism. A bitter opponent of the philosophical works of **Viscount Bolingbroke**. Chaplain to **Frederick, Prince of Wales** from 1738. His edition of Shakespeare (1746) was intended to supplant the work of his former friend and collaborator **Lewis Theobald**, but for the most part, it has not convinced later scholars. Dean of Bristol, 1757–60; Bishop of Gloucester from 1760 to his death.

Warburton first set himself up as the defender and expositor of AP's poetry with *A Vindication of Mr. Pope's Essay on Man* (1738–39), a riposte to the attacks on its orthodoxy by **Jean-Pierre de Crousaz**. The two men met in 1740, and the clergyman quickly worked his way into the poet's good graces. He became AP's principal agent in reformulating the canon and was made literary executor in his **will**. He also acquired directly or indirectly the major part of AP's **library**. In 1746 Warburton married Gertrude Tucker, the twenty-year-old niece of **Ralph Allen**, and he spent long periods at **Prior Park**. There he was one of those who made life difficult for **Martha Blount**, of whom he disapproved. He lived long enough to gain the friendship of younger men such as Laurence Sterne and to launch an attack on David Hume. After his death he was criticized by Edward Gibbon.

Warburton has fared badly at the hands of posterity. In his controversial books he adopts a combative and even hectoring tone. His main bequest, along with *The Divine Legation*, was his edition of AP's works (1751), which remained the basis of most subsequent versions of AP's works for a century or more. Warburton's text is often irritating in its lack of scholarly scruple and its readiness to "improve" the poet in the interests of orthodoxy or conventional taste, and his attempts to reshape *An Essay on Man* and the *Moral Essays* are generally thought to be misguided. However, the edition does proceed from extensive firsthand contact with AP in his last years, notably during the preparation of the so-called **deathbed edition**. In addition, Warburton planned a biography of AP, and though, he did not carry this through he supplied a large body of materials to **Owen Ruffhead**. He gave **Joseph Spence** some anecdotes but little bearing on AP. Looking on himself as the guardian of the poet's reputation, he erected a bulky monument in **Twickenham parish church**.

A substantial new treatment is needed. The most recent coverage is in a slender book, R.M. Ryley, *William Warburton* (Boston: Twayne, 1984).

Ward, Edward (1661–1731). Miscellaneous writer, usually known as Ned Ward. His most famous production was *The London Spy* in eighteen parts (1699–1700). He often dealt in his work with travel and colonial themes. With no apparent provocation, AP included his name in *The Art of Sinking*, chapters 6 and 9. He then turned up in *The Dunciad*, with references in Books 1 and 3, later augmented with wickedly precise details. Ward complained that he kept not an "alehouse" in Moorfields, as the poem suggested, but a "tavern." He was responsible for two **pamphlet attacks** in retaliation, *Durgen* (1728) and *Apollo's Maggot in his Cups* (1729): see Guerinot 157–59, 177–79. AP

did not have enough on Ward to move much beyond general satire of a popular writer of no great delicacy but considerable gusto.

See H.W. Troyer, *Ned Ward of Grubstreet: A Study of Sub-Literary London in the Eighteenth Century* (Cambridge, MA: Harvard University Press, 1946; reprint, London: Cass, 1968).

Ward, John (d. 1755). Brother of **Joshua Ward**. A merchant sometimes known as "Ward of Hackney," regarded by AP as a swindler. He was an MP from 1701 to 1726, but his various constituencies, ending with the venal borough of Weymouth, were merely "commodities to be bought" (Paul Baines). He had been steward to the **Duke of Buckinghamshire**'s estates at Mulgrave in North Yorkshire. In 1717 the Duke discovered that Ward had embezzled the entire stock of alum produced there. After the Duke's death in 1721 his widow the **Duchess of Buckinghamshire** brought an action against Ward in Chancery. With progress in the case predictably slow, the young Duke's trustees enlisted the help of AP's friends **Lord Bathurst**, **Orrery**, and others to present a petition to Parliament to help recover the assets. Despite an appeal by Ward to the House of Lords, he was defeated in the Chancery suit, a decree issued, and costs awarded against him. The Attorney General (later Lord Hardwicke) then brought an action for forgery in the Court of the King's Bench, and eventually in February 1727 (after Ward, not for the first time, had absconded) he was convicted and sentenced to a fine of £500 and the pillory. He was also expelled from Parliament. In years to come, he was to continue to make a nuisance of himself.

Ward's career provided abundant copy for AP. His spell in the pillory even figures briefly in *The Dunciad*, Book 3 (*TE* 5: 152). The fullest treatment occurs in a note to l. 20 of the *Epistle to Bathurst*, where he is linked to **Peter Walter** and **Francis Charteris**. This note draws attention to further suspect behavior on Ward's part, involving an attempt to syphon off money from the estate of **Sir John Blunt**, which had been declared forfeit in the aftermath of the **South Sea Bubble** (see *TE* 3.ii: 85, 104).

In the case of Ward, AP's natural interest in the depredations of such financial operators was abetted by his friendship with the Duke and Duchess. In fact, the Duchess kept him abreast of developments in the case: See *Corr* 2: 286–87. The last blow from the poet's hand came in the *Epilogue to the Satires*, and characteristically the verse does not confine its animus to the obvious malefactor: "Shall *Ward* draw Contracts with a Statesman's skill?" (*TE* 4: 306).

See P. Baines, *The House of Forgery in Eighteenth-Century Britain* (Aldershot: Ashgate, 1999), 61–80.

Ward, Joshua (1685–1761). Brother of **John Ward**. Quack doctor. Briefly an MP. After being accused of fraud, he fled to France. There he developed his two popular universal nostrums, known as "Ward's Drop and Pills." The former consisted of an antimony salt dissolved in wine. The latter was a medicine made with an antimony salt and an East Indian extract called Dragon's Blood. It apparently contained arsenic and may well have done more harm than good. It was said to induce purging, sweating, and vomiting at the same time. However, on his return to England in 1734 Ward received considerable patronage from the great and even from **George II** himself. He was also defended by **Henry Fielding**. At the same time he was often satirized in the press and figures in a famous print by **William Hogarth**. He was known as "Spot" because of a birthmark on his face.

AP capitalized on the quack's notoriety with a couplet in the *Epistle to Augustus*: "He serv'd a 'Prenticeship, who sets up shop; / Ward try'd on Puppies, and the Poor, his Drop." A note reads, "A famous Empirick, whose Pill and Drop had several surprizing effects, and was one of the principal subjects of Writing and Conversation at this time" (c. 1737). There is another reference in *The Sixth Epistle of the First Book of Horace Imitated*. See *TE* 4: 211, 241. **Viscount Bolingbroke** wanted to call in Ward during AP's final illness, but this does not seem to have been done (*Corr* 4: 519).

War of the Spanish Succession. An involved and long-lasting international conflict dividing the major powers of Europe. It began in 1701, after the throne of Spain had been settled on Philip, Duke of Anjou, a grandson of Louis XIV of France. The Bourbon claimant was supported by France and Spain, and ranged against these nations was the Grand Alliance, comprising Britain, the Holy Roman Empire, and the United Provinces (Holland). The main theater of war was situated in the Low Countries, but action spread to Germany, Italy, and Spain. In reality, one of the main causes of the war was the need to control trade with the New World, something disputed by France, British, and Spain, in particular. There were some notable British victories on land and sea, particularly those of the **Duke of Marlborough**. However, these tended to dry up as time went on, and there were some reverses in the Spanish campaign.

In general the war was opposed by British Tories, who distrusted the Dutch and wished to keep open lines of communication with the French. In addition, they believed that the conflict had been allowed to go on longer than necessary in order to fill the coffers of army contractors and city magnates (who provided the credit for the military operations) and that another motive was to provide for the greater glory of Marlborough. Whigs represented an opposite point of view, as they stressed the continuing threat provided by France. After extensive peace negotiations, the war was eventually ended by the **Treaty of Utrecht** in 1713. (Some of the combatants stood outside the agreement until 1714.) In his poem *Windsor-Forest*, AP lauded this peace and alluded to some of the main features of the war. Other references suggest that AP accepted the view set out by his friend **Jonathan Swift**, in a series of trenchant pamphlets such as *The Conduct of the Allies* (1711).

Warren, Austin (1899–1986). Critic and influential teacher at the University of Michigan. He was an early student of literary theory and a pioneer of the New Criticism, with interests in both British and American literature. His main work on AP is *Alexander Pope as Critic and Humanist* (1929), a study in some ways in advance of its time. See also an essay on AP in *Rage for Order* (1949).

Warton, Joseph (1722–1800). Clergyman, poet, and critic. Brother of the literary historian and Poet Laureate Thomas Warton (1728-90), who was also Professor of Poetry at Oxford. Both the Wartons were members of the Literary Club along with **Samuel Johnson**. Joseph served as headmaster of Winchester school from 1766 to 1793. His two-part *Essay on the Writings and Genius of Pope* (1756–82) was one of the harbingers of more critical attitudes toward AP. In 1797 he published a substantial edition of the *Works* in nine volumes, which was largely supplanted by the later editions of **William Lisle Bowles** and **William Roscoe**.

See J. Pittock, *The Ascendancy of Taste: The Achievement of Joseph and Thomas Warton* (London: Routledge, 1973). The most up-to-date biographical account is D. Fairer, "Joseph Warton," in *The Dictionary of Literary Biography: The Eighteenth-Century British Poets*, ed. J. Sitter (Detroit: Bruccoli Clark Layman, 1991), 262–70.

Warwick, Edward Rich, seventh Earl of (1697–1721). He was the stepson of **Joseph Addison**, after his mother's remarriage in 1716—an unhappy match, according to AP (*Anecdotes* 1: 79). He had succeeded to the earldom at the age of three. A wild young man who is said to have encountered AP on his ventures about town, c. 1714, and to have warned the poet about Addison's growing hostility. According to **Colley Cibber**, there was a meeting between Warwick and himself at **Button**'s coffeehouse, probably in 1715, when a joke was played on AP, who was taken to a brothel near the Haymarket; Warwick "staid tittering without." A friend of **John Gay**, he subscribed for ten copies of the latter's *Poems* in 1720. Gay introduced him into the poem *Mr. Pope's Welcome from Greece* in the same year. AP mentions Warwick several times in his letters, sometimes in a context of rakish behavior. He figures in *A Farewell to London* and *Sandys's Ghost*.

Wasserman, Earl Reeves (1913–73). Scholar who taught at Johns Hopkins University from 1948. He wrote widely on English poetry. His book *The Subtler Language* (1959) contains one of the most influential studies of AP's *Windsor-Forest*. In 1960 he published *Pope's Epistle to Bathurst: A Critical Reading with an Edition of Manuscripts*. Among his essays on AP is a well-known article, "The Limits of Allusion in *The Rape of the Lock*," *Journal of English and Germanic Philology*, 65 (1966), 425–44, reprinted in *PRE* 224–46. See also *Ode for Musick on St. Cecilia's Day*.

Watts, John (c. 1678–1763). Printer. Apprenticed, 1698; freed, 1707. One of the most celebrated figures in the history of eighteenth-century printing, he was eulogized by John Nicholls: "The fame of Mr. John Watts for excellently good printing will endure as long as any public library shall exist." He was especially admired for editions of Greek and Latin classics, published by **Jacob Tonson senior**, featuring elegant design and skilled typographic layout. Watts was also responsible for splendid editions of English writers including **Addison** and **Congreve**. His printing house stood in Bow Street and then near Lincoln's Inn Fields, where Benjamin Franklin worked for him from about September 1725 to June 1726. Watts printed *The Guardian* paper of **Richard Steele**. He often printed libretti and occasionally music. Together with **William Bowyer senior**, he advanced money to William Caslon (1692–1766) to set up the first great English type foundry in 1720.

Most of AP's early works were printed by Watts, whether the publisher was Tonson, **Bernard Lintot**, or someone else. The connection was resumed with the *Odyssey* and the **Shakespeare edition**. There is evidence from the correspondence that AP dealt with Watts personally, but they cannot have been intimate acquaintances.

Welsted, Leonard (1688–1747). Poet and translator. A product of Westminster School and Trinity College, **Cambridge**, generally nurseries of Whig talent. Clerk in the office of the Secretary of State, then Clerk in the Ordnance Office, 1725–47, in which post he occupied a residence in the Tower of London. His first wife was Frances (1688–1724), daughter of the composer Henry Purcell. His translation of *Longinus on the Sublime* (1712) was prefaced by an essay of complacent faith in modern writers such as **Ambrose Philips**. **Jonathan Swift** suggests in his poem *On Poetry: A Rhapsody* that Welsted's version was in fact "translated from **Boileau**'s translation," rather than from the Greek. In AP's anti-Longinian satire *The Art of Sinking*, Welsted predictably receives some attention and figures in chapter 6 as one of the "didappers," that is, "authors that keep themselves long out of sight, under water, and come up now and then when you least expect them." He is also listed among the "eels," that is "obscure authors, that wrap themselves up in their own mud" (*Prose* 2: 197).

Hostilities began several years earlier. In *Palaemon to Celia, at Bath* (1717), Welsted had launched a few thrusts at the Scriblerians. AP waited, as was his habit, and then followed up *The Art of Sinking* with a damaging passage in Book 2 of *The Dunciad*. Here the dunce excels in the mud-diving sports: "No crab more active in the dirty dance, / Downward to climb, and backward to advance" (2: 297–98). Even more cruel were the lines that parodied a famous passage in *Cooper's Hill* by **Sir John Denham**:

> Flow Welsted, flow! Like thine inspirer, Beer,
> Tho' stale, not ripe; tho' thin, yet never clear;
> So sweetly mawkish, and so smoothly dull;
> Heady, not strong, and foaming tho' not full. (3: 163–66)

Understandably riled, Welsted responded with a vigorous retort, *One Epistle to Mr. A. Pope* (1730), possibly cowritten with **James Moore Smythe**. In this a number of charges are leveled against AP, some familiar and some new. The most intriguing is that **Charles Gildon** "was dismissed from the D[uke of Buckingham]'s Pension and Favour, on Account of his Obstinacy in refusing to take the Oaths to P—pe's Supremacy" (see Guerinot 188–93). A still more bizarre accusation turned up in a verse satire that Welsted brought out soon afterward, *Of Dulness and Scandal* (1732). This suggested that a certain "Victoria" (whose identity remains a mystery) had died as a result of reading AP's *Iliad*. In the same year Welsted produced *Of False Fame*, a poem satirizing AP as the unjustly celebrated scribbler "Bavius."

Three years later AP made his own reply. In the *Epistle to Arbuthnot* he caricatured Welsted as "Pitholeon," a feeble libeler (ll. 49–54). Later in the poem, the *coup de grâce* is administered in a lethal verse, "Three thousand Suns went down on *Welsted*'s Lye" (l. 376). This cannot relate to the story that "Mr. P. had occasion'd a *Lady's death*" or to a charge that AP had taken a gift of £500 from the **Duke of Chandos**, as a note suggests, insofar as these "lies" did not surface until 1732. Perhaps AP had in mind some lost allegation by his antagonist. Deceived by AP's ruse in publishing the *Essay on Man* anonymously, Welsted wrote to the unknown author, praising the work to the skies (*Corr* 3: 355–56).

See D.A. Fineman, *Leonard Welsted: Gentleman Poet of the Augustan Age* (Philadelphia: University of Pennsylvania Press, 1950). *One Epistle to Mr. Pope* has been edited in *Two Poems against Pope*, ed. J.V. Guerinot (Los Angeles: Augustan Reprint Society, 1965).

Wesley, Samuel junior (1691–1739). Clergyman and poet. Brother of the founders of Methodism, John and Charles Wesley. Studied at Westminster and Christ Church, **Oxford**. Head usher at Westminster, 1713; Master of Blundell's School, Tiverton, Devon, from 1733. His schoolboy poem about the indignities suffered by **Edmund Curll** in 1716, *Neck or Nothing*, is couched in rough octosyllabics: it has allusions to AP, **Lintot**, and **Tonson**. A more serious offering was an elegy in heroic couplets, to the memory of Mary Morice, daughter of **Francis Atterbury** (1730), which AP praised as a "good deed & good work as a poet" (*Corr* 3: 105).

In 1735 he published *Dissertationes in librum Job*. AP was active in promoting the **subscription** campaign, as emerges from his letter to Wesley on 21 October 1735 (*Corr* 3: 504).

Among those listed among the subscribers are "Bishop Atterbury" (a posthumous entry), **John Barber**, **Lord Bathurst**, **Hugh Bethel**, **Viscount Bolingbroke**, Dr. **Patrick Delany**, General **James Dormer**, **John Knight** (also posthumously), **Erasmus Lewis**, **Richard Mead**, **William Morice**, **William Stukeley**, **Jonathan Swift**, and **Sir William Wyndham**, as well as three Earls close to AP—**Burlington**, **Orrery**, and **Oxford**. Also in this year came his *Poems on Several Occasions*, with several flattering references to AP and poems to Oxford, **James Oglethope**, and others. Three surviving letters indicate cordial relations between Wesley and AP, which suggests that AP's lines "To the Right Honourable the Earl of Oxford," referring to Wesley (*TE* 6: 294–95), were written in a mood of good humor and tolerance.

West, Gilbert (1703–56). Author. Educated at Eton and Christ Church, **Oxford**, he was well connected socially. His maternal uncle was **Viscount Cobham** and his first cousin **George Lyttelton**. His reputation, though quite slender, was enough to earn him a place in the *Lives of the Poets* and a few respectful comments by **Samuel Johnson**. He produced a metrical version of the *Odes of Pindar* (1749): AP had suggested to him that he select a few of the odes to translate (*Anecdotes* 1: 225). West's father Dr. Richard West had helped to edit the works of Pindar in 1697. Other works by the son included imitations of **Spenser**. He had early been recruited to the cause of the **opposition to Walpole**; it is said that Cobham offered him a cornetcy in his own regiment if he did not study divinity at Oxford and thus kept his Whig principles clean. West's *The Institution of the Order of the Garter* (1742) is one of the better "patriot" poems, designed to bestow on **Frederick, Prince of Wales** a mythological dignity as an inheritor of Arthurian power and virtues—*Comus* seen through the lens of *The Idea of a Patriot King*. David Garrick turned this masquelike production into an entertainment for **Drury Lane Theatre** in 1771, by which time its political message would have been unreadable.

West probably announced himself to AP by what is today his most accessible work, *Stowe: The Gardens of the Right Honourable Richard Viscount Cobham* (1732). The poem opens: "To Thee, great Master of the vocal String, / O Pope, of Stowe's Elysian Scenes I sing." It celebrates the famous garden at **Stowe**, the seat of his uncle. West regularly visited AP in the last decade of the poet's life, sometimes in company with Lyttelton. In AP's **will** he was left £5 for a mourning ring, as well as £200 after the decease of **Martha Blount** (who in fact would outlive him).

West's *Poetical Works* have been reprinted (Southsea, Hampshire: Bardon, 1999).

Weston, Elizabeth (d. 1724). She was a member of an ancient Catholic family, the sister of the first Viscount Gage and the adventurer Joseph Gage (c. 1678–c. 1753), who figures in the *Epistle to Bathurst*. Her marriage to John Weston (d. 1730), of Sutton Court in Surrey, proved unhappy. AP made himself unpopular by the support he gave her and by his opposition to her abusive husband, who was on good terms with AP's brother-in-law Charles Rackett and his family (see **Rackett family**). She seems to have considered entering into a convent but did not do so. Somewhat implausibly identified as the "real-life" heroine of the *Elegy to the Memory of an Unfortunate Lady*. See the pioneering research of C.W. Dilke, *Papers of a Critic* (London: Murray, 1875), 1: 131–40.

Wharton, Philip, first Duke of (1698–1731). An unstable and unpredictable figure. He was the son of the Whig grandee Thomas, Earl of Wharton (who was among those to read AP's *Pastorals* in manuscript), but became a Jacobite and high-flying Tory. A leading freemason, he ended his days as a Catholic convert in a Spanish monastery. A notorious libertine, he is supposed to have been involved in the so-called Hellfire Club. Created a Duke in 1718 in a vain attempt to retain his loyalty to the regime. In 1722 he came to live at **Twickenham**, in the house formerly occupied by **James Craggs junior**. AP probably saw something of him in the following years, especially as Wharton was involved with **Lady Mary Wortley Montagu**, pursuing her with an ardor she seems not to have returned. He also conducted a Tory journal called the *True Briton*. In 1725 financial pressures forced him to decamp to the Continent, where he devoted himself for a time to the cause of the **Pretender**, and he never returned to England.

Understandably, AP disliked Wharton. Although many of the Duke's political opinions were congenial to him, and he recognized some talent for writing and public speaking in the precocious young man, AP rightly saw that no steadiness or loyalty could ever be expected in his character. The outcome was an extraordinary passage in the *Epistle to Cobham* (ll. 174–209), which renders the contradictions in Wharton's mercurial nature in one of AP's most brilliant psychological studies. For Wharton, the "ruling passion" was "the Lust of Praise," to which he sacrificed his wife, his friends, his cause, and his country. AP's antithetical style is seldom put to such expressive service as in the portrait of this complex individual. See *TE* 3.ii: 30–33.

There is no adequate life of Wharton. M. Blackett-Ord, *Hell-Fire Duke* (Shooter's Lodge, Windsor: Kensal Press, 1982), contains some useful information, but is neither complete nor accurate.

What d'ye Call It, The. A comedy by **John Gay**, described as a "Tragi-Comi-Pastoral Farce." It was first performed at **Drury Lane Theatre** on 23 February 1715 and enjoyed great success. The Prince and Princess of Wales (later **George II** and **Queen Caroline**) were in the first audience. It was a riotous and anarchic piece of fun, directed mainly against the stiffer conventions of contemporary tragedy, and it aroused great mirth. Some were unable to understand the jokes, notably AP's friend **Henry Cromwell**, who was now deaf (see *Corr* 1: 282–83). The play gave rise to *A Complete Key* (1715), possibly coauthored by **Lewis Theobald**, and other attacks, which is no doubt what the author had expected.

Most hostile commentators assumed that AP was at least in part the author of this play. In fact it is certain that Gay had primarily respon-

sibility for its composition, although AP and **Dr. John Arbuthnot** may have supplied some passages to the script. AP is said to have carried a part of the play in his own handwriting to **Colley Cibber** (*Anecdotes* 1: 103).

Whiston, William (1667–1752). Mathematician and theologian. A clergyman who succeeded **Sir Isaac Newton** as Lucasian Professor of Mathematics at Cambridge in 1703. His Arian (Unitarian) views led to his dismissal on the grounds of heresy in 1710. Thereafter he became increasingly notorious for wild theories and bizarre speculative schemes: he proposed that the Tartars were the lost tribes of Israel and began a movement for "primitive christianity." One of his best-known projects was one to find the longitude by anchoring fire-ships at intervals round the meridian, each setting off rockets at noon each day to signal the time to all shipping within earshot. The Scriblerian group produced a verse satire on this proposal. It also receives a mention in *Memoirs of Martin Scriblerus*, where Whiston's argument that Halley's comet might have been responsible for the biblical Flood is also ridiculed. Another episode in which Whiston became involved was the affair of the rabbit-woman Mary Tofts, which also attracted the attention of AP (see *The Discovery*). The mathematician contended that the monstrous births fulfilled the prophecy of Esdras concerning the Last Judgment. **John Arbuthnot** seems to have taken particular pleasure in making fun of Whiston; however, it was probably **John Gay** who wrote *A True and Faithful Narrative* (c. 1714), which incorporates a botched prophecy by the mathematician concerning the imminent end of the world.

As a religious fanatic who scorned orthodoxy and drew up elaborate projects for the reformation of mankind, Whiston would seem a natural target for AP's satire. However, the picture is more complicated. Under the sponsorship of **Addison** and **Steele**, Whiston began in 1713 to give subscription lectures on astronomy, first at **Button's** coffeehouse and then at Steele's new "Censorium," a public venue for entertainment and education. AP attended the lectures, and he was captivated imaginatively and intellectually by the vistas opened up by Whiston's cosmic speculations. The approach of a total eclipse of the sun in April 1715 led to a popular obsession with astronomy, in which AP was caught up— not surprisingly, in view of the fact that Edmond Halley was one of the main public spokesmen in this area. Like others of his time, AP was at once excited, enthralled, and appalled by the questing scientific theories of his day. References in AP's letters, notably one to **John Caryll senior** in August 1713 (*Corr* 1: 185–86), show the extent of his engagement in scientific matters, along with his collaboration in Scriblerian pieces like *Mr. Joanidion Fielding, His True and Faithful Account of the Comet* (1716) and *Annus Mirabilis* (1722). Some of AP's acquaintances, such as **Stephen Hales** and **William Stukeley**, had studied under Whiston at Cambridge.

See *This Long Disease* 133–235; and G. Sherburn, "Pope and 'The Great Shew of Nature,' " in R.F. Jones et al., *The Seventeenth Century* (Stanford: Stanford University Press, 1951), 306–15.

Whitehill House. The Popes' home in **Binfield** from 1700 to 1716. It was sold to AP's father in June 1698 by Charles Rackett, (see **Rackett family**), who had married the poet's half sister. However, the family did not take up residence until 1700. Here AP grew up in the heart of **Windsor Forest**, not far from the small market town of **Wokingham**. The transaction was strictly illegal, in view of the Popes' Catholic religion, and two years later, it was conveyed to Protestant relatives of AP's mother, in trust for the young Alexander. However, fresh anti-Catholic legislation made it prudent for the property to be sold after the **Hanoverian accession**, in order to avoid special taxes. The house was sold on 1 March 1716, and the family moved to **Chiswick**. Thus AP was deprived of his "paternal cell," a traumatic loss of his boyhood home to which he refers in the *Epistle to Arbuthnot* and *The Second Epistle of the Second Book of Horace*. He movingly describes a farewell visit to his youthful haunts in a letter to **John Caryll senior** on 20 March 1716 (*Corr* 1: 336–37).

Whitehill House was a small structure, probably of brick, suitable to a yeoman farmer rather than a member of the gentry. It has been enlarged and remodeled several times since, and the present-day building on this site better fits the name, Pope's Manor, which was bestowed on it in recent years. There were about fourteen acres of land attached to the house, with two small parcels separately held. Nothing is known of the interior of the house.

Whiteknights. Estate in **Berkshire** of AP's friends the **Englefield family**. It lay at Earley, southeast of Reading, on the site of a medieval manor, which was purchased in 1606 by Sir Francis Englefield for £7,500. This was the main family residence of the Englefields, an ancient Catholic family in the county, until they sold it to the Marquis of Blandford in 1798. The Marquis (later fifth Duke of Marlborough) spent extravagant amounts on the house and gardens but bankrupted himself in the process. The house was demolished in 1840. Since 1947 the estate, containing some 300 acres of parkland, has been occupied by the main campus of the University of Reading. The city now surrounds the park.

AP often stayed at the house in his earlier years, for example, in 1711 and 1713. Sometimes he used Whiteknights, about seven miles from **Binfield**, as a staging place on his way to and from **Mapledurham**, during visits to the Blount family. According to **Martha Blount**, it was here that she first met AP (*Anecdotes* 1: 42). AP planned to revisit the house on a sentimental trip to **Windsor Forest** in 1734, as he told Martha, but it is not clear whether he fulfilled his hopes (*Life* 622).

Whiteway, Martha (1690–1768). She was the great-niece of **Jonathan Swift**, as the daughter of his niece Anne Perry. Married first to Rev. Thophilus Harrison and after his death to Edward Whiteway. She moved to Dublin, and in the last fifteen years of the Dean's life, she became his most loyal companion and friend. In 1738 Swift described her to AP as "a very worthy, rational, and judicious Cousin of mine, and the only relations whose visits I can suffer"

(*Corr* 4: 116). Appropriately her name is commemorated in the Martha Whiteway Day Hospital for psychiatrically sick elderly people, based at St. Patrick's Hospital, Dublin, founded by Swift. Through her contacts with **William King** and the **Earl of Orrery**, she became an important agent in the publication of the letters of Swift and AP. She regarded AP with some suspicion, and in her efforts to protect the interests of an increasingly senile Swift, she proved a match for the poet in her use of subterfuge and delay. Her daughter Mary married Deane Swift (1707–83), great-nephew and biographer of Jonathan. Three letters between Mrs. Whiteway and AP survive.

Whitton. Village adjoining **Twickenham** to the west. It was the home of **Sir Godfrey Kneller** who demolished an earlier structure and built Whitton Hall in 1709–11, probably to his own designs, with decorative work by the painter **Louis Laguerre**. It was a large house with a frontage of nine bays, surrounded by an extensive park. It was extensively remodeled more than once before it became the home of the Royal Military School of Music in 1857, as it remains today under the name of Kneller Hall. When AP first moved to Twickenham, he was on easy social terms with Sir Godfrey and seems to have visited the house for cards and conversation.

Nearby lay the estate of Whitton Park, acquired by the **Earl of Islay** in 1722. From about 1725 the Earl built the state, acquiring more land as he went on. The house (not much larger than AP's own **villa**), designed by Roger Morris, was built c. 1737–38. There were also a stone "greenhouse" with Corinthian pilasters by **James Gibbs** and a large Gothick tower at the end of a canal. With added parcels the estate was increased to over fifty acres. The gardens were famous for their exotic plant specimens. Later on, part of the estate was owned by the architect Sir William Chambers. Around 1847 the main house was demolished. Many plants from the park were taken to nearby Kew, to help from the nucleus of the Royal Botanical Gardens. There are now scarcely any traces of the former estate. AP certainly visited the house, but it was too close at hand for a major trip to be recorded.

It was on a bridge over the River Crane, where Whitton met Twickenham, that AP almost drowned and suffered a bad injury to his hand in 1726 (see **accidents**).

See P. Foster and D.H. Simpson, *Whitton Park and Whitton Place* (Twickenham: Borough of Twickenham Local History Society, 1999).

Wife of Bath's Prologue, The. One of AP's youthful **imitations** of **Chaucer**, written as early perhaps as 1704–5. The poem may have been revised after a comedy by AP's new friend **John Gay** titled *The Wife of Bath* had a two-night run in May 1713. Its first appearance in print came with *Poetical Miscellanies*, published on 29 December 1713; the editor was **Richard Steele** and the publisher **Jacob Tonson senior** (Griffith 24). Reprinted in the *Works (1717)* and subsequently, but without extensive revision by AP. As in his other versions of Chaucer, AP was building on the modernizations of **Dryden**.

The poem reduces the original prologue from 828 lines to 439. AP abridges, combines, and telescopes various sections. A clear-cut comparison can be made between some passages, for example, lines near the opening (Chaucer, ll. 9–29; AP, ll. 9–18). The Augustan wife is less blowsy and more urbane than her medieval counterpart: AP aims for speed, polish, and wit rather than the rendition of deep human experience. His poem may lack the spontaneity and earthiness that Chaucer's wife often achieves, substituting a more bland and controlled voice. However, the language is at times colloquial and easy, especially in its free use of proverbs.

For the text and annotation, see *TE* 2: 56–78.

Wild, Jonathan (1683–1725). Criminal organizer who arranged for thefts, received stolen goods, and laid information with the authorities. One of the principal models for the character of "Peachum" in ***The Beggar's Opera***. One of the instant lives of Wild published after his death was probably by **Daniel Defoe**. The subject of a satiric biography by **Henry Fielding** (1743). AP mentions his case in the *Epilogue to the Satires* (2: 39, 54–56). See G. Howson, *Thief-Taker General: The Rise and Fall of Jonathan Wild* (London: Hutchinson, 1970); and L. Moore, *The Thieves' Opera: The Remarkable Lives and Deaths of Jonathan Wild, Thief Taker, and Jack Sheppard, House Breaker* (London: Viking, 1997).

Wilks, Robert (c. 1665–1732). Actor. He achieved success in both tragic and comic roles. Joint manager with **Colley Cibber** (from 1710) and **Barton Booth** (from 1714) at **Drury Lane Theatre**. Wilks delivered the prologue by AP at the famous first night of *Cato* in 1713. AP was certainly acquainted with Wilks (who subscribed to the *Iliad*), but nothing is known of their relations. He escaped mention in *The Dunciad*, Book 3, where Cibber and Booth came in for ridicule.

will. AP drew up his last will and testament on 12 December 1743, six months before his death. The document was witnessed by his neighbor, the **fourth Earl of Radnor**, along with the scientist **Stephen Hales** and the scholar **Joseph Spence**, both clergymen. It was proved in the consistory court in London on 14 June 1744, attested by his executors **Lord Bathurst**, **Marchmont**, **William Murray**, and **George Arbuthnot**.

The will requests that his body be buried near the monument of his parents at **Twickenham parish church**, with a bare addition of the date of his death to be added to the tablet. It asks for the body to be carried to the grave by six of the poorest men of the parish, who were to be given mourning clothes for the purpose. AP names **Bolingbroke** as his literary executor. Various books and possessions were bequeathed to friends. Monetary requests were made to **Ralph Allen** (in return for outstanding loans) and to members of the **Rackett family**, including his half sister **Magdalen Rackett**. Also remembered was his gardener **John Serle**, who was further requested to divide £20 among the poor of the parish. A sum of £1,000 was given to **Martha Blount**, who was also named

as the residuary legatee, "out of a sincere Regard, and long Friendship for her." The will was published in a life of AP, issued by Charles Corbett shortly after the poet's death.

It is possible that Magdalen Rackett attempted to challenge the will by launching an appeal in Doctors' Commons, which oversaw probate in the see of Canterbury (*EC* 5: 345). If so, proceedings appeared to have been dropped.

For the text, see *Garden and City* 263–65; or *Prose* 2: 501–15 (with helpful annotation).

William III (1650–1702). King of England from 1689. A grandson of Charles I, who was Prince of Orange from 1672. He reigned jointly until 1694 with his wife Mary, daughter of James II and sister of **Queen Anne**. She was also his first cousin.

AP spent his earliest years under the rule of a man regarded by some as an opportunistic invader. The King's main aim was to keep England free from the influence of Catholicism, regarded as the nurse of arbitrary power, and his foreign policy furthered this end, as in the inception just before he died of the **War of the Spanish Succession**. William's death, following a riding accident, was greeted with relief by many Tories, who looked for a more favorable dispensation under Queen Anne. It is generally thought that AP's treatment of the cruel tyrant William the Conqueror serves (as often in Tory polemic) as cover for an attack on William III, here depicted as an alien monarch remote from the concerns of his people. There are few other references to the King, and none seems favorable. In *The Second Epistle of the Second Book of Horace*, there is a bitter recollection of the harsh laws imposed on Catholics in the 1690s, "While mighty WILLIAM's thundering Arm prevail'd" (*TE* 4: 169).

Will's. A coffeehouse established after the Restoration, possibly by William Urwin. It was located on the northwest corner of Bow Street and Russell Street, a few yards east of Covent Garden, London. The coffeehouse was upstairs, above a draper's shop. It was a haunt of poets, associated principally with **John Dryden**, who is said to have had a chair reserved for his own use. **Jonathan Swift** refers ironically in *A Tale of a Tub* to his "brethren and friends" at Will's. The essential facts were reported by AP: "It was Dryden who made Will's Coffee-House the great resort for the wits of his time. After his death Addison transferred it to Button's, who had been a servant of his. They were opposite to one another—by Tom's in Russel Street, Covent Garden" (*Anecdotes* 1: 29).

The reputation of the house declined after the death of Dryden. In an early issue of *The Tatler*, **Richard Steele** asserted that the tone had gone down since Dryden's time: "This place is very much altered since Mr. Dryden frequented it; where you used to see Songs, Epigrams, and Satires, in the hand of every man you met, you have now only a pack of cards; and instead of the Cavils about the turn of expression, the elegance of the style and the like, the learned now dispute only about the truth of the game." In fact, the literary gossip in *The Tatler* was avowedly sent out from Will's. Some commentators were less impressed with what they saw at the house: "Ah, pox confound that Will's coffee-house," a character in **Congreve**'s *Love for Love* (1695) astringently remarks, "it has ruined more young men than the Royal Oak lottery. Nothing thrives that belongs t' it." In his *Hints towards an Essay on Conversation* (c. 1711), Swift declared, "The worst conversation I ever remember to have heard in my life, was that at Will's coffeehouse, where the wits (as they were called) used formerly to assemble; that is to say, five or six men, who had writ plays, or at least prologues, or had share in a miscellany, came thither, and entertained one another with their trifling composures, in so important an air, as if they had been the noblest efforts of human nature, or that the fate of kingdoms depended on them."

According to a report made in 1730 by **Jonathan Richardson senior**, AP claimed to have set eyes on Dryden only once, at Will's, when he was a very young boy ("New Anecdotes" 347). This must have been around 1698 or 1699. The scene is depicted in a Victorian genre piece by Eyre Crow (1824–1910). Nevertheless, AP as an adolescent gained the ac-

quaintance of men like **Thomas Betterton**, **Henry Cromwell**, **George Granville**, **Samuel Garth**, and **William Wycherley**, all of whom frequented Will's in the early years of the century. It was here that he gained some of his earliest contact with living authors and the discussion of books. But he too affected disdain: "I have now chang'd the Scene from the Town to the Country," he wrote to Wycherley in 1705, "from *Will's* Coffee-House to *Windsor* Forest. I find no other difference than this, betwixt the common Town-Wits, and the downright Country Fools" (*Corr* 1: 11). It may be that AP attended lectures on astronomy by **William Whiston** in 1713, as well as at the rival house of **Button**'s: see **John Gay**'s letter of April 1715. Henry Cromwell was evidently still loyal to Will's at this date (*Corr* 1: 288).

Wimpole. Estate in Cambridgeshire, about ten miles southwest of the city of Cambridge, belonging to the Harley family in AP's day. The house was built c. 1640 and sold in 1686 to Sir John Cutler, a miser who figures in the *Epistle to Bathurst*. It passed in 1693 to Cutler's son-in-law the second Earl of Radnor, who spent as much as £20,000 in improvements before he sold it to the Duke of Newcastle in 1710. After the Duke's death a year later, his daughter Lady Henrietta Cavendish-Holles married the son of the Lord Treasurer, Robert Harley, **first Earl of Oxford**. It was Harley's son the **second Earl of Oxford** who took over the reins at Wimpole and whom AP knew intimately.

Soon after his marriage, the younger Harley began to make plans for his new home, involving his own favorite architect **James Gibbs**. It took time to carry out the work, but by 1721 Gibbs and **Charles Bridgeman** were busy seeking to make the house and grounds "the finest and noblest thing in England." The original red-brick mansion was extended, with additions including a chapel and a library, designed to hold the magnificent collection of books and manuscripts known as the **Harleian library**. Unfortunately the second Earl ruined himself in assembling these treasures, so that the estate had to be sold in 1738 and the collection was put in storage at Welbeck Abbey.

The new owner, Lord Hardwicke, remodeled Wimpole Hall to designs by Henry Flitcroft, and his son later employed Capability Brown to fashion a new landscape in the park. Along with the chapel and library, the house survives, but it has been much altered since AP's time. It is in the care of the National Trust and is open to the public.

A frequent visitor at Wimpole was **Matthew Prior**, one of the Earl's private circle of artists. AP planned to visit the house on a number of occasions, but a stay in July 1727 is the only one to which a firm date can be attached. He refers several times to Wimpole in his correspondence with the Earl.

See *Earls of Creation* 212–18; and D. Souden, *Wimpole Hall, Cambridgeshire* (London: National Trust, 1991).

Wimsatt, William Kurtz (1907–75). Scholar who taught at Yale University from 1939. Best known for his work on critical theory and on **Johnson** and Boswell, he also wrote the standard account of the **portraits** of AP (1965). In addition, he was the author of important articles on AP, including "One Relation of Rhyme to Reason," *Modern Language Quarterly*, 5 (1944), 323–38; reprinted in *The Verbal Icon* (1954), 153–68 (also in *EA* 63–84). The same volume contains his essay "Rhetoric and Poems: Alexander Pope," 152–66, which first appeared in *English Institute Essays 1948*, ed. D.A. Robertson (1949). Wimsatt edited *Selected Poetry and Prose* of AP (1951). See also **ombre**.

Winchilsea, Anne Finch, Countess of (1661–1720). Sometimes spelled "Winchelsea." Poet. She was the daughter of Sir William Kingsmill (d. 1661) of Sydmonton, near Newbury. In 1683 she became one of the **maids of honor** to Mary of Modena, Duchess of York. She was married in 1684 to Colonel Heneage Finch, who was a member of the household of the Duke of York (later James II). She addressed her husband in poems and verse epistles, in which he figures as Daphnis and she as Ardelia. After the Revolution in 1688–89, Heneage Finch refused the oath of allegiance to the new monarchs (see **William III**); the couple had no fixed home until they were invited in 1690 to Eastwell Park, Kent, by Finch's nephew Charles, fourth Earl of Winchilsea. On the death of his uncle in 1712 Heneage Finch succeeded to the earldom. Lady Winchilsea died on 5 August 1720, leaving no issue; her husband survived until 1726. He was still regarded by some **Jacobites** as their "chief" in Kent when an uprising was being planned in 1721.

A selection of Lady Winchilsea's poems was published by Benjamin Tooke in 1713 (the printer may have been **John Barber**), and she contributed to a number of miscellanies, including those of **Jacob Tonson senior** and **Lintot**. A prolific and versatile writer of poetry and drama, she composed in forms as varied as elegy and fable and produced a number of translations. She also wrote verses on the model of those of **Matthew Prior** and addressed a poem to **Charles Jervas**. Among the best known of her works were "The Spleen," "Petition for an Absolute Retreat," and most widely admired of all, "A Nocturnal Reverie." Many of her poems circulated in manuscript, and some have been published only in recent years. See her *Poems*, ed. M. Reynolds (Chicago: University of Chicago Press, 1903); and *The Anne Finch Wellesley Manuscript Poems*, ed. B. McGovern and C.H. Hinnant (Athens: University of Georgia Press, 1998). A complete modern edition is still needed. She is now regarded as one of the outstanding lyric poets of the age.

Poems by AP had appeared alongside those of Lady Winchilsea in various collections, and she contributed commendatory verses at the start of *Works* (1717). In addition, her "Answer" to AP's *Impromptu, to Lady Winchelsea* was included in *Poems on Several Occasions*, a miscellany that AP himself is thought to have edited. AP dined with the Countess in 1713 (*Corr* 1: 203). It remains uncertain whether she supplied lineaments to the character of Phoebe Clinket in *Three Hours after Marriage*, although she is the likeliest candidate. She and her husband both subscribed to the *Iliad*, as they did to the poems of Prior. "*Winchelsea* still Meditating Song" appears in *Mr. Pope's Wel-*

come from Greece. She was an "old acquaintance" of **Jonathan Swift**.

See B. McGovern, *Anne Finch and Her Poetry: A Critical Biography* (Athens: University of Georgia Press, 1992).

Windsor Forest. Medieval hunting area in the county of **Berkshire**, with its heart about twenty-five miles from the center of London. It had been set aside for royal use, its borders extending at least fifteen miles from the River Thames to Bagshot in a north-south direction, and from Windsor to Reading in an east-west direction. In the early eighteenth century it comprised something like 100,000 acres. Most of the area enclosed was subject to forest law, as that had evolved over the course of several centuries since the Norman Conquest (and beyond), administered by a sizable legal bureaucracy. Such places were defined by their use and their legal status, not by their geographical character: originally, "a Forest was a place of deer, not necessarily a place of trees" (Oliver Rackham). However, by a later date forest law restricted unauthorized tree-felling as much as it precluded the poaching of deer.

The Crown was most obviously represented at Windsor Castle—the Home or Little Park adjoining it, and the larger Great Park stretching toward the heart of the forest. For the rest, the landscape was made up of mixed regions of woodland, arable land, pasture, and scrub. Especially on its edges, the forest included areas of marginal heathland unfit for regular agricultural use, and these had been occupied by squatters and itinerant workers. On the southeast corner was found an area of barren soil leading to the desolate stretches of Bagshot Heath. The gentry were settled in a number of districts: some of the larger estates lay just outside the limits of the forest, and their pleasure grounds were not subject to the same restrictions on hunting. Among the largest settlements were Maidenhead, Cookham, and Bray at the northern edge. In the heart of the forest there was only one market town, **Wokingham**; AP's home at **Binfield** lay close by. However, the significant towns were Windsor, the seat of royal authority, and (just beyond the western

fringe) Reading, the county town of Berkshire. It is hard to give an accurate figure for the total population, but in all there may have been something like 10,000 residents in the time of AP.

The poet had contacts throughout most of the forest. His immediate ties were with Binfield and **Easthampstead**, the seat of his patron **Sir William Trumbull**. On the border, in the direction of London, lay the home of the Racketts, the family of his half sister **Magdalen Rackett** (see also **Rackett family**). At **Whiteknights**, just short of Reading on the western perimeter, lived his close friends **the Englefield family**. AP visited here often, sometimes en route to the Blount residence at **Mapledurham**, a little way beyond Reading.

In his youth the forest became an important element in AP's private world of the imagination. He often uses it as an emblem of retirement, peace, and inspiration. But he was aware of the social and political tensions that had come to affect the area. Consequently his poem *Windsor-Forest* shows a double awareness: While it celebrates the literary and historical associations of the castle and the river, it portrays the landscape as fragile and vulnerable—open to "ravishment" by unsympathetic rulers like **William III**. The scenery described by AP is on the surface poetic or symbolic, and yet it contains a curiously realistic element. Thus, the wastelands peopled by squatters are present, and so in the allegorical set piece of the mythical "Lodona" is the real Loddon river, running into a loop of the Thames between Wokingham and Reading. A year after this poem was published, there occurred the death of **Queen Anne**, who had retained a special affection for Windsor and its surroundings. This event paved the way for the **Hanoverian accession** and fresh rivalries within the forest community, notably the episode of the **Waltham Blacks** in 1722–23, in which AP's own family was caught up.

Windsor-Forest. A poem by AP begun in his teenage years and published when he was twenty-four. The first edition appeared on 7 March 1713 as a folio of twenty pages (Griffith 9; Foxon P987). The publisher was **Bernard**

Lintot, who paid AP £32.5.0 (£32.25) for the copyright. On the title page appear the lines: "To the Right Honourable / George Lord Lansdown" (see **George Granville**). A second edition came out on 9 April of the same year. It was included in a miscellany issued by Lintot in 1714, probably edited by AP (see *Miscellaneous Poems and Translations*). When the poem went into the *Works* **(1717)** a number of significant changes were made. There were several other reprints in AP's lifetime, with a version in 1736 the most important. The standard text consists of 434 lines in **heroic couplets**.

AP gave slightly conflicting accounts of the genesis of *Windsor-Forest*. In 1736 he appended a note at the head of the text, "This poem was written at two different times: the first part of it which relates to the country, in the year 1704, at the same time with the Pastorals: the latter part was not added till the year 1710 [*sic*], in which it was publish'd" (*TE* 1: 148). The year "1710" here appears to be not a deliberate obfuscation, but a simple error. On the **manuscript** (described below) AP inscribed a different note: this was undoubtedly added long after the poem was written out, perhaps as late as 1736. "This Poem was writ mostly in ye year just after ye Pastorals. The author was then years of age. But the last hundred lines beginning with ye Celebration of ye Peace, were added in ye year 1 soon after ye Ratification of ye Treaty at Utrech_ It was first printed in folio ye same year, & afterwards in Octavo ye next." The poem certainly had some shape or form by October 1707, when **Ralph Bridges** was in correspondence with his uncle, **Sir William Trumbull**. Bridges mentioned AP's plans to publish his *Pastorals* and added that one was to be dedicated to Trumbull: if this did not happen, the "verses upon Windsor Forest" were to carry the dedication instead. In the event the opening pastoral, "Spring," would be inscribed to AP's mentor, and so the later dedication went to Lord Lansdowne. When *Windsor-Forest* was published, Trumbull wrote to Bridges that AP had played "a slippery Trick" on him, for "I had long since put him upon this subject, have severall hints & at last w^n he brought it & read it, & made some little

Alterations &c. not one word of putting in my Name till I found it in print" ("New Anecdotes"). This refers to the allusion to Trumbull within the text (l. 258).

There are signs that AP may have prepared this early version of *Windsor-Forest* for the press in the spring of 1712. At some point in time he changed his plans and set to work on the more expansive form of the poem, no doubt revising in the process the sections already written. Progress on this can be tracked in letters to his friend **John Caryll senior** on 29 November and 5 and 21 December 1712 (*Corr* 1: 157, 162, 168). In February 1713 he told Caryll that the poem had been dispatched to the press. By this date AP had written to Lord Lansdowne, thanking the peer for allowing him to make the dedication (*Corr* 1: 172–73). Many years later AP told **Joseph Spence** that Lansdowne "insisted on my publishing my Windsor Forest" (*Anecdotes* 1: 43), but we need not take this form of words too literally. It is possible that AP sent **Joseph Addison** a prepublication copy, acknowledged by the latter on 11 February (see *Life* 274).

A manuscript is preserved in the library of Washington University, St. Louis. It was written out with extreme care in AP's most polished "print hand" (see **handwriting**). There are nonetheless several corrections and erasures. It is likely that this was prepared around the end of 1712, but it does not seem to have been used as printer's copy, as a number of further alterations were introduced into the printed text. A leaf containing the last forty or so lines is missing. At some later date AP gave this holograph version to **Jonathan Richardson junior**, apparently to help in revising the text for the printing in 1736: various markings were made on it to indicate the nature of changes. For a transcript and careful survey of the issues surrounding this manuscript, see the admirable edition by **Robert Morell Schmitz**, *Windsor Forest, 1712: A Study of the Washington University Holograph* (1952).

According to a note by AP in 1736, the original pastoral poem extended up to line 290 in the text as it was printed. The remainder, except for a few concluding verses, "was not added till the year 1710," again an error for 1713 (*TE* 1: 175). This new section was designed explicitly to celebrate the **Treaty of Utrecht**, which was signed on 31 March 1713, Old Style (but was widely known to be imminent). **Thomas Tickell** had already struck an early blow with his poem *The Prospect of Peace*, which AP necessarily saw as a potential rival to his own work (see *Corr* 1: 157). Other writers, great and small, weighed in with their own effusions in this moment of national relief and rejoicing. The superiority of AP's creation lies in a number of features but especially the way in which he integrates the two portions of the work. It owes much also to the manner in which he transcends the topical theme by opening up a much more universal perspective on the larger issues of war and peace, trade and empire, time and place.

In fact *Windsor-Forest* belongs to no single genre. It draws less on pastoral than on **georgic**, and in this respect it constitutes AP's Virgilian career move from pure idyll to a poetry of real life. It is an intensely patriotic work, confronting the past, present, and future of the British people. At the same time, it culminates in a vision of a harmonious world order, where the nation's preeminence is to be earned by its adherence to noble values of cooperation and humanity—another idea taken from **Virgil**. AP uses some of the motifs of panegyric, not unnaturally in a poem that explicitly glorifies **Queen Anne** as the notional peacemaker. Others commended are the dedicatee Lansdowne and AP's mentor Trumbull, a neighbor during his boyhood in the environs of Windsor. Implicitly the work serves to pay homage to the **first Earl of Oxford**, leader of the government and recently founder of the South Sea Company, and **Viscount Bolingbroke**, who had directed the peace negotiations. Prophetic overtones are added by reference to the Book of Isaiah and seventeenth-century providential writing. Initially the poem obeys the rules of local or topographical verse, but it gradually sweeps out to a national and international compass. Here AP specifically recalls the idiom of *Annus Mirabilis* (1667) by his mentor **John Dryden**. In one section AP pays tribute to the poets associated with the Thames around Windsor, including the Earl of Surrey, **Sir John Denham** and **Abraham Cowley**. Other elements in this complex design are chivalric lore, linked to the court at Windsor; the iconography of country sports, especially hunting; and a masquelike dramatization of the mythology of rivers, based on **Spenser** and **Drayton**. AP's interest in landscape painting and in **gardening** also enhances the texture of the verse. At the center of the poem comes an Ovidian myth concerning the nymph Lodona, stressing the fragility of the precious environment AP has been describing.

Windsor-Forest is one of AP's most carefully wrought compositions. For a long time it was treated in a patronizing way, either because of its seemingly "split level" construction or because of its ornate diction. Today we can see that its various parts are united by a number of devices. In particular, its political theme of open support for the Stuart dynasty runs through each section of the work: AP portrays **William III** as an invader in the mold of William the Conqueror and as one bent like Oliver Cromwell on destroying the integrity of the nation as he allows the forest to fall prey to "foreign" interests. The interrelated symbols of forest, river, and castle permit AP to exploit Windsor as both microcosm and macrocosm.

The standard edition, with an excellent introduction and commentary, is *TE* 1: 125–94. For a political perspective on the work, involving the so-called **Waltham Blacks**, see E.P. Thompson, *Whigs and Hunters: The Origin of the Black Act* (Harmondsworth: Penguin, 1977). For some of the intellectual components, see E.R. Wasserman, *The Subtler Language* (Baltimore: Johns Hopkins University Press, 1959), 101–68. For some of the historical content, see J.R. Moore, "*Windsor-Forest* and William III," *Modern Language Notes*, 66 (1951), 451–54, reprinted in *EA* 242–46.

Wise, Henry (1653–1738). Landscape gardener. Partner with George London (c. 1640–1714) at Brompton Nursery from 1687. Served as royal gardener to **Queen Anne** and **George I** between 1701 and 1727. His main achievement was probably the remodeling of the gardens at **Hampton Court**. His other main tasks for the Queen included laying out the new garden at Kensington Palace and overhauling the park at St. James's Palace and Windsor Castle. Wise was responsible for the original landscape design at **Blenheim** along with **John Vanbrugh**. In addition, he worked at Chelsea Hospital, Chatsworth, Longleat, Castle Howard, and many other famous estates, most of which were visited by AP. He eventually retired to the Priory at Warwick, which he had acquired in 1709. His pupil and successor was **Charles Bridgeman**.

See D. Green, *Gardener to Queen Anne: Henry Wise, 1653–1738, and the Formal Garden* (London: Oxford University Press, 1956).

Wise, Thomas James (1859–1937). Famous rogue book collector, forger, thief, and vandal whose practices were ultimately exposed. His main work concerning AP, *A Pope Library* (1931), has not done quite as much damage as some of his other productions, but it muddied the waters of **bibliography** for a time. Equally unreliable is *A Catalogue of the Library of the Late John Henry Wrenn* (1920), which is based on many of Wise's rash ascriptions.

wit A difficult and complicated notion. According to **Samuel Johnson**, the "original signification" was mental power, or intellect. A newer meaning that had evolved was "imagination, or quickness of fancy." In this sense, *wit* had been contrasted by John Locke with *judgment*. Wit consisted of putting congruent ideas together and forming agreeable and fanciful connections. Judgment lay in discriminating and keeping different ideas separate in the mind. As time went on, wit came to be increasingly identified with jocular wordplay and socially adroit badinage. In addition, the noun *wit* could also apply to " 'a man of fancy' " (Johnson), that is, someone who exhibited powers of ready invention in conversation or writing. A major reappraisal of the concept can be found in Johnson's life of **Cowley** in *The Lives of the Poets* (1779–81).

In his early manhood, AP aspired to the con-

dition of a sophisticated intellectual, in the manner that had prevailed at **Will's** coffeehouse, and his letters are full of strenuous attempts at wit. This phase came to an end after he had written *An Essay on Criticism*, which explores the several senses of the term with remarkable ingenuity. It is an attack on shallow wit conducted with the aid of true wit. See W. Empson, "Wit in the *Essay on Criticism*," in *The Structure of Complex Words* (London: Chatto & Windus, 1951), reprinted in *EA* 208–26, for a virtuoso discussion of the ambiguity of AP's usages. More generally, see J. Sitter, *Arguments of Augustan Wit* (Cambridge: Cambridge University Press, 1991).

Withers, Henry (c. 1651–1729). Soldier. A lieutenant in the Queen's regiment of Foot, 1683. Withers served in the **War of the Spanish Succession** and became a Lieutenant-General in 1707. He was one of the principal commanders of the **Duke of Marlborough** at the battle of Malplaquet in 1709 and later acted as governor of Sheerness fort. A friend of **Henry Disney**, who signed a prose epitaph to Withers, perhaps written by AP. This accompanies a set of verses (twelve lines of **heroic couplets**) for the monument in Westminster Abbey, which were certainly the work of AP. Together with Disney, he is the first to greet AP in *Mr. Pope's Welcome from Greece*. A subscriber to the *Iliad*.

Wokingham Often known in former times as "Ockingham," this was the local market town during AP's youth in **Berkshire**. It lay some three miles southwest of **Binfield**. AP certainly knew the town well, but none of the legends connecting him with local inns and the like has any basis in fact. It was at the heart of the activity surrounding the **Waltham Blacks** about 1723.

women From early on, interest has been expressed in AP's relations with women. Biographically, this has concerned his supposed attraction to the sisters **Teresa** and **Martha Blount** and his violently oscillating dealings with **Lady Mary Wortley Montagu**. In recent years more attention has been given to his other women friends, including **Mary Caesar**, **Judith Cowper**, and **Sarah, Duchess of Marlborough**. A fuller appraisal has been made of AP as son and brother (see **Edith Pope**; **Magdalen Rackett**). Within both of these categories, the most important contribution has been that of Valerie Rumbold. At the same time, a new wave of criticism inspired by feminist ideas has laid special emphasis on certain poems, in particular, the *Epistle to a Lady*, as well as the perennial favorite *The Rape of the Lock*, which has been subjected to scrutiny from radically different angles. Further light has been cast on the reactions of AP's early women readers.

Misogyny was once not commonly attributed to AP, even when his reputation stood at its lowest. However, this has been widely diagnosed of late. Felicity Nussbaum has connected AP's work to other satires on women written in the later seventeenth and early eighteenth century. Ellen Pollak described AP's **Belinda** as a passive sexual object, the victim of male gaze, and ultimately doomed to "nonexistence" as a subject "on the margins of the text." AP's sexist attitudes have been contrasted unfavorably by Margaret Doody and others with the outlook of his friend **Swift**; his relatively "gentle" approach has been seen as condescending and his vein of gallant compliment judged to be enmeshed in the historical patronization of chivalry. Critics seeking a less biased view of Augustan womanhood have set his work alongside that of female authors such as Mary Leapor and further connections forged between AP and **Anne Finch, Countess of Winchilsea**. Admirers of **Eliza Haywood** have objected to AP's brisk and unkind treatment of the novelist in *The Dunciad*, whose monstrous titulary goddess also inspires widespread commentary. Vigorous debate continues: it is clear that AP's best poems interrogate many of the issues of gender now under constant review.

The most complete survey of issues related to this theme is V. Rumbold, *Women's Place in Pope's World* (Cambridge: Cambridge University Press, 1989). Also concerned with matters of gender are E. Pollak, *The Poetics of Sexual Myth: Gender and Ideology in the Verse of Swift and Pope* (Chicago: University of Chicago Press, 1985); and C.D. Williams, *Pope, Homer, and Manliness: Some Aspects of Eighteenth-Century Classical Learning* (London: Routledge, 1993). An influential article is C. Fabricant, " 'Binding and Dressing Nature's Loose Tresses': The Ideology of Augustan Landscape Design," *Studies in Eighteenth-Century Culture*, 8 (1979), 109–35. For other articles, see *Pope, Swift, and Women Writers*, ed. D.C. Mell (Newark: University of Delaware Press, 1996). On the tradition of misogyny, see F. Nussbaum, *"The Brink of All We Hate": English Satires on Women 1660–1750* (Lexington: Kentucky University Press, 1984). For AP's audience, see C.N. Thomas, *Alexander Pope and His Eighteenth-Century Women Readers* (Carbondale: Southern Illinois University Press, 1994).

Woodward, John (1665–1728). A noted geologist and physician who became a frequent butt of the Scriblerians (see **Scriblerus Club**), chiefly on account of his adventures and misadventures as an **antiquarian**. In the battles of the **Ancients and Moderns** he was an uncompromising devotee of modernism. Professor of Physic at Gresham College, 1692; FRS, 1693. **Dr. John Arbuthnot** had opposed his geological theories concerning the effects of the biblical Deluge. He is given a major role in the farce *Three Hours after Marriage* as "Dr Fossile," a credulous antiquarian. He also receives brief and scornful reference in AP's *Fourth Satire of Dr. John Donne* (*TE* 4: 29, 37), both for his ragbag collection of curiosities and for his fondness as a medical man for prescribing emetics. However, the major onslaught on Woodward by the satirists came as a result of his deluded belief that he had acquired an ancient Roman shield, a discovery he trumpeted forth in many publications. Subsequently the shield has been identified as of sixteenth-century German origin. The episode forms the basis of an early section of the *Memoirs of Martin Scriblerus*. Woodward stands for a new breed of speculative scientist, commonly ridiculed by writers like **Swift** and AP. Today they are recognized for their pioneering (if sometimes misconceived) attempts to extend the range of investigations of the natural world.

See a highly informative and well-organized study, J.M. Levine, *Dr. Woodward's Shield: History, Science, and Satire in Augustan England* (Berkeley, University of California Press, 1977). For Arbuthnot's role, see L.M. Beattie, *John Arbuthnot: Mathematician and Scientist* (Cambridge, MA: Harvard University Press, 1935; reprint, New York: Russell and Russell, 1967).

Woolf, Virginia (1882–1941). Novelist and critic. The daughter of **Sir Leslie Stephen**, she was deeply versed in the eighteenth century. Among her works are essays on **Joseph Addison**, **Jonathan Swift**, **Daniel Defoe**, and **Eliza Haywood**. AP figures, along with Addison and Swift, in the adventures of the heroine in Woolf's fantastic story *Orlando* (1928).

Wordsworth, William (1770–1850). Poet. Wordsworth claimed late in life that he could repeat, "with a little previous rummaging of my mind, several thousand lines of Pope." His early work shows some signs of influence by AP, but he soon came to find the poet's balanced and sententious style a vicious one. In his "Essays on Epitaphs" (1810) he analyzed AP's work in this genre, concluding that these poems "cannot well be too severely criticized," on account of their artificial language and "unmeaning antithesis." Most famously, Wordsworth wrote in the "Essay Supplementary to the Preface" (to *Lyrical Ballads*) of AP's failure to depict nature at firsthand and of his "false and contradictory" descriptions in the translations of **Homer**. In general, Wordsworth considered that AP's inability to achieve the beautiful, the sublime, and the pathetic placed his achievement "almost at the foot of Parnassus."

M.L. Peacock, Jr., *The Critical Opinions of William Wordsworth* (Baltimore: Johns Hopkins Press, 1950), remains at this point the fullest conspectus of Wordsworth's views over his lifetime. See also R.J. Griffin, *Wordsworth's Pope* (Cambridge: Cambridge University Press, 1995).

Works of Buckingham, The. Around 1721 AP was asked to edit the literary works of his patron **John Sheffield, first Duke of Buckinghamshire**, probably at the instance of his widow (see **Kathleen Sheffield, Duchess of Buckinghamshire**). This was a touchy affair, as some of these works carried an obvious Jacobite flavor, and in September 1721 AP wrote to **Jacob Tonson junior** that he had decided to remove himself from the "business of the impression" and to take no share in the profits (*Corr* 2: 81). These would be left to **John Barber**, who had been granted a royal license by the Secretary of State in April 1722 and was superintending the publication. While these preparations were going on, **Edmund Curll** announced the appearance of his own unauthorized version of the Duke's works, to be garnished with a life by **Lewis Theobald**. A complaint was made to the House of Lords, and on 23 January 1723 Curll admitted that he had no permission for his proposed work. In high dudgeon the Lords made Curll apologize on his knees before the bar of the House and forbade publication. Moreover, a ruling was issued on 30 January, stating that it was a breach of privilege for anyone to print the works, life, or will of a deceased peer (Curll's stock in trade). The response was characteristic. Curll simply removed the life and the will and added a note that the works had been revised by the Duke himself and given to **Charles Gildon** to be published. Otherwise, the works, backdated to 1721, remained in the state they had probably always been.

Meanwhile the Barber version, of which AP remained the clandestine editor, appeared on 24 January and ran into immediate trouble. Three days later, the King's messengers (officers employed by the Secretary of State) carried out a search of Barber's printing shop and seized copies of the work as "a seditious and scandalous Libel." One press story claimed that AP himself had been taken in for questioning. AP seems to have thought that his old enemies in the Whig circle at **Button's** were to blame, especially **Thomas Tickell** (see *Corr* 2: 159). In any case, AP had to tread very carefully at this juncture, since the prosecution of his friend

Francis Atterbury was currently being set up. Delicate negotiations went on with the Secretary of State, **John, Baron Carteret**. On 9 March the *London Journal* reported that AP was reediting the volumes in order to "expunge all those Passages which have given Offence" (*Early Career* 226–27). The doctored book went back on sale, although several copies survive in which the suppressed portions are present. It was left for Curll to capitalize on events in his usual fashion: He issued a forty-page pamphlet, *The Castrations*, which printed the two offending essays in full. In 1726 the cuts were restored in the Barber edition. There was also a piracy in that year by the notorious T. Johnson in The Hague. AP changed his mind about taking the profits and received about £200. Barber was also under suspicion by the ministry, and it was apparently Tonson who carried the publication through.

The first edition came out in two handsome quarto volumes, running to 476 pages and 312 pages, respectively (Griffith 137). The full title reads *The Works of John Sheffield, Earl of Mulgrave, Marquis of Normanby, And Duke of Buckingham*. Later editions appeared in AP's lifetime. The best account of this episode remains *Early Career* 220–28.

Works (1717). The first major collection of the poems of AP. It appeared on 3 June 1717 as *The Works of Mr. Alexander Pope* and was stated to be printed by **William Bowyer** for **Bernard Lintot**. There are versions in folio (442 pages) and quarto (470 pages), each available in larger or standard page sizes (see Griffith 79–83). Shortly afterward **Jacob Tonson senior** somehow asserted his rights in certain of the items included, and the title page was altered to carry his name along with that of Lintot. A curious contract was drawn up, mysteriously dated as late as 28 December 1717, by which AP was reimbursed through the gift of 120 copies of the quarto edition on royal paper (a few of these presentation copies survive): see *Book Trade* 239–41. A frontispiece consists of a portrait by **Charles Jervas**, engraved by **George Vertue**. This portrait (*Portraits* 2.1) had been painted in 1714 and engraved in 1715.

There are nine headpieces engraved by the Huguenot artist Simon Gribelin (1661–1744), who had also provided the illustrations to *The Rape of the Lock*.

The volume gathers together all of AP's important work so far published, with the exception of the early volumes of his translation of the *Iliad*. It also contains several major new items that had not previously appeared in print. Finally, there is a significant preface, setting out the poet's considered view of his career and his role as a poet, the nearest AP had come to an *apologia pro sua vita*, together with a short essay on pastoral.

The contents may be summarized as follows:

1. A series of complimentary poems by friends of AP, namely, the **Duke of Buckinghamshire**, **Lady Winchilsea**, **William Wycherley**, **Elijah Fenton**, **Thomas Parnell**, and **Simon Harcourt**. There is also an unknown "Knapp," possibly a minor poet named Francis Knapp.

2. The preface. This has been edited from AP's manuscript by **Maynard Mack** in *CIH* 159–78.

3. The *Discourse on Pastoral Poetry*, now printed for the first time.

4. Previously printed items, including the *Pastorals*; *Messiah*; *Windsor-Forest*; *An Essay on Criticism*; *The Rape of the Lock* (expanded version of 1714); *The Temple of Fame*; *Epistle to Jervas*; and various translations.

5. New items, most notably *Verses to the Memory of an Unfortunate Lady*; *Epistle to Miss Blount, on her Leaving the Town, after the Coronation*; and *Eloisa to Abelard*.

Overall, this handsome and impressive volume constitutes AP's attempt to define his achievement up to this point and to set out his credentials as a writer of "classic" status. For a full assessment, see V. Caretta, " 'Images Reflect from Art to Art': Alexander Pope's Collected Works of 1717," in *Poems in Their Place: The Intertextuality and Order of Poetic Collections*, ed. N. Fraistat (Chapel Hill: University of North Carolina Press, 1986), 195–233.

Wren, Sir Christopher (1632–1723). Architect. AP added a note to the second book of

The Dunciad, expressing great indignation that Wren, "who had been Architect to the Crown for above fifty Years," should have been displaced by the incompetent **William Benson** (*TE* 5: 188). This occurred not long after Wren had seen its greatest enterprise, St. Paul's Cathedral in London, brought to virtual completion. Wren was a colleague of **Dr. John Arbuthnot** on committees of the Royal Society. He subscribed to the *Iliad*, but there is no evidence that AP knew him personally.

Wright, John (d. 1754). "Pope's printer." He was probably apprenticed to John Streeter and freed in 1693. By 1713 he was working as a journeyman for **John Barber**. When Barber went abroad in 1722, most likely to relay funds to the **Pretender**, Wright was left in charge of the business. He began to work in his own capacity c. 1728, beginning with the *Miscellanies* of AP and **Swift**. Further printing assignments for AP included *The Dunciad Variorum*, most of the *Imitations of Horace*, and the *Moral Essays*, as well as volumes of *Works* and letters. The association continued virtually up to AP's death. Sometimes a bookseller such as **Lawton Gilliver** is named on the title page of these books, but it appears that AP generally acted as his own publisher, paying the printer and distributor and reaping the profits himself. Wright printed books by members of AP's circle such as **Walter Harte** and **George Lyttelton** but by few others. He was also involved in the clandestine printing of *The Idea of a Patriot King*.

See J. McLaverty, *Pope's Printer, John Wright: A Preliminary Study* (Oxford: Oxford Bibliographical Society, 1976).

Wycherley, William (1641–1715). Dramatist. Best known for his comedies *The Country Wife* (1675) and *The Plain Dealer* (1677), after which his fortunes went into a steep decline. A member of the circle of **John Dryden** at **Will's** coffeehouse, his friends included **William Congreve**, **Henry Cromwell**, **Thomas Southerne**, and **William Walsh**. His unsuccessful volume of *Miscellany Poems* (1704) may have made him hospitable to the literary overtures of AP,

who sought him out at the age of about sixteen. They began a lengthy correspondence in which the young man paid his elder stately compliments but also undertook to revise Wycherley's sometimes clumsy verses. This led to periodic spells of misunderstanding and coolness: The dramatist was now suffering from the effects of age and had lost much of his power of memory. However, the two were reconciled, and Wycherley received several invitations to **Binfield**, at least one of which he accepted.

A week before his death, the senile Wycherley was inveigled by a cousin, Thomas Shimpton, a skilled con artist, into marrying a young woman named Elizabeth Jackson and into making a will in her favor. Three months later, the con man married Elizabeth. AP had been to see Wycherley twice in his final days but did not fully realise what had happened (see *Corr* 1: 328). Wycherley's nephew and namesake brought a suit in Chancery but failed to have the will overturned. The Shimptons gained control of the family property in Shropshire. Acting on their behalf was the young attorney **Lewis Theobald**, who later edited a volume of Wycherley's *Posthumous Works* (1728). AP was greatly incensed by this action and responded with a second volume of these *Works*. In his collection AP printed a number of poems that he had himself revised and corrected for publication, as well as including some of the early letters he had exchanged with Wycherley. About forty letters survive between the two.

Throughout his life AP continued to think well of his mentor. He defended Wycherley against **John Ozell** in one poem (*TE* 6: 37). When the old man died, AP recorded the event in his private obituary list (see **Memorial List**), although he misplaced the event from 31 December 1715 to March 1716: "a writer famous for his knowledge of human nature, the first to gain my affection" (*EC* 1: ix). He told **Joseph Spence** several good-humored stories concerning his relations with Wycherley (*Anecdotes* 1: 32–41). A portrait hung at AP's house.

See B.E. McCarthy, *William Wycherley: A Biography* (Athens: Ohio University Press, 1979).

Wyndham, Sir William (1687–1740). Tory politician who represented Somerset in Parliament for thirty years. He came to the fore in the **Harley administration**, holding the offices of Secretary at War (1712) and Chancellor of the Exchequer (1713). His friend **Bolingbroke** had earmarked a major role in government for him, until the death of **Queen Anne** blighted the hopes of his party. A leader of the planned rising in the West Country in 1715, he was arrested and sent to the Tower of London on suspicion of treason. No charges were finally brought, and he was released in 1716. After the rise of **Sir Robert Walpole**, Wyndham renounced his **Jacobite** loyalties and became a leader of the Hanoverian Tories. As such he took a leading part in the Opposition campaign supported by AP (see **opposition to Walpole**).

Wyndham became a member of the **Brothers Club** on its formation in 1711. AP was not a member, but many of his closest allies were, notably **Swift**. It is probable that the two men were first acquainted soon afterward. In August 1715 AP was planning to visit Wyndham's home near Williton in Somerset, in company with **Dr. John Arbuthnot**, **Jervas**, and **Henry Disney**; but the trip was curtailed, owing to the political crisis. In fact, Wyndham had to go into temporary hiding, and it was in the following month that officers arrived at his home to arrest him. Later on, in the 1720s, AP along with **Gay** kept in contact with Wyndham, who saw Swift when the Dean came over to England in 1726. During the 1730s AP and Wyndham were often in consultation regarding Opposition strategy. AP paid his friend warm tributes in poetry, notably the second dialogue of the *Epilogue to the Satires*. An equally warm but more personal remembrance occurs is AP's *Verses on a Grotto* (*TE* 6: 308). The death of Wyndham in July 1740 hit AP very hard, as he had now lost faith in many of the **Patriots**' leaders (*Corr* 4: 249). Wyndham's son Charles became the second Earl of Egremont, while his grandson George, third Earl, was the patron of the artist **Turner** at the family home of Petworth.

Υ

Yonge, Sir William (1693–1755). Politician. An MP who held high government posts under **Sir Robert Walpole**. He had a few poetic trifles published and later wrote an epilogue to **Samuel Johnson**'s tragedy *Irene* (1749). Yonge earned a surprise admission to *The Art of Sinking*, chapter 6. AP also satirized him as "Sir William Sweet-Lips" in *A Master Key to Popery* (*Prose* 2: 416–19). He was on the end of brief thrusts in the *Epistle to Arbuthnot* and the *Epilogue to the Satires* and appears as "frontless Young" in *One Thousand Seven Hundred and Forty*, l. 54 (*TE* 4: 334). Despite all this, Yonge subscribed to the *Odyssey* and the **Shakespeare edition**.

York. On his maternal side, AP's forebears had long been settled around York. However, he seems to have visited the city only once, around September or October 1716. This was in company with the **Earl of Burlington**, whose seat at Londesborough lay not far away. It was the furthest north AP ever ventured. Through the Earl and **Hugh Bethel**, who often stayed in lodgings at York, AP knew a fair selection of people linked with the area and received news of doings such as Burlington's new Assembly Rooms in 1732.

Young, Edward (1683–1765). Clergyman and writer. Originally held a law fellowship at Oxford (Doctor of Civil Law, 1719). He established a reputation as a poet and dramatist, besides gaining the patronage of the **Duke of Wharton**. When already into his forties, he took orders and quickly became chaplain to **George II** (1728) and Rector of Welwyn in Hertfordshire (1730), where he spent the remainder of his life. His seven satires known as *The Universal Passion* or *The Love of Fame* came out in 1725–28, dedicated to notable patrons such as **Sir Robert Walpole** and **George Bubb Dodington**. Their wit and technical assurance may have encouraged AP to embark on his own later verse satires. Young's outstanding success was the series of blank verse meditations *Night Thoughts*, sometimes titled *The Complaint* (1742–45), which achieved international fame and was translated into several languages. It continued to be a potent influence on some of the French Romantic writers two generations later. Young was a friend of Samuel Richardson and **Samuel Johnson**, who cites his works on about 100 occasions in the *Dictionary of the English Language*. Young also figures in the *Lives of the Poets*. His *Conjectures on Original Composition* (1759), in prose and addressed to Richardson, have been seen as raising the status of "originality" as a critical watchword.

It is not known exactly when AP and Young met, although it must have been by 1715, when Young was acting as the poet's distribution agent in **Oxford** for his *Iliad* (*Corr* 1: 294). A friend of **Joseph Addison** and **Thomas Tickell**, he introduced **Aaron Hill** to AP. He attempted to keep lines open both to the ministry and to the **opposition to Walpole**, where AP's friends were concentrated. **Swift** alludes in *On Poetry: A Rhapsody* to a pension of £100 that Young had accepted from Walpole. In 1730 Young produced two *Epistles to Mr. Pope concerning the Authors of the Age*, in which Young resolutely declines to name real names. The amusing start of the first of these poems may have given AP a lead for the *Epistle to Arbuthnot*. Many readers thought that *An Essay* *on Man* was the work of Young. Among these was Swift, who seems to have interpreted the *Essay* as a satire and wrote to AP that the work was "too Philosophical for me. . . . The Doctor is not merry or angry enough for the present age to relish as he deserves" (*Corr* 5: 11–12). Young himself wrote to AP urging him "to write something on the side of Revelation" as a counterpart to the supposedly deistic *Essay* (see *Anecdotes* 1: 136). Young gave **Joseph Spence**, a fellow Wykehamist, a number of sto-ries about literary figures of the time. A bountiful subscriber: his name is found on the list for both the *Iliad* and **Odyssey**.

See H. Forster, *Edward Young: Poet of the Night Thoughts* (Alburgh, Norfolk: Erskine, 1986); and *The Correspondence of Edward Young, 1683–1765*, ed. H. Pettit (Oxford: Clarendon, 1971). Hardly any of his letters to and from AP survive. The *Night Thoughts* have been published, ed. S. Cornford (Cambridge: Cambridge University Press, 1989).

zeugma. A rhetorical term for "yoking," that is, using one word in combination with two others that relate in unequal ways to the first. A common example is, "She arrived in a temper and a new hat." The most famous example in all literature is found in AP's line about **Queen Anne** from *The Rape of the Lock*: "Dost sometimes Counsel take—and sometimes *Tea*" (*TE* 2: 169). According to strict grammarians, this usage is more properly regarded as exemplifying another figure, *syllepsis*, but it is almost always described as zeugma. There are numerous other examples in AP's works, in *The Rape* especially: see, for example, "Or stain her Honour, or her new Brocade" and "Or lose her Heart, or Necklace, at a Ball" (*TE* 2: 166).

❧ Selected Bibliography ❧

REFERENCE

Bibliographical

Griffith, R.H. *Alexander Pope: A Bibliography.* 2 vols. Austin: University of Texas Press, 1922–27.

Catalogs

Alston, R.C., and M.J. Jannetta. *Bibliography Machine Readable Cataloguing and the ESTC . . .* [containing] *A Catalogue of the Works of Alexander Pope Printed between 1711 and 1800 in the British Library.* London: British Library, 1978.

Foxon, D.F. *English Verse, 1701–1750: A Catalogue of Separately Printed Poems with Notes on Contemporary Collected Editions.* 2 vols. Cambridge: Cambridge University Press, 1975.

Mack, M. *The World of Alexander Pope.* New Haven, CT: Beinecke Library and Yale Center for British Art, 1988.

General Reference

Berry, R. *A Pope Chronology.* Boston: G.K. Hall, 1988.

A Concordance to the Poems of Alexander Pope. Ed. E.G. Bedford and R.J. Dilligan. Detroit: Gale, 1974.

Guerinot, J.V. *Pamphlet Attacks on Alexander Pope 1711–1744: A Descriptive Bibliography.* London: Methuen, 1969.

Kowalk, W. *Alexander Pope: An Annotated Bibliography of Twentieth-Century Criticism 1900–1979.* Frankfurt: Peter Lang, 1981.

Lopez, C.L. *Alexander Pope: An Annotated Bibliography, 1945–1967.* Gainesville: University of Florida Press, 1970.

Tobin, J.E. *Alexander Pope: A List of Critical Studies Published from 1895 to 1944.* New York: Cosmopolitan Science and Art Service Co., 1945.

Aids to Study

Baines, P. *The Complete Critical Guide to Alexander Pope.* London: Routledge, 2000.

Pope: The Critical Heritage. Ed. J. Barnard. London: Routledge, 1973.

Wimsatt, W.K. *The Portraits of Alexander Pope.* New Haven, CT: Yale University Press, 1965.

EDITIONS

Collected Works

Pope: Poetical Works. Ed. H. Davis. Introduction by P. Rogers. Oxford: Oxford University Press, 1980.

The Prose Works of Alexander Pope. Vol. 1, *The Earlier Works, 1711–1720.* Ed. N. Ault. Oxford: Blackwell, 1936. Vol. 2, *The Major Works, 1725–1744.* Ed. R. Cowler. Hamden, CT: Archon, 1986.

The Twickenham Edition of the Works of Alexander Pope. Ed. J. Butt et al. 11 vols. London: Methuen, 1938–68.

The Works of Alexander Pope. Ed. W. Elwin and W.J. Courthope. 10 vols. London: John Murray, 1871–89.

Annotated College Texts

Alexander Pope: The Oxford Authors. Ed. P. Rogers. Oxford: Oxford University Press, 1993.

Poetry and Prose of Alexander Pope. Ed. A. Williams. Boston: Houghton Mifflin, 1969.

Selected Bibliography

Selected Poetry. Ed. P. Rogers. Oxford: Oxford University Press, 1996.

Selected Poetry and Prose. Ed. W.K. Wimsatt. 2nd ed. New York: Holt, Rinehart and Winston, 1972.

Selected Works

Literary Criticism of Alexander Pope. Ed. B.A. Goldgar. Lincoln: University of Nebraska Press, 1965.

Selected Prose of Alexander Pope. Ed. P. Hammond. Cambridge: Cambridge University Press, 1987.

Separate Works

The Art of Sinking in Poetry. Ed. E.L. Steeves. New York: King's Crown Press, 1952. Reprint, New York: Russell & Russell, 1968.

The Dunciad in Four Books. Ed. V. Rumbold. Harlow, Essex: Longman, 1999.

The Iliad. Ed. S. Shankman. London: Penguin, 1996.

Pope's Dunciad of 1728: A History and Facsimile. Ed. D.L. Vander Meulen. Charlottesville: University Press of Virginia, 1991.

Pope's Own Miscellany. Ed. N. Ault. London: Nonesuch Press, 1935.

The Rape Observ'd: An Edition of Alexander Pope's Poem "The Rape of the Lock." Ed. C. Tracy. Toronto: University of Toronto Press, 1974.

The Rape of the Lock. Ed. C. Wall. Boston: Bedford Books, 1998.

Collaborations

The Memoirs of the Extraordinary Life, Works, and Discoveries of Martinus Scriblerus. Ed. C. Kerby-Miller. New Haven, CT: Yale University Press, 1950. Reprint, New York: Oxford University Press, 1988.

Three Hours after Marriage. Ed. J.H. Smith. Los Angeles: Augustan Reprint Society, 1961.

Manuscripts

The Last and Greatest Art: Some Unpublished Poetical Manuscripts of Alexander Pope. Ed. M. Mack. Newark: University of Delaware Press, 1984.

Pope's "Essay on Criticism," 1709: A Study of the Bodleian Manuscript Text with Facsimiles, Transcripts, and Variants. Ed. R.M. Schmitz. St. Louis: Washington University Press, 1962.

Pope's "Windsor Forest" 1712: A Study of the Washington University Holograph. Ed. R.M. Schmitz. St. Louis: Washington University Press, 1952.

Wasserman, E.R. *Pope's "Epistle to Bathurst": A Critical Reading with an Edition of the Manuscripts.* Baltimore: Johns Hopkins University Press, 1960.

Letters

Alexander Pope: Selected Letters. Ed. H. Erskine-Hill. Oxford: Oxford University Press, 2000.

The Correspondence of Alexander Pope. Ed. G. Sherburn. 5 vols. Oxford: Clarendon, 1956.

Sherburn, G. "Letters of Alexander Pope." *Review of English Studies,* n.s., 9 (1958), 388–406.

BIOGRAPHY

Mack, M. *Alexander Pope: A Life.* New Haven, CT: Yale University Press, 1985.

Root, R.K. *The Poetical Career of Alexander Pope.* Princeton, NJ: Princeton University Press, 1938.

Rosslyn, F. *Alexander Pope: A Literary Life.* London: Macmillan, 1990.

Sherburn, G. *The Early Career of Alexander Pope.* Oxford: Clarendon, 1934.

Spence, J. *Anecdotes, Observations, and Characters of Books and Men.* Ed. J.M. Osborn. 2 vols. Oxford: Clarendon, 1966.

CRITICISM

Collections: Published Works

Alexander Pope: A Critical Anthology. Ed. F.W. Bateson and N.A. Joukovsky. Harmondsworth: Penguin, 1972.

Critical Essays on Pope. Ed. W. Jackson and R.P. Yoder. New York: Hall, 1993.

Critics on Pope. Ed. J. O'Neill. London: Allen & Unwin, 1968.

Discussions of Alexander Pope. Ed. R.A. Blanchard. Boston: Heath, 1960.

Essential Articles for the Study of Alexander Pope.

Ed. M. Mack. Rev. ed. Hamden, CT: Archon, 1968.

Modern Critical Interpretations: "The Rape of the Lock." Ed. H. Bloom. New York: Chelsea House, 1988.

Pope. Ed. B. Hammond. Harlow, Hertfordshire: Longman, 1996.

Pope: A Collection of Critical Essays. Ed. J.V. Guerinot. Englewood Cliffs, NJ: Prentice-Hall, 1972.

Pope: Recent Essays by Several Hands. Ed. M. Mack and J.A. Winn. Hamden, CT: Archon, 1980.

The Rape of the Lock: A Casebook. Ed. J.D. Hunt. London: Macmillan, 1968.

Twentieth Centenary Interpretations of "The Rape of the Lock." Ed. G.S. Rousseau. Englewood Cliffs, NJ: Prentice-Hall, 1969.

Collections: New Works

Alexander Pope: Essays for the Tercentenary. Ed. C. Nicholson. Aberdeen: Aberdeen University Press, 1988.

Alexander Pope: World and Word. Ed. H. Erskine-Hill. Oxford: Oxford University Press, 1998.

The Art of Alexander Pope. Ed. H. Erskine-Hill and A. Smith. London: Vision Press, 1979.

The Enduring Legacy: Alexander Pope Tercentenary Essays. Ed. G.S. Rousseau and P. Rogers. Cambridge: Cambridge University Press, 1988.

Pope and His Contemporaries: Essays Presented to George Sherburn. Ed. J.L. Clifford and L.A. Landa. Oxford: Clarendon, 1949.

Pope: New Contexts. Ed. D. Fairer. Hemel Hempstead, Hertfordshire: Harvester, 1990.

Writers and Their Background: Alexander Pope. Ed. P. Dixon. London: G. Bell, 1972.

Monographs: General

Aden, J.M. *Pope's Once and Future Kings: Satire and Politics in the Early Career.* Knoxville: University of Tennessee Press, 1978.

Atkins, G.D. *Quests of Difference: Reading Pope's Poems.* Lexington: Kentucky State University Press, 1986.

Ault, N. *New Light on Pope.* London: Methuen, 1949.

Bogel, F.V. *Acts of Knowledge: Pope's Later Poems.* Lewisburg: Bucknell University Press, 1981.

Boyce, B. *The Character Sketches in Pope's Poetry.* Durham: University of North Carolina Press, 1962.

Brower, R.A. *Alexander Pope: The Poetry of Allusion.* Oxford: Clarendon, 1959.

Brown, L. *Alexander Pope.* Oxford: Basil Blackwell, 1985.

Damrosch, L. *The Imaginative World of Alexander Pope.* Berkeley: University of California Press, 1987.

Deutsch, H. *Resemblance and Disgrace: Alexander Pope and the Deformation of Culture.* Cambridge, MA: Harvard University Press, 1996.

Edwards, T.R. *This Dark Estate: A Reading of Pope.* Berkeley: University of California Press, 1963.

Erskine-Hill, H. *The Social Milieu of Alexander Pope: Lives, Example and the Poetic Response.* New Haven, CT: Yale University Press, 1975.

Fairer, D. *Pope's Imagination.* Manchester: Manchester University Press, 1984.

Ferguson, R. *The Unbalanced Mind: Pope and the Rule of Passion.* Brighton: Harvester, 1986.

Griffin, D.H. *Alexander Pope: The Poet in the Poems.* Princeton, NJ: Princeton University Press, 1978.

Jackson, W. *Vision and Re-Vision in Alexander Pope.* Detroit: Wayne State University Press, 1983.

Keener, F.M. *An Essay on Pope.* New York: Columbia University Press, 1974.

Knight, G. Wilson. *The Poetry of Pope: Laureate of Peace.* New York: Barnes & Noble, 1965.

Mack, M. *The Garden and the City: Retirement and Politics in the Later Poetry of Pope 1731–1743.* Toronto: University of Toronto Press, 1969.

Morris, D.B. *Alexander Pope: The Genius of Sense.* Cambridge, MA: Harvard University Press, 1984.

Noggle, J. *The Skeptical Sublime: Aesthetic Ideology in Pope and the Tory Satirists.* Oxford: Oxford University Press, 2001.

Rogers, R.W. *The Major Satires of Alexander Pope.* Urbana: University of Illinois Press, 1955.

Russo, J.P. *Alexander Pope: Tradition and Identity.* Cambridge, MA: Harvard University Press, 1972.

Tillotson, G. *Pope and Human Nature.* Oxford: Clarendon, 1958.

Warren, A. *Alexander Pope as Critic and Humanist.* Princeton, NJ: Princeton University Press, 1929.

Selected Bibliography

Weinbrot, H.D. *Alexander Pope and the Traditions of Formal Verse Satire*. Princeton, NJ: Princeton University Press, 1982.

Williams, C.D. *Pope, Homer, and Manliness: Some Aspects of Eighteenth-Century Classical Learning*. London: Routledge, 1993.

Essays

Butt, J. *Pope, Dickens and Others: Essays and Addresses*. Edinburgh: Edinburgh University Press, 1969.

Mack, M. *Collected in Himself: Essays Critical, Biographical, and Bibliographical on Pope and Some of His Contemporaries*. Newark: University of Delaware Press, 1982.

Rogers, P. *Essays on Pope*. Cambridge: Cambridge University Press, 1993.

Tillotson, G. *Augustan Studies*. London: Athlone Press, 1961.

Monographs: Introductory

Clark, D.B. *Alexander Pope*. Boston: Twayne, 1977.

Fairer, D. *The Poetry of Alexander Pope*. London: Penguin, 1989.

Gordon, I. *A Preface to Pope*. Harlow, Essex: Longman, 1993.

Hammond, B. *Pope*. Brighton: Harvester, 1986.

Rogers, P. *An Introduction to Pope*. London: Methuen, 1976.

Monographs: Specialized Topics

Batey, M. *Alexander Pope: The Poet and the Landscape*. London: Barn Elm, 1999.

Brownell, M.R. *Alexander Pope and the Arts of Georgian England*. Oxford: Clarendon, 1978.

Goldstein, M. *Pope and the Augustan Stage*. Stanford: Stanford University Press, 1958.

Hammond, B. *Pope and Bolingbroke: A Study of Friendship and Influence*. Columbia: University of Missouri Press, 1984.

Martin, P. *Pursuing Innocent Pleasures: The Gardening World of Alexander Pope*. Hamden, CT: Archon, 1984.

Nicolson, M.H., and G.S. Rousseau. *"This Long Disease, My Life": Alexander Pope and the Sciences*. Princeton, NJ: Princeton University Press, 1968.

Thornton, F.B. *Alexander Pope: Catholic Poet*. New York: Pellegrini & Cudahy, 1952.

Monographs: Feminist Issues

Knellwolf, C. *A Contradiction Still: Representations of Women in the Poetry of Alexander Pope*. Manchester: Manchester University Press, 1998.

Pollak, E. *The Poetics of Sexual Myth: Gender and Ideology in the Verse of Swift and Pope*. Chicago: University of Chicago Press, 1985.

Pope, Swift, and Women Writers. Ed. D.C. Mell. Newark: University of Delaware Press, 1996.

Rumbold, V. *Women's Place in Pope's World*. Cambridge: Cambridge University Press, 1989.

Thomas, C.N. *Alexander Pope and His Eighteenth-Century Women Readers*. Carbondale: Southern Illinois University Press, 1994.

Monographs: Books and Publishing

Foxon, D. *Pope and the Early Eighteenth-Century Book Trade*. Ed. J. McLaverty. Oxford: Clarendon, 1991.

McLaverty, J. *Pope, Print, and Meaning*. Oxford: Oxford University Press, 2001.

Pope's Literary Legacy: The Book-Trade Correspondence of William Warburton and John Knapton, with Other Letters and Documents 1744–1780. Ed. D.W. Nichol. Oxford: Oxford Bibliographical Society, 1992.

Monographs: Style

Adler, J.H. *The Reach of Art: A Study in the Prosody of Pope*. Gainesville: University of Florida Press, 1964.

Jones, J.A. *Pope's Couplet Art*. Athens: Ohio University Press, 1969.

Parkin, R.P. *The Poetic Workmanship of Alexander Pope*. Minneapolis: University of Minnesota Press, 1955.

Spacks, P.M. *An Argument of Images: The Poetry of Alexander Pope*. Cambridge, MA: Harvard University Press, 1971.

Tillotson, G. *On the Poetry of Pope*. Oxford: Clarendon, 1938.

Monographs: Reputation and Afterlife

Amarasinghe, U. *Dryden and Pope in the Early Nineteenth Century: A Study of Changing Literary Taste, 1800–1830.* Cambridge: Cambridge University Press, 1962.

Griffin, R.J. *Wordsworth's Pope.* Cambridge: Cambridge University Press, 1995.

MacDonald, W.L. *Pope and His Critics: A Study in Eighteenth Century Personalities.* London: Dent, 1951.

Rennes, J.J. *Bowles, Byron and the Pope-Controversy.* Amsterdam: H.J. Paris, 1927.

Studies of Individual Works

Aden, J.M. *Something Like Horace: Studies in the Art and Allusion of Pope's Horatian Satires.* Nashville: Vanderbilt University Press, 1969.

Brooks-Davies, D. *Pope's "Dunciad" and the Queen of the Night: A Study of Emotional Jacobitism.* Manchester: Manchester University Press, 1985.

Contexts 2: The Rape of the Lock. Ed. W. Kinsley. Hamden, CT: Archon, 1979.

Cunningham, J.S. *Pope: The Rape of the Lock.* London: Arnold, 1961.

Dixon, P. *The World of Pope's Satires: An Introduction to the "Epistles" and "Imitations of Horace."* London: Methuen, 1968.

Erskine-Hill, H. *Pope: "The Dunciad."* London: Arnold, 1972.

Fuchs, J. *Reading Pope's "Imitations of Horace."* Lewisburg: Bucknell University Press, 1989.

Halsband, R. *The Rape of the Lock and Its Illustrations, 1714–1896.* Oxford: Clarendon, 1980.

Jones, W.L. *Talking on Paper: Alexander Pope's Letters.* Victoria, BC: University of Victoria, 1990.

Kallich, M. *Heav'n's First Law: Rhetoric and Order in Pope's "Essay on Man."* DeKalb: Northern Illinois University Press, 1967.

Knight, D. *Pope and the Heroic Tradition.* New Haven, CT: Yale University Press, 1951.

Leranbaum, M. *Alexander Pope's "Opus Magnum," 1729–1744.* Oxford: Clarendon, 1977.

Maresca, T.E. *Pope's Horatian Poems.* Columbus: Ohio State University Press, 1966.

More Solid Learning: New Perspectives on Alexander Pope's "Dunciad." Ed. C. Ingrassia and C.N. Thomas. Lewisburg: Bucknell University Press, 2000.

Nuttall, A.D. *Pope's "Essay on Man."* London: Allen & Unwin, 1984.

Shankman, S. *Pope's Iliad: Homer in the Age of Passion.* Princeton, NJ: Princeton University Press, 1983.

Sitter, J.E. *The Poetry of Pope's "Dunciad."* Minneapolis: University of Minnesota Press, 1971.

Solomon, H.M. *The Rape of the Text: Reading and Misreading Pope's "Essay on Man."* Tuscaloosa: University of Alabama Press, 1993.

Stack, F. *Pope and Horace: Studies in Imitation.* Cambridge: Cambridge University Press, 1985.

Sühnel, R. *Homer und die englische Humanität; Chapmans und Popes Übersetzungskunst im Rahmen der humanistischen Tradition.* Tübingen: Niemeyer, 1958.

White, D.H. *Pope and the Context of Controversy: The Manipulation of Ideas in "An Essay on Man."* Chicago: University of Chicago Press, 1970.

Williams, A. *Pope's "Dunciad": A Study of Its Meaning.* London: Methuen, 1955.

Winn, J.A. *A Window in the Bosom: The Letters of Alexander Pope.* Hamden, CT: Archon, 1977.

Local Studies

Brownell, M.R. *Alexander Pope's Villa.* London: Greater London Council, 1980.

Willson, A.B. *Alexander Pope's Grotto in Twickenham.* Twickenham: Garden History Society, 1998.

———. *Mr Pope & Others at Cross Deep, Twickenham in the 18th Century.* Twickenham: For the author, 1996.

Background and Comparison

Brown, L. *Ends of Empire: Women and Ideology in Early Eighteenth-Century English Literature.* Ithaca: Cornell University Press, 1993.

Carretta, V. *The Snarling Muse: Verbal and Visual Political Satire from Pope to Churchill.* Philadelphia: University of Pennsylvania Press, 1983.

Chalker, J. *The English Georgic: A Study of the Development of a Form.* London: Routledge, 1969.

Selected Bibliography

Erskine-Hill, H. *The Poetry of Opposition and Revolution: Dryden to Wordsworth.* Oxford: Clarendon, 1996.

Fussell, P. *The Rhetorical World of Augustan Humanism: Ethics and Imagery from Swift to Burke.* Oxford: Clarendon, 1965.

Gerrard, C. *The Patriot Opposition to Walpole: Politics, Poetry, and National Myth, 1725–1742.* Oxford: Clarendon, 1994.

Goldgar, B.A. *Walpole and the Wits: The Relation of Politics to Literature, 1722–1742.* Lincoln: University of Nebraska Press, 1976.

Hagstrum, J.H. *The Sister Arts: The Tradition of Literary Pictorialism and English Poetry from Dryden to Gray.* Chicago: University of Chicago Press, 1958.

Hammond, B. *Professional Imaginative Writing in England, 1670–1740: "Hackney for Bread."* Oxford: Clarendon, 1997.

Ingram, A. *Intricate Laughter in the Satire of Swift and Pope.* Basingstoke: Macmillan, 1986.

Jack, I. *Augustan Satire: Intention and Idiom in English Poetry, 1660–1750.* Oxford: Clarendon, 1952.

Kernan, A. *The Plot of Satire.* New Haven, CT: Yale University Press, 1965.

Kramnick, I. *Bolingbroke and His Circle: The Politics of Nostalgia in the Age of Walpole.* Cambridge, MA: Harvard University Press, 1968. Reprint, Ithaca: Cornell University Press, 1992.

Lees-Milne, J. *Earls of Creation: Five Great Patrons of Eighteenth-Century Art.* London: Hamish Hamilton, 1962.

Nicholson, C. *Writing and the Rise of Finance: Capital Satires of the Early Eighteenth Century.* Cambridge: Cambridge University Press, 1994.

Nokes, D. *Raillery and Rage: A Study of Eighteenth Century Satire.* Brighton: Harvester, 1987.

Nussbaum, F. *The Brink of All We Hate: English Satires on Women 1660–1750.* Lexington: University of Kentucky Press, 1984.

Rawson, C. *Order from Confusion Sprung: Studies in Eighteenth-Century Literature from Swift to Cowper.* London: Allen & Unwin, 1985. Reprint, Atlantic Heights, NJ: Humanities Press, 1992.

———. *Satire and Sentiment, 1660–1830: Stress Points in the English Augustan Tradition.* Cambridge: Cambridge University Press, 1994. Reprint, New Haven, CT: Yale University Press, 2000.

Rawson, C., and J. Mezciems, eds. *Pope, Swift, and Their Circle. The Yearbook of English Studies, Special Number.* London: Modern Humanities Research Association, 1988.

Rogers, P. *Grub Street: Studies in a Subculture.* London: Methuen, 1972. Abridged as *Hacks and Dunces: Pope, Swift, and Grub Street.* London: Methuen, 1980.

———. *Eighteenth-Century Encounters: Studies in Literature and Society in the Age of Walpole.* Brighton: Harvester, 1985.

———. *Literature and Popular Culture in Eighteenth-Century England.* Brighton: Harvester, 1985.

Todd, D. *Imagining Monsters: Miscreations of the Self in Eighteenth-Century England.* Chicago: University of Chicago Press, 1995.

Weinbrot, H. *Augustus Caesar in "Augustan" England: The Decline of a Classical Norm.* Princeton, NJ: Princeton University Press, 1978.

———. *Eighteenth-Century Satire: Essays on Text and Context from Dryden to Peter Pindar.* Cambridge: Cambridge University Press, 1988.

———. *The Formal Strain: Studies in Augustan Imitation and Satire.* Chicago: University of Chicago Press, 1969.

Woodman, T. *Politeness and Poetry in the Age of Pope.* Rutherford, NJ: Fairleigh Dickinson University Press, 1989.

❋ Index ❋

Page numbers for each main article are in **bold** type. Headings in SMALL CAPITALS indicate that a main article is found in the *Encyclopedia* under this name. The abbreviation AP is used for Alexander Pope.

Topics directly related to AP will be found under POPE, ALEXANDER, and not in the main sequence of the index: thus, the entry for his LIBRARY appears within the group of entries under POPE. Book titles are entered under the author's name.

ABBERLEY, Worcestershire, **1**, 239. *See also under* POPE, visits

ABBOTT, EDWIN (1808–82), writer, **1**, 67

ABSCOURT, Surrey, **1**, 263. *See also under* POPE, visits

ACIS AND GALATEA, **2**, 53, 135, 149, 161, 294, 296

ADDERBURY, Oxfordshire, **2**, 10, 212, 216, 240. *See also under* POPE, visits

ADDISON, JOSEPH (1672–1719), author, **2–3**, 6, 26, 40, 47–50, 57, 68, 73, 79, 83, 88–89, 110–11, 117, 135, 137, 144, 147, 149, 161–62, 164, 169, 171, 176, 195, 198, 200, 204, 209–12, 227, 241, 248, 261, 273, 275, 278–80, 284, 286, 288, 293, 299–302, 310, 317, 322, 325, 329, 332, 336, 340; quarrel with AP, 14, 49, 110–11, 120, 299, 301. *Works*: *The Campaign*, 2–3, 227; *CATO*, 2–3, 26, 40, **57**, 135, 204, 209, 211, 258, 266, 294, 328. *See also GUARDIAN, THE*; *SPECTATOR, THE*; *TATLER, THE*

ADEN, JOHN MICHAEL (1918–93), scholar, **3**

AITKEN, GEORGE ATHERTON (1860–1917), scholar, **3**, 29

Algarotti, Francesco (1712–64), author, 168, 198

ALLEN, RALPH (1693–1764), philanthropist, **4**, 20, 35, 42, 61, 71, 95, 123, 143, 152, 158–59, 182, 202, 210, 233, 240, 262, 265, 279, 309, 310, 328. *See also* PRIOR PARK

AMESBURY, Wiltshire, **4**, 24, 43, 236, 240. *See also under* POPE, visits

"AMICA," pseudonym, **4**

ANCESTRY, **4–5**, 86, 104, 229–30, 304

ANCIENTS AND MODERNS, **5–6**, 13, 21, 25, 37, 86, 175, 215, 294, 335

ANECDOTES, **6**, 31, 215, 250, 276

ANNE, QUEEN (1665–1714), **6–7**, 8, 13, 15, 20, 33–34, 46, 54, 58, 63–64, 69, 79, 83, 93, 141, 148,

150–51, 161, 176, 188–91, 193, 210, 232, 238, 244, 256, 260, 271, 273, 285, 288, 319, 328, 331, 333–34, 342; death of, 7, 10, 38, 135–36, 149, 180, 217, 223, 262, 269–70, 317, 339

ANSTIS, JOHN (1669–1744), herald, **7–8**, 286, 310

ANTIQUARIANS, **8**, 99, 150, 154, 185, 216, 225, 319, 335

ARBUTHNOT, ANNE (d. 1751), daughter of John, 6, **8**, 81

ARBUTHNOT, GEORGE (1703–79), son of John, **8**, 9, 26, 44, 328

ARBUTHNOT, DR. JOHN (1667–1735), writer, 2–4, 6–7, **8–10**, 11, 15, 19–20, 40, 44, 53, 59, 61, 110, 119, 130, 135, 139, 144–45, 149, 154, 160, 180, 190, 192–94, 197, 200, 203, 205, 212, 221, 225, 254, 283, 287–89, 298, 310–11, 314, 325, 335, 338–39; connections with the Scriblerian group, 9, 15, 171, 193, 214, 262, 288; *THE HISTORY OF JOHN BULL*, 9, 144, **171**

ARBUTHNOT, ROBERT (1669–1741), brother of John, 9, **10**

ARGYLL, JOHN CAMPBELL, SECOND DUKE OF (1680–1743), 2, **10–11**, 40, 59, 72, 168–69, 212–13, 253, 257, 274, 315

ARISTARCHUS, pedant, **11**, 25

ARNOLD, MATTHEW (1822–88), author, **11**, 245, 249, 265

Arran, Charles Butler, second Earl of (1671–1758), 44, 147–48

ASHE, SIR JAMES (1683–1733), Twickenham resident, **12**

ATOSSA, character sketch by AP, **12–13**, 47, 82, 86, 109, 190

ATTERBURY, FRANCIS (1662–1732), churchman, 5, **13–14**, 18, 71, 115, 150, 170, 194, 201, 203, 210, 260, 268, 278, 323–24

Index

Index

Index

Index

Index

About the Author

PAT ROGERS is DeBartolo Chair in the Liberal Arts at the University of South Florida. He is the author of more than 200 articles, and his many books include *The Samuel Johnson Encyclopedia* (Greenwood, 1996), *Essays on Pope* (1993), *The Oxford Illustrated History of English Literature* (editor, 1987), and *Literature and Popular Culture in Eighteenth-Century England* (1985).